# CHILDREN AND LITERATURE

**HOUGHTON MIFFLIN COMPANY** · Boston

Dallas   Geneva, Illinois   Princeton, New Jersey   Palo Alto

# CHILDREN AND LITERATURE

## Second Edition

### JOHN WARREN STEWIG

The University of Wisconsin–Milwaukee

Cover illustration by N. C. Wyeth from *The Boy's King Arthur* by Sidney Lanier. Copyright 1917 Charles Scribner's Sons; copyright renewed 1945 N. C. Wyeth. Reproduced by permission of Charles Scribner's Sons, a division of Macmillan, Inc.

Acknowledgments begin on page 708.

Printed in the U.S.A.

Library of Congress Catalog Card Number: 87-80337

ISBN: 0-395-42950-1

CDEFGHIJ-H-9987654321

# CONTENTS

## 5 · WORDLESS BOOKS: UPDATING AN ANCIENT FORM

166

## 10 · CONTEMPORARY FICTION: VIEWS OF LIFE    431

# PREFACE

I was delighted with the children's room in the old stone Carnegie library that sat in our downtown park when I was a small child. I am still intrigued, thousands of books later, when reading a new children's book. Many people and experiences have shaped my reading habits, as they have yours. But for me—and I hope for you—the joy of books remains. And so I want to share my enthusiasm for children's books and encourage you to share your enthusiasm with the children you teach.

## AUDIENCE

The Second Edition of *Children and Literature* is a balanced, objective introduction to the range of literature available for children. The text integrates the study of children's books with techniques teachers can use to evoke students' responses to the literature, and is thus appropriate for undergraduate students in both English and Education departments.

## PURPOSE

It is not enough for teachers and librarians simply to know children's books; they must also know what to do with them. This text treats children's involvement with and appreciation of books as an integral part of the study of literature.

- *Children and Literature* provides a comprehensive survey of both traditional and contemporary children's literature, arranged by genre. Each of the books mentioned is discussed fully enough to give students an understanding of its contents and to encourage them to want to find and read the book. My experience teaching undergraduate students suggests that just listing titles with brief descriptions is not likely to interest them in the books.

- Criteria provided for evaluating the books in each genre enable readers to move from selected examples in the chapter to apply the criteria to books not mentioned in the text. Thus, students will be able to select and evaluate books for children effectively.
- In addition to providing a literary analysis of children's books, this text concentrates on ways to use literature with children. Specific suggestions for presenting literature to children and for using art, drama, creative writing, storytelling, and other activities in the classroom are described in each chapter.
- To discuss teaching strategies realistically, I have gone into schools, used books with children, and then reported the children's responses. Child development has been integrated and discussed in the context of the discussion of particular books and children's responses to those books. Rather than give specific recommendations for appropriate ages for the books discussed, I have given a general recommendation for primary, intermediate, or junior high readership. Really fine books can draw readers younger or older than narrow age ranges indicate. When an author's skill sparks a reader's interest, the combination can successfully transcend limited academic considerations of difficulty level.

## NEW IN THIS EDITION

The Second Edition has been greatly expanded and updated. The number of children's titles discussed is more than double the number in the first edition. Approximately a quarter of these titles were published since 1980. To make this text as current as possible, I continued to read the latest children's books until just before the manuscript went to press; some were not yet in bound form. A discussion of the best of the most recently published books was added to the text at the last possible moment.

- More than half of the black-and-white and four-color illustrations are new to this edition; seventy-one new illustrators have been introduced. The distribution of the illustrations has been improved to demonstrate more effectively the role of art in relation to the story text. To acknowledge their influence on illustration today, art from historic children's books has been used to introduce each chapter. These illustrations are by artists such as L. Leslie Brook, Howard Pyle, Beatrix Potter, M. Boutet de Monvel, Edward Lear, John Batten, and John Tenniel.
- To emphasize the point that to build a successful curriculum you have to think about how books relate to one another, I have included ad-

ditional integrated units of study in this edition. These units demonstrate how to build a unit around several books from different genres that deal with the same topic.

- The suggestions for further study that follow each chapter have been developed to present students with specific activities for observing and evaluating children's responses to literature. Many new suggestions have been added and those that appeared in the first edition have been expanded to include references for the student to consult.
- The annotated bibliographies of related readings at the end of each chapter give the reader a look at current available periodical literature and a view of what other people in the field have written.
- The list of professional references found at the end of each chapter gives the reader a convenient way to see in one place the references cited in the chapter.
- The titles listed in the bibliography of children's books at the end of each chapter have been alphabetized by author in this edition to make it easier to locate bibliographic information.

## ACKNOWLEDGMENTS

I would like to thank the many teachers, in both public and private schools, who patiently tried my ideas with their students and carefully gathered samples of the responses. Their work helps give this text the validity that can come only from ideas that have been tried out with real boys and girls.

I would also like to thank the following reviewers for their helpful comments on the revision of this book: Richard Ammon, Penn State University; Vanita Gibbs, Indiana State University; James W. Mittelstadt, University of North Florida; Ben F. Nelms, University of Missouri–Columbia; Marilou Sorenson, University of Utah; and Joan M. Tieman, Simmons College.

Finally, my thanks to the Cooperative Children's Book Center, the Milwaukee and Muskego Public Libraries, and the Curriculum Collection and the Interlibrary Loan Service at the University of Wisconsin–Milwaukee for their help with gathering the illustrations for this project. My special thanks to Holly Sanhuber, whose tireless searching, exemplary literary judgment, and persistent good humor helped bring this book to publication the first time around. I am equally indebted for her help in this Second Edition. Although any errors in this text are my responsibility, the fact that the book became a finished product is in no small part due to her enthusiasm.

J.W.S.

# CHILDREN'S LITERATURE: WHAT, WHY, HOW?

## WHAT IS CHILDREN'S LITERATURE?

What is a children's book? The answer to that question varies according to the time and place being considered. To better understand the variety of forms children's books take today, it is helpful to know something about how they have evolved.

In the beginning, there were no books. Tribal storytellers served as custodians of a culture's mores, values, and history. Stories, told primarily to instruct and less often to entertain, were linear: flows of beguiling speech that lasted a finite time and then ceased to exist except in the memories of listeners, until the next retelling. Quite different from the bound books we know today: physical objects occupying space, ready whenever the reader wants them.

Later, after books as we know them had begun to be printed and accumulated, children appropriated for their own such adult books as *Robinson Crusoe* by Daniel Defoe and *Gulliver's Travels* by Jonathan Swift. Yet it was not until 1744 that John Newbery published *A Little Pretty Pocketbook*, written especially for children (Norton, 1987).

Books specifically written for children included some made up by individual writers. Mrs. Sarah Trimmer and other authors writing in the last half of the eighteenth century continued the didactic, or teaching, tradition begun earlier. Other books for children were collections that brought together stories from the oral tradition and thus made widely available the German tales written down by the Brothers Grimm as well as the English tales preserved by Joseph Jacobs.

Topics of children's books widened during the nineteenth century: Louisa May Alcott's *Little Women* popularized family stories, and Robert Louis Stevenson's *Treasure Island* did the same for adventure stories. Just before the twentieth century began, animal stories like *Black Beauty* by Anna Sewell and fantasies like *Alice in Wonderland* by Lewis Carroll further expanded the type of books available. Magazines especially for children began to appear toward the end of the nineteenth century. Mary Mapes Dodge edited *St. Nicholas*, which exemplified her belief that writing for the young needn't be didactic. She published such authors as Lucretia Hale (*The Peterkin Papers*) and poet Laura E. Richards (whose poems are still anthologized today). In so doing, she produced literature we would today recognize as being specifically aimed at children.

At the beginning of the twentieth century, *The Here and Now Story Book* by Lucy Sprague Mitchell was one manifestation of adults' new interest in and respect for children as separate beings, no longer to be considered as merely little adults. The variety in children's literature continued to expand.

Early in this century, C. B. Falls's *ABC* included quality reproductions of woodcuts and led the way for other picture books that had become possible because of new technology. Rudyard Kipling knew that humor was important to children; his *Just So Stories*, published in 1902, remain popular today. In the same year, Beatrix Potter introduced the animal story with *The Story of Peter Rabbit*, which has been a children's favorite ever since.

A specific example from one genre indicates one significant way in which literature for children has changed through the years. The tales of Grimm and Perrault, served up today with lavish illustrations for children's pleasure, were not originally designed for that purpose. The folk tales we now consider particularly appropriate for young children were originally tales for adults. These simple stories of conflict between good and evil dramatically outlined cause and effect for the benefit of the illiterate adults who listened to the storyteller. The tales were designed to impart the mores and social customs of the group. (See Chapter 6.) Comparing an updated version of the "Twelve Brothers" with one of the original versions shows how these tales have changed over time. The original Grimm version ended very differently from the adapted version, which was softened to make it more appropriate for children. The original read as follows:

> . . . the wicked old mother-in-law was taken before the judge, and tried, and he condemned her to be put in a jar of boiling oil, in which there were poisonous snakes and so she died a miserable death. (*Grimm, 1917*)

In comparison, the adapted version minimizes the unpleasantness.

> . . . the wicked mother-in-law was very unhappy and died miserably. (*Grimm, 1945*)

## A LITERATURE OF VARIETY

The diversity of children's literature today is probably its most striking characteristic. *Children's literatures* perhaps more accurately describes this field of myriad facets. There are many kinds of variety in literature for the young, including variety in genre, format, and subject.

**VARIETY IN GENRE.**   The *genres* (or categories) of children's literature vary widely. Writers create both historic and modern fiction for children. By reading *The Witch of Blackbird Pond*, by Elizabeth Speare, children can journey up the Connecticut River in 1687. The retribution visited upon the frivolous but innocent heroine by her stern and determined neighbors seems very real. In contrast, children can enter, vicariously, the contemporary world of a rich adolescent boy, as depicted by John Ney in *Ox*. Ox tries to solve his problems of being overweight and unpopular amid such trappings of wealth as private airplanes.

Fantasy and biography are also available. Many children have enjoyed *The Borrowers*, Mary Norton's delightful tale of a tiny family living in snug comfort under the floorboards of a rambling old house. The adventures of the Clock family take place in a milieu of miniature items cleverly adapted from the human world. Biography includes Ingri and Edgar Parin d'Aulaire's sympathetic story of our Civil War president, *Abraham Lincoln*, written for primary grade children and illustrated with strong stone lithographs.[1] Biography also includes complex treatments of important minority figures, such as Sojourner Truth, in *Journey Toward Freedom*, written for middle school children by Jacqueline Bernard.

Children can also choose poetry or folk literature. Some poetry is fairly traditional, such as the ever popular poems of David McCord in *Every Time I Climb a Tree*. Poetry can also take an untraditional form, as it does in a book for older children, *Reflections on a Gift of Watermelon Pickle . . .*, by Stephen Dunning, Edward Lueders, and Hugh Smith. Folk literature is available in fine collections—for instance, *Favorite Fairy Tales Told in Scotland*, a compilation of six stories translated by Virginia Haviland and illustrated by Adrienne Adams with whimsical orange and blue drawings. Equally valuable are the many excellent illustrated editions containing a single old tale bound as an independent volume. One example is *The Funny Little Woman*, retold by Arlene Mosel, a delightful Japanese tale about an old woman who falls through her kitchen floor into underground caverns. Her adventures below ground are portrayed in sensitive watercolors; the goings on above ground at the same time are depicted in smaller, black-line drawings.

Picture books and information books are produced in great numbers each year. Some new picture books find an immediate audience. Despite its remote location and unfamiliar culture, *King Island Christmas* by Jean Rogers appeals to many children. The illustrations by Alaska native Rie Munoz are highly patterned designs outlined in light blue. The rhythm of these designs subordinates small details to the overall effect of movement. Other older picture books retain a wide following among children long after their initial publication. *Madeline*, which chronicles the appealing adventures of a little girl living in a Paris convent, remains a favorite, despite the fact that it was written by Ludwig Bemelmans almost forty years ago.

---

[1]Lithography is the art of putting designs on stone with a grease crayon, etching away part of the surface with acid, and then printing a picture from the remaining raised portions of the stone. Further explanation is included in Chapter 2.

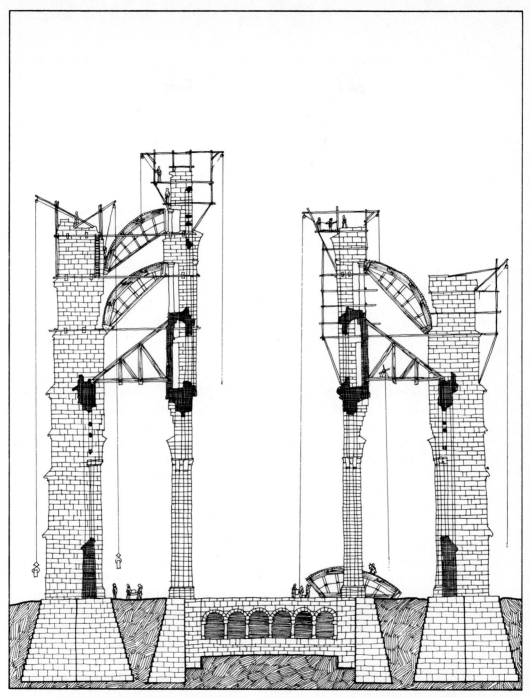

***Using a very precise black-ink line to depict the architectural details, artist David Macaulay also includes human figures to establish the scale.*** From *Cathedral* by David Macaulay. Copyright © 1973 by David Macaulay. Reprinted by permission of Houghton Mifflin Company.

In contrast to the lush imagination displayed by creators of picture books is the finely controlled imagination employed by the creators of information books. A particularly impressive example is *Cathedral* by David Macaulay. Named a Caldecott honor book, this superb combination of words and line drawings evokes the determination of medieval people to build a tribute to their God. Although they provide a great deal of technical information, the author's words and pictures go beyond simple facts to vividly re-create a lifestyle quite unlike our own.

**VARIETY IN FORMAT.**  Children's books range in size from miniatures like *The Nutshell Library* by Maurice Sendak to oversized books like *Milton the Early Riser* by Robert Kraus. The former consists of four tiny (measuring about 3 inches by 4 inches) books enclosed in a box. Especially designed to be intimately shared by a reader and a child sitting on the reader's lap, these small volumes are crammed with details to be examined and savored. Another example of miniature books is *The Little Box of Fairy Tales*, four folk tales retold by Olive Jones and illustrated by Francesca Crespi. The bold illustrations are whimsically bordered with flowers and other designs. The oversized book about Milton, illustrated by Jose Aruego and Ariane Dewey, features large (about 8 inches by 12 inches) splashy pictures that a teacher can easily share with the entire class. The oversized format is also utilized in *A Day in the Life of Petronella Pig*, a wordless book by Tatjana Hauptmann. Each page, or partial page (with much of the original cut away to enhance the design), turns to reveal more of the extensively crosshatched pastel drawing on the succeeding page. The generous size of this book allows ample room for the drawings and their plain borders.

Children's books also vary greatly in shape. Pages can be vertical rectangles, as in *The Tall Book of Mother Goose* by Feodor Rojankovsky, which has enjoyed wide popularity since its publication in 1942. Rojankovsky created the illustrations using lithograph stones, designing each page to accentuate the book's tall shape. Pages can also be horizontal rectangles, as in *Jack Jouett's Ride* by Gail E. Haley, a retelling of the historical events of 1781. Using double-page spreads (arranging one picture across two facing pages), the illustrator created powerful linoleum-block prints that extend almost twenty-two inches from one edge to the other. Still other books are almost square in shape. In *The Juniper Tree* (tales from Grimm translated by Lore Segal and Randall Jarrell), illustrator Maurice Sendak's black-ink drawings are placed squarely in the middle of each page to reinforce the book's shape.

Style of illustration is another variable aspect of format in children's books. Some books feature line drawings with little or no color. In the

**Evaline Ness's work is always characterized by the juxtaposition of strong patterns and the use of unusual color combinations.** Illustration by Evaline Ness from *Tom Tit Tot.* Illustrations copyright © 1965 Evaline Ness. Reprinted with the permission of Charles Scribner's Sons.

popular *Frog Goes to Dinner,* by Mercer Mayer, the wordless story is told in humorous brown line illustrations. In other cases, the illustrator purposely chooses a limited color scheme, sure to attract attention because it is unusual. For *Tom Tit Tot,* a retelling of the old Rumplestiltskin tale, Evaline Ness created woodcuts in which light blue, dull gold, and two shades of brown are combined with much heavy black. The combination may sound uninteresting when described in words but is impressive in actuality. Other books are ablaze with bright colors designed to delight the eye. In *The Little Old Lady Who Was Not Afraid of Anything,* by Linda Williams, the highly saturated[2] illustrations by artist Megan Lloyd depict the incremental refrain and the imaginative solution the old lady develops. Still other books employ sensitively conceived photographs, as in *They Call Me Jack,* by Sandra Weiner. Life in New York is not easy for twelve-year-old Jacinto, who cherishes

---

[2]The term *saturation,* in relation to color, refers to the intensity of the color. A highly saturated color is more intense than a color whose original strength has been diluted.

***Figures and trees printed in heavy black ink show through translucent pages to form new designs in which elements are of varying intensity.*** Reproduced with the permission of William Collins Publishers from *The Circus in the Mist* by Bruno Munari. Copyright © 1963 by Bruno Munari.

memories of his native Puerto Rico. Adjusting to a new life in a big city where friends are few is difficult, but Jack—as he is called in New York— finds some rewards.

Despite the added production expense involved, some books feature individually cut pages. In *The Very Hungry Caterpillar* by Eric Carle, designed in paint and tissue paper, the caterpillar "eats" his way through the pages of the book. In *Look Again!*, author/photographer Tana Hoban uses the cut- page device to encourage children to notice details in the everyday things around them.

*The Circus in the Mist,* by Bruno Munari, is an experiment with different kinds of paper. Translucent pages are used at the beginning and end of the story and heavier colored paper (similar to construction paper) is used for the inner pages, giving readers the sense of passing through a mist to enter and leave the story. The printing of designs and words on both sides of translucent pages results in an unusual visual overlapping that allows readers to see through the "mist."

The variety in construction details raises a question: what is a book? Customarily, we think of flat pages stapled or sewn conventionally, though in fact publishers experiment with a variety of forms that do not fit this usual pattern. Accordian-fold construction, in which the pages are attached to one another and unfold into a long connected strip, has become commonplace. *Little People's Book of Baby Animals,* by Susan Jeffers, features miniature (about 2 inches square) panels, each showing a single animal and its name. The twenty-six animals depicted in loving detail are worth studying over and over. But is this a book *per se?* A larger format (about 6 inches square) was used by Erika Schneider for the potato prints in *The Twelve Days of Christmas.* The overlapping, highly stylized illustrations for the popular song are presented on the front side of the accordian fold; the music and words, without background, are on the reverse side. Consciously designed to be stylish, *The Twelve Days of Christmas* once again challenges our conventional beliefs about what a book is. A variation of the accordian-fold format is found in the recent reproduction of *The Doll's House.* When it is unfolded, some of the pages form the walls of the rooms. This book, originally published in 1890, is by Lothar Meggendorfer, considered to be the father of the pop-up book.

Publishers have recently produced many different kinds of movable and pop-up books. *A Day in the Zoo* is a reissue of a late-nineteenth-century accordian-fold book. On each page, one reads the sentence, then pulls out the flap to activate the pop-up feature. These features are elaborate cutouts, some as many as four layers deep. The aquarium illustration even incorporates clear acetate to create a watery effect. Other recent books combine different ways of making pictures move. For example, in Brian Froud's *Goblins,* some of the pictures move as the page is turned; on other pages, the reader must pull a tab or rotate a wheel. McGee and Charlesworth (1984) argue that such books are immensely appealing to today's video- and movie-oriented generation. If by using such books teachers can motivate students to read, both reading and language benefits will accrue.

Separate component parts of varying sizes and shapes are included in *The Jolly Postman or Other People's Letters,* by Janet and Allan Ahlberg. The human postman brings letters to a variety of storybook folk. For instance, the three bears receive a letter of apology from Goldilocks, done in childlike handwriting; the witch in the gingerbread house receives an advertisement from Hobgoblin Supplies; the giant receives a postcard from Jack, who is off on vacation. Each letter is in its own envelope, to be lifted out and read as one does a real letter. This is one of the most imaginative uses of paper construction in a children's book in recent years.

**VARIETY IN SUBJECT.**  Today, books for children deal with topics that previously were considered taboo. These topics range from birth to death and include almost every subject in between.[3]

Children can find very frank books about human birth, such as *Making Babies* by Sara Bonnett Stein, as well as honest, detailed descriptions of animal birth, such as *My Puppy Is Born* by Joanna Cole. *It's a Baby!* follows the physical development of Pablo, the photographer's son, from birth to age one. Author George Ancona uses black-and-white pictures to focus attention on the content. The book is candid, but the two modest pictures of breast-feeding should not offend. It is also complete. The pictures of spoon-feeding are realistically messy, not prettified. Such books serve a valuable purpose in helping parents answer some of the difficult questions children ask.

Death has come to be an acceptable topic for children's books. *The Dead Bird*, by Margaret Wise Brown, broke publishing ground when it was released nearly thirty years ago. The author, creator of many lyrical books with minimal plots, describes the brief though tender attention some children give a dead bird they find. Pages of simple, hand-lettered text alternate with full-color illustrations. In a more recent book, *Annie and the Old One*, Miska Miles gives children an impressive look at how the Navajo culture views death as integral to the cycle of life. The grandmother accepts her approaching death with equanimity, trying to help her granddaughter see its inevitability. Not all treatments of death are as gentle as this one. Startling realism is found in a collection of short stories for junior high students, *Mr. Death; Four Stories*, by Anne Moody. These stories deal with the raw edges of death that comes unexpectedly and with macabre force.

Among the topics formerly considered inappropriate for children's books but now treated with frankness are several related to sex. Blossom Elfman deals with premarital pregnancy in *A House for Jonnie O*. In *I'll Get There. It Better Be Worth the Trip*, John Donovan views homosexuality dispassionately within the context of a boy's growth toward manhood.

Children's authors examine family problems of many types, including the difficulties of living with a sibling who is different. In *Take Wing*, by Jean Little, a young girl is sometimes overwhelmed by a feeling of responsibility for her younger brother, who is mentally retarded. *My Dad Lives in*

---

[3]Many critics maintain that although the range of children's topics has broadened to include some not formerly addressed, the pervasive tone of much fiction remains didactic. See Lou Willett Stanek, "The Maturation of the Junior Novel: From Gestation to the Pill," in *Issues in Children's Book Selection*, ed. Lillian Gerhardt (New York: R. R. Bowker, 1973), pp. 174–184.

**The not-so-subtle exaggeration of these figures matches the humor in the story.** From *Hey, What's Wrong with This One?* by Maia Wojciechowska. Illustrated by Joan Sandin. Illustration copyright © 1969 by Joan Sandin. Reprinted by permission of Harper & Row, Publishers, Inc.

*a Downtown Hotel*, by Peggy Mann, telis of Joey's adjustment when his mother and father end their marriage and helps the reader sense Joey's awkwardness and pain. In *Hey, What's Wrong with This One?* Maia Wojciechowska descirbes the problem of living in a single-parent household with household. She does not, however, underestimate the difficulties; the three children in the book all feel that life would be better if their father remarried.

Other books focus on physical problems. *Follow My Leader*, by James B. Garfield, describes a blind eleven-year-old child's difficulties as he begins to deal with his anger about the accident that caused his blindness. *Don't Feel Sorry for Paul*, by Bernard Wolf, catches readers off guard with its objective and candid treatment of a topic rarely discussed—birth defects. Paul's equanimity in dealing with problems others might consider overwhelming is impressive. The book is compassionately illustrated in black and white.

**VARIETY IN INTENDED AUDIENCE.** The dividing line between a book for adults and one for mature youngsters with well-developed reading skills has always been difficult to discern. Indeed, before authors began producing books specifically for children, youngsters who were interested in reading simply read adult books. Such books as *Gulliver's Travels* by Jonathan Swift and *Robinson Crusoe* by Daniel Defoe were in fact adult books appropriated by children for their own delight.

Authors continue today to produce very sophisticated books that challenge child readers to the utmost. The work of black author Virginia Hamilton presupposes a literate child reader. Few upper-grade readers will find her work easily accessible, but those who persist will be richly rewarded. Although author Susan Cooper has done some simpler books more readily identifiable as children's books, her *The High King* series yields its richly textured rewards to only a small group of mature child readers. A teacher at the middle school level might choose to read these books aloud to the class, allowing less able readers access to the series.

There has recently been a notable proliferation of books at the other end of the spectrum of children's literature. Designed to be used with children from birth until they begin to read, most of these books are in "board book" format: heavy cardboard pages with a slick surface for easy cleanup. The single word or few words on each page for the most part identify the object being shown. Among the simplest of this type is the series by Helen Oxenbury: *I can, I hear, I see,* and *I touch*. Of an easy-to-hold shape (about 5 inches square), each book contains six double-page spreads. The same male baby inhabits all the books, accompanied by even younger siblings, a bearded daddy, and various small animals. A single word is featured on one side of the double-page spread, and the facing page is wordless. Designed for slightly older children are four books by Betsy and Giulio Maestro, *Harriet at Work, Harriet at Home, Harriet at Play*, and *Harriet at School.* Harriet, an elephant, is a simple white shape outlined in black, who performs various activities against simplified backgrounds. Each page contains one sentence (with the verbs and nouns in heavier type) and a picture. The visual language is indeed easy for very young children to comprehend, but in these books—as in many others of their type—the illustrations are utilitarian rather than inspired.

## WHAT IS NOT A CHILDREN'S BOOK

Each year more than 2400 new children's books are published in the United States and distributed to libraries and retail stores. Some of the books that get printed in formats usually associated with children's books and distributed through the children's divisions of publishing houses, however, are not really children's books. This chapter will consider some general evaluative criteria for judging a book's appropriateness for children. Later chapters provide additional guidelines for evaluating a particular type, or genre, of children's literature. The crucial question is whether a book is really a child's book. To answer this question about a specific book, a teacher or librarian should consider the following issues.

1. ***Does the book deal honestly and forthrightly with children, portraying them candidly and accurately as children?***

   *A Hole Is to Dig* by Ruth Krauss should probably be identified as a book for adults, because it presents a whimsical view of children's understanding of the world. Idealized, somewhat abstract sentiments accompany stylized visual representations of children that appeal to adults but seldom hold children's interest. Other books present highly sentimentalized views of what children are like. Tasha Tudor's work, immensely popular with adults, holds little interest for most children. Racks in drugstores and supermarkets are full of thin volumes in which pretty children do kind things and voice sweet sentiments. The relation of these books to childhood realities is minimal. Such books appeal to memories adults have of childhood and are not children's books.

2. ***Does the book expect children to make associations or perform mental processes of which they are not capable?***

   *The Inner City Mother Goose* by Eve Merriam is not a child's book. The

*The figures extend outside the frame of the picture, and the sweep of the garment leads the viewer's eye between the old woman and the king, emphasizing the transformation.* Reproduced with permission of Macmillan Publishing Company from *The King of the Pipers* by Peter Elwell. Copyright © 1984 by Peter Elwell.

book is a clever satiric treatment of the inconsistencies and inequalities of ghetto life, but most children of the age its picture book format seems intended for will not appreciate it. The book requires knowledge few children have. In addition, it depends for its effect on satire, a sophisticated form of humor to which few children can respond.

Similarly, the fantasy account of *The Shrinking of Treehorn*, by the talented Florence Parry Heide, appeals to adults' sense of irony. In her description of the reaction to Treehorn's discovery that he is getting tinier, Heide aptly captures the indifference of some parents and the conventionality of some teachers. Few children find it as funny as adults do, simply because they take it seriously. Hurst (1984) suggests using this book as the base for a unit on satire with children in fourth through sixth grade.

Peter Elwell's book *The King of the Pipers* abounds with droll humor that adults can enjoy but that child readers find perplexing. The humor, of which the following passage is an example, is too subtle for youngsters.

Jack was known far and wide for his ability to play the bagpipes. In fact, no one could play quite as badly as Jack, which is why, when he decided to walk out into the world and seek his fortune, his parents were not entirely displeased. So with a song in his heart and not the slightest idea of how to play it, Jack strolled off down the dusty road.

Jack does find a beautiful maiden and bests the devil to get her back from him. Sir Giles, typical of the inept folk Jack encounters along the way, acts ". . . with a bravery bred of too many dents to the helm . . . ," which is clever word play for adults, who bring a sophisticated understanding to Elwell's prose. The black-ink and wash drawings that accompany this wry prose are as full of small, quirky details as the story is.

Another book in which the humor is not really for children is *Millicent the Monster*, by Mary Lystad. The story line may well appeal to children: Millicent likes the idea of becoming a monster, but when she stops being a monster she enjoys the fact that other people then like her. The visual humor, however, is clearly adult. Millicent's unruly thatch of hair, beady eyes, quasi-Victorian clothes, and exaggerated stereotyped gestures of despair are all funny to adults, but children are likely to take them seriously.

## THE GOOD, THE BAD, AND THE INDIFFERENT

**THE TEACHER AS BOOK EVALUATOR.** An elementary teacher must be both a selector and a recommender of books.

1. Teachers need to select books to use in a daily period of group sharing, planned as a continuing part of the language arts curriculum. Children should be read to each day both at the primary level, where reading aloud is fairly common, and at the intermediate level, where it is less common (Root, 1967).
2. Teachers need to be able to recommend fine books to individual children who have a special interest. Such a special interest might be an emotional interest—perhaps a concern about the physical problems of growing up. Reading *Are You There, God? It's Me, Margaret*, by Judy Blume, and understanding that Margaret had the same doubts may be comforting to a preadolescent girl fearful of the bodily changes she will soon experience. A special interest may also be cognitive: for a child fascinated by animals, a teacher might recommend *A Natural History of Giraffes*, with the lucid text by Dorcas MacClintock and elegant silhouette illustrations by Ugo Mochi. Equally specialized is *African Images*, by the same two collaborators. Whatever the special interest, it

*The elegance of these animals is captured by using the silhouette technique, which eliminates extraneous detail and thus focuses attention on the shapes themselves.* Illustration by Ugo Mochi from *African Images* by Dorcas MacClintock. Illustrations copyright © 1984 Estate of Ugo Mochi. Reprinted with the permission of Charles Scribner's Sons.

is important that teachers be able to recommend good books to individual children.

3. Teachers should be aware of new books so that they can recommend additions to the school library's collection. In becoming involved in library selection, a teacher is not questioning the school librarian's competency but simply acknowledging that greater diversity results when input comes from several sources.

4. Teachers should be able to recommend books for use at home. Many parents' knowledge of children's books is essentially limited to those they see in drugstores and supermarkets; trips to a bookstore or library are rare. If a parent is to use the best books with a child, a recommendation from the teacher is often necessary.

Given the number of new children's books published each year, how is the teacher to separate the great from the gruesome, the inspired from the inadequate? What is acclaimed today may be ignored or criticized a few years from now. One obvious answer to this dilemma is to wait until a book

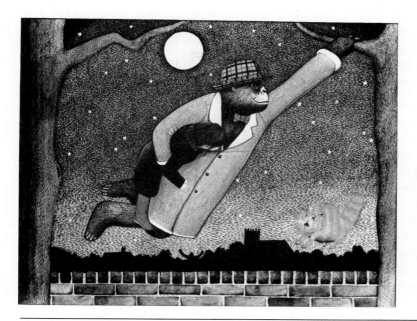

*The realistic way in which the gorilla is depicted contrasts with the curious flatness of the trees and the wall. The lack of any sense of deep space, despite the buildings in the background, sets up an interesting visual tension.* From *Gorilla* by Anthony Browne. Copyright © 1983. Reprinted by permission of Alfred A. Knopf, Inc.

has stood the test of time before declaring it good.[4] To follow this course of action, however, is to limit severely what one selects or recommends. If a child is interested in animal stories, we know we are on solid ground with comfort-loving Ratty, obstreperous Toad, and taciturn Mole, from Kenneth Grahame's *The Wind in the Willows*. Similarly, given the book's enduring popularity, we are sure of the quality of *Charlotte's Web*, E. B. White's book about ingenious Charlotte the spider, crafty Templeton the rat, and friendly Wilbur the pig.

We cannot apply this criterion of endurance, though, to such books as John Donovan's *Family*, since his adventure story about intelligent chimpanzees—powerful Moses, appealing Lollipop, and gabby Myrtle—is too new. Should we recommend *Gorilla*, by Anthony Browne, an even newer book with a similar main character, for intermediate grade readers? This strangely surrealistic story, with its visual allusions to such things as the painting of Whistler's mother, is problematic. To newer books such as these, we need to apply other criteria. Some general guidelines follow. Specific suggestions for evaluating individual genres appear in subsequent chapters.

---

[4]The bestowing of the Lewis Carroll Shelf Awards, given annually for a number of years by the University of Wisconsin (Madison) School of Education, represented one attempt to identify books that stood the test of time. Award books were selected from those nominated by publishers as "worthy to sit on the shelf with *Alice in Wonderland*," an enduring favorite.

**EVALUATION SOURCES.** Evaluating books is a challenging, enjoyable task. The two basic types of evaluation, based on the source of the information, are *internal evaluation* and *external evaluation.*

Internal evaluation involves the teacher's reading a children's book and evaluating it according to a set of criteria such as the following:

1. ***Characterization.*** How convincing are the characters? Do they seem real, even if they are unlike anyone we have ever met? Are they believable, even if they are fantasy characters? Do we care about the characters, responding to them in some way because of the author's skill in bringing them to life? Would we like to know more about them or read another book about them?

2. ***Dialogue.*** Dialogue shows the author's skill in making conversation sound as if it were taking place between actual people. What do we learn of the characters' thoughts, beliefs, and feelings through their conversation? What insights can we gain into how characters interact from the ways they talk with each other? Is there something about the conversation of each character that sets him or her apart from the other characters?

3. ***Setting.*** Do we get a definite sense of place from the author's description of the setting? Even if it is a place we have never been, we should have a vivid, convincing sense of the location. Can we see, hear, and feel the environment in which the action takes place?

4. ***Plot.*** Is the plot an exciting one that carries us along? Is it simple enough that we can follow it yet complex enough to hold our interest? Do we want to continue reading to find out what happens? Is what happens logical, even if the story is a fantasy?[5]

5. ***Conflict.*** The driving force that makes things happen is the conflict. Conflict is often physical, but it can be mental. Is the conflict believable and understandable? Whatever the type of conflict, it must be convincing; the reason for the disagreement must ring true.

6. ***Resolution.*** In some genres, such as folk literature, conclusions are easy to anticipate: evil is punished; the good are rewarded and "they live happily ever after." Such is not the case in other genres, where endings may be equivocal or even sad. To evaluate a story's resolution, we need to ask if the ending could have happened. Given what the author establishes in the book, is what happens a logical consequence? Does

---

[5]As one writer notes, there are definite limits to what can happen in a story, even if it is fantasy. Fantasy is not, as one might suspect, an anything-goes genre. See Sam Leaton Sebesta and William J. Iverson, *Literature for Thursday's Child* (Chicago: Science Research Associates, 1975), p. 179. This idea will be discussed at length in Chapter 11.

the resolution bring naturally to an end what the author set in motion?

7. **Theme.**  After all the details of which people, what places, and when the story happens are stripped away, what a reader is left with is the theme. The theme is the underlying idea, the foundation upon which particular information rests. Theme deals with major issues, such as the importance of standing up for what one believes. Specific details may set the story in the sixteenth or the twenty-first century; the main character may be a young woman or an old man; the environment may be here or in another world. But when these particulars are set aside, the theme of two apparently diverse books may in fact be the same. Many experts have written about theme. Cohen (1985) took the single most pervasive theme in literature—the quest—and analyzed its components (problem, struggle, realization, and achieving the goal), demonstrating her categories in the context of three popular books.

8. **Style.**  Style is a complex, rather ephemeral aspect of writing, determined to a large degree by the author's use of language. (Language use is discussed in Chapter 12 on information books.) Words may flow in long, convoluted phrases or march jerkily in telegraphic sentences. The book's pacing also affects style: events may pile upon one another quickly, or description may extend the time between events. Finally, the author's choice of narrative voice affects whether readers get the more personal view of first-person narration or the more impersonal view of third-person narration.

9. **Mood.**  Two contrasting books, both loosely taken from Chaucer's work and presented in picture-book format, show how different authors create varying moods. In *Pinchpenny John*, Lee Lorenz created a Rabelaisian tale that is jaunty despite mishaps and cheerfully optimistic. Although unfamiliar vocabulary (like "perish") is not eschewed, the language is direct, and the syntax is kept simple to aid readability. In sharp contrast to *Pinchpenny John* is Ian Serraillier's retelling of *The Franklin's Tale*. Serraillier's book is actually slightly shorter (27 pages versus 30) than Lorenz's, but its elegant language and the corresponding formality of Philip Gough's pictures make clear its suitability for older readers. Readers are kept at a distance from the characters by the language, which moves at as measured a pace as the people must have moved in their floor-length gowns. The problem is presented more seriously and the final happiness is more melancholy than in the Lorenz book. (To better understand mood, you might read and then contrast other children's books. In *A Ring of Endless Light*, Madeline L'Engle creates a secure, content feeling for her family. Quite different is the sense of suspense and ominous foreboding created by H. M. Hoover in

*The Rains of Eridan.* That suspense, in turn, is unlike the aura of supernatural mystery John Bellairs creates in *Revenge of the Wizard's Ghost.*)

External evaluation of books involves looking up the opinions of others in lists of award-winning books, standard bibliographic sources, and evaluative reviews in magazines and newspapers.

1. ***Lists of award-winning books.*** Many organizations award prizes regularly to meritorious children's books.[6] The two best-known awards are the Newbery Medal and the Caldecott Medal, both presented annually by a committee of the Association for Library Service to Children (ALSC) of the American Library Association. The Newbery Medal is named for John Newbery (1713–1767), a London publisher who broke new ground in children's publishing (Doyle, 1971). He is credited with publishing the first book written especially to entertain children, *The History of Little Goody Two-Shoes,* a sharp contrast to the didactic, solemn books then available. Each year the award is given for the original work published during the preceding year that is considered the most distinguished contribution to American literature for children. The Caldecott Medal, named for the prolific and influential British illustrator Randolph Caldecott (1846–1886), is given for the most distinguished picture book of the year. One of the first artists to make a name illustrating children's books, Caldecott was known for the action, vitality, and humor of his picture books. Lane (1986) gives a more detailed description of Caldecott's work.

Other awards, such as those given by the American Institute of Graphic Arts and the Children's Book Council, recognize excellence in various aspects of fine bookmaking, such as size and shape, paper, typography, and page layout. (See Chapter 4.) Jones (1983) provides a comprehensive listing of awards. This source describes both current awards (Coretta Scott King Award) and discontinued awards (Lewis Carroll Shelf Award); both limited awards (Indiana Author's Day Award) and awards that are wider in scope (International Board of Books for Young People); both awards given by children (Georgia Children's Book Award) and awards given by adult experts (Art Books for Children Citation). Part Two of Jones's book is an alphabetical list of authors and illustrators, with their award-winning books. For those

---

[6]A complete listing of awards is available in *Children's Books: Awards and Prizes,* a yearly paperback compilation published by the Children's Book Council, 67 Irving Place, New York, NY 10003.

interested in critical reaction to and analysis of the awards themselves, a bibliography of professional journal articles is also included.

2. **Standard bibliographic sources.**   General sources provide information about and comment on the worth of books.

*Children's Books in Print* (*CBIP*), published annually by the R. R. Bowker Co., New York, is a bibliographic tool containing information about all the children's books (both hard-cover and paperback) currently in print. *CBIP* indexes books according to author, title, and illustrator, including much helpful information in its brief entries. A companion volume is *Subject Guide to Children's Books in Print*, which is helpful for locating books about a specific topic. These two volumes do not recommend books but simply provide information about their availability. They are often needed, however, in external evaluation to supplement other sources that tell which books are good.

*The Elementary School Library Collection*, published annually by Bro-Dart Foundation, New Brunswick, New Jersey, recommends films, filmstrips, and other media in addition to books. This source gives short plot summaries and an order of priority for library purchasing, as well as the type of bibliographic information included in *CBIP*.

*Children's Catalogue* is published annually, with a cumulative revision every five years, by H. W. Wilson Co., New York. This selective source is divided into two parts. In Part I books are arranged according to a modified Dewey Decimal system; Part II is an author, title, subject, and analytic index. In addition to standard bibliographic information, entries in this source include the Dewey classification number and an excerpt of a review from some reviewing source. For readers who do not know specific authors' names or titles, there is also a subject entry.

*The Elementary School Library Collection* and *Children's Catalogue*, as well as over fifty other sources of information about children's books, are themselves annotated in a list prepared by the Reference Books Committee of the Association for Childhood Education International (1983).

3. **Magazine reviews.**   Many periodicals, both professional and popular, publish reviews of new books. Because such publications have limited space for reviews, almost all reviews are positive. An additional problem is that some reviews fail to go beyond simple plot summaries. (Policies and the nature of the reviews for publications may well change as column or general editors change.) The following magazines may be helpful.

*Booklist*, published by the American Library Association, is issued twice monthly except in August, when there is only one issue. All books included are recommended, and most reviews venture beyond plot summary into criticism. Composed almost entirely of reviews, this publication evaluates adult, young adult, and children's books. Special sections include high-interest/low-vocabulary books, easy-to-read books, and audiovisual materials.

*Bulletin of the Center for Children's Books*, published monthly by the University of Chicago, contains critical evaluations and a helpful rating code, including "marginal" and "not recommended."

*The Horn Book*, published bimonthly, features insightful articles on a variety of book-related topics. In addition, the carefully selected reviews focus at greater length on criticism than do reviews in other journals.

*The Kirkus Reviews*, the first publication in a loose-leaf format, has been providing lengthy critical reviews of adult and children's books since 1933. Issued twice monthly, the critiques appear well in advance of publication of the books reviewed.

*Language Arts* (formerly *Elementary English*) is published eight times a year by the National Council of Teachers of English. This periodical includes a monthly column in which an editor notes recent publications, providing primarily plot summaries.

*The Reading Teacher*, a journal of the International Reading Association, includes a limited number of reviews of children's books. The reviews tend to include some evaluative comments in addition to plot summaries.

*School Library Journal*, published by R. R. Bowker Co., includes many reviews that go beyond simple synopses. A variety of people throughout the United States do the reviews, which therefore represent a diversity of opinion not offered by other reviewing periodicals.

*Wilson Library Bulletin*, published monthly by the H. W. Wilson Co., New York, features an insightful column on picture books written by two authors who seldom rely on plot descriptions, but rather analyze the visual elements of the books they discuss.

*Young Children*, published by the National Association for the Education of Young Children, does not regularly feature a book column but occasionally publishes articles about children's books.

4. ***Newspaper reviews.***  Several national newspapers review new children's books. Reviewers for *The New York Times* and *Christian Science Monitor*, among others, regularly write review sections about new children's books.

To locate reviews of a particular book, see the *Book Review Index*, published by Gale Research Co., Detroit. It gives information about where and when a book has been reviewed. This periodical includes references to reviews in all the major reviewing sources.

Reviewers bring different competencies to their jobs, and as a result the evaluations vary greatly. You might find it interesting to analyze a book, applying the criteria suggested earlier, and then read several reviews of that book to see how the reviews and the analyses compare. For instance, you might read *Charlie and the Chocolate Factory*, by Roald Dahl, in which the pathetic main character rises to prominence after finding the golden ticket to a place where chocolate flows like water. After evaluating the book yourself, you could read the interchange of letters between the author and a respected critic who was less than delighted with the book.[7]

To be well informed about books, teachers and librarians must read criticism as well as reviews. The distinction between reviewing and criticism is explained by Hearne (1978). Reviewing lets readers know the book exists: "Speed, brevity and currency are the essence. . . ." Reviewers must sift through all the books published in order to determine, as soon as they are available, which will be reviewed. In contrast, criticism, which focuses on fewer books, can be more leisurely, considering the chosen books in their publishing or social context. The critic can think about the book as it compares to others by the same author or similar ones by other authors. We read reviews in sources such as those mentioned above in order to begin forming judgments about books. Then we must seek longer, more thoughtful criticism from the pens of such authorities as John Rowe Townsend and Eleanor Cameron. They give us more insightful comments than reviews can provide.

**THE GOOD OR THE USEFUL BOOK?**   The amount of time children spend reading appears to be diminishing yearly; statistics on increases in television viewing are not encouraging. Although it is important to evaluate books in order to find the very best ones to share with children, there are times when the habit of reading is best encouraged by recommending that a child read a book that is useful, even if it is not of the best quality (West, 1978).

Perhaps a book is particularly appropriate for a child because of an interest or problem he or she has at a particular time. A child may be dealing

---

[7]Eleanor Cameron, "McLuhan, Youth and Literature," *The Horn Book* (October 1972), pp. 433–440; (December 1972), pp. 572–579; and (February 1973), pp. 79–85. Roald Dahl's reply is in "Charlie and the Chocolate Factory" (February 1973) pp. 77–78. Cameron's response is in the April 1973 issue, pp. 127–129. Further comments are in the "Letters to the Editor" columns from February to October 1973.

with insecurities due to an impending divorce at home or to the intrusion of an unwanted younger sibling. For such a child, retreat into one of the series books about the adventures of a cardboard hero or heroine may be a necessary escape. An intermediate-grade child may be having a problem with schoolwork. Retreat into one of the myriad undistinguished horse or mystery stories cranked out by the hundreds may provide needed contact with the familiar. When a child is having a personal problem is not the time to try to sell the child on one of the "good" books on the Newbery list.

A book may be useful simply because it is the only one or one of very few available on a topic. Although today a teacher may, quite rightly, want to search for a more realistic book, *Two Is a Team*, by Lorraine and Jerrold Beim, in which the main characters are a black child and a white child interrelating in a natural way, was the only one of its kind available when it was published. If a teacher needs an information book on praying mantises, fiction about a child with hemophilia, or a collection of cinquain poetry, he or she must be satisfied with what is available. The search for the very best in children's books should not stop, but at times some book— any book—may keep a child reading.

## WHY LITERATURE FOR CHILDREN?

Why is literature for children such a sturdy plant? Publishing houses continue to bring out a great variety of children's books because these books are avidly consumed by children who understand their lure. But why do children read?

**FOR SIMPLE ENJOYMENT.**   Anyone who has ever experienced the pleasure of following a character through a series of adventures knows the delight of simple enjoyment. Things happen to the adventuresome doll in *Miss Hickory*, by Carolyn Bailey, though this doll is by no means as passive as her construction might suggest. In *Ronia, the Robber's Daughter*, a more extended story than this author's popular *Pippi Longstocking*, Astrid Lindgren tells a tale to be savored. Ronia is taught by her father to live fearlessly in the forest, and child readers follow her adventures with joy. Adults will be aware of the Romeo and Juliet motif that forms the base of this story, but children will simply and delightedly attend to the action. There are countless other examples of books children read for enjoyment alone, a prime purpose of reading.

**TO ESCAPE FROM PRESENT SITUATIONS.**   For many children, reading offers a temporary diversion, a means of getting away from problems that seem insoluble (Jacobs, 1985). In *Johnny Lion's Book*, Edith Thacher Hurd creates a charming story within a story. The young protagonist can read, and he goes adventuring through the book his parents give him when they go hunting. As the story proceeds, the pages in his book get larger, and when he makes the transition into the story itself, they fill the pages of the actual book. The adventure almost becomes a misadventure, but his parents' welcoming arms at last enfold the little lion, who is warned not to leave the safety of home. There is no reason to look down on the escape function of literature; even mature adults need to escape from the intensity of current problems. Too few know how effective reading can be in serving this purpose.

**TO STIMULATE THE IMAGINATION.** Effective fiction makes both children and adults wonder about the nature of a character, the look of an environment, the reason behind a twist of plot, or the nature of an unspecified outcome. Blair Lent's book *Bayberry Bluff*, set so convincingly on Martha's Vineyard, raises questions about how the people who live there during the summer manage to arrange their lives so they can do so. Effective nonfiction also stimulates wonder, generating new questions as questions are answered. Nelly Munthe's fine book for intermediate-grade students, *Meet Matisse*, may lead its readers to explore this French painter's predecessors and disciples.

**TO GAIN UNDERSTANDING OF THEMSELVES.** Children whose determination sometimes gets them into trouble can read a message about this quality incorporated skillfully into the saga of *Rufus M*, by Eleanor Estes. Though some of the referents in this book are now dated (for example, Rufus falls into the library basement through the coal chute), the author tapped into universal qualities of childhood when she created her main character. A child who feels neglected because his or her physical appearance is unlike other children's can read *A Girl Called Al*, by Constance C. Greene. At the book's end, Greene shows, rather than tells, that Al ends up feeling good about herself despite her appearance. The character proved so popular with child readers that her adventures were continued in *I Know You Al*, *Your Old Pal*, *Al*, and *Al(exandra) the Great*. All are characterized by a breezy text composed mostly of dialogue, with little description to interrupt the flow of action.

**TO GAIN UNDERSTANDING OF OTHERS.** Lewis, who is ten, finds out what it is like to be old when he encounters Mr. Madruga in Paula Fox's *A Likely*

***The unvarying thinness of the ink line and the absence of shading produce symbolic rather than realistic images.*** Illustration by Byron Barton from *A Girl Called Al* by Constance Greene. Copyright © 1969 by The Viking Press, Inc. Reproduced by permission of Viking Penguin Inc.

*Place*. He also discovers that, despite the disparity in their ages, they can be friends. Children come closer to understanding what it would be like to be blind by reading the hauntingly beautiful *Sound of Sunshine, Sound of Rain*, by Florence Parry Heide. Blindness seems natural to the unnamed boy in this story. As Katherine Paterson (1982) comments, "There are plenty of American children adventurous enough imaginatively to read about characters who are not carbon copies of themselves."

**TO GAIN UNDERSTANDING OF THE NATURE OF LANGUAGE.**  Children can learn about the dialects of people in different parts of our country through such books as *Strawberry Girl*, by Lois Lenski. The author reproduces in detail the dialect of the Florida Crackers, a group of Anglo-Saxon descent who first lived in the Carolinas. At one point, the main character comments,

> Pa . . . iffen that cow laps her tongue around the new leaves, she'll twist the bark loose and pull it off. Do we stop her, she might could eat up all them orange trees.

Several authors use dialects from other countries. Among these is a black author and translator, Lorenz Graham, who provides a strong version of the David and Goliath story told in Liberian English in *David He No Fear*. The accompanying woodcut illustrations by Ann Grifalconi are as spare and strong as the language. Other titles by Lorenz Graham include *Every Man Heart Lay Down* and *God Wash the World and Start Again*.

Books can also show other kinds of language differences, such as the ways in which language changes as people grow older. In Clara I. Judson's *Abraham Lincoln*, Lincoln's language changes from the simple, untutored language of his childhood home to the more polished, slightly formal dialect he spoke when he was president.

Nonverbal language is the focus of other books. *Talking Without Words*, by Marie Hall Ets, provides charming lithograph illustrations that show common uses of gesture, the nonverbal language that accompanies spoken words. Children can learn about the stylized use of gesture perfected by mimes in *The Marcel Marceau Alphabet Book*, by George Mendoza. *Sign Language*, by Laura Greene, is a more comprehensive treatment of nonverbal language, examining differences of opinion about the relative merits of finger-spelling, sign language, and the oral method.

Children can become aware of the qualities of words by reading *Sparkle and Spin*, a unique book handsomely illustrated with pictures that reinforce the qualities discussed. The authors, Ann and Paul Rand, use big words and small words, as well as comforting, whispering, and sound-alike words. The qualities of each are depicted in sophisticated collages combining cut paper, newspaper, ink, and photographs.

A poet, Mary O'Neill, captured word qualities memorably in *Words Words Words*. These poems for boys and girls in sixth grade or above should be read aloud so that children can concentrate on the concepts encoded in the fairly sophisticated language. In her poem titled "Forget," O'Neill likens that word to a hider in a long black cape, for "nothing that happens goes truly away."

Finally, children can learn about other forms of written language through such books as *The Sioux Indians*, by Sonia Bleeker, in which ideographs are used to record a winter hunt.

**TO LEARN ABOUT OTHER TIMES AND PLACES.** Students can travel through time to other eras in books that give insights into the ways people lived and the problems they encountered. Such books are available for even the youngest readers. *Thy Friend, Obadiah* and other books about this character provide a vivid picture of the sights, sounds, and smells of Nantucket Island in its early Quaker days. Children will discover that Obadiah's problems, as described by author Brinton Turkle, are common ones, despite the remoteness of the time.

Children can travel to various geographical locations in books that give a clear sense of another place. The appeal of the rocky shores of New England becomes real for children when they read *One Morning in Maine*, by Robert McCloskey, who, in this distinctive environment, captures with authenticity a child's reaction to a loose and then lost tooth. In *Dragonwings*, a sensitive novel of a young boy's adjustment to an alien culture, boys and girls move vicariously through the crowded streets of San Francisco's Chinatown. Lawrence Yep's Newbery honor book contrasts the two distinct environments of Chinatown and Nob Hill, both of which may be unfamiliar to readers.[8]

Some authors provide penetrating glimpses into life in other countries. In *The Wheel on the School*, children get a detail-packed view of life in the Netherlands from Meindert DeJong, who has used reminiscences of his own childhood. Half a world away, in *Ash Road*, by Ivan Southall, the mood is quite different as a fire accidentally set by three boys in the parched Australian bush causes an inferno that threatens the lives of hundreds. The desperation of the boys draws readers relentlessly into the fast-moving plot.

---

[8]In "Language and Cognitive Development Through Multi-Cultural Literature" (*Childhood Education*, November/December 1985, pp. 103–108), Donna E. Norton recommends using this book, as well as several others, for developing students' evaluation skills. She asserts that "historic fiction is excellent for investigating, discussing, and evaluating the authenticity of characters, plots, and settings."

*Artist Brinton Turkle uses a soft, fluid crayon line over his watercolors to give definition to the shapes. There is enough detail in such things as the clothing to give historic authenticity without detracting from the action in the picture.* Illustration from *Obadiah the Bold* by Brinton Turkle. Copyright © 1965 by Brinton Turkle. Reproduced by permission of Viking Penguin Inc.

**IN QUEST OF INFORMATION.** The information in trade books is often more compelling than similar material in textbooks. Trade books offer writers more freedom in writing than do textbooks, which are usually conceived in sequential order with concepts and vocabulary carefully controlled for maximum readership. Authors of trade books can afford to be more selective in the concepts they present, more imaginative in their treatment of subjects, and more sophisticated in the vocabulary and language patterns they use.

Information books are available to help children in all subject-matter areas. In science, books about animals present facts and figures compellingly. Holling C. Holling, the author of *Pagoo*, writes clearly and concisely about sea animals and provides both four-color and black-and-white drawings. In social studies, a wealth of books, such as *Sidewalk Story,* by Sharon Bell Mathis, deal with minority groups with which all children should be familiar. In mathematics, new books abound, including easy-to-understand books like *Meter Means Measure,* by S. Carl Hirsch. Many exciting new books about the arts are discussed in Chapter 12.

# THE HOW OF CHILDREN'S LITERATURE

In addition to knowing about children's literature, teachers must know what to *do* about books if they are to be effective in bringing children and books together.

A basic premise of this book is that all students at all levels should hear fine literature read aloud every day. This means reading to four-year-olds who are not yet fluent readers. It also means reading to eighth graders, who may be fluent readers but who can still benefit from hearing literature presented orally. Many primary-level teachers do read to children. Unfortunately, teachers of older students, pressured to present more and more content, often do not read aloud regularly. A recent nationwide study showed that only 60 percent of middle-grade teachers read to their students (Koeller, 1981). Following are some guidelines for effectively sharing literature with children and sensitively using literature to evoke responses from children. The organized sharing of books and eliciting of student response will be further considered in the final chapter of this book.

## INTRODUCING A BOOK

Many books require no introduction. The teacher simply must make sure children are ready to listen, tell them the author and the title, and begin to read; children will be carried away almost instantly. It takes no more than a page to get into the conflict between Dave and his dad in *It's Like This, Cat,* by Emily Neville. The author ensures easy entry with these opening sentences: "My father is always talking about how a dog can be very educational for a boy. This is one reason I got a cat." In these two sentences, the author skillfully sets up the universal conflict between a growing child and parental dictum. The children don't need to know any more—they just want to find out what happens next. Similarly, girls and boys don't need a long introduction to *I Never Saw . . . ,* a picture book that features a dynamic opening page with a huge orange sun, a wide blue tree, and a white bird. Judson Jerome planned that visual opening, as well as the opening words of the book, to attract children's attention immediately, so that they want to see what happens next.

Not all books are as easy as these to get into, however. For some, teachers will need to present a skillful introduction. Perhaps the book requires some information the children do not have. Students may lose interest in *A Proud Taste for Scarlet and Miniver,* by E. L. Konigsburg, unless the teacher briefly introduces the historic facts involved. The musings of an impatient Eleanor of Aquitaine as she awaits the long-delayed entry of her errant husband Henry into heaven take many pages. A teacher can sustain listeners' interest through this beginning by providing information about who these characters are.

At times, teachers may need to identify the people involved in a story and clarify their relationships. To appreciate the moving drama recounted in *Susette La Flesche: Voice of the Omaha Indians*, by Margaret Crary, children need to know who Susette is and understand her relationships with her brother Francis, her uncle Standing Bear, and the crusading journalist named Thomas Tibbles who later becomes her husband. A brief identification of Susette as the first woman of the Omaha tribe to crusade for Indian rights and some mention of the support she received from her husband will help interest children in the book.

Teachers may need to clarify the places in certain stories. For example, a teacher can capture children's interest for *The Fearsome Inn*, by Isaac Bashevis Singer, by showing them where the story takes place. Poland will seem remote to child readers/listeners unless the teacher takes a few minutes to locate the cities mentioned in the story on a map. Even parts of their own country may seem remote to children, despite the ease of travel today. For full appreciation of the folkways described by Katherine Milhous in *The Egg Tree*, children should know where the Amish live in Pennsylvania. The fact that the Amish maintain their customs even though surrounded by modern society can heighten children's sensitivity to the uniqueness of this cultural group.

## SHARING A BOOK

Sharing a piece of literature orally can be a magical experience. It is inspiring to listen to Ruth Sawyer, a master of vocal interpretation, share the fantasy story of Tikipu, the apprentice who walks into a painting done by his master, Wiowani. In *The Storyteller* (Weston Woods, cassette #701-C), Wiowani, jealous of his student's talent, bricks up the door. For five years nothing is heard of Tikipu. In his studio, the evil master pridefully shows the painting to visitors, until one day—in an ending reminiscent of Poe— a tiny hand appears over the garden wall in the painting and starts to remove the bricks, one by one! With just a voice—no props, no lights, no setting— Sawyer shares an enchantment that goes far beyond the written word. She captures listeners' attention and, through her artistry, holds their interest throughout the story. Although few will achieve the perfection of such a reader as Ruth Sawyer, all teachers can become more effective readers if they think about the act of reading to children.

It is imperative that teachers read a story themselves before they read it to children. Even the simplest picture book must be read through in its entirety before it is read aloud in class. For example, only someone familiar with the fey story of *Mr. Grumpy's Motor Car,* by John Burningham, would be able to read smoothly a sentence like "They pushed and shoved and heaved and strained and gasped and slipped and slithered and squelched." For maximum aural effect, the sentence needs to be read smoothly, with a small accent on each verb and a gradual increase in tempo toward the end. The involved sentence structure, which provides a necessary rhythm, is not suitable for reading at first sight.

More complex literature may require more than one rehearsal. The alliteration and rhyming words in a terrifying tale based on Grimm need to be carefully studied before the tale is shared with children. The words in Ian Serraillier's *Suppose You Met a Witch?* must be spoken fluidly to convey the sense of impending disaster. Often the arrangement on the page doesn't indicate pauses. The reader must read ahead to determine where the juncture goes in

> *. . . and the witch will-nilly—*
> *each prickle and pin*
> *as it skewered her in*
> *was driving her silly.*

In the first line, the author indicates a pause with a dash. Although no further pauses are indicated, a slight pause at the end of the third line will increase anticipation about the pin's effect and heighten the humor of that line. Decisions like these cannot be made while one is reading to students.

Beyond simply rehearsing to make sure words are pronounced correctly, it is important to think consciously about three aspects of oral language: pitch, stress, and juncture. *Pitch* refers to the highness or lowness of sounds; it provides variation that holds listeners' attention. *Stress* is the emphasis a reader places on particular words to call attention to them. *Juncture* refers to the positions and the lengths of the pauses. Creative use of these three aspects of oral language adds drama to a reading. Crucial when reading complex material to older children, they are also necessary for effective reading of a simple Mother Goose rhyme. A record titled *Mother Goose Rhymes* (Caedmon Records, #TC1091) features three accomplished verbal interpreters: Cyril Ritchard, Celeste Holm, and Boris Karloff. As Karloff reads "There Was a Crooked Man," he progressively lowers the pitch, uses emphasis to stretch out some words, and exaggerates pauses between words to contribute to the feeling of chilly apprehension.

Gesture can also be used effectively to reinforce a story. The possibilities for gesture when reading aloud are notably limited, simply because the reader must hold the book. But simple one-handed gestures and movements of eyes and head can help accent the action. A reader can mime the villager anxiously pushing aside the huge sunflower leaf in Shan Ellentuck's *A Sunflower as Big as the Sun* and use accompanying facial expression to reinforce the nervousness of the angry peasant people. Or a searching gesture can indicate the anxiety of the young boy looking for his lost pet in *The Little Brown Hen*, by Patricia Miles Martin. More extensive gestures are possible in storytelling, when the teller works without a book, as described in Chapter 6.

Readers must decide how much and what they will read from a piece of literature. In most cases, it is best to share the entire book, for the book was conceived as a unit to be savored in its entirety. But sometimes teachers may read to an exciting place and stop, allowing those children who wish to do so to finish reading by themselves. Teachers of upper grades, reading longer works appropriate for older students, often make use of this technique in order to share a greater variety of stories with students. For example, teachers might read *A Matter of Spunk*, by Adrienne Jones, only to the point (page 77) at which Margy, the narrator, discovers that her little lead dog, a gift from her older sister Blainey, has disappeared. At this point, it is clear to Margy that tough Pauline, one of the charity students in the private school Margy attends, has stolen the beloved figurine. Interested children can then finish the book on their own, and the teacher can move on to group sharing of some other book.

In other cases, teachers may synopsize parts of the story, reading only particularly interesting parts to their listeners. In reading *Ramona the Pest*, by Beverly Cleary, the reader might skip over the first several pages, which detail six-year-old Ramona's getting ready at home and walking to school. The more interesting part of the story begins when Ramona walks into the kindergarten to encounter Miss Binney, who was "so young and pretty she could not have been a grownup very long."

## FOLLOWING UP A BOOK

A teacher can plan many kinds of follow-up activities for children. One is *not* to follow up at all! Some books are so special to readers that to insist on a culminating activity may spoil the effect. Virtually all of us have read books to which we have responded simply by sitting silently for a while. In quietly rethinking, questioning, or reacting, we are making the only response necessary. After reading *The Gift of Sarah Barker*, a teacher would be unwise to spoil the intensely compelling story of Sister Sarah and Brother Abel, young teenagers, with a discussion. Author Jane Yolen transports readers into a Shaker community in the middle of the nineteenth century as she describes the poignant conflict between two youngsters who fall in love, in contradiction to their sect's beliefs. The lovers make the difficult choice to go out into the world; they set off into a new life, as alien to them as any we can imagine. The book infuses readers with hope; we want Sarah and Abel to thrive because of their choice. To talk about these feelings would only intrude on the tale Yolen has written with such rare skill.

At other times, teachers and children can follow up a piece of literature in a variety of ways.

1. **Orally.**  Teachers can discuss with children their reactions to a piece, asking them questions to help them go beyond the story. Valuable discussion can be elicited with a facilitating question, such as "What were you thinking as you listened to the story?" More extended verbal responses can be obtained by having children make up a radio play based on the story, translating from the author's words into their own. Or teachers can have children do interviews between a reporter and a book character. For example, pairs of young listeners could take the roles of a radio interviewer and Captain Toad, featured in *Captain Toad and the Motorbike*, by David McPhail. In this wacky tale, the captain, happily retired to a bucolic country cottage after a long and successful naval career, finds himself and his neighbors pestered by invading motorcyclists. His jumping ability inadvertently contributes to his winning the race and dispersing the cyclists.

2. **Orally and physically.**  Teachers can encourage children to dramatize part of a story they have read. Many books contain a scene or series of scenes that can serve as a basis for dramatization. After reading *A Ride on High*, by Candida Palmer, children could dramatize scenes such as the ride on the el, the baseball game, and the point at which Chet and Tony solve their problem. Or students could make their own puppets and some simple scenery to enact a story (see Schlansky, 1985).

3. **Visually.**  Teachers can encourage children to make a model of a building crucial to a story, to illustrate their favorite part of a story, or to make a "movie" out of a continuous roll of paper wound on two dowels. *Violett*, by Julia Cunningham, is a compelling tale of a thrush who cannot sing, illustrated with rather nondescript black-and-white drawings. A teacher could read this story to children and then ask them to paint a picture of the part of the story they like best.

4. **Musically.**  Teachers can encourage children to set the verses in a story to song, working with the music teacher to create a simple melody. Traditional literature often includes repeated refrains or verses that can readily be made into songs. Several are included in "The Widow's Lazy

Daughter," in *Favorite Fairy Tales Told in Ireland*, edited by Virginia Haviland.

5. ***In writing.*** Teachers can encourage students to write something about a piece of literature. Students might be asked to create another story along the same plot lines as a sample, to complete a story, or to rewrite a story from a different character's point of view. A teacher could introduce children to haiku and ask them to write a poem of their own. (Several of these ideas are expanded upon in later chapters.)

Every child will respond with zest to one of these techniques at one time or another. We all like to share with others something we have read that has touched us. But no child will respond with anything but dutiful compliance if asked to follow up every reading with some sort of culminating activity. The decision as to which project is best for a particular child at a particular time is an intuitive one.

## PROVIDING TIME TO READ

In addition to group literature time, a complete literature program in the elementary school includes time set aside for children to read *real* books on their own.

We cannot be content with the condensations of literature included in reading texts; the reading of basal reading texts does not constitute a literature program. It is true that both the amount and the quality of the literature in basal reading texts has increased dramatically in the last ten years. Nonetheless, as one respected authority contends, "it is *not* a question of the basal reader *or* the library book. It is more a matter of how the basal reader leads unerringly to daily reading of library books" (Manning, 1985). In other words, after teaching the skills of reading (most commonly through the use of a basal reading series), teachers must also provide time every day for every child to apply those skills in a meaningful context by reading a book he or she has chosen. Only in such a context can we be sure the skills have been internalized to the point where children will choose to use them later. A complete literature program, therefore, includes both components— the planned group and free reading time.

## *SUMMARY*

To the uninitiated adult, children's literature may seem a simple matter, but closer inspection reveals enormous variety in genre, format, and subject.

There is indeed a bewildering array of books for young readers—some excellent, some mediocre. Students have a limited number of years in which to read this body of literature, and during this time they will encounter only a limited number of books. Thus those who work with children must be able to direct them to the best selections available.

Literature is not simply a harmless diversion. Rather, it serves very specific purposes for readers. In planning literature programs, teachers must provide books that will accomplish the purposes of providing enjoyment; escape; stimulation of the imagination; knowledge of people, places, and other times; and an understanding of the nature of language.

A teacher must also know how to use literature for maximum effect. There are many times when no related experiences are necessary—the effect of the book on the reader is sufficient. At other times, the teacher must enhance or extend the literary experience by planning meaningful oral, nonverbal, written, or visual experiences. The rest of this book will suggest ways in which teachers can develop skill in handling these responsibilities within the context of various genres.

## Suggestions for Further Study

1. The section dealing with books that are not children's books referred to Ruth Krauss. One critic declares that books by Joan Walsh Anglund are really not for children either but play on the nostalgia adults have for their childhood. See "Greenaway Went Thataway," by Selma G. Lanes, in *Down the Rabbit Hole* (New York: Atheneum, 1971, pp. 31–34). Do you agree with Lanes's contention about Anglund?

2. *Wind in the Willows*, mentioned in this chapter as an enduring favorite of children, may not appeal to many children at first encounter. Because of the extensive description, Britishisms, and leisurely pace, it may need careful introduction to attract children's interest. Read the book yourself, and plan how you would introduce it to make it interesting to children.

3. This chapter refers to Arlene Mosel's *The Funny Little Woman* (see page 4). Read it to a group of children, and then ask them to write another adventure about the little woman, telling what happened to her after she returned safely from her adventure with the Oni.

4. This chapter refers to books about birth. Read *Wind Rose*, by Crescent Dragonwagon (New York: Harper and Row, 1976), which deals with conception in a lyrical way. Despite the evocative language, some readers may be offended. What is there about the book that some people might find objectionable? How would you defend the book against their objections?

5. Some thirty years after its publication, *The Borrowers*, by Mary Norton, "is widely regarded as a children's classic" (Kuznets, 1985). Is it still interesting to children? Read the first chapter to your class. Focus on the

description of the Clocks' home beneath the floorboards. Then have children write descriptions of their own homes. If your students are interested in the problems and rewards of being miniscule, introduce them to *The Wall People* (*In Search of a Home*) by Joseph J. DiCerto (New York: Atheneum, 1985). The book derives from Norton's earlier one but puts more emphasis on action than on reflection.

6. After reading *Cathedral* by David Macaulay to intermediate-grade children, invite an architect to your classroom to talk about contemporary building practices. Boys and girls find it interesting to hear about materials, processes, and problems involved in architecture today.

7. In the section on internal evaluation of books, this chapter suggested several questions to ask, including questions about such elements as characterization, plot, and setting. Examine this year's Newbery Medal and honor books to determine how the authors used these elements. The books represent, according to the committee that selected them, the best available. Do you agree or disagree?

8. After using the *Marcel Marceau Alphabet Book*, by George Mendoza, with children, encourage them to think of actions or objects they could mime for each letter of the alphabet. It might be interesting to have them think about and use language to talk about their reactions to the question "Which is easier to show in mime—actions or objects?"

## Related Reading for Adults

Bamman, Henry A., Mildred A. Dawson, and Robert J. Whitehead. *Oral Interpretation of Children's Literature*. Dubuque, Iowa: William C. Brown, 1964.

The authors, in 119 pages and five chapters, deal concretely with a wide range of oral activities related to literature. The chapter on oral reading is particularly useful. The only disadvantage is the unimaginative format; the book is better than it appears at first glance.

Blishen, Edward, ed. *The Thorny Paradise: Writers on Writing for Young Children*. Harmondsworth, Eng.: Kestrel Books, 1975.

Twenty-two essays by noted children's authors are divided into two types: (1) assertions that children's literature is a valid literary genre and writing for children is a respectable literary profession, and (2) expanded analyses of individuals, sources of ideas, processes of writing, and other professional concerns. Among the most provocative are essays by John Gordon and Joan Aiken.

Bouchard, Lois K. "A New Look at Some Old Favorites." *Interracial Books for Children*, Winter/Spring 1971, pp. 3 and 8.

The author gives reasons why *Charlie and the Chocolate Factory* by Roald Dahl is inappropriate for children. She describes at length her reaction to the portrayal of the Oopma-Loompas, which she feels is racist. Because of such pressure, the publisher brought out another edition in which they are described quite differently. Locate a copy of each edition, and compare to see how Dahl changed the description.

Carlson, Ruth Kearney. "Sparkling and Spinning Words." *Elementary English*, January 1964, pp. 15–22.

In *Sparkle and Spin*, again available from Gregg Press, authors Ann and Paul Rand examine the qualities of words. Carlson identifies ways teachers may help children write creatively by exploring vocabulary and using literature as a base for writing. She believes that children's writing will sparkle when it grows from exposure to adult poetry, figurative language, and beautiful rhythms.

*Early Children's Books and Their Illustration.* New York: The Pierpont Morgan Library, 1975. This elegantly designed and beautifully printed and bound volume will interest bibliophiles. A preface, foreword, and essay by three authorities precede the chapters by G. Gottlieb on different types of early books. These range from editions of fables through primers and readers to religious books. Each descriptive entry, about a paragraph in length, includes details about the author and circumstances of publication, and sometimes a plot summary.

Egoff, Sheila. "If That Don't Do No Good, That Won't Do No Harm: The Uses and Dangers of Mediocrity in Children's Writing." *School Library Journal*, October 1972, pp. 93–97. In this ironic, well-written article, Egoff asserts that someone must determine what is good in children's books and raises a question: Who is better equipped to do it, the child or the professional? She refutes the notion that reading something is better than reading nothing, replying that there are various grades of something. She believes that "whatever mediocre books do, good books can also do—and much better." Egoff would probably disagree with Ed Carroll and Larry Dorrell in "Spider-Man at the Library" (*School Library Journal*, August 1981, pp. 17–19). These authors enthusiastically endorse using comics as a way to entice junior high students into the library. Which of the two articles do you find more convincing?

Ellis, Alec. *How to Find Out About Children's Books.* Oxford, Eng.: Pergamon Press, 1973. Ellis discusses ways to find out about children's literature by looking at library collections and organizations and gives some general keys to selection, including criticisms of children's literature. The book contains brief surveys of historic and contemporary fiction and a useful chapter on poetry. Although primarily British in orientation, this work does consider some American books, authors, and organizations.

Fisher, Margery. *Who's Who in Children's Books.* New York: Holt, Rinehart and Winston, 1975. If you don't know who Milo or Mowgli or Mary Anne is, this reference work will tell you. Milo is from *The Phantom Toll Booth*, by Norton Juster; Mowgli is from *The Jungle Book*, by Rudyard Kipling; and Mary Anne is from *Mike Mulligan and His Steam Shovel*, by Virginia Lee Burton. That type of knowledge by itself has limited use, but the commentary with each entry makes interesting reading. The book provides not only plot synopses but also fascinating evaluative comments and the author's personal responses to the materials.

Jan, Isabelle. *On Children's Literature.* New York: Schocken, 1974. Jan, a noted French critic, discusses various genres of children's literature and shares her insights concerning didacticism. She believes that children's literature exhibits special characteristics, has antecedents, and is continually evolving. She does not discuss many writers who are considered important in the United States and at times includes others not generally deemed worthy of serious criticism. The book, written in articulate style, abounds in intellectual challenges.

Scott, Jon C. "Anatomy of a Masterpiece: *The Borrowers.*" *Language Arts*, May 1976, pp. 538–544. Scott provides an extensive analysis of Mary Norton's fantasy to help readers better understand why it is a book of "unquestioned, timeless genius." Although he acknowledges the author's consummate skill in characterization, style, and detail, Scott is most interested in the element of unity that the concept of seeing provides. An analysis of visual images demonstrates how crucial seeing and avoiding being seen are for the Borrowers.

Shattuck, Roger. "How to Rescue Literature." *The New York Review of Books*, April 17, 1980, pp. 29–35.

Although the author is writing about the various schools of literary criticism prevalent in the teaching of literature at the college level, he provides a compelling rationale for reading aloud at all grade levels. He states that oral interpretation restores freshness and urgency to literature, as it requires listeners to "register literary works first in linear human time, with its subtle aspects of evanescence." Shattuck closes with the contention that "most teachers are potential performers, and all of us can develop our skills in that direction." The article is difficult to read, but well worth the effort.

Sueling, Barbara. *How to Write a Children's Book and Get It Published*. New York: Scribner's, 1984.

This succinct handbook guides the intended writer along an often precarious path, from defining his or her goals as a writer to promoting the published book. One of the most interesting chapters is "Lessons from the Past," a brief but careful look at how such people as Ludwig Bemelmans, Eleanor Estes, and Else Holmelund Minarik changed the nature of writing for children. After the body of the text, eight appendixes provide additional information.

Townsend, John Rowe. "Didacticism in Modern Dress." *The Horn Book*, April 1967, pp. 159–164.

Townsend, a noted writer of modern fiction for young adults, claims that many works of modern fiction are heavily didactic, despite protests to the contrary. This didacticism appeals, albeit unconsciously, to the adults involved in book selection. The three dangers of this didacticism are that ordinary, unliterary children lose interest in books, that we come to expect from authors what it is not right to expect, and that we judge books by the wrong standards.

## Professional References

Cohen, Caron Lee. "The Quest in Children's Literature." *School Library Journal*, 31 (August 1985), 28–29.

Doyle, Brian. *The Who's Who of Children's Literature*. New York: Schocken, 1971.

Hearne, Betsy. "Reviewing and Criticism: A World of Difference." *Booklist*, 75 (September 1, 1978), 46–48.

Hurst, Carol O. "Picture That! Using Picture Books in the Fourth Through Eighth Grades." *Early Years*, March 1984, 31–34.

Jacobs, Leland B. "A Thousand Guesses, My Dear Children." *The Advocate*, 5 (Fall 1985), 10–14.

Jones, Dolores Blythe. *Children's Literature Awards and Winners: A Directory of Prizes, Authors and Illustrators*. Detroit: Neal-Schuman, 1983.

Koeller, Shirley. "25 Years Advocating Children's Literature in the Reading Program." *The Reading Teacher*, February 1981, 552–556.

Kuznets, Lois R. "*The Borrowers*: Diaspora in Miniature." In *Touchstones: Reflections on the Best in Children's Literature.* Ed. Perry Nodelman. West Lafayette, Ind.: Children's Literature Association, 1985, pp. 198–203.

Lane, Lisa. "Caldecott. New Look at a Picture-Book Pioneer." *Christian Science Monitor,* February 21, 1986, 16–17.

Manning, John C. "Integrating Reading with Other Subjects." *Reading Today,* October 1985, 4.

McGee, Lea M., and Rosalind Charlesworth. "Books with Movables: More than Just Novelties." *The Reading Teacher,* May 1984, 853–859.

Norton, Donna E. *Through the Eyes of a Child, An Introduction to Children's Literature.* Columbus, Ohio: Merrill, 1987.

Paterson, Katherine. "The Aim of the Writer Who Writes for Children." *Theory into Practice,* 21 (Autumn 1982), 325–331.

Reference Books Committee. "Selected References for an Elementary School Library." In *Books for Children Bibliography.* Washington, D.C.: Association for Childhood Education International, 1983.

Root, Sheldon. "What's Wrong with Reading Aloud?" *Elementary English,* December 1967, 929–932.

Schlansky, Marilyn A. "The Patterson Players." *VOYA,* June 1985, 112.

West, Elizabeth. "Good Clean Trash." *Parents' Choice,* November/December 1978, 6.

## Bibliography of Children's Books

Ahlberg, Janet, and Allan Ahlberg. *The Jolly Postman or Other People's Letters.* Boston: Little, Brown, 1986.

Ancona, George. *It's a Baby*! New York: Dutton, 1979.

Anonymous. *A Day in the Zoo.* New York: Viking, 1980.

Bailey, Carolyn S. *Miss Hickory.* New York: Viking, 1946.

Beim, Lorraine, and Jerrold Beim. *Two Is a Team.* New York: Harcourt, Brace, 1945.

Bellairs, John. *Revenge of the Wizard's Ghost.* New York: Dial, 1985.

Bemelmans, Ludwig. *Madeline.* New York: Viking, 1939.

Bernard, Jacqueline. *Journey Toward Freedom.* New York: Grosset and Dunlap, 1967.

Bleeker, Sonia. *The Sioux Indians.* New York: William Morrow, 1962.

Blume, Judy. *Are You There, God? It's Me, Margaret.* New York: Scribner's, 1970.

Brown, Margaret Wise. *The Dead Bird.* New York: Young, Scott, 1958.

Browne, Anthony. *Gorilla.* New York: Knopf, 1983.

Burningham, John. *Mr. Grumpy's Motor Car.* New York: Thomas Y. Crowell, 1973.

Carle, Eric. *The Very Hungry Caterpillar.* New York: World Publishing, 1968.

Cleary, Beverly. *Ramona the Pest.* New York: Morrow, 1968.

Cole, Joanna. *My Puppy Is Born.* New York: Morrow, 1973.

Cooney, Barbara (ill.). *The American Speller.* New York: Thomas Y. Crowell, 1969.

Crary, Margaret. *Susette La Flesche: Voice of the Omaha Indians.* New York: Hawthorn Books, 1973.

Cunningham, Julia. *Violett.* New York: Pantheon, 1966.

Dahl, Roald. *Charlie and the Chocolate Factory.* New York: Knopf, 1964.

d'Aulaire, Ingri, and Edgar Parin d'Aulaire. *Abraham Lincoln.* Rev. ed. Garden City, N.Y.: Doubleday, 1957.

DeJong, Meindert. *The Wheel on the School.* New York: Harper and Row, 1964.

Donovan, John. *Family.* New York: Harper and Row, 1975.

———. *I'll Get There. It Better Be Worth the Trip.* New York: Dell, 1969.

Dunning, Stephen, Edward Lueders, and Hugh Smith. *Reflections on a Gift of Watermelon Pickle* . . . . Glenview, Ill.: Scott, Foresman, 1969.

Elfman, Blossom. *A House for Jonnie O.* Boston: Houghton Mifflin, 1976.

Ellentuck, Shan. *A Sunflower as Big as the Sun.* Garden City, N.Y.: Doubleday, 1968.

Elwell, Peter. *The King of the Pipers.* New York: Macmillan, 1984.

Estes, Eleanor. *Rufus M.* New York: Macmillan, 1967.

Ets, Marie Hall. *Talking Without Words.* New York: Viking, 1968.

Fox, Paula. *A Likely Place.* New York: Macmillan, 1967.

Froud, Brian. *Goblins.* New York: Macmillan, 1983.

Garfield, James B. *Follow My Leader.* New York: Viking, 1957.

Graham, Lorenz. *David He No Fear.* New York: Thomas Y. Crowell, 1971.

———. *Every Man Heart Lay Down.* New York: Thomas Y. Crowell, 1970.

———. *God Wash the World and Start Again.* New York: Thomas Y. Crowell, 1971.

Grahame, Kenneth. *The Wind in the Willows.* New York: Scribner's, 1908.

Greene, Constance C. *A Girl Called Al.* New York: Viking, 1969.

———. *Al(exandra) the Great.* New York: Viking, 1982.

———. *I Know You Al.* New York: Viking, 1975.

———. *Your Old Pal, Al.* New York: Viking, 1979.

Greene, Laura. *Sign Language.* New York: Franklin Watts, 1981.

Grimm, Jacob, and Wilhelm Grimm. *Grimms' Fairy Tales.* Trans. Mrs. Edgar Lucas, Lucy Crane, and Marian Edwards. New York: Grosset and Dunlap, 1945, p. 47.

———. *Grimms' Fairy Tales: Stories of Elves, Goblins and Fairies.* New York: Books, Inc., 1917, p. 58.

———. *The Juniper Tree.* Trans. Lore Segal and Randall Jarrell. New York: Scribner's, 1965.

Haley, Gail E. *Jack Jouett's Ride.* New York: Viking, 1973.

Hauptmann, Tatjana. *A Day in the Life of Petronella Pig.* New York: Holt, Rinehart and Winston, 1982.

Haviland, Virginia. *Favorite Fairy Tales Told in Ireland.* Boston: Little, Brown, 1961.

———. *Favorite Fairy Tales Told in Scotland.* Boston: Little, Brown, 1963.

Heide, Florence Parry. *The Shrinking of Treehorn.* New York: Holiday House, 1971.

———. *Sound of Sunshine, Sound of Rain.* New York: Parents' Magazine Press, 1970.

Hirsch, S. Carl. *Meter Means Measure.* New York: Viking, 1973.

Hoban, Tana. *Look Again!* New York: Macmillan, 1971.

Holling, Holling C. *Pagoo.* Boston: Houghton Mifflin, 1957.

Hoover, H. M. *The Rains of Eridan.* New York: Viking, 1977.

Hurd, Edith Thacher. *Johnny Lion's Book.* New York: Harper and Row, 1985.

Jeffers, Susan. *Little People's Book of Baby Animals.* New York: Random House, 1980.

Jerome, Judson. *I Never Saw* . . . . Chicago: Albert Whitman, 1975.

Jones, Adrienne. *A Matter of Spunk.* New York: Harper and Row, 1983.

Jones, Olive (reteller). *The Little Box of Fairy Tales.* New York: Dial, 1983.

Judson, Clara I. *Abraham Lincoln.* Chicago: Follett, 1950.

Konigsburg, E. L. *A Proud Taste for Scarlet and Miniver.* New York: Atheneum, 1973.

Kraus, Robert. *Milton the Early Riser.* New York: Windmill Books, 1972.

Krauss, Ruth. *A Hole Is To Dig: A First Book of First Definitions.* New York: Harper and Row, 1952.

L'Engle, Madeline. *A Ring of Endless Light.* New York: Farrar, Straus and Giroux, 1980.

Lenski, Lois. *Strawberry Girl*. Philadelphia: J. B. Lippincott, 1950.

Lent, Blair. *Bayberry Bluff*. Boston: Houghton Mifflin, 1987.

Lindgren, Astrid. *Ronia, the Robber's Daughter*. New York: Viking, 1983.

Little, Jean. *Take Wing*. Boston: Little, Brown, 1968.

Lorenz, Lee. *Pinchpenny John*. Englewood Cliffs, N.J.: Prentice-Hall, 1981.

Lystad, Mary. *Millicent the Monster*. New York: Dial, 1974.

Macaulay, David. *Cathedral*. Boston: Houghton Mifflin, 1973.

MacClintock, Dorcas. *African Images*. New York: Scribner's, 1984.

———. *A Natural History of Giraffes*. New York: Dell, 1973.

Maestro, Betsy, and Giulio Maestro. *Harriet at Work*. New York: Crown, 1984.

Mann, Peggy. *My Dad Lives in a Downtown Hotel*. Garden City, N.Y.: Doubleday, 1973.

Martin, Patricia Miles. *The Little Brown Hen*. New York: Thomas Y. Crowell, 1960.

Mathis, Sharon Bell. *Sidewalk Story*. New York: Viking, 1971.

Mayer, Mercer. *Frog Goes to Dinner*. New York: Dial, 1974.

McCloskey, Robert. *One Morning in Maine*. New York: Harcourt Brace, 1957.

McCord, David. *Every Time I Climb a Tree*. Boston: Little, Brown, 1971.

McPhail, David. *Captain Toad and the Motorbike*. New York: Atheneum, 1978.

Meggendorfer, Lothar. *The Doll's House*. New York: Viking, 1979.

Mendoza, George. *The Marcel Marceau Alphabet Book*. Garden City, N.Y.: Doubleday, 1970.

Merriam, Eve. *The Inner City Mother Goose*. New York: Simon and Schuster, 1969.

Miles, Miska. *Annie and the Old One*. Boston: Little, Brown, 1971.

Milhous, Katherine. *The Egg Tree*. New York: Scribner's, 1950.

Moody, Anne. *Mr. Death; Four Stories*. New York: Harper and Row, 1975.

Mosel, Arlene. *The Funny Little Woman*. New York: E. P. Dutton, 1972.

Munari, Bruno. *The Circus in the Mist*. New York: World Publishing, 1968.

Munthe, Nelly. *Meet Matisse*. Boston: Little, Brown, 1983.

Ness, Evaline (illustrator). *Tom Tit Tot*. New York: Scribner's, 1965.

Neville, Emily. *It's Like This, Cat*. New York: Scholastic, 1963.

Ney, John. *Ox*. Boston: Little, Brown, 1970.

Norton, Mary. *The Borrowers*. New York: Harcourt, Brace, 1953.

O'Neill, Mary. *Words Words Words*. Garden City, N.Y.: Doubleday, 1966.

Oxenbury, Helen. *I can*. New York: Random House, 1986.

———. *I hear*. New York: Random House, 1986.

———. *I see*. New York: Random House, 1986.

———. *I touch*. New York: Random House, 1986.

Palmer, Candida. *A Ride on High*. Philadelphia: Lippincott, 1966.

Rand, Ann, and Paul Rand. *Sparkle and Spin*. New York: Harcourt Brace, 1957.

Rogers, Jean. *King Island Christmas*. New York: Greenwillow, 1985.

Rojankovsky, Feodor. *The Tall Book of Mother Goose*. New York: Harper and Row, 1942.

Schneider, Erika. *The Twelve Days of Christmas*. Natick, Mass.: Picture Book Studio, 1974.

Sendak, Maurice. *The Nutshell Library*. New York: Harper and Row, 1962.

Serraillier, Ian. *The Franklin's Tale*. New York: Frederick Warne, 1972.

———. *Suppose You Met a Witch?* Boston: Little, Brown, 1973.

Singer, Isaac Bashevis. *The Fearsome Inn*. New York: Scribner's, 1967.

Southall, Ivan. *Ash Road*. New York: St. Martin's, 1965.

Speare, Elizabeth George. *The Witch of Blackbird Pond*. Boston: Houghton Mifflin, 1958.

Stein, Sara Bonnett. *Making Babies*. New York: Walker, 1974.

Turkle, Brinton. *Thy Friend, Obadiah*. New York: Viking, 1969.

Weiner, Sandra. *They Call Me Jack*. New York: Pantheon, 1973.

White, E. B. *Charlotte's Web*. New York: Harper and Row, 1952.

Williams, Linda. *The Little Old Lady Who Was Not Afraid of Anything*. New York: Thomas Y. Crowell, 1986.

Wojciechowska, Maia. *Hey, What's Wrong with This One?* New York: Harper and Row, 1969.

Wolf, Bernard. *Don't Feel Sorry for Paul*. Philadelphia: Lippincott, 1974.

Yep, Lawrence. *Dragonwings*. New York: Harper and Row, 1975.

Yolen, Jane. *The Gift of Sarah Barker*. New York: Viking, 1981.

# STUDYING BOOK
## ILLUSTRATION:
### LOOKING
#### WITH INSIGHT

Books for children present an astoundingly wide spectrum of visual stimulation. Choices range from the bright, full-color illustrations in *Morris's Disappearing Bag*, by Rosemary Wells, to the effective use of a single color with black and white in *The Lace Snail*, by Betsy Byars, to books in which the artist simply uses the contrast of black and white, as in *The Owl-Scatterer* by Howard Norman. In addition to the variety in color use, there is an almost infinite array of styles (from realistic to abstract) and designs (from highly patterned to restrained and understated). Zena Sutherland (1977, p. 54) comments aptly on children's book illustration: "Sharing such books with children, adults will find themselves as charmed with the pictures as are the children . . . a wonderful way to teach art appreciation would be through children's picture books which run the whole gamut of styles and techniques."

To study the range of illustrations in children's books as well as the media and methods used by the illustrators, it is necessary to distinguish among picture books, picture storybooks, and illustrated books.

**PICTURE BOOKS.** In picture books, the pictures carry the entire message. This category includes alphabet books, counting books, and concept books (as well as wordless books; see Chapter 5). In these kinds of books, different objects or ideas appear on each page, linked by the artist's style but not necessarily by a sequential story line.

There are alphabet books for all ages, although we usually consider these books to be for beginning readers. *Ben's ABC Day*, by Terry Berger, features almost full-page color photographs, by Alice Kandell, showing a boy and his family and friends engaged in a variety of activities throughout the day. It is a book for beginners; most children will be familiar with the commonplace activities portrayed. In contrast, *The Museum of Modern Art ABC*, by Florence Cassen Mayers, is clearly intended for a more sophisticated audience; much of the art included is highly abstract.

Counting books are plentiful. *Up to Ten and Down Again*, by Lisa Campbell Ernst, opens with a solitary duck floating in its pond and continues on to a page packed with picnickers, who begin to disappear when rain threatens. Large, full-color, bordered illustrations on facing pages provide much to look at. Brown line focuses the details in the pictures. Some counting books are appropriate for the youngest viewer. In *Night Counting*, by Ann Morris and Maureen Roffey, the young children are plainly drawn, and what is to be counted is quite evident. In contrast, in *When Sheep Cannot Sleep*, by Satoshi Kitamura, the author/illustrator was obviously aiming at an older audience; the complex, unrealistic pictures require a more developed eye and counting skills.

*Sharp edges and intense contrasts are possible with wood etching, a very precise technique appropriate for creating a wealth of detail.* From *The Owl-Scatterer* by Howard Norman. Illustrations copyright © 1987 by Ed Young. By permission of Little, Brown and Company.

Margaret Wise Brown's *The Important Book* is an example of a concept picture book. She identifies an object, notes its most salient characteristic, lists several of its other qualities, and at the bottom of the page repeats the first-mentioned characteristic. Brown describes in poetic fashion a spoon, the rain, an apple, shoes, and, at the end of the book, the reader. The illustrations by Leonard Weisgard are still fresh despite the fact that this book was first published in 1949.

**PICTURE STORYBOOKS.** In picture storybooks, the artist must show characters, settings, and actions in a way that will relate to and advance a plot. An example is James Skofield's *All Wet! All Wet!*, illustrated by Diane Stanley. On each page are meticulously executed, detailed pictures that are indeed integral to the story. The story is stronger because of the pictures, and in the same way the pictures benefit from the author's words. The words focus on the main objects and events in the picture; the picture then elaborates on the words. Because they combine words and pictures, picture storybooks present an interesting evaluation problem: those who select books for children must make both a visual and a verbal judgment.

**ILLUSTRATED BOOKS.** Illustrated books have fewer illustrations than do picture storybooks and what they do have are often printed in limited color or just black and white. The illustrations are extensions of the text and may add to the interpretation of the story but are not necessary for understanding it. These books are intended for children who have developed fluent reading skills. An example is *The Ghost of Windy Hill* by Clyde Robert Bulla, which contains ink-wash and line drawings by Don Bolognese. These drawings accompany the strange and exciting adventure of a family that is not sure whether its house is haunted. A more recent example is Martin Waddell's *Harriet and the Haunted School.* The black-and-white illustrations by Mark Burgess break up the text, for the most part paralleling rather than expanding on the story. The hilarious adventures of Harriet, the troublemaker of her school, are conveyed effectively through the words.

# BOOK ILLUSTRATION TODAY

Book illustration today differs significantly from that in earlier children's books for several reasons. First, the technology is highly developed: new laser technology and computer-set type are only two examples. One cannot but marvel, when watching the sheets of a book being propelled through four-color presses at an astounding speed, at the advances that make such means of production possible. Many effects are achieved that were not even considered just a few years ago. Second, the field of book illustration attracts immensely talented artists. Whereas at one time illustration of children's books was a limbo into which the professional artist did not venture, the same cannot be said of the field today. Impressive recognition from various professional groups is accorded the artist who successfully illustrates children's books. In addition, a fair percentage of the selling price is passed on to the illustrator; in view of the large printing runs common today, the financial remuneration a talented and recognized artist receives makes illustrating books worthwhile.

Teachers should consciously study the illustrator's art so that they can introduce children to the wealth of inventive, imaginative pictures in books today. Teachers and librarians can help children study illustrations as independent visual artifacts, created by someone, reproduced by some means, designed to create some specific effect on the intended audience.

## STUDYING ARTISTS' TECHNIQUES

One way to sensitize children to the quality of book illustrations is to focus on the media, the materials the artist used to make the original artwork.

Several media used by artists are simple enough for even very young children to understand and may be utilized for children's own creative artwork.

**WATERCOLOR.** Watercolor is an artist's medium often used by book illustrators. An artist mixes a pigment—either in dry form or bound with gum arabic and glycerine (a water-soluble solution)—with water. The pigment may be mixed with a lot of water and washed onto the paper to create a very fluid, loose effect having flowing forms and undefined edges. Or the pigment may be mixed with very little water and applied with an almost dry brush to create a brilliant, highly controlled effect having precise edges and strong colors.

Another factor determining the final appearance of watercolor painting is the paper. Unlike painters' canvas, which has a minimal texture, or the kind of smooth papers used in fingerpainting, watercolor paper usually has a very noticeable *tooth*, or irregularity in the surface texture. High ragged peaks, resulting from the large amount of cloth incorporated in the papermaking process, catch the brush and prevent it from laying down the color smoothly, unless the watercolorist uses a great deal of water or applies the paint in a very determined manner. As a result, some of the surface area of the watercolor paper remains untouched by the brush; small flecks of white paper usually show through the color, increasing what painters call the "sparkle." The whiteness of the paper contrasts with the intensity of the watercolor, increasing the brilliance of the image.

The watercolor illustrations of several artists are well worth studying for what children can learn from them about technique. The illustrations by William Stobbs in *Greyling*, by Jane Yolen, show the effect of tooth in paper. There are many places in each illustration where the white shows through, accentuating the brilliance of the colors. Stobbs also mixes many shades of color in his illustrations. For example, the colors of the sea and rocks in the scene where the villagers watch the grey seal dive into the sea make this particular illustration as impressive as any formal watercolor painting.

Berthe Amoss uses watercolor to evoke realistically the shady recesses of the bayou in her book *Old Hasdrubal and the Pirates*. As Billy and Old Hannibal fish, the old man tells about an encounter his adventuresome grandfather Hasdrubal had with Jean Lafitte. Amoss employs the sparkle of watercolor by applying paint so that the white paper shows through. She mixes many subtle shades of color and uses soft brown ink line in a few places to help define shapes.

Watercolor is often used with ink line, which adds definition to the forms. In one watercolor illustration in *Little Tim and the Brave Sea Captain*,

***Edward Ardizzone skillfully uses crosshatching to create darker areas, giving the impression of depth.*** Illustration from *Little Tim and the Brave Sea Captain*, copyright © 1955 by the Estate of Edward Ardizzone. Permission granted by the Edward Ardizzone Estate.

Tim and the Captain survey the stormy waters from the ship's bridge just as it seems they are about to go under. Author/illustrator Edward Ardizzone uses watercolors to create the wave, the ship, and the figures themselves and ink line to further define the forms. In other illustrations in this book, it is notable how Ardizzone's use of crosshatched ink lines alone gives very sharp, well-defined images.

Sometimes an artist creates illustrations in which the color itself defines the form or the line is so incidental that it goes almost unnoticed. In Aileen Fisher's *Listen, Rabbit!*, Symeon Shimin uses soft, gentle colors to create pictures that shimmer with enchantment and require only minimal addition of line. The straw and the nest, for example, are three-dimensional forms created only with color.

Few art education textbooks recommend using watercolor with children in elementary school. Watercolor can be frustrating to work with. First, it is difficult to control because of the large amount of water in the medium. Second, if misused, watercolor can become very hard-edged and may inhibit children's creativity. Teachers can, however, incorporate watercolor into art experiences for intermediate-grade children.[1]

**WOODCUT.** Woodcut and its more recent descendant, linoleum-block printing, are media well worth children's study. The Japanese used woodcuts as early as A.D. 800 to make art prints. In addition, woodcut has a long history as a medium for book illustration.[2] As early as 1493, woodcuts were used to produce illustrations for a book entitled *Der Ritter vom Turn*, published in Switzerland.[3] These first black-and-white illustrations contrast sharply with the brilliant full-color reproductions found in current children's books. Working in linoleum is not as formidable as working in wood, which has a hard, resistant grain, so recently more artists have been using linoleum blocks, which give a finished effect very similar to woodcuts. Whether the artist works in wood or linoleum, the finished product has a recognizable "look."

When making a woodcut or linoleum block, the artist works with a surface thick enough to be cut into several different levels. First, the artist draws a design on the surface of the wood or linoleum, in reverse of the desired final effect. Using a small sharp gouge, the artist then cuts away everything except what is to be printed. (Small bits of the surface often remain outside the desired areas, giving the characteristic appearance to the print.) After cutting the design, the artist is left with a two-level block. Areas that have been cut away, and will thus not print on the paper, are deeper than the raised portions, which will print. The ink is applied to the top surface of the block with a small roller called a *brayer*. Because both the brayer and the wood have hard surfaces, the ink does not reach the

---

[1]In *Children and Their Art* (New York: Harcourt Brace Jovanovich, 1975, p. 196), Charles D. Gaitskell and Al Hurwitz maintain that experience with watercolor should follow experiences with other media that are more predictable. Muscular control and manipulative ability are necessary if watercolor is to be appealing rather than frustrating to children.

[2]Michael Rothenstein's *Linocuts and Woodcuts* (New York: Watson-Guptill, 1962) is a book for adult artists that is written clearly enough for the novice to understand. Chapters on materials and processes are liberally illustrated with many black-and-white and a few color photographs. These show details of processes involved; reproductions of linoleum-block prints and woodcuts by such artists as Pablo Picasso and Paul Gauguin are also included. Of direct use to teachers is the chapter titled "Print Methods for Schools."

[3]Henry C. Pitz's *Illustrating Children's Books* (New York: Watson-Guptill, 1963) is a handsome book intended for artists interested in illustrating for children. It includes a strong section on the history of illustrating and comprehensible sections on techniques and materials.

*The technique of wood engraving allows the artist to provide many small and precise indications of texture, as in the fur of the hare, and shape, as in the head of the flower.* From *Berry Woman's Children* by Dale DeArmond, © 1985 by Dale DeArmond. By permission of Greenwillow Books (A Division of William Morrow).

deeper, cutaway portions. The artist places a piece of paper on the inked surface and rubs, transferring the ink to the paper. After examining the print, the artist may decide to alter the image by cutting away more of the block's printing portion. Obviously, adding anything at this stage of the process is impossible.

The artist repeats the process of cutting and inking blocks and lifting prints for each color to be included in the print. Only one color, except in instances where two areas are widely separated on the block, can be printed from each block, although the artist may overlap colors to create new colors. Most block-printing inks are opaque, so mixing colors is harder to do than it is with transparent watercolors.

Many illustrators use block printing. Nonny Hogrogian, a gifted woodcut artist, employs this technique in *Hand in Hand We'll Go*, a collection of ten poems by Robert Burns. Using just four colors—brown, black, grey, and mustard yellow—she creates bold silhouette shapes, angular details, and strong patterns to augment the poems. The shapes are essentially two-dimensional, but because of the strong body positions the characters take, there is no lack of movement. Two figures—the old man and woman in "John Anderson My Jo"—for instance, make a powerful visual statement because of the contrast between their sturdy bodies and the empty spaces surrounding them.

Blair Lent provides more complex illustrations, slightly less angular than those of Nonny Hogrogian but also in limited color, for an old Japanese tale, *The Wave*, by Margaret Hodges. These illustrations are done in cardboard print, which looks much like block print. The author, a noted storyteller and children's librarian, adapted a story first brought to America in the late nineteenth century. Lent's illustrations in brown, grey, and black reflect both the initial tranquility of life in a house above a valley and the later uproar as the convoluted shape of the tidal wave gathers force and strikes the village below.

Evans G. Valens combines linoleum cuts with lift (or transfer) prints to illustrate his dramatic book *Wildfire*. Valens first transferred the grain of the wood and the design of small plant and leaf forms to paper. He applied paint to the surface of the objects, placed a piece of paper over them, and rubbed the paper to lift the design (similar to the way children do a pencil rubbing of a penny). The small animals were cut in linoleum blocks and printed in the usual manner. Many pages are printed in black and white, but some also include red and green. The full-page spreads convey the extent of the forest and the magnitude of the damage done by the fire very effectively.

Block printing is beyond the capabilities of most young children, primarily because of the danger involved in using sharp gouges to prepare the blocks. With careful instruction and close supervision, however, fifth- and sixth-grade students can create their own linoleum cuts. The action of cutting the block and the ability to make many copies of one design appeal to children.

**COLLAGE.**  The term *collage*,[4] from the French *papier collé* (meaning "glued papers"), refers to the process of attaching fragments of printed matter, colored papers, photographs, fabrics, and other materials to a solid background to make a composite picture. The desired arrangement can be sketched in pencil beforehand, or the entire creation may be spontaneous. The technique of collage was first used in 1912 by the painter Pablo Picasso, who was attempting to break from more traditional approaches to painting in vogue at the time. Since then, it has become an accepted medium for artists.

Several children's illustrators use collage. For example, Leo Lionni has created many popular books for children. In *Frederick*, his gentle story about

---

[4]*Collage* by Herta Wescher (New York: Abrams, 1968) is an exhaustive text. On every third page are full-color, full-page reproductions of collages, from early works by Georges Braque and Juan Gris to works by contemporary artists.

a mouse, Lionni uses grey torn-paper shapes with cut-paper ears and tails to depict Frederick and his friends. The large and blocky designs, spread across facing pages, are simple but effective.

Another well-known collage illustrator was Ezra Jack Keats, whose *The Snowy Day* won a Caldecott Medal (see Chapter 1). Bold shapes and interesting surface textures characterize this innovative book, which pioneered in the portrayal of black children in natural settings (Hopkins, 1983). Keats also used collage in the minimal but pleasant story of *Jennie's Hat*. (See Plate C in the color section.) Endpapers with an intricate design introduce Jennie, whose dress is of the same material. Birds decorate her plain hat with a variety of printed papers, painted shapes, leaf-vein forms, and Victorian cutouts of flowers, hearts, and photographs, turning it into a "garment of brightness" (Lanes, 1984).

Eric Carle uses transparent tissue papers, lightly streaked with paint, to form collages for his counting book *1, 2, 3 To the Zoo*. It features brightly colored creatures transported by minimal train cars. The lions are suitably fearsome, the crocodiles flash their teeth, and the monkeys' curved tails intertwine in Carle's sharp-edged collages. In George Mendoza's *The Scarecrow Clock*, Carle again uses tissue papers streaked with paint to illustrate a story about a scarecrow, a wobbly ant, a rock spider, a sprightly grasshopper, a windup mouse, and other imaginatively described animals. The bodies of the scarecrow and the animals are rendered in vibrant shades of transparent color that overlap in interesting ways. Carle combines his familiar full-color collage with paper engineering in *The Honeybee and the Robber*. On each page, there is something that moves. In the center of the book is the most spectacular display—a butterfly with opened wings that springs up when the pages are spread. Though the story itself is fiction, Carle provides two pages of factual information about honeybees inside the back cover.

Young children enjoy the tactile experience of arranging bits of fabric, ribbon, paper, cardboard, etc. on paper to create their own collages. Junior high school students may enjoy creating *montages*, combinations containin only photographs.

**FABRIC.** It is not common for artists to use fabric as the major element in their pictures. One artist who does use fabric effectively is Edda Reinl, who works in *batik*, a Javanese hot-wax resist technique that involves painting designs with wax and dying the fabric in several stages. Her book *The Three Little Pigs* is a swirl of color. The opening endpapers feature dancing pigs that are appealing without being cloying; the concluding endpapers feature the decorative designs of the pigs' houses. On the pages in between, Reinl uses batik impressively: each picture is exuberant and filled with details that add to the total effect rather than calling attention to themselves. The artist's palette ranges from the warm yellow/orange/red range used most often in depicting the pigs to the chilly blue/green/purple combination used in showing the fearsome wolf as he stalks his quarry, huffs at their house, and finally explodes startlingly. An equally effective gathering of jewellike colors and designs by the same author/illustrator is found in *The Little Snake*. The text is a retelling of a nature myth and is less impressive than the illustrations. Even though the pictures for the most part simply illustrate and do not expand or extend the text in significant ways, the colors are so joyous and the partitioning of space is so effective that the book is a delight.

**STONE LITHOGRAPHY.** *Lithography,* a term derived from the Greek word *lithos* (meaning "stone"), is a technique devised by the Bavarian dramatist Senefelder in 1798. The artist draws with a greasy crayon on the smooth surface of a heavy limestone slab. The stone is then treated with a mixture of gum arabic and nitric acid, which eats away areas not protected by the crayon. When the stone is inked, the ink sticks only to areas containing grease deposits from the original drawing. The artist places paper on the inked stone and forces both through a press, transferring ink from the stone to the paper. The process is both strenuous and messy, and therefore few artists use it. Though artists can now use lighter-weight materials such as zinc and aluminum, many printmakers still savor the older slabs of limestone.

Among the best-known lithographers are Ingri and Edgar Parin d'Aulaire, who used this medium in many large books—including their *Book of Greek Myths*, *Norse Gods and Giants*, and *d'Aulaires' Trolls*—which alternate monochrome with full-color lithographs. Another author/illustrator who uses lithography is Robert McCloskey, winner of a Caldecott Medal for *Make Way for Ducklings*. Reproduced in soft brown, his illustrations show the casual, sketchy, and grainy quality of lithographs.

Lynd Ward creates realistic lithographic character studies in two books by his wife, May McNeer. In *The Canadian Story*, he depicts the rugged strength of the Indian, French, English, and Eskimo people who shaped the Canadian frontiers. In a companion book, *The Mexican Story*, Ward's illustrations are similar lithographs but their colors are harsher and less interesting. Felix Hoffman also uses lithography to portray people in two traditional tales by the Brothers Grimm, but his work is very different from that of Ward. Hoffman creates historically clothed wisewomen, among others, in retelling *The Sleeping Beauty;* the figures advance the story but never become the highly individualized people represented in lithographs

*Few picture book artists use the technique of etching, in which the design is formed when part of a metal plate is eaten away by acid.* Reprinted with permission of Macmillan Publishing Company from *About Wise Men and Simpletons* by Elizabeth Shub, illustrated by Nonny Hogrogian. Illustration copyright © 1971 by Nonny Hogrogian.

by Ward. Hoffman also illustrated *The Seven Ravens*, about a brave little girl who sets out alone to free her brothers from imprisonment as birds.

**PHOTOGRAPHY.** An increasing number of children's books are being published with photographs as illustrations.[5] Like other photographers, those who illustrate books for children often prefer to work in black and white, because they believe that color can be a distraction from the dramatic quality of an image.

Tana Hoban is one well-known photographer whose work helps children see the drama in everyday objects. In *Push-Pull Empty-Full*, her photos of children, objects, animals, and birds illustrate a book of antonyms for young readers. Clear black-and-white photographs of contrasting concepts (up/

---

[5]An interesting comparison of photography versus illustrations can be made using the live-action film version of *Paddle to the Sea* (National Film Board of Canada) with the book of the same name by Holling C. Holling (Boston: Houghton Mifflin, 1941), which contains full-color paintings.

down, front/back) face each other across double-page spreads. The photographs catch every wrinkle, blemish, light, and shadow and thus bring out details people often miss when looking at well-known objects.[6] In *Shapes and Things*, Hoban uses *photograms*, shadowlike photographs made by placing objects between light-sensitive paper and a light source. The technique yields a high-contrast outline with no interior details.

Recently, Hoban has moved into color photography. *Is It Rough? Is It Smooth? Is It Shiny?* presents full-page, full-color photographs of, for the most part, single objects evoking a sensory response. A child's hand holding pennies is shot so close up that the many fine creases in the palm form an interesting contrast to the metallic, lettered coins. The photo of a girl in a foil costume contrasts that texture with the softer texture of the girl's hair, and the grainy texture of the pillar against which she leans. *A Children's Zoo*, by Hoban, is even more elegantly produced. Black high-gloss pages contrast vibrantly with stark white lowercase letters, which spell out two adjectives and a verb. These words are in the upper right-hand corner of the page; in the middle, in the same typeface but in all capital letters, the animal's name is given. On the facing page is a single photograph of the animal, bordered in white and set on black.

Photographs by George Ancona have an impressive, direct honesty. In *Faces*, a book by Barbara Brenner, the minimal text calls attention to the wonder of a face and what it can do. Ancona's black-and-white photographs—including both closeups and longer shots—are the most interesting part of the book.

Shirley Glubok, an artist who has earned respect for her impressive series of books on the art of various cultures, has often used black-and-white photography not to interpret but to record with clarity. *The Art of the Vikings* is typical of Glubok's high-quality photography and tasteful design. In *The Art of Photography*, Glubok turns her attention to the art of "writing with light," to make a permanent image. The first photograph included is from 1837 and the last from 1961, though the majority of those featured are from the earlier years considered. Glubok's usual stylish production prevails in this volume from cover to cover. The binding contrasts pale beige with warm brown, in a vertically divided, off-center arrangement featuring a particularly distinctive sans serif lettering in black. The endpapers show

---

[6]A teacher working on antonyms with her or his class might use Hoban's book in conjunction with one by John Burningham called *Opposites*. Burningham's book features a single word on each page accompanied by a watercolor and crayon drawing. For example, one left-hand page shows a small boy pushing a hippopotamus uphill in a wicker vehicle, and the facing right-hand page shows him pulling a pair of cows uphill.

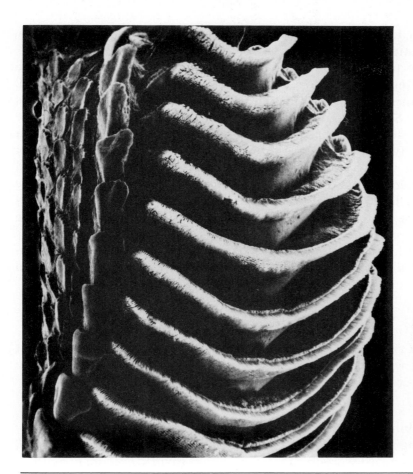

*This black-and-white photograph was shot at such close range that it presents a totally mystifying (but intriguing) view of an unfamiliar object—the underside of a gecko's toe (the gecko is a southeast Asian climbing lizard).* From Lisa Grillone and Joseph F. Gennaro, *Small Worlds Close Up*, Crown Publishers, Inc., 1978.

Eadweard Muybridge's horse-and-rider studies, which represented a major breakthrough in photographic technique. This innovative photographer is described in a double-page spread, as are more than sixteen other important photographers, such as Alfred Steiglitz and Edward Steichen. There is never more than one photograph on each generous (nearly 10 inches square) page; as a result, all the photos are large enough to show details clearly.

*Small Worlds Close Up,* by Lisa Grillone and Joseph Gennaro, is an effort to make viewers more aware of their environment. The book is illustrated with pictures taken with a scanning electron microscope (in which an electron gun bombards an object with a thin stream of millions of electrons). These *micrographs,* as they are called, are arranged in three categories: animal, vegetable, and mineral. A brief explanatory paragraph introduces each section, followed by closeup views of common objects (such as needles, hair, and cotton) and less common objects (such as dolphin skin, an opal, and a xylem tube). The dramatic black-and-white micrographs are captivating, causing the viewer to marvel anew at objects in the everyday world.

Sometimes photography is used with other media to add interest, as in *The Secret Seller* by Betty Jean Lifton. Black-and-white, almost full-page photographs introduce the story of Ken, an upper-class child living in a New York City apartment across from Central Park. Ken wants a secret of his very own. One day he encounters the secret seller on a park bench, and from that point the book bursts with brilliant, full-color paintings, as the minuscule seller with a mushroom-shaped hat shows Ken the many small delights of the world around him. These imaginative illustrations by Eugene Delessert are crammed with fanciful designs.

Information concerning other books that contain photographs is included in Paulin (1982), in a compendium that is descriptive rather than evaluative.

## STUDYING VISUAL ELEMENTS

Any work of art, whether it is the most delicate of watercolors or the most dramatic of woodcuts, uses at least one of the following visual elements: shape, line, color, proportion, detail and space (Harlan, 1970).

**SHAPE.**   Any artist will pay attention, either consciously or subconsciously, to the possibilities inherent in shape.[7] Shapes may be flat and two-dimensional, giving no impression of thickness or substance, as in *Curl Up Small* by Sandol Stoddard Warburg. This is a pleasant rhymed account of mothers relating to their babies. A prolific illustrator and Caldecott Medal winner, Trina Schart Hyman, painted the shapes in soft watercolors—browns and greens with some yellow accents. Even though they are two-dimensional, the shapes of the pointy mother bird, the blocky mother bear, and the rounded human mother are effective.

In *Clocks and More Clocks*, Pat Hutchins provides the same type of flat shapes, but dressed in brighter colors and decorated with black line. Be-

---

[7]A helpful book for introducing the concept of shapes—what they are and where they are found in nature—is Ed Emberley's *The Wing on a Flea* (Boston: Little, Brown, 1961). Two other useful books are Karen Gundersheimer's *Shapes to Show*, a small, mice-inhabited volume with just a word on each page (New York: Harper and Row, 1986), and Leonard Everett Fisher's *Look Around!* (New York: Viking/Kestrel, 1987), which has the kind of full-color paintings this artist has been doing recently.

fuddled Mr. Higgins, whose determination to know the right time leads him into a frenzy, inhabits a flat world of orange, green, yellow, and brown shades. The decorative patterns enhance the essentially two-dimensional landscape.

In contrast, an artist might create fully rounded shapes, which give an impression of three-dimensional substance and weight, usually because the artist made them look rounded through shading. C. W. Anderson provides very realistic horse drawings in his *Complete Book of Horses and Horsemanship*. Many different kinds of horses, seen from a variety of angles and in various positions, are meticulously drawn and defined with line. This artist, who completely understands the body structure of horses, creates shading through a buildup of small strokes. We see the lift of an ear, the droop of an eyelid, and the ripple of a cord in a neck because of the artist's skill. All of these details, however, are successfully subordinated to the total impression.

Realistic human shapes are found in the illustrations Trina Schart Hyman did for *Rapunzel*, written by Barbara Rogasky. Because of her thorough understanding of the underlying anatomy of the human figure, Hyman's people are always convincingly three-dimensional. They come to life on the two-dimensional page as they move through the deep space in which she places them. We sense, for example, the depth of a built-in bedchamber because of the realism of the two people she shows inhabiting this space.

**LINE.** Line is another element artists employ in various ways to achieve a final effect. Line may be a thin, barely perceived whisper to enhance subtle color. Or it may be a heavy, dark stroke to boldly define forms and create shapes. Line may be regular, maintaining the same form throughout a book, without variation. Or it may be flexible and fluid, varying from thick to thin.

An unvaryingly thin line may have an elegant quality, and a precise yet flowing line can not only outline form but also create mass without the use of color. In *The Aeneid for Boys and Girls*, by Alfred Church, artist Eugene Karlin provides a detailed, self-assured line that creates shapes with the precision of an etching.

Steven Kellogg uses a spidery, black line with a variety of crosshatchings and dots to evoke the unreal, the bizarre, and the eccentric in *Gwot! Horribly Funny Hairticklers*, written by George Mendoza. Kellogg's drawings of the scrawny farmer with fiendish eyes, the squatty old lady with a voracious appetite, and the cross-eyed, taloned Gumberoo echo the macabre short stories.

*James Stevenson's fluent line doesn't vary much in thickness. The forms are pulled into sharp focus in his cartoonlike style.* From *Worse Than Willy* by James Stevenson, © 1984 by James Stevenson. By permission of Greenwillow Books (A Division of William Morrow).

Edward Gorey uses another kind of thin line to create his easily recognizable drawings in *The House with a Clock in Its Walls*, by John Bellairs. This fantasy features a haunted house with a ticking clock counting the hours to doomsday. Crosshatched black line creates placid, fusty creatures who seem unaware of what may happen to them. The artist presents assorted textures and patterns of light and dark, and a shallow sense of space.

A very energetic line pervades the work of James Stevenson. For example, *Worse Than Willy* and other books form a series about Grandpa—in his current form as an elderly man and in his amusing childhood personification (also replete with mustache!). Stevenson's line is everywhere, leading to a "super-charged, frenetic cartoon-like" quality, recommended by Richard and MacCann (1984) as a particularly effective example of this kind of line.

In *The Two Reds*, by William Lipkind and Nicholas Mordinoff, robust line crams the page with energetic detail. The pictures spill off the edges of the pages in this story of a small boy and a cat named Mr. Furpatto Purrcatto. Intense reds and yellow are splashed here and there; sometimes the color defines a form, and at other times it only lands generally in the area of the character. This use of color, only generally contained within the lines, is similar to the French painter Raoul Dufy's technique.

For further discussion of line, see the article by Moebius (1986), which considers a variety of visual codes found in picture books.

*This full-page picture vibrates with highly saturated color, and energetic patterns are juxtaposed.* From *Parade* by Donald Crews, © 1983 by Donald Crews. By permission of Greenwillow Books (A Division of William Morrow).

**COLOR.** Some artists prefer to work within the limited range offered by black and white (including intermediate shades of gray). In *The Garden of Abdul Gasazi*, a Caldecott honor book by Chris Van Allsburg, we see this subtle palette used to impressive effect. When asked by Miss Hunter to care for her incorrigible dog, Alan tries his best, but only the retired magician Abdul Gasazi is able to outwit the small, peevish creature, who bites everything. Van Allsburg creates a surreal world where illusion blends into reality. His pencil illustrations are realistic, and he uses light, shadow, and perspective to evoke strong impressions of space and density.

Many artists work with a broader spectrum of color than just the shades available from black and white. An artist may use just one or two subtle hues to underlie or understate an idea. This is apparent in the ink-line illustrations done by William Wiesner for *The Gunniwolf*, by Wilhelmina Harper. Wiesner's simple aqua and orange washes modestly complement his ink drawings for this tale of a little girl living next to a dense jungle.

Donald Crews's *Parade*, which won an IRA Children's Choice Award, shows how effective high-intensity, saturated color can be when printed on a shiny, clay-coated paper. Crews provides flat, decorative shapes that serve as symbols for the people and objects he is portraying. The complete array of colors he uses is more effective than words would be in capturing the excitement of the outdoor, public event of a parade.

Another example of color use is the restrained, highly sophisticated technique of concentrating on two or more unusual shades. Barbara Cooney uses color this way in her illustrations for William Wise's humorous rhymed account titled *The Lazy Young Duke of Dundee*. Cooney uses shades of blue-green for the duke and his family and magenta for the attacking MacClane and his horde. To complete her palette, she adds grey and some small accents of yellow. Even more restricted color use appears in the illustrations for Joseph Jacobs's retelling of an old tale, *The Buried Moon*. Susan Jeffers limited her palette to purple, lavender, beige, and black to illustrate this complex fantasy in which the moon is trapped by the Quicks and Bogles and Things that dwell in the bog. The evil qualities of these beings are well depicted, and the flowing black line augments the somber pages.

Fionna French, author/illustrator of *The Blue Bird*, places figures and other elements formally in her pictures, balancing areas of pattern with large plain areas. The only color other than blue is the peach and yellow of the main character's gown. After the denouement, the pictures burst into color. The pattern becomes more enveloping and the illustration on the last page is reminiscent of the pattern-packed paintings of the French painter Henri Matisse.[8] (For another comment about French's work, see the annotation on the Hannabuss article in "Related Reading for Adults" at the end of this chapter.)

The use of color may be highly realistic when the artist wants to create a natural effect. Master watercolorist Robert McCloskey used color to this effect in pictures for *Time of Wonder*, his Caldecott Medal–winning book depicting weather changes. McCloskey's color varies from the crisply contrasting blues and greens of a bright early morning through the deep-hued blacks, blues, and purples of a storm at its height. Although the shapes themselves are not clearly defined and the brush line adds few details, the color creates the desired realism.

An artist may make use of arbitrary color that does not depict objects naturally. In *The Christmas Birthday Story*, by Helen Lucas, for example, abstract line drawings are highlighted with large, simplified blocks of color, which divide the page into segments, rather than coloring in particular parts of the drawing. The handsome result is art as surely as is any literal representation.

**PROPORTION.** Proportion in illustrations may be highly realistic: parts of bodies are shown in correct relation to the whole body, and objects are kept

---

[8]When intermediate-grade children are studying hue (pure color), tint (varied by adding white to a color), and shade (varied by adding black to a color), they might try creating a painting using just tints and shades of one hue the way the artist did in this book.

*In many subtle shades of gray, artist Charles Mikolaycak creates his usual finely rendered, realistic depiction of a person and an environment.* Reprinted with permission of Macmillan Publishing Company from *The Cobbler's Reward* by Barbara Reid and Ewa Reid, illustrated by Charles Mikolaycak. Illustration copyright © 1978 by Charles Mikolaycak.

in accurate scale relative to the environment. Charles Mikolaycak is one artist whose work is stronger because of the absolute accuracy of his proportions, yet the imagination in his illustrations far transcends simple accuracy. Several of his books have been honored by the American Institute of Graphic Artists. His pictures for *The Cobbler's Reward*, by Barbara and Ewa Reid, are typical of his draftsmanship. Whether portraying the handsome, young cobbler or the fat, old peasant woman, Mikolaycak is equally at home, using realistic proportions to create scenes we find believable despite the fantasy elements in the story itself.

On the other hand, artists may exaggerate proportion to create funny or fantastic effects. An example is the exaggerated forms created by Dennis Lyall for a modern tall tale, *So You Shouldn't Waste a Rhinoceros* by Nathan Zimmelman. Lyall exaggerates the amount of hair on the characters' heads, the roundness of their body shapes, and the bend in their spines. He also exaggerates size—a huge, green telephone sprawls across a double-page spread, a soap-bubble pipe stretches to the size of a head, and a soap bubble with one of the characters inside becomes as big as a standing police officer.

Dr. Seuss, a favorite with children, often uses exaggerated proportions to create humor in his drawings. Seuss's color is unexceptional, and his line is for the most part uninteresting. As can be seen in *One fish two fish red fish blue fish*, Seuss takes proportions beyond realism in the convoluted horns of the Gack, the funny roundness of Joe's body, or the comical sway-back of the cow.

**DETAIL.** Artists may also vary the amount of detail to create desired effects. A cluttered illustration, straining against its borders, with objects literally packed in, can be used to reflect the state of mind of one of the characters or to comment on a crowded plot. The illustrations for Mary Norton's *Borrowers Aloft* were created by artists Beth and Joe Krush to evoke the tiny world of the Clock family. The detail-packed drawings executed in thin black line show every shingle on the roof, every brick in the chimney, and every leaf on the tree.

In contrast, illustrations with relatively few details are appropriate for characters who lead a calm life or for peaceful, ordered environments. Horizontal bands in soft shades of blue and green lead the reader on in Uri Shulevitz's *Dawn*. The artist begins the story with a soft-edged oval shape that increases in size and includes more and more objects until finally becoming a verdant image of the world turning green as sunrise hits a lake.

Where an artist places the detail may also be of interest, such as in *The Girl Who Loved the Wind*, by Jane Yolen. Ed Young, a native of China, uses watercolor and collage, arranging the details in various places. Pages that have much detail alternate with pages that have large plain spaces to provide needed balance. Even on the title page, space is broken up geometrically and pattern relegated to only one part of the design. The formal placement of the text and illustrations within a wide gold band emphasizes the story's formal nature.

Sometimes the amount of detail increases gradually to add emphasis to the story line, as in *An Invitation to the Butterfly Ball*, a counting rhyme by Jane Yolen. The artist, Jane Breskin Zalben, adds objects and animals page by page, from one mouse looking for a floor-length dress to ten porcupines disagreeing over a velvet evening jacket, until the last page where all the animals arrive at the ball.

**SPACE.** Finally, artists may manipulate space in a variety of ways. Some artists use a flat plane in their pictures, providing no sense of a third dimension. Janet McCaffery's imaginative two-dimensional illustrations in Mary Calhoun's *The Witch of Hissing Hill* combine cut and torn paper shapes, crayon lines, and overlapping transparent papers to establish a two-dimensional environment for Sizzle, a wicked old witch. On the other hand,

*Often an artist enhances the viewer's sense of space by employing an unusual point of view. In this case, looking down upon the scene makes the space seem more real.* Reprinted with permission of Macmillan Publishing Company from *A Country Tale* by Diane Stanley. Copyright © 1985 by Diane Stanley Vennema.

some artists arrange three-dimensional objects in perspective, one behind another, to give the impression of deep space. In *The Brook*, by Carol and Donald Carrick, watercolor, ink-line, and charcoal drawings encourage the reader to wander visually among the trees, all the way back toward high rocks in the distance.

Most artists probably do not think consciously about these six elements—shape, line, color, proportion, detail, and space—when planning and executing illustrations. However, examining each of these elements separately can help children appreciate the artist's skill in creating a final effect.

# THE INFLUENCE OF ART MOVEMENTS

Understanding the effect of artistic antecedents on book illustration can enhance children's appreciation of illustrations. Many ideas, techniques, and themes of painting have been incorporated into book illustration.[9]

All art forms a continuous flow, a largely unbroken stream of influences and followers. Techniques and concepts artists use today will lead to new techniques and concepts for future artists. A group of German painters working near the end of the nineteenth century can be lumped together and called expressionists, and we can study the phenomenon of expressionism. But the work of the expressionists didn't exist in a vacuum; it grew out of the movements that went before and it led into the movements that followed. Teachers can help children sense this flow by pointing out the links that exist between art movements and the art in children's books.

## IMPRESSIONISM

Impressionism, an art movement centered in France between 1860 and 1920, probably had more effect on more artists than any other single art movement (Gaunt, 1970). Exemplified by such widely known painters as Claude Monet (1840–1926) and Auguste Renoir (1841–1919), impressionism influences painting and book illustration even today. Impressionism was revolutionary, growing up largely as a reaction against the conventional art of that time. Impressionists were rebelling against the naturalistic style of such artists as Camille Corot (1796–1875), who painted landscapes in realistic colors. The work of the impressionists bursts with unmixed color and with unusual subjects. These artists were concerned with the changing effect of light on surfaces at different times of day and under different atmospheric conditions. They used anything for subject matter, and their asymmetrical compositions presented an unusual view of temporary events. A fine, though brief, explanation of impressionism intended for children is given by Marshall B. Davidson in *A History of Art*.

Nonny Hogrogian, although known for her woodcuts, has also worked in an impressionistic manner. In her book *Apples*, she uses light, bright crayon colors in a pleasantly hazy rendition of objects and the environment.

---

[9]Marlene Linderman, *Art in the Elementary School* (Dubuque, Iowa: William C. Brown, 1979), pp. 53–68. One section, "Teaching Art Heritage in the Elementary Classroom," presents a rationale for sharing art with children and accounts by teachers of specific techniques for encouraging children to look at and talk about art.

The strokes of several different shades of color define the forms, rather than line.

Maurice Sendak prepared as beautiful an example of impressionism in children's literature as any in his illustrations for the gentle story of *Mr. Rabbit and the Lovely Present*, by Charlotte Zolotow. Using soft, wonderfully varied shades of watercolor, Sendak creates a pastoral environment. The muted blues, greens, and purples in the illustration showing the main characters standing at the edge of a lake are evidence of a gentle approach to watercolor that is characteristic of impressionism. The work may be overshadowed by some of Sendak's later, better-known books, but it is among the very best of his work in this style.

## POINTILLISM

The pointillists, also called neoimpressionists, carried the idea of placing strokes of pure color side by side as far as it could go without the subject's disappearing entirely. They broke up large surfaces into countless small, separate dots (or points) of complementary color—a tedious, time-consuming process. The viewer's eye mixes these colors visually. Pointillism attracted few followers. The best known were Georges Seurat (1859–1891) and his student Paul Signac (1863–1935). Interest in pointillism waned after Signac died. Book illustrators do occasionally use the technique, however.

Children will enjoy the opportunity to learn about the paintings of Seurat, many of which are splendidly reproduced in a book for adults by Fry (1965). Seurat's best-known painting, *La Grande Jatte*, is a precisely organized, solidly planned composition depicting the afternoon excursion of a great number of people. These solid citizens, so weightily arrayed, seem like figures carved of wood. The close-ups in the book of this and other paintings show the thousands of tiny color daubs Seurat used to create the images. Signac's work is available in a book for adults by Cachin (1971). Though these books are for adults, children will enjoy their large, full-color reproductions.

Although few illustrators today use pointillist techniques to any great extent, many do use small dots of color to build up form. On the "r is for rain" page of *Gyo Fujikawa's A to Z Picture Book*, the author/illustrator uses many round dots of different shades of green and brown to suggest, rather than literally depict, the tree leaves.

Ellen Raskin modified the pointillist technique by using black dots in *Spectacles*, a humorous account of the problems Iris Fogel has because she resists wearing glasses. The author/illustrator, generally acknowledged as one of the best illustrators for children, alternates full-color pages with others featuring only black-ink pointillist designs made up of thousands of tiny dots. For example, the giant pigmy nuthatch on Iris's front lawn, depicted in black dots on a solid green background, turns out—in full color on the next page—to be Iris's good friend Chester.

Author/illustrator Rachel Isadora, in *City Seen from A to Z*, incorporates pointillist techniques in black-and-white drawings depicting the many environments and inhabitants of an urban area. Some of the drawings are richly complex, and others are interestingly spare. For example, the "p" (for pigeon) page provides many people, buildings, and objects to study, all done in myriad tiny black and white dots, but the "h" (for hat) page is dramatically understated, with no background at all. Throughout the book, Isadora presents fully rounded, three-dimensional forms, created as the dots converge to create shadows. (See the reproduction of one of her illustrations in Chapter 3, page 111.)

## LES FAUVES

Following in the footsteps of Vincent Van Gogh and Paul Gauguin, some painters achieved eminence as part of a French group called *les fauves* (di San Lazzaro, 1971). This name translates as "wild beasts," and art critics used it scornfully to reject paintings these artists submitted to an important exhibit in 1905. Today, the label is neutral and simply describes a group whose works share certain visual similarities, as well as a stylistic verve that incorporates lively linear effects and boldly clashing colors.

Georges Roualt (1871–1958) was one of the best known of *les fauves* but used a more somber palette than the others. The most distinctive characteristic of his paintings is the heavy black lines that enclose each color area. These lines and the austere forms create an effect much like stained glass, a craft Roualt pursued as a young man.

John Steptoe, some of whose work is similar to Roualt's, is a contemporary illustrator for children. A young black man, Steptoe has written realistic stories about black children and illustrated them in vibrant shades of color separated into areas by heavy black line. *Stevie* is the universally appealing story of a young child who feels displaced when a younger child comes to stay in his home. The book has been praised by Tremper (1979/1980) for the authenticity of its Black English. The illustrations are done in brilliant chalk, with one color skillfully layered over the one below to increase the intensity of both. In *Uptown*, two boys contemplate what they will be when they grow up. *Train Ride* tells of four adventuresome boys who find that sneaking onto a train is not an unalloyed joy. The illustrations in *Uptown* and *Train Ride* are done in opaque watercolor. In addition to black line, Steptoe skillfully uses applied white. For example, in *Train Ride*, the decorative use of white smudges to depict the lights of movie marquees in one illustration contrasts starkly and yet pleasingly with the darker color range of the background. Steptoe's more recent work has taken a different direction visually; for an example, see page 143.

In Fiona French's *City of Gold*, the stiff figures with stylized faces, done in brilliant color and outlined heavily in black, recall the stained-glass windows that influenced Roualt's work. Author/illustrator French uses brighter colors than Steptoe does and mixes them less frequently.

## FOLK ART

Unlike formal art movements, whose originators were localized in a particular time or place, folk art is the naive, unselfconscious creations of untrained artists of any time or place. These people, often engaged in other work to earn a living, paint because they feel impelled to express themselves in this way. Folk art is often characterized by imaginative use of color, repeated stylized patterns, lack of perspective, and simple, childlike forms.

Henri Rousseau (1844–1910) is a striking example of a self-taught artist who painted because he felt compelled to (Vallier, 1964). Unschooled in formal approaches to painting, Rousseau used strong lines to fill his canvases of jungle scenes with wildly imaginative plant forms and animals. His flat patterns evoke an unworldly but appealing landscape in which all natural detail is subordinate.

Rousseau-like patterning is evident in the illustration for the "l is for lullaby" page in *Gyo Fujikawa's A to Z Picture Book*. The artist used basic plant forms and, by accenting the curves and repeated aspects of their lines, made a pattern that is more a symbol for the plants than a realistic representation.

Margot Zemach's illustrations for a variation of an old Swedish tale, *Nail Soup*, by Harve Zemach, capture the quality of folk art. Zemach's humorous ink and wash drawings show a squatty tramp and a rotund old lady, whose tiny house is stuffed with hidden food. Using only watercolor shades of brown, gold, and pink and applying them loosely, the artist creates charming peasant patterns on the clothes of the lady and the tramp. The black outline of the trees and the lack of perspective in the house add to the folk-art quality.

Lester Abrams created decorative patterns in his illustrations for *The Four Donkeys*, by Lloyd Alexander. These patterned pastel illustrations successfully evoke a different time and place. Abrams also added many unusual, unsymmetrical borders made up of repeated decorative patterns in related

*The flat, patterned shapes and lack of any attempt to create depth in this painting mark it as folk art, as does the fact that all the elements of the scene are given equal importance.* Illustration from *My Little Island* by Frane Lessac (J. B. Lippincott). Copyright © 1984 by Frane Lessac. Reprinted by permission of Harper & Row, Publishers, Inc.

colors; Whalen-Levitt (1986) believes these borders to be so significant artistically that she analyzes them at length.

Brightly colored, highly simplified decorative shapes abound in *My Little Island*, by Frane Lessac. This book tells of the visit of the narrator and his best friend to the little Caribbean island on which the narrator was born. The figures are all two-dimensional; the patterns in the clothes they wear are delightful. The waves in the water, leaves on the trees, scales on the fish—all show a similarity to the works of the American primitive painter Grandma Moses.

*Flat geometric shapes in highly saturated colors create a two-dimensional world; Leonard Weisgard manipulates patterns for the decorative effect.* Illustration from *The Noisy Book* by Margaret Wise Brown. Illustrated by Leonard Weisgard. Copyright © 1939 by Margaret Wise Brown. Renewed 1967 by Roberta Brown Rauch. Reprinted by permission of Harper & Row, Publishers, Inc.

The paintings of Mattie Lou O'Kelley in *From the Hills of Georgia* and *Circus* also present flat, decorative patterns, which are delightful for their own sake, rather than for any attempt to represent the world realistically. In both books, the text simply serves to string the pictures together, but O'Kelley's folk art—especially the richly luminous night scenes—will quickly engage children's attention.

## ABSTRACTIONISM

Stuart Davis (1884–1964) was an American painter who painted so abstractly that the shapes of objects become more important than their details. Davis's colorful landscapes juxtapose flat but lively patterns against other patterns (Goosen, 1959).

An artist who works in a style reminiscent of Davis's is American illustrator Leonard Weisgard. For both *The Noisy Book* and *The Winter Noisy Book*, by Margaret Wise Brown, Weisgard painted bold blocks of solid, unshaded colors. He uses these blocks of color to create illustrations that stand for but do not realistically depict his subject matter. In the two cityscapes in *The Noisy Book*, solid orange, light blue, yellow, and black geometric shapes represent buildings. These bold abstractions capture the essence of the buildings without showing details. Individual details are eliminated or made into patterns that are subordinated to the overall design of the page. In the same way, the artist abstractly portrays fathers coming home in *The Winter Noisy Book*. These two books, with their fine abstract illustrations, were introduced during the 1940s, when most books were firmly anchored in the realistic representational style.

Similar to Weisgard's work are illustrations by Marcia Brown, an artist whose work has been characterized by continuous experimentation in various styles and mediums. In her *Henry—Fisherman*, Brown creates pleasant, abstract forms that tell a tale of a young boy growing up in the Caribbean. Though Stuart Davis portrayed a different geographic area, the visual similarities between his work and Brown's are impressive. A teacher might share Brown's book with students and then present reproductions of Davis's work, encouraging the children to notice how they are alike.

A kinetic energy similar to that found in Stuart Davis's paintings is evident in *Little Chicks' Mothers and All the Others*, by Mildred Luton. The handsome endpapers feature strong geometric patterns in highly saturated colors that vibrate against one another. The animals inside the book are equally intense: the curved line of the goat, the straight lines of the horse's blanket, and the teardrop-shaped feathers on the chicken are juxtaposed to produce a greater intensity than any of the patterns would have by itself. The effect is further intensified by the latticelike patterns that border the pages. The rhyming text facing the full-page illustrations has less impact than the visual qualities of the pictures.

A rather sophisticated book, both visually and textually, is *Sun Moon Star*, written by Kurt Vonnegut and illustrated by Ivan Chermayeff. This handsomely produced oversized volume has a black linen cover, stamped in gold, silver, and black, that opens to reveal black endpapers with an impressive heft. Inside, the glossy, coated paper sets off the highly saturated colors used by Chermayeff, who made the pictures before Vonnegut wrote the words. *Sun Moon Star* is one of a small number of books described by Dressel (1984), who examines the appropriateness of abstract art for young children. It is often asserted that abstract art is inappropriate for children, but Dressel believes that they can indeed deal with abstraction, but "in a concrete way."

## SURREALISM

Surrealists juxtapose contrasting realistic elements to create a vague, dreamlike world of surprises; their paintings are usually puzzling and sometimes shocking. The imaginative qualities of such paintings do not appeal to viewers who want to feel firmly grounded in reality.

A Spanish painter, Salvador Dali (b. 1904) is undoubtedly the best-

*The luminous, jewellike colors are enriched by the contrast with black. The flatness of the buildings and the unexpectedly large size of the cat add to the surrealistic effect.* Illustration from *The Moon Jumpers* by Janice May Udry. Illustration by Maurice Sendak. Illustration copyright © 1959 Maurice Sendak. Reprinted by permission of Harper & Row, Publishers, Inc.

known surrealist. Although his paintings are seminal to the surrealist movement, the work of another Spaniard, Joan Miró (1893–1983), and that of the Swiss painter Paul Klee (1879–1940) hold more appeal for children. A book written for adults about Miró by Rowell (1970) and one about Klee by Grohmann (1967) could be used to introduce boys and girls to surrealism. Clark (1986) wrote about Klee for children in one of a series of articles on art that appear regularly in the magazine *Highlights for Children*.

Surrealism has not had an extensive impact on children's book illustration, though sometimes surrealistic elements appear in books of fantasy. An interesting example is *The Moon Jumpers*, by Janice Udry. Pictures by Maurice Sendak set a surreal mood, as on the title page, which features a cat that is as big as the house. Framed by sunflowers, his tail tightly encircling a moon, the cat stares with unequal almond-shaped eyes at the reader. In full-color, double-page spreads, Sendak creates an eerie, otherworldly environment, using the sharp contrast between rich deep purples and blues and the light cast by the moon. Such intense *chiaroscuro*[10] is not common in children's books but is a usual feature in surrealistic paintings. The recurring figure of the cat, in one case peering from the crotch of a tree, is reminiscent of the Chesire cat in *Alice in Wonderland*. This book represents Sendak's finest work in surrealistic interpretation, but, like his work in *Mr.*

---

[10]*Chiaroscuro* is the intensification of light and dark in a painting to provide greater contrast.

*Rabbit and the Lovely Present*, it has been overshadowed by his more popular books.

*Story Number 4*, by the absurdist playwright Eugene Ionesco, tells of an inquisitive little girl, who searches for her father under the kitchen table and other peculiar places. Illustrations by Jean-Michel Nicollett are as strange and otherworldly as the almost plotless tale about a father who wants to elude his daughter while he gets ready to go to work. The illustrations are modestly in the tradition of Salvador Dali—not as complex but equally surreal. What is real and what is a dream is not resolved either in the illustrations or in the story. Another story by Ionesco that also moves from dreamlike states to apparent reality and back again is *Story Number 1*, which has illustrations by Etienne Delessert designed for children under three (according to the author).

Recently, Henrik Drescher has incorporated a feeling of surrealism in his *Look-Alikes*, which chronicles one unexplainable happening after another, beginning when a boy and his obstreperous monkey flee the dinner table for the treehouse. In the treehouse, they play with toy look-alikes that suddenly run across the lawn and up to the treehouse, just as Rudy and Buster did. The boy and his monkey are drawn into the toys' adventure— or are the toys drawn into theirs? Reality and fantasy merge in the full-color illustrations, and the book is decorated throughout with tiny black ink drawings reminiscent of the work of Klee.

## ILLUSTRATOR OF THE MONTH

An effective way to expand children's awareness of illustrators and their work is to plan and present an illustrator-of-the-month program. This approach is effective at all grade levels and is simple enough even for kindergarteners (Hansen and Hansen, 1973; Pippel, 1984). The teacher selects an artist whose work will interest students. On a bulletin board the teacher features a large, full-color reproduction of one of the artist's paintings or illustrations, and around this central focus the teacher can arrange smaller reproductions of some of the artist's other works. On a table nearby, books featuring the work of the artist can be displayed. To initiate discussion of the artist and his or her work, the teacher may want to make a few introductory statements about the artist, being careful not to give a formal lecture inappropriate for children. The teacher should ask children to share their observations about what they see in the art and encourage them to speculate as to why the artist painted something in a particular manner, emphasizing that more than one speculation is always possible. After several months of studying one artist a month, the teacher can ask children to comment on how what they are viewing is like or unlike something they saw earlier.

## THE ILLUSTRATOR AS A PERSON

One goal of studying illustrators is to help children understand each illustrator as a person and thereby become sensitive to the full range of his or her work. Too frequently children may feel that artists work in only one given style. Teachers should help children understand that an illustrator's visual expression often varies depending on the book: a particular story may evoke a kind of illustration very different from what the illustrator has previously produced. In addition, a painting created at the height of an illustrator's powers may be quite different from one produced in younger years. By locating and sharing as much as possible of one illustrator's work, the teacher shows children a wide range of visual expression.

## THE DEVELOPMENT OF AN ILLUSTRATOR

If teachers at every grade level in a particular school utilize illustrator-of-the-month experiences, the work of particular artists can be returned to at different times during elementary school, and children will, as a result, develop a deeper understanding and appreciation of artists' work. Marcia Brown, for example, is an artist whose illustrations could be studied at several different grade levels for the differences in media and style they represent. Brown's many books illustrated in paint, ink line, and chalk are probably the most familiar. Her *Cinderella* in this combination medium won the artist her first Caldecott Medal. Other of her books show an equally competent use of this mix. For *Skipper John's Cook*, the artist did bold ink-line and dry-brush paintings of the skipper and the dog. In *The Little Carousel*, she paints the adventures of Anthony and Mr. Corelli with flat shades of red, green, blue, and yellow. Though the environments of these two stories are different, children can see similarities in the use of flat, solid-color shapes and of dry brush and chalk. Other books in which Brown uses a similar technique are *Felice*, *The Neighbors*, and *Tamarindo*.

Very different from this style is Brown's work in woodcut. She uses just one color—a soft sage green—in a book for intermediate-grade students, *Backbone of the King*. Appearing on every other page or so, the half- and full-page woodcuts make extensive use of the wood's grain and are predictably angular. The artist uses silhouette shapes and different textures to evoke an island world. Another example of this style is *Dick Whittington and His Cat*.

In two books about animals, Brown uses a wider color spectrum in her woodcuts. She also uses the print of the uncut board to create backgrounds. The pattern is strong and angular, but not overwhelming. Light and dark olive green and burnt orange evoke the jungle setting in a retelling of an old Indian fable, *Once a Mouse*, for which Brown won her second Caldecott Medal. The wood grain and the gouges themselves are incorporated in the design. A white silhouette of a dog barking in the woods is a fine use of negative shape; the feline grace of the tiger stretching to fill the page makes a convincing two-dimensional rendition. In a nonstory format, in *All Butterflies*, the artist used woodcuts of animals, domestic and wild, to present the alphabet via linked pairs of words (*cat dance, mice nibbling*).

With the publication of *Listen to a Shape, Touch Will Tell*, and *Walk with Your Eyes*, Brown's fans became aware of her interest in photography. Her beautiful photos are taken from an amazing variety of perspectives. Closeup and wide-angle shots are displayed in full-, half-, and quarter-page sizes on clay-coated paper. The subjects are nearly all from the natural world, though the pictures include a wide variety of shapes, colors, forms, and textures. This visually stimulating series of books is somewhat marred by inept and clumsy text. Poetic language is interspersed with pedestrian language, and inappropriate words jar the reader's ear. Readers may become confused trying to determine what is text and what is caption. Nonetheless, these books should be shared with children to expand their sense of Brown's development as an artist.

With *Shadow*, a story originally written in French by Blaise Cendrars, Brown returns to the medium of woodcut. (See Plate I in the color section.) There is the same interesting use of transparency and subtle color that marked her earlier efforts. In addition, in several places she utilizes an unusual effect produced by putting a blank piece of paper on top of a piece with wet paint and then removing it. The sharp outline and intense blackness contrast well with the highly saturated and pastel colors. This book, Brown's third Caldecott Medal winner, provoked widely varying responses. *The Bulletin of the Center for Children's Books* (1982) was one of several reviewing sources that commented positively on the book, noting especially its "strong use of pure color . . . eerie wisps of superimposed images . . . strong silhouettes, all in handsome double-page spreads that are remarkable in their composition." In contrast, the *Interracial Books for Children Bulletin* (1983) was highly critical of the text ("presents no authentic cultural clues" and "reinforc[es] the idea of Africa as 'The Dark Continent' ") and of the illustrations (the figures do not "reflect the actual grace of an African dance"

**PLATE A.** *Ed Young uses jewel-like colors to create richly detailed forms that contrast effectively with large areas of plain color. The pastel and watercolor pictures are often framed with a thin line, giving them a formal quality reminiscent of oriental folding screens.* Illustration by Ed Young reprinted by permission of Philomel Books from *Yeh-Shen* by Ai-Ling Louie, illustrations copyright © 1982 by Ed Young.

PLATE B. *Many soft shades of watercolor blend subtly to evoke a significant moment in this tale. In Ivan Gantschev's watercolor illustrations, shapes are not as important as is the play of various tonalities.* Illustration taken from *Noah and the Ark and the Animals* © 1984 Picture Book Studio. By Andrew Elborn, illustrated by Ivan Gantschev.

PLATE C. *Ezra Jack Keats created striking collages using such diverse materials as cardboard, photographs, paint, and gummed stickers.* Illustration from *Jennie's Hat* by Ezra Jack Keats. Copyright © 1966 by Ezra Jack Keats. Reprinted by permission of Harper & Row, Publishers, Inc.

PLATE D. *Some artists create two-dimensional images utilizing the plane of the page—here Patricia Hutchins has combined a variety of shapes.* Reprinted with permission of Macmillan Publishing Company from *Changes, Changes* by Pat Hutchins. Copyright © 1971 by Pat Hutchins.

PLATE E. *David McPhail's intensely dark watercolors are brought to life by the "sparkle" from the white paper beneath, which shows through here and there throughout the painting.* Illustration from *Farm Morning* by David McPhail. Copyright © 1985. Reproduced by permission of Harcourt Brace Jovanovich, Inc.

PLATE F. *Eric Carle used images of letters found in the real-world environment for his illustrations for an alphabet book.* From the book *All About Arthur* by Eric Carle. Copyright © 1974 by Eric Carle. Reprinted with permission of Eric Carle and published by Franklin Watts.

and there is "casual use of African spiritual/religious symbols"). Which represents the more accurate assessment? Teachers may want to examine the book themselves in light of these varying points of view, which illustrate that even award-winning books are by no means universally accepted.

No school library is likely to have copies of all books by a single illustrator, but a teacher interested in doing illustrator-of-the-month programs for children will have no trouble securing a selection of books using the interlibrary loan services available either through the school library or the local public library. By encountering an array of books at appropriate times during elementary school, students will gain a firmly established sense of the range of possibilities within one artist's work. A coordinated study similar to that outlined for the work of Marcia Brown is possible for other illustrators, such as Trina Schart Hyman, Roger Duvoisin, and Maurice Sendak. Indeed, a classroom teacher has described in detail her work highlighting Sendak for children (McKay, 1982). The variety in the works of such artists as Paul Cezanne, Pablo Picasso, and Georges Braque makes them also particularly fitting for such study.

## BOOKS ABOUT ART AND ARTISTS

A number of high-quality books about art and artists are available today. These books are typically written by experts who are well acquainted with the art forms they describe. They bring art to life, through clarifying descriptions, helpful photographs, and/or imaginative illustrations. Teachers should seek out and utilize appropriate books about art and artists; a brief annotated list of such titles appears on pages 82–84.

## *SUMMARY*

A separate chapter on book illustration might seem strange in a textbook on children's literature, since illustrations are always seen in the context of a story line. The purpose of this chapter is to emphasize the possibility of studying illustration as an independent visual artifact. The outcome of such conscious study is the development of children's visual sensitivity so that they can be knowledgeable consumers of illustrative art in books.

Book illustrators are often influenced by different art movements, such as impressionism, pointillism, and abstractionism. Teachers can help children develop their visual awareness by leading them in studying the relationship between art movements and their parallels in book illustration (Purves and Monson, 1984).

Classroom teachers need to share art experiences with children. Since many students attend schools that offer no separate art program staffed by trained teachers, they will only be exposed to an array of art experiences if their classroom teachers provide such experiences.[11] Many fine books describe for classroom teachers how to offer an art-making program. Fewer discuss how to share art books with children or suggest books to use. The "Related Reading for Adults" section includes books that may help teachers give boys and girls exposure to works of art.

## Suggestions for Further Study

1. Trina Schart Hyman, a prolific artist, has illustrated books for children of different ages. Locate as many of her books as you can. Study these to see what differences are apparent. Has her style changed? If so, in what ways? A very thorough analysis of the backgrounds on which she draws and the changes in her work over time is presented by Michael Patrick Hearn in "The 'Ubiquitous' Trina Schart Hyman" (*American Artist*, May 1979, pp. 36–43ff). After doing your own analysis of her books, read Hearn to see how his opinions agree or disagree with your observations. For a simple, first-person account by the author, with illustrations— though not including reproductions from her books—see *Self-Portrait: Trina Schart Hyman* (Reading, Mass.: Addison-Wesley, 1981). This book, like others in the *Self-Portrait* series, is a chatty, personalized account of Hyman's life, designed to interest children in the artist's work, not a serious study of the nature of the art itself.

2. Read Margaret Wise Brown's *The Important Book* to children. Have them choose several objects, identify the salient characteristics of each, illustrate these characteristics, and make an "important" book of their own. Alternatively, read the suggestions about using this book to motivate compositions in an article by Gerry M. Palmer and George E. Coon, "Writing Excellence Through the Literature Connection," *The Advocate*, 5 (Fall 1985), pp. 30–34.

3. To observe how book illustration has changed since publishers began to create books especially for children, see *The Collector's Book of Children's Books* by Eric Quayle (New York: Clarkson N. Potter, 1971). In what ways do older illustrations differ from those in books today? What can we learn about the cultures that produced them by studying these illustrations? Another resource for answering these questions is *When We Were Young* by William Feaver (New York: Holt, Rinehart and Winston, 1977). This book includes an ample number of full-color illustrations covering nearly two centuries—from an etching by William Blake to Maurice Sendak's *In the Night Kitchen*.

4. Read "Children, Books and Collage," by

---

[11]In "Are Those Children Reading in the Art Room?" (*Wilson Library Bulletin*, March 1971, pp. 681–684), John Warren Stewig suggests ways to introduce books and some techniques for managing the independent use of books. The article includes an annotated bibliography. In "Making Is Not Enough" (*Art Teacher*, Fall 1974, pp. 31–33), Stewig identifies a new interest— aesthetic awareness—that utilizes art books to make children aware of art others create.

Linda Lamme (*Language Arts*, November/December 1976, pp. 902–905). Do you agree with her contention that an illustration medium should never be discussed before children have had a chance to work with the medium? Why or why not?

5. Art-supply houses carry the type of transparent tissue papers used by Eric Carle. In final effect, these somewhat resemble watercolors. Try working with both watercolors and tissue papers. Which do you find more satisfying? How does your choice relate to the nature of the medium?

6. Michael Foreman did surrealistic illustrations for *War and Peas* (New York: Thomas Y. Crowell, 1974), a fantasy about King Lion, whose country is in desperate straits because of a lack of wood. Locate a copy of this book and share it with children. What kinds of comments, if any, do they make about the surrealistic illustrations?

7. Woodcut is a medium used fairly frequently in children's books. Another artist who used this medium is Naomi Bossom in *A Scale Full of Fish and Other Turnabouts* (New York: Greenwillow, 1979). Compare her work in this book with that in some of the books discussed in the chapter. Then find a copy of *The Silent One*, by Joy Cowley (New York: Knopf, 1981), which is illustrated with wood engravings, rather than woodcuts. Wood engravings are made using the end, not the side, grain of the wood. How does the final visual effect differ with these two techniques?

8. Three techniques not mentioned in this chapter are infrequently used in children's books. Silkscreen (or serigraphy) is used in *Sand Dollar, Sand Dollar*, by Joyce Audy dos Santos (New York: Lippincott, 1980). Etching is used in *Teddy*, by Enid Warner Romanek (New York: Scribner's, 1979). Scratchboard is used in *All Times, All Peoples*, by Milton Meltzer (New York: Harper and Row, 1980). Read about these techniques, and then examine the books and try to describe the visual differences in writing.

9. Read "Art Through Children's Literature" by Marilyn Locke (*Arts and Activities*, April 1986, pp. 50–51), in which she describes having children illustrate their favorite books, after seeing how the published versions are illustrated. Try her technique with a class and evaluate its effectiveness.

## Related Reading For Adults

Bonnefoy, Yves. *Miró*. New York: Viking, 1967.
Large pages (more than a foot square) feature full-color reproductions of Miró's work, and some fold-out pages allow for even larger reproductions. The artist's inventive use of shapes and lines, which float unpredictably through backgrounds, giving little indication of depth, should intrigue children.

Coody, Betty. *Using Literature with Young Children*. Dubuque, Iowa: William C. Brown, 1983.
In the chapter "Books That Lead to Art Experiences," the author presents art projects that derive from reading books to children. She describes murals, friezes, collages, montages, mosaics, and easel paintings, listing specific books that may be useful in motivating children to work on such projects. An annotated list provides useful information about each book mentioned.

Doonan, Jane. "Talking Pictures: A New Look at 'Hansel and Gretel.'" *Signal*, September 1983, pp. 123–131.
This article is an in-depth study of a single

book, beginning with the premise that pictures "may be experienced both with the conscious and the un-conscious mind: while they entertain the former, they carry important messages to the latter." Doonan insightfully examines the *Hansel and Gretel* of surrealist artist Anthony Browne, who made the unconventional decision to set the tale in contemporary dress. She discusses the fact that in Browne's work, what we do *not* see reminds us of the inner consciousness we occupy. His obsessive use of pattern destroys material reality as he does not decorate but rather penetrates the tale. This article is difficult reading, but delivers insightful criticism well worth the effort.

Hannabuss, Stuart. "Sources of Information for Children's Book Illustration." *Journal of Librarianship.* 13 (July 1981), 154–171.

Hannabuss has compiled an exhaustive listing of books, periodical articles, and occasional papers and included brief indications of their contents. Many of the books are British and old, but the serious student of book illustration will find this a useful compilation of leads to further reading. The most interesting material is in a final section that considers two often overlooked sources of information on illustration: the books themselves, and the children. The author raises some important issues (for example, the frame of reference expected, as in the work of Fiona French, which often is "adult-based").

Kingman, Lee, Grace Allen Hogarth, and Harriet Quimby, eds. *Illustrators of Children's Books, 1967–1976.* Boston: The Horn Book, 1978.

A continuation from three earlier volumes (1744–1945, 1946–1956, and 1957–1966) by the same publisher, this volume provides succinct biographies of major illustrators. Each paragraph begins with a short quote from the illustrator, then provides biographic information and a brief description of the materials used by the illustrator. The information is descriptive, with no attempt at evaluating the subject's work. A bibliography is helpful in locating all the work of any particular artist.

Klemin, Diana. *The Art of Art for Children's Books: A Contemporary Survey.* New York: Clarkson N. Potter, 1966.

Providing only minimal introductory text, the author launches a study of contemporary illustrators. The reproductions—unfortunately, mostly in black and white—are large, sometimes spread across two pages, and meant to be studied in detail. A brief evaluative paragraph accompanies each reproduction. Compare Klemin's evaluation of Joan Walsh Anglund with the comments by Selma G. Lanes in *Down the Rabbit Hole* (New York: Atheneum, 1971).

Lanes, Selma G. *The Art of Maurice Sendak.* New York: Abrams, 1980.

Fans of Sendak will greatly enjoy this extensive (273 pages) and lavishly illustrated (something on nearly every page) book. John Cech, in "Sendak's Mythic Childhood" (*Children's Literature*, 10, 1982, 178–182), suggests caution, however. Although he acknowledges the service Lanes provides in turning her attention to the "primary innovator and extender of the . . . [picture book]," Cech feels she is reluctant to function as a critic.

Larkin, David. *The Fantastic Kingdom.* New York: Ballantine Books, 1974.

Using intriguing, full-page, color reproductions, the editor presents fourteen illustrators whose names are too often unknown and whose paintings are too often forgotten. Born in the last half of the nineteenth century, these illustrators created a unique world of fantasy infused with elements of Art Nouveau. Despite that common element, the remarkable diversity among the works will delight the student of children's book illustration.

Meyer, Susan E. *A Treasury of the Great Children's Book Illustrators*. New York: Abrams, 1983.

An extended introduction considers the time setting, including social and economic conditions, that influenced the flowering of children's book illustration. The author augments this background with chapters on thirteen specific illustrators. This admittedly idiosyncratic book leaves living contemporary illustrators to the children's literature specialists from whom Meyer is careful to distance herself. In a discussion of the social ferment during Victorian times, which changed the face of England forever, Meyer identifies antecedents of modern publishing, albeit briefly (the two paragraphs on nursery rhyme origins are interesting but incomplete), and details, in easily understood language, the dramatic changes that took place in publishing and printing techniques. The chapters devoted to individual illustrators, which range from fourteen pages on Caldecott to twenty-two pages on Howard Pyle, are lavishly illustrated with full-color reproductions; in fact some chapters have almost more pictures than words. Detailed consideration is given to the careers, influential acquaintances, and important commissions of these artists, but less attention is paid to critical comments on why these artists are in fact "great" illustrators.

Ovenden, Graham. *The Illustrators of Alice in Wonderland*. New York: St. Martin's, 1972.

This volume sketches briefly the history of Carroll's classic book from its publication in 1865, through the work of many illustrators, to the illustrations produced in 1970 by Peter Blake. Many of the black-and-white reproductions are of illustrations long out of print. Since the publication of Ovenden's book, publishers have continued to make available various editions of *Alice*. A recent example is *Alice's Adventures Under Ground*, the script facsimile of the 1864 version with Carroll's own illustrations and a foreword by Mary Jean St. Clair, the original Alice's granddaughter (New York: Holt, Rinehart and Winston, 1985).

Richard, Olga. "The Visual Language of the Picture Book," in *Jump Over the Moon*, ed. Pamela Barron. New York: Holt, Rinehart and Winston, 1984.

The author opens her extended consideration of art elements by acknowledging that the categories vary according to which author one is reading. She discusses color, shape, line, texture, and arrangement in depth, linking each element to artists such as Cezanne and to examples from books. In addition, Richard considers other components of book art such as typeface and placement. Richard states in her conclusion that "... illustrations belong to the realm of visual art and are appropriately judged by criteria coming from the fine arts."

Rumpel, Heinrich. *Wood Engraving*. New York: Van Nostrand Reinhold, 1972.

Despite its title, this book's subject matter is not limited to engraving but deals widely with a variety of printing processes using wood. The book includes useful descriptions of the processes, many photographs of artists making prints, and reproductions of woodcuts. The reproductions are too small to use with children; the book functions best as a resource for broadening the teacher's knowledge of relief printing.

Schwarcz, Joseph H. *Ways of the Illustrator*. Chicago: American Library Association, 1982.

Schwarcz presents a serious analysis of fourteen topics in chapters that draw their material not only from American but also from international children's book publishing. The author takes a scholar's in-depth approach to these topics, which are discussed at length, based on many sources, and accompanied by documenting footnotes. The chapter on visible sound, "the attempt to represent pictorially various aspects of sound, and especially letters, words and mu-sic notes signifying sound," is one of the most interesting chapters. A particularly helpful device used by Schwarcz is the jux-taposing of several different versions of the same tale. One chapter draws on fifty dif-ferent editions of *Cinderella*, for example, but an eighteen-page chapter on versions of the Jonah tale may be more than most read-ers need. One drawback of the book is that some of the sample illustrations are so small as to be virtually useless. Also, the many references to international editions mean that some books will not be easily available. Nonetheless, even the casual reader will find much of interest.

Stewig, John Warren. "Assessing Visual Ele-ments Preferred in Pictures by Young Children." *Reading Improvement*, Summer 1975, pp. 94–97.

This article investigates the preferences ex-pressed by 285 preschool, kindergarten, and first-grade children for visual elements in realistic or unrealistic color, three-dimen-sional or flat shapes, realistic or unrealistic proportions, much or little detail, and shal-low or deep space.

## Related Reading for Children

Batterberry, Michael, and Diane Ruskin. *Chil-dren's Homage to Picasso*. New York: Abrams, 1970.

Children of the tiny, ancient village of Val-lauris, in southern France, were well ac-quainted with Picasso because he spent a lot of time there. The children's fondness for him resulted in this collection of paintings given to him on his eighty-fifth birthday.

Carle, Eric. *My Very First Book of Colors*. New York: Thomas Y. Crowell, 1974.

This wordless book for very young children features heavy cardboard pages divided in half so that both halves flip on the spiral binding. The lower halves feature animals, natural objects like trees and foods, and syn-thetic objects. The upper halves are solid blocks of color that children can match with the colors of objects on the lower halves.

Dobrin, Arnold, *I Am a Stranger on the Earth*. New York: Frederick Warne, 1975.

Both drawings and completed paintings are included in this simplified version of Van Gogh's life for middle school or junior high students. The easy-to-read text is fairly self-contained. Full-color illustrations always al-ternate with black-and-white ones; both types are rather small, however.

Downer, Marion. *Children in the World's Art*. New York: Lothrop, Lee and Shepard, 1970.

Taking one strong, unifying idea—artists' varying portrayals of children—the author creates a capsule view of art history from an Egyptian wall painting (1450 B.C.) to a Pi-casso painting (1961). The text is most ap-propriate for late-intermediate-grade or junior-high-school readers. The very clear reproductions are unfortunately all in black and white.

Fisher, Leonard Everett. *The Shoemakers*. New York: Franklin Watts, 1967.

One of many fine volumes in the *Colonial American Craftsmen* series, this volume fol-lows the history of shoemaking beginning in 1629 when Thomas Beard, the first shoe-maker in New England, started to ply his trade. An explanation of the techniques, ter-minology, and tools of the craft follows. Although suitable for upper-elementary students, the picture book format may turn away older children who might otherwise be interested.

Gladstone, M. J. *A Carrot for a Nose, The Form of Folk Sculpture*. New York: Scribner's, 1974.

A visual delight, this book inspires readers

to notice the art of commonplace things surrounding us all. From a snowman with a carrot for a nose to manhole covers in the street to weathervanes on country barns, many forms of folk art are of high quality and unjustly ignored. The illustrations are superb and the book's design exemplary.

Hofsinde, Robert. *Indian Arts.* New York: Morrow, 1971.

The survey of American Indian art from earliest times to the present focuses on the media used: horn, bone, shell, quill, roots, grasses, clay, and metal. The book is profusely illustrated in pen-and-ink drawings.

Holme, Bryan. *Enchanted World: Pictures to Grow Up With.* New York: Oxford University Press, 1979.

The author's background as scion of an art-publishing firm has clearly influenced this elegant and expensively produced volume. Nearly half of the ninety-six illustrations are reproduced in strikingly accurate full color. Margins are narrow and the print small to allow room for reproductions larger than in many similar books. Subject matter varies from an oil landscape by Fragonard to "Lady Mouse in a Mob Cap" by Beatrix Potter. The book spans a time period from the eleventh to the twentieth century. In several places paintings on the same subject face each other to facilitate comparisons. The text assumes no previous art background and avoids art-world jargon. In another book, *Creatures of Paradise* (London: Thames and Hudson, 1980), Holme focuses on common and extraordinary animals as depicted by such diverse artists as Edward Hicks and Joan Miró. The lavish use of color and the large size of the pictures make the details easy to study.

Macaulay, David. *Cathedral: The Story of Its Construction.* Boston: Houghton Mifflin, 1973.

This large-format, visually impressive book employs an imaginary example to describe the process used during the fourteenth century to build Gothic cathedrals. Detailed line drawings, precise and regular, present both straight-on and bird's-eye views. The wealth of detail does not become clutter but fits together to make an artistic unit.

Myller, Rolf. *From Idea into House.* New York: Atheneum, 1974.

This consideration of house construction from an architect's point of view is unique among children's books. The mathematical computations included do not obscure the graceful illustrations by Henry Szwarce.

Peterson, Harold L. *A History of Body Armor.* New York: Scribner's, 1968.

This technical book is as concerned with the mechanics of how armor works as with its aesthetic qualities. Nevertheless, it reveals that early armor was highly decorative. Many small, black-ink drawings show with precision the details involved in protecting the soldier.

Tobias, Tobi. *Isamu Noguchi. The Life of a Sculptor.* New York: Thomas Y. Crowell, 1974.

Twelve full-page and nineteen smaller black-and-white photographs augment the textual account of this famous, if reclusive, sculptor's life. Details are plentiful, but, as in many biographies, they don't fully explain such perplexing events as Noguchi's father's early desertion, his American mother's decision to remain in Japan, and the sculptor's feeling "angry and hurt" when as an adult artist his plans for a project were not accepted. Tobias attempts to depict Noguchi's visual statements in words: "He got excited when he just looked at a piece of wood or metal. . . . He felt that locked inside . . . were great adventures. As a sculptor he could make them happen." Such statements accompany but do not really illuminate the visual works. The book is valuable, however, as one of few children's books about the three-dimensional art of sculpture.

# Professional References

*The Bulletin of the Center for Children's Books*, 35 (July–August 1982), 203.

Cachin, Francoise. *Paul Signac.* Greenwich, Conn.: New York Graphic Society, 1971.

Clark, Hattie. "Paul Klee." *Highlights for Children*, January 1986, 20–21.

di San Lazzaro, G. *Homage to Georges Roualt.* New York: Tudor, 1971.

Dressel, Janice Hartwick. "Abstraction in Illustration: Is It Appropriate for Children?" *Children's Literature in Education*, 15 (Summer 1984), 103–112.

Fry, Roger. *Seurat.* London: Phaidon Press, 1965.

Gaunt, William. *Impressionism.* New York: Praeger, 1970.

Goosen, E. C. *Stuart Davis.* New York: George Braziller, 1959.

Grohmann, Will. *Paul Klee.* New York: Abrams, 1967.

Hansen, Harlan, and Ruth Hansen. "The Arts in the Kindergarten?" *Instructor*, January 1973, 57ff.

Harlan, Calvin. *Vision and Invention.* Englewood Cliffs, N.J.: Prentice-Hall, 1970.

Hopkins, Lee Bennett. "Remembering Ezra Jack Keats." *School Library Media Quarterly*, 12 (Fall 1983), 7–9.

*Interracial Books for Children Bulletin*, 14 (1983), 34.

Lanes, Selma G. "Ezra Jack Keats: In Memoriam." *The Horn Book*, September/October 1984, 551–558.

McKay, Jo Ann. "Making the Most of Maurice." *The Reading Teacher*, October 1982, 90–91.

Moebius, William. "Introduction to Picturebook Codes." *Word and Image*, 2 (April–June 1986), 141–158.

Paulin, Mary Ann. *Creative Uses of Children's Literature.* Hamden, Conn.: Library Professional Publications, 1982.

Pippel, Midge. "Guess Who Visited Our Class? Artist Appreciation with Flair." *Early Years*, April 1984, 25.

Purves, Alan C., and Dianne L. Monson. *Experiencing Children's Literature.* Glenview, Ill.: Scott, Foresman, 1984.

Richard, Olga, and Donnarae MacCann. "Picture Books for Children." *Wilson Library Bulletin*, 59 (October 1984), 128–129.

Rowell, Margit. *Miró.* New York: Abrams, 1970.

Sutherland, Zena. *Children and Books.* Glenview, Ill.: Scott, Foresman, 1977.

Tremper, Ellen. "Black English in Children's Literature." *The Lion and the Unicorn*, 3 (Winter 1979/1980).

Vallier, Dora. *Henri Rousseau.* New York: Abrams, 1964.

Whalen-Levitt, Peggy. "Breaking Frame: Bordering on Illusion." *School Library Journal*, March 1986, 100–103.

# Bibliography of Children's Books

Alexander, Lloyd. *The Four Donkeys.* New York: Holt, Rinehart and Winston, 1972.

Amoss, Berthe. *Old Hasdrubal and the Pirates.* New York: Parents' Magazine Press, 1971.

Anderson, C. W. *C. W. Anderson's Complete Book of Horses and Horsemanship.* New York: Macmillan, 1963.

Ardizzone, Edward. *Little Tim and the Brave Sea Captain.* New York: Henry Z. Walck, 1955.

Bellairs, John. *The House with a Clock in Its Walls.* New York: Alfred A. Knopf, 1964.

Berger, Terry. *Ben's ABC Day.* New York: Lothrop, Lee and Shepard, 1982.

Brenner, Barbara. *Faces*. New York: E. P. Dutton, 1970.

Brown, Marcia. *All Butterflies*. New York: Scribner's, 1974.

———. *Backbone of the King*. New York: Scribner's, 1966.

———. *Cinderella*. New York: Scribner's, 1954.

———. *Dick Whittington and His Cat*. New York: Scribner's, 1950.

———. *Felice*. New York: Scribner's, 1958.

———. *Henry—Fisherman*. New York: Scribner's, 1949.

———. *Listen to a Shape*. New York: Franklin Watts, 1979.

———. *The Little Carousel*. New York: Scribner's, 1946.

———. *The Neighbors*. New York: Scribner's, 1967.

———. *Once a Mouse*. New York: Scribner's, 1961.

———. *Shadow*. New York: Scribner's, 1982.

———. *Skipper John's Cook*. New York: Scribner's, 1951.

———. *Tamarindo*. New York: Scribner's, 1960.

———. *Touch Will Tell*. New York: Franklin Watts, 1979.

———. *Walk with your Eyes*. New York: Franklin Watts, 1979.

Brown, Margaret Wise. *The Important Book*. New York: Harper and Row, 1949.

———. *The Noisy Book*. New York: Harper and Row, 1939, 1967.

———. *The Winter Noisy Book*. New York: Harper and Row, 1947, 1975.

Bulla, Clyde Robert. *The Ghost of Windy Hill*. New York: Thomas Y. Crowell, 1964.

Burningham, John. *Opposites*. New York: Crown, 1985.

Burns, Robert. *Hand in Hand We'll Go*. New York: Thomas Y. Crowell, 1965.

Byars, Betsy. *The Lace Snail*. New York: Viking, 1975.

Calhoun, Mary. *The Witch of Hissing Hill*. New York: William Morrow, 1964.

Carle, Eric. *The Honeybee and the Robber*. New York: Philomel Books, 1981.

———. *1, 2, 3 To the Zoo*. Cleveland: World Publishing, 1968.

Carrick, Carol, and Donald Carrick. *The Brook*. New York: Macmillan, 1967.

Church, Alfred. *The Aeneid for Boys and Girls*. New York: Macmillan, 1962.

Crews, Donald. *Parade*. New York: Greenwillow, 1983.

d'Aulaire, Ingri, and Edgar Parin d'Aulaire. *Book of Greek Myths*. Garden City, N.Y.: Doubleday, 1962.

———. *d'Aulaires' Trolls*. Garden City, N.Y.: Doubleday, 1972.

———. *Norse Gods and Giants*. Garden City, N.Y.: Doubleday, 1967.

Davidson, Marshall B. *A History of Art*. New York: Random House, 1984.

Drescher, Henrik. *Look-Alikes*. New York: Lothrop, Lee and Shepard, 1985.

Ernst, Lisa Campbell. *Up to Ten and Down Again*. New York: Lothrop, Lee and Shepard, 1986.

Fisher, Aileen. *Listen, Rabbit!* New York: Thomas Y. Crowell, 1964.

French, Fiona. *The Blue Bird*. New York: Henry Z. Walck, 1972.

———. *City of Gold*. New York: Henry Z. Walck, 1974.

Fujikawa, Gyo. *Gyo Fujikawa's A to Z Picture Book*. New York: Grosset and Dunlap, 1974.

Glubok, Shirley. *The Art of Photography*. New York: Macmillan, 1977.

———. *The Art of the Vikings*. New York: Macmillan, 1978.

Grillone, Lisa, and Joseph Gennaro. *Small Worlds Close Up*. New York: Crown, 1978.

Harper, Wilhelmina. *The Gunniwolf*. New York: E. P. Dutton, 1967.

Hoban, Tana. *A Children's Zoo*. New York: Greenwillow, 1985.

———. *Is It Rough? Is It Smooth? Is It Shiny?* New York: Greenwillow, 1984.

———. *Push-Pull Empty-Full*. New York: Macmillan, 1972.

———. *Shapes and Things*. New York: Macmillan, 1970.

Hodges, Margaret. *The Wave*. Boston: Houghton Mifflin, 1964.

Hoffman, Felix. *The Seven Ravens*. New York: Harcourt Brace, 1962.

———. *The Sleeping Beauty*. New York: Harcourt Brace, 1959.

Hogrogian, Nonny. *Apples*. New York: Macmillan, 1972.

Hutchins, Pat. *Clocks and More Clocks*. New York: Macmillan, 1970.

Ionesco, Eugene. *Story Number 4*. New York: Harlan Quist, 1973.

———. *Story Number 1*. New York: Harlan Quist, 1967.

Isadora, Rachel. *City Seen From A to Z*. New York: Greenwillow, 1983.

Jacobs, Joseph. *The Buried Moon*. Englewood Cliffs, N.J.: Bradbury, 1969.

Keats, Ezra Jack. *Jennie's Hat*. New York: Harper and Row, 1966.

———. *The Snowy Day*. New York: Viking, 1962.

Kitamura, Satoshi. *When Sheep Cannot Sleep*. New York: Farrar, Straus and Giroux, 1986.

Lessac, Frane. *My Little Island*. New York: Lippincott, 1985.

Lifton, Betty Jean. *The Secret Seller*. New York: W. W. Norton, 1968.

Lionni, Leo. *Frederick*. New York: Pantheon Books, 1967.

Lipkind, William, and Nicholas Mordinoff. *The Two Reds*. New York: Harcourt Brace, 1950.

Lucas, Helen. *The Christmas Birthday Story*. New York: Alfred A. Knopf, 1980.

Luton, Mildred. *Little Chicks' Mothers and All the Others*. New York: Viking, 1983.

Mayers, Florence Cassen. *The Museum of Modern Art ABC*. New York: Abrams, 1986.

McCloskey, Robert. *Make Way for Ducklings*. New York: Viking, 1941.

———. *Time of Wonder*. New York: Viking, 1957.

McNeer, May. *The Canadian Story*. New York: Ariel Books, 1958.

———. *The Mexican Story*. New York: Ariel Books, 1953.

Mendoza, George. *Gwot! Horribly Funny Hairticklers*. New York: Harper and Row, 1967.

———. *The Scarecrow Clock*. New York: Holt, Rinehart and Winston, 1971.

Morris, Ann, and Maureen Roffey. *Night Counting*. New York: Harper and Row, 1986.

Norman, Howard. *The Owl-Scatterer*. Boston: Little, Brown, 1986.

Norton, Mary. *The Borrowers Aloft*. New York: Harcourt Brace, 1961.

O'Kelley, Mattie Lou. *Circus*. Boston: Atlantic Monthly Press, 1986.

———. *From the Hills of Georgia*. Boston: Atlantic Monthly Press, 1983.

Raskin, Ellen. *Spectacles*. New York: Atheneum, 1972.

Reid, Barbara, and Ewa Reid. *The Cobbler's Reward*. New York: Macmillan, 1978.

Reinl, Edda. *The Little Snake*. Boston: Neugebauer USA, 1982.

———. *The Three Little Pigs*. Natick, Mass.: Picture Book Studio, 1983.

Rogasky, Barbara. *Rapunzel*. New York: Holiday House, 1982.

Seuss, Dr. *One fish two fish red fish blue fish*. New York: Random House, 1960.

Shulevitz, Uri. *Dawn*. New York: Farrar, Straus and Giroux, 1974.

Skofield, James. *All Wet! All Wet!* New York: Harper and Row, 1984.

Steptoe, John. *Stevie*. New York: Harper and Row, 1969.

———. *Train Ride*. New York: Harper and Row, 1971.

———. *Uptown*. New York: Harper and Row, 1969.

Stevenson, James. *Worse Than Willy*. New York: Greenwillow, 1984.

Udry, Janice. *The Moon Jumpers*. New York: Harper and Row, 1959.

Valens, Evans G. *Wildfire*. Cleveland: World Publishing, 1963.

Van Allsburg, Chris. *The Garden of Abdul Gasazi*. Boston: Houghton Mifflin, 1979.

Vonnegut, Kurt, and Ivan Chermayeff. *Sun Moon Star*. New York: Harper and Row, 1980.

Waddell, Martin. *Harriet and the Haunted School*. Boston: Atlantic Monthly Press, 1984.

Warburg, Sandol Stoddard. *Curl Up Small*. Boston: Houghton Mifflin, 1964.

Wells, Rosemary. *Morris's Disappearing Bag*. New York: Dial Press, 1975.

Wise, William. *The Lazy Young Duke of Dundee*. Chicago: Rand McNally, 1970.

Yolen, Jane. *The Girl Who Loved the Wind*. New York: Thomas Y. Crowell, 1972.

———. *Greyling*. Cleveland: World Publishing, 1968.

———. *An Invitation to the Butterfly Ball; A Counting Rhyme*. New York: Parents' Magazine Press, 1976.

Zemach, Harve. *Nail Soup*. Chicago: Follett, 1964.

Zimmelman, Nathan. *So You Shouldn't Waste a Rhinoceros*. Austin, Tex.: Steck-Vaughn, 1970.

Zolotow, Charlotte. *Mr. Rabbit and the Lovely Present*. New York: Harper and Row, 1962.

# THE ALPHABET BOOK: FORMS AND POSSIBILITIES

Covering everything from alleycat[1] and Amanda[2] to zemmi[3] and zoom,[4] the ubiquitous alphabet book forms part of the environment of every nursery school and kindergarten. Some alphabet books are also appropriate for older children. The genre is not new: the *New England Primer*, which was published in 1683, contained alphabet rhymes. This early book not only taught children the alphabet but also contained strong moralistic admonitions designed to save their souls.

In the following years, alphabet books remained popular. In *The Adventures of A Apple Pie*, by George Burgess, first published in 1835, two small children dressed as adults cavort around the apple pie. The diminutive size of the book and the authentic details of the full-color illustrations capture children's interest today. Although some of the vocabulary may be unfamiliar (for instance, "... y yeomaned it ..."), the book is well worth sharing with children.

In 1871, Edward Lear, whose limericks have kept their appeal to the present, published *ABC*, an alphabet book that was very funny, in contrast to the *New England Primer*. A new edition of this work, printed as penned in Lear's own hand, is available; *A Was Once an Apple Pie* is embellished with pictures by William Hogarth. More of Lear's rhyming is available in *An Edward Lear Alphabet*, with compellingly fresh and imaginative illustrations by Carol Newsom. Much white space (with only minimal backgrounds) enhances her intricately designed watercolors. This particular book is not suitable for teaching letter forms because each pair of lower- and upper-case letters is different in style, and some are even deliberately eccentric. Despite this, the book is appealing because Newsom is able to depict animal characters without making them self-consciously cute.

Another reprint of an early alphabet book provides some insight into such books published in the last decade of the nineteenth century. *A Moral*

---

[1]Soft impressionistic illustrations in charcoal and watercolor wash effectively evoke the fur of different kinds of cats in Clare Turlay Newberry's *The Kitten's ABC* (New York: Harper and Row, 1965). The author/illustrator had a very successful career in designing and illustrating a series of books about the appealing qualities of cats.

[2]Kathleen Hague wrote *Alphabears*, illustrated by Michael Hague (New York: Holt, Rinehart and Winston, 1984). This book portrays a collection of bears—some alone, others in groups—doing mostly homey activities in a slightly British atmosphere.

[3]In *All in the Woodland Early*, by Jane Yolen (New York: Philomel Books, 1979), meticulously detailed watercolor drawings of birds, animals, and insects are effective because they are set (for the most part) against the crisp white page.

[4]Tony King wrote *The Moving Alphabet Book* (New York: Putnam, 1982), in which a large, black, upper-case letter, surrounded by smaller illustrations of objects beginning with that letter, is presented on a white background. Two small holes cut into each page mask an internal, moveable wheel the child turns to reveal other objects beginning with the same letter.

Open

*A concept, a word, and a letter establish the message of this large, full-color illustration in natural colors outlined in black ink.* Illustration from *The Guinea Pig ABC* by Kate Duke. Copyright © 1983 by Kate Duke. Reproduced by permission of the publisher, E. P. Dutton, a division of NAL Penguin Inc.

*Alphabet,* by Hilaire Belloc, contains verses about careless people who don't pay attention. The moral at the end of each small tale sums up the advice to the reader.

Despite its age, the genre of the alphabet book shows no sign of dying out; each year brings several new books to add to the already wide selection available. Newer books may be simple yet charming, like *The Guinea Pig ABC* by Kate Duke, which features full-color illustrations and is designed for preschool children or beginning readers. On each page, a letter fills up nearly the whole space, and the illustration fits around or behind the letter, with the word below. Other new books are more complex and seem intended for intermediate grades. For example, *If There Were Dreams to Sell*, by Barbara Lalicki, has selections for each letter taken from a variety of sources, such as Mother Goose, Emily Dickinson, and John Keats, among others. Margot Tomes's droll pictures in monochromatic colors are worthy of as much study as the words. There are many large-sized books with full-color pictures, such as *Alfred's Alphabet Walk*, by Victoria Chess, in which an odd-looking little animal encounters a variety of other animals on his excursion. Small pictures (less than 5 inches square) are executed as paper cutouts in *ABC*, by Elizabeth Cleaver. In *A Folding Alphabet Book*, by Monika Beisner, small pictures are enhanced by the high-gloss board-book format. This book unfolds to show each upper-case outlined letter accompanied by carefully crafted details.

What accounts for this continuing interest in alphabet books and the variety in their styles and formats?

# PURPOSES OF ALPHABET BOOKS

Early childhood educators use alphabet books for several purposes. Most alphabet books can be used to teach letter sequence, letter form, letter style, and sound-symbol correspondence. In addition some alphabet books teach concepts. Alphabet books also help children achieve visual and verbal literacy.

## LEARNING ABOUT LETTERS

Most often, teachers use alphabet books to teach children letter sequence. The bright colors and interesting items for each letter attract and hold children's interest. Listening to the teacher read the books and paging through the books by themselves can be recurring activities that give the children great pleasure.

Most alphabet books proceed in strict sequence through the alphabet, but at least two are arranged nonalphabetically. No rationale is given for the out-of-order sequence presented in *The Sesame Street Book of Letters*, by the Children's Television Workshop: A, H, S, Z, X, K, Y, O, C, G, I, T, L, J, E, F, D, B, P, R, M, W, N, U, V. Jane Thayer does give a reason for the nonalphabetical sequence in *Timothy and Madam Mouse*—the "easiest and most useful letters" appear first. Thayer's fanciful story about mice follows this sequence: M, S, A, B, F, T, L, P, I, H, J, N, O, R, G, D, U, C, W, V, K, Y, Q, E, Z, X. Both books should probably not be introduced until after children have the correct sequence of the letters firmly in mind, but they should not be eliminated just because they are nonalphabetic. Children will enjoy the humorous characters in the Sesame Street book and the charming adventures of the mice in the second one.

In addition to letter sequence, alphabet books teach letter form. Some books feature only capital letters. In *Still Another Alphabet Book,* by Seymour Chwast and Martin Stephen Moskof, the author/illustrators have used a variety of typefaces, but limited the letters to capitals. The impressively imaginative illustrations, in highly saturated, flat colors, feature strong patterns and unexpected placement, reminiscent of the best of commercial art. Across each page is run a string of letters, some of which are highlighted in contrasting color. These letters spell out a word—forming a puzzle for children to solve.

In *Annie, Bridget, and Charlie,* by Jessie Townsend, large, open-outline capital letters in pastel shades face illustrations that are fresh and vibrant. The illustrator, Jan Pienkowski, created letter shapes that cover three-quarters of the page; their softly rounded serifs and thick-and-thin lines will entice children to trace the shapes with their fingers.

Another important alphabet book is *Alphabet,* illustrated by Sonia Delaunay, a painter and costume designer who was at the forefront of avant-garde art movements throughout much of this century. In *Alphabet,* Delaunay's vibrant patterns seem to leap off the page in exuberance. Because the shapes of the capital letters are more imaginative than literal, teachers may prefer to use this book after children have learned to identify the letters.

More commonly, alphabet books include both capital and lower-case letters. *The Golden Happy Book of ABC* has large, white, silhouette capital letters that entirely fill the page. On these block-letter forms, artist Helen Frederico superimposed color illustrations and words printed in both upper-case and lower-case letters. Although neither the objects nor the style of illustration is noteworthy, the page design is imaginative.

Alphabet books can teach differences in letter form in addition to the distinction between upper case and lower case. Once children have grasped the basic letter forms (or shapes), teachers can help them focus on the style of letters. Style is the way the illustrator or type designer varies elements of the basic letter form. The letter *P* is basically made up of a straight line and a half-circle to the right of the line, but, as the following examples show, there is great stylistic variety possible in this basic form:

$$\mathscr{P} \quad \mathrm{P} \quad \mathbf{P} \quad \mathbf{P} \quad P \quad \mathrm{P} \quad \boldsymbol{P} \quad P \quad \mathrm{P} \quad \boldsymbol{P}$$

To help sensitize children to such stylistic differences among typefaces, teachers might ask them to compare all the lower-case letters (or all the upper-case ones) in *Letters and Words*, a useful book for alerting children to type differences. David L. Kreiger, the author/illustrator, included a wide variety of types: tall and short, thin and thick, serif and sans-serif, cursive and manuscript. The limited color helps focus attention on the style of the letters.

By calling attention to such differences, teachers can alert children to variety in letter form; this makes them more sensitive to qualities of typefaces. The process of looking at several different styles of type for the same letter and discussing how they are alike or different can be a valuable activity. This activity is, however, not appropriate for young children, primarily because it would be confusing during their initial learning of letter forms. Once students know the basic letter forms, teachers can help them study typefaces for the variety they present. Putting what is perceived visually about form into words is a useful challenge for children.

Teachers can encourage experimentation in letter form with three books that appeal to intermediate-grade students. In *Add-a-Line Alphabet*, Don Freeman has incorporated each letter into the body of a zoo animal. In *The Alphabeast Book*, Dorothy Schmiderer takes each letter form (all lower-case letters) and in a sequence of four panels transforms it into an animal. For example, she uses white silhouette shapes on a red rectangle to transform the *l* into a llama. A more recent variant of this idea was executed by Suse MacDonald in *Alphabatics*, in which each full-color letter transforms into an object on the facing page. The stylish simplicity of this book is dramatically impressive. A logical follow-up to any of these books is to have children work in the manner of the artist. After seeing the Freeman book, children could incorporate a letter shape into the body of an animal. Following Schmiderer's or MacDonald's technique, students could choose a letter and in a sequence change it into an animal or object.

Many teachers also use alphabet books to help students make the connection between each letter and the sound commonly associated with it. Learning sound/symbol correspondences is especially crucial for English, because it is such an irregular language.

## LEARNING ABOUT CONCEPTS

Alphabet books also teach concepts. *ABC of Cars and Trucks*, by Anne Alexander, presents a fairly conventional view of occupations related to transportation. In *26 Ways to Be Somebody Else*, Devorah Boxer uses a more imaginative and playful approach to describing occupations. The artist provides strong, simple woodcuts with much black and limited use of color.

The unnamed, freckle-faced little boy featured in this book tries out occupations ranging from acrobat to zookeeper.

Visually impressive yet understated design qualities enhance the concept development in *We Read: A to Z*, by Donald Crews, which explores such ideas as *almost, horizontal, inside,* and *whole*. First published more than twenty years ago and for some time out of print, this book has been reissued in almost the original format. Large and square-shaped, it features nonliteral designs rendered in flat, intense colors. The concepts are illustrated with a dramatic impact few other such books achieve. The book is a noteworthy example of the inherent value of fine design. Kiefer (1985) asserts that it "stands clean and free of convention, like a Balanchine ballet, or the Museum of Modern Art, a paragon in design choice."

A newer but equally distinguished book is *Action Alphabet*, by Marty Neumeier and Byron Glaser. Done exclusively in black and white, this book features, on each left-hand page, just the upper- and lower-case letter and one word in a serif-style lettering. On the facing right-hand page is a black-and-white graphic, which uses the entire page to show one concept. For example, on the *r* page, a large black umbrella is bombarded with rain consisting of diagonal lines of *r*'s. The *h* page shows a huge, sans-serif letter *h* hanging from a washline. Other equally dramatic depictions of concepts combine to make this book a convincing demonstration that color is not a mandatory ingredient in effective bookmaking for children.

*Space Alphabet*, by Irene Zachs, presents a different kind of information. Including material dating back to the beginning of space exploration, this book associates a person, place, or object involved in space travel with each letter. One might expect this book, now more than twenty years old, to be out of date; interestingly, because of the introductory level of simplicity at which it is written, it is still usable. Illustrations consisting of pleasant blocks of colors with a unifying line are easily understood and artistically designed.

The way in which letters can be used to write down sounds from the world around us is shown in *Arf Boo Click* by Bijou Le Tord. Some of the onomatopoeic examples are predictable, for instance, "vroom" as the jalopy roars away; others are more imaginative, such as "ubble gubble" to represent the sound of barnyard fowls scrabbling for food. Some of the examples, however, stretch one's credibility; "jabber jabber" is used for two female pigs knitting, rocking, and gossiping. The pleasant crispness of every page in this small book is the result of the intensely colorful, sharp-edged illustrations. This is one of several recent alphabet and counting books recommended by Schoenfeld (1982), who gives criteria for evaluating such books.

# hanging

*Very clear black-and-white close-ups of boys and girls from various ethnic groups give momentary glimpses into the world of children's movements.* Illustration from *A-B-C-ing: An Action Alphabet* by Janet Beller. Copyright © 1984 by Janet Beller. Used by permission of Crown Publishers, Inc.

Alphabet books generally include a mix of objects (nouns) and a few actions (verbs), but in *ABC Say with Me*, Karen Gundersheimer has included only verbs—from "asking" to "zooming." A small child, the main character, is involved in such actions as hiding, pretending, and rocking. As a follow-up for this book, children could make a list of all the action words they can think of. Each child could then choose one word and draw a picture to illustrate it. When finished, the pictures could be put together to make a composite alphabet of verbs.

Another book with an emphasis on verbs is *Magic Monsters Act the Alphabet*, by Jane Belk Moncure. Full-color cartoon illustrations of monsters giggling with a ghost and riding a rocket are nearly too cute, but they are usable as a way to involve children in thinking of action words and/or making their own alphabet books. Compare Moncure's book with the verb-filled *Teddy Bears ABC*, by Susanna Gretz, whose bright illustrations are enhanced by the white backgrounds on which they appear.

The concept of alphabets themselves can be explored, as children discover that an alphabet can be conveyed in ways other than writing it down and that different cultures have different alphabets. *A Show of Hands*, by Mary Beth Sullivan and Linda Bourke, shows the sign language alphabet. Sign language for numbers and words is included in *Handtalk Birthday*, by Remy Charlip, Mary Beth, and George Ancona. In *The Alphabet of Creation*, the distinguished artist Ben Shahn has retold and illustrated an ancient legend that accounts for the twenty-two letters of the Hebrew alphabet.

Still other alphabet books can augment the curriculum by teaching concepts in particular areas of study. For example, *Jambo Means Hello*, written by Muriel Feelings and illustrated by Tom Feelings, could extend learning in social studies. A one-page introduction accompanies a map of Africa that shows where Swahili in its various dialects is spoken by 45 million people. Feelings presents the twenty-four letters of the Swahili alphabet, from "a for arusi" (ah·roo·see), which means wedding, to "z for zeze" (zay·zay), a stringed instrument. The information is presented on double-page spreads using a capital letter, the word in dark-green lower-case letters, a phonetic pronunciation, and two or three sentences defining or explaining the word. In a full page at the end of the book, artist Tom Feelings explains how the art was done, using a complex printing technique called *double-dot*. Two photographs of the art are made, a key plate that prints in black and a second plate that prints in another color (in this case ochre), which doesn't show but enriches the image. Both *Jambo Means Hello* and a similar number book, *Moja Means One*, were Caldecott honor books. Talking about his work in these books, Feelings (1985) said, ". . . I tried to incorporate flowing rhythmic lines of motion, like the feel of a drum beat, a vivid luminosity, and a style that incorporated a dance consciousness."

Another book useful in social studies is *A Is for Aloha*, by Stephanie Feeney. Black-and-white, full- and sometimes double-page photos depict elements of Hawaiian culture. Some of the subjects pictured are universal concepts (such as "e is for eat"); others (such as "i is for ipu," a musical instrument made from a gourd) are particular to this culture.

Children who are interested in science can learn much from *Anno's Magical ABC*, by Mitsumasa and Masaichiro Anno. This book is actually two alphabets in one, both depending on the visual trick of anamorphosis, a word first used in the seventeenth century to describe negative perspective. The artist draws something in a warped, or misshapen way, so that when

*A full-page black-and-white photograph faces the page on which the text for the word appears. This is for "D is for Daddy."* Photo © Hella Hammid. Reprinted from *A Is for Aloha* by Stephanie Feeney, © 1980 by University of Hawaii Press.

the drawing is reflected in a distorted mirror, the object looks normal. (A flexible piece of metallic paper to be bent into a cylinder is provided with this book.) Reading from front to back, a child finds an alphabet of people and created objects from angel to zipper; turning the book over and reading from the back—now the front—a child discovers another alphabet, this time of animals and birds, from anteater to zebra. The book also includes instructions on how to do this kind of drawing, an interesting challenge for junior high students. The Annos have created an alphabet book that reminds teachers that the genre is a flexible one, appropriate for children of varying ages.

## ACHIEVING VISUAL AND VERBAL LITERACY

Those who teach children to read are well aware that literacy is frequently elusive. Most definitions of literacy include being able to read and write.

Language-arts specialists spend much time helping children achieve such literacy, but these efforts are incomplete because they do not encompass two important components: visual and verbal literacy.

Visual literacy is the ability to decode and to utilize what is decoded. To be truly literate today, children must be able to decode the messages in pictures and encode their findings in language. About 80 percent of received information comes to us visually (Debes and Williams, 1974). We are so universally bombarded by visual images that they hardly evoke comment. Yet where in the curriculum do children learn to read such visual input—to examine it carefully part by part, extract meaning, and interact with what is extracted? Such processes are central to programs that teach children to read language, but few children learn to read pictures effectively.

Verbal literacy is the ability to put coherent thoughts into words, words into sentences, and sentences into larger units. Most people spend more time communicating orally than reading or writing. Yet where in elementary schools do children learn to express in words what they have taken in through their senses? The teaching of picture reading and oral communication should begin with the youngest children who—as they are enjoying alphabet books—are ready and able to learn to see with discrimination and to put into words what they see.

**VISUAL AND VERBAL SKILLS.** Achieving visual and verbal literacy requires three skills, which range from simple to complex. Children should be allowed to develop each of these skills fully before moving to the next.

1. *Children must be able to describe objectively—clearly, concisely, concretely—what they see.*

Children should study an object that provides visual input and then translate this input into words. Children should be able to look at an illustration in an alphabet book and accurately describe what they see.

2. *Children must learn to compare two objects using common descriptors.*

Young children should be asked to observe related things and describe what they observe. What are the visible physical differences, for example, between two classmates? Or, what do two pictures have in common, and what sets them apart from each other? A teacher might show the pages for the same letter in two alphabet books and ask the children to describe how the illustrations are the same or different.

### 3. Children must learn to value one of several objects.

Children should develop the ability to say which picture or object they prefer and why. This verbal ability is an important skill, yet few people are capable of formulating an articulate and convincing description of a visual preference. Children should be encouraged to state and defend such preferences.

**MATERIALS TO USE.**  Some writers recommend using films for developing visual literacy (Stewig, 1983). Films are indeed an exciting possibility but should be used only *after* preparatory experiences. For children who are just beginning this process, the visual images on film move too quickly and are not conducive to study and reflection. Additional drawbacks are the cost and relative inconvenience of films.

A plentiful, convenient, and relatively inexpensive source of material for developing visual and verbal skills is illustrated children's books. A teacher can use any type of picture or illustrated book for this purpose (see discussion in Chapter 4). Alphabet books are especially accessible as a basis for practicing each of the three visual and verbal skills with young children.

**CLASSROOM STRATEGIES.**  In using illustrations from alphabet books as stimuli, teachers can help children study the illustrations for the sake of visual interpretation—not for letter forms, alphabet sequence, or concepts. Teachers should encourage students to examine each illustration as an independent visual artifact, with meaning of its own. It makes little difference whether a teacher uses the black-ink fantasy drawings of *From Ambledee to Zumbledee*, by Sandol Warburg; the subdued color washes of *A is for Annabelle*, by Tasha Tudor; or the sharply delineated photography of *Alphabet World*, by Barry Miller. Such books naturally attract children's interest. What child could resist talking about Leo Lionni's fuzzy mauve caterpillar, searching for words in a lush, stenciled design of leaves in *The Alphabet Tree*, or discussing Dahlov Ipcar's toothy carpenter, one of a varied assortment of people and animals in *I Love My Anteater with an A?*

The teacher should begin very simply by using one illustration and asking students to describe what they see, to detail what they take in visually. For example, she or he might start with *Curious George Learns the Alphabet*, by H. A. Rey. The bold black lines enclosing vibrant primary colors are a suitable background for George, whom children delight in describing. Asking boys and girls "What do you see?" will generally elicit a simple enumeration of items. To begin, especially if working with children who are verbally reticent, the teacher might model the response quite specifi-

J j

Jackrabbit

**The artist uses lithography to create fur so soft it looks real.** Illustration from *Animals in the Zoo* by Feodor Rojankovsky. Copyright © 1962. Reproduced by permission of Alfred A. Knopf, Inc.

cally, giving an example: "I see a giraffe eating grapes. What do you see?" In *A for Angel*, a giraffe is only one of many creatures that Beni Montressor juxtaposes to unusual effect in darkly handsome pictures, crammed with many unexpected items.

After simple identification, the teacher should encourage children to describe the nature of the object more specifically. The meticulously detailed quetzel, by Feodor Rojankovsky, in *Animals in the Zoo*, might elicit a response such as, "I see a brown bird with a long tail feather." In attempting to describe an illustration in *Animal ABC*, by Celestino Piatti, one child said, "I see an orange monkey with a funny white face hanging in a tree." The child's description of the illustration includes colors (orange and white), objects (monkey and face), actions (hanging), and spatial relationships (in a tree). To further develop describing skills, the teacher might ask this child, "What makes a face look 'funny'?" Such a question helps children confront the issue of what they really mean when they use generalizations that lack concrete meaning.

In dramatic contrast to the fanciful treatment of animals in the above books, is the compelling realism of Bert Kitchen's animals in *Animal Alphabet*. Through accurate details, Kitchen draws students into close scrutiny of the pictures. Each large, white, glossy page (approximately 9 inches by 12 inches) is an effective foil for the single painting of an animal intertwined with a large, black, capital letter. The plain white background and the crisp black letter set off nicely the minutely detailed animals: every feather, hair, and scale are shown in biologically accurate detail. The book was chosen for inclusion in Children's Choices for 1985, a list of newly published books that children themselves like, compiled jointly by the International Reading Association and the Children's Book Council. The acknowledgment of this book is a testimony to children's inherent, though untutored, good taste.

Once children can describe what they see, the next step is encouraging them to compare two or more illustrations. The teacher can choose two quite different books so that the contrast is apparent. In *C is for Circus*, Bernice Chardiet's fluid, curving black lines, enclosing dots of color, are a world away from the evocative realism of the clear, black-and-white photographs in Isabel Gordon's *The ABC Hunt*. Or, during the first stages of comparing, a teacher might use Amelia Frances Howard-Gibbon's illustrations for *An Illustrated Comic Alphabet;* her thin black line details with precision another time and place.[5] Howard-Gibbon's style contrasts with the simplified geometry of John Burningham in *ABCDEFGHIJKLM-NOPQRSTUVWXYZ*. Burningham's stolid queen in bright, bold color and heavy outline is stylistically very unlike Howard-Gibbon's nobleman. Kate Greenaway's delicately drawn pastel renditions of children in *A Apple Pie* contrast dramatically with the round-faced children in Charlotte Steiner's *Annie's ABC Kitten*. Teachers, however, should not use *Peter Piper's Alphabet*, by Marcia Brown, at the same time as *Hilary Knight's ABC*, because it is difficult for young children to discern any differences between the styles. The use of color and line is too similar in these two books; children need greater contrast when beginning to learn to compare. Likewise, teachers should save Brian Wildsmith's *ABC* and Bruno Munari's *ABC* for later in the sequence, when children have developed their seeing and comparing skills, since the subtle differences between the two books are not readily apparent.

---

[5]This book is of historic interest: it is believed to be the first Canadian picture book and contains reproductions from a Victorian manuscript of 1859.

*Wanda Gag produced her own lithographic illustrations for this sequential alphabet story.*
Illustration reprinted by permission of Coward, McCann & Geoghegan from *The ABC Bunny* by
Wanda Gag, copyright 1933 by Wanda Gag, copyright renewed © 1961 by Robert Janssen.

When developing the third skill, valuing, the teacher must respect a
child's reason for choosing an illustration, even when it doesn't seem like
a good reason. Referring to *The Big Golden Animal ABC*, by Garth Williams,
one child said, "I like this one because the fish has a silly smile." This may
not seem like a good reason because it ignores the qualities of the fluid
watercolor with subtle mixed hues that the artist uses. Nevertheless, the
child understood the process of verbalizing the reason for his choice. A
fourth-grade child said of an illustration in *The ABC Bunny*, by Wanda
Gag, "I like the rabbit because he looks happy dancing with his feet off the
ground." This comment is closer to the goal of a fluent oral response. The
same is true of a sixth-grader's evaluation after examining Katharina
Barry's *A Is for Anything*: "I like the lion because of the way the *l*'s overlap
to make a nice repeat." Barry's use of stenciling and stamping techniques
caught this child's attention, and she went on to compare the lion favorably
to a jaguar from C. B. Falls's *ABC*: "I like it better than the jaguar because
you can imagine more with the lion." This child may lack an appreciation
of the strength of Falls's illustration, but the teacher must respect her judgment.

As children move from the simple monochrome illustrations in *Crictor*,
by Tomi Ungerer, to the intricacies of *Mary Poppins from A to Z*, by P. L.
Travers, they sharpen their visual judgments and their ability to describe.

**OTHER VISUAL POSSIBILITIES.** In some alphabet books, the pictures shown
do not stand for the first letter of a word. Rather, each picture illustrates

the shape of the letter as found in some object. For example, in *The Alphabet Symphony*, by Bruce McMillan, the letter *u* is represented by the shape of a tuning fork. The fork is being held by a kettledrummer, so there is no intrinsic relationship between the letter being featured and the instrument being played. The letters are white silhouettes lifted from the photographs, rather than typeset letters. McMillan's book, elegantly designed with the photographs set against large, plain, dark-colored backgrounds, should be used with upper-primary students who have the letter shapes firmly in mind. They will be able to enjoy this imaginative approach to finding letter forms in the visual world.

As a contrast with *The Alphabet Symphony*, the teacher might use *Arlene Alda's ABC*. It, too, presents photographs—in this case in color—of objects in the world that have shapes similar to letters. For example, the illustration for the letter *s* in this book, which uses the sound hole in the violin for the *s*, can be compared with the photo in McMillan's book for the letter *c*, which shows the outer edge of a violin's case. Both illustrations show a violin: in one case, the external shape is used for the letter *c*; in the other case, the shape cut into the instrument is used for the letter *s*.

## *TYPES OF ALPHABET BOOKS*

Alphabet books typically fall into three general types: related-topic books, potpourri books, and sequential-story books. To gain a sophisticated understanding of the genre, boys and girls should encounter all three types of alphabet books. The teacher might call this organizational difference to children's attention, thus giving them a fuller understanding of the books they have been experiencing.

### RELATED-TOPIC BOOKS

Probably the most common type of alphabet book is the related-topic book, in which the items chosen to illustrate the letters are in some way related. The alphabet book comprising only animals is common. Peggy Parrish leads children through the alphabet with a collection of unusual animals engaged in even more unusual activities in *A Beastly Circus*. What probably distinguishes the book more than its sentences is the array of visually intriguing beasts created by the talented illustrator Peter Parnall.

*A Beastly Collection*, by Jonathon Coudrille, is more likely than Parrish's book to interest students above the primary grades because of the vocabulary and the sophisticated humor in the illustrations. Children can read, for example, about "Licorice the lamb [who] leans languidly on Laurence the Lion . . ." while enjoying the accompanying black-line illustrations.

Black line is also used in *Adam's Book of Odd Creatures*, but the thick and robust brush line is applied over watercolor washes of pink, green, gold, and brown. Joseph Low's verses are humorous but minimal; his illustrations deserve the greater attention. (See Plate L in the color section.)

Jan Garten created *The Alphabet Tale*, in which the reader/viewer is led through the book by the unusual page arrangement. The author's verse describes an animal, the tail of which appears in the lower right-hand corner of the page. The child is encouraged to guess the animal being described but must turn the page to see the entire picture.

In *On Market Street*, simple colored borders encase (and are breached by) individual fantasy figures, bedecked with things bought. Anita Lobel's introductory picture shows a young child contemplating the newly opened stores, which display "such wonders." The child makes purchases from apples to zippers, with hats, noodles, toys, and vegetables in between. The fantasy figures are arrayed in each of these in turn.

The diverse items in *On Market Street* are unified because of their location, and the diverse activities and objects in *By the Sea* are also united by the environment. Ann Blades shows all the adventures children can have at the seashore in a large book illustrated with watercolors. Opening with endpapers having a wave design, the book follows through with mostly sea and sand colors. The simplified illustrations have a pleasant calm quality, and no extraneous details.

## POTPOURRI BOOKS

Less common among alphabet books are ones with a potpourri organization, including a little of everything and with the alphabet forming the only structure. For example, *Puptents and Pebbles*, by poet William Jay Smith, presents a collection of unrelated people (pirate), animals (zebra), natural objects (cabbage), manufactured objects (jack-in-the-box), birds (owl), and geographic features (volcano). Simple, nonliteral illustrations accompany the verses.

Another potpourri alphabet book, *Certainly, Carrie, Cut the Cake*, by Margaret and John Moore, features odd-looking small creatures (both human and animal) whose activities are described in verse. The illustrations, meticulously detailed in brown ink, feature crosshatching and a use of dots that is similar to pointillism.[6]

---

[6]Pointillism, an art movement that originated in France during the late nineteenth century, is the process of painting tiny dots (or points) of pure color closely together so that the eye blends the colors. See pages 67–68 in Chapter 2 for further explanation of the technique.

Softly he walks, pitter pat.

This tail is the tail of the meowing ___

John Burningham's *ABC* features both common and uncommon animals (a bear and a newt, for example) as well as such human characters as a juggler and a queen. An example for each letter is accompanied by drawn upper-case and lower-case versions of the letter and a single word (in lower-case black letters). The pale watercolor-and-crayon drawings are connected through the ongoing use of scratchy line and the youngster in a hat who appears on each page.

*On the right-hand page, only the upper-case letter, the tail, and a description of the animal whose tail it is appear. The child turns the page to see which animal is being described.* From *The Alphabet Tale* by Jan Garten. Illustrated by Muriel Batherman. Copyright © 1964. Published by Random House, Inc. Reprinted by permission of Muriel Batherman.

In some potpourri books, the creator does attempt to make links between disparate objects. For example, *What's Inside?*, by Satoshi Kitamura, includes a variety of objects: animals (hippopotamus), created objects (guitar), natural phenomena (morning), and produce (apple). These items are

***Most of the children in this
alphabet book are rendered
in black line with minimal,
patterned backgrounds.***
Reprinted with permission
of Macmillan Publishing
Company from *Certainly,
Carrie, Cut the Cake* by
Margaret Moore and John
Travers Moore, illustrated
by Laurie Anderson.
Illustration copyright ©
1971 by Laurie Anderson.

linked together, however, by clues the artist hides in each picture as to the
identity of the two objects on the following page. For example, on the page
with letters *c* and *d*, where the dog is threatening the cat, we see the smoke
from a fire and huge footprints heading down the street toward it. On the
next page, we find an elephant watching a fire engine approach a burning
building. The pleasantly quirky drawings are filled to the edge of the page
with details children will want to look at again and again.

## SEQUENTIAL-STORY BOOKS

Least common of the organizational patterns for alphabet books is the sequential-story form. This form is rare simply because it is the most difficult to do: to tie twenty-six appropriate words into a meaningful sequence is not easy. Kate Greenaway, an influential early British illustrator, fashioned a loose sequence of events in her *A Apple Pie,* omitting the letter *i.* Wanda Gag's lithographed rabbit has a sequential adventure in *The ABC Bunny,* but some of the word choices are a bit strained. The example for *x* is of the rabbit exiting his burrow, although the word *enter* would have been more appropriate to the story line. Probably one of the most successful of these sequential stories is *Apricot ABC,* by Miska Miles, who designs the life cycle of an apricot tree from seed to seed within the structure of the twenty-six letters. The elegantly restrained illustrations with effectively used white space, by Peter Parnall, add much to this book.

One sequential-story alphabet book is distinguished by its illustrations. *All About Arthur,* by Eric Carle, is a loosely constructed tale about a lonely ape who travels from city to city to meet animal companions. The striking illustrations feature linoleum cuts of the animals, printed in black, combined with (and often superimposed on) full-color photographs of the letters as they appear in the environment. (See Plate F in the color section.)

The physical format distinguishes a gentle pair of sequential alphabet stories in *The City-Country ABC,* by Marguerite Walters. The child reads the city tale through to its completion and then turns the book upside down to read the country tale from back to front. Full-color illustrations alternate with black line drawings.

Another book with a unified story line is *Applebet,* by Clyde Watson. This story follows the adventures of the apple from being picked from the tree by Bet to going home with Bet and her mother, who zigzag all the way. The book includes such related items as a farmer at work as they journey to the fair, lollipops sold there, and the velvet ribbons given for prizes. Wendy Watson illustrates the rhymed text with simplified drawings showing round-faced rural folks.

*Victoria's ABC Adventure,* by Cathy Warren, is another sequential tale, this time about a brown garden snake who doesn't fit in with her siblings. An outcast, young Victoria slithers into a cookout, causing predictable damage. Only in the end, when she saves her mother and sisters, does Victoria's family come to recognize that being different is acceptable.

## *EVALUATING ALPHABET BOOKS*

Because the alphabet book is a kind of picture book, the criteria suggested in Chapter 4 (pages 126–139) for judging illustrations, binding and paper, page layout, and typefaces, among other items in the physical design of a book, are also appropriate in evaluating this genre. In addition, a few criteria specifically for alphabet books are useful.

### 1. The book design and illustrations should be appropriate for the intended age level.

Some books are for prereaders. Sue Dreamer's *Circus ABC* is one example; it has the board-book format, with only eight leaves containing pleasantly decorative, flat illustrations of commonplace objects and people at the circus. *The Bears' ABC Book*, by Robin and Jocelyn Wild, is for slightly older readers/listeners. Three bears, in compellingly fuzzy, variegated shades of brown, explore bicycles, jars of honey, and ladders. The lack of background only enhances the tactile quality of these adventuresome animals, who express their thoughts in cartoon balloons. Other books, because of their subtle illustrations and content references, are obviously designed for intermediate-grade children. *Twenty-Six Starlings Will Fly Through Your Mind*, by Barbara Wersba, assumes a child reader sophisticated enough to not be put off by its confusing references and not immediately accessible illustrations. *L* whirls in a languid lagoon, and *M* imitates mice who scamper on marmalade hills. Swirling illustrations by David Palladini are only loosely anchored to reality, and yet do not provide a coherent fantasy. What is going on here? It is difficult to tell, but self-confident readers may find this book an interesting variation on the alphabet genre.

In some cases, it is not clear who the intended audience is, as, for example, in *Mouse Writing* by Jim Arnosky. Two characters, LC and Cap, set out to go skating. In black and white with the sole addition of blue, they cut cursive letters into the ice. Children old enough to be learning the cursive alphabet may find the characters a bit silly. Teachers may also be concerned about visual interference: there are times, such as on the *g* page, when the page is cluttered enough to obscure the letter form.

### 2. There should be a good match between the visuals and the content references.

Simple books for preschool children need common referents. *Apple* and *dog* appropriately accompany simple, easy-to-recognize pictures for two- to five-year-olds. However, *aardvark* and *dromedary* are more complex words and would appropriately accompany visually sophisticated illustrations in books designed for middle-grade readers. Also, the pictures and the words should match in difficulty level. With *Faint Frogs Feeling Feverish,* by Lilian Obligado, one is not sure of the intended audience. The pictures are simple, colored cartoons, but many of the animals included, such as alpacas, ferrets, pangolins, and voles will probably be unfamilar to young readers. The book thus may be useful to stimulate curious children to further research.

This criterion raises two other issues for adults to think about when selecting alphabet books. First, how clearly are the pictures presented? For example, assuming that a child reader knows what a guitar is, is the picture of a violin in a book clearly enough depicted that the child will notice it is a different instrument? Second, will the book be used by the child alone or with an adult? Some books may present simple objects distinctly, allowing the child to use the book alone. Other books may require adult interpretation so that the child can get the full benefit of the visuals.

### 3. There should be a balance between the known and unknown.

Every alphabet book should strike a balance between words (and pictures) children will know and others that will extend their world. If the words reflect only what a child already knows, a major opportunity for concept and language learning is lost. A good balance between known and unknown is struck in *A My Name is Alice*, by Jane Bayer, with Steve Kellogg's usual slightly frenetic pictures. Children will know such words as bear, frog, and hamster, but may be unfamiliar with condor, emu, and unaus. The animals come from strange places and do unusual things in this text, which the author adapted from a playground game. For example, "My name is Queenie and my husband's name is Quentin. We come from Quebec and we sell question marks. Queenie is a quail. Quentin is a quahog." Child readers thus encounter much that is familiar, but also much that will cause them to wonder about the unfamiliar. In recommending this book, Richard and MacCann (1985) comment that the "incredibly detailed costumes, absurd posturings and the slapstick dilemmas" compound so that "the silliness becomes contagious." They also note that Kellogg's work is more interesting on the *X* page, where the illustration is loose and fresh, than on the other pages, where the pictures are more like his usual work.

## SHARING ALPHABET BOOKS WITH CHILDREN

Once the teacher has selected alphabet books to use she or he must determine the specific methods of presentation, the types of questions to ask to encourage observation and discussion, the number of illustrations to use, and how long the sessions should be to best suit a particular group.

One kindergarten class, without previous experience in structured oral discussion, delighted in describing what they saw in *Gyo Fujikawa's A to Z Picture Book*. These children were developing the first skill, describing or

**J**azz

**Rachael Isadora masses together many tiny black dots to create both texture and shading in this drawing. Note the strong verticals and diagonals in the window frame and the instruments.**
Illustration from *City Seen from A to Z* by Rachel Isadora, © 1983 by Rachel Isadora. By permission of Greenwillow Books (A Division of William Morrow).

enumerating. The initial experience began simply with one illustration and a few questions:

1. What do you see in the picture?
2. What colors has the artist used?
3. Where is this happening? How can you tell?

Children who have had a variety of previous oral experiences and practice in describing, are able to do quite well in valuing. One classroom teacher used three books for a unit on describing. She included Marcia Brown's *All Butterflies*, Miska Miles's *Apricot ABC*, and Maurice Sendak's *Alligators All Around*. The books were available in the room for a few days so that children could read them. It became a challenge for these fourth-grade students to see how closely they could observe what was there. In the first discussion session about the books, children described what they had noticed. The second discussion centered on comparing two of the illustrations. During the third session, each child chose the book he or she liked best and wrote a statement about the choice. Teresa wrote:

> I like *All Butterflies* because it has a lot of colors and Marcia Brown mixed the colors. She made some strange creatures. I think this is a wonderful book for little children. In the book it has lots of animals. She made them look silly. It's a good book. You should read it.

David wrote:

> I really enjoyed *Apricot ABC* by Miska Miles. I think the way the author hides the letters makes the book exciting and fun to read. This book also has very good poetry and great animal pictures. It gives me a warm and quiet feeling. The pictures are very realistic and have fantastic backgrounds. It also tells an action-packed story to make it even more exciting. *Apricot ABC* is a fun way to learn the alphabet.

Having chosen *Alligators All Around* as his favorite, Jeremy wrote:

> I like the words because they are real funny and I like funny words. Because some of the animals look human and I like to read books that have human animals. The colors of the book because they keep showing the same colors on each page and they are my favorite colors. At the beginning of each word the letters are the same. And some of the words rhyme.

Most alphabet books, despite the text included, are essentially visual. In addition to asking children to use words to encode their reactions to these books, teachers can also ask students to create visual responses through art media. One kindergarten teacher has had success in using Brian Wildsmith's *ABC* book with her children. After sharing the book and en-

H is the HEATHER, red, purple, and grey,
Which reminds the poor Swiss of his home far away.

I is the IVY, that gives the cool shade,
Where John eats the soup that his daughter has made.

J is the JONQUIL, that grows by the brook,
At which Ellen and Caroline longingly look.

K is the KING-CUP, as yellow as gold,
Which Katherine prizes as treasure untold.

**These reproductions of illustrations created many years ago show children how books used to look.** "Alphabet of Flowers," from *100 Nineteenth Century Rhyming Alphabets*, by Ruth M. Baldwin. Copyright © 1972 by SIU Press. Reprinted by permission of the publisher.

couraging boys and girls to look at the pictures as much as they like, the teacher asks the students to list as many other animals as they can think of for each of the letters. Once the chalkboard is filled with lists of animals, each child chooses and then paints a bold picture of one animal. The resulting pictures are as splashy as the ones by Wildsmith that inspired the activity.

*Pigs from A to Z*, by Arthur Geisert, features full-page, complicated etchings, showing pigs engaged in building a treehouse. Rendered in the hard-edged line typical of etching, the pigs chop down a birch tree, nap in the partially finished house, raise the rafters, and dream about tomorrow in their aerie. The book is a visual puzzle to challenge intermediate-grade students: on each page seven pigs (some hidden) cavort, and the subject letter appears five times. In addition, carefully hidden among the many lines are the preceding letter and the following letter. After searching for the hidden pigs and letters in this book, children could make drawings of their own, concealing letters and animals of their choice.

Adults often assume that alphabet books are of interest only to young children, although these books frequently depict objects unfamiliar to pre-school and kindergarten children and employ sophisticated language to describe the objects. Upper-grade children may need encouragement to read alphabet books, because, like adults, they will probably feel that anything with an alphabet is only for the very young. Some uses of even simple alphabet books are appropriate for older children. An effective technique in stimulating intermediate-grade children to write creatively is to ask them to write an alphabet story. The teacher can explain that although the students are too mature to read alphabet books they should try their hand at writing such a book for the kindergarten children down the hall. This ploy allows older children to listen with interest and then write with concentration.

One teacher of intermediate grades recently used Wanda Gag's *ABC Bunny* as a motivator of creative writing. She read the book to the group of fourth- through sixth-grade students and explained that she had received a request from the first-grade teacher for more alphabet stories to use with the younger children. In response, a student named Mary wrote the following:

### The ABC Pussy Cat

*A is for Alley, an alley cat.*
*B is for Ball that she plays with.*
*C is for Catnip which she eats.*
*D is for Dog which chases it.*
*E is for Ear, an ear on the cat.*
*F is for Food, the food she eats.*
*G is for Good, good as a treat.*

*H is for Happy, a happy cat.*
*I is for Ice Cream which melts into milk.*
*J is for Jokes which children play.*
*K is for Kitten, which she is.*
*L is for Lick. She licks your hand.*
*M is for Mitten on her hand.*
*N is for Nice, which they are.*
*O is for Open. Open the door and let her in.*
*P is for Pine tree which she lays under.*
*Q is for Quiet, which they are.*
*R is for Rain which they get clean from.*
*S is for Slide, slide on their tummies.*
*T is for Two of them.*
*U is for Under a bed.*
*V is the View which they see.*
*W is for Welcome. We welcome you.*
*X is for X-ray, a picture of happiness.*
*Y is for Yikes!, it's time to go!*
*Z is for Zero, that's the end.*

After the class had completed their writing, each student was paired with a listener in the first-grade classroom, providing a live audience. Such cross-grade grouping as this adds vitality to the literature-based composition program. A major focus in recent professional writing about composition instruction is the need of student writers to develop a sense of audience by writing for real people, in addition to the teacher, who is most often the only audience.

## SUMMARY

The alphabet book is a staple in every early-education classroom. When using such books, teachers often focus on their function, rather than on their organizational format. In order to enhance literature programs, teachers should make sure boys and girls encounter the three organizational forms of alphabet book: related-topic books, potpourri books, and sequential-story books. Presenting these three types of organizational patterns and encouraging children to talk about them serves two purposes: (1) to do a more mature, in-depth study of alphabet books than is usually done, and (2) to make children aware of the many options available to them when creating alphabet books of their own.

## Suggestions for Further Study

1. *Certainly, Carrie, Cut the Cake* is one of those books whose format seems to make it a children's book but whose content contradicts that classification. Share this book with children and get their reactions to it. Do they find it amusing?

2. Provide students with paints, brushes, pens, sticks, stencil paper, and scissors; encourage them to make a single letter in as many different ways as they can devise. Variations in size, thickness (visual weight), and shape should be apparent in the results. Encourage children to note and discuss these variations.

3. Do a study of the history of letter shapes with boys and girls, examining how different cultures make the same letters. *The 26 Letters*, by Oscar Ogg (New York: Thomas Y. Crowell, 1971), contains much useful information, presented on an adult level but adaptable for use with children.

4. Find several different typefaces in magazines. (*The New Yorker* is a good source because of the variety of advertisements it includes.) Mount the examples on construction paper, and show them to children, using an overhead projector to enlarge them for easy viewing. Ask children to point out similarities and differences.

5. Some books mentioned in this chapter are illustrated with photographs, and much is being written about the use of photography with children (see, for example, *Children Are Centers for Understanding Media*, eds. Susan Rice and Rose Mukerji, Washington, D.C.: A.C.E.I., 1973). Secure several inexpensive cameras. Teach your students to use the cameras, and then have them take pictures of objects in the classroom or around the school to make a photographic alphabet book.

6. Use *Q Is for Duck*, by Mary Elting and Michael Folsom (New York: Clarion Books, 1980), with second, third, or fourth graders. The book's concept is one that children will enjoy trying to duplicate in their own examples. One page provides a statement about a letter and the question "Why?"; the following page provides the riddle's answer. For example, "H is for owl. Why? Because an owl hoots." The pictures are undistinguished, but the word play will fascinate boys and girls.

7. Involve children in a group effort to construct a collage alphabet book, after showing them *Have You Ever Seen . . . ?*, by Beau Gardner (New York: Dodd, Mead, 1986). Highly saturated colors printed on a coated paper depict, in simplified, patterned shapes, a range of animals from the alligator with antlers through the zebra with a zipper. Done without backgrounds, these illustrations show that less can indeed be more.

8. Children can use their bodies to make the letters of the alphabet, as in *I Can Be the Alphabet*, by Marinella Bonini (New York: Viking/Kestrel, 1986). This accordion-fold book shows one or more children, brightly dressed in a variety of costumes, shaping the letters with their arms, legs, and torsos. As a follow-up, you might photograph the children in your class doing the same thing.

# Related Reading for Adults

Baldwin, Ruth M. *One-hundred Nineteenth Century Rhyming Alphabets in English*. Carbondale, Ill.: Southern Illinois University Press, 1972.

A two-page preface is the only text in this extensive survey of early alphabet books, reproduced in sharply contrasting black and white. The illustrations in these books are small and full of detail, and the moral tone of the texts is likely to amuse today's readers. The range of topics and vocabulary is impressive—but many of the ideas and words will be unfamiliar to children.

Cataldo, John W. *Words and Calligraphy for Children*. New York: Reinhold, 1969.

Cataldo provides a lavishly illustrated record of the ways words and art materials can be unified into a finished visual expression. Examples of art by children from six to seventeen years of age demonstrate how words and letter forms can become integral parts of paintings, drawings, and other art forms. Although some of the techniques (for example, batik) are not explained in sufficient detail, most of the projects are well within the capabilities of an interested classroom teacher. Though now out of print, this older book is well worth the effort of locating in a library or borrowing via interlibrary loan.

Holt, John. *What Do I Do Monday?* New York: Dutton, 1970.

Holt, a provocative writer on education, turns his attention to the dullness of penmanship instruction. In an exciting section dealing with ways to help children explore letter form, he suggests focusing on the proportion, slant, and weight of letters. This challenging approach, to be used after children have learned the alphabet, is still a fresh one—despite its age.

Hopkins, Lee Bennett, and Misha Arenstein. "From Apple Pie to Zooplankton." *Elementary English*, November 1971, pp. 788–793.

In a short introduction, the authors discuss the proliferation of alphabet books that are creative, unusual, and complex. In the past, one or two simple objects appeared on a page. Now many exotic objects or concepts may appear, and the books motivate new interest in language on nearly every grade level. For each book, the article includes an excerpt, full bibliographic information, and a short annotation.

Jones, Marian. "AB (by) C Means Alphabet Books by Children." *The Reading Teacher*, March 1983, pp. 646–648.

Identifying Kate Greenaway's alphabet book, published in 1886, as the first of this genre, Jones recommends those of its descendants that have been named Caldecott honor books. She then describes many group and individual activities that can grow from experiences with alphabet books, including composition (oral and written) and art activities. Several activities are based on specific books such as Marcia Brown's *All Butterflies* (described in this chapter).

Pellowski, Anne. "AaBbCc." *Top of the News*, 30 (January 1974), pp. 144–149.

Although young children are usually fascinated by the sound of language, they are too often conditioned to consider people who speak other languages "different." Children should be made aware of the many forms of language. The article describes three films about alphabets and provides a short bibliography of non-English alphabet books. After explaining how to run an alphabet program, the author appends a list of ways to arouse children's interest in other languages and alphabets.

## Related Reading for Children

Farber, Norma. *As I Was Crossing Boston Common*. New York: Dutton, 1973.

> In rhyme with a definite rhythm, Farber tells the fanciful story of a menagerie following a leader across the common. The names are intriguing; from *angwantibo* to *zibet*, the sounds tickle children's ears. Ink drawings, in soft gold and green, and in Arnold Lobel's predictably whimsical style, evoke a historical ambiance. All the names are actual terms for rare species of animals; a glossary is provided.

McGinn, Maureen. *I Used to Be an Artichoke*. St. Louis: Concordia, 1973.

> Full color contrasts with liberal expanses of white paper to create a humorous tale about an artichoke who was completely happy until someone criticized him. The former artichoke becomes something for every letter of the alphabet. The imaginative use of pattern and bold color results in art that is better than the poetry that tells the story.

Mendoza, George. *The Alphabet Boat*. New York: American Heritage, 1972.

> The author, a prolific writer whose output reached 100 books with this one, explores a variety of boats and the alphabetic needs they have, from anchor to zephyr winds.

> Two Sendakesque children inhabit the detailed, pastel pictures of boats and waters.

Milgrom, Harry. *ABC of Ecology*. New York: Macmillan, 1972.

> Milgrom depicts people and objects, primarily from the urban environment, in clear black-and-white photographs. The pictures are almost full-page; the brief text tells something about an aspect of ecology and poses parallel questions that ask children to perform some activity (such as a simple experiment) or think about some problem.

Milne, A. A. *Pooh's Alphabet Book*. New York: Dutton, 1975.

> The characteristics and philosophies of childhood are portrayed in limericks, and dolls and teddy bears animate the alphabet. Children old enough to comprehend the subtle humor will be charmed by this addition to the Pooh library.

Ruben, Patricia. *Apples to Zippers*. Garden City, N.Y.: Doubleday, 1976.

> Ruben pictures objects in an urban child's environment in sometimes humorous but always unambiguous black-and-white photographs. Two to four large pictures for each letter fill the page in a pleasant layout.

## Professional References

Debes, John L., and Clarence M. Williams. "The Power of Visuals." *Instructor*, December 1974, 32–39.

Feelings, Tom. "Illustration Is My Form; The Black Experience My Story and My Content." *The Advocate*, 4 (Winter 1985), 76.

Kiefer, Barbara. "Critically Speaking. Literature for Children." *The Reading Teacher*, January 1985, 458–463.

Richard, Olga, and Donnarae MacCann. "Picture Books for Children." *Wilson Library Bulletin*, 59 (May 1985), 608–609.

Schoenfield, Madalynne. "Alphabet and Counting Books." *Day Care and Early Education*, 10 (Winter 1982), 44.

Stewig, John Warren. *Exploring Language Arts in the Elementary Classroom*. New York: Richard C. Owen Publishers, 1983, pp. 147–150.

# Bibliography of Children's Books

Alda, Arlene. *Arlene Alda's ABC*. Millbrae, Calif.: Celestial Arts, 1981.

Alexander, Anne. *ABC of Cars and Trucks*. Garden City, N.Y.: Doubleday, 1971.

Anno, Mitsumasa, and Masaichiro Anno. *Anno's Magical ABC*. New York: Philomel Books, 1980.

Arnosky, Jim. *Mouse Writing*. New York: Harcourt Brace Jovanovich, 1983.

Barry, Katharina. *A Is for Anything*. New York: Harcourt Brace, 1961.

Bayer, Jane. *A My Name Is Alice*. New York: Dial, 1984.

Beisner, Monika. *A Folding Alphabet Book*. New York: Farrar, Straus and Giroux, 1979.

Beller, Janet. *A-B-C-ing*. New York: Crown, 1984.

Belloc, Hilaire. *A Moral Alphabet*. New York: Dover, 1961. (Original version published in 1899.)

Blades, Ann. *By the Sea*. Toronto: Kids Can Press, 1985.

Boxer, Devorah. *26 Ways to Be Somebody Else*. New York: Pantheon, 1960.

Brown, Marcia. *All Butterflies*. New York: Scribner's, 1974.

———. *Peter Piper's Alphabet*. New York: Scribner's, 1959.

Burgess, George. *The Adventures of A Apple Pie*. New York: Dover, 1973 (1835).

Burningham, John. *ABC*. New York: Crown, 1985.

———. *ABCDEFGHIJKLMNOPQRSTUVWXYZ*. New York: Bobbs-Merrill, 1964.

Carle, Eric. *All About Arthur*. New York: Franklin Watts, 1974.

Chardiet, Bernice. *C Is for Circus*. New York: Walker, 1971.

Charlip, Remy, Mary Beth, and George Ancona. *Handtalk Birthday*. New York: Four Winds, 1987.

Chess, Victoria. *Alfred's Alphabet Walk*. New York: Greenwillow, 1979.

Children's Television Workshop. *The Sesame Street Book of Letters*. Boston: Little, Brown, 1969.

Chwast, Seymour, and Martin Stephen Moskof. *Still Another Alphabet Book*. New York: McGraw-Hill, 1969.

Cleaver, Elizabeth. *ABC*. New York: Atheneum, 1984.

Coudrille, Jonathon. *A Beastly Collection*. London: Frederick Warne, 1974.

Crews, Donald. *We Read: A to Z*. New York: Greenwillow, 1984.

Delaunay, Sonia. *Alphabet*. New York: Thomas Y. Crowell, 1970.

Dreamer, Sue. *Circus ABC*. Boston: Little, Brown, 1985.

Duke, Kate. *The Guinea Pig ABC*. New York: Dutton, 1983.

Falls, C. B. *ABC*. Garden City, N.Y.: Doubleday, 1923.

Feelings, Muriel. *Jambo Means Hello*. New York: Dial, 1974.

———. *Moja Means One*. New York: Dial, 1974.

Feeney, Stephanie. *A Is for Aloha*. Honolulu: University Press of Hawaii, 1980.

Frederico, Helen. *The Golden Happy Book of ABC*. New York: Golden Press, 1963.

Freeman, Don. *Add-a-Line Alphabet*. San Carlos, Calif.: Golden Gate Junior Books, 1968.

Fujikawa, Gyo. *Gyo Fujikawa's A to Z Picture Book*. New York: Grosset and Dunlap, 1974.

Gag, Wanda. *The ABC Bunny*. New York: Coward McCann, 1933.

Garten, Jan. *The Alphabet Tale*. New York: Random House, 1964.

Geisert, Arthur. *Pigs from A to Z*. Boston: Houghton Mifflin, 1986.

Gordon, Isabel. *The ABC Hunt*. New York: Viking, 1961.

Greenaway, Kate. *A Apple Pie*. London: Frederick Warne, n.d.

Gretz, Susanna. *Teddy Bears ABC*. New York: Four Winds, 1986.

Gundersheimer, Karen. *ABC Say With Me*. New York: Harper and Row, 1984.

Howard-Gibbon, Amelia Frances. *An Illustrated Comic Alphabet*. New York: Henry Z. Walck, 1967.

Ipcar, Dahlov. *I Love My Anteater with an A*. New York: Alfred A. Knopf, 1964.

Kitamura, Satoshi. *What's Inside?* New York: Farrar, Straus and Giroux, 1985.

Kitchen, Bert. *Animal Alphabet*. New York: Dial, 1984.

Knight, Hilary. *Hilary Knight's ABC*. New York: Golden Press, 1961.

Krieger, David L. (ill.). *Letters and Words*. New York: Young Scott Books, 1969.

Lalicki, Barbara (selector). *If There Were Dreams to Sell*. New York: Lothrop, Lee and Shepard, 1984.

Lear, Edward. *ABC*. New York: McGraw-Hill, 1965. (Originally published in 1871.)

———. *A Was Once an Apple Pie*. New York: Scholastic Book Services, 1969.

LeTord, Bijou. *Arf Boo Click*. New York: Four Winds, 1981.

Lionni, Leo. *The Alphabet Tree*. New York: Pantheon, 1968.

Lobel, Anita. *On Market Street*. New York: Greenwillow, 1981.

Low, Joseph. *Adam's Book of Odd Creatures*. New York: Atheneum, 1962.

MacDonald, Suse. *Alphabatics*. New York: Bradbury, 1986.

McMillan, Bruce. *The Alphabet Symphony*. New York: Greenwillow, 1977.

Miles, Miska. *Apricot ABC*. Boston: Little, Brown, 1969.

Miller, Barry. *Alphabet World*. New York: MacMillan, 1971.

Moncure, Jane Belk. *Magic Monsters Act the Alphabet*. Elgin, Ill.: Child's World, 1983.

Montressor, Beni. *A for Angel*. New York: Alfred A. Knopf, 1969.

Moore, Margaret, and John Moore. *Certainly, Carrie, Cut the Cake*. New York: Bobbs-Merrill, 1971.

Munari, Bruno. *ABC*. Cleveland: World Publishing, 1960.

Neumeier, Marty, and Byron Glaser. *Action Alphabet*. New York: Greenwillow, 1985.

Newsom, Carol (ill.). *An Edward Lear Alphabet*. New York: Lothrop, Lee and Shepard, 1983.

Obligado, Lilian. *Faint Frogs Feeling Feverish*. New York: Viking, 1983.

Parrish, Peggy. *A Beastly Circus*. New York: Simon and Schuster, 1969.

Piatti, Celestino. *Animal ABC*. New York: Atheneum, 1966.

Rey, H. A. *Curious George Learns the Alphabet*. Boston: Houghton Mifflin, 1963.

Rojankovsky, Feodor. *Animals in the Zoo*. New York: Alfred A. Knopf, 1962.

Schmiderer, Dorothy. *The Alphabeast Book*. New York: Holt, Rinehart and Winston, 1971.

Sendak, Maurice. *Alligators All Around*. New York: Harper and Row, 1962.

Shahn, Ben. *The Alphabet of Creation*. New York: Schocken, 1965.

Smith, William Jay. *Puptents and Pebbles*. Boston: Little, Brown, 1959.

Steiner, Charlotte. *Annie's ABC Kitten*. New York: Alfred A. Knopf, 1965.

Sullivan, Mary Beth, and Linda Bourke. *A Show of Hands*. New York: Harper and Row, 1980.

Thayer, Jane. *Timothy and Madam Mouse*. New York: Morrow, 1971.

Townsend, Jessie. *Annie, Bridget, and Charlie*. New York: Pantheon, 1967.

Travers, P. L. *Mary Poppins from A to Z*. New York: Harcourt Brace, 1962.

Tudor, Tasha. *A Is for Annabelle*. New York: Henry Z. Walck, 1954.

Ungerer, Tomi. *Crictor*. New York: Harper and Row, 1958.

Walters, Marguerite. *The City-Country ABC*. Garden City, N.Y.: Doubleday, 1966.

Warburg, Sandol. *From Ambledee to Zumbledee.* Boston: Houghton Mifflin, 1968.

Warren, Cathy. *Victoria's ABC Adventure.* New York: Lothrop, Lee and Shepard, 1984.

Watson, Clyde. *Applebet.* New York: Farrar, Straus and Giroux, 1982.

Wersba, Barbara. *Twenty-Six Starlings Will Fly Through Your Mind.* New York: Harper and Row, 1980.

Wild, Robin and Jocelyn Wild. *The Bears' ABC Book.* New York: Harper and Row, 1985.

Wildsmith, Brian. *ABC.* New York: Franklin Watts, 1962.

Williams, Garth. *The Big Golden Animal ABC.* New York: Simon and Schuster, 1957.

Zachs, Irene. *Space Alphabet.* Englewood Cliffs, N.J.: Prentice-Hall, 1964.

# PICTURE BOOKS: A SUBTLE BALANCE

. . . once or twice she had peeped into the book her sister was reading, but it had no pictures . . . in it, "and what is the use of a book," thought Alice, "without pictures . . .?"[1]

Many children since Alice have echoed her sentiments. To meet their demands, the picture storybook was developed and has proliferated. Today the picture storybook is a recognized genre, and there are awards to honor the best examples. More of these books are published each year than most teachers and librarians can become familiar with. Because picture storybooks are such a pervasive part of children's early education, it is important to consider what they are, the purposes they serve, and the nature of children's responses to them.

## A BOOK WITH PICTURES

A picture storybook is a book in which the story and pictures are of equal importance. The two elements together form an artistic unit that is stronger than either of them would be alone.

Sometimes such books have few words because they are designed for the very youngest readers. An example is *Drummer Hoff*, by Barbara Emberley, an adaptation of a Mother Goose rhyme that is illustrated by Ed Emberley with solid woodcuts in bright colors. The cumulative, rhyming story contains only thirty words, but the highly complex pictures, which culminate in a vibrant red, pink, and purple double-page explosion of "kahbahbloom," are intriguing.[2]

Other picture books are more complex than *Drummer Hoff* and are obviously appropriate for intermediate-grade readers. *Brave Janet Reachfar*, by Jane Duncan, is the story of a girl's attempts to rescue sheep from an unexpected spring snow. The characters, the animals, and the environment in the Scottish Highlands are realistically depicted. The author uses a sophisticated vocabulary and lengthy sentences (one sentence has fifty-four words, more than in all of *Drummer Hoff*). However, this impressive story of courage and ingenuity is well worth the demands it makes on the reader/

---

[1]There are numerous versions of *Alice in Wonderland*, with illustrations by artists working in a variety of styles.

[2]See Barbara Bader's article "Picture Books, Art and Illustration" (in *Newbery and Caldecott Medal Books, 1966–1976*, Boston: The Horn Book, 1975, pp. 278–280). Bader is not impressed with this award winner, and she offers acerbic comments on most of the others. Her educated eye prompts her to plead for more discrimination in making the awards.

listener. Pictures in this book occur less frequently than in *Drummer Hoff*; the text is pleasantly augmented by the pictures but does not rely on them.

Some picture books represent a collaboration between an author and an illustrator. Adrienne Kennaway did the striking, full-page pictures, bled to the page edge, for *Hot Hippo*, by Mwenye Hadithi. This *pourquoi* (tell-me-why) tale recounts how the hippo finds its special place in nature. The simple langauge is augmented by the intense and varied watercolors, which do not add much factual detail but do provide a pleasant accompaniment.

Other picture books are written and illustrated by just one person. An example is *Burt Dow, Deep-Water Man*, written and illustrated by Robert McCloskey. Burt sets out to sea one day in his leaky old double-ender. McCloskey's pictures show Burt's encounter with a huge whale, who saves him from a storm only to get him into more trouble in a school of whales. The opaque watercolor illustrations bleed off the edges of the pages, resulting in large, bright images that clarify and extend the text.

Picture books may be illustrated in black and white, in a few colors, or in many hues. Leonard Everett Fisher demonstrates the expressiveness of simple black and white in *The Great Wall of China*. His monumental paintings use applied white to achieve an array of grey tones that further contrast with the more stark white of the page itself.

One of the most talented illustrators in the use of black and white is Chris Van Allsburg. In his *The Garden of Abdul Gasazi*, Van Allsburg creates a surreal world where illusion blends into reality. The pencil illustrations are realistic, but he uses intensified light, shadow, and perspective to create unusual impressions of space and density. This book, his first, marked the beginning of an impressive succession of high-quality picture books.

Just a few colors are used by Peter Parnall in *Winter Barn*. This book features more realistically detailed drawings with less undesigned space than is usual in Parnall's work. Faint touches of brown and red direct the eye in these drawings. Another example of effective use of a few colors is found in Mary Calhoun's *The Witch Who Lost Her Shadow*. With three colors, artist Trinka Noble defines the village and the characters. This simple story is about a good witch whose constant companion, her "silent-sipping wisp of a cat," disappears. The book is an admirable combination of low-keyed art and graceful, unobtrusive writing.

Unlike artists who work with few colors, Eric Carle utilizes many hues, both primary and pastel, in his collage pictures for *Why Noah Chose the Dove*. This Bible story was retold from the animals' viewpoint by Isaac Bashevis Singer. The animals, bragging about their good qualities, are depicted in blocky, page-filling shapes, cut from paper and streaked with paint. More than a decade later, perennially popular Carle again uses the same

*Using just pencil, the artist creates an amazing variety of shades of black and grey, evoking a sense of immensely deep space. The unusual perspective, looking up the tunnel through the trees, is echoed elsewhere in other unusual points of view.* From *The Garden of Abdul Gasazi* by Chris Van Allsburg. Copyright © 1979 by Chris Van Allsburg. Reprinted by permission of Houghton Mifflin Company.

technique in *The Foolish Tortoise,* by Richard Buckley. In this case, the artist's considerable talent perhaps overmatches the rather slight fable, but his pictures are as appealing and as "readable" as ever.

Picture-book stories may be realistic or fantastic. In spare prose, often no more than a sentence or two per page, Donald Carrick tells the poignant story of *The Deer in the Pasture* who "adopted" a human but later had to be returned to the wild. The author provides pleasantly casual watercolor paintings in many subtle shades of brown, green, gold, and orange. The open ending is also realistic; children will wonder what happens to the deer, and hope. After reading this book to children, a teacher might ask them to write an ending to the story.

In contrast to Carrick's kind of realism, picture books often feature fantastical tales about either animals or people. Barbara Lucas's *Sleeping Over* is a story about a bear and a frog, which ends happily when the frog finds a comfortable place to sleep (a toothbrush glass full of water). Stella Ormai's watercolor-and-ink paintings convincingly depict the frog's trouble and the resolution.

A pleasant fantasy about a human is Jenny Thorne's *My Uncle*, featuring a round-faced gentleman nattily attired in black-and-yellow checked knickers. His desire to go mountain climbing first gets him into trouble with a big-billed bird; later he gets lost in a forest inhabited by strange creatures and finally barely escapes an octopus in the water. The dry, pragmatic language is in interesting contrast to the fantasy of the drawings.

## PHYSICAL FORMAT OF PICTURE BOOKS

Beyond the quality of the illustrations themselves, several considerations influence the final look of a picture book. Some of these components are rather subtle. In choosing books to use with children, a teacher should assess the effectiveness of the book designer's decisions concerning: (1) shape and size, (2) binding, endpapers, and paper, (3) typefaces, and (4) page layout.

**SHAPE.** A book designer carefully chooses a book's shape to enhance the text and pictures. Although constraints are imposed by the practicalities of printing and the problem of shelving unusually shaped books, the designer has a range of options.

The most common shape for books is the rectangle. Some books that are rectangular are taller than they are wide. For example, the tall shape of *Up Goes the Skyscraper!*, by Gail Gibbons, effectively ties in with the subject, but the solid colors and pervasive thin, black line of the illustrations are utilitarian, merely providing the necessary factual details about the construction of buildings. A tall, thin shape was used also by the book designer for *Jack and the Beanstalk*, retold by Walter de la Mare. The artist, Joseph Low, stretched the illustrations (especially the one of the beanstalk) to the full height of the page. Using black crayon with bold splashes of color, Low created pleasantly casual illustrations to accompany the detailed story. (A different approach to the same story is a square-shaped version with illustrations by Matt Faulkner, who uses soft, pastel-hued crayon.)

**These blocky woodcut illustrations show a dramatic combination of heavy line and big bulky areas of color.** Illustration from *A Boy Went Out to Gather Pears* by Felix Hoffman. Copyright © 1963 by Verlag Sauerlander, Aarau (Switzerland) and Frankfurt am Main (Germany). Reproduced by permission.

The book designer, on the other hand, may choose a rectangular shape that is longer in the horizontal dimension. In *Carol Barker's Birds and Beasts*, Barker uses darkly intense colors with swirling patterns to develop a menagerie of wild beasts. The illustrations spread across facing pages, giving an impression of extended horizontal space. The chameleon, with rotating eyes and spotted skin, extends the full width of the open book, nearly 21 inches. Several other animals are almost as long. The horizontal dimension is also exploited effectively in *A Boy Went Out to Gather Pears*, by Felix Hoffman. The text is an old verse about a boy who, instead of picking pears, waits for them to fall; his master sends out a dog, a stick, fire, and four other messengers to stir the boy to action. The artist fills the 17-inch-wide horizontal spreads with angular illustrations in limited but cheerful shades of orange, yellow, blue, green, brown, and black.

More elegant illustrations appear in the realistic story *Toad*, by Anne and Harlow Rockwell. This almost square book (about 8 inches by 8 inches) tells of the dangers and pleasures of a year in the life of a toad. Illustrations that are both rectangular and square are mostly placed rather formally on the pages, with a border of color surrounding them. (This book could be used in conjunction with a more recently published work by the Rockwells, such as *In Our House* so children can notice changes in the artists' style.)

Another alternative for a book designer is to choose a square shape. *The Fish* is a square book (about 6 inches on a side) containing a not very believable story about a fish who rescues a little girl. Prolific artist Dick Bruna rendered the fish, swans, ducklings, and little girl in flat, intense colors boldly outlined with a uniform black line. The illustrations' blocky shapes are well suited to the book's square format.

**The elaborate illustrations of bumpy toads and the simple typeface used for the authors' names complement each other.** Illustration by Harlow Rockwell, from *Toad* by Anne and Harlow Rockwell, published by Curtis Brown Ltd. Reproduced by permission of Anne and Harlow Rockwell.

**SIZE.** Within certain limits, publishers will experiment with book size to create specific effects. However, very small or very large books are difficult to print, mail, and shelve. A designer considers the topic, the potential audience, and the total visual presentation desired when selecting a size.

Undoubtedly the best-known creator of small books is Beatrix Potter. Although Potter's stories are usually accompanied by her own illustrations, *The Tale of Tuppenny* is available with pictures by another artist, Marie Angel. Angel's pictures are softer than Potter's but are quite appropriate to the story. This book's miniature size, similar to those illustrated by Potter herself, reinforces the charm of the story.

Another small book (about 5 inches square) is *Hooray for Us*, by Sandol Stoddard Warburg, which is illustrated with detailed black-ink drawings of homely children, animals and older people. Effective in enhancing children's self-concept, this book's small size makes it most effective when shared with one child at a time.

Large size can also be utilized to make a book more effective. Tomi Ungerer, the author and illustrator of over fifty books, chose a large, rectangular shape (9 by 12 inches) for the humorous story of *Zeralda's Ogre*. The innocent farmer's daughter uses her culinary skill to win over the grumpy ogre and solve the villagers' problem. Ungerer takes full advantage of the generous space the large size affords.

Another large book, the same size as *Zeralda's Ogre*, is William Steig's pleasant story *Roland the Minstrel Pig*. Roland, who has a beautiful voice, aspires to be rich and famous but falls in with bad company—a voracious

**This gothic display typeface would be difficult to read if many words were involved, but it reinforces the quasi-medieval mood of the story.** Illustration from *Zeralda's Ogre* by Tomi Ungerer. Copyright © 1967 by Tomi Ungerer. Reprinted by permission of Harper & Row, Publishers, Inc.

fox. Until the king fortuitously passes by and rescues him, he is in danger of being roasted and eaten. The illustration for the crisis point in the story gains in intensity by being spread across two pages. A wide variety of pastel shades are employed in the detailed illustrations.[3]

**BINDING.**  The binding is carefully chosen by the designer to give a book an attractive and durable exterior. In planning a cover, the designer gives careful consideration to the visual impression that will be created. To ensure that the cover is representative of the book, a designer will sometimes use a design motif or picture that appears elsewhere in the book, or will tie in the color.

Higher-quality picture books may be hardbound with a cloth cover. A very handsome black linen cover with a gold-stamped ship's wheel,[4] a design element that is repeated on the title page, introduces *Steamboat in a Cornfield,* by John Hartford. Black was an appropriate color choice for this cover, given the thin black line that borders the sepia-toned photographs in the book. These photographs were taken during the first decade of this century, when the steamboat *Queen City* traveled from Pittsburgh to New Orleans. A brown linen cover would have been the more obvious but less effective choice.

Sometimes the cover is a combination of cloth and paper. The designer of *Half a Moon and One Whole Star,* by Crescent Dragonwagon, chose dark blue paper with a linen spine edging of even darker blue. Visually, this cover leads directly into the book, in which artist Jerry Pinckney's richly interesting watercolors show a similar midnight blue. A cloth-and-paper binding in two shades of orange, one bright and one burnt, introduces *A Regular Rolling Noah,* by George Ella Lyon. Throughout the book, artist Stephen Gammel's full-page watercolors in a variety of browns, golds, and other oranges echo the introductory colors.

Because of increasing production costs, books are often bound in a paper-over-boards format. A particularly well-done example of this less expensive binding is *Wallaby Creek,* by Joyce Powzyk. The high-gloss finish of the cover sets off its deep blue border, lighter aqua type, and naturally colored animal painting.

---

[3]William Steig is a master at personifying animals. In *Who's Who in Children's Books* (New York: Holt, Rinehart and Winston, 1975, p. 336), Margery Fisher comments that "larger animals do not as a rule humanize well in visual terms, but [Steig] . . . has overcome the inherent difficulties" in turning animals into recognized suburban families.

[4]Such color designs are stamped under pressure using a brass die. If no ink is used, the sunken image is referred to as *blind-stamped*. An example of a blind-stamped design is found on the vivid purple cover of *A Color of His Own,* by Leo Lionni (New York: Pantheon, 1975).

**ENDPAPERS.** Opening a book's cover, readers discover another important visual element, the endpapers.[5] These may have a design that comes from a motif or an illustration used elsewhere in the book, or they may simply be a solid color.

A very simple endpaper design that is nonetheless effective is found in *Ruff Leaves Home*, by Anne Carter. A blue silhouette of a fox faces left on the front endpapers and right on the back endpapers, nicely framing the story in between. The blue is repeated as the background color on the title page and in the book's realistic paintings by John Butler.

More elaborate endpapers are found in *Katie Morag and the Two Grandmothers*, by Mairi Hedderwick. The front endpapers show the Isle of Struay by day, with the buildings labeled. Pleasant watercolors are enhanced by a liberal use of white. The back endpapers show the same scene at night, without the labels, in the glow of moonlight. Hedderwick's illustrations within the book are also done in watercolors that are pleasantly kinetic, using much white for contrast and a thin brown line to define shapes. The same endpapers are used again in *Katie Morag and the Tiresome Ted*, which is also characterized by Hedderwick's light, bright palette.

In *Mike Mulligan and His Steam Shovel*, author/illustrator Virginia Lee Burton makes the endpapers into a teaching tool. Since children may not know the parts of a steam shovel, the endpapers provide a diagram. It shows, in bright colors, a side view of the steam shovel, with each part labeled; small drawings to one side show the steam shovel at work. Though nearly fifty years old, this story remains a favorite.[6]

More recently, another illustrator, Peter Spier, often designs endpapers that set the tone for or expand upon the story within a book. For example, for his extended wordless retelling in *Noah's Ark*, Spier presents from one to three illustrations on each page. The opening endpaper alludes to the events that led up to Noah's task, and the closing endpaper shows what Noah did after he left the ark.

Whether or not they are illustrated, endpapers are frequently of a color that is the same as or in contrast to the cover. The color of the endpapers can also reflect the book's mood. A dark grey stock is used for the endpapers

---

[5]Endpapers are the first and last spreads of a book. One side of each spread is glued to the inside of the cover; the other side is not pasted down. Endpapers are usually of heavier paper than are the printed pages.

[6]In a rare commentary on a children's book within a children's book, Beverly Cleary lets the main character in *Ramona the Pest* (New York: Morrow, 1968) give her reaction to this book during her first day in kindergarten. Ramona's delight in the story is shared by many real children.

in *The Something*, by Natalie Babbitt. Ugly Milo and his uglier mother live in a cavelike home. Milo is afraid of an unknown thing, which he believes will invade his bedroom. Babbitt creates an ominous effect on the endpapers with fine, black lines. She does not outline the shapes of the interlocking trees but rather uses the fine lines to create the background in a reverse effect. After listening to this story, children may enjoy discussing their own fears and comparing them to Milo's.

In *The Sign in Mendel's Window*, the plain lavender endpapers pick up shades and tints of purple that appear in, but do not dominate, author/ illustrator Margot Zemach's watercolors. Similarly, in *Henry's Fourth of July*, the light blue endpapers reflect various shades of that color used by Holly Keller throughout the book.

**PAPER.** Since children are very sensorily oriented, they should have the luxury of fine paper in their books. The smell and feel of good-quality paper can be a delight to them, just as it often is to adults.

Papers basically have one of two finishes: matte or shiny. A matte finish is a dull surface. Matte-finish paper is often heavy, with an interesting texture that does not reflect but rather absorbs light. The kind of pleasurable delight to be derived from fine, matte-finish paper is apparent in the thick, cream-colored stock used for *Grandmother's Pictures*, reminiscences of Sam Cornish, a major black poet. The heavy paper has a velvety surface and is completely opaque; no hint of an illustration on the reverse side of a page ever shows through. *Under the Green Willow*, by Elizabeth Coatsworth, was first published in 1971 and was recently reissued. Janina Domanska's geometric drawings, alive with repeated patterns in shades of just green and yellow, show up well on the heavy, white, textured matte paper. Also printed effectively on heavy, white matte paper, but very different stylistically from Domanska's drawings are Brock Cole's realistic watercolors for *The Winter Wren*.

In contrast to matte-finish papers are those with a shiny, light-reflecting surface, technically called *coated* papers because they are created in a complex process in which a coating of clay and adhesive is applied. The smooth, glazed surface creates a very different effect than does a matte-finish surface.

*The Golem*, a picture book for older children, was named a Caldecott honor book in 1976. Author/illustrator Beverly Brodsky McDermott used massive, rather abstract shapes to illustrate this retelling of a Jewish legend. The paper's high sheen and the light that it reflects deepen and intensify the dark colors McDermott uses. Heavy black line, which liberally outlines many of the objects, is kept from being oppressive by the paper. Lydia Dabcovich tells of the hibernation of *Sleepy Bear* in less than fifty words.

Her bold but limited-color illustrations are enhanced by the coated paper on which they are printed. Lillian Hoban's casual pictures for Miriam Cohen's book *Starring First Grade* are similarly enriched by glazed paper.

An extended but interesting technical consideration of binding and paper is provided by Groban and Lowe (1982), who base it on their experiences working in publishing.

**TYPEFACES.** Although few readers will ever pause to consider the typefaces selected by a book's designer, the type chosen does affect the final look of a book. Typefaces are basically of two kinds: text faces and display faces.

Text faces are those used to set the body of the book's copy and are usually much simpler than display faces. Text faces feature easy-to-read shapes that do not tire the reader's eye. These are examples of text faces:

Old Mother Hubbard
Went to the cupboard,
To give her poor dog a bone,

Old Mother Hubbard
Went to the cupboard,
To give her poor dog a bone,

Old Mother Hubbard
Went to the cupboard,
To give her poor dog a bone,

Old Mother Hubbard
Went to the cupboard,
To give her poor dog a bone,

Old Mother Hubbard
Went to the cupboard,
To give her poor dog a bone,

Close observation of the above text types will reveal subtle differences. Take one letter and compare its form in the five samples. How are the *a* forms, the *w* forms, or the *g* forms the same or different?

Display faces often have unusual shapes that will attract and hold readers' attention. Display faces are used on the title page and for chapter and section headings. Since fewer words are set in display faces than in text faces, readability is not the prime consideration. When selecting a display face, the book designer searches for a type that will enhance the message of the book.

# Children and Literature

# CHILDREN AND LITERATURE

# Children and Literature

# Children and Literature

# Children and Literature

Compare the letter forms of the display types above, noting ways they are alike or different. Can you make any inferences about the reasons why a book designer might choose one or another of these typefaces?

Typefaces are either *serif* or *sans serif* (without serif). Serif letters have short extensions off the extremities of the basic letter forms, as in the first, third and fifth examples of display faces above.[7] Sans serif letters, however, are unadorned; the lines forming each letter just end, with no flourish, as in the second and fourth examples.

Some children's books utilize reproductions of hand-lettering rather than being set in type. Hand-lettering adds to the cost of a book's production, but is sometimes considered worth it for the diversity it brings. In *Brownies— Hush!*, by Gladys L. Adshead, an appealing story of a little old woman and man and the imaginary creatures who help them, letters in brown ink are arranged in a variety of ways. The artist also varies the quality of the letters themselves for emphasis. This book is reminiscent of the works of Wanda Gag, who hand-lettered her enduringly popular *Millions of Cats*, as well as her other picture books. (Gag is one of many authors and illustrators whose brief biographies are included in Carpenter and Prichard, 1984). In *Panda*, artist Susan Bonners uses soft-edged watercolor, dark and very wet looking, to portray the life cycle of a young cub. The text is hand-lettered in a precise fashion that gives it the look of print.

Jean de Brunhoff wrote the text to *The Story of Babar* in script (cursive

---

[7]A serif is "the short finishing stroke set across or projecting from the end of a letter stem," according to Geoffrey Glaister in *An Encyclopedia of the Book* (Cleveland: World Publishing, 1960). This book includes many terms, arranged alphabetically, related to papermaking, printing, binding, and publishing.

They took the kitten into the house, where the
very old woman gave it a warm bath and brushed
its fur until it was soft and shiny.

*The hand-lettered text complements the illustration and adds interest to the page.* Illustration by Wanda Gag reprinted by permission of Coward-McCann, Inc., from *Millions of Cats* by Wanda Gag, copyright 1928 by Coward-McCann, Inc., copyright renewed © 1956 by Robert Janssen.

---

or connected writing), which is used in children's books even less often than hand-lettering. This story of an elephant and his adventures is truly captivating, and children enjoy the challenge of reading the script. Originally published in 1933, *The Story of Babar* has been reissued using the original plates and the oversized pages (more than a foot square) that were used in the first but not subsequent editions. *The Travels of Babar* by the same author has also been reissued with the original cursive text.

If a book designer decides that a book should be set in a conventional typeface, he or she then must specify the type size and placement. Typefaces come in different sizes, called *points*.[8] Some picture books for beginning readers feature type that is thirty-six points high, but books for mature readers may use type that is one-third that size or smaller.

---

[8] There are seventy-two points in an inch. Points are used to measure both the size of typefaces and the space between lines of type.

| | |
|---|---|
| H | 6-point |
| H | 8-point |
| H | 10-point |
| H | 11-point |
| H | 12-point |
| H | 14-point |
| H | 18-point |

H 24-point

H 30-point

H 36-point

H 42-point

H 48-point

The amount of white space between the lines of type is controlled by the *leading*. Originally, pieces of lead of different heights were used to determine the space between lines of hand-set type. Today, this spacing is controlled by computer, but it is still called leading. The amount of white space between lines (together with the width of the margins) determines whether the page will have an open, airy look or a tight, compressed appearance.

**PAGE LAYOUT.** Where the type is placed on the page is another important design consideration. In some children's books, the type occurs in the same place on every page; in some, it is placed in the same relative position on alternate pages. For example, in *One Was Johnny,* by Maurice Sendak, all the type is arranged in the bottom two inches of each right-hand page. The room in which Johnny sits comfortably reading his book becomes increasingly crowded as he is joined by all sorts of animals. In *All the Way Home,* by Lore Segal, a pleasant, cream-colored paper sets off James Marshall's humorous three-color illustrations of a parade of caterwauling animals that follow a girl and her mother home. The illustrations are formally placed on the right-hand pages, surrounded by a colored border, and the type always appears on the left-hand pages, adding to the book's predictable progression. This story is a literary cumulative tale, meaning that characters or action are added in sequence and it was written by an identifiable author. It is interesting because of its similarity to folk cumulative tales like *Jack and the Beanstalk,* which have the same general additive form but are from the oral tradition and have no identifiable author.

In some books, the type is placed in a variety of locations. In *Parade,* by Tom Shachtman, the type appears above and below as well as to the left and right of the full-color photographs. In addition, the type is placed on both left-hand and right-hand pages, presenting more variety than is evident in other books.

Picture book designers must also decide where to place the illustrations. Several types of page placement are possible. In some cases, the designer simply puts one picture on each page. The entire picture is contained on the page, creating a particular effect. Wanda Gag, who illustrates most of her own work, uses this placement technique. *Gone is Gone* is a petite book meant for sharing with a single listener, in which Gag tells the whimsical story of an old man who wants to swap jobs with his wife.

The illustrations for *The Princess and the Froggie*, three short tales for very young children, by Harve and Kaethe Zemach, are examples of self-contained pictures. Margot Zemach provides pleasant pastel sketches, located below or above brief lines of type and surrounded by generous white margins.[9] Each picture, which generally has a minimal background and no border, can stand alone.

Sometimes the illustrator places the picture within a formal frame, a device that Dooley (1980) identifies as one of the oldest conventions in book art. Dooley examines frames, visual points-of-view, and captioning as options available to artists. She opens with a consideration of various framing devices, including formal ones such as curtains or stage architecture, parts of the picture itself, and decorative frames. In framing a picture, an artist calls special attention to its boundaries, creating in the process a more formal effect than when a picture is bled to the page edge.

Derek Collard creates a somber effect in his detailed linoleum cuts for the highly original *The Squirrel Wife*, by Philippa Pearce. Collard's brown leaf-and-flower border is printed on light brown paper. On some pages, the border sets off a full page of type; on others, it frames complex illustrations reminiscent of the Norwegian expressionist painter Edvard Munch.

Geometric and curvilinear plantlike forms are combined in the imaginative frame for the illustrations in *Whinnie the Lovesick Dragon*, by Mercer Mayer. Artist Diane Dawson Hearn has breached the frame in a variety of ways (for example, one character rests his elbows on it; another lifts a leg to crawl over it; on one page a boy holding a flag actually becomes part of the frame).

A different kind of framing is present in *The Story of Chicken Licken*, by Jan Ormerod, a book in which the entire story is recreated by child actors in costume, watched by an audience presented in silhouette. Above, the performers on stage are in full-color costumes, their words in cartoon-strip balloons. Below, the silhouettes making up the audience vary on each page, so a continuing "story" develops there, too. Children may need to look at

---

[9]A lot of the real-life characters described in *Self-Portrait: Margot Zemach* (Reading, Mass.: Addison-Wesley, 1978) turn out to look very similar to the fictional characters in the artist's illustrations for her books. These are homey, somewhat dumpy, but charming characters.

these illustrations more than once to perceive the dual stories. This presentation is an effective way of framing the pictures, even though there is no all-around border.

The book designer may spread an illustration across facing pages, creating a double-page spread, which has two advantages. First a double-page spread enhances the dimensions established by the book's shape. For example, a double-page spread in a book with a horizontal rectangular shape makes that rectangle wider, changing its proportions dramatically. In *Two Hundred Rabbits*, by Lonzo Anderson, Adrienne Adams used soft, sometimes transparent watercolor to create serene, pastoral landscapes and richly detailed court scenes for the story in which a young boy tries to think up a way to entertain the king (the rabbit narrator finally helps solve the boy's problem). In several places, the illustrations extend all the way across the 19-inch double-page spread, with the type arranged below.

The second advantage offered by the double-page spread is that it allows the artist to use both vertical and horizontal pictures in one book. For example, in *George's Garden*, by Gerda Marie Scheidl, illustrator Bernadette Watts fully utilizes the potential of the book's shape, which is a vertical rectangle. On some pages, upright pictures stretch the full height (almost 12 inches). This height is particularly effective, for example, for the picture showing the high wall separating the two gardens. In other cases, pictures extend horizontally across two pages, for a width of more than 16 inches. This layout allows Watts plenty of space in the picture showing the variety of birds, animals, and flowers in George's garden.

There is an intrinsic bookmaking problem with double-page spreads, however. The place where two facing pages come together is called the *gutter*, and careful bookmaking is necessary to ensure that the two halves of an illustration match up exactly across this division. The designer must take into account the portion that will disappear into the binding when the pages are sewn together. Children have a clear eye for detail and will notice any missing parts or misalignment in pictures that extend across the gutter. The illustrator and book designer must weigh the gains of using double-page spreads against the added problem presented by this arrangement.

Instead of containing the illustration totally within the page area, book designers sometimes use another type of placement, called a *bleed*, in which the illustration extends all the way to the edge of the page and then seems to fall off of it.[10] Placing illustrations in this manner can be very effective.

---

[10]The illustration is actually printed slightly larger than the final page size. When the paper is trimmed to the page size, so is the illustration. This effect is described with clarity by Henry C. Pitz in *Illustrating Children's Books* (New York: Watson-Guptill, 1963).

Sometimes the bleeds are so unobtrusive that they are almost unnoticeable. *Bang Bang You're Dead*, by Louise Fitzhugh and Sandra Scoppettone, is illustrated in black line with much cross-hatching to create realistically shaded boys with exaggeratedly homely faces. The pictures sometimes extend off the page, but what bleeds off is not of any real significance to the pictures. Parts of a room, rocks, and tree branches extend off the edge, but the figures of the characters are usually contained on the page.

Other artists make more noticeable use of bleeding. In *While the Horses Galloped to London*, by Mable Watts, the bleeding of the illustrations creates a sense of people being jammed into a carriage. The fussiness of the ink line and the close-up view taken by the illustrator increase the effect of crowdedness in these pictures.

Even more innovative use of bleeds is made by Ezra Jack Keats in his bold, colorful illustrations for *The King's Fountain*, written by Lloyd Alexander. All the pictures bleed off the page, and often only parts of the characters are contained on the page. Several illustrations show only the characters' torsos and heads. On the page showing three merchants in a warm beige-and-brown close-up painting, the tops of their heads are cut off by the page edge. Keats's technique is reminiscent of that used by such French painters as Edgar Degas and Henri de Toulouse-Lautrec, who often included only part of a figure or object within the frame of a painting.

Some books show a variety of page placements. In *One Monster After Another*, Mercer Mayer at times contains his aggressive, crowded illustrations within a black-line edge, surrounded by a white border. In other places, the picture is bounded on the bottom by a black line but spills off the top and sides. In still other places, no border at all contains the picture, which simply takes the shape of the objects in it.

## CHILDREN'S AWARENESS OF PHYSICAL FORMAT

Details of physical format are important to book designers, to teachers who share books with children, and, eventually, to the children themselves. When teachers share books with children, they can call attention to such details as an interesting paper color, a striking typeface, or an unusual page layout. There is no need to talk at length about these details; casual comments will make children aware that a book is more than just the story.

A teacher can also heighten children's awareness of physical format by asking incidental questions such as the following when sharing a book with children:

1. Did you notice the paper in this book? Feel it with your fingertips, and think of a word that tells how the paper feels.

2. Where have you seen a color like the one in this endpaper? What does this color suggest to you about the kind of story that may be in this book?

3. Did you notice the letters used for the title of this book? Based on the typeface what idea do you have about the kind of person the main character is?

4. Where are the illustrations placed on the pages in this book? Can you think of a book in which the illustrations were placed in another way? Why is there a difference in where the illustrations are placed?

## THE LANGUAGE OF WORDS AND PICTURES

A good picture book is an effective synthesis of pictures and words. This means, ideally, that both elements should be strong. Although neither the words nor the pictures would be as effective apart, there should be something distinguished about each. The problem in selecting picture books is that not all combine both distinguished writing and distinguished illustration.

*Of Witches and Monsters and Wondrous Creatures*, by Lisl Weil, is an example in which quite competent text is presented in the context of illustrations that range from inept to consciously ugly. The book itself is a generous size (approximately 10 inches square), the matte paper has a pleasant heft, and the lavender endpapers are a positive introduction. The weakness is in the illustrations, which are done in pen line and watercolor wash in purple, lavender, blue, and gold. The pen line is awkward, varying in width for no apparent artistic reason; the crosshatching is merely nervous, not atmospheric; and the forms, human and animal, are clumsy. The reason for all this conscious ugliness cannot be the subject. Although some of the creatures are indeed unpleasant (for example, the Minotaur), other artists have depicted such creatures with far more vigor and grace than does Weil (for example, Weil's version of Baba Yaga is so inferior to that by Blair Lent in Ernest Small's *Baba Yaga* that it does not deserve comparison). The words, strong enough to interest children on their own merit, unfortunately get lost among the pictures.

Sometimes a book will have strong pictures, but the words will be undistinguished. Such a book is *Coco Can't Wait!*, by Japanese author/illustrator Taro Gomi. The book is a horizontal rectangle that opens to a 20-inch width, providing ample room for the boldly simplified shapes. The carefully chosen, restricted range of highly saturated colors (including purple and magenta set off against several shades of brown) is intensified by the bright white background. Richard and MacCann (1985) comment on the "exquisite and accessible" art work, with "many ingenious scale

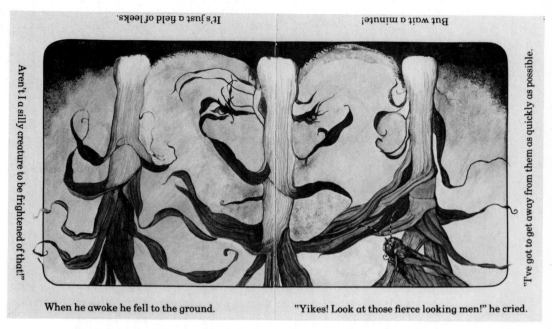

*The full-color painting must be looked at both upside down and right side up to see the two different designs.* From *If at First You Don't See* by Ruth Brown. Copyright © 1982 by Ruth Brown. Reprinted by permission of Henry Holt and Company, Inc.

changes." This book should be used with children despite the fact that the language is pedestrian at best, the kind of language experts rail against when they encounter it in basal readers: "Dear me! Coco is not here!" "Oh no! Grandma is not here!"

It is a happy occurrence when both the pictures and words are equally distinguished. The language used in *Wildfire*, by Evans G. Valens, is equally as good as the pictures (described in Chapter 2):

The heat of the long western summer lay stagnant on the forest when the first raindrops tumbled from the sky. They rattled the dry needles and spanked hot rocks on the ridge above. A chipmunk scuttling for shelter left a wisp of red dust hanging in the drowsy air.

The sky cracked open, a quick electric slit of light running from a cloud to a towering fir. The crack was mended with a clump of thunder, and the echo rolled and ricocheted.

In the clearing dead brush lay dry and hot. The manzanita leaves were ripe with oil. When the flames reached them, the bushes withered. Then they blossomed in a wave of yellow flame. A sound like loud breathing mingled with the snapping and whistling of separate leaves.

*Wildfire* is among the books recommended by Cianciolo (1981). She includes this title in the second edition of her text, despite its being out of print, because it still exemplifies the best possible in picture books.

The language in *Little Silk*, by Jacqueline Ayer, shows what language-sensitive authors can achieve:

> *Deep back in a night-black closet,*
> *hidden behind a tumble of boxes,*
> *boots and bundles,*
> *a faded silk doll*
> *sits and dreams and waits for the closet door to open.*

Note the choice of words "deep back" instead of the more common "way back" or "far back." "Night-black" is a fine choice, since it intensifies the darkness of a closet in a particularly effective way. The doll is hidden in a "tumble" of boxes, an unusual word choice that unconsciously attracts a reader's notice. The alliteration of *b*oxes, *b*oots, and *b*undles is natural. From among all the objects that might be in a closet, the writer has chosen three beginning with the same sound. The triplet construction "sits and dreams and waits" parallels the three words beginning with *b*. Ayer uses lines of varying lengths to tell the story, until the point at which the family reaches the market, where she changes the style somewhat, creating a heavily accented, shorter, and more regular line, with near rhymes at the ends of lines two and four:

> *Cabbages and kumquats,*
> *Chestnuts on the fire,*
> *"Virtuous and Prosperous,"*
> *Fried squid, rubber tires,*
>
> *Peppered eels and crab claws,*
> *Chicken-noodle hot pot,*
> *"Constant Joy Harmonious,"*
> *Wong Lee Barber Shop.*

The rhythmic difference of these lines sets apart the market scene very effectively.

Introduced by dramatic, dark blue endpapers with a stylized floral design, the illustrations by Ayer combine flat blocks of intense orange, blue, and black paint with softer, contrasting areas of pencil, sharpened in places with ink line of delicate, unvarying thickness. The pictures are in perfect harmony with the words.

The effective use of language does not have to be limited to standard

*Very different from his earlier, heavily painted work, this drawing is a delicate array of subtle shades of grey, black and white, showing John Steptoe's ability to switch mediums and styles to suit the story he is illustrating.* From *The Story of Jumping Mouse*, by John Steptoe, copyright © 1984 by John Steptoe. By permission of Lothrop, Lee & Shepard (A Division of William Morrow).

English but may include dialect in order to better create a character. In *All Us Come Cross the Water*, by Lucille Clifton, a small black boy is talking:

> I got a sister name Rose. She studying to be a practical nurse. When she get home I ask her, "Rose where we from?" She come talking about, "Mamma was from Rome, Georgia and Daddy from Birmingham."
> "Before that," I say . . .
> "They wasn't no way back before that. Before that we was a slave."
> I could a punched her in her face. Rose make me sick.

Clifton's book is one of several recommended by Sunal and Hatcher (1985) as being particularly effective in helping children understand the kinds of changes that occur in their lives.

Another distinguished example in which words and pictures are equally strong is found in the Caldecott honor book *The Story of Jumping Mouse*, by John Steptoe. Retelling a Plains Indian tale, the author/illustrator provides large pencil drawings, sometimes stretched to all four edges of a page. The patterns of natural and animal shapes are presented in an impressive array of light and dark shading. Richard and MacCann (1984) comment that the artist is "able to animate the surfaces and depict a rich environment with more success than most artists can achieve with a full range of color."

The language in Steptoe's book is equally strong:

> To his joy he began to see the wondrous beauty of the world above and below and to smell the scent of earth and sky and living things.

Note the dynamic tension in these words—the contrast of the two-part construction ("world above and below") with the three-part construction ("scent of earth and sky and living things"). Steptoe's syntax is mature and accomplished, the mark of a skilled writer. Children will not necessarily notice the syntax, but it does contribute to the quality of the writing and thus has an influence on them.

## EVALUATING PICTURE BOOKS

Not all picture books embody the necessary balance between vigorous language and imaginative pictures. When one or the other of these elements is missing, the book may not be worth sharing with children. Teachers and librarians selecting picture books will do well to examine the candidates carefully, to weed out books that do not combine effective words and effective pictures. Despite the bright colors, John Stadler's cartoon characters in *Snail Saves the Day* are devoid of appeal. The words are written for beginning readers but do not have the wry charm of Arnold Lobel's books, for example, *Owl at Home*, for the same age group. In sum, nothing to recommend here. Similarly, Denys Cazet's rabbits, in *December 24th*, frolic and cavort but never manage to make real magic. The bespectacled grandfather rabbit entertains his grandchildren, and some child readers may find this funny. But there's nothing to recommend the pedestrian language or the overly bright pictures, which are cute without being appealing and rather predictable in their humor.

Often a picture book is unsuccessful because the topic is one that has been treated many times before. It is difficult, for example, to come up with an imaginative treatment of monsters (Stewig, 1977). Despite his recognized success as one of the key innovators in picture books, Maurice Sendak turned out a book that is undistinguished when he tried his hand at monsters—in *Seven Little Monsters*.

Another major consideration when evaluating picture storybooks is how well the words and the pictures mesh. There may be such distinct contradictions between the text and the illustrations that it becomes doubtful that children will accept the book. Though an artist should be free to interpret words imaginatively, pictures that contradict the words can only serve to confuse child readers. An unfortunate example comes from the drawing board of a talented illustrator, Susan Jeffers, whose pictures for *Cinderella* don't bear out the words of translator Amy Ehrlich. The text asserts that "he became a fat coachman with a most imposing beard." The beard Jeffers shows seems rather unremarkable, and the young man is clearly thin, without a trace of extra poundage on him. Further, Jeffers's predilection for drawing beautiful people has here led her astray. The text states that Cinderella is "yet a hundred times more beautiful than her stepsisters." However, the sisters aren't ugly! They may not be as beautiful as Cinderella is, but they are definitely not just plain; they are in fact very comely.

There is another factor teachers must consider in selecting picture books to share with children—the issue of gender representation. Do these books present an equitable balance of male and female characters? Stewig and Knipfel (1975) found that picture books available a decade ago featured male characters far more often than was necessary to reflect their actual representation in life. Noting the widely accepted contention that "picture books probably play a part in early sex-role development," Engle (1981) concluded that, even though there was a slight shift toward gender equality in the 1976–1980 period covered in her study of nineteen Caldecott Medal and honor books, "greater change is needed." It may be perfectly logical, within the fictional context set up by an individual author, for a boy to be the main character in a particular book and for girls to be nonexistent or relegated to a minor role. (See, for example, *The Chocolate Chip Cookie Contest*, by Barbara Douglas.) In the same way, it is logical in some books for a girl to be the main character and for there to be no boys or for boys to be relegated to minor roles. (See, for example, *Battle Day at Camp Delmont*, by Nicki Weiss.) An observation of gender bias may obscure how well a particular book intrinsically meets the other criteria for a fine picture book. Nonetheless, in considering the total array of picture books to be shared with the class, the teacher will want to keep this issue in mind.

## BOOKS WITH MINIMAL STORIES

Picture storybooks must be evaluated according to the quality of both the pictures and the stories, but a problem arises with those books that do not really tell a story—that is, an organized series of events that move from an interesting beginning through a series of actions to a climax and a conclusion. Many picture storybooks that have minimal stories are memorable nevertheless. These mood pieces, which may describe an environment, a feeling, or some people, are not really stories in the usual sense. They are important, however, because, through their use of language and illustrations, they convey a lasting impression.

Tobi Tobias's *Jane, Wishing* is made more interesting because of the alternation of double-page spreads in color (what Jane wishes) with double-page spreads in black pencil (Jane's reality). There is not a lot of dramatic action here. The spread on which Jane wishes for a room of her own shows, in lovely pastel shades, a frilly, feminine, beflowered hideaway. The following spread shows her mother with laundry in hand, her sister bedecked with curlers, her brother reading comics, and her father looking in from the door, bemused. The black-and-white reality, cluttered and not beautiful, is in sharp contrast to the colored fantasizing. Each alternation is more effective because of the difference. The pictures, by Trina Schart Hyman, are especially interesting to viewers since she won a Caldecott Medal for a later book: these earlier pictures can be compared with her later illustrations.

*The Desert Is Theirs* is by Byrd Baylor, who knows the Southwest intimately and conveys her delight to the reader. Another impressive combination of words and pictures, this book does not necessarily tell a continuous story but rather describes evocatively an environment and its inhabitants in Baylor's usual prose/poetry style.

> *The desert's children*
> *learn to be patient.*
> *Hidden in his burrow,*
> *Kangaroo Rat*
> *Spends each long day*
> *waiting*
> *for the heat to fade,*

> *waiting*
> *for darkness*
> *to cool the desert*
> *where he runs.*
> *Just so he runs sometime . . .*

Peter Parnall's understated but elegant drawings match the author's spare writing. He makes impressive use of negative, or empty, space; with a thin black line he carves bold abstract rock shapes in the white paper. Even though it is not a storybook, this book's impressive combination of words and pictures makes it well worth sharing with children.

# FUNCTIONS OF PICTURE BOOKS

In order to understand why picture books need to be a pervasive part of the environment for young children, it is important to identify some purposes these books serve. Like other categories of books, picture storybooks are valuable because they allow children to experience environments unlike their own, to travel to another time, to confront situations unlike their own, or to empathize with a character who shares a common problem. There are, in addition, three unique functions of picture storybooks.

### 1. Picture storybooks provide language input for children.

Because of the vocabulary and the syntax they include, picture books provide models that can influence children's language. Authors of picture books use the words necessary to deal with their topics.[11] Writers usually do not limit their word choices, knowing that children's listening comprehension is more extensive than their speaking and reading vocabularies. The context often provides clues to word meanings; a child can figure out what a word means by listening to the sentence in which the word occurs:

*Hoarfrost* coated their eyebrows as they set out on the slow, *wobbly* ride homeward.

John would undo the *stanchions* in late afternoon and chase the whole herd into the bitter cold outside.

---

[11]In contrast, another type of picture book that has become very common is that type specifically designed to be read by beginning readers themselves. Called by various titles (the *Ready-to-Read* series of Macmillan, the *I Can Read* series of Harper and Row), these series are valuable for children who are eager to read because they have just mastered beginning reading skills. In these books, both vocabulary and syntax are stringently controlled.

In both these sentences, children can determine at least approximate meanings for the unfamiliar words because of the context.

Authors also use whatever syntax is necessary to create a desired effect. The following sentence, which is in inverted form (main clause following a subordinate clause) and is longer (twenty-two words) than is usual in picture books, is a model of mature, adult language:

> On the frozen sea of snow that stretched across farmlands broken only by barbed-wire fences, prairie boys would find jack-rabbit trails.

*A Prairie Boy's Winter*, from which these examples come, is told in third-person narrative, despite the fact that author William Kurelek is relating events from his own boyhood. Although each section can be read independently, the short episodes about different aspects of winter are roughly sequential. Each episode is arranged on one page, with a full-color painting facing it. This format is also used in this author's *A Prairie Boy's Summer*. An interesting comparison for children to make would be to compare Kurelek's descriptions with Laura Ingalls Wilder's accounts of seasons in her *Little House* books.

Students need to experience language more complex than what they generally use if they are to improve in language use. The influence adult language has on children's language is commented on in an article describing uses of books. Schmidt (1977) warns that teachers must beware of attempting to "protect the child from the frustration of a too rich language environment, a language too different for him to fully understand."

### 2. Picture storybooks provide visual input for children.

Picture storybooks can heighten visual sensitivity by exposing students to fine illustrations on a regular basis. In contrast to the indifferent visual quality of much television for children and the banal art found in the thin books sold in supermarkets and drugstores, the illustrations in quality children's books are a feast for the eyes.[12] This exceptional art is available in a variety of styles. Some of it is realistic, for example, that in *The Mare on the Hill*, by Thomas Locker. These full-page paintings are full of details, which combine to create a lifelike effect seldom presented in children's books. Some of this impressive artwork is somewhat surrealistic, such as

---

[12]In *Illustrations in Children's Books* (Dubuque, Iowa: William C. Brown, 1976), Patricia Cianciolo describes different styles in art and comments on the importance of sharing the best book designs with children. The book is a comprehensive examination of styles and media. Suggestions for using illustrations found in books are included in Chapter 4.

*This full-color painting, full of detail, convinces viewers of the roundness of the forms and the depth of space, despite the flatness of the page.* Illustration from *The Mare on the Hill* by Thomas Locker. Copyright © 1985 by Thomas Locker. Reproduced by permission of the publisher, Dial Books for Young Readers.

that in *Maria Theresa*, by Petra Mathers. Despite its picture-book format, this book is for third- through sixth-grade readers; some of the Italian referents and the theme are clearly beyond very young children. Richard and MacCann (1985), two of the most insightful reviewers of children's books working today, comment on the flat, primitive style that produces "a consistently engaging, other-worldly quality." No matter what style is involved in a particular book, teachers must help children learn, essentially, to "read" the pictures.

### 3. *Picture storybooks stimulate the visual and verbal fluency of children.*

Even when the words in picture books are not particularly distinguished, these books may serve as a source for the language development of children if they are carefully used. As teachers use picture books with classes, they can encourage students to notice and comment on the following things:

*what* the illustrator includes in the picture: the people, objects, and settings

*where* things are in the picture: the location of objects can illustrate, among other things, their relative importance the *colors:* children can be led to sense the mood of a book because of the colors the artist uses

what *changes* are evident in succeeding illustrations: how a character or object changes or doesn't change as the story progresses

their *reaction* to what they see

By asking questions and by commenting on students' reactions, teachers can encourage a flow of language, a habit of reacting to books that will help children sharpen their ability to express in words what they notice and how they feel about it. Jalongo and Bromley (1984) develop this idea more fully with respect to dialectically different, language-delayed, and linguistically advanced children. They recommend specific books appropriate for each group of children.

## STIMULATING CHILDREN'S RESPONSES TO PICTURE BOOKS

A natural thing for students to talk about is the illustrations in books. Some examples of teachers' use of picture books to stimulate verbal language will illustrate the potential that these books have.

One teacher shared an old favorite, *Animal Babies*, by Arthur Gregor (now fortunately available in an inexpensive paperback reprint), which has clear, black-and-white, close-up photographs of animals. The teacher showed the book to children in a group and gave them the opportunity to tell their reaction to one of the pictures in the book. Two five-year-old kindergarteners contributed the following stories:

I like the elephants. They are big animals. They have long legs, a trunk and big ears. The baby elephants are small. They are going to grow up into big elephants.
*Michael*

Polar bears are my favorite animals. I like polar bears because my uncle has one. Polar bears are one of my favorite animals because they swim in the water. Polar bears are my favorite because they splash and because they sit funny.
*Heather*

These represent the kind of beginning story dictation that results when children study an illustration and comment on it. When this activity is repeated with other books at intervals over an extended period of time, it can sharpen children's observation of what artists portray on the page and their ability to respond verbally to it. Three other books by Gregor, more specifically focused on one kind of animal, include *The Sleepy Little Lion,* *Two Little Bears,* and *The Little Elephant.* Each book features the same large format and clear, appealing black-and-white photographs by Ylla as in *Animal Babies.*

Two teachers of first-graders presented traditional literature in picture-book format, sharing more than one version of the same story and asking children to comment on the illustrations. They asked children to respond to pictures in versions of *Little Red Riding Hood.* Some commented on the Bernadette version:

> The colors made things look real. They looked like they were made with Craypas.
>
> *Mikaela*

> I don't like this wolf, because he looks like a dirty mouse. No one would be afraid of him, but he doesn't look right.
>
> *Drew*

About the Paul Galdone version, other children commented:

> There were lots of interesting patterns, like in the quilt and in the flowers in the grass.
>
> *Jodie*

> In this one the grandmother looks more like a grandmother, because she's dressed the way they should dress.
>
> *Alex*

Two other versions of this story that teachers might use in doing a comparison/contrast activity with children include Lisbeth Zwerger's version, *Little Red Cap,* which has soft-edged watercolors that make effective use of negative space. She focuses our attention on character detail by eliminating almost all extraneous background detail. Entirely different in effect from Zwerger's illustrations are the black-and-white, superrealistic, contemporary photographs by Sarah Moon in an edition of *Little Red Riding Hood* that won the grand prize at the Bologna International Book Fair. Moon's book differs from Zwerger's in more than just the illustrations; the completely different emotional tone of the former is also due to the fact that the text is based on Perrault rather than Grimm. There are also notable differences in shape, size, binding, endpapers, paper, typeface, and page layout.

Working with third-grade children, one teacher read two versions of the Hans Christian Andersen tale *The Nightingale,* introducing them by saying they were different but not pointing out how. She encouraged the children to study the illustrations as she was reading but did not comment on the art herself. She then made the books available in the classroom for the

*These essentially two-dimensional ink paintings by Nancy Ekholm Burkert reflect the flatness of earlier oriental paintings on silk. Areas of intricate detail alternate with larger areas of plain color, showing up more effectively because of the contrast.* Illustration from *The Nightingale* by Hans Christian Andersen. Translated by Eva LeGallienne. Illustrated by Nancy Ekholm Burkert. Illustration copyright © 1965 by Nancy Ekholm Burkert. Reprinted by permission of Harper & Row, Publishers, Inc.

rest of the week and asked the children to write descriptions of the books. One student wrote the following response to the version illustrated by Nancy Burkert:

> The picture of the castle and garden looks more Chinese and the colors are much softer and more delicate. It looks more like the story itself. The porcelain castle looks realistic with its gardens and forest and the ocean rushing in on the beach. The people look more Chinese and more like real people. The outfits of the people are so delicate and the people stand out. The artificial bird is pretty with its diamonds and rubies, and the real nightingale looks very beautiful, even though it is not so colorful as the artificial bird.
>
> *Michelle*

Another student described the illustrations by Fulvio Testa:

> The garden and the castle don't look very real and around the picture is just white. There is no real background for the picture. The pictures aren't as soft and delicate as in the other book. The castle looks fake as does its surrounding. The people don't look Chinese, and they don't really fit into the Chinese story. The pictures look like any American pictures would. The real bird looks artificial just as the artificial bird really does, and the pictures of the birds don't really catch someone's eye with all the white showing around and in it.
>
> *Liz*

In doing such an activity with children, teachers might like to try using a newer version of this tale with pictures by Beni Montressor. (See Chapter 11, page 532.) A more complete description of this methodology is available (Stewig, 1986).

## PICTURE BOOKS IN OTHER MEDIA

Several manufacturers produce film versions of favorite stories. There are differences between the film and book formats. The advantages of using a book include the following:

1. The child can shift position to examine a picture more closely or from some distance to perceive the total effect.
2. The child can adjust the reading to his or her own pace, moving slowly to savor a particularly enjoyable section or moving more quickly in an exciting part of the story.
3. The child can go back to a previous page to check details, to compare illustrations, or to enjoy a description in relation to what she or he is currently reading.

The child, in essence, remains in control of the experience (Shaw, 1985).
In contrast, film viewing has certain disadvantages:

1. The filmmaker controls the point of view, what is seen, and the distance from which a scene is viewed.
2. The pace is preestablished and cannot be varied.
3. It is not possible to go back, unless the entire film is rewound and started over.

Despite these drawbacks, film versions of picture books also offer several advantages:

1. Sound effects, skilled narrators, and music can enhance the printed word.
2. Children can experience the film as a group, and valuable discussion can follow.
3. Many visual effects—superimposition of images, closeups, perspective views, and animation of static images—provide visual experiences the average book cannot achieve.

Teachers should be aware that several different types of filmed literature for children are available. Nancy Larrick identified four basic kinds of films about children's books: live action (an example is *Rapunzel*, Tom Davenport Films, Delaplane, VA, 22025); puppets (*Dick Whittington and His Cat*, Sterling Films); animation (*Anansi the Spider*, Landmark Educational Media); and iconography (*Andy and the Lion*, Weston Woods).[13]

When teachers choose a media version of a book, they need to consider fidelity to the original. Fidelity does not mean complete correspondence with the original version, which is impossible, but rather a sensitive adaptation of it to a new mode. Blair Lent (1974), an artist who made puppets for a film based on one of his books, comments, "I do not think that the filmed version of a story should correspond exactly with that of the book. Film is a different medium, and it is most effective when telling a story in its own way." He believes that what is added in the film must be sympathetic to the book content and should not overshadow the original concept.

Teachers could help intermediate-grade youngsters compare Lent's ideas about filmmaking with those of Tom Davenport (1981), who describes how he made the live-action film *Rapunzel* (mentioned above). Davenport's fascinating account might encourage teachers to attempt live productions of fairy tales in the classroom, because his rules of production could be applied to informal drama. One of his basic precepts is that "how an actor looks and moves is more important than his voice or facility with dialogue." In addition, Davenport talks of the need to understand the story thoroughly and seriously, to follow the original story as carefully as possible, and to look for the intrinsic dramatic elements in the story.

Most film versions retain the original artwork and avoid distorting the story. Unfortunately, some companies pirate stories and add artwork they feel is more appealing. Shoddy artwork is more likely to occur in filmstrip versions; these need to be evaluated carefully to make sure their quality is good enough to make them worth sharing with children. In this area, as in other areas of children's literature, there are valuable resource books that provide comprehensive information to help teachers make selections. May (1981) annotated nearly three hundred films and filmstrips produced in the last decade; presented alphabetically, these are indexed by subject and theme.

Today, even more than film, videotape has become a pervasive visual

---

[13]In *A Parent's Guide to Children's Reading* (Garden City, N.Y.: Doubleday, 1975, pp. 155–156), author Nancy Larrick includes a complete list of different kinds of audiovisual adaptations of children's books. This popular resource book is available in an updated version—with new annotated children's titles—from Bantam (1982), but the film material has been dropped.

*Stocky, peasantlike characters, doing a wide variety of rural tasks, are portrayed in a direct fashion in high-contrast woodcuts printed in black on cream paper. (See the discussion on page 156).* From *A Farmer's Alphabet* by Mary Azarian. Copyright © 1981 by Mary Azarian. Reprinted by permission of David R. Godine, Publisher.

medium. Children are influenced by the adaptations of literature they see on commercial television. In addition, several manufacturers are offering video adaptations of literature. Some of these efforts rise to the quality teachers have come to expect from such suppliers as Weston Woods; other efforts have met with less success in making an effective transfer from book to media.

## SUMMARY

Picture storybooks must combine strong visual features with memorable language. In a truly fine picture storybook, both illustrations and words are equally strong.

Though picture storybooks serve the same general purposes as other kinds of fiction, this genre has three additional instructional functions. These books can provide language input for children. Second, they provide visual information students can reflect upon. Third, picture storybooks can serve to stimulate verbal response, as children talk or write about their observations and reactions.

---

## An Integrated Unit of Study

As a start in building an integrated unit on farms for primary-grade students, a teacher might introduce *A Farmer's Alphabet*, by Mary Azarian. The vertical rectangular format provides an appropriate shape for the artist's strong woodcuts, patterned in a quasi-primitive style that complements the general topic. (See the illustration on page 155.) She makes impressive use of silhouette (on the "M for Maple Sugar" page, trees interlace in a dramatic pattern). Some pages are full of action (on the "J is for Jump" page, the farm children jump in the haymow); others are essentially static (on the "Q is for Quilt" page, the pattern is explored for its own sake).

After using Azarian's book to introduce the unit, the teacher could use Donald Carrick's *Milk*. The simple four-color, full-page watercolors with an unobtrusive line show a mechanized view of one modern type of farm. Simple language, set in bold type, faces the pictures, and both describe the processes of producing milk—from the farm to the supermarket. Children will deduce from the pictures what some words, such as *udders*, mean; the words are not explained. A more extensive look at the milk-producing process is provided by Gail Gibbons in *The Milk Makers*. She pictures, with labels, the five most common breeds of dairy cows and gives simple diagrams of the four parts of a cow's stomach. Her schematics of the machines that package, seal, and date the milk are all very clear. The illustrations are not particularly exciting as art, but this is a useful book for teaching the information involved.

After these books, it would be appropriate to move on to *Our Animal Friends at Maple Hill Farm*, which has pleasantly simplified and stylized illustrations in ink and watercolor by Alice and Martin Provensen. The Provensens explore many aspects of different kinds of farms, with both single pictures spread over the entire double-page spread and with as many as twelve small pictures crammed onto facing pages. The Provensens (1984) have written about their art in general (though not about this book in particular) in an article that focuses on how they try to achieve certain artistic effects.

Also appropriate for primary-grade children in this context is *Farm Morning*, by David McPhail. A father and his young daughter enjoy being and working together: she is absorbed in helping to feed the animals; he is bemused by the extra work she causes. A simple early-morning routine is portrayed in McPhail's pleasantly modulated watercolors, which contain lots of shades of color, sparkled with white, and pulled into more defined shapes with ink line. (See Plate E in the color section.)

Teachers of intermediate grades might begin a farm-based unit with the Azarian book and then move directly into *Joel: Growing Up a Farm Man*, by Patricia Demuth. Featuring black-and-white photos by Jack Demuth on almost every page, this book evokes a life-style that is rapidly becoming less and less common in America. A contemporary biography of a thirteen-year-old Illinois native, living in the house built by his great-grandfather gives details of what it requires to manage a hog-raising operation that grosses $40,000 a year. For city dwellers, operating front loaders, grinding corn in a mixer mill, and supervising a farrowing house are unfamiliar tasks. For Joel, they are simply part of his daily routine, work to be done when he isn't at school. Strongly implicit in the book are messages about the value of work and the sense of self-worth that comes from doing it well. Demuth wisely avoids stating these messages explicitly. Instead, she lets Joel's life story speak for itself.

Teachers of either primary or intermediate grades might choose to read parts of *Early Farm Life*, by Lise Gunby, to their classes. This fascinating collection of old photographs and etchings, supplemented by small drawings and other decorations in the margins, is printed in brown and burnt orange on a cream paper. Rather than a coherent story or a carefully laid out exposition, this book is a pleasantly eccentric collection of miscellany that moves, for example, from workhorses to poultry feed, to cows, to thirsty cats, to razorback hogs. *Early Farm Life* is appropriate for selective reading and viewing, rather than sustained, whole-book sharing. A complementary book is *Farming Today Yesterday's Way*, by Cheryl Walsh Bellville. Full-color photographs on nearly every page show processes, such as threshing, and objects, such as a stoneboat, that are involved in farming with horses instead of tractors. The book follows the life of a family on a Wisconsin dairy farm from summer, through the winter logging chores, to the birthing of foals the next spring. Embedded throughout the text are reasons why a family would choose to live this way, relying on draft horses instead of gasoline-powered tractors.

## *Suggestions for Further Study*

1. The chapter mentions *Bang Bang You're Dead*, by Louise Fitzhugh and Sandra Scoppettone. When published, this book was attacked by many critics, who felt it might be a bad influence on children. Read some reviews written then and see if you agree or disagree with them. (See *Elementary English*, March 1970, pp. 427–428; and *Kirkus Reviews*, April 15, 1969, p. 434.)

2. Compare the words in Barbara Emberley's *Drummer Hoff* with those in *The Annotated Mother Goose* by William S. and Ceil Baring-Gould (New York: Bramhall House, 1962). Note that the differences begin with the opening line: the Baring-Goulds' "John Ball shot them all" as opposed to Emberley's "Drummer Hoff fired it off." Which do you prefer? Read both books to children and see whether their preferences match yours.

3. In *Zeralda's Ogre*, by Tomi Ungerer, the heroine and the ogre apparently live happily ever after. Children could speculate on what happened to the couple after the story ends. Does the ogre contentedly settle down? Who or what might come along to interrupt such bliss? Ask children to write another adventure for the ogre.

4. The illustrations by Derek Collard for *The Squirrel Wife*, written by Philippa Pearce, are stylistically similar to the work of Edvard Munch, a Norwegian expressionist painter. Find a book about Munch's work. What similarities exist between his paintings and Collard's illustrations?

5. Popular stories are often translated into a variety of formats (records, tape, filmstrip, and film). Select a picture book you enjoy, and then find out whether it is available in a film version. To do this, consult the NICEM *Index to 16mm Educational Films*, available from the National Center for Educational Media, University of Southern California, University Park, Los Angeles, 90007.

6. Prepare for gathering some data about pre-school youngsters by reading Maureen and Hugh Crago's "Order from Chaos: Learning to Read Pictures" (in *Prelude to Literacy*, Carbondale, Ill.: Southern Illinois Press, 1983, pp. 143–162). Using some of the picture books the Cragos used, gather information

about children's ability to comprehend the concepts of up and down, figure/ground relationships, changing sizes of objects on different pages, color accuracy and con-

sistency, and bleed-off versus self-contained pictures. Do your observations support or disagree with what the Cragos report about their daughter's visual learning?

## Related Reading for Adults

Abrahamson, Richard F. "An Analysis of Children's Favorite Picture Storybooks." *The Reading Teacher*, November 1980, pp. 167–170.

The author analyzes fifty books among those chosen as favorites by children who participated in the 1979 International Reading Association "Children's Choices" award. He analyzes the books according to: (1) story structure, (2) genre represented, and (3) literary elements such as humor. He also indicates the most commonly chosen favorite illustrator. Abrahamson's article, however, suffers from a problem found in many articles about picture books: it provides no indepth analysis of the visual nature of the illustrations.

Alderson, Brian. *Looking at Picture-Books, 1973; an Exhibition Prepared by Brian Alderson and Arranged by the National Book League*. Distributed in the United States by the Children's Book Council, 1973.

The annotations in this catalogue are refreshing because they are critical rather than simply descriptive. Though primarily British in focus, the work includes a large number of books also published in the United States, making it a valuable resource.

Bader, Barbara. *American Picturebooks from Noah's Ark to the Beast Within*. New York: Macmillan, 1976.

Generously sized, clear illustrations in lavish quantity and an articulate commentary mark this as the definitive text on picture books. Bader writes convincingly, sharing

the results of years of study. Her book regards today's picture books in the light of historical antecedents that are all too often inaccessible to anyone but scholars.

Colby, Jean Poindexter. *Writing, Illustrating and Editing Children's Books*. New York: Hastings House, 1974.

The author presents a general view of children's book illustration, including the interests of various age groups, editorial and production requirements, and advice for starting out in the field. The steps in illustrating and producing a picture book are described in detail.

Cott, Jonathan. "Maurice Sendak, King of All the Wild Things." *Rolling Stone*, December 30, 1976, pp. 50–59.

In a series of one-page features, the author examines Sendak's early life, working style, environmental milieu, and thoughts about his work. Drawn from several interviews Cott had with the artist, this series is liberally sprinkled with provocative quotes and many small illustrations.

Egoff, Sheila A. "Picture Books." In *Thursday's Child*. Chicago: American Library Association, 1981, pp. 247–274.

Contending that the picture book is subjected to closer scrutiny and more judgments than any other genre, Egoff goes on to assert a paradox: though it seems to be the "coziest and most gentle of genres," it actually produces the greatest social and aesthetic tensions in all of children's literature. Setting this argument in the context of changes that occurred during the fertile period of 1930 through 1960, she notes a balance between words and pictures that now seems to have given way to excessive emphasis on the pictorial. In addition to her comments about visual aspects of the genre, Egoff notes the psychological changes that have taken place in it over the years and the positive effect on picture books of the economic recession of the 1970s. In closing, she notes the widening audience for picture books and the fact that this form seems to be leading the way in innovations, although some artists (such as John Burningham, James Marshall, and Bernard Waber) continue to produce satisfying works in the established tradition.

Gainer, Ruth Straus. "Beyond Illustration: Information about Art in Children's Picture Books." *Art Education*, March 1982, pp. 16–19.

An elementary art teacher, Gainer recommends picture books as a source of information for children who are feeling frustrated as they make comparisons between what they intended to do visually and what they accomplished. Too often children evaluate their own art as inadequate, get discouraged, and give up. If picture books were used systematically in art programs, teachers could suggest specific titles, different representations of the problems the children are trying to solve, as resources. Discussion on how artists solved a problem differently would give children a plan of action. Helping children seek their own visual solutions self-reliantly will improve their grammar and syntax as they structure visual forms.

Lucas, Barbara. "Picture Books for Children Who Are Masters of Few Words." *Library Journal*, May 15, 1973, pp. 1641–1645.

The author discusses the problems of creating picture books (for instance, rising costs of paper and printing) and the need for reviewers to keep these problems in mind when examining books. She also identifies the most important task for artists: not merely to relate a story line through pictures but to interpret it in an unpedestrian manner.

MacCann, Donnarae, and Olga Richard. *The Child's First Books; a Study of Pictures and Texts*. New York: H. W. Wilson, 1973.

The authors, who write the column "Picture Books for Children" in *Wilson Library Bulletin*, discuss provocatively the state of art in modern illustrated books. They spotlight some artists whose work they consider superior; many award winners are notably absent. The incisive opinions held by MacCann and Richard may disturb some readers, but these authors never take the easy way out—lapsing into mere commentary on plot —as too many writers do.

Moss, Elaine. *Picture Books for Young People, 9–13*. Stroud, Gloucestershire, Eng.: Thimble Press, 1985.

Making no attempt to provide a comprehensive survey of all available material, the author instead annotates 101 picture books presented in four general categories that include "A Wry Look at Ourselves" and "Cosmorama: A Relative Look at Ourselves in Time and Place." Although it was published in Britain, this overview includes such well-known Americans as Maurice Sendak and Ezra Jack Keats and some British authors that are published in the United States, such as Roy Gerrard. As is often the case, plot summary predominates, but there is enough critical evaluation to make this book worthwhile.

Norsworthy, James A. "In Search of an Image: The Adult Male Role in Picture Books." *Catholic Library World*, December 1973, pp. 220–226.

Much attention has been given to the roles of women as portrayed in all sorts of children's books, but Norsworthy believes men's roles should be given similar attention. This study analyzes picture books to see whether men are portrayed positively.

Orr, Nancy Young. "The Internationalism of Picture Books in the United States." *Bookbird*, 9 (June 1971), 15–18.

> The author discusses the vigorous tradition of picture books that exists in other countries. She believes that this tradition in the United States has been enriched by influences from abroad. To substantiate her contention, Orr includes a lengthy bibliography of successfully translated books, including ones by Jean de Brunhoff, Bruno Munari, and Celestino Piatti.

Roxburgh, Stephen. "A Picture Equals How Many Words? Narrative Theory and Picture Books for Children." *The Lion and the Unicorn*, 7/8 (1983–84), pp. 20–33.

> In an extended and articulate analysis, Roxburgh demonstrates why he feels Maurice Sendak's *Outside Over There* is "a seminal book in the genre." He points out such easily overlooked visual details as the sequence of shadows in succeeding pictures, which indicate that chronological time has stopped, a detail not duplicated in the word narrative. Roxburgh identifies the reasons for many visual clues to the story's reality. Roxburgh also documents the three narratives he feels Sendak is pursuing in this book. Roxburgh's analysis is one of thirteen articles in this issue of *The Lion and the Unicorn* by various authorities on a variety of artists and types of picture books.

Shulevitz, Uri. *Writing with Pictures: How to Write and Illustrate Children's Books*. New York: Watson-Guptill, 1985.

> The author states that visual thinking is the key to "writing with pictures," creating the flow of graphic images that is crucial in picture books. Illustrations must be readable, coherent, and obviously related to the text. Shulevitz's book is divided into four parts. To begin, he distinguishes between the true picture book and the storybook with pictures. Part 2 deals with technical matters, such as storyboards and dummies, and more general concerns of a book's physical structure, including size, scale, and shape. In Part 3, Shulevitz analyzes both the purposes of illustrations and the art of drawing. In Part 4, he becomes more technical again, focusing on how books are made. Over six hundred illustrations accompany text that is logical and written in language that communicates clearly.

Taylor, Mary Agnes. "In Defense of the Wild Things." *The Horn Book*, December 1970, pp. 642–646.

> Taylor rebuts Bruno Bettelheim's article criticizing Maurice Sendak's book, *Where the Wild Things Are* ("The Care and Feeding of Monsters," *Ladies Home Journal*, March 1969, p. 48). For his article Bettelheim talked with three mothers about the book, even though he hadn't seen it. He writes of the need three to five year olds have for a clear, definite message and of his perception that being sent to bed without dinner is twofold desertion. In contrast, Taylor offers a valuable distinction between the primarily verbal and aural experiences in traditional folk tales and the basically visual experience in modern picture books, designed to help very young children transcend their verbal limitations. She maintains that Bettelheim's attribution of psychological purposes to Sendak is erroneous.

Walp, Esther S. "Thirty Years and Three Thousand Picture Books Later." *Ohio Library Association Bulletin*, April 1975, pp. 13–15.

> This article describes the Walp Family Juvenile Collection, a book-selection center that is unique in that it contains more than a hundred original signed drawings. Its holdings include complete sets of the work of Ed Emberley, Robert Lawson, and Ludwig Bemelmans, and the only woodblocks and lithographic stones not retained by the families of Emberley and the d'Aulaires.

## Professional References

Carpenter, Humphrey, and Mari Prichard. *The Oxford Companion to Children's Literature.* New York: Oxford Univ. Press, 1984, p. 184.

Cianciolo, Patricia. *Picture Books for Children.* Chicago: American Library Association, 1981.

Davenport, Tom. "Some Personal Notes on Adapting Folk-Fairy Tales to Film." *Children's Literature*, 9 (1981), 107–115.

Dooley, Patricia. "The Window in the Book: Conventions in the Illustration of Children's Books." *Wilson Library Bulletin*, October 1980, 108–112.

Engle, Rosalind E. "Is Unequal Treatment of Females Diminishing in Children's Picture Books?" *The Reading Teacher*, March 1981, 647–652.

Groban, Betsy, and Robert G. Lowe. "Book Binding Considerations." *School Library Journal*, October 1982, 101–104.

Jalongo, Mary Renck, and Karen D'Angelo Bromley. "Developing Linguistic Competence Through Song Picture Books." *The Reading Teacher*, May 1984, 840–845.

Lent, Blair. "How the Sun and the Moon Got into a Film." *The Horn Book*, 47 (December 1971), 589–596.

May, Jill P. *Films and Filmstrips for Language Arts.* Urbana, Ill.: National Council of Teachers of English, 1981.

Provensen, Alice, and Martin Provensen. "Caldecott Medal Acceptance." *The Horn Book*, 60 (August 1984), 444–448.

Richard, Olga, and Donnarae MacCann. "Picture Books for Children." *Wilson Library Bulletin*, 59 (September 1984), 50–51.

———. "Picture Books for Children." *Wilson Library Bulletin*, 59 (January 1985), 338–339.

———. "Picture Books for Children." *Wilson Library Bulletin*, 59 (June 1985), 686–687.

Schmidt, Sheldon. "Language Development and Children's Books in Intermediate Classrooms." *Insights into Open Education*, March 1977, 2–10.

Shaw, Francine Shuchat. "The Limitations of Motion Picture Adaptations to Contribute to Reading Development in Pre-Schoolers." *The Advocate*, 5 (Fall 1985), 36–46.

Stewig, John Warren. "Books in the Classroom." *The Horn Book*, 62 (May/June 1986), 363–365.

———. "Still Another Monster/Talking Animal Book?" *Wisconsin English Journal*, April 1977, 37–38.

Stewig, John Warren, and Mary Lynn Knipfel. "Sexism in Picture Books: What Progress?" *Elementary School Journal*, December 1975, 151–155.

Sunal, Cynthia Szymanski, and Barbara Hatcher. "A Changing World: Books Can Help Children Adapt." *Day Care and Early Education*, 13 (Winter 1985), 16–19.

## Bibliography of Children's Books

Adshead, Gladys L. *Brownies—Hush!* New York: Oxford University Press, 1939.

Alexander, Lloyd. *The King's Fountain.* New York: E. P. Dutton, 1971.

Anderson, Lonzo. *Two Hundred Rabbits.* New York: Viking, 1968.

Ayer, Jacqueline. *Little Silk.* New York: Harcourt Brace, 1970.

Azarian, Mary. *A Farmer's Alphabet.* Boston: David Godine, 1981.

Babbitt, Natalie. *The Something.* New York: Farrar, Straus and Giroux, 1970.

Barker, Carol. *Carol Barker's Birds and Beasts.* New York: Franklin Watts, 1971.

Baylor, Byrd. *The Desert Is Theirs.* New York: Scribner's, 1975.

Bellville, Cheryl Walsh. *Farming Today Yesterday's Way.* Minneapolis: Carolrhoda Books, 1981.

Bernadette (ill.). *Little Red Riding Hood.* Cleveland: World Publishing, 1969.

Bonners, Susan. *Panda.* New York: Delacorte, 1978.

Bruna, Dick. *The Fish.* Chicago: Follett, 1963.

Buckley, Richard. *The Foolish Tortoise.* Natick, Mass.: Picture Book Studio, 1985.

Burkert, Nancy (ill.). *The Nightingale.* New York: Harper and Row, 1965.

Burton, Virginia Lee. *Mike Mulligan and His Steam Shovel.* Boston: Houghton Mifflin, 1939.

Calhoun, Mary. *The Witch Who Lost Her Shadow.* New York: Harper and Row, 1979.

Carrick, Donald. *The Deer in the Pasture.* New York: Greenwillow, 1976.

———. *Milk.* New York: Greenwillow, 1985.

Carter, Anne. *Ruff Leaves Home.* New York: Crown, 1986.

Cazet, Denys. *December 24th.* New York: Bradbury, 1986.

Clifton, Lucille. *All Us Come Cross the Water.* New York: Holt, Rinehart and Winston, 1973.

Coatsworth, Elizabeth. *Under the Green Willow.* New York: Greenwillow, 1984.

Cohen, Miriam. *Starring First Grade.* New York: Greenwillow, 1985.

Cole, Brock. *The Winter Wren.* New York: Farrar, Straus and Giroux, 1984.

Cornish, Sam. *Grandmother's Pictures.* Scarsdale, N.Y.: Bradbury, 1974.

Dabcovich, Lydia. *Sleepy Bear.* New York: E. P. Dutton, 1982.

Dalgliesh, Alice. *The Little Wooden Farmer.* New York: Macmillan, 1968.

de Brunhoff, Jean. *The Story of Babar.* New York: Random House, 1984.

———. *The Travels of Babar.* New York: Random House, 1985.

de la Mare, Walter. *Jack and the Beanstalk.* New York: Alfred A. Knopf, 1959.

Demuth, Patricia. *Joel: Growing Up a Farm Man.* New York: Dodd, Mead, 1982.

Douglas, Barbara. *The Chocolate Chip Cookie Contest.* New York: Lothrop, Lee and Shepard, 1985.

Dragonwagon, Crescent. *Half a Moon and One Whole Star.* New York: Macmillan, 1986.

Duncan, Jane. *Brave Janet Reachfar.* New York: Seabury, 1975.

Ehrlich, Amy (trans.). *Cinderella.* New York: Dial, 1985.

Emberley, Barbara. *Drummer Hoff.* Englewood Cliffs, N.J.: Prentice-Hall, 1967.

Faulkner, Matt (ill.). *Jack and the Beanstalk.* New York: Scholastic, 1986.

Fisher, Leonard Everett. *The Great Wall of China.* New York: Macmillan, 1986.

Fitzhugh, Louise, and Sandra Scoppettone. *Bang Bang You're Dead.* New York: Harper and Row, 1969.

Gag, Wanda. *Gone Is Gone.* New York: Coward, McCann, 1935.

———. *Millions of Cats.* New York: Coward, McCann, 1928.

Galdone, Paul (ill.). *Little Red Riding Hood.* New York: McGraw-Hill, 1974.

Gibbons, Gail. *The Milk Makers.* New York: Macmillan, 1985.

———. *Up Goes the Skyscraper!* New York: Four Winds, 1986.

Gomi, Taro. *Coco Can't Wait!* New York: Morrow, 1984.

Gregor, Arthur. *Animal Babies.* New York: Harper and Row, 1959.

———. *The Little Elephant.* New York: Harper and Row, 1956.

———. *The Sleepy Little Lion.* New York: Harper and Row, 1975.

———. *Two Little Bears.* New York: Harper and Row, 1954.

Gunby, Lise. *Early Farm Life*. Toronto: Crabtree, 1983.

Hadithi, Mwenye. *Hot Hippo*. Boston: Little, Brown, 1986.

Hartford, John. *Steamboat in a Cornfield*. New York: Crown, 1986.

Hedderwick, Mairi. *Katie Morag and the Tiresome Ted*. Boston: Little, Brown, 1986.

———. *Katie Morag and the Two Grandmothers*. Boston: Little, Brown, 1985.

Hoffman, Felix. *A Boy Went Out to Gather Pears*. New York: Harcourt, Brace and World, 1963.

Keller, Holly. *Henry's Fourth of July*. New York: Greenwillow, 1985.

Kurelek, William. *A Prairie Boy's Summer*. Boston: Houghton Mifflin, 1975.

———. *A Prairie Boy's Winter*. Boston: Houghton Mifflin, 1973.

Lobel, Arnold. *Owl at Home*. New York: Harper and Row, 1975.

Locker, Thomas. *The Mare on the Hill*. New York: Dial, 1985.

Lucas, Barbara. *Sleeping Over*. New York: Macmillan, 1986.

Lyon, George Ella. *A Regular Rolling Noah*. New York: Bradbury, 1986.

Mathers, Petra. *Maria Theresa*. New York: Harper and Row, 1985.

Mayer, Mercer. *One Monster after Another*. New York: Golden Press, 1974.

———. *Whinnie the Lovesick Dragon*. New York: Macmillan, 1986.

McCloskey, Robert. *Burt Dow, Deep-Water Man*. New York: Viking, 1963.

McDermott, Beverly Brodsky. *The Golem*. Philadelphia: J. B. Lippincott, 1976.

McPhail, David. *Farm Morning*. San Diego: Harcourt Brace Jovanovich, 1985.

Moon, Sarah (ill.). *Little Red Riding Hood*. Mankato, Minn.: Creative Education, 1983.

Ormerod, Jan. *The Story of Chicken Licken*. New York: Lothrop, Lee and Shepard, 1985.

Parnall, Peter. *Winter Barn*. New York: Macmillan, 1986.

Pearce, Philippa. *The Squirrel Wife*. New York: Thomas Y. Crowell, 1971.

Potter, Beatrix. *The Tale of Tuppenny*. New York: Frederick Warne, 1971.

Powzyk, Joyce. *Wallaby Creek*. New York: Lothrop, Lee and Shepard, 1985.

Provensen, Alice, and Martin Provensen. *Our Animal Friends at Maple Hill Farm*. New York: Random House, 1984.

Rockwell, Anne. *In Our House*. New York: Thomas Y. Crowell, 1985.

Rockwell, Anne, and Harlow Rockwell. *Toad*. Garden City, N.Y.: Doubleday, 1972.

Scheidl, Gerda Marie. *George's Garden*. New York: North-South Books, 1985.

Segal, Lore. *All the Way Home*. New York: Farrar, Straus and Giroux, 1973.

Sendak, Maurice. *One Was Johnny (Nutshell Library)*. New York: Harper and Row, 1962.

———. *Seven Little Monsters*. New York: Harper and Row, 1975.

Shachtman, Tom. *Parade*. New York: Macmillan, 1985.

Singer, Isaac Bashevis. *Why Noah Chose the Dove*. New York: Farrar, Straus and Giroux, 1974.

Small, Ernest. *Baba Yaga*. Boston: Houghton Mifflin, 1966.

Spier, Peter. *Noah's Ark*. Garden City, N.Y.: Doubleday, 1977.

Stadler, John. *Snail Saves the Day*. New York: Thomas Y. Crowell, 1985.

Steig, William. *Roland the Minstrel Pig*. New York: Windmill Books, 1968.

Steptoe, John. *The Story of Jumping Mouse*. New York: Lothrop, Lee and Shepard, 1984.

Testa, Fulvio (ill.). *The Nightingale*. New York: Abelard-Schuman, 1974.

Thorne, Jenny. *My Uncle*. New York: Atheneum, 1982.

Tobias, Tobi. *Jane, Wishing*. New York: Viking, 1977.

Ungerer, Tomi. *Zeralda's Ogre*. New York: Harper and Row, 1967.

Valens, Evans G. *Wildfire*. Cleveland: World Publishing, 1963.

Van Allsburg, Chris. *The Garden of Abdul Gasazi*. Boston: Houghton Mifflin, 1979.

Warburg, Sandol Stoddard. *Hooray for Us*. Boston: Houghton Mifflin, 1970.

Watts, Mable. *While the Horses Galloped to London*. New York: Parent's Magazine Press, 1973.

Weil, Lisl. *Of Witches and Monsters and Wondrous Creatures*. New York: Atheneum, 1985.

Weiss, Nicki. *Battle Day at Camp Delmont*. New York: Greenwillow, 1985.

Zemach, Harve, and Kaethe Zemach. *The Princess and the Froggie*. New York: Farrar, Straus and Giroux, 1975.

Zemach, Margot. *The Sign in Mendel's Window*. New York: Macmillan, 1985.

Zwerger, Lisbeth (ill.). *Little Red Cap*. New York: Morrow, 1983.

# 5

# WORDLESS BOOKS:
# UPDATING AN
# ANCIENT FORM

Oone might rephrase Alice's question, "What is the use of a book without pictures?" and ask, "What is the use of a book without words?" Indeed, it may seem that a wordless book is a contradiction in terms: how can something be a book if it hasn't any words?

# PICTURES WITHOUT WORDS

Many children's books tell their stories using only pictures. The idea of telling a story without words is not new. More than thirty thousand years ago, primitive people dwelling in caves in France and Spain decorated the walls with monumental drawings of hunts and other events of daily life.[1] Nine centuries ago, after the Norman invasion of England, William the Conqueror's brother, Bishop Odo, commissioned a tapestry depicting the military incursion.[2] This linear strip, more than two hundred feet long and magnificently embroidered in limited colors, is essentially a cartoon strip in which the pictures speak for themselves. Medieval artisans used lead strips and thick chunks of glass to create stained-glass windows recounting Bible stories for peasants who could not read.

With the advent of printed books and rising literacy, wordless story-telling diminished, becoming less important to maintaining society. Words in books became the accepted norm (Herman, 1976). However, the number of wordless books currently being published for young "readers" is growing. Rarely seen even twenty years ago, wordless books now form, in the United States at least, a sturdy new genre, well represented in many classrooms and other early learning environments.

Two characteristics set wordless picture books apart from other picture storybooks for the young: a majority of wordless books feature animals as the main characters, and many are fantasies.

## CHARACTERIZATION IN WORDLESS BOOKS

Conventional picture storybooks frequently feature animals, but in wordless books, animal main characters seem to predominate.

---

[1]A description and pictures of this early form of recording events is given by V. M. Hillyer and E. G. Huey in *Young People's Story of Our Heritage/Fine Art* (New York: Meredith Press, 1966). Another description of cave painting is in Hans Baumann's *The Caves of the Great Hunters* (New York: Pantheon, 1954).

[2]The tapestry is reproduced clearly, with easy-to-read commentary, in *The Bayeux Tapestry* by Norman Denny and Josephine Filmer-Sankey (New York: Collins/Merrimack, 1984). The reproductions are printed on pleasant matte paper, and the descriptions—laid out with wide margins—do not overpower the artwork.

Sometimes these animals are completely realistic. *The Spider Web*, by Julie Brinckloe, shows the painstaking process by which a spider creates a web. The precarious nature of the web and the suddenness with which it can be destroyed are conveyed convincingly and realistically. Thin connected lines of unvarying thickness, a great deal of disconnected crosshatching, and dot accumulation to build up depth and roundness of shape characterize the ink drawings in this book.[3]

Often animals are given human qualities. In *Psst! Doggie* (not strictly a wordless book since there are three lines of text), a shaggy dog and his lanky feline partner dance imaginatively. Ezra Jack Keats shows the pair dancing in wild abandon in front of suitable though minimal backgrounds, attired in a variety of ethnic costumes. Mostly painted in full color, with some use of collage, these illustrations are visually not as interesting as others of Keats. The artist uses this visual style again in *Kitten for a Day*. Although there are single words on many of the pages, the pictures function very well without them. To use this book as a stimulus for young children's storytelling, the teacher might cover up the author's words and let the children tell the story themselves.

In *Little Mops At the Seashore*, by Elzbieta, the author/illustrator presents three characters and an environment that is a fanciful but convincing creation. A bird is not careful enough of her egg, so an anteater absconds with it, but eventually responds to the mother's pleading that her property be returned. The egg then hatches, and the three animals journey off together. The drawings are simple, essentially two-dimensional creations. The artist clearly subscribes to the theory that "less is more." The humor that is found here may appeal to viewers willing to look carefully, although the drawings do not have immediate appeal for children.

Some author/illustrators endow animal characters with human attributes, but others create imaginary creatures whose identity is difficult to determine. Using thin, connected black line, reminiscent of the work of Ernest H. Shepard in his books about Winnie the Pooh, Lilo Fromm creates stuffed animals of indeterminate species. It is difficult to tell, without referring to the dust jacket, the difference between the two animals in *Muffel and Plums* because they look so much alike. The book relates nine short

---

[3]If children get interested in this topic, Faith McNulty's *The Lady and the Spider* (New York: Harper and Row, 1986) is useful reading. In both words and Bob Marstall's pictures, the perspective of the spider itself is well-represented; these people clearly understand what it would be like to be small and helpless. They present the idea appealingly, without resorting to personification. Another resource is Joanne Ryder, *The Spiders Dance* (New York: Harper and Row, 1981), written lyrically but without sentimentality.

***Using only brown line on cream paper, artist Mercer Mayer creates a humorous, three-dimensional world.*** Illustration from *A Boy, a Dog, and a Frog* by Mercer Mayer. Copyright © 1967 by Mercer Mayer. Reproduced by permission of the publisher, Dial Books for Young Readers.

adventures of these two animal friends. The gentle stories, with minimal plots, mostly consist of encounters with bigger animals.

Some wordless books do include human characters, most successfully those found in the realistic tales of Mercer Mayer. In *A Boy, a Dog, and a Frog*, this author/illustrator presents his well-known cast of characters via soft, brown illustrations, gently crosshatched to create a naturalistic effect. The book tells the pleasant tale of a small boy, an inquisitive dog, and an elusive frog, who decides eventually that he does not want to be captured at all. The adventures continue in *A Boy, a Dog, a Frog and a Friend*, by Mercer and Marianna Mayer. Other titles in this series are *Frog Goes to Dinner* and *One Frog Too Many*.

In *Clementina's Cactus*, published almost a decade after *Psst! Doggie*, Keats returned to the wordless book format. Using richly varied water-colors, Keats tells of a bonneted little girl and a thin scraggly man who together enjoy the desert blossoming as anticipated. The color in this book

**Bright watercolors show the unusual pair of friends; the casual pictures tell the story of everyday life together, being friends.** Illustration from *Clementina's Cactus* by Ezra Jack Keats. Copyright © 1982 by Ezra Jack Keats. Reproduced by permission of Viking Penguin Inc.

is lighter and brighter than in some of Keats's earlier work, such as *Apt. 3*, in which the tonality is much darker and the paint is applied more thickly.

*The Hunter and the Animals* is a tastefully designed wordless book by Tomie de Paola. The author broke up the space of the page by dividing it into separate panels, similar to comic strip panels. In addition, the panels are further subdivided by elements like trees. The cheerful colors, with much show-through of those underneath, and the decorative shapes make this style easily identifiable as de Paola's. A very natty hunter sets out early in the day, replete with striped tights and a matching feather in his hat. He becomes slightly less confident as the many animals cleverly tucked into the tree forms continue to elude him. An owl awakens him from his ex-

*The unrealistic, two-dimensional figures of the hunter, the animals, and the plants together create a pleasing repeated design.* Illustration copyright © 1981 by Tomie de Paola. Reprinted from *The Hunter and the Animals* by permission of Holiday House.

hausted snooze; finally, the compassionate animals lead him safely home. The artist is obviously intrigued with two-dimensional patterns on the page; the final effect is pleasantly naive and folklike. A similar patterning is apparent in de Paola's *Sing, Pierrot, Sing*, in which full-page illustrations and double-page spreads alternate with half-page illustrations. The simple line forming the borders and the relatively untextured colors add to the air of tranquility in these pictures.

*The Yawn*, by Barney Saltzberg, is another book that features both people and animals. Old people, young people, an elephant, a duck, and a snake pass along a contagious yawn from one to another. Eventually the yawn is passed to the moon, who puts a boy to sleep with it. Not much happens here; a gentle, insignificant story is presented pleasantly enough in simple black and white.

A few wordless books feature only people. In *Lost*, by Sonia O. Lisker, a small boy's fear is realistically depicted in soft shades of brown, yellow, and orange. The boy is accidentally separated from his family during a visit to the zoo. As he searches frantically for his family, everything begins to seem threatening, until he meets another lost child. Attempting to calm the other, he loses his own fear, and when the two rediscover their families, they sit down to picnic in newfound friendship. One third-grade teacher discussed with children their memories of and reactions to being lost. Following this introduction, she shared the book *Lost* with her students, picture by picture, in sequence. Afterward, she left the book out where children could examine it more fully at their leisure. The following day, while students were doing independent reading, she called them to her individually and took dictation from those who wanted to retell the story in their own words. Aline retold the story as if it were happening to her:

> We are going to the zoo today. It is going to be my brother's first time. A man took a picture of us. Then we got something to eat. Finally we went to the Murry Zoo and saw the elephants. Then we saw the lions, the tigers, and then the monkeys. Finally, we went to the children's zoo. There we saw the lambs and geese. I got to feed them. There was one I especially liked. I hugged him. Then all in a black magic poof! everybody disappeared. I was lost! I met some people. They were very nice to me. I went out looking for my family. I went in the out, and out the in. I passed the monkeys, tigers, and lions. The daddy lion growled at me. I was very scared. I thought about all the scary things I saw. It just made matters worse. I sat down and cried. Then I walked around. I saw another boy. He was lost and crying too. Then I remembered my puppet. I showed it to him. He really liked it. We went around the whole zoo looking for our families. Instead of us finding them, they found us! The little boy's daddy picked him up. Then he picked me up. My dad saw me. Then I ran to him. After that we all had a picnic together.

Dictation experiences are valuable at all ages or grade levels because they

1. help children understand the sequential nature of plot,
2. encourage the invention of detail and the making of inferences, and
3. provide the teacher with valuable insights into the language abilities of children.

Not all boys and girls will dictate fluent stories on their first tries. The exercise is valuable, nevertheless. Perhaps such experiences are even more valid for children with limited language skills, although the results may not be as satisfying for the teacher.

In addition to simple stories such as the ones above, there are many complex wordless books appropriate for intermediate-grade students. In *The Joneses*, Corinne Ramage uses thin, unvarying black line with restrained touches of solid pink, orange, green, and yellow to tell about a family with thirty-one children. The family is liberated: the father stays home to iron, feed the baby, and play with the children; the mother goes off to her job driving a submarine. The activities of the father and children are shown in small framed drawings on the left-hand page, and the mother's adventures are simultaneously recorded in similar but larger drawings on the right-hand page. Mother goes through the enclosing line to rescue her children when they carelessly fall out of the picture. All return home happily to be met by Father—in apron—grinning at the door. This book is one of a long list of titles recommended by Ellis and Preston (1984) in an article about establishing a cross-grade tutoring program. Fifth-graders were trained to use these books with first-graders to stimulate fluency in oral language.

## A WORDLESS WORLD OF FANTASY

Many picture books with words intended for the youngest readers deal with the everyday events, people, and places that children know or can empathize with. In contrast, few wordless books describe in realistic ways places and experiences with which children will be familiar. More often wordless picture books deal with unusual main characters doing unusual things in unusual places; in other words, they are fantasies.

An example, for primary-grade children, is *Sebastian and the Mushroom*, by Fernando Krahn. A round-faced, button-nosed hero drawn in dark-brown ink, Sebastian is innocently picking mushrooms one day when he notices something is dripping. It turns out to be paint from the brush of a gentleman painting a huge mushroom over Sebastian's head. When he climbs a ladder lowered to him, Sebastian enters the mushroom and is led to other galaxies, stars, and the mushroom planet before falling off the edge of the moon into his room. (This story is an interesting parallel to Max's journey in *Where the Wild Things Are*, by Maurice Sendak.)

Mercer Mayer creates another hero of a wordless fantasy in *Bubble Bubble*. A small boy who purchases the Magic Bubble Maker discovers that the bubbles take the forms of some animals he is not overjoyed to see. Each succeeding threatening animal drives away the one before, until the boy pours out the rest of the bubble liquid. As he walks happily away, a forlorn-looking, serpentlike animal arises from the spilled liquid! A dictation experience for primary-grade children might consist of asking them to extend this story by creating an adventure for the animal: where does it go, who does it meet, and what happens? Ways to use Mayer's book are included in a useful teacher's guide by Jett-Simpson (1976), which gives suggestions on prediction, artistic and chain storytelling, and discussion for this and three other books.

One fantasy for primary-grade children, *Elephant Buttons*, by Noriko Ueno, consists of soft black-pencil illustrations depicting a sequence of an-

***The round-bodied, button-nosed main character is typical of Fernando Krahn's artistic style.***
Excerpted from the book *Journeys of Sebastian* by Fernando Krahn. Copyright © 1968 by
Fernando Krahn. Reprinted by permission of Delacorte Press/Seymour Lawrence.

imals, in which each is unbuttoned to reveal another animal inside. An
invisible hand unbuttons four buttons on the elephant's tummy, and a horse
steps out of the opening. The horse is unbuttoned to reveal a toothy lion,
who in turn is unbuttoned to reveal a seal, and so on. In the end, the minute
mouse is unbuttoned to reveal . . . an elephant!

Fantasy for intermediate-grade children is presented equally imaginatively in some wordless books. In *The Journeys of Sebastian*, Fernando
Krahn created three engaging voyages into a child's imagination. Sebastian,

round of head, eye, and body, is curious about everything and therefore has interesting adventures because he notices things most people would miss. His journey with a bee leads to such wondrous places as the inside of a flower; stepping into a mirror, he becomes a king; after pulling the monster through a small hole, he rides it to victory and wins a trophy, into which the monster disappears. Each story is told in black-line drawings with small touches of color that increase as the plot gathers momentum.

Another imaginative fantasy is *In the Eye of the Teddy,* by Frank Asch. The reader is brought closer and closer to Teddy's eye until the black pupil engulfs the page. Then a naked boy and a pocket watch with attached paraphernalia appear: the boy descends, and, on the facing page, the watch ascends. To what purpose is never made clear. Following this episode, the reader/viewer journeys back out of the pupil to discover a pleased-looking little boy holding Teddy. Strongly contrasting black-and-white drawings convey the fragmentary incident. Whalen-Levitt (1980) analyzes more completely the ambiguous realities in this book, pointing out how Asch explores figure/ground relationships. Dominant objects are shown against subdued backgrounds, but often this relationship reverses, with the object becoming less substantial than the background, as the artist moves between reality and fantasy.

In *The Grey Lady and the Strawberry Snatcher,* by Molly Bang, an extraordinary use of negative space pervades the entire book from the beginning (the shopkeeper handing the box of strawberries to the lady) to the end (only the empty box and the stems are left). In between is the ebb and flow of pursuit, with the lady and the purple-hatted snatcher dancing closer together and farther apart, becoming larger and smaller, in richly complex pictures. The lady, the road, and the tree are all shown as negative shapes. The objects themselves are not depicted, but rather the background comes up to the place where each object would be, and ends. These shapes are not outlined, which further challenges children's sense of figure/ground relationships. Also, the viewpoint varies in interesting ways. For example, sometimes the viewer looks up the sidewalk one way, sometimes the other, and sometimes straight on from the side. The distance between the viewer and the viewed object changes in succeeding pictures: in one picture, the lady is at a great distance; in another, she is right at the front of the picture plane. All of this demands complex visual skills not usually required by wordless picture books. Bang's book is one of several recommended by Greenlaw (1984) in an article describing how books can facilitate play behavior, stimulating children to act out part of a story. Campbell (1980) also responded very favorably to this book, although MacCann reacted negatively in the same issue of the same journal.

## REALITY WITHOUT WORDS

In contrast to imaginative fantasies like those described above, a few word-less books are reality-based. A particularly effective story is *The Wrong Side of the Bed*, by Edward Ardizzone. This author's first wordless book is about a small boy whose day goes from bad to impossible. After alienating his entire family, he seeks solace outside, only to be mistreated by older children. The artist uses thin, black line and extensive crosshatching over salmon and green to create naturalistic illustrations. The experience of having a bad day is one many children have had, and several books have been written about it.[4]

*The Apple and the Moth*, by Iela and Enzo Mari, is not a fictionalized story but rather a sequence of details concerning a natural event. The beautifully understated illustrations employ large, hard-edged blocks of color to tell a circular tale, beginning with an egg hatching into a worm and ending with a full-grown moth laying her egg. Silhouettes are accented here and there with thin ink line, and the colors change with the seasons. This book is one of several recommended by D'Angelo (1981) as being particularly effective in developing sequence and prediction skills in language-disabled children.

*Dandelion Year*, by Ron McTrusty, also utilizes silhouette shapes to recount a natural event. Green leaf shapes on a rich brown background make an effective foil for the softer brown line that details the life cycle of the weed. Skillfully applied brown dots and crosshatching show the girl, the animals, and the trees in the dandelion's environment as the seasons change. The abruptness of the changes and overpowering quality of the sun are difficult to understand, but the book's bold graphic quality is impressive.

## PICTURES THAT DON'T TELL STORIES

Instead of presenting a sequential story line, some wordless books contain intriguing illustrations that are related to each other but do not follow any conventional literary form. A striking example of this type is an award-winning book by Mitsumaso Anno, *Topsy-Turvies*. Gnomelike creatures in peaked hats inhabit an environment that bends and turns in impossible ways. What is the top at one end becomes the bottom at the other; what is

---

[4]It is interesting to contrast Ardizzone's story with Judith Viorst's *Alexander and the Terrible, Horrible, No Good, Very Bad Day* (New York: Atheneum, 1972). A suitably irritated Alexander is rendered by illustrator Ray Cruz. Although Alexander does not manage to bring his day to a pleasant conclusion, his mother helps him realize that some days are just like that.

inside strangely becomes outside; what seems to be front turns out to be back. These full-color optical illusions feature outlines in thin black line. They are humorous, in part because the gnomes seem unaware of (or unperturbed by) these shifts in perspective. Since the structural changes are subtle, this book is appropriate for intermediate- and upper-grade students.

*Snail, Where Are You?* is by the talented Tomi Ungerer, who has written many conventional books for children. This one features a series of brilliantly colored and highly stylized paintings of a tuba player, a jester, a pig on a ball, a violinist, and two birds fighting for a worm, among others. A visually sophisticated child will realize it is the circular snail shape that relates these seemingly disparate objects. Ungerer's illustrations are distinguished. In one, the black background is incorporated into the owl's shape in a superb design. After using this book with intermediate-grade children, a teacher might ask them to paint a picture containing a hidden shape.

## WORDLESS BOOKS FOR OLDER CHILDREN

Teachers and librarians tend to consider wordless picture books appropriate for only very young children. The visual complexity of a few, however, makes them more suitable for older children. One complex and extended wordless book, *The Silver Pony*, is done in tempera; the resulting paintings are characterized and unified by a unique tonality. Lynd Ward (whose lithographic illustrations were discussed in Chapter 2) here tells a tale about a lonely young boy growing up on a farm. One day he sees a winged silver pony, but his father does not believe him. When the pony reappears, the boy rides off on it. After an extensive journey and various earthly adventures, the pair visit the stars, where the pony is struck by a rocket, and the two plummet to the ground. In a literal ending that provides a striking contrast to the earlier fantasy, the boy is treated for shock by a country doctor and receives a real pony from his parents. One of the most extensive of wordless books, *The Silver Pony* contains eighty drawings divided into "chapters."

Another extended wordless story is *The Wonder Ring* by Holden Wetherbee. Silhouettes, hand-cut from paper, are less complex than those done by Arthur Rackham for his *Mother Goose Nursery Rhymes* but are effective nonetheless. The young hero, after befriending a beggar, finds that others befriend him, and their assistance enables him eventually to vanquish the giant. Because of the limitations of the medium, the emphasis is on action rather than character development. The book is particularly effective in stimulating children to make inferences about what is happening in the pictures.

Because it deals with emotions in an impressionistic way, *Vicki*, by

***Lynd Ward creates very realistic illustrations using lithography.*** From *The Silver Pony* by Lynd Ward. Copyright © 1973 by Lynd Ward. Reprinted by permission of Houghton Mifflin Company.

Renate Meyer, is probably most easily understood by children in inter-mediate grades. Striking *string print*[5] endpapers in maroon and dark brown introduce the story of an introspective girl who wants a friend. She has one, loses her to another child, approaches a group and is rejected, and finally creates her own friend. The art, done as prints lifted from natural plant forms, is unusual. The story itself is a slender thread, not completely de-veloped but simply a means of connecting the visuals.

Each of the wordless books for older readers considered so far includes a main character with whom students can empathize. In contrast, *Anno's Britain*, by Mitsumaso Anno, is full of many tiny characters engaged in a variety of actions—there is no single main character. Full-color, double-page spreads contain watercolors bled to the edge and sharpened with a black-ink line. The book contains many referents that may be unfamiliar even to upper-grade students: scenes from the play *Romeo and Juliet* and from paintings by John Constable and Jean Millet, for example. Other re-ferents may be more familiar: children engaged in playing nursery-rhyme games and characters from such books as *Dr. Doolittle*. This book is an intriguing puzzle for children to decipher. An equally complex book is *Anno's Journey* for which Jett-Simpson (1984) has provided activities in drama, associations, prediction, and studying the time period.

# EVALUATING WORDLESS PICTURE BOOKS

As is true of any genre, some wordless books are impressive examples of the form. Others—though not memorable—are probably usable; still others are poor and not worth children's time.

## PICTURE QUALITY

Because wordless picture books are primarily visual, teachers or librarians must make educated judgments about the quality of the pictures. In eval-uating such books, it is important to think about how effectively the illus-trator has utilized such elements as line, color, proportion, detail, and space (see Chapter 2).

As an example of the use of these elements, the work of a single illus-trator, John S. Goodall, is noteworthy. His small, rectangular books are

---

[5]String is dipped into paint, and paper is placed on top of the string and rubbed, which transfers the design to the paper.

*This picture is like many in John S. Goodall's books—very completely painted, bled to the page edges, and making little use of the color of the paper itself.* Illustration by John S. Goodall from *Paddy to the Rescue.* Copyright © 1985 John S. Goodall. (A Margaret K. McElderry Book) Reprinted with the permission of Atheneum Publishers, a division of Macmillan, Inc.

unusual in including half-pages bound in between the full pages. As the central half-page is flipped from right to left, the action advances in smaller steps than is possible when only full pages are used.

Line is very important in Goodall's work. In *The Adventures of Paddy Pork*, he uses heavy black line and a lot of crosshatching to create depth and roundness of form on cream-colored paper. The line breaks up the double- and half-page spreads so that few surfaces remain undecorated.

Goodall is also skilled in using color. Lavish full color is apparent in *Paddy's Evening Out*, in which two friends, the personifications of porcine elegance, encounter troubles at the theater. Careful bookmaking was necessary to match and align the half-pages that flip to advance the action. Skillful color matching contributes to the book's unity. The popular main character's adventures are continued in *Paddy's New Hat, Paddy Pork Odd Jobs, Paddy Under Water,* and *Paddy to the Rescue.*

Goodall's realistic depiction of proportion is apparent in *Jacko*, the tale of a resourceful monkey who goes from serving an organ grinder to final bliss in the arms of another monkey on a desert island. All along the way, the artist has paid careful attention to naturalistic proportions in the bodies of the peruke-wearing colonial gentlemen and the saber-flashing pirates.

Goodall's work is packed with details, as the pleasant accumulation in *Shrewbettina's Birthday* shows. Her bedroom is authentic, right down to the sloping ceiling and poster bed. These interior details are replaced by the many tiny plants and flowers of the countryside as this appealing heroine sets out on a shopping excursion. A pleasant coziness is the direct result of this homey assemblage.

Finally, this artist's use of space to create a three-dimensional environment through which characters move is apparent in the beguiling tale *Naughty Nancy*. Nancy is a small mouse who causes a lot of trouble. She moves convincingly around the house, out the door, into an automobile, down the church aisle, and up the side of a tent because of Goodall's ability to create three-dimensional space. Using line and color, he creates an environment that transcends the flatness of the printed page.

## STORY QUALITY

Despite the lack of words, teachers or librarians evaluating wordless picture books can apply some of the criteria they would use in evaluating other kinds of stories.

### 1. Are the characters interesting? Do they engage and hold the reader's attention? Do they do things consistent with the situation?

The bear and the mouse in *Ernest and Celestine's Patchwork Quilt*, by Gabrielle Vincent, are indeed interesting characters. They care for each other: Ernest looks after Celestine, but together they accomplish more than either could alone. They cooperate: after she selects and arranges fabric samples, he sews them together. The quilt that results inspires Celestine to make one for herself, and once again the friends collaborate.

### 2. Are the settings intriguing? Are they appropriate to the characters and the plot the author has created?

There is only one setting in *Snow*, by Isao Sasaki, but it changes visually, and the changes are a major part of the story. The time of day, the characters, the presence or absence of mechanical things (the train and its cargo), all change to make significant differences in how this single setting looks. The large paintings are in full color, and heavy use of applied white intensifies the colors. The soft gray borders are an attractive foil for the paintings.

### 3. Is the plot exciting enough to hold the reader's interest? Is it logical (which is not the same as realistic)?

There are actually three plots in *The Happy Dog*, by Hideyuki Tanaka. The first short story, encapsulated in cartoon panels, ends with the disheveled little dog wandering unhappily off. The middle tale comes to a happy conclusion as the dog solves the problem posed by an enticing mud puddle. The final tale results in the loss of a balloon, but nothing more

*Artist Peter Parnall plays one black-line pattern against another. His use of negative, or white, space in the waves is unusual.* Illustration by Peter Parnall from *The Inspector* by George Mendoza. Copyright © 1970 by Peter Parnall. Reprinted by permission of Doubleday & Company, Inc.

serious, and the dog goes whistling off. The cartoon panels help hold children's attention to the plot lines of these brief stories.

**4. Does the book have any message or theme? Is the author successful in helping the reader sense something new or experience something old in a new way?**

Without words, Hanne Turk communicates a message about adaptability in *The Rope Skips Max.* On 6-inch-square pages, simple pictures with

no background show Max trying to make use of his rope. Foiled in one way, he perseveres in another. The watercolor illustrations are pleasant without being cute. Children who enjoy this book will want to follow Max's adventures in the several other books that are available.

**5.  *What is the readability level of the pictures? Can the child piece together the elements in the individual pictures to extract meaning from the total presentation?***

The easily readable visual language is part of the charm in *Picnic* and *First Snow,* both by Emily Arnold McCully. The author's mouse family is quite large, and all its members engage in human activities and gestures (for instance, wringing hands in despair) but wear only minimal human clothing. What makes the stories accessible is that the events (such as sailing a toy boat) and themes (such as the value of gathering up courage to try something unfamiliar) are commonplace to children. Since each story takes place in a familiar environment and includes many recognizable objects, most children will have no trouble deciphering the visual story.

Sometimes a book appears at first glance to be impressive but proves on further examination not to be. A striking title page and pleasant vertical-striped endpapers promise better things to come in *The Knitted Cat*, by Antonella Bollinger-Savelli, but the illustrator does not deliver. The story line is minimal, and the pictures, though strongly designed with simplified and accentuated patterns, are disappointing. As the book progresses, the pattern and color become so dominant that the viewer has no sense of what is more and less important. There is no emphasis and subordination in the pictures; they all function at such a high level of visual intensity that no space is left for the viewer to "step back" and reflect on what has been seen. As a result, the book does not draw viewers in, to become emotionally or cognitively involved, but functions on a surface level, to be appreciated only for its visual decorativeness.

## SUITABILITY

Teachers must also assess whether a book is really a children's book or a book for adult readers that has a children's book format. Teachers who are squeamish might object to *The Inspector*, by George Mendoza. However, the question is not whether children should be protected from the bloody conquests this book depicts, but whether it holds any intrinsic interest for most children. The inspector, in cape and hat, is oblivious to the dangers threatening him on succeeding pages. His appealing dog, happily scratching itself in the beginning, takes on one after another of the beastly monsters that stalk the inspector. But with each bloody attack, the dog grows more sinister, evolving into a monster.

*The Package*, by Laurie Anderson, is another wordless book that may not be suitable for children. The pictures are rendered in black line with closely spaced black dots to create depth and substance. The package is passed from hand to hand until a bizarrely garbed fisherwoman puts it into her bicycle basket and pedals off over the hill. The drawings are complex and imaginative but will probably not interest the age group usually attracted to wordless books. The humor is not apparent to children: it is based on subtle exaggerations of adult physical features. The monk is funny to adults because of his pointy big feet, beady eyes, and emphatically flat hat. Few children will notice these details; those who do won't be amused by them.

*Above and Below Stairs* by John Goodall is an adult book in children's book format. The book is a horizontal rectangle bound along the top, so the pictures are oriented horizontally. The unusual relationship between the pictures clearly requires an almost adult audience. In each case, using the half-pages that have become his trademark, the artist shows those who are ministered to and those who minister. The book begins in the Middle Ages with a royal banquet and those who prepare the feast. For the time of Richard III, it shows both the knights jousting and the stablemen shoeing a horse. The final scene is a somewhat jarring one-page view of an attic apartment, complete with posters of Marilyn Monroe and Elvis Presley. An adult might find this a charming, though superficial, look at nearly a thousand years of history. The book, however, requires more interest in and knowledge of historic periods than most children have.

# REASONS FOR THE POPULARITY OF WORDLESS BOOKS

Why have wordless picture books, recently enjoying much popularity, been so enthusiastically accepted by children and the adults who work with them? Children find wordless books intriguing. One reason is that the author/illustrator has created compelling characters who do interesting things. This most basic motivation for reading, however, does not identify the particular appeal of wordless books. There are three factors that make wordless books particularly attractive to young "readers."

### 1. Children today are visually oriented.

Television is such a pervasive element in our society that when most students graduate from high school they have spent more time viewing television than they have spent in school. Influenced almost from birth by this medium, students have been unconsciously inculcated with the importance of the language of images. However, such awareness does not necessarily guarantee the ability to evaluate visual images. In fact, many boys and girls seem particularly uncritical consumers of visual images. Nonetheless, it is logical to assume a direct relation exists between children's immersion in television and their attraction to wordless books.

### 2. Wordless picture books are more accessible than are more complex genres.

It is not necessary to be able to read to derive pleasure from following the plot of a wordless book. These books tend, on the surface at least, to be plot-oriented, and children like action. The immense popularity of series books, lacking in other literary elements but heavy on plot, testifies to children's consuming interest in plot.[6]

Who could resist the plot in brightly imaginative *Changes, Changes,* by Pat Hutchins? The book features two inventive puppetlike people, a man and a woman, who build an assortment of wooden shapes into a house and then rebuild them into a fire engine when the house catches fire. Too much water from the engine makes a lake, so they rebuild the shapes into a boat and sail across the lake toward other adventures.[7] The book is also noteworthy for its impressive illustrations, in which a very regular black line tightly encircles each shape.

Some wordless books are accessible because they deal with experiences many children have had. Boys and girls enjoy *The Snowman,* by Raymond Briggs, because building a snowman and then pretending to have adventures with him are commonplace experiences. Briggs imaginatively links reality with fantasy in his book, which functions effectively as a visual unit. *Walking in the Air, The Party, Dressing Up,* and *Building the Snowman* are the result of repackaging parts of the original book as board books. Each of these four books includes ten approximately 6-inch-square closeups of various parts of the story. The lack of continuity between pages is disconcerting: body parts are lopped off arbitrarily, and one scene (page) does not bear any apparent sequential relationship to the next.

*Dreams,* by Peter Spier, reflects the common childhood pastime of looking at clouds and imagining they are specific objects. Double-page watercolor spreads, with less persistent ink line than is usual in Spier's work, show children "seeing" unicorns, dragons, people, dolphins, and steam engines, among other things. There is no story line, as such, but rather a gentle recapturing of possibilities in the sky.

---

[6]To locate succeeding books when children have enjoyed the first in a series, see Susan Roman, *Sequences: An Annotated Guide to Children's Fiction in Series* (Chicago: American Library Association, 1985).

[7]To see how another author uses a danger-escape motif, look at *Pig Pig and the Magic Photo Album,* by David McPhail (New York: E. P. Dutton, 1986). Pig Pig is human in porcine form, and the hairbreadth escapes, before he ends up in the haven of home, delight readers.

**3.** ***Wordless books allow wider interpretation of the author's message than books with words usually do.***

Children are not held too closely to the author's specific intent when the story is presented pictorially. In *Frog Goes to Dinner,* by Mercer Mayer, it is possible to extract the meaning of *dinner* without knowing that word or the related word *supper.* From the pictures, a child can see that the family is going out to eat a meal. Similarly, in *First Snow,* by Emily Arnold McCully, mentioned earlier in this chapter, the mouse family might be either sledding or sliding down the hill. They could be wearing scarves or mufflers. In a conventional story, extracting the author's meaning might well depend on understanding word distinctions. When the information is presented visually, the ability to decode the exact words the author intended isn't critical.

# *SHARING WORDLESS BOOKS WITH CHILDREN*

## DEVELOPING ORAL AND WRITING ABILITIES

Teachers commonly use wordless books to stimulate oral or written composition. Many authors have pointed out ways these books can motivate children to retell stories in their own words.

One could begin with a set of very simple books for preschool viewers. *When?, What?, Where?,* and *Who?* by artist/illustrator Leo Lionni are board books without words. His usual appealing mice explore the seasons, common objects, locations, and other creatures. A variety of papers are used in the collage illustrations to engage the eye and mind of the young child, and start the child talking about the objects shown. The teacher can use these books to encourage language generation. *Where?* illustrates concept words such as *on, in,* and *behind.* After talking about these concepts, the teacher can encourage children to list other location words, such as *above, between,* and *below.* After developing this list, children can make their own pictures to show locations.

One kindergarten teacher provides recurring opportunities for her girls and boys to share a wordless book and then dictate a story as a group. One day she used Jack Kent's *The Egg Book* with six children. The pictures, in bright yellow, red, and orange, tell of a befuddled hen who searches for an egg to tend. She discovers several, but in each case what hatches out follows after its real mother. Finally, almost accidentally, she discovers she has laid an egg of her own and is delighted when it hatches a chick that needs her care. After looking carefully at the pictures, the group dictated this composite story:

> One day a chicken looked for her egg. "I'm looking for my baby chicken." She looked all day. She looked everywhere. She found another hen who had an egg in a yellow nest. It was her own, she thought. It hatched because it was so warm. She said to the other chicken, "Do you know what? There's a crack in your egg." Then she went past it.
>
> "I found my chicken that cracked out of the egg. Hello, chick."
>
> The chick was yellow. It was so cute. It walked out of the egg. It followed the mother. She couldn't find her egg.
>
> Now she found another egg. She sat on this one and thought it was her egg. It wasn't her egg. It really wasn't. A different animal came out. It was a turtle. She thought it was her egg again. She kept thinking that over and over. The egg cracked. Instead of her chick it was a tiny alligator. HELP! She thinks this is her egg. "I hope this is my egg." It's cracking. "This is my egg, I think." The mother ostrich came to take her baby home to her house or nest. They left the chicken.
>
> She found an egg this time that was hers, she thought. She walked away from it. Then it hatched. It was her chick, all wet. No one else can have her baby chick. No one else can use it except her. No one can be its babysitter but her. It followed Mother everywhere.

The children's story is sturdy oral language, a careful recounting of many sequential details. In addition, it also includes children's

1. personal responses: "It was so cute."

2. expression of feelings: "I hope this is my egg." "This is my egg, I think."

3. ideas about the hen's rights: "No one else can have her baby chick. No one else can use it except her. No one can be its babysitter but her."

A newer book by Jack Kent, *The Scribble Monster,* is one of five recommended by Arthur (1982) in an article that includes suggestions for using it in developing language-based reading skills.

When a teacher divides the total group into several smaller ones, each child gets to contribute more to a dictation experience. If the teacher has two or three versions of the same wordless book, dictated by different groups of children, the students can be encouraged to compare and contrast the resulting stories. McGee and Tompkins (1983), writing about intermediate-grade students, suggest that this process allows children to discuss the authors' different styles.

As part of her composition program, one second-grade teacher regularly lets students look through wordless books and retell the stories in their own words. In one case, the motivating book was the humorous story, *Who's Seen the Scissors?*, by Fernando Krahn. In this story, a balding tailor possesses flying scissors that escape through an open window and set off on a journey, causing a series of mishaps. A suitor's flowers are beheaded, a lady's dog escapes with its leash cut in two, and a Japanese lantern crowns a restaurant patron. Finally, the scissors return to the tailor, who finds just the right place to store them. The second-grade teacher, aware that children's abilities to tell stories often outstrip their abilities to write down their thoughts, makes provision for children to dictate into a cassette recorder. A clerk then types the stories and gathers them in a book that is featured in the reading corner. The stories represent the children's *oral* language abilities.

Craig not only retold Krahn's story but added some interesting details of his own:

Once there was a tailor with magic scissors. One day when the tailor was making a suit the magic scissors flew out the door and it cut a girl's hair. Then it cut a man's newspaper, a girl's dress, a man's tie and then it flew into a circus. It cut the tightrope when someone was on it. Then it cut the lion's hair. It went out of the circus tent and it cut the feathers from an eagle and then it cut the tailor's clothes. It went into the tailor shop and sat on the table. The tailor put the scissors in a cage so it couldn't get out. But the scissors did not like the cage so it cut the cage and got out. The tailor was so scared he said, "Help!" But the scissors just sat on the table. The tailor was surprised because he thought that the scissors would make more trouble but the scissors just sat on the table. When the tailor wanted to make clothes all he had to do is tell the scissors what to do and it would do it. They were happy till one morning when the tailor woke up, he noticed that the scissors was gone. He started to cry because he didn't have any more scissors. So now he couldn't make any more clothes. He called the police but they never saw the scissors. One day the mayor came over to buy some clothes but the tailor didn't have any clothes so he was scared to death. But then he remembered the clothes he made during the night. So he got his clothes and gave his clothes to the mayor. But the tailor was still scared because he thought that the scissors would make more trouble, but the scissors was hiding in the closet. When the tailor saw the scissors he was laughing instead of being mad. Every day something good happened to the scissors and the tailor. One day it was the tailor's birthday. Then the scissors made him the best suit. It fit him. He was so surprised. He invited all his friends. He had a happy birthday and the scissors and the tailor had a happy life.

Instead of tape recording her oral story, Lynn, proud of her ability to print, insisted on writing her story. She apparently also enjoys using punctuation:

> A man was getting ready to go somewhere. But suddenly, his scissors flew out doors. It cut a girl's hair off! A man's tie off! This time a flower pot fell on somebody's head! And then the man from this morning was happy. He forgot about the scissors. He was making a speech, off his trousers go. That scissors! A lady was walking her dog but the scissors came. The scissors found something . . . A circus trapeze. Oh, no! There it goes. Now the lion's cage . . . he let the lion out! Mrs. Mrs. WATCHOUT! Pick up your clothes. That scissors broke the clothes line. Mister, a scissors is flying through your door. It cut off the strings of the violin. I don't believe it. That man is reading a newspaper. I hope the scissors doesn't come? It did . . . and it cut the newspaper. Right after that the man found the scissors (what a relief!). Well, he put the scissors in a cage and the scissors couldn't get out.

## DEVELOPING LITERARY JUDGMENT

*April Fools*, by Fernando Krahn, is about two small boys with big imaginations who fashion a long-necked but bodiless monster. Using it to frighten the townsfolk, they carelessly allow themselves to become lost. Their own cleverness results in their being rescued, and they return to town in a triumphant motorcade. The drawings are in black and white, with soft gold used only for the monster. A first-grade teacher asked children to react to this story. Brad's reaction was very positive:

> It was good. It had interesting things happening. Brian and Brad had a spooky-hooky board thing to scare people. It was sort of neat to scare them like that. I like stories where people get scared.

Sara declared her disbelief in monsters, perhaps to reassure herself:

> I liked the story. I liked it when they put it on the roof and turned it upside down. They fooled the father. It looked like a monster, even though there is no such thing.

*April Fools* is one of several books Jalongo (1985) analyzed and used as examples of the types of humor that appeal to children. She describes three theories used to explain humor and details how what children think is funny changes as they grow.

*Pastel watercolors depict whimsical characters performing actions against only a minimal background.* Illustration from *Mighty Mizzling Mouse* by Friso Henstra (J. B. Lippincott). Copyright © 1983 by Friso Henstra. Reprinted by permission of Harper & Row, Publishers, Inc.

## MIMING THE ACTION

An interesting challenge for children is translating literature from one mode to another. One possibility is to translate a wordless book into a pantomime, though shifts to other modes are also possible. Teachers can use *The Midnight Adventures of Kelly, Dot and Esmeralda*, by John S. Goodall, as a basis for mime.[8] Mime, fundamental to informal drama, does not rely on words to express ideas. Students will need much experience in solving mime problems in order to develop their skills in this area. Goodall's book, about the adventures of three friends and their narrow escape from danger, provides ample opportunity for children to practice miming. The action includes

opening the door,

welcoming the guests,

making and serving tea,

climbing into a picture frame,

---

[8]See John Warren Stewig, *Informal Drama in the Elementary Language Arts Program* (New York: Teachers College Press, 1983). The book develops a rationale for including drama in the curriculum and a sequence of activities of increasing difficulty, beginning with pantomime, leading through story drama, into improvisation.

getting into and rowing a boat,

warming hands before a fire,

eating soup,

helping someone climb onto the back of a wagon,

playing a game of skill at a carnival,

grabbing a small animal,

playing a bass drum, and

running with a small animal under one arm.

These actions are roughly in sequential order, although a teacher leading a drama session need not necessarily present them this way. Some of the actions, like eating soup, are relatively simple to mime. Others, like helping someone climb on the back of a wagon, are more difficult to show without words. The teacher must assess the difficulty level of the pantomimes when planning a lesson.

After sharing the pictures with the children, the teacher can involve them in miming the actions, presenting the actions in order, from simple to complex. The teacher should let all the children do each mime at the same time; this is called *simultaneous playing*. After the children are finished, the teacher can lead a discussion, asking such questions as

"What was difficult to do in that action?"

"How was this action like or different from the previous one?"

"Is there something you need to add to make it more convincing?"

Encouraging children to think about ways to make the pantomime more effective is an important part of building mime skills.

Once the pantomimes are convincing, they can be arranged sequentially, with every child doing each action at the same time. Only after much experience with simultaneous play should children be divided into groups and assigned parts. The emphasis in *informal classroom drama* should be on the value of individual participation and not on performing for an audience.

## ASSESSING COMPREHENSION AND LANGUAGE ABILITY

The previous sections considered the use of wordless books as an instructional vehicle to motivate oral, written, and nonverbal language. Wordless books also have diagnostic uses; they can help teachers measure and monitor children's thinking and language abilities.

Teachers have long been concerned with how well children comprehend what they have read. One aspect of comprehension is inference making. Children can make inferences about either text or pictures. Teachers see skill in making inferences about text as an indication of inference-making ability in general. Typically, teachers measure comprehension using responses to questions about printed material, but comprehension may be limited in such situations by children's lack of understanding of syntax or their inability to decode words. A procedure that allows children to respond orally to wordless books gives teachers the opportunity to observe natural patterns of inferential comprehension.

Jett-Simpson (1976) investigated children's comprehension using a wordless book (*Frog Goes to Dinner*, by Mercer Mayer). She developed a classification system to describe inferential comprehension of a picture narrative based on children's oral responses. The system analyzes inferences about plot (cause/effect, elaborated events, added events), setting (place/object, refinement, time) and character (identification, refinement, external and internal behavior). Jett-Simpson's subjects, representing three levels of reading readiness scores in kindergarten and three levels of reading scores in second and fourth grades, participated in warm-up activities that included tape recorder play with the researcher. Then children individually recorded original stories for the wordless book. Each child also answered five inference questions about the book.

Inferences about conversation, plot, setting, and character increased as grade level increased. The number of *T-units*[9] and the number of inferences per T-unit also increased. The number of correct responses to inference questions also increased with grade level. Children made more inferences about character and plot than about other elements. The author concluded that children's verbalized responses during picture-stimulated storytelling can reveal comprehension. The study demonstrates the usefulness of wordless picture books; teachers interested in measuring comprehension in other than traditional ways might use Jett-Simpson's scale.

Wordless books can also be used to assess children's productive language ability. Children's competency in generating language has long con-

---

[9]A T-unit is a measure of language maturity consisting of one main clause with all the subordinate clauses (if any) attached to it. The unit was developed by Kellogg W. Hunt, *Grammatical Structures Written at Three Grade Levels* (Champaign, Ill.: National Council of Teachers of English, 1965, p. 20). It is a more accurate assessment of language maturity than sentences are.

*A pebbly texture combined with thin pencil line yields a pleasant drawing contained within a dramatic, thin orange-red border.* Illustration from *Up a Tree* by Ed Young. Copyright © 1983 by Ed Young. Reprinted by permission of Harper & Row, Publishers, Inc.

cerned educators, but in-school measurement of language has too frequently taken the form of standardized tests emphasizing analysis. In this era of increasing demands for accountability, use of such tests of children's analyzing abilities is increasing. Teachers need other measures to determine how children's language abilities are growing.

A teacher might use a wordless book to elicit samples of language in September. She or he could show the book to children and then record (by writing down or tape recording) their retellings. These samples can be analyzed for the following elements:

1. ***Total word output.*** Quantity of language is one measure of language maturity.
2. ***Total number of communication units.*** This measure is similar to, but more precise than, the sentence (Loban, 1963).
3. ***Mean length of communication units.*** Dividing the total number of words by the total number of communication units gives the average length of the units.

4. **A type/token ratio.**   This is a measure of the number of different words (types) per given sample (tokens). This ratio is computed by choosing a sample consisting of a hundred words and determining how many different words it includes (Jensen, 1973).

For the sample below, the type/token ratio is 64:100 (of the one-hundred-word sample sixty-four are different). The repeated words are italicized so that the different words can be counted easily.

Once there was a little boy named Jonathan. He *was* going to sleep. The next morning *he* woke up *he* got out on *the* wrong side of *the* bed. *He got* dressed. Then *he* went downstairs for breakfast. *He was* reaching *for the* doughnuts *the* pitcher fell but *he* took *a doughnut. Then* when *he was* done *he* kicked his chair and pulled *his* sister's hair. *Then he* went *to* their shed *and* started *to* make *a* plane *out of* wood. *Then his* dad came in *and* said, "I've told you not *to* play here." So *he* left. *Then he* . . .

Having measured oral language ability in September, the teacher can repeat the assessment at mid-year and again in June (Buckley, 1976). Comparing this information for any child should give the teacher an idea of the growth in language production skills that occurred during the year. This procedure measures a critical area not often assessed on standardized tests and therefore gives the teacher important additional information about children's language abilities.

## SUMMARY

Storytelling with pictures has ancient antecedents; today's wordless picture books are the latest in a long line of visual encodings. Animal characters and fantasy prevail in recent wordless books. Although the absence of words may seem to indicate that these books are for prereaders only, in fact, some are complex and require sophisticated skills in visual comprehension and inference making.

Story dictation or composition (either as a group or individually) is a logical way to stretch children's abilities in verbal or written language. Many wordless books can also be used for developing the skills of pantomime, which leads into drama. Wordless books provide valuable material with which to assess comprehension and determine how effectively children can make inferences about plot, setting, and character. Using the procedure described in the chapter, teachers can monitor the growth of children's language abilities, assessing progress at different times during the year.

## Suggestions for Further Study

1. Nancy Larrick (see Related Reading for Adults, page 197) claims that some wordless books may be too confusing for many children to understand. She refers specifically to *Paddy's Evening Out*, by John S. Goodall. Use a copy of this book with preschool, kindergarten, and primary-grade children. At what age do children seem able to retell this story, indicating an understanding of the plot?

2. After using several wordless books with children and talking with them about the process of telling a story with pictures alone, ask them to draw or paint a wordless story of their own, or help them translate a simple traditional tale (like *The Three Bears*) into a sequence of pictures.

3. *In the Eye of the Teddy*, by Frank Asch, is a perplexing book. Look at it and try to put into words what you think it is about. Read the review in *Kirkus Reviews* (41, July 1, 1973, p. 679), which says the book might be the seed of a short film fantasy, representing a high order of ingenuity. The review in *Library Journal* (98, October 15, 1973, p. 3135) compares it to Sendak's *In the Night Kitchen*, contending that Sendak's fantasy is in the end "pure, frolicsome, and joyous" and that Asch's, in contrast, borders on the bizarre. *Publisher's Weekly* (204, July 12, 1973, p. 80) reports that children with whom the book was shared found it silly, not funny.

4. Authors often do sequels to books (see, for example, *A Boy, a Dog, and a Frog*, by Mercer Mayer, and *A Boy, a Dog, a Frog, and a Friend*, by Mercer and Marianna Mayer). Share *Lost*, by Sonia O. Lisker, with your children. Then ask them to plan an adventure for the two new friends, as a sequel, and tell it in pictures.

5. Read reviews that appeared when Antonella Bollinger-Savelli's *The Knitted Cat* was published in 1971. Compare and contrast them to the evaluation in this chapter. Look at the book itself, and form your own opinion. How does your opinion compare to these others?

6. After studying *The Inspector*, by George Mendoza, role-play two opposing viewpoints concerning its suitability. One role can be that of a librarian justifying its inclusion in the school's book collection; another can be that of a parent objecting to it. On what grounds might the two points of view be based?

7. This chapter described Molly Bang's *The Grey Lady and the Strawberry Snatcher* and mentioned both positive and negative reactions to the book. Examine the book, read the reviews mentioned in this chapter, and then compare them to Barbara Kiefer's reactions ("Fantasy in Children's Picture Books," *The Dragon Lode*, 5, Fall 1986, pp. 2–7). She reports very positive reactions from children to this sophisticated visual book. Use the book with a group of children to see what their responses are.

8. John Goodall's wordless books incorporate half-pages that flip from right to left to advance the action. Goodall's books are small in scale, but Brian Wildsmith, in *Pelican* (New York: Pantheon, 1982) and *Daisy* (New York: Pantheon, 1984), uses the half-page device in a larger size. Compare Wildsmith's vivid and consciously patterned books with Goodall's, and note any other differences in how the two artists use half-pages.

# Related Reading for Adults

Children's Book Council, Inc. "Wordless Book List." *Library Journal*, October 1974, pp. 2711–2712.

> This list of seventy-nine wordless books was compiled for a conference sponsored by Children's Book Council and the National Council of Teachers of English. Capsule summaries are included.

Cianciolo, Patricia. "Use Wordless Picture Books to Teach Reading, Visual Literacy and to Study Literature." *Top of the News*, April 1973, pp. 226–234.

> Pictures speak a universal language, but to understand it "one must be able to bring meaning/significance to the shapes, positions, and movements depicted by the book artist as he tells his story in pictures." The author recommends a language-experience approach to reading, basing written or dictated compositions on wordless books.

Fagerlie, Anna M. "Using Wordless Picture Books with Children." *Elementary English*, January 1975, pp. 92–94.

> The wordless books Fagerlie discusses stimulate language development, especially in shy children and those of limited background who may not have much to talk about. These books also help children discover the enjoyment of books because children can easily discern the plots.

Groff, Patrick. "Children's Literature Versus Wordless Books." *Top of the News*, April 1974, pp. 294–303.

> Groff says that Patricia Cianciolo's claim that the characteristics of visual literature and conventional literature are so similar that children move naturally from one to the other constitutes faulty logic. If it were true, children highly experienced in understanding picture plots on television would have keen sensibilities for literary conventions. One cannot assume that the lifelike, easygoing experiences children have with television prepare them for purposely ambiguous, difficult-to-follow literary plots. Groff believes the "harsh mental break" from viewing pictures to reading print must be made eventually, so it should not be delayed by providing children with wordless books.

Herman, Gertrude B. "Books Without Words: Picture Stories Bring Thought, Imagination, Delight." *Wisconsin Library Bulletin*, July 1976, pp. 151–152.

> The antecedents of today's wordless books include temple friezes, ancient Japanese scrolls, "catchpenny prints," "metamorphoses," and comic strips. Herman comments on the uses of wordless books, including instruction and entertainment, observational and aesthetic response, and stimulation of inference and other intellectual abilities. She believes these books can sometimes be more subtle and evocative than verbal messages.

Larrick, Nancy. "Wordless Picture Books and the Teaching of Reading." *The Reading Teacher*, May 1976, pp. 743–746.

> This author wondered if children really liked wordless picture books and how the books gave positive support to reading. To answer these questions, she interviewed four teachers and their pupils. She concluded that for four-year-olds such books are a boon: the children enjoyed looking at the pictures and talking about them. They learned to handle books and to proceed from front to back and left to right. The sixth-graders in Larrick's sample, even though they were poor readers, preferred books with words.

Read, Donna, and Henrietta M. Smith. "Teaching Visual Literacy Through Wordless Picture Books." *The Reading Teacher*, 35 (May 1982), pp. 928–933.

> Opening with a discussion of the pervasiveness of visual symbols in American culture, the authors move to a consideration of what they believe to be the most significant elements in the genre of wordless picture books. Shapes, space, color, and symbolism are each discussed in the context of a particular wordless book. The authors point out that even though 98 percent of children in the United States learn to read from basal readers, pictures in these books are "flat, not always intellectually challenging and of limited artistic quality." Consequently, students' perception and comprehension skills can be better developed using wordless trade books. Read and Smith conclude by identifying six skills that can be taught via such books; each is discussed in the context of a recommended book.

Salley, Colleen C., and Karen H. Harris. "The Bizarre in Children's Books." *Top of the News*, November 1974, pp. 95–99.

> The authors identify a trend characterized by violence, callousness, and brutality. Bizarre concepts that play upon the subconscious fears of children have crept into juvenile literature. The world depicted is unpredictable, incomprehensible, and threatening. Adults behave erratically; chaos abounds. For example, about *The Inspector*, by George Mendoza, they write: "The obvious theme of innocence corrupted by evil, and clever satirical treatment of dogged single-mindedness are suitable for mature audiences."

## *Professional References*

Arthur, Sharon V. "What Can You Do with a Book Without Words?" *The Reading Teacher*, 35 (March 1982), 738–740.

Buckley, Marilyn Hanf. "A Guide for Developing an Oral Language Curriculum." *Language Arts*, September 1976, 625–626.

Campbell, Patty. "The Young Adult Perplex." *Wilson Library Journal*, October 1980, 136–138.

D'Angelo, Karen. "Wordless Picture Books and the Young Language-Disabled Child." *Teaching Exceptional Children*, 14 (1981), 34–37.

Ellis, DiAnn Waskul, and Fannie Wiley Preston. "Enhancing Beginning Reading Using Wordless Picture Books in a Cross-Age Tutoring Program. *The Reading Teacher*, 37 (April 1984), 692–698.

Greenlaw, M. Jean. "Facilitating Play Behavior with Children's Literature." *Childhood Education*, 61 (May/June 1984), 339–344.

Herman, Gertrude B. "Books Without Words: Picture Stories Bring Thought, Imagination, Delight." *Wisconsin Library Bulletin*, July 1976, 151–152.

Jalongo, Mary Renck. "Children's Literature: There's Some Sense to Its Humor." *Childhood Education*, 62 (November/December 1985), 109–114.

Jensen, Julie M. "A Comparative Investigation of the Casual and Careful Oral Language Styles of Average and Superior Fifth Grade Boys and Girls." *Research in the Teaching of English*, 7 (Winter 1973), 338–350.

Jett-Simpson, Mary. *Anno's Journey*. Weston, Conn.: Weston Woods, 1984.

———. "Children's Inferential Responses to a Wordless Picture Book: Development and Use of a Classification System for Verbalized Inference." Ph.D. dissertation, University of Washington, 1976.

———. *Creative Approaches to Non-Verbal Film-strips*. Weston, Conn.: Weston Woods, 1977.

Loban, Walter. *The Language of Elementary School Children*. Champaign, Ill.: National Council of Teachers of English, 1963, pp. 17–21, 58–61, 85.

MacCann, Donnarae. "Picture Books for Children." *Wilson Library Bulletin*, October 1980, 132–135.

McGee, Lea M., and Gail E. Tompkins. "Wordless Picture Books Are for Older Readers, Too." *Journal of Reading*, 27 (November 1983), 120–123.

Whalen-Levitt, Peggy. "Picture Play in Children's Books: A Celebration of Visual Awareness." *Wilson Library Bulletin*, October 1980, 102–107.

## Bibliography of Children's Books

Anderson, Laurie. *The Package*. Indianapolis: Bobbs-Merrill, 1971.

Anno, Mitsumaso. *Anno's Britain*. New York: Philomel Books, 1982.

———. *Topsy-Turvies*. New York and Tokyo: Weatherhill, 1970.

Ardizzone, Edward. *The Wrong Side of the Bed*. Garden City, N.Y.: Doubleday, 1970.

Asch, Frank. *In the Eye of the Teddy*. New York: Harper and Row, 1973.

Bang, Molly. *The Grey Lady and the Strawberry Snatcher*. New York: Four Winds, 1980.

Bollinger-Savelli, Antonella. *The Knitted Cat*. New York: Macmillan, 1971.

Briggs, Raymond. *Building the Snowman*. Boston: Little, Brown, 1985.

———. *Dressing Up*. Boston: Little, Brown, 1985.

———. *The Party*. Boston: Little, Brown, 1985.

———. *The Snowman*. New York: Viking, 1978.

———. *Walking in the Air*. Boston: Little, Brown, 1985.

Brinckloe, Julie. *The Spider Web*. Garden City, N.Y.: Doubleday, 1974.

de Paola, Tomie. *The Hunter and the Animals*. New York: Holiday House, 1981.

———. *Sing, Pierrot, Sing*. San Diego, Calif.: Harcourt Brace Jovanovich, 1983.

Elzbieta. *Little Mops at the Seashore*. Garden City, N.Y.: Doubleday, 1972.

Fromm, Lilo. *Muffel and Plums*. New York: Macmillan, 1972.

Goodall, John S. *Above and Below Stairs*. New York: Atheneum, 1983.

———. *The Adventures of Paddy Pork*. New York: Harcourt Brace, 1968.

———. *Jacko*. New York: Harcourt Brace, 1971.

———. *The Midnight Adventures of Kelly, Dot, and Esmeralda*. New York: Atheneum, 1972.

———. *Naughty Nancy*. New York: Atheneum, 1975.

———. *Paddy Pork Odd Jobs*. New York: Atheneum, 1983.

———. *Paddy's Evening Out*. New York: Atheneum, 1973.

———. *Paddy's New Hat*. New York: Atheneum, 1980.

———. *Paddy to the Rescue*. New York: Atheneum, 1985.

———. *Paddy Under Water*. New York: Atheneum, 1984.

———. *Shrewbettina's Birthday*. New York: Harcourt Brace, 1970.

Hutchins, Pat. *Changes, Changes*. New York: Macmillan, 1971.

Keats, Ezra Jack. *Apt. 3*. New York: Macmillan, 1971.

———. *Clementina's Cactus*. New York: Viking, 1982.

———. *Kitten for a Day*. New York: Franklin Watts, 1974.

———. *Psst! Doggie*. New York: Franklin Watts, 1973.

Kent, Jack. *The Egg Book*. New York: Macmillan, 1975.

———. *The Scribble Monster*. New York: Harcourt Brace Jovanovich, 1981.

Krahn, Fernando. *April Fools*. New York: E. P. Dutton, 1974.

———. *Journeys of Sebastian*. New York: Delacorte, 1968.

———. *Sebastian and the Mushroom*. New York: Delacorte, 1976.

———. *Who's Seen the Scissors?* New York: E. P. Dutton, 1975.

Lionni, Leo. *What?* New York: Pantheon, 1984.

———. *When?* New York: Pantheon, 1984.

———. *Where?* New York: Pantheon, 1984.

———. *Who?* New York: Pantheon, 1984.

Lisker, Sonia O. *Lost*. New York: Harcourt Brace Jovanovich, 1975.

Mari, Iela, and Enzo Mari. *The Apple and the Moth*. New York: Pantheon, 1969.

Mayer, Mercer. *A Boy, a Dog, and a Frog*. New York: Dial, 1967.

———. *Bubble Bubble*. New York: Parents' Magazine Press, 1973.

———. *Frog Goes to Dinner*. New York: Dial, 1974.

Mayer, Mercer, and Marianna Mayer. *A Boy, a Dog, a Frog, and a Friend*. New York: Dial, 1971.

———. *One Frog Too Many*. New York: Dial, 1975.

McCully, Emily Arnold. *First Snow*. New York: Harper and Row, 1985.

———. *Picnic*. New York: Harper and Row, 1984.

McTrusty, Ron. *Dandelion Year*. New York: Harvey House, 1975.

Mendoza, George. *The Inspector*. Garden City, N.Y.: Doubleday, 1970.

Meyer, Renate. *Vicki*. New York: Atheneum, 1969.

Ramage, Corinne. *The Joneses*. Philadelphia: J. B. Lippincott, 1975.

Saltzberg, Barney. *The Yawn*. New York: Atheneum, 1985.

Sasaki, Isao. *Snow*. New York: Viking, 1982.

Sendak, Maurice. *Where the Wild Things Are*. New York: Harper and Row, 1963.

Spier, Peter. *Dreams*. Garden City, N.Y.: Doubleday, 1986.

Tanaka, Hideyuki. *The Happy Dog*. New York: Atheneum, 1983.

Turk, Hanne. *The Rope Skips Max*. Natick, Mass.: Alphabet Press, 1982.

Ueno, Noriko. *Elephant Buttons*. New York: Harper and Row, 1973.

Ungerer, Tomi. *Snail, Where Are You?* New York: Harper and Row, 1962.

Vincent, Gabrielle. *Ernest and Celestine's Patchwork Quilt*. New York: Greenwillow, 1982.

Ward, Lynd. *The Silver Pony*. Boston: Houghton Mifflin, 1973.

Wetherbee, Holden. *The Wonder Ring*. Garden City, N.Y.: Doubleday, 1978.

# TRADITIONAL
# LITERATURE:
# THE MISTS
# OF TIME

Once, so the story goes, there were seven children . . .
*"Misfortune," by Italo Calvino*

Long ago, when wishes often came true, there lived a king . . .
*"The Frog Prince," by Joanna Cole*

Once upon a time, when pigs were swine, a King and a Queen had one son . . .
*"Billy Begg and the Bull," by Virginia Haviland*

A long time ago, when pretzels still fell from the sky like rain . . .
The Hedgehog Boy, *by Jane Langton*

Though their wording varies, introductions such as these signal for listeners an engrossing time to follow; characters we empathize with will perform deeds we admire, and good will triumph over adversity. What accounts for the attraction of such folk or fairy tales, one type of traditional literature?

A preliterate tribe gathers around a campfire to hear again the familiar and loved tale of how a hero conquered evil. A group of third-graders form a circle on the carpeted floor of the media center as the librarian introduces an unfamiliar version of *Stone Soup,* by Ann McGovern. Though to all outward appearances the differences outnumber the similarities, in one respect the groups are alike: they are responding to a common stimulus, the lure of a traditional story told orally. Even though centuries of human development separate the two groups, they are alike in their enthusiastic response to an oral story.

The creation of forms of traditional literature—folk and fairy tales, myths, legends, and others—is difficult to describe, since they have only recently been studied. In most cases, it is not possible to pinpoint a date of origin or even to determine which is the original version, for in the handing down of this rich verbal legacy, many groups have used the same or similar ideas.

## KINDS OF FOLK LITERATURE

The vast body of traditional literature was shaped verbally by generation after generation, simply because oral language was then the only language.[1] This material has been recorded only in its old age. Traditional literature

---

[1] Even today, writing is far from universal. Of 2796 languages in the world, all have an oral form, but only about 153 have a written form.

also differs in purpose from composed literature. Written compositions are conceived as art forms, expressive ways of communicating ideas and providing pleasure; traditional literature typically has more consciously utilitarian purposes.

### 1. Folk tales were a convenient way of passing down cultural history to the next generation.

Among preliterate people, oral storytelling was a natural way of sharing the group's heritage with children. Stories from Ireland, Hungary, Greece, Iran, and Finland, among others, in *Hero Tales from Many Lands*, by Alice I. Hazeltine, are examples of histories of a cultural past. These are primarily stories of heros of great courage. They are not history as we know it from textbooks—organized, sequential, and panoramic—but rather glimpses into the particular time and culture in which the person lived.

### 2. Folk literature served to inculcate a culture's current mores, informing the young of the accepted behaviors of the group.

In recounting clearly the conflicts between good and evil and the outcomes of such conflicts, storytellers prescribed for listeners the behavior that was acceptable to the society. For example, industry and perseverance are rewarded in *The Shoemaker and the Elves*, retold by Ann Herring (and illustrated with full-color photographs of carved wooden dolls set against three-dimensional backgrounds).

Although there are some exceptions, these two cultural elements—history and mores—recur with regularity in the diversity of forms that make up traditional literature. These forms include nursery rhymes, proverbs, fables, folk and fairy tales, written tales, and such longer forms as myths and legends.

## NURSERY RHYMES

Most children first encounter traditional literature in the form of Mother Goose rhymes.[2] Parents frequently use these rhymes with preschoolers, and collections of them are a staple in nursery schools and kindergartens. These

---

[2]Various fanciful reasons for this title and differing opinions about how the rhymes began are contained in Katherine E. Thomas's *The Real Personages of Mother Goose* (New York: Lothrop, Lee and Shepard, 1930).

short, rhythmic, and usually rhymed forms are a type of poetry, and will therefore be described more fully in Chapter 7.

## PROVERBS

Proverbs, consisting of one or two succinct sentences about some aspect of life, represent the conventional wisdom of a culture. Proverbs contain kernels of truth, often more than meets the eye. Because they should be interpreted on other than the literal level, children may need help in understanding them. For example, "The early bird catches the worm" can be interpreted in different ways:

1. The student who gets up early and studies will learn and get good grades.
2. The first person in line at a store having a sale will get the best bargain.
3. The first applicant for a job has the best chance of getting it.[3]

Some proverbs, like the early bird one, are quite familiar. Another well-known one is "You can lead a horse to water, but you can't make him drink." Others may be quite unfamiliar, such as "It is sure to be dark if you close your eyes." American children today probably encounter these proverbs less often than did children in earlier eras. In order to understand this form, children need to hear or read proverbs, speculate about their meanings, and write their own proverbs. A helpful book for introducing proverbs is *Everything Is Difficult at First*, by Robert Sargent. The book includes, among others,

Divide an orange—it tastes just as good.

All that trembles does not fall.

Fishes see the worm, not the hook.

Kinetic black-ink line drawings are accompanied by watercolor applied loosely with brush and sponge.

*They Say Stories*, by Warren Chappel, consists of two- to four-page stories that illustrate proverbs from around the world. The homely, humorous wisdom is apparent in such sayings as "Two pieces of meat confuse the mind of the fly" and "Raindrops can't tell broadcloth from jeans." D'Angelo

---

[3]Duncan Emrich collected material in *The Hodgepodge Book* (New York: Four Winds, 1972). This is an almanac of curious, interesting, and out-of-the-way information culled from American folklore.

(1978) suggests that a teacher might introduce this book by reading several of the stories and their accompanying proverbs to children. Then the teacher can ask the children to write their own stories to illustrate a different saying. To further broaden children's acquaintance with this form, the teacher might share some African proverbs, reading *Speak to the Winds*, by Kofi Asare Opoku.

## FABLES

Fables are succinct, didactic tales that have a stated or implied moral. These short stories are often traced to a man named Aesop. He was supposedly a Greek slave who lived in Asia Minor around 600 B.C.; however, as with the origins of much traditional literature, this information is difficult to substantiate (Muggeridge, 1973). The animals in such fables as "The Hare and the Tortoise" personify human virtues and failings. The hare represents the devil-may-care, flippant, and self-assured nature of some humans. The tortoise, in contrast, represents the steady, conscientious, striving nature of other humans. The stated moral of this fable is "Slow but steady wins the race," which sums up the story's message in one sentence.

*The Fables of Aesop*, by Joseph Jacobs, includes "The Hare and the Tortoise" and features black-line and brown-wash illustrations by Kurt Wiese. Another collection that includes this fable is *Aesop's Fables*, with pictures by Heidi Holder. The single, full-page illustration for each fable is executed in subdued shades dominated by browns and set in a formal frame with decorative detailing. These intricate paintings are set pieces that will attract the attention of children who enjoy romantic realism.

Today, teachers share fables with children not so much for the messages they contain as for their literary qualities. They are admirable models of concise language: within the short scope of a single fable, children can laugh at the foolishness and admire the earnestness of the various animal characters.

One third-grade teacher used *Three Aesop Fox Fables*, by Paul Galdone. On three succeeding days, the teacher read one fable and wrote the moral on the chalkboard. Then she asked each student to choose one of the three morals and write a fable of his or her own to fit it. The following are two of the responses to her request:

### The Giraffe and the Raccoon

One day a giraffe met a raccoon. The raccoon was digging up beets. The giraffe said, "Are those good?" And the raccoon said, "Yes, they are good." The giraffe said, "Will you get me one?" The raccoon said, "Get it yourself." When the

**Heidi Holder's minutely detailed full-color paintings are bordered with elaborately figured frames, which contain almost as much content as the pictures themselves.** Illustration by Heidi Holder from *Aesop's Fables*. Illustration copyright © 1981 by Heidi Holder. Reproduced by permission of Viking Penguin Inc.

*Done in artist Paul Galdone's recognizable style, this pen and watercolor drawing incorporates shades of green, pink, and brown.* From *Three Aesop Fox Fables* by Paul Galdone. Copyright © 1971 by Paul Galdone. Reprinted by permission of Clarion Books/Ticknor & Fields, a Houghton Mifflin Company.

giraffe bent over he missed the beets, because he could not bend over that far. He kept missing the beets. So the giraffe walked away and said to himself, "I bet those beets were tough anyhow."

It is easy to scorn what you cannot get.

*Jared*

### The Sheep and the Rabbit

A sheep and a rabbit met at a hollow log one day. The rabbit said, "Oh, dear, dear wooly sheep, you're such a wooly sheep, so soft and cuddly." "Oh, yes, yes, yes, indeed. Do you like my beautiful soft wooly white fur?" requested the sheep. "Yes, of course," said the rabbit. "I'm sure my farmer and his children and all the other animals will love you, for I live on a farm. Please, oh please come with me to my farm. You can stay and live with us too, if you want," coaxed the wise rabbit. "Oh, do you really think so? I mean with all my beautiful, lovely, wooly, fluffy, nice, soft, and cuddly, white wool?" asked the sheep. "I'm almost positive. They'll love your beautiful, lovely, wooly, fluffy, nice, soft and cuddly, white wool. Well, I mean with all your magnificent wool," said the rabbit. So the sheep went with the wise little rabbit.

At first sight of the sheep, the farmer sheared the sheep right down to his skin, and made a nice little wool rug for the wise little rabbit. The rabbit said to the sheep, "Never trust a flatterer!"

*Jill*

Usually a fable has a deliberately stated moral, though some do not. The short (one-page) tales in *Berry Woman's Children* do not, but are described by the publisher as fables. This collection features strong wood engravings by Dale DeArmond (see page 51) and a handsomely designed picture-book format. The opening three pages introduce Grandmother, who has gathered her grandchildren around her to tell them of Raven, who made the animals, and Berry Woman, into whose care the animals were entrusted. Although the short fables are not as completely developed into story form as are those of Aesop, they are nonetheless interesting, especially in the context provided. Dramatic black endpapers lead into text on left-hand pages (highlighted with a dark red initial letter) facing DeArmond's patterned engravings, set in a luxurious amount of white space and with no background. Share this book with children in a group, as it is too fine to be overlooked; on the shelf, it may not be immediately appealing to children.

After reading some traditional fables to children, a teacher might share *Two More Moral Tales,* a wordless book by Mercer Mayer. "Sly Fox's Folly" and "Just a Pig at Heart" follow conventional fable form. Children can be encouraged to translate these tales into their own words. This book, as well as *Fables,* by Arnold Lobel, represent literary fables: fables not drawn from ancient sources but rather patterned after them. *Fables* was one of ten books singled out for special mention by Kanfer (1980). Lobel's twenty fables follow traditional form but deal with some unusual animals and modern settings. In "The Crocodile in the Bedroom," an obsession with orderliness in wallpaper turns the crocodile "a very pale and sickly shade of green." In "The Ostrich in Love," the main character tries for seven days but never does succeed in letting his beloved know his feelings. In "The Bad Kangaroo," the small kangaroo is only reflecting the equally outrageous conduct of his parents. A full-page, full-color illustration faces each one-page fable.

Fables are usually short, but there are exceptions. In *The Tale of the Golden Cockerel,* Patricia Lowe translates Russian poetry by Aleksandr Pushkin into smoothly moving prose. This literary fable, modeled on earlier oral forms, tells of an elderly czar who finds defending his kingdom more problematic than it was in his youth. The court magician provides a magic golden cockerel that protects the kingdom for some time, and in return, the czar agrees to give the magician whatever he wants. Later, however, the czar is unwilling to part with what the magician asks for. The czar's greed results in his and the magician's death and the queen's disappearance. The moral is "Do not make a promise that you are not willing to keep." The illustrations are reproductions of paintings done early in this century by the great Russian painter Ivan I. Bilibin.

## FOLK TALES

Because so many of them are available, folk tales are a staple of literature programs for children. Some experts divide this form of literature into several subtypes, with fairy tales as one division. Huck, Hepler, and Hickman (1987) provide an exhaustive analysis of the different types of folk tales. Here the general term *folk tale* will be used with the understanding that it covers all of these types.

No matter the type or country of origin, most of these traditional stories share several characteristics.

### 1. *Conventional introductions and conclusions predominate in folk tales.*

A formalized beginning, the simplest being "Once upon a time . . . ," sets a story in the indeterminate past and an unspecified place. Some of these beginnings are more elaborate, for example, "In the olden time, when wishing was some good . . . ." The conventional openings of folk tales set them off from contemporary realistic fiction in which the author sets the story in a single time and place and specifically defines the characters. In a folk tale, the ending tells listeners the tale has come to a satisfactory, unequivocal conclusion: for example, ". . . [they] rejoiced because they could now live out their days in peace and happiness" (from *Floating Clouds, Floating Dreams,* by I. K. Junne), or the more detailed "And so it came about that they ruled the land in friendship and prosperity that year and in peace and tranquility the next" (from *Welsh Legends and Folk-Tales,* by Gwyn Jones). These finishes also differentiate folk tales from contemporary, composed literature in which endings often leave what will happen next to the reader's imagination.

### 2. *Folk tales are characterized by their brevity.*

For example, "A Pig on the Road," in *Irish Folk Tales,* by Henry Glassie, is only three paragraphs long—less than a full page in some contemporary fiction.

### 3. *Folk tales have simple, direct plots and seldom include a subplot.*

An example is *It Could Always Be Worse,* by Margot Zemach, about a beleaguered man who is oppressed by life in his too small house with too many children. Seeking advice, he goes to the rabbi, who tells him to take the fowls, the goat, and the cow into the house. The obedient man does so, and things get worse. In despair, he returns to the rabbi, who advises him to take all the animals out. By contrast, the peace is overwhelming!

### 4. Setting is only minimally described in folk tales.

A particular place is not essential, since environment seldom has a significant influence on the story line of a folk tale. In *Arab Folktales*, by Inea Bushnaq, "A Trip to Paradise" is set "in the desert," and "The Ring of the King" is set "neither here nor there."

Two exceptions to this rule about generalized settings are tales about distant cultures. *Let's Steal the Moon*, by Blanche Luria Serwer, is a collection of Jewish stories set in specific locations and including references to particular people instead of types of people. One tale is set in Ascalon, an ancient city in Israel, and tells how Rabbi Simon rids the city of a plague of eighty witches. Black-ink line illustrations by Trina Schart Hyman with pale-yellow and brown wash depict the highly individualized humans effectively. A collection of Mexican tales, *The Wonderful Chirrionera*, by David L. Lindsey, also relates the adventures of named characters in definite locations. Four stories recount clashes of wit as wily people outsmart one another. The black and orange woodcuts are strong, if not immediately appealing.

### 5. Folk tales are notable for one-dimensional characters.

Authors of contemporary fiction usually create well-rounded, three-dimensional characters, believable because readers know their mental and emotional states as well as what they do to advance the plot. In contrast, folk tales are peopled with certain stock characters, often described in a simple phrase or two.

The beautiful daughter is the oppressed, even-tempered girl who prevails in the end. Sweet Little Sister in *Little Sister and the Month Brothers*, by Beatrice Schenk de Regniers, is a variant of Cinderella, doing all the work while the pointy-nosed stepmother and stepsister order her around. This Slavic version has no grand ball as in Perrault's *Cinderella;* instead, the stepsister and stepmother venture into the wintry cold greedily searching for the strawberries and flowers Little Sister has gotten from the Month Brothers and are never seen again.

The weak father cannot take command of the situation. An example is the father in "Hansel and Gretel," who twice allows himself to be talked into abandoning his children to the unknown dangers of the forest. Simple line etchings by Nonny Hogrogian, printed in sepia, accompany the version of "Hansel and Gretel" in *About Wise Men and Simpletons*, by Elizabeth Shub. More elaborate, full-color pictures by Paul Zelinsky for another version of this tale are commented on in an article by Marantz and Marantz (1986).

The wicked stepmother, in addition to being evil, is often greedy. A typical example is found in the title story of *The Well at the World's End*, a collection of Scottish tales by Norah and William Montgomerie. The evil stepmother wants to get rid of the king's daughter, who is extraordinarily good-natured and likeable. The stepmother sends the girl a great distance to fetch water. However, because of her kindness to creatures she meets along the way, the daughter not only succeeds, but returns from her mission more beautiful than ever. Also, each time she speaks, a ruby, a diamond, and a pearl drop from her mouth; each time she combs her hair, she combs a peck of gold and a peck of silver out of it. In a variant of this tale, "Diamonds and Toads," by Charles Perrault, the details are somewhat different, but the same greedy stepmother presides. The good daughter receives her reward, and the lazy one receives serpents and toads. The Norwegian version, "The Two Stepsisters," is included in *A Time for Trolls*, by Joan Roll-Hansen.

The clever brother uses his wits to get the best of situations. In "Jack and His Master," from *Celtic Fairy Tales*, by Joseph Jacobs (available as a reprint of the original 1892 edition), the youngest son proves to be the clever one. Thought simple by his two older brothers, Jack finally outwits the Gray Churl, who has overworked and underpaid the brothers and tricked them into giving up a strip of skin from their backs. By paying meticulous attention to the Churl's careless use of language, Jack comes home with double wages and enough extra money to support his hapless brothers.

The simpleton is barely able to cope with the exigencies of everyday life. Sometimes the foolishness is only an inconvenience or embarrassment; at other times, the results are more grave. *Favorite Folktales from Around the World*, edited by Jane Yolen, features an entire section on "Numbskulls and Noodleheads." An English tale about Lazy Jack is typical: for a while it appears he will never get his day's earnings safely home, until inadvertently he wins himself a beautiful wife. An interesting, extended analysis of simpletons is given by Tatar (1985), who contrasts them with heros and with female main characters.

### 6. Many folk tales, despite their brevity, are cumulative.

One idea, person, or object is added to the story at a time, until at the end an extended list has been compiled. *The House That Jack Built* is an example of a story in which one thing affects another. In such a *chaining tale*, the main character often wants something and asks another for help. That person (or object or animal) will help only if another person (or object or animal) does something else. Finally, the main character accomplishes the goal after each of the others does, in order, what was asked of them. Rodney Peppé did a version of this tale featuring boldly colored, decorative collages that evoke quasi-Victorian costumes and architecture.

A cumulative story in rhyme, *A Boy Went Out to Gather Pears*, by Felix Hoffman, can be traced back to the Middle Ages. Henry Bett (1974) discovered a Swahili version from Zanzibar that also relates the death of a man killed by a falling tree, as well as a Kabyle story from Algeria that tells of an obdurate child who refused to eat his dinner. Such cumulative rhymes are found in many cultures.

A modern chaining tale is *The Rose in My Garden*, by Arnold Lobel. This story starts simply enough with "This is the rose in my garden," accompanied by a botanically accurate illustration by Anita Lobel. It accumulates, "This is the bee that sleeps on the rose in my garden," until the cat with the "tattered ear" chases the field mouse "shaking in fear." Finally, the awakened bee undoes all the accumulation; the last page, like the first, shows the rose in solitary tranquility.

### 7. In most folk tales, cause and effect relationships are quite apparent.

The evil receive their just reward, trickery is foiled, the meek are exhalted, and the modest, self-effacing hero or heroine triumphs. Wrongdoing, carelessness, and disobedience are inevitably punished. In fact, "the remorseless sequence of events in nature [is] an essential ingredient in the 'true' fairy and folk story" (Storr, 1976). This is so, despite the fact that "there was never any feeling in the old fairy tales . . . of Good being more powerful than Evil. It was the very evenness of the match which gave these tales their powerful narrative hold over the reader" (Lanes, 1971).

**ENGLISH TALES.** Almost all English-speaking children are exposed to folk tales from Great Britain and northern European countries, which are widely available because they were the first to be collected and distributed.

Among the most popular folk tales enjoyed by children are those from England. A collection of these tales by Joseph Jacobs, titled *English Fairy Tales*, is available as a facsimile edition of the original version published in 1898. The book includes Jacobs's preface explaining how he gathered these tales, comments on why they are called fairy tales, despite the absence of fairies, and remarks about his language use in recording the stories. Further details of Jacobs's life and work are described by his daughter (Hays, 1978).

Examples of tales Jacobs collected include "The Story of the Three Little Pigs," "Mr. and Mrs. Vinegar," and "Henny Penny." This last can be compared with a variant by Veronica Hutchinson and also with a variant entitled *Chicken Licken*, by Kenneth McLeish. Jacobs also collected "Cap of Rushes," which is a British version of the French "Cinderella," and a much-loved English tale, "Jack and the Beanstalk."

Many different versions of "Jack and the Beanstalk" have been published. *The History of Mother Twaddle and the Marvelous Adventures of Her Son Jack*, by Paul Galdone, uses a rhyme first published in 1807 as the text:

> *A peddler cried out,*
> *"Buy this Bean for a farthing.*
> *It possesses such virtues*
> *That sure as a gun,*
> *Tomorrow it will grow*
> *Near high as the sun!"*

Galdone pictures an appropriately dim-witted Jack, decked out in neck scarf with hair combed by mother, going to the fair with a sixpence she found under the floor.

An impressive version of this tale was written and illustrated by Gail Haley, the only artist to win both a Caldecott Medal and a Kate Greenaway Award. *Jack and the Bean Tree* is full of interesting language, such as "Jack clomb the tree...," and "Bedad, this is strange." Haley's giant is "so mean and hairy that his head looked like a busted hay stack." The giant's wife, Matilda, is stylishly dressed. In this version, Jack steals a tablecloth that lays itself with a banquet, a dancing hen that lays golden eggs, and a singing harp. When the giant is pursuing Jack down the beanstalk, Haley changes the orientation of the book from a wide horizontal rectangle to a vertical one; children must turn the book sideways to "read" this picture.

Lorinda Bryan Cauley also illustrated this tale, using much texture in full-color, full-page illustrations. Each of these faces a page of text. Cauley uses some lighter colors, but the overall tonality of the paintings is dark. The giant's wife seems less of a fashionable vamp than the one in Haley's depiction; the giant, although just as large, seems somewhat less threatening.

Interesting language variation is found in the version in *The Jack Tales*, by Richard Chase, who recorded tales in western North Carolina. Jack, "a real teensy boy," notes that his tree has "done growed plumb out-a-sight." He plays with the giant's knife "a right smart while." The story here differs in details as well as language. Jack doesn't get the bean from an old man, as is more usual, but from his mother, who swept it up from the floor of

*Artist Gail E. Haley often juxtaposes swirling, curved lines with straight lines. The resulting tension makes for an intensely active picture.* Reprinted from *Jack and the Bean Tree* by Gail E. Haley. Copyright © by Gail E. Haley, 1986. Used by permission of Crown Publishers Inc.

their house. In this version, Jack takes the giant's "rifle-gun," his "skinnin' knife," and his "bed coverlid with bells on it."

A delightfully quirky retelling by Tony Ross adds an enormous amount of off-beat detail: "Jack Trotter lived with his mum, his sister Polly and his cat Bodger on an old, run-down farm." Their cow, in addition to giving milk, also pulls the plow and digs up potatoes with her horns. Ross proceeds through the story this way, dropping details in his wake, but somehow these don't sidetrack readers. It is the giant's housekeeper (not wife) who meets Jack outside and leads him to the house. The giant, who has bad breath, eats fifty-six pounds of potatoes at a sitting. Some visual details, such as Jack lolling on a befringed Victorian chaise lounge, may not be as amusing to children as they are to adults who know the historic referents. Nonetheless, Ross makes us look with new pleasure at an old tale.

**FRENCH TALES.** French folk tales, among the first to be preserved in writing, were recorded—it is believed—by Charles Perrault. Near the end of the seventeenth century, this member of the elite French Academy, a body that functioned as guardian of the language, published an edition of these tales. The stories include such popular ones as "Little Red Riding Hood," "Sleeping Beauty,"and "Puss in Boots."

"Cinderella" is clearly the best-known French tale.[4] In 1955, Marcia Brown won her first Caldecott Medal for her illustrations for this tale, done in ink line, paint, and chalk in muted shades of blue, rose, and yellow. Irregular thin line emphasizes the sisters' eccentricities and the fragile beauty of Cinderella (called Cinderseat in this version).

In contrast to Brown's illustrations are the very elegant, detailed black-pencil drawings that accompany a translation of *Cinderella* by John Fowles. Fowles uses contemporary British idiom and provides parenthetical explanations of some terms. Even though these explanations interrupt the narrative flow, the book should be shared with children for its fine pictures. This version is probably most appropriate for intermediate-grade children.

Not a simple retelling of the folk tale, but rather an expansion or elaboration of the story, is *The Glass Slipper*, by Eleanor Farjeon, who is an unrivaled language stylist. In this version, the innocent Ella talks to clocks, dishes, and chairs, among other inanimate objects. A distinguishing feature of Farjeon's tale is this childlike naiveté that the heroine retains throughout, even when attired as a regal lady at the ball. The accompanying illustrations are by Ernest H. Shepard.[5]

The title of Farjeon's work brings up a minor scholarly controversy of the type that are common because folk tales evolved over a long period of time. Whether or not Cinderella's slipper was in fact glass is analyzed at length by John White (1976), who explores the disagreement over the slipper's being made of glass (the French word is *verre*) or of fur (*vair*).

Any of the print versions of "Cinderella" might be used with a media version from Miller-Brody Productions (#SMB 100/101), which consists of two filmstrips and a teacher's manual with pre- and post-viewing suggestions. The narrator's voice is particularly pleasant.

In selecting a version of "Cinderella," teachers should keep in mind that the tale has often been softened to minimize the sisters' "ruthlessness and greed." Meer (1984) points out a tendency during the 1930s, in this country, to edit out the more gruesome aspects of folk tales. But he notes that today, in contrast, psychologists feel it is critical to show children that

---

[4]Versions of this tale are listed by Norma O. Ireland in *Index to Fairy Tales, 1973–1977* (Westwood, Mass.: F. W. Faxon, 1979). This reference volume, arranged by subject, title, and author, continues the *Index to Fairy Tales* (and supplements) by M. H. Eastman (same publisher, 1926, 1937, 1952) and by N. O. Ireland (same publisher, 1973). The two newest volumes include other kinds of folk literature, such as myths and legends.

[5]Ernest H. Shepard's pen-and-ink drawings brought him fame as the first illustrator for A. A. Milne's *Pooh* books, and for Kenneth Grahame's *Wind in the Willows*. In each case, these illustrations set a standard against which later ones were measured.

*Trina Schart Hyman's pictures include sufficient details to create a believable environment and are done in a full array of colors.* Illustration copyright © 1983 by Trina Schart Hyman. Reprinted from *Little Red Riding Hood* by permission of Holiday House.

" 'the punishment for the bad guy must equal the crime,' even if it offends adult sensibilities."

"Little Red Riding Hood" is another popular tale first published in Paris by Perrault in 1697 (Mavrogenes and Cummins, 1984), and now also available in translations from the German. The evolution of this tale has been widely studied. Mavrogenes and Cummins analyze what is known of the changes and present interesting quotes from earlier editions.

**GERMAN TALES.** Most German folk tales were first written down by Jacob and Wilhelm Grimm. These brothers were raised in poverty by their widowed mother. They obtained law degrees and eventually settled into jobs as university librarians. Their first collection of *Kinder-und-Hausmarchen* (Nursery and Household Tales) was published in 1812, and reflected their careful transcription of the stories they were told.

One folk tale derived from three early German sources is about dancing princesses whose nocturnal activities frustrate their father. One version features a princess who wears out twelve pairs of shoes every night; another, from Westphalia, features three princesses instead of twelve. The unsuccessful suitors die in the original German versions; to suit late Victorian sensibilities, Andrew Lang disposed of the unsuccessful candidates by having them disappear.[6]

In the Grimm brothers' *Twelve Dancing Princesses*, Uri Shulevitz's pictures are highly simplified but show a wide array of pastel colors. The princesses are locked into their room each night, yet each morning their dancing shoes are worn to shreds. The king offers to reward whoever discovers their secret with the hand of one of them in marriage. The princes all lose their lives trying to discover the secret. With the help of an old woman, who gives him a cloak of invisibility, an unprepossessing poor soldier discovers the hidden castle where the princesses dance.

Adrienne Adams's version of *Twelve Dancing Princesses* focuses not on the princesses but on Michael, a young peasant. Adams uses a translation by Andrew Lang, a longer and more romantic version than the Grimm one. After having visions of a beautiful woman who advises him to go to the castle, Michael sets off. Only after Michael's arrival at the castle is the princesses' elusive behavior introduced. Adams's pictures are in full color,

---

[6]Valuable historic information, including the date and circumstances of the tale's first appearance and a comparison with similar tales of different names, appears in Iona and Peter Opie's *The Classic Fairy Tales* (London: Oxford University Press, 1974). The book contains a fascinating collection of full-color reproductions of obscure original illustrations and variants of each tale.

more robust than Shulevitz's, and are not outlined. Her princesses seem less formidable, perhaps because they are more realistic.[7]

Another German tale, "Rapunzel," is included in *The Juniper Tree*, a collection of Grimm tales translated by Lore Segal and illustrated by Maurice Sendak.[8] Rather than many lavish color illustrations, Sendak produces a single black-ink line drawing for each story in this two-volume set.

One of the best-known Grimm tales is "Snow White," reprinted in many versions since the Grimm Brothers' first collection was published. An edition translated from the German by Paul Heins and illustrated by Trina Schart Hyman features dark, lushly brooding illustrations on every page, overlaid in some cases by text in white panels. Snow White's pale ivory skin contrasts dramatically with her lustrous black hair. The evil queen's beauty is just sufficient to make her envy seem plausible. Details of architecture and garb make the environment believable. As always, Hyman's masterful understanding of underlying bone structure makes her people convincing. Her impressive technical skill supports her interpretation, without ever drawing attention to itself. (Analysis of this version, and one by Nancy Burkert, is given on page 256.)

**EASTERN EUROPEAN TALES.** Many other European countries have folk tales equally as interesting as the French, British, and German stories but not nearly as well-known. One Rumanian tale, *The Enchanted Pig*, is illustrated with cartoonlike drawings by Jacques Tardi. The story is interesting, but the pictures are not as imaginative as is usual in this series of folk tales published by Creative Education, Inc. This publisher is doing experimental work sure to stimulate controversy, because their books contrast with conventional views of traditional tales. It is interesting to compare Tardi's version with the same title featuring pictures by Tony Ross.

Russian tales tend to be more violent than those from other countries.

---

[7]P. L. Travers classified these princesses in one of six categories of women found in folk and fairy tales. See "Grimm's Women," *New York Times Book Review*, November 16, 1975, p. 59. Her analysis identifies the apparently passive heroines, beauties, apparent simpletons, heroic women, worldly women, and women with occult knowledge. The princesses are in the last category.

[8]For Sendak's comments about what he was trying to accomplish with these illustrations, see "Maurice Sendak," by Justin Wintle and Emma Fisher, in *The Pied Pipers: Interviews with the Influential Creators of Children's Literature* (New York: Paddington, 1974), pp. 20–34. Sendak feels these stories are not as simple as they appear; his illustrations attempt to capture the moments of most intense emotion in each story.

*Maurice Sendak's finely cross-hatched ink line creates depth and shadows, yielding a three-dimensional space that extends from the front of the picture plane to the far-distant buildings.* Illustration by Maurice Sendak from *The Juniper Tree*, translated by Lore Segal and Randall Jarrell. Copyright © 1973 by Maurice Sendak. Reprinted by permission of Farrar, Straus & Giroux, Inc.

*Baba Yaga*, by Ernest Small, a compilation of elements from many traditional Russian sources, is noticeably so (though all ends happily):

> "Whenever the terrible-tempered old woman is restless," Marusia's mother had warned, "her hut roams through the woods on chicken legs, so Baba Yaga may search for bad Russian children to cook in a stew."

Blair Lent's imaginative illustrations in black, pink, orange and gold reinforce Baba Yaga's menace and the power of the flying mortar in which she travels. The child Marusia, in both story and visuals, seems dim-witted and oblivious to danger.

A more lighthearted Russian tale, *The Woman of the Wood*, by Algernon Black, is about a woodcarver, a tailor, and a teacher. Done by Evaline Ness in subdued shades of brown, green, and blue, the illustrations show her usual asymmetrical balance and exaggerated body forms. Three common men with uncommon abilities meet at an inn and decide to travel together. They spend a night in a tree to escape wolves; to keep from falling asleep, the woodcarver fashions a beautiful woman from the tree. The tailor clothes her, and the teacher educates her. All three then argue about whose she is. A wise man considers each claim and comes up with an unexpected solution. The woman's change from wood to human and the wise man's change from old to young are interesting transformations.

Another lighthearted Russian tale is *Bubba and Babba*, by Maria Polushkin. The misadventures of two foolish bears, each of which tries to be lazier than the other, are recounted. This tale is illustrated, in three shades of pale pastel charcoal, by Diane de Groat.

Seven long tales about tsars and their sons, about orphaned brothers and sisters, and about old men and their daughters are found in *Russian Folk Tales*, by Robert Chandler. Several full-color pictures by Ivan I. Bilibin are included for each tale; these and the text pages are bordered with folk motifs. Treachery is everywhere: the evil witch "had a smooth tongue, and when she wanted to, she could be very charming," and she uses this charm to deceive the innocent Alyonushka. Transformations abound: Grey Wolf "leapt into the air, stamped against the ground" and turned into the "spitting image" of Elyena the Beautiful. Also in this book is "Vasilisa the Beautiful," in which the heroine receives from her dying mother a magic doll that does her work and feeds her. This comes in handy when Vasilisa's widowed father marries a cruel woman with ugly daughters. The same tale is available in book form. *Lovely Vassilisa*, retold by Barbara Cohen, features black-and-white pencil pictures by a Russian emigré, Anatoly Ivanov.

**ORIENTAL TALES.** A clever female character is the main attraction in *The Funny Little Woman*, by Arlene Mosel. A cheerful dumpling maker finds that following an escaped dumpling leads to trouble. Falling through her earth floor, she lands below ground on a road lined with statues of the gods. Her continued pursuit of the dumpling takes her into an involved adventure. Blair Lent's pleasant, soft watercolors, augmented with ink line, depict the main events. In the upper corners of the illustrations, small ink-line drawings show the seasons passing while the little woman is away from home. Another version of this tale is available in *Clever Cooks*, by Ellin Greene. In this collection of traditional tales about cooks or bakers who get into trouble, the stories are interspersed with recipes and riddles about foods.

*The Five Chinese Brothers*, by Claire Bishop, features brothers with highly differentiated abilities. Pictured by Kurt Wiese, the brothers look identical, but each has a unique and valuable ability that helps save the first brother from execution.

The large influx of Vietnamese refugees to the United States makes it important to have some of their folk tales available for the Vietnamese children themselves as well as for others unfamiliar with Vietnamese culture. *Toad Is the Uncle of Heaven* is retold and illustrated by Jeanne M. Lee. Toad goes to the King of Heaven, seeking relief from the drought. Along the way, the bees, a rooster, and a tiger decide to accompany Toad. Naturally, these characters in their own ways help Toad accomplish his purpose when the King sets various of his aides against him. Flat color and simple shapes are enclosed in pen line. Lee also adapted *Legend of the Milky Way* and *Legend of the Li River* from the Vietnamese culture.

**AFRICAN TALES.**   Traditional tales from many African tribes are being translated into English. A recurring character in Ashanti tales from Ghana is Anansi, the spider. The spider tales show small, defenseless men or animals outwitting others and succeeding against great odds. A teacher might introduce Anansi and the tales describing his cunning by reading *A Story, A Story*, by Gail E. Haley, which tells how Anansi obtained his stories from Nyame, the Sky God. As a condition for getting stories, Nyame sets a seemingly impossible task: he asks Anansi to obtain Osebo the leopard-of-the-terrible-teeth, Mmboro the hornet-who-stings-like-fire, and Mmoatia the fairy-whom-men-never-see. Through his cunning, Anansi captures these elusive creatures and wins his stories. The book's woodcuts are highly patterned, swirling designs in multiple vibrant hues. They are symbolic rather than realistic but are not simplified into abstract symbols like the illustrations by Caldecott-winner Gerald McDermott. In an unusual reversal of the norm, McDermott created *Anansi the Spider* from an animated film he did earlier. The highly abstract, symbolic pictures are vibrantly rendered in intense, highly saturated colors and printed on coated paper with a sheen that accentuates the color. The clever father spider Anansi relies on each of his six sons in turn to get him out of assorted dangers. Each has a specialized ability useful in returning the father to safety. (A teacher might use *Anansi the Spider* and *The Five Chinese Brothers* to highlight contrasting though equally useful abilities of characters.)

Another African trickster, Rabbit, trades one thing for another and loses, before all ends well. *Behind the Back of the Mountain* is a Thonga tale retold by Verna Aardema. It relates how Rabbit deceives Ostrich, a man, a woman, ants, and a lion before convincing Ostrich to extricate him from his scheming. As he goes from encounter to encounter, his cumulative lament grows:

> *Oh, my sour milk is gone,*
> *The milk I got for my meat.*
> *The meat I got for my feather.*
> *The feather I got for my berries,*
> *The berries that are all eaten up,*
> *Oh, now I have nothing.*

A talented husband-and-wife team, Leo and Diane Dillon, provided dramatic full-page pictures patterned in shades of black and grey and bordered by three lines of varying thickness.

Animal stories with a very different flavor are found in *Black Folktales*, by Julius Lester, which incorporates current brand names and contemporary items into the retelling of African tales. "How Snake Got His Rattles" features an obliging Mr. God who listens to both sides of an argument. The book also includes several stories with human main characters.

Included in *Catlore*, by Marjorie Zaum, "Dividing the Cheese," is a very short tale of how clever monkey duped the hungry cats. (Zaum's book contains eleven short tales from as many different countries and illustrates for boys and girls the idea that similar tales come from different parts of the world.) Read "Dividing the Cheese" to children and then share with them the longer but similar tale, *Two Greedy Bears*, by Mirra Ginsburg. Jose Aruego and Ariane Dewey's simplified drawings for Ginsburg's tale are done in flat colors with some ink line to give detail but no depth. "Dividing the Cheese" also appears in a different context in Eleanore Schmid's *Cats' Tales*, a lavishly produced, oversized book with illustrations in soft-stroked pastels. Other comparisons are possible using "Why the Black Monkey and the Crocodile Are Enemies," which is a variant of the Aesop fable "The Fox and the Stork." Ross (1975) collected this and other animal tales from Zaire; the stories were gathered orally and written down in the Lonkundo language.

Other African tales were gathered in the Americas and collected by Jaqueline Shachter Weiss in *Young Brer Rabbit*. These are short tales (up to five pages in length) told by generations of Africans brought to Venezuela, Brazil, Columbia and other countries as slaves. A recurring motif is Brer Rabbit's trickery and the gullibility of the other animals. Weiss's introduction is full of fascinating details; for instance, the tales from Brazil contain a queen, Sis Jaguar, who is present in tales from no other land.

**NORTHERN EUROPEAN TALES.**　Large and rather fearsome creatures populate tales from the chilly fjords of Norway, where a rich heritage of folk literature grew. The best known interpreters of this heritage are Ingri and Edgar Parin d'Aulaire. One favorite old tale, *The Terrible Troll Bird*, features trolls, red-capped gnomes, and green-clad sprites called *hulder-maidens*. The exciting story focuses on the adventures and resourcefulness of Ola, Lina, Sina, and Trina. Each time a danger lurks, the children solve the problem. Healthy measures of tension and release lead listeners to the satisfying end when the children go boating in the troll bird's beak. The illustrators' usual, easily identified pictures are here in the form of black-and-white lithographs with colored acetate overlays.

**AMERICAN TALES.** Last, but certainly not least, is the diverse bounty of American folk tales. After sharing *Arrow to the Sun*, by Gerald McDermott, with children, a teacher might let them paint costumes and masks so that they can be characters in the story.

In addition to native American tales, there is an extensive body of tall tales about well-known heros such as Paul Bunyan and Pecos Bill as well as lesser-known heros such as Joe Magarac and Febold Feboldson. May (1980) recommends these as a particularly rich source of information about American political beliefs, social change, regionalism, and humor.

*The Song of Paul Bunyan and Tony Beaver*, by Ennis Rees, features wry black-and-white illustrations by cartoonist Robert Osborn. *Ol' Paul, The Mighty Logger*, by Glen Rounds, originally published in 1936 and in print ever since, was reissued in 1976 in a larger size with new illustrations. Steven Kellogg's *Paul Bunyan* has pictorial endpapers that are different in front and back. A set of loosely linked adventures starts when baby Paul (weighing in at 156 pounds at birth) bursts on the scene and ends when a surprisingly young-looking Paul "gave up lumbering and rambled north searching for new areas of untouched wilderness." Kellogg's usual detail-packed illustrations are a delight for the child who likes lots to look at.

*Pecos Bill, the Greatest Cowboy of All Time*, by James Cloyd Bowman, contains stories collected during the last three decades of the nineteenth century, when "great armies of singing cowboys galloped into the range Country of the Southwest, [where] they created Pecos Bill." Compare this book with the one with pictures by Steven Kellogg. These tall tales are commonly regarded as folk tales, though one source (Trustees of the Boston Public Library, 1979) argues that they are "fakelore," not really authentic tales coming from the oral tradition.

**USING FOLK TALES FOR CULTURAL COMPARISONS.** In addition to presenting individual folk tales, Norton (1985) suggests that teachers do a comparative unit on ones from different countries. She sees this unit as a way to explore values with children. When students think about which actions are rewarded, which are punished, and what rewards are given—among other questions—they will begin to see the cultural similarities and differences the tales embody.

**SEXISM IN FOLK TALES.**  One criticism of folk tales is that they present unrealistic views of male and female roles. Some educators believe such tales should therefore not be shared with students. It is true that young women in these tales are often portrayed as beautiful but not terribly bright or resourceful. As Rosemary Minard (1974) says, "Snow White was pretty stupid to disregard the dwarf's advice and allow herself to be duped by the stepmother-witch three times. And then all she had to do to win the prince was to be beautiful." Conversely, young men most frequently solve the problems and win both the hand of the young maiden and wealth. Such narrow role presentations do not reflect modern life.

Even though folk and fairy tales often portray sexist roles, teachers can still share them with children for the following reasons:

1. Because of their conventional nature, most children perceive these tales, at least unconsciously, as unrealistic. Psychologists contend that children clearly understand the fanciful nature of the tales as one of the literary conventions of this genre.[9]
2. Because teachers present a balanced literature program, children experience these folk tales with a wide variety of other types of literature, containing more true-to-life role presentations.

No one would advocate using only fairy tales with children. Since boys and girls are also exposed to contemporary realistic fiction, they understand that there are many ways to look at male and female roles. The ways fairy tales present roles reflect the views of the societies that created them, not the view of our society.

Some folk tales do provide examples of strong, resourceful heroines. *Womenfolk and Fairy Tales* features clever, inventive women who do not sit about pining until Prince Charming arrives but strike out independently to solve problems needing attention. Author Rosemary Minard tells these short, pithy stories with humor and appeal. The tale about the husband who takes a turn minding the house is one widely included in other collec-

---

[9]Bruno Bettelheim's *The Uses of Enchantment: The Meaning and Importance of Fairy Tales* (New York: Alfred A. Knopf, 1976) is a significant study of the genre that draws heavily on Freudian psychology for the interpretation of the tales' symbols. The author describes similarities between fantastic events in fairy tales and those in adult dreams and daydreams. For comparison, see Carl-Heinz Mallett's *Fairy Tales and Children* (New York: Schocken, 1984).

*In Suzanna Klein's pencil illustration for the tale "Molly Whuppie," viewers are given an unusual perspective on Molly and the giant.* Illustration by Suzanna Klein from *Womenfolk and Fairy Tales* by Rosemary Minard. Copyright © 1975 by Rosemary Minard. Reprinted by permission of Houghton Mifflin Company.

tions. He was "so surly and cross he never thought his wife did anything right," but he discovers, after an attempt to do her work, that she is more competent than he thought. Others, such as the tale of "Three Strong Women"—Amazons who befriend a famous wrestler—are probably unfamiliar to most readers. The heroines run the gamut from pretty young women, who differ in some way from their more conventional counterparts, to mature women in the fullness of their powers. In one story, a young woman uses five items in a small bag in searching for her sister who has disappeared. She uses her thinking abilities to calmly outwit a wizard, and then finds handsome young men for herself and her sister to marry. An example of an older, powerful heroine is Unanana, who rescues her helpless children from the evil one-tusked elephant that swallowed them whole. One of the most engaging aspects of these heroines is that even though they are clearly capable and in control, they are not without small flaws.

Similarly capable heroines are found in *Tatterhood and Other Tales*, by Ethel Johnson Phelps, representing the oral tradition of such diverse cultures as the Ivory Coast (Africa), the Sudanese region of the Nile River valley, and the Yun-nan tribes of southwest China. The tales themselves range from the comic to the eerie; they feature both nubile young women of marriageable age ("The Squire's Bride") and women long past the age of adventures but yet still capable ("The Hedley Kow"). Other collections featuring strong women are recommended by Rigg (1985) in an article analyzing female characters in all genres.

Segel (1983) concludes her consideration of the debate over whether folk tales contain any strong female role models by noting that such tales do exist but do not often enough find their way into the large collections of tales designed for popular audiences. A major way to evaluate collections of fairy tales is to note how many of them go beyond such well-known tales as "Cinderella" to present other tales containing more positive and active female images.

Some tales of resourceful females are presented individually in picture-book format, rather than in collections. *Mollie Whuppie*, retold by Walter de la Mare, is available in a book with illustrations by Errol Le Cain. Clever and daring Mollie, the youngest daughter, not only saves her sisters from the giant, but also finds husbands for them. Le Cain's elegant, highly patterned, full-color pictures decorate the story effectively, creating a faraway land.

**FOLK TALES AND READING INSTRUCTION.**  This section has been primarily concerned with advocating the use of folk tales for the literary value they have. Focusing on a different purpose, Matthias and Quisenberry (1986) develop an interesting argument for using these tales as a base for reading instruction. They are particularly concerned with describing reasons these tales are appropriate for children in developing countries where literacy rates are often low.

## MYTHS

A variety of longer works, which in their complexity of character and plot approach adult literature in difficulty, can be used with older students. Teachers should be aware that many myths and legends are not readily accessible to average or slow readers. However, through careful preparation, by introducing the unfamiliar characters and describing the setting, and by reading some of these works aloud to students, the teacher can make myths and legends more accessible than they usually are.

Myths represent societies' attempts to deal with the three most crucial mysteries of life: creation, the nature of life itself, and death. Many myths provide accounts of the beginning of the world; others explain natural phenomena or prescribe desirable behaviors for members of a particular society; still others describe death and the afterlife.

The following table, condensed from extended expository material in Bettelheim (1976), provides some specific points of contrast between myths and folk tales.

|  | *Myths* | *Folk Tales* |
|---|---|---|
| **Characters** | centers on one strong character who is named | more familiar and thus more universal, seldom named |
| **Events** | unique experiences that could not have happened to anyone else or in any other setting, certainly not to anyone mortal | although out of the ordinary, presented as something that could happen to the listener |
| **Endings** | almost always tragic | despite adversities, almost always happy |
| **Tone** | pessimistic | optimistic; no matter how terrifyingly serious some events may be |

The characters in myths are gods or goddesses, the best known being those from Greek mythology. These immortals are capable of amazing deeds and possess unusual powers. Nearly forty myths (and the legend of Odysseus) are included by Alice Low in *Greek Gods and Heroes*. The book contains some readily available myths, such as those of Pandora and Persephone. It also includes myths children won't know, such as those of Io and Europa, and Daedalus. Arvis Stewart's full- and half-page watercolors are augmented by black-line drawings on other pages. Low's book—despite its handsome details—will probably not, on its own, attract a lot of individual child readers; the many unfamiliar names can be a stumbling block to average students. But with skilled oral interpretation of the stories, the teacher can interest students in the myths simply by reading the book aloud in class.

Children are usually not familiar with Norse mythology because it is difficult to understand; the characters and the relations between them are complex. One collection for intermediate-grade children, *Norse Gods and Giants*, simplifies and explains the gods and their roles. Each separate story, although it can be enjoyed independently, is carefully linked to the others. The illustrations by Ingri and Edgar Parin d'Aulaire are exemplary stone lithographs. A "Readers Companion" that explains unfamiliar terms and an index make the book easy to use.

Mythology is not only of European origin, however. There is an impressive though hard-to-access body of native American mythology. Eskimo and American Indian myths are not nearly as well known as are Greek and Norse tales because (1) native American cultures are not as homogeneous as Greek and Norse cultures,[10] (2) western society is more closely related to the Greco-Roman culture, and (3) attempts to study native American cultures have been recent and are as yet incomplete. Neither the Eskimo nor the American Indian culture has a pantheon of gods as did the Greek and Norse cultures; instead, almost everything (including trees and animals) has a spirit.

**CREATION MYTHS.** One of the most common types of myth is that which explains the creation of the world. Almost all cultures have offered some description of the way the earth came into being.

In preparing *At the Center of the World*, a combination of Papago and Pima Indian myths, Betty Baker studied the earliest versions recorded by anthropologists, incorporated elements of several, and added portions of her own. In Baker's account of creation, Earth Magician tries to make the world four times, but each time there is something wrong. The language introducing the tale has an impressively primal feeling:

> Dark was all. There was no moon, no sun, no stars. But the dark hid nothing, for there was no earth.
>
> Then the darkness began to gather. Slowly, slowly, it turned on itself, coiling deeper than dark, working power and magic. Until out of the deep and heavy dark came Earth Magician.

*The First Morning*, by Margery Bernstein and Janet Kobrin, is a creation myth of the East African Sukuma people, accompanied by semiabstract black-and-white illustrations by Enid Romanek. In simple but expressive prose, the authors tell of four creatures—Lion, Mouse, Spider, and Fly—who cooperate in obtaining light. Together they perform the difficult tasks set by the Sky King, who continuously tries to trick them and keep the light for himself. When the friends return in chagrin to earth, it appears the Sky

---

[10]The term *Indian* is inaccurate: it refers to several hundred distinct cultural units. This is one reason the study of American Indian myths is so complex.

*In this abstract illustration, the artist groups the faces of the animals and uses some of their arms and legs to tie them together visually.* By Margery Bernstein and Janet Kobrin, illustration from *The First Morning.* Copyright © 1976, 1972 Margery Bernstein and Janet Kobrin. Reprinted with the permission of Charles Scribner's Sons.

King has won. However, they joyfully discover that they have succeeded when the cock's crowing summons the sun.

**MYTHS ABOUT NATURAL PHENOMENA.** Primitive peoples commonly devised explanations for natural events: why the sun rises each day, why the cold of winter comes, why certain animals behave in particular ways. In addition to enjoying these myths as literature, readers can gain insights into the thinking of the people who created them.

*How the Sun Made a Promise and Kept It,* by Margery Bernstein and Janet Kobrin, is a myth of the Bungee Indians of central Canada. It recounts how the god Weeseka-jak captured the sun in a net and held it close to the earth so earth would always be warm and light. He miscalculated, however, and the earth became too hot. Though others try in vain, it is brave Beaver who eventually succeeds in freeing the sun from the net.

A more extended explanation of a natural phenomenon—the changing seasons—is given in a Greek myth. Demeter's beautiful daughter Persephone is captured by Hades, who wants her for his bride. He takes her to his underworld home and forces her to stay there. When he finally releases Persephone, he decrees she must return to him for one month for each pomegranate seed she has eaten. Teachers can help older students compare the three versions of this myth provided by Olivia Coolidge (in *Greek Myths*), Anne Terry White (in *The Golden Treasury of Myths and Legends*), and Ingri and Edgar Parin d'Aulaire (in *Book of Greek Myths*). A number of points are summarized in the table below. Gerald McDermott used a Roman version of this myth for his story of Proserpina, who was kidnapped by Pluto, lord of the underworld. His *Daughter of the Earth* has full-color, double-page spreads done in *gouache*, or opaque watercolor.

| | Coolidge Version | White Version | d'Aulaire Version |
|---|---|---|---|
| **Introduction** | not included | introductory episode with Aphrodite and son Eros, who shot arrow at Pluto, making him fall in love | not included |
| **Mother** | Demeter | Demeter | Demeter |
| **Daughter (captive)** | Persephone | Persephone | Persephone |
| **Captor** | Hades | Pluto | Hades |
| **Asked Zeus for permission to take her** | yes | no | no |
| **How he got her** | while she was gathering flowers with her maidens, she saw a narcissus; earth opened in front of her | with a sweep of his arm he caught her up and drove swiftly away | she strayed into a yawning crevice; herd of pigs also tumbled in; swineherd saw it |
| **Vehicle** | golden chariot drawn by coal-black horses; earth closed after them | he drove to the River Cyone, struck bank with trident, earth opened and swallowed them | dark chariot with black horses |

| | Coolidge Version | White Version | d'Aulaire Version |
|---|---|---|---|
| **Hades' (Pluto's) home** | not included | not included | extended description of underworld |
| **Demeter's response** | veiled self as a dark cloud; sped for nine days over land and water searching | sought her daughter from end to end of earth | ran about searching and all earth grieved with her |
| **How she found out what happened** | Apollo told her | a river nymph sent Persephone's girdle on waves to Demeter | turned into gray-haired old woman, returned to field; asked sun and the swineherd's brother |
| **Subplot** | meets Metaneira, looking for nurse for child; begins to make child immortal | not included | not included |
| **Effect of losing her daughter** | no harvests | famine | called to Zeus that she would never again make the earth green |
| **Zeus' response** | sent Iris (rainbow) to appeal to Demeter; Zeus sends Hermes to Hades to fetch Persephone | sends gods and goddesses to appeal to Demeter | sends Hermes to Hades |
| **Hades' entreaty to Persephone to eat** | she eats seven pomegranate seeds | eats four seeds | does not specify how many seeds she eats |
| **Return to her mother** | Hermes took her with him, and she came into the upper air | Hermes drives her back to Demeter's temple in Pluto's golden chariot | not included |
| **Conclusion** | not included | not included | Demeter lent her chariot loaded with grain to Triptolemus, who is told to teach people how to sow and reap grain |

**MYTHS AS PRESCRIPTIONS OF BEHAVIOR.** The Greek tale about Midas is an example of a myth that prescribes behavior. This familiar story of a rich king who desires even more wealth is clearly didactic. A version of this tale, including considerable dialogue that adds to its interest, is in *The Scott, Foresman Anthology of Children's Literature*, by Zena Sutherland and Myra Cohn Livingston. This extensive (almost a thousand pages) collection of selections—some complete and others excerpted—is a fine source for reading aloud. By doing so, the teacher or librarian may interest some children in going to other sources to read more themselves.

Native American myths frequently prescribe acceptable behavior. "The Forbidden Mountain," a tale included in *Windigo and Other Tales of the Ojibways*, by Herbert T. Schwartz, describes the conflict between Grey Beaver and his grandsons Stone, Water, and Sky. They do not give him the respect due to tribal elders. When Grey Beaver asks them to accompany him to sacred rites, they refuse and go hunting instead. They find nothing, however, and climb the mountain that all Ojibways have been told to avoid. At the top, they are charmed by a beautiful woman who feeds them blue eggs and red juice. After they eat, she disappears, and they begin turning into dreadful thunderbirds. Only after their grandfather listens to the medicine man's instructions are Stone, Water, and Sky saved from their fate. From that time on, they treat Grey Beaver with proper respect.

The prescription is directly stated in Paul Goble's picture book *The Great Race of the Birds and Animals*. In this tale of a competition between the four-legged animals and the two-legged ones, the buffalo is pitted against man, but it is the magpie who wins. The tale ends with this moral:

> We can all be a little like the birds: they leave the earth with wings, and we can also leave the world by letting our thoughts rise as high as the birds fly.

Drawn from the mythologies of the Cheyenne and Sioux peoples who lived on the Great Plains, the tale is illustrated by Goble in highly saturated, flat colors.

**MYTHS AND DEATH.** "The Death of Baldur," in *Thunder of the Gods*, by Dorothy Hosford, is a myth that tries to explain death. The hero, fairest and most beloved of the gods, is wise in judgment, gracious in speech, and pure in deed. He relates his perilous dreams to his mother, who extracts an oath from all the things in the world that they will not harm her son. The god Loki, taking the form of an old woman, finds that only a small mistletoe, which Baldur's mother thought was too young to take an oath, has not agreed. Loki tricks Baldur's brother into throwing the fatal mistletoe at Baldur.

*These unrealistic, two-dimensional figures are heavily outlined in black, to emphasize the repeated patterns.* Illustration by Norval Morrisseau from *Windigo and Other Tales of the Ojibways* by Herbert T. Schwartz. Copyright © 1969. Published by McClelland and Stewart Ltd.

Edna Barth, in *Balder and the Mistletoe*, bases her retelling of this myth on the thirteenth-century Icelandic *Prose Edda*, retaining the unsoftened ending: Balder must remain in the spectral abode of Hel, ruler of the world of the dead, until the final battle and the world's end. After three winters with no intervening summers, the earth will rise from the seas, fresh and green again. The ink-and-wash drawings by Richard Cuffari were among the last this prolific artist (almost two hundred books) did before his death.

In addition to versions in books, this tale is available as a cassette recording in *Baldur: A Norse Myth* (American Library Association, Chicago), a stirring retelling by Gudrun Thorne-Thompsen, a master storyteller. Thorne-Thompsen's clear enunciation, sensitive use of pauses, and flexible voice

*Artist Richard Cuffari uses a thin ink line and cross-hatching to create naturalistically rendered humans who are somewhat idealized, appropriate for this story of gods and goddesses.* Illustration by Richard Cuffari from *Balder and the Mistletoe* by Edna Barth. Illustration copyright © 1979 by Richard Cuffari. Reprinted by permission of Clarion Books/Ticknor & Fields, a Houghton Mifflin Company.

qualities are heard here without distracting background music or sound effects.

**CHILDREN'S COMPOSITIONS.** Following a unit on myths with a group of sixth-grade children, a teacher asked the students to write their own explanation of some natural phenomenon. One child wrote an explanation of how the equator came to be.

### Equatorus and the Middle of the World

Once there was a fair maiden named Equatorus. She was the daughter of King Qualdis. She married a prince named Prince Metaphorus. She had a beautiful baby which they named Prince Sratus, and her husband became King of the Country, Nalis. Now Equatorus was very full of curiosity. Equatorus went on a trip around the world to find the answer to a question that had been bothering her for a long time: "Where is the center of the earth?" Equatorus traveled to all parts of the world. She went to Africa and met a big famous chief named Maula of a big tribe called Hitawa and since he knew a lot Equatorus asked him, "Where is the middle of the world?" Maula thought and thought but couldn't answer her. Equatorus went to South America and asked a chief named Pano and he knew a lot also, and she asked him: "Where is the center of the earth?" Pano thought and thought but he couldn't answer her. Equatorus went all over the world, but she heard the same answer, "I don't know!" Now there were only two gods who knew Equatorus' answer, Jupiter and Uranus. They were feeling sorry for Equatorus, because she was getting tired and discouraged and was about to give up. So Jupiter and Uranus turned her into a marker that went around the world in the middle, and they called it the equator after her name Equatorus. Then everybody knew the answer to Equatorus' question . . . including Equatorus.

*Tisha*

Wolfe (1972) recommends studying myths in the intermediate grades and encouraging children to write their own myths explaining how certain things got to be the way they are. He suggests various possible topics, such as "Why the Sea Is Salty," and the sample stories by children that he includes are convincing proof that the motivation works. In describing how to use comic books and their mythic heroes as a stimulus for writing, Kohl (1974) talks about his work with uninterested five- and six-year-olds. His technique should also be usable with more academically inclined students.

## LEGENDS

Legends, another longer form of traditional literature, are imaginative reconstructions of an earlier period by authors of a later age. Authors and poets who make legends usually create a perfect hero who is able to overcome a monster or other dangers. Often such a hero is an amalgamation of several real people.

A simple legend, suitable as an introduction to this form, is *The Little Juggler*, retold and illustrated by Barbara Cooney. This legend is derived from the earliest written version, which is seven hundred years old. The poignant story is about an orphaned minstrel, befriended by monks when it becomes too cold for him to make his living entertaining outside. It saddens the boy that all the monks are working for God while he is not. He juggles before an altarpiece depicting Mary and Jesus, and she descends to wipe his brow. Using scratchboard technique for her illustration, Barbara Cooney includes many small details of medieval dress and environment, transporting readers to another time and place.

Lonzo Anderson retells an old Greek legend in *Arion and the Dolphins*, with pictures by his wife, Adrienne Adams. This version focuses mostly on the action with little description, but Adams's visual details of setting and costumes support the words. Pleasant, full-page watercolors are overprinted with or surround the text.

A Shawnee legend describes Waupee, or White Hawk, a hero with superhuman qualities, in *The Ring in the Prairie*, by John Bierhorst.

> Tall and manly, with the fire of youth shining in his eye, he walked unafraid through the gloomiest woods and could follow a track made by any of the numerous kinds of birds and beasts. Every day he would return to his lodge with game, for he was one of the most skillful and celebrated hunters of his tribe.

Waupee could also change his form. Beguiled by the beauty of the youngest of twelve dancing sisters, he changes into a mouse so he can observe them unnoticed. His plan allows him to capture the youngest, but the others escape back into the sky. Despite his loving ministrations, his wife longs to return to her father, the star. She eludes Waupee and flees with their son to the heavens. Finally, Waupee achieves happiness by going to the sky to join his family. The illustrations rendered in clear, bright colors by Leo and Diane Dillon are highly decorative: their rhythmic pattern creates a sense of movement.

*The Fire Plume*, also by John Bierhorst, is a legend from the Algonquin tribe that describes the conflict between winter and spring. Peboan, old man of winter, and Seegwun, young man of spring, confront each other. Peboan, whose locks are white with age, trembles in every joint. Seegwun, whose cheeks are red with the blood of youth, strides into Peboan's tent with a light, quick step. After they share a ceremonial tobacco pipe, Peboan yields to Seegwun.

The hero must search for his family in an Eskimo legend, *Kiviok's Magic Journey*, by James Houston. Kiviok marries a beautiful girl whose white feather coat is snatched by a wicked raven one day while she and her sisters are bathing in a lake. The sisters turn into snow geese and soar away into the sky. The rest of the story tells of the hero's efforts to find his lost family.

Both North American Indian and Eskimo material is included by Virginia Hamilton in *North American Legends*. She uses the term *legends* to mean "any stories coming from the past . . . selected from a large body of folklore that has become an integral part of American literature . . . ." This is perhaps a more inclusive definition of the word than most. Legends of Plains, Southwestern, and Northern Pacific Indians are included here, as well as Eskimo legends such as "Sedna the Sea Goddess." The tales are well worth sharing orally with children.

Legends have sprung up in all parts of the world. One tale from *Legends of Hawaii*, by Padraic Colum, illustrates several characteristics of the form. Au-ke-le, a hero with superhuman qualities, is the youngest son of the king of Ku-ai-he-lani, "The Country That Supports the Heavens." He is loved by his father more than the other children, and their resentment causes them to cast him into a pit. Fortunately, the pit is also inhabited by his grandmother, who has taken on the form of a serpent. She sends him on a quest for wisdom, giving him magic gifts to help him. On the quest, Au-ke-le conquers the four brothers of the warlike queen into whose land he has wandered. Amazed by his powers, the queen agrees to be his wife. He becomes lonely for his now-dead brothers, however, so his wife sends him to find the Water of Everlasting Life. Au-ke-le succeeds in this quest, and his brothers are restored to life.

**KING ARTHUR AND ROBIN HOOD.** Historians differ on whether King Arthur really lived in the sixth century, united England, and led its armed forces against Saxon invaders.[11] Nevertheless, the stories remain exciting. As Arthur's followers retold the tales during exile in Brittany and Wales, they elaborated on them and added other tales. The version in *The Book of King Arthur and His Noble Knights*, by Mary MacLeod, is introduced by Angelo Patri, who describes five different versions published prior to the one by Sir Thomas Malory in the latter part of the fifteenth century. The Malory version, a "great and joyous book . . . written in English prose so simple and so beautiful that it set a standard to which great writers will always turn," is the version on which MacLeod based her book. The book includes handsome but restrained illustrations in subdued shades of orange, olive green, yellow, and black by the master illustrator, Henry C. Pitz.

The archaic language in many versions of the Arthur legend presents reading problems. The following excerpt from *The Story of King Arthur and His Knights*, by Howard Pyle, is illustrative:

> Merlin, so far as my death is concerned—when my time cometh to die I believe God will give me grace to meet my end with entire cheerfulness; for, certes, my lot is in that wise no different from that of any other man who hath been born of woman. But touching the matter of this young child, if thy prophecy be true, then his danger is very great, and it would be well that he should be conveyed hence to some place of safe harborage as thou dost advise.

---

[11]A helpful explanation of the country, politics, and social conditions during Arthur's time is included in *Bulfinch's Mythology* (New York: Thomas Y. Crowell, 1970). The description of a knight's training, which began at seven years of age, may be of special interest to children.

With this book, as with other books like it, a skilled teacher/reader can interpret the material to make it interesting to students who would not ordinarily be able to read and comprehend it themselves.

In illustrating *The Knight of the Lion*, Gerald McDermott has used only black and white, in a strongly designed but less geometric style than in his earlier work. McDermott explores the way calligraphic pen, India ink, and lithographic crayon can evoke texture through high-contrast light and dark. The story is interestingly retold in first person by Yvain, a dark-haired youth with an adventurous spirit, who sets out to vanquish the Black Knight.

Some seven centuries after King Arthur's time, Robin Hood, another legendary British hero, is supposed to have lived in Sherwood Forest with his Rabelaisian band. Robin, a magnanimous figure, shares with the poor the contraband that he steals from the rich. Skillful reading of the archaic language by a teacher or librarian will interest children in the stories, which are full of adventure and good humor. To begin, a teacher can share "How Robin Hood Met Friar Tuck," in *Some Merry Adventures of Robin Hood*, by Howard Pyle. This hilarious account of two men trying to best each other will appeal to students because of the similarity to two small boys fighting.

This same episode is one of several collected in an exceptional book, *The Song of Robin Hood*, edited by Anne Malcolmson, which includes eighteen airs and ballads. Virginia Lee Burton did the illustrations in pen, ink, and scratchboard. Despite the hundreds of verses and as many as nine illustrations on a page, Burton has masterfully designed the pages and subordinated the abundant details to prevent a cluttered appearance.

*Robin Hood*, by Paul Creswick, has been reissued with illustrations from the original canvases done by N. C. Wyeth. Born in 1882, this prolific artist produced more than four thousand illustrations, murals, and easel paintings; during his lifetime, he was recognized as one of the most distinguished living artists.

No matter which version of the Robin Hood legend is used, it is the "escape to freedom" that will intrigue child readers, as it intrigued a distinguished writer of fantasy, Philippa Pearce (1985). In sharing her childhood recollections of this engrossing tale, Pearce comments that the "foremost appeal . . . has always been the spaciousness" of the stories.

**WOMEN IN LEGENDS.** Although legends typically feature male main characters, *The Stolen Fire*, by Hans Baumann, a collection of stories from Europe, Siberia, Africa, Asia, Australia, and America, also includes tales with heroines.

In "Kara Khan's Daughter," Altyn Aryg shows herself worthy of inheriting her father's possessions by defeating the Snake Prince. Inside the Snake

**The symmetry in this very detailed illustration is left/right as well as top/bottom.** Illustration by Virginia Lee Burton from *Song of Robin Hood*. Copyright © 1947 by Anne Burnett Malcolmson and Virginia Lee Demetrios. Copyright © renewed 1975 by Grace Castagnetta, George Demetrios, Michael and Aristides Demetrios. Reprinted by permission of Houghton Mifflin Company.

Prince, Altyn Aryg strikes at the beast's heart with the swords of captured heros, but to no avail. Finally, using her own blade, she " . . . inflicted such a deep wound that the Snake Prince gasped and opened his mouth in terror. The open mouth remained, even after he was dead."

In "Nana Miriam," a Nigerian tale, the main character displays similar bravery in the face of intimidating animal power. Nana, tall, strong, and beautiful, learned magic powers from her father. A monster rampaging through the area takes the form of a hippopotamus, and " . . . huge pots of fire were hung around the animal's neck." Using her magic powers, Nana outwits the hippo, and in a final show of strength, she flings it across the river, where it " . . . crashed against the opposite bank, its skull was split, and it was dead."

## THE BIBLE AS LITERATURE

Using the Bible in school as literature is far more difficult today than previously. Aggressive action by those intent on maintaining a wide gulf between the public schools and religion has been an ongoing deterrent to such use. Religious fundamentalists have more recently begun to work against what they see as blatant secularism by trying to influence materials for children. To date, efforts have centered primarily on textbooks, though both groups also want to influence trade books in school libraries. Because of these two diverse, but growing influences, most teachers stay away from books having an identifiable religious theme. In the process, much fine literature is lost.

The Bible is written in a variety of literary formats, including poetry (discussed in Chapter 7). In order to ensure that children are not denied access to the wealth of tales included in the Bible, teachers must themselves understand and be able to articulate to parents the important distinction between the promulgation of the beliefs or customs of a particular religion and the study of the Bible as literature in the oral tradition.

To introduce Bible stories to young children, a teacher can use Helen Dean Fish's *Animals of the Bible*, winner of the first Caldecott Medal and featuring pictures by Dorothy Lathrop. The illustrations show Lathrop's versatility. Some, like the hart (mentioned in one of the Psalms), are soft and appealing; others, like the leviathan (Job 41), are frightening. In between these extremes, the artist shows foxes (Matthew 8), ravens (I Kings), and rams (Genesis 22), among others. The text, usually no more than one page for each story, is taken from the King James version.

Much of the literature in the Bible is complex, but talented writers have managed to present many of the stories in a form simple enough for children to enjoy. Only part of the life of Jesus is recounted, in words from the King James version, in *A Child Is Born*, by Elizabeth Winthrop. What distinguishes this book is the characteristically fine draftsmanship of artist Charles Mikolaycak. Although he is also a sensitive colorist, Mikolaycak's strength is his ability to subtly delineate the bone structure that underlies flesh. His people and animals are always solidly conceived, but the technique never intrudes on the overall effect of a page.

A different view of the life of Jesus is found in Sandol Stoddard's *Five Who Found the Kingdom: New Testament Stories*. Two women (Naomi and Susannah) and three men (Joshua, Nathan, and Michael) narrate their own life stories and describe how knowing Jesus affected them. The author uses a lot of authentic details to establish credibility but does not get bogged down in excessive facts. Reading the account of Jesus' birth told from Joshua's point of view makes the reader view this familiar story with new freshness. Naomi tells of knowing Jesus when they were both youngsters. Nathan describes being healed by Jesus when they were both young men. Susannah welcomed Jesus to her uncle's home when Jesus was at the peak of his ministry. Michael, a slave, tells how he came to follow Jesus and was present when Jesus was entombed. For middle-grade readers, this book presents stories that function as literature rather than as bases of religious belief.

A well-known male character from the Bible is the focus of *I Am Joseph*, by Barbara Cohen. The author uses a first-person narrative to bring the seventeen-year-old Joseph to life. He is not without character flaws: "We were twelve brothers, and we were all handsome, but I was the handsomest and I knew it." The account ends with the reconciliation, when Joseph and his brothers are together at last. Charles Mikolaycak's realistic pictures, in colored pencils with oil glazes, evoke the costumes and architecture of ancient Egypt. Set formally within a border, the pictures are especially well-designed to lead the eye beyond the frame, because Mikolaycak shows only part of many figures and objects. His use of this device is similar to the use of partial figures by such painters as Henri Toulouse-Lautrec and Edgar Degas.

Two different versions of the same Bible tale can be compared to illustrate how differently one story can be visualized. Beverly Brodsky uses first-person narration in *Jonah*. Large, boldly executed watercolors full of swirling motion permeate the book. Using only minimal line, she defines form via color and leads the viewer's eye with strong, repeating patterns. Much more restrained in color is Warwick Hutton's *Jonah and the Great Fish*. This is also illustrated in watercolor but has a softer and more distant mood than Brodsky's version.

Lisl Weil, in *Esther*, relates indirectly the background of the Hebrew feast of Purim, which commemorates the time that Queen Esther saved her people from the duplicity of her husband's evil advisor. Weil's casual ink-and-wash drawings are highlighted in blue. This book is important because it is about a female Biblical character.

Focusing not on a particular Biblical character but rather on a series of events is *Genesis. The Story of Creation*, by Allison Reed. This book uses the King James version's words and is noteworthy for Reed's illustrations. Double-page spreads bleed to the edge of the paper, and the words are superimposed on the pictures. Richly detailed, muted pastels with spatter effects overlaying background colors show insubstantial things (for instance, God moving upon the waters) as well as tangible things (such as Adam and Eve). Each time viewers return to a page, they will notice new details. The layouts are interestingly varied: on some pages, detail is evenly distributed; on other pages, it is concentrated in one part.

The often-illustrated tale of the flood is recounted fairly conventionally in *Noah and the Ark and the Animals*, by Andrew Elbourn. There are some enlivening turns of phrase: "The water covered the earth for one hundred and fifty days! That is a very long time to be swaying around in a floating barn." But it is the pictures by the talented Ivan Gantschev that will capture and hold children's interest. (See Plate B in the color section.) The artist uses a pleasantly loose watercolor technique; areas of color are often enriched by the many related tones used nearby. Ink line gives definition to shapes, but it is the interaction of various colors that makes the pictures compelling. The tale itself is set within the frame of another: the book opens as a mare is relating the Noah tale to her colt and closes just as the rainy weather clears, so the colt can go outside. (Additional comments about this book are included in Chapter 14; see page 688.)

# *SHARING TRADITIONAL LITERATURE WITH CHILDREN*

Storytelling, dramatization, comparison of variants, and retelling through composition can all be used to encourage children to respond to literature in intensely personal ways.

## TELLING TALES

Because of their brevity and clarity of incident, folk tales are particularly appropriate for storytelling. Children enjoy hearing such tales read aloud but respond even more enthusiastically when a teacher retells them. Although many talk about the art of storytelling, few practice it. Why are children so seldom exposed to the joy of a well-told story?

First, storytelling requires patience. Most elementary classroom teachers experience inordinate demands on their time. They are busy preparing materials, planning learning experiences, ministering to and conferring about children's emotional and cognitive needs, evaluating success, and planning new strategies where success has been elusive. These and other demands limit the time a teacher has for learning a story and sharing it. Even finding a few minutes to rehearse a story before reading it to children sometimes seems like an impossible task. However, forces are at work that may make storytelling more possible in elementary schools in the next few years. Among these is decreasing enrollment. As pupil-to-teacher ratios diminish, more time may be available for such activities as storytelling. Changing organizational patterns, such as the open classroom and individual instruction, as well as changing ideas about teachers' roles, with decreasing emphasis on teachers as presenters of information, may provide opportunities for storytelling.

Second, few teachers know how to develop storytelling skills. There are current materials available to the teacher who wants to become adept at telling stories. Periodicals include such articles as one by Groff (1977), who offers simple, usable suggestions for potential storytellers. More extended treatments are available in books, such as the one by Livo and Reitz (1985). For teachers who become really committed to storytelling, membership in The National Association for the Perpetuation and Presentation of Storytelling may be a useful way to further their skills.

Some specific techniques can help anyone become an acceptable storyteller.

**1. *The storyteller can read several stories when it is time to learn a new one.***

After reading perhaps a half-dozen unfamiliar stories, the storyteller should wait at least a week. Usually one of the stories will keep coming back to mind; that is the one to learn.

**2. *The storyteller can divide a story by identifying separate scenes, or units of action, into which the plot can be segmented.***

Action sequences can be found in any story, once the descriptive material is separated from the bare bones of the plot. After segmenting the plot into units, the storyteller should learn them in order. This does not mean memorizing word for word; it means learning the sequence necessary to move the story ahead. As the storyteller practices saying what must happen in the first unit to lead into the second, the story will be learned, not memorized. A storyteller should not worry about trying to use the same words during each practice session (Nessel, 1985). Part of the charm of a story that is told aloud is the differences in language that occur as the teller responds to various audiences.

One storyteller thinks not about units of action as described here, but rather of division of a story into a beginning, middle, and end. Labeling each part with an emotion helps her remember them, and learning the progression of emotions helps her let go of the words and think of the story as a memory to be shared (Schwartz, 1985).

### 3. *The storyteller can identify those sections of the story that do need to be memorized verbatim.*

Usually sections that must be memorized are not extensive and can easily be learned. There is an example in the charming tale "The Cat and Chanticleer," from *Ukranian Folk Tales*, by Marie Halun Bloch. The chanticleer calls for help as the fox captures him:

> *Pussy dear! Brother dear!*
> *The fox is taking me*
> *Beyond the green woodlands,*
> *Over the yellow sands,*
> *Beyond the rapid waters,*
> *Over the lofty mountains!*
> *Pussy dear! Brother dear!*
> *Save me, I pray!*

This passage needs to be incorporated into the retelling word for word as it stands because the words contribute to the story's mood. Likewise, in "Snowdrop," from *Grimm's Fairy Tales*, the superb version of the Snow White tale translated by Arthur Rackham, the interchange between the wicked queen and her mirror should be repeated using the exact words provided. The queen questions the mirror, using the familiar words:

> *Mirror, mirror, on the wall,*
> *Who is fairest of us all?*

And the mirror's reply is notable for its poetic beauty:

> *Queen, thou are fairest here*
> *But Snowdrop, over the fells*
> *Who with the seven dwarfs dwells*
> *Is fairest still, by far.*

The third line has such rich euphony that it demands to be heard exactly as translated.

**4. *The storyteller can practice the story once or twice a day, incorporating verbatim sections into the sequence of action.***

She or he should rehearse in a place that is comfortable for saying the story aloud and should become accustomed to the sound of his or her own voice.

**5. *A storyteller can monitor his or her progress by tape-recording a practice session.***

The storyteller should not listen to the tape immediately. Waiting a few days will ensure the objectivity necessary to evaluate the work. While listening to the tape, the storyteller should answer the following questions:

a. What parts of the story do I need to practice more to achieve greater fluency?
b. What parts of the story should be changed (expanded or condensed) for greater effectiveness?
c. Are there places where a different word will evoke a mood more clearly?
d. Are there places where a change in paralinguistic elements—pitch, stress, pause, and tempo—will produce greater effectiveness?

After some thoughtful analysis and resultant repractice, the storyteller is ready for the reward of sharing the story with children.

**VALUE OF STORYTELLING.** Becoming a competent storyteller is personally rewarding for the teacher, but this is scarcely sufficient justification for recommending that all teachers develop storytelling skills. What value does storytelling have for children? There are three reasons why students should experience literature that is told rather than read.

**1. *Hearing literature teaches children to understand the oral tradition.***

In earlier times, young people in many societies were entertained and instructed when elders regularly shared tales. These tales taught moral lessons, perpetuated the group's belief system, and also provided diversion. Listening to stories, the young learned through example that the basic thread of the plot remained the same, even though details and words varied from teller to teller. More recently, grandparents entertained children growing up in our culture, although they were limited to recounting childhood adventures and a small number of well-known stories and rhymes. The context for telling stories shifted from the group to the family unit, and the diversity of the stories diminished. Today, few children encounter any live storytelling experiences; they must usually settle for a story read from a book. When a parent or teacher reads "Cinderella," few children understand that the tale being read is one version, but not necessarily the only one.

### 2. Telling stories provides for the active involvement of children.

Once teachers have learned a tale to tell and are free of dependence on a book, they can employ creative ways to involve children. Many stories include refrains children can repeat as they help the teacher tell the story. Involving students in such oral participation bridges the gap between storytelling and choral speaking and is more satisfying than passive listening to stories (Swanson, 1985).

A teacher can also involve children in storytelling by developing and incorporating gestures. For "Jack and the Beanstalk" the teacher can climb the beanstalk and encourage the children to do so as well. For *Hansel and Gretel*, by Yoshitaro Isaka, a version that takes its story line from E. Humperdinck's opera rather than from the original Grimm source, the children can pantomime scattering the crumbs, nibbling on the house, and shutting the oven door, among other actions. In telling "The Cat and Chanticleer," the teacher can have children mime the cat hitting the foxes with his club. Children revel in such physical involvement: it makes them feel they are an active part of the experience and holds their attention even through long stories.

A teacher can also involve boys and girls by incorporating music in stories where it is appropriate. At first, the teacher may make up simple melodies and teach them to children using tone bells or a guitar. The song the cat sings to entice the foxes out of their house in "The Cat and Chanticleer" is an example of the type of musical opportunity that exists in many stories. Eventually, the teacher can ask the children to make up a simple melody themselves. Children can contribute melodies line by line, as the teacher jots down in notation what they sing. Later these notes can be written on the board for older children or taught by rote to younger ones. This process is more fully described, with a song created by children, on an in-classroom tape by Stewig (n.d.). Such experiences with simple melodic composition help children develop a sense of themselves as creators of music not simply reactors to someone else's composition. These experiences also help them see how a story can be enriched beyond a simple verbal telling. In a modest way, children can carry on the tradition of music in storytelling that Pellowski (1977) describes so thoroughly.

*Charles Mikolaycak's usual superb draftsmanship is here enriched with full color, underscoring his ability to create believable three-dimensional forms.* Illustration by Charles Mikolaycak from *Peter and the Wolf* by Sergei Prokofiev. Copyright © 1982 by Charles Mikolaycak. Reproduced by permission of Viking Penguin Inc.

If a teacher is not able to lead children in an informal dictation of melody lines, he or she can speak to the music teacher, who will be pleased to have an additional opportunity to incorporate music into the curriculum. A suggestion by Morrow (1979) about matching musical motifs to characters, as is done in *Peter and the Wolf*, might provide another occasion for collaboration between the classroom teacher and a trained music specialist.

### 3. Telling stories is valuable for the stimulus it provides for children's retelling.

Seeing the teacher—a significant adult—engaged in storytelling helps children perceive this art form as a worthwhile activity. Thus, children will also want to tell stories. The teacher can encourage children to retell a favorite story they have heard. Initial efforts will be primarily rote retellings; only after several attempts will children begin to embellish. As children use the language they have heard, they are imitating language more complex in both vocabulary and syntax than that which they ordinarily use. This is an important developmental stage leading to mature language independence.

The following is a retelling by Charissa, a young black child.[12] The teacher read Paul Galdone's *The Three Bears* to a group of first-grade children and left the book on the classroom library table near the storytelling booth. This booth was a large refrigerator carton equipped with a small table, chair, and cassette recorder. Children were encouraged to go into the booth any time thay wanted to retell a story they had heard or to tell an original story. Several days after hearing the teacher read *The Three Bears*, Charissa told this:

> There was a poppa bear, and there was a mother and the baby, that lived in this little house. They went out for to get some flowers. The mother, she, the baby and the poppa went out to the woods.
> This little girl named Goldilocks, she came in and then she ate the poppa bear's gruel, it was too hot. Then she ate the mother bear's gruel, it was too cold. She ate the baby bear's gruel. She ate it all up.
> She sat in the poppa bear's chair, it was too hard. She sat in the mother bear's chair, it was too soft. She sat in the baby bear's chair and she broke it.
> She got in the poppa bear bed, it was too hard. She got in the mother bear bed, it was too soft. She got in the baby bear bed, it was just right.
> "Somebody been eatin' my porridge."
> "Somebody been eatin' my porridge."
> "Somebody been eatin' my porridge and they eat it all up."
> "Somebody been in my chair."
> "Somebody been in my chair."
> "Somebody been in my chair, and they broke it."
> "Somebody been in my bed."
> "Somebody been in my bed."
> "Somebody been in my bed, and they still in it."
> They woke Goldilocks up. Scared she jumped out the window.

(As a followup to *The Three Bears*, a teacher might share with students the clever reversal found in *Deep in the Forest*, by Brinton Turkle. This wordless picture book about a family living in a forest in frontier America depicts what happens when a little black bear comes for a visit.)

Once students have mastered retelling favorite stories, teachers can encourage them to invent a new ending for an old favorite and eventually

---

[12] The transcription is from a tape provided by Joan Groth, Burbank School, Milwaukee, Wisc.

to make up an original story. One kindergarten teacher shared variants of "The Gingerbread Boy" with her class. On successive days, she told different versions, encouraging the children to notice similarities and differences. The children told which story they liked best and gave reasons for their choices. The culminating activity was to tell a variation of the story to the class. One child decided to make the runaway a hamburger from a well-known fast-food chain. The hamburger rolled out of the shop, eluded a police officer, a mail carrier, some shoppers, and a delivery boy before rolling into the child's school. There it avoided the principal, the secretary, and the janitor while rolling down the hall. The willful burger, which the child personified with gusto, finally met its untimely end by rolling into the kindergarten, where it was devoured by the children. This is just one example of the type of creativity that results when children see the teacher as storyteller and are encouraged to emulate this activity.

**FACILITATING CHILDREN'S STORYTELLING.** How does a teacher encourage girls and boys to tell stories beyond simply serving as a model? The teacher should provide several specific aids to facilitate children's storytelling.

1. *A time and place for practice.* A storyteller needs to get used to the sound of his or her voice telling a story. Perhaps an unused classroom, an alcove under the steps, even a large closet might serve as a secluded place where anyone who wants to practice may go. In addition, children must have time, because it is only through repeated retellings that they decide which details to include and which words to select.

2. *Feedback to the child.* The availability of inexpensive, simple-to-operate cassette recorders makes it easy for children to listen to their storytelling and analyze it. Children will need help in evaluating their oral storytelling. A teacher begins the process by discussing with youngsters what makes a told tale interesting. Such a discussion can result in a simple set of evaluation questions against which the young storyteller can check his or her telling:

   Did I remember to include all the important things that happen (units of action)?

   Did I include enough details so my listeners can see the story in their minds?

   Did I use my voice differently in different parts of the story?

3. *An audience when the child storyteller wants one.* A regular time should be set aside for story sharing in the classroom. For those who are hesitant, opportunities can be provided to tell a story to a group of younger children.

The teacher does not have to be the initiating storyteller; parents can also be involved. Paulson (1981) describes a community-based program, started more than a decade ago, of which one of many outcomes is that the parents "pass on their values . . . and their heritage" through an organized storytelling guild and annual festival. A city-wide program, in which thousands of New York City children participate, is described by Walton (1982).

## DRAMATIZING TRADITIONAL LITERATURE

Because of their simple, action-oriented plots, folk tales are logical bases for informal drama experiences. It is easy to take a simple folk tale and plan a session in which children translate its words into action. In the process of enacting a piece of literature, children develop a deeper understanding of it, express their reactions to it, and learn about the process of dramatization. In addition, Sparks (1984) points out that their ability to predict increases, as does their vocabulary and syntactic flexibility.

In story dramatization, children plan how to use their bodies and voices to enact a story they have read or heard. The group comes up with effective ways of translating the story from the printed page into a living mode, incorporating voice, gesture, and body movement. The purpose of such activity is to teach children about literature and drama and how the two are related. The purpose is not to teach children lines written by adults so they can put on a finished performance for the enjoyment of an audience.

Story dramatization is only one type of drama experience. Creative dramatics includes a variety of activities such as rhythmic movement, pantomime, characterization, and sophisticated story creation; improvisation goes beyond the initial material provided.

**COMPONENTS OF DRAMA.** All types of drama sessions, including story dramatization, are made up of four basic components:

1. *Material.* Effective drama leaders use many kinds of material to stimulate dramatic activity: pictures, real objects, conflict lines, and minimal situations, among others. As we have seen, literature can be the motivating material.
2. *Discussion-questioning segment.* As leaders present the material, and afterward, they encourage spontaneous discussion by asking questions that will uncover the possibilities for dramatization.
3. *Playing an idea.* The actual playing of an idea varies in complexity depending on the children's age and previous drama experience. Some-

times playing is a simple pantomime of a single activity (opening a box containing a birthday present); at other times it is more complex (playing an entire story the children have created).
4. *Evaluation.* Leaders should encourage children to consider what they have done, to decide which aspects they were pleased with and which could have been more effective. Self-evaluation is a basic goal of drama.

**LEVELS OF DRAMATIZING.** The two levels of the dramatic treatment of a story or poem are interpretation and improvisation. The term *interpreting* is another way of saying "acting out." There is an important distinction between interpreting a story and improvising one. In interpreting, the story is translated from the author's written words into movement and oral language, retaining most of the ideas of the author. In *improvising*, the story is used as a base from which to develop further ideas, extending the story in ways not included in the original. For example, a teacher might use "The Fox and the Grapes," from *Aesop's Fables*, by Louis Untermeyer, and ask the children how they could convey the anger of the thwarted fox by using sounds and body movements. But, if the teacher asks children to imagine what might have happened if the grapes had fallen into the fox's paws, she or he is then asking them to extend, to extrapolate, to enrich the basic material with their own ideas. At this point, the group goes beyond simple interpreting to more sophisticated improvising.

Allowing children to choose parts and enact a story is doubtlessly valuable. With "The Midas Touch," in Edith Hamilton's *Mythology*, children take great pleasure in impersonating the greedy king and his pathetic daughter. The theme of this story provides a variety of questions on which children could easily improvise:

1. Why do you imagine the king was so greedy? What might have made him this way?
2. How did the king react to other people? (In the story, he is not seen interacting with others.) What do you think he was like to his servants or to the townspeople?
3. In what other ways could he have solved this problem?

One second-grade teacher used *The Little Red Hen*, with pleasantly bright illustrations by Margot Zemach. The teacher opened with an examination of the language of the story. The hen "worked hard to keep her family well fed." The teacher asked the class to suggest things the hen did to look after her family; the suggestions were listed on the chalkboard. All the children worked on pantomime at the same time, choosing a task and practicing miming it. The teacher then led children through each action in sequence, reading the words, and exploring with the class what they thought the hen did, and how they could show it. For example, the hen planted the wheat: How did she do this? Did she need any tools? What kinds? Where did she get them? How did she help the wheat grow?

In order, the children talked about, and then pantomimed, planting the wheat, harvesting the wheat (including discussion of what a scythe is), threshing the wheat, putting the wheat into a sack, and carrying the heavy sack to the mill. Discussion about the equipment needed and processes involved in baking the bread followed. Children then mimed setting the table, lifting the baked loaves from the oven, sitting down at the table, and eating the bread.

Activities to develop the verbal dialogue involved pairing children, with one child playing the hen and the other one of the friends (the goose, the cat, or the pig) the hen tries to convince to help her. After children practiced both action and dialogue, they shared their interpretations with one another. This example indicates how rewarding translating the printed page into spoken word and gesture can be for both children and teacher.

## COMPARING VARIANTS

One of the richest possibilities in studying folk literature with children is the comparison of different versions. Unlike contemporary literature written by a single author, folk tales appear in many mutations, formed as anonymous, long-forgotten storytellers added, changed, and deleted details. A teacher should deliberately select and use several variants of one tale so children understand the concept that there is no single right version. Teaching this concept is especially critical since the story children think of as the original is often in fact a highly modified, or prettified, retelling that lacks the integrity of the version that came from the oral tradition. MacDonald (1982) facilitates the locating of variants by providing a bibliographic index listing over five hundred collections and over three hundred individual picture books. However, the individual titles of one story may be quite different.

Contact with folk literature from many different countries helps children understand that all people have created such stories, that the impetus to tell tales is universal, although details, characters, and events vary in different societies. Almost all children will recognize Charles Perrault's *Cinderella;* few will know the Armenian version in *One Hundred Armenian Tales,*

***Margot Zemach's pleasantly informal watercolor-wash drawings, unified with a scratchy ink line, match the casual, simple language used to tell the story.*** Illustration from *The Little Red Hen* by Margot Zemach. Copyright © 1983 by Margot Zemach. Reprinted by permission of Farrar, Straus & Giroux, Inc.

by Susie Hoogasian-Villa. This theme of the young girl imposed upon and abused by stepsisters and stepmother until she is rescued by a handsome prince appears in many cultures. *Yeh-Shen. A Cinderella Story from China,* by Ai-Ling Louie, presents a version that includes a beautiful fish with golden eyes. Ed Young's understated, jewel-colored illustrations for this book prove that richness does not depend on the inclusion of a lot of details; large areas of white space contrast with and set off the color. (See Plate A in the color section.)

Similarly, the story about food that runs away from the old person who prepared it ("The Gingerbread Boy") is a universal theme. In Norway, it is a pancake that runs away; in Russia, it is a bun; in Scotland, it is an oatmeal cake (a bannock); in Japan, it is a rice cake. Who pursues the escaping food and its eventual end vary according to the country; in any case, children should understand recurring folk-tale themes.

Listening to or reading variants of the same tale impresses on children the idea that there is no one right version. Oral tradition is characterized by variety, and it is sometimes difficult for children to understand, especially in this age of mass media, that there is not a single "correct" variant. Children are positive they know the "right" names for the dwarves in "Snow White," for example, but the cute appellations were added relatively recently by Walt Disney. The dwarves had distinctive qualities for many years before Disney decided they needed to be christened.

Chambers and Lowry (1975) explain that children should be encouraged to examine the differences in folk tales because of the influence it may have on their writing abilities:

> Literary analysis does not just belong at the university level. Elementary school students are capable, at their level, of analyzing literature to better understand how an author uses language to produce a work of art. When [a student] begins to understand the technique of writing by examining good models of writing, the probability of his [or her] growth with that written language is certainly better than before.

**STORIES DIFFER.** It is wise to begin the comparing and contrasting of folk tales as early as kindergarten. One kindergarten teacher uses "The Gingerbread Boy" with her children each year, sharing several variants of it for the language-stimulating discussion it provokes. A teacher can choose any of the more common folk tales and ask children to think about the details and identify ways in which the stories are alike and different.

A third-grade teacher read *Rumplestiltskin*, by Jacqueline Ayer, and *Tom Tit Tot*, by Evaline Ness, to her class. She introduced the stories by telling students that they would be hearing two variations of the same tale and that they would then be asked to tell how the stories were alike or different. Since this was the children's first experience with this type of lesson, they were encouraged to notice anything they could about the tales. In the discussion that followed the reading, boys and girls made the observations collected in the table on the next page.

After reading and discussing these two books, the teacher showed a film of the same story. Afterwards, the teacher encouraged the children to compare the film to the two book versions. They noticed differences in the following elements:

1. *The ending.* When his name was discovered, Rumplestiltskin fell on the floor and vanished in the film (see item 4 in table).
2. *Who discovered the name.* In the film, the entire village went to look for the man (see item 10 in table).

| Rumplestiltskin | Tom Tit Tot |
|---|---|
| 1. language is simple | language is strange |
| 2. main character is a man | main character is "That" |
| 3. straw was spun into gold | flax was changed to five skeins |
| 4. Rumplestiltskin split apart | "That" flew away |
| 5. miller told king that his daughter could spin gold | woman's daughter ate five pies; woman said her daughter spun five skeins |
| 6. girl had only a father | girl had only a mother |
| 7. characters look Chinese | characters look like poor village folk |
| 8. Rumplestiltskin didn't have wings | "That" had wings |
| 9. Rumplestiltskin wanted the baby if she didn't guess his name | "That" wanted the girl if she didn't guess his name |
| 10. hunter went to look | king happened to find "That" |
| 11. girl had to spin right away | girl had to spin after eleven months |
| 12. spun for three nights | spun for an entire month |

3. **The motivation.**   In the film, the miller needed the money for taxes; no reason is given in the books.

4. **The characterization of the girl.**   The girl was not as pretty or as clever in the film as she was in the books.

5. **The behavior of the neighbors.**   They drank wine to celebrate at the end of the film; this behavior is not included in the books.

To follow up, teachers might read Eleanor Farjeon's literary retelling of this story in *The Silver Curlew*. She develops the story at an almost unbelievably leisurely pace. On page 46, she finally gives the reason the king is out riding (searching for a wife, to take him off the hands of his devoted but aging nurse). The pages before this are devoted to charming introductory portraits of mother Codding, her sons, "good strong lads with enormous appetites, who said little and thought less," and other interesting characters both central and peripheral. Farjeon's strength is clearly characterization, as shown in her description of Charlee Loon, the amiable, if dim, fisherman who provided mother Codding with her fish.

> Sometimes he caught things and sometimes he didn't. Sometimes he went out to fish without his nets, and sometimes he forgot where he had set his lobster pots. But other times he came back with his nets full of slippery silvery herrings or flat white flounders.

The story itself, when Farjeon comes back to it from her digressions, is essentially the same one as presented in the more bare-bones retellings. The "Spindle-Imp," whose name she must guess, gives the young woman nine guesses, rather than the more usual three.

Another choice for a follow-up is the variant entitled "Whuppity Stourie," as found in *The Other Country*, retold by Marion Lochhead. The Goodwife of Kittlerumpit was a practical sort. The widow, living alone with her wee bairn, was "a sensible woman who made the best of things, brave too and quick witted." When she discovered her pig was sick she "sat down and cried. That did not help much, and very soon she was on her feet again. . . ." She encounters one of the Other People, a tiny woman no bigger than a child but with an old face. When the woman cures the pig, the Goodwife finds to her dismay that the price is the wee bairn. As in Rumplestiltskin, the only way to prevent the loss is to discover the old lady's name, which the Goodwife does. There are no multiple guesses here—she gets the name right the first time—and "with a skirl of rage . . . that was the last sight and sound of" the old lady.

**ILLUSTRATIONS DIFFER.**    Teachers and librarians can help children enjoy the full pleasure of folk literature by sharing with them several artists' pictures for the same story. For most well-known tales, several versions are available.

Nodelman (1984) provides an extended analysis of two versions of Snow White. In the process, he extends our thinking about this old tale, cast into two very different visual forms by Nancy Burkert and Trina Schart Hyman. In talking about style (not what is shown, but how it is shown), Nodelman points out that in Burkert's version viewers look at the heroine, not with her. She is seen as part of a larger picture. The woman is an object, Nodelman asserts, to be admired as the other objects are to be admired. In contrast, in Hyman's pictures, viewers are taken inside the events. We see and feel as she sees and feels, and we empathize with her as a fellow human, with no intervening distance of the type evoked by Burkert. Obviously, this kind of adult analysis of pictures is not developmentally appropriate for children. However, it is important to share more than one version, so children may observe and comment on visual differences they notice. Asking children to look at and talk about stories illustrated by different artists helps develop their visual and verbal abilities.

Artists have depicted "Puss in Boots" in a variety of ways. Marcia Brown creates a flamboyant cat in dry paint, chalk, and hard black-ink line in her book *Puss in Boots*. The cat is a swashbuckler through and through—from the flare of his coral-colored boots to the sweep of his black hat's brim. Quite different is the cat in *Puss in Boots* by Hans Fischer. This cat strides with chest puffed out in black knee-high boots, carrying his yellow sack confidently across his shoulder. The crayon drawings, in places augmented with blue, orange, and lemon yellow, are pleasantly relaxed. Nicola Bayley's meticulously detailed cat is attired in an embroidered and bejeweled cape in her pictures for the story as retold by Christopher Logue. The flat pages in this book have small elaborate drawings in the corners; the pop-up pages are more intricately detailed than is usual.

A pair of books provides further comparison and contrast of illustrations. Leo and Diane Dillon won a Caldecott Medal for their illustrations in *Why Mosquitoes Buzz in People's Ears*, by Verna Aardema, a tale in which what one animal does affects another. The illustrations are highly patterned, double-page spreads done with an airbrush technique. A more extended analysis of this and thirteen other picture books is provided by Moss and Stott (1986). In Benjamin Elkin's *Why the Sun Was Late*, a different version of the same tale, Jerome Snyder creates darkly handsome illustrations that need to be studied at close range.

**USING VIDEOTAPES.** In addition to books, teachers or librarians can also use videotapes to work with children on the concept of variants of stories. In "Who Is the Real Cinderella?" from the series *The Folk Book*, by Eileen Littig, the multisource origin of the folk tale is explored. Variants of this tale include "Turkey Girl" (native American), "Nitokris and the Gilded Sandals" (Egyptian), and "Kari Woodencoat" (Norwegian). The guide to these tapes is very well developed, including a summary of the tales, cultural notes, activities, and a bibliography that includes stories for young children, stories for teachers and older children, and nonprint materials. The visual aspect of comparing variants is presented in the program "Jim and the Beanstalk," from the series *Magic Pages*, by Judy Wimmer. Opening with an original variant presented by a female storyteller with no visuals, the video then moves on to a presentation of the story by Raymond Briggs, with his illustrations. The guide pages provided are extremely helpful. (Both of these videotape series are available from Agency for Instructional Television, Bloomington, Ind.)

## RETELLING A TALE THROUGH COMPOSITION

A useful project for intermediate-grade children is to have them rewrite a tale from the point of view of one of the characters. Typical of most folk tales is the omniscient, all-seeing observer who relates the story. Once children have moved from the self-centeredness of their early years, they enjoy the challenge of "becoming" one of the characters.

When introducing this activity, it is usually necessary to stress that characters cannot know that certain events have happened or how they have happened, unless it is made clear in the rewriting that someone told them. For example, Snow White cannot know what happens after she eats the poisoned apple unless someone tells her.

One teacher asked third-grade students to write a different version of Snow White. One child chose to retell the story from Snow White's point of view, and another retold it from the prince's point of view.

I am Snow White and this is what happened in my life. I'll start at the beginning. I was born and then my mother died. My father remarried a mean, mean lady. She was my stepmother. She wanted to be the prettiest in all the land, and she was until I grew up a little. I was very beautiful. I got prettier every day. Once stepmother asked her magic mirror: "Mirror, mirror, on the wall, who is the fairest of us all?" The mirror replied: "Thou art fairest in this hall but Snow White's the fairest of us all." She was very mad with envy. She was so mad she sent for a huntsman and ordered him to take me to the forest and bring back my liver and lung. He did take me to the forest but he spared my life. Instead he killed a boar and took its liver and lung. He told me to run away and never come back. I did. I ran and ran and then I saw a little cottage. Inside it had seven places set at the table and seven little beds. I was so tired I went to sleep. When I woke up I saw seven dwarfs. They were kind to me. I stayed with them a very long time. One day the queen asked her mirror who the fairest was, and it answered that Snow White was the fairest. She was so mad. She tried to kill me. First with lace and second with a poisonous comb. But both times the dwarfs saved me. Then she made a poison apple. This time the dwarfs couldn't save me. They made a glass coffin for me and kept it. One day a prince came and told the dwarfs that he just had to have the coffin. The dwarfs took pity on him and gave it to him. He called his servants to put the coffin on a horse to take it back to the palace. They did. When they were riding to the palace, the horse hit a rock. The bump made the piece of apple come out of my mouth. I was alive again. The prince and I married and lived happily ever after.

*Michele*

I come in in the middle of the story. I think you should have some background. The evil stepmother gave Snow White an apple. Half of it was poisoned.

I was riding along in the woods when I noticed a glass coffin. There was a girl inside of the coffin. She was locked in. It puzzled me why she didn't try to get out. She didn't look dead.

I saw a little man walking around. I asked him, "What's wrong with this girl?" He told me the story. I felt sad. He also said that he was one of the seven dwarfs. I was very puzzled. I offered him some money for the coffin with the girl. He turned me down. She was so beautiful I had to have her. I offered him anything for it. He said "No." Then I said I would cherish it forever. He called his brothers. They decided that they would give her to me on one condition. It was that I must keep her outside until I die. I said OK.

At that instant I ordered my servants to carry the coffin and whoever dropped it, "Off with their head!" They just started walking along and one of the front guards dropped it. I was just about to yell, "Off with his head," and she seemed to come awake.

The apple that was in her mouth was somehow forced to come out. She sat up. The beautiful girl awakened. I jumped off my horse. Only it was love at first sight. Both of us got on my horse. I ordered the servants to carry the coffin back to the dwarves and give them the good news.

On the night of our wedding we asked her evil stepmother to come. When she arrived she had to place metal shoes that were in a hot fire and dance until she was dead. She arrived and after dancing for 16 minutes she dropped dead!

*Tim*

## SUMMARY

Describing fully the immense body of traditional literature in one brief chapter is an impossible task. At best, this chapter serves as an introduction to the array of forms some scholars spend a lifetime studying.

A major part of the traditional literature teachers share with children should be folk tales. As teachers and students enjoy this form together, students gain an understanding of historic cultures unlike their own, with different beliefs, different dangers and problems, and different solutions. In so doing, children grow beyond their innate self-centeredness to a larger awareness of human diversity.

## Suggestions for Further Study

1. Catherine Storr (see page 212) comments that consciously invented stories lack a "remorseless sequence of events," which she feels is necessary. Bruno Bettelheim comments more specifically on this lack in *Little Toot*, by Hardie Gramatky (New York: G. P. Putnam's, 1939). Read Bettelheim's *The Uses of Enchantment: The Meaning and Importance of Fairy Tales* (New York: Alfred A. Knopf, 1976), and tell what your reaction is to his and Storr's contentions.

2. Teachers may avoid sharing myths with children because they see them as being remote from contemporary life. Read *Myth and Modern Man*, by Raphael Patai (Englewood Cliffs, N.J.: Prentice Hall, 1972), which identifies links between ancient myths and many aspects of modern life. How would you plan

a lesson for children that would involve them in studying the uses of myth in modern advertising? Intermediate- and upper-grade children could identify mythic parallels in product advertising.

3. There are many other kinds of heros besides those in myth and legend. American folk heros include Johnny Appleseed, Davy Crockett, and Pecos Bill. Anne Malcolmson presents a collection of American folk tales, arranged by geographic regions, in *Yankee Doodle's Cousins* (Boston: Houghton Mifflin, 1941). Read several of these. In what ways are the heros like and unlike the heros described in this chapter?

4. Compare reviews of Bruno Bettelheim's book *The Uses of Enchantment* (mentioned above). "The Meaning of Fairy Tales" (*Newsweek*, May 24, 1976, pp. 88 and 91) is a different response than that of reviewer Paul Heins in *The Horn Book* (June 1976, pp. 301–302). Which of the two reviews is closer to your own opinion? Nicholas Tucker provides a far more extensive critical analysis in "Dr. Bettelheim and Enchantment" (*Signal*, January 1984, pp. 33–41). Tucker talks not only about internal strengths and weaknesses he perceives in this book, but also about the effect it has had since its publication on children's literature and education in general.

5. *Stone Soup*, by Ann McGovern, was mentioned early in this chapter. You could use several editions of this story with a group of children to see which they enjoy most and why. The edition mentioned on page 202 is probably not as well known as the edition with pictures by Marcia Brown (New York, Scribner's, 1947), in which three soldiers, returning from war, are portrayed in almost monochromatic shades of brown and orange. In a variant, retold by Willis Lindquist, a poor farm boy, Pell, is the main character (New York: Western, 1970). This is presented in a large vertical rectangular format with simplified, humorous illustrations by Bob Shein, done in bright watercolor contained within a firm black ink line.

6. At what age do children begin to understand parody? Jane Yolen's *Sleeping Ugly* (New York: Coward, McCann, 1981) is a take-off on the better-known "Sleeping Beauty" that adults find humorous. Do students? Read this book to a first-, third-, and sixth-grade class, and note the differences in comments made during discussion following the reading. With a group of intermediate-grade boys and girls, you might use *Sleeping Ugly* as the base for having them select another old tale and do a similar sort of parody.

7. Try using *Jelly Belly*, by Dennis Lee (New York: Peter Bedrick Books, 1983) as a contrast with conventional Mother Goose rhymes. Do children respond any differently to Lee's updated rhymes?

8. In *It Could Always Be Worse* (New York: Farrar, Straus and Giroux, 1976), illustrator Margot Zemach uses many shades of brown and grey, warmed with rose-colored accents. The ink-line-defined peasants and animals are strewed casually across facing pages. Compare Zemach's version (discussed on pages 209–210) with one entitled *Too Much Noise*, by Ann McGovern (New York: Scholastic, 1968). Although the tale is similar, the illustrations are notably different. Illustrator Simms Taback produced flat, decorative paintings in orange, blue, and brown with a sharp black pen line. Their simple, somewhat untutored aspect is quite in keeping with the folklike quality of this tale. A third version, *Could Anything Be Worse?*, by Marilyn Hirsch (New York: Holiday House, 1974), presents this Yiddish tale with double-page, wordless spreads in full color alternating with double-page black-and-white spreads containing text and drawings.

# Related Reading for Adults

Bosma, Bette. *Fairy Tales, Fables, Legends, and Myths*. New York: Teachers College Press, 1986.

Subtitled "Using Folk Literature in Your Classroom," this book includes chapters on critical reading, writing from literature, and creative activities. A major portion of each chapter is devoted to suggested lesson descriptions, including an objective, materials needed, and procedures. One chapter recounts the experiences a class of fifth- and sixth-graders had with a variety of literature-based activities. The book ends with a long annotated list of recommended books whose publication dates range from 1924 to 1985.

Colum, Padraic. *Orpheus: Myths of the World*. New York: Macmillan, 1930.

Of interest to teachers because of its complete yet succinct examination of the myths of many civilizations, this large book is handsomely illustrated with black-and-white wood engravings by Boris Artzybasheff in a high-contrast art deco style. Beginning with Egyptian mythology, the book ranges through the classic Greco-Roman period and includes Polynesian, Peruvian, and Zuni sections.

Guirand, Felix. *Greek Mythology*. London: Paul Hamlyn, 1963.

Rather than a collection of myths, this book is a conveniently organized and extensive description of characters and events in myths. The material is arranged according to three categories of myths, making it easy to locate information about a particular hero.

Jennings, Tim, "Storytelling, a Nonliterate Approach to Teaching Reading." *Learning*, 9 (April/May 1981), pp. 49–52.

The author, a professional storyteller, set up and ran an alternative educational program for problem children, most of whom were nonreaders. Jennings taught reading by telling stories to his students, who then told stories to each other. Their writing improved as they wrote their own stories. The step from listening to reading and writing was neither automatic nor easy, but it did occur. Another article describing professional storytellers' work with more typical students is "Storytellers in the Classroom," by Stewart Marsden, *Teacher*, 98 (December 1980), pp. 33–36.

Sawyer, Ruth, *The Way of the Storyteller*. New York: Viking, 1962.

This book has two equally useful parts: one describing storytelling as an art, and the other comprising stories adapted for telling. Rather than an organized exposition of techniques, the book is an intimate reminiscence of the long, successful career of a master storyteller.

Schrank, Jeffrey. "Mythology Today." *Media and Methods*, April 1973, pp. 22–38.

Comparisons of television advertisements point out ways these ads appeal to age-old desires to have powers beyond the ordinary. The author shows how commercials are mini-myths that borrow characters from classical mythology. His analysis of politics explains why some public figures become heros while others, equally able, never receive such adulation.

Shedlock, Marie L. *The Art of the Storyteller*. New York: Dover, 1951.

This version of a classic work merits attention as much for its legible, attractive format as for its content. Although written many years ago, both the section explaining the author's ideas and the section containing stories adapted for telling are unique. A more recent volume does not attempt to replace the inspirational words of Marie Shedlock or Ruth Sawyer, but rather concentrates on a systematic approach to the skills of storytelling. See *Once Upon a Time* by Lucille N. Breneman and Bren Breneman (Chicago: Nelson-Hall, 1983). This well-written handbook shows that its authors understand what beginning storytellers need.

Toothaker, Roy E. "Folktales in Picture Book Format." *Library Journal*, 99 (April 15, 1974), pp. 1188–1194.

The author introduces his bibliography by contending that folklore mirrors culture and provides a way for people to know other cultures. Each book was selected because it is folklore with a clearly defined ethnic setting and provides a literary text that preserves the cultural and stylistic integrity of the ethnic group from which it came.

Walker, Virginia, and Mary E. Lunz. "Symbols, Fairy Tales and School-Age Children." *The Elementary School Journal*, November 1976, pp. 94–100.

The authors point out that interest in fairy tales is pervasive because these tales emphasize action. Because fairy tales are symbols, they should be heard, not read. Listening to a tale is a powerful experience because the archetypes activate images from the listener's collective unconscious.

Willard, Nancy. "The Well-Tempered Falsehood: The Art of Storytelling." *Top of the News*, Fall 1982, pp. 104–112.

Willard reminisces about storytelling in her childhood and about how telling tales makes her a better writer. Using an example from "Snow White," she points out the "miracle of economy" in which a year passes, one character dies, another is born, and a third remarries, all "so simply yet so concretely that I think nobody could wish for more details." The writer who also tells stories orally becomes more able to (1) create characters who are not just individuals but also types, (2) describe not only situations but also the forces that caused them, (3) use fewer adjectives and more verbs, which makes the story move, and (4) become less important than the story told.

## Professional References

Bett, Henry. *Nursery Rhymes and Tales.* London: Methuen, 1924 (Folcroft Library Editions, 1974).

Bettelheim, Bruno. *The Uses of Enchantment: The Meaning and Importance of Fairy Tales.* New York: Alfred A. Knopf, 1976.

Chambers, Dewey W., and Heath W. Lowry. *The Language Arts: A Pragmatic Approach.* Dubuque: William C. Brown, 1975, p. 354.

D'Angelo, Frank J. "Fables in the Composition Classroom." *Arizona English Bulletin*, February 1978, 21–24.

Groff, Patrick. "Let's Update Storytelling." *Language Arts*, March 1977, 272–277.

Hays, May Bradshaw. "Memories of My Father, Joseph Jacobs." In *Folk Literature of the British Isles.* Ed. Eloise Speed Norton. Metuchen, N.J.: Scarecrow, 1978, pp. 86–92.

Huck, Charlotte S., Susan Hepler, and Janet Hickman. *Children's Literature in the Elementary School.* New York: Holt, Rinehart and Winston, 1987, pp. 160–164.

Kanfer, Stefan. "A Lively, Profitable World of Kid Lit." *Time*, December 29, 1980, 62–65.

Kohl, Herbert. "Comics and Myths." *Teacher*, 92 (November 1974), 6.

Lanes, Selma G. *Down the Rabbit Hole.* New York: Atheneum, 1971, pp. 103–104.

Livo, Norma, and Sandra Reitz. *Storytelling: Process and Practice.* Littleton, Colo.: Libraries Unlimited, 1986.

MacDonald, Margaret Read. *Storyteller's Source*

*Book: A Subject, Title and Motif Index to Folklore Collections for Children.* Detroit: Gale Research, 1982.

Marantz, Sylvia, and Kenneth Marantz. "Interview with Paul O. Zelinsky." *The Horn Book,* May/June 1986, 295–304.

Matthias, Margaret, and James D. Quisenberry. "Toward Increasing Literacy in Developing Countries." *Childhood Education,* 63 (January/February 1986), 186–190.

Mavrogenes, Nancy A., and Joan S. Cummins. "What Ever Happened to Little Red Riding Hood? A Study of a Nursery Tale." In *Jump Over the Moon.* Ed. P. Barron. New York: Holt, Rinehart and Winston, 1984, pp. 305–309.

May, Jill P. "Using Folklore in the Classroom." *English Education,* 11 (February 1980), 148–155.

Meer, Jeff. "Terrifying Tales." *Psychology Today,* October 1984, 21.

Minard, Rosemary. "The Forgotten Fairy Tales." *Instructor,* November 1974, 54–55.

Morrow, Lesley Mandel. "Exciting Children about Literature through Creative Storytelling Techniques." *Language Arts,* March 1979, 236–243.

Moss, Anita, and Jon C. Stott. "Appendix A: Picture Books." In *The Family of Stories.* New York: Holt, Rinehart and Winston, 1986, pp. 581–619.

Muggeridge, Kitty. *Fables from la Fontaine.* London: Collins, 1973.

Nessel, Denise D. "Storytelling in the Reading Program." *The Reading Teacher,* January 1985, 378–381.

Nodelman, Perry. "How Picture Books Work." In *Image and Maker.* Ed. Harold Darling and Peter Neumeyer. LaJolla, Calif.: Green Tiger, 1984, pp. 1–12.

Norton, Donna E. "Language and Cognitive Development Through Multicultural Literature." *Childhood Education,* 62 (November/December 1985), 103–108.

Paulson, Jeannette. "Storytelling in Jackson County." *Childhood Education,* 58 (March/April 1981), 209–212.

Pearce, Philippa. "Robin Hood and His Merry Men: A Rereading." *Children's Literature in Education,* 16 (Autumn 1985), 159–164.

Pellowski, Anne. *The World of Storytelling.* New York: R. R. Bowker, 1977.

Rigg, Pat. "Those Spunky Gals: An Annotated Bibliography." *The Reading Teacher,* November 1985, 154–160.

Ross, Mable. "Folktales from Zaire." *Instructor,* March 1975, 82–88.

Schwartz, Marni. "Finding Myself in My Stories." *Language Arts,* 62 (November 1985), 725–729.

Segel, Elizabeth. "Feminists and Fairy Tales." *School Library Journal,* January 1983, 30–31.

Sparks, Christopher W. "Using Fairy Tales with Younger Children." *The Reading Teacher,* April 1984, 803.

Stewig, John Warren. "Literature and Young Children: Classroom Approaches." Urbana, Ill.: National Council of Teachers of English, n.d., stock no. 72636J.

Storr, Catherine. "Why Folk Tales and Fairy Stories Live Forever." In *Suitable for Children? Controversies in Children's Literature.* Ed. N. Tucker. Berkeley: University of California Press, 1976, pp. 64–73.

Swanson, Barbara. "Participation Storytelling." *School Library Journal,* 31 (April 1985), 48.

Tatar, Maria. "Tests, Tasks, and Trials in the Grimms' Fairy Tales." *Children's Literature,* 13 (1985), 31–48.

Trustees of the Boston Public Library. *Proceedings of Children's Books International IV,* 1979, 13–14.

Walton, Susan. "Telling Tales Out of School—and In." *Education Week,* June 2, 1982, 7.

White, John. "New Slippers for Cinderella?" *Harvard Magazine,* September 1976, 42–46.

Wolfe, Don M. *Language Arts and Life Patterns.* New York: Odyssey Press, 1972, pp. 130–131.

# Bibliography of Children's Books

Aardema, Verna. *Behind the Back of the Mountain*. New York: Dial, 1973.

——. *Why Mosquitoes Buzz in People's Ears*. New York: Dial, 1975.

Anderson, Lonzo. *Arion and the Dolphins*. New York: Scribner's, 1978.

Ayer, Jacqueline (ill.). *Rumplestiltskin*. New York: Harcourt, Brace and World, 1967.

Baker, Betty. *At the Center of the World*. New York: Macmillan, 1973.

Barth, Edna. *Balder and the Mistletoe*. Boston: Houghton Mifflin, 1979.

Baumann, Hans. *The Stolen Fire*. New York: Pantheon, 1974.

Bernstein, Margery, and Janet Kobrin. *The First Morning*. New York: Scribner's, 1976.

——. *How the Sun Made a Promise and Kept It*. New York: Scribner's, 1974.

Bierhorst, John. *The Fire Plume*. New York: Dial, 1969.

——. *The Ring in the Prairie*. New York: Dial, 1970.

Bishop, Claire. *The Five Chinese Brothers*. New York: Coward, McCann, 1938.

Black, Algernon. *The Woman of the Wood*. New York: Holt, Rinehart and Winston, 1973.

Bloch, Marie Halun. *Ukranian Folk Tales*. New York: Coward, McCann, 1964.

Bowman, James Cloyd. *Pecos Bill, The Greatest Cowboy of All Time*. Chicago: Whitman, 1972.

Brodsky, Beverly. *Jonah*. Philadelphia: J. B. Lippincott, 1977.

Brown, Marcia. *Cinderella*. New York: Scribner's, 1954.

——. *Puss in Boots*. New York: Scribner's, 1952.

Bushnaq, Inea (trans.). *Arab Folktales*. New York: Pantheon, 1986.

Calvino, Italo (selector). "Misfortune." In *Italian Folktales*. New York: Pantheon, 1980.

Cauley, Lorinda Bryan (ill.). *Jack and the Beanstalk*. New York: G. P. Putnam's, 1983.

Chandler, Robert (trans.). *Russian Folk Tales*. New York: Shambhala/Random House, 1980.

Chappel, Warren. *They Say Stories*. New York: Alfred A. Knopf, 1960.

Chase, Richard. *The Jack Tales*. Boston: Houghton Mifflin, 1971.

Cohen, Barbara. *I Am Joseph*. New York: Lothrop, Lee and Shepard, 1980.

——. *Lovely Vassilisa*. New York: Atheneum, 1980.

Cole, Joanna (selector). "The Frog Prince." In *Best-Loved Folktales of the World*. Garden City, NY: Doubleday, 1982.

Colum, Padriac. *Legends of Hawaii*. London: Oxford University Press, 1937.

Coolidge, Olivia. *Greek Myths*. Boston: Houghton Mifflin, 1949.

Cooney, Barbara. *The Little Juggler*. New York: Hastings House, 1961.

Creswick, Paul. *Robin Hood*. New York: Macmillan, 1984.

d'Aulaire, Ingri, and Edgar Parin d'Aulaire. *Book of Greek Myths*. Garden City, N.Y.: Doubleday, 1962.

——. *Norse Gods and Giants*. Garden City, N.Y.: Doubleday, 1967.

——. *The Terrible Troll Bird*. Garden City, N.Y.: Doubleday, 1976.

De Armond, Dale. *Berry Woman's Child*. New York: Greenwillow, 1985.

de la Mare, Walter. *Mollie Whuppie*. New York: Farrar, Straus and Giroux, 1983.

de Regniers, Beatrice Schenk. *Little Sister and the Month Brothers*. New York: Seabury, 1976.

Elbourn, Andrew, and Ivan Gantschev. *Noah and the Ark and the Animals*. Natick, Mass.: Picture Book Studio, 1985.

Elkin, Benjamin. *Why the Sun Was Late*. New York: Parent's Magazine Press, 1966.

Farjeon, Eleanor. *The Glass Slipper*. New York: Viking, 1956.

———— . *The Silver Curlew*. New York: Viking, 1954.

Fischer, Hans. *Puss in Boots*. New York: Harcourt, Brace, 1957.

Fish, Helen Dean. *Animals of the Bible*. Philadelphia: J. B. Lippincott, 1937.

Fowles, John, *Cinderella*. London: Jonathan Cape, 1974.

Galdone, Paul. *The History of Mother Twaddle and the Marvelous Adventures of Her Son Jack*. New York: Seabury, 1974.

———— . *Three Aesop Fox Fables*. New York: Seabury, 1971.

———— . *The Three Bears*. New York: Seabury, 1972.

Ginsburg, Mirra (adaptor). *Two Greedy Bears*. New York: Macmillan, 1976.

Glassie, Henry. *Irish Folk Tales*. New York: Pantheon, 1985.

Goble, Paul. *The Great Race of the Birds and Animals*. New York: Bradbury, 1985.

Greene, Ellin. *Clever Cooks*. New York: Lothrop, Lee and Shepard, 1973.

Grimm, Jacob and Wilhelm. *Twelve Dancing Princesses*. Trans. Elizabeth Shub. New York: Scribner's, 1966.

Haley, Gail E. *Jack and the Bean Tree*. New York: Crown, 1986.

———— . *A Story, A Story*. New York: Atheneum, 1970.

Hamilton, Edith. "The Midas Touch." In *Mythology*. Boston: Little, Brown, 1942.

Hamilton, Virginia. *North American Legends*. New York: Philomel, 1979.

Haviland, Virginia. "Billy Beg and the Bull." In *Favorite Fairy Tales Told Around the World*. Boston: Little, Brown, 1985.

Hazeltine, Alice I. *Hero Tales from Many Lands*. New York: Abingdon, 1961.

Heins, Paul (trans.). *Snow White*. Boston: Atlantic Monthly Press, 1974.

Herring, Ann. *The Shoemaker and the Elves*. Tokyo: Gakken, 1971.

Hoffman, Felix. *A Boy Went Out to Gather Pears*. New York: Harcourt, Brace and World, 1966.

Holder, Heidi (ill.). *Aesop's Fables*. New York: Viking, 1981.

Hoogasian-Villa, Susie. *One Hundred Armenian Tales*. Detroit: Wayne State University Press, 1966.

Hosford, Dorothy. "The Death of Baldur." In *Thunder of the Gods*. New York: Henry Holt, 1952.

Houston, James. *Kiviok's Magic Journey*. New York: Atheneum, 1973.

Hutchinson, Veronica. *Henny Penny*. Boston: Little, Brown, 1976.

Hutton, Warwick. *Jonah and the Great Fish*. New York: Atheneum, 1983.

Isaka, Yoshitaro. *Hansel and Gretel*. Tokyo: Gakken, 1971.

Jacobs, Joseph. *Celtic Fairy Tales*. New York: Dover, 1968.

———— . *English Fairy Tales*. New York: Dover, 1967.

———— . *The Fables of Aesop*. New York: Macmillan, 1950.

Jones, Gwyn. *Welsh Legends and Folk-Tales*. New York: H. Z. Walck, 1955.

Junne, I. K. (ed.). *Floating Clouds, Floating Dreams*. Garden City, N.Y.: Doubleday, 1974.

Kellogg, Steven. *Paul Bunyan*. New York: Morrow, 1984.

———— . *Pecos Bill*. New York: Morrow, 1986.

Lang, Andrew (trans.). *Twelve Dancing Princesses*. New York: Holt, Rinehart and Winston, 1966.

Langton, Jane. *The Hedgehog Boy*. New York: Harper, 1985.

Lee, Jeanne M. *Legend of the Li River*. New York: Holt, Rinehart and Winston, 1983.

———— . *Legend of the Milky Way*. New York: Holt, Rinehart and Winston, 1982.

———— . *Toad is the Uncle of Heaven*. New York: Holt, Rinehart and Winston, 1985.

Lester, Julius. *Black Folktales*. New York: Richard W. Baron, 1969.

Lindsey, David L. *The Wonderful Chirrionera.* Austin, Tex.: Heidelberg Publications, 1974.

Lobel, Arnold. *Fables.* New York: Harper and Row, 1980.

——— . *The Rose in My Garden.* New York: Greenwillow, 1984.

Lochhead, Marion. "Whuppity Stourie." In *The Other Country.* London: Hamish Hamilton, 1978.

Logue, Christopher. *Puss in Boots.* New York: Greenwillow Books, 1977.

Louie, Ai-Ling. *Yeh-Shen. A Cinderella Story from China.* New York: Philomel, 1982.

Low, Alice. *Greek Gods and Heroes.* New York: Macmillan, 1985.

MacLeod, Mary. *The Book of King Arthur and His Noble Knights.* Philadelphia: J. B. Lippincott, 1949.

Malcolmson, Anne (ed.). *The Song of Robin Hood.* Boston: Houghton Mifflin, 1947.

Mayer, Mercer. *Two More Moral Tales.* New York: Four Winds, 1974.

McDermott, Gerald. *Anansi the Spider.* New York: Holt, Rinehart and Winston, 1973.

——— . *Arrow to the Sun.* New York: Viking, 1974.

——— . *Daughter of the Earth.* New York: Delacorte, 1984.

——— . *The Knight of the Lion.* New York: Four Winds, 1979.

McGovern, Ann. *Stone Soup.* New York: Scholastic, 1968.

McLeish, Kenneth. *Chicken Licken.* Scarsdale, N.Y.: Bradbury, 1973.

Minard, Rosemary. *Womenfolk and Fairy Tales.* Boston: Houghton Mifflin, 1975.

Montgomerie, Norah, and William Montgomerie. *The Well at the World's End.* London: Bodley Head, 1975.

Mosel, Arlene. *The Funny Little Woman.* New York: Holt, Rinehart and Winston, 1973.

Ness, Evaline. *Tom Tit Tot.* New York: Scribner's, 1965.

Opoku, Kofi Asare. *Speak to the Winds.* New York: Lothrop, Lee and Shepard, 1975.

Peppé, Rodney. *The House That Jack Built.* New York: Delacorte, 1985.

Perrault, Charles. *Cinderella.* New York: H. Z. Walck, 1970.

——— . "Diamonds and Toads." In *Famous French Fairy Tales.* New York: Franklin Watts, 1959.

Phelps, Ethel Johnson. *Tatterhood and Other Tales.* Old Westbury, N.Y.: Feminist Press, 1978.

Polushkin, Maria. *Bubba and Babba.* New York: Crown, 1976.

Pushkin, Aleksandr. *The Tale of the Golden Cockerel.* Trans. Patricia Lowe. New York: Thomas Y. Crowell, 1975.

Pyle, Howard. *Some Merry Adventures of Robin Hood.* New York: Scribner's, 1954.

——— . *The Story of King Arthur and His Knights.* New York: Scribner's, 1954.

Rackham, Arthur. "Snowdrop." In *Grimm's Fairy Tales.* New York: Viking, 1973.

Reed, Allison, *Genesis. The Story of Creation.* New York: Schocken, 1981.

Rees, Ennis. *The Song of Paul Bunyan and Tony Beaver.* New York: Pantheon, 1964.

Roll-Hansen, Joan (selector). *A Time for Trolls.* Oslo: Tanum-Norli, 1983.

Ross, Tony (ill.). *The Enchanted Pig.* New York: Peter Bedrich Books, 1983.

Ross, Tony. *Jack and the Beanstalk.* London: Methuen, 1980.

Rounds, Glen. *Ol' Paul, the Mighty Logger.* New York: Holiday House, 1976.

Sargent, Robert. *Everything Is Difficult at First.* New York: Scribner's, 1968.

Schmid, Eleanore. *Cats' Tales.* New York: North-South, 1984.

Schwartz, Herbert T. "The Forbidden Mountain." In *Windigo and Other Tales of the Ojibways.* Toronto: McClelland and Stewart, 1969.

Segal, Lore (trans.). *The Juniper Tree.* New York: Farrar, Straus and Giroux, 1973.

Serwer, Blanche Luria. "The Witches of Ascalon." In *Let's Steal the Moon.* Boston: Little, Brown, 1970.

Shub, Elizabeth. *About Wise Men and Simpletons*. New York: Macmillan, 1986.

Small, Ernest. *Baba Yaga*. Boston: Houghton Mifflin, 1966.

Stoddard, Sandol. *Five Who Found the Kingdom: New Testament Stories*. Garden City, N.Y.: Doubleday, 1981.

Sutherland, Zena, and Myra Cohn Livingston. *The Scott, Foresman Anthology of Children's Literature*. Glenview, Ill.: Scott, Foresman, 1984.

Tardi, Jacques (ill.). *The Enchanted Pig*. Mankato, Minn.: Creative Education, 1984.

Turkle, Brinton. *Deep in the Forest*. New York: E. P. Dutton, 1976.

Untermeyer, Louis. *Aesop's Fables*. New York: Golden, 1966.

Weil, Lisl. *Esther*. New York: Atheneum, 1980.

Weiss, Jaqueline Shachter. *Young Brer Rabbit*. Owings Mills, Md.: Stemmer House, 1985.

White, Anne Terry (adaptor). *The Golden Treasury of Myths and Legends*. New York: Golden, 1959.

Winthrop, Elizabeth. *A Child Is Born*. New York: Holiday House, 1983.

Yolen, Jane (ed.). *Favorite Folktales from Around the World*. New York: Pantheon, 1986.

Zaum, Marjorie. *Catlore*. New York: Atheneum, 1985.

Zemach, Margot. *It Could Always Be Worse*. New York: Farrar, Straus and Giroux, 1976.

———. *The Little Red Hen*. New York: Farrar, Straus and Giroux, 1983.

# POETRY:
# EXPANDING
# PERCEPTIONS

HEY DIDDLE · DIDDLE

Copyright 1897 by F. Warne & Co.

## The Wind

*One day I went outside*
*And heard the wind whisper—*
*It made the leaves wave.*

*I whistled and the wind whistled back—*
*It went up, down, around,*
*And made a chair for me.*

*I sat down and suddenly*
*I rose high in the air—*
*I rose smooth and the wind was gentle.*

*I looked down and saw the world—*
*It was beautiful.*
*I kept going higher and higher—*
*It was beautiful.*

*Then I heard a voice,*
*A calming voice,*
*It was the wind—*
*And it said to me,*
*"This is what is to come. . . ."*

*It brought me back,*
*And now every time*
*I hear the wind*
*I'm not afraid—*
*I'm glad.*

                              *Jim*


Young children react eagerly to rhyme, repeating with delight the lines of Mother Goose, singing enthusiastically the poetry in songs they are taught,[1] and responding sensitively to the rhythmic pulse of poems read by their teachers. Most young children seem to have a natural appetite for poetry. A few students, like the one whose poem is printed above, continue to express ideas freely in poetic form beyond the middle grades.

---

[1]An example of a fine collection of poetry set to music is John Bierhorst's *Songs of the Chippewa* (New York: Farrar, Straus and Giroux, 1974). Collected originally on the western shores of the Great Lakes during the early part of the twentieth century, these songs are characteristically clear and brief; many are in minor key, and the words are plaintive.

# KINDS OF POETRY FOR CHILDREN

The array of poetic forms available to primary-grade children includes Mother Goose rhymes, poems set to music in folk songs, and poetry in picture books. Narrative poetry, limericks, free verse, and concrete poetry challenge intermediate-grade children.

## MOTHER GOOSE RHYMES

Many children are first introduced to poetry when parents and others share Mother Goose rhymes with them. Collections of these traditional nursery verses form a large part of the literature found in preschool and kindergarten classrooms. Given their great age, the continuing popularity of these poems is rather amazing. This popularity is documented in a recent edition of *Children's Books in Print*, which lists fifty-three different collections of Mother Goose rhymes.

Mother Goose rhymes are part of the oral tradition, having sprung from the spoken language of common folk and nobility. Widely known as early as the seventeenth century, they are so old that their origins are uncertain.[2] What accounts for their long life?

Walter de la Mare, himself a poet, introduced his *Nursery Rhymes for Certain Times* by saying that rhymes "free the fancy, charm tongue and ear, delight the inward eye, and many of them are tiny masterpieces of word craftsmanship . . . they are a direct short cut into poetry itself."

**THE APPEAL OF MOTHER GOOSE.** Mother Goose rhymes in particular appeal to the young for several reasons.

### 1. Mother Goose rhymes often include repeated refrains.

The pleasure of anticipating something familiar or of saying the refrain along with others accounts for the popularity of some of the verses. An example is the simple "fa la, la la lal de," which is repeated after each of the four lines in the rhyme about two birds sitting on a stone. This is one

---

[2]An extensive analysis of the history of Mother Goose rhymes, *The Real Personages of Mother Goose* by Katherine E. Thomas (New York: Lothrop, Lee and Shepard, 1930), includes details about the real people involved, such as Thomas Fleet, reputed to have published an edition of the verses, and Dame Goose, thought to have lived in Boston. A briefer treatment is in *Children Experience Literature* by Bernard Lonsdale and Helen K. Mackintosh (New York: Random House, 1973, pp. 184–197).

of several verses included in *And So My Garden Grows*, by Peter Spier. The illustrator links the unrelated verses via the device of two children who take an extended walk through the lush greenness of the Italian countryside. Because of this device, the unrelated verses seem to tell a coherent, if not completely sequential, story.

### 2. *Many of these rhymes tell interesting stories.*

"The farmer went trotting," is the first line of a pleasant verse in *Fee Fi Fo Fum*, by Raymond Briggs, which recounts a sequence of events— something that could have happened. Drawings by Briggs show vigorous action as the dappled horse, head down toward the cobblestones and rear feet in the air, bucks off the farmer: the portly gentleman sails through the air to the left; the daughter flys off to the right.

### 3. *Many of these rhymes are sheer nonsense, lacking logic but not needing it.*

A strong rhyme and rhythm make these verses a delight to the ear, enjoyable solely for the flow of sound they provide. The following rhyme included in Briggs's *The White Land*, is a good example:

> *Barber, barber, shave a pig.*
> *How many hairs will make a wig?*
> *Four and twenty, that's enough.*
> *Give the barber a pinch of snuff.*

This one can be found in *One Misty Moisty Morning*, by Mitchell Miller:

> *Baby and I*
> *Were baked in a pie,*
> *The gravy was wonderful hot.*
> *We had nothing to pay*
> *to the baker that day*
> *And so we crept out of the pot.*

Children can appreciate the rhyme scheme and the bouncing rhythm even though the words don't make sense. This is one of twenty-one lesser-known verses in Miller's collection, which is illustrated with soft pencil drawings in a quasi-medieval style. The book is best used with an individual child: the pictures are too faint to be seen at a distance.

Many children grow up listening to "Jack and Jill" or "Humpty-Dumpty" again and again. Hearing verses like these is like meeting old friends.

In *Quentin Blake's Nursery Rhyme Book,* there are a number of the familiar rhymes, such as "Goosey, Goosey Gander." But there are also unfamiliar characters, such as "Robin the Bobbin the big-bellied Ben," "Jeremiah" who blew the fire, and "Pretty John Watts." All are brought to visual life in Blake's eccentric watercolors.

**A DIFFERENT SOCIETY.** Though they are commonly shared in schools today, Mother Goose rhymes were not originally intended for the young. Many are strikingly unsuitable for those of tender years, even by today's relaxed standards. Describing the centuries in which these verses were created, Opie and Opie (1951) have pointed out that

> . . . children were treated as "grown-ups in miniature." In paintings we see them wearing clothes which were replicas of those worn by their elders. The conduct and the power of understanding we find expected of them were those of an adult. Many parents saw nothing unusual in their children hearing strong language or savouring strong drink. And behavior was not as abashed as it is today. The spectacle of their fathers asleep under the table and in other "even more lamentable positions" would not be unfamiliar to them.

Most versions of Mother Goose rhymes published today omit the more controversial verses. Some collections do contain poems teachers may not want to read to children; teachers should therefore screen these books carefully. *Cakes and Custard,* by Brian Alderson, includes several verses whose violence is typical of the era in which they were originally written.

> *Old Mother Roundabout*
> *Knocking all the kids about*
> *Outside Elsie's door.*
> *Up comes Elsie with a great big stick*
> *And lets her know what for.*

Alderson chose verses that do not minimize the unpleasant aspects of life: a child is boiled in a pot; a husband shoves an unloved wife up a chimney; someone throws a man downstairs; a child has a drunken father. Helen Oxenbury uses pastel colors and subtle exaggeration of body shapes in her illustrations. However, the pictures are reminiscent of the cartoons of Charles Addams in their humor; the wit will escape most children.

*Mother Goose Lost,* by Nicholas Tucker, is another collection. In both verses and illustrations, this book does not take the conventional, bland approach. On the title page, Mother Goose squints through a pince-nez and her bewhiskered chin thrusts forward to almost meet her hooked, bony nose.

Full-color pictures by Trevor Stubley illustrate the verses. One shows a dissolute couple about to enter a shop marked "Wine and Spirits":

> *Oh my dear, what a cold you've got,*
> *Come with me to the brandy shop;*
> *There you shall have something hot*
> *To cure that very bad cold you've got.*

These verses and others illustrate the tension between good and evil, a central fact of life commented on by Lynn (1985), who provides an extended eleven-page analysis of them. She sees the verses as being rooted in a particular time and culture, yet exemplifying universal life experiences.

**FORM IN THE RHYMES.**　Mother Goose rhymes vary noticeably in form. Many are miniature jewels that recount a story in four brief lines:

> *Hark, hark! the dogs do bark!*
> 　*Beggars are coming to town:*
> *Some in jags and some in rags,*
> 　*And some in velvet gowns.*

In *The Real Mother Goose*, from which this comes, several verses are arranged on each page. The illustrations by Blanche Fisher Wright, in black line and simple pastel colors, have only minimal backgrounds. This particular edition is still in print seventy years after its first publication.

Sometimes such minimal verses are fleshed out with pictures. *This Little Pig*, by Leonard B. Lubin, has many full-color, full-page illustrations interspersed between lines of text. In the quasi-historical, detail-crammed pictures, elaborately garbed pigs, ducks, and frogs act out the verse but also extend it. For example, the poem line is simply "This little pig stayed home"; but the pictures show that while at home, he hauled water in the wheelbarrow, hoed radishes, clipped hedges, talked with friend Frog, and went fishing. This book should be shared with children with adult guidance because the involved visual style may not be immediately appealing to them.

In contrast to shorter rhymes, "The Fox's Foray," included in *The Oxford Dictionary of Nursery Rhymes*, is an extended narrative, telling a complete story that begins

> *A fox jumped up one winter's night,*
> *And begged the moon to give him light,*
> *For he'd many miles to trot that night*
> *Before he reached his den O!*
> 　*Den O! Den O!*

*Using a limited array of colors (shades of green, brown, gold, and rust), Leonard B. Lubin creates a highly patterned, two-dimensional world. The forms are arranged for their decorative value, not as a realistic rendering of objects.* From *This Little Pig* by Leonard B. Lubin. Copyright © 1985 by Leonard B. Lubin. By permission of Lothrop, Lee & Shepard Books (A Division of William Morrow).

Several verses later, the story ends happily for the fox and his family; they are picking the bones of the goose over which Old Mother Slipper Slopper had despaired earlier. This tale is part of *The Mother Goose Treasury*, by Raymond Briggs. The book opens with a picture of stout Mother Goose, a round-chinned lump of a woman in lavender dress and hat (firmly attached with a long hat pin), determinedly riding a white goose through the sky.

**KINDS OF RHYMES.** At first glance, the rhymes in Mother Goose collections may seem fairly homogeneous, but a more careful look reveals that there are several different kinds.

### 1. Some verses are ones children repeat while playing active games.

*Peas porridge hot,*
*Peas porridge cold,*
*Peas porridge in the pot*
*Nine days old.*[3]

A variation of this rhyme appears in *The Rooster Crows,* a collection featuring realistic lithographs in full color by Maud and Miska Petersham, who won the Caldecott Medal for this work.

### 2. Some verses are counting-out rhymes.

An example of this type comes from *Brian Wildsmith's Mother Goose:*

*One, two, three, four, five,*
*Once I caught a fish alive,*
*Six, seven, eight, nine, ten,*
*But then I let it go again.*

For some of the rhymes in this volume, illustrator Wildsmith created an almost full-page painting in his usual, pleasantly casual watercolor and crayon style. The bright colors are intensified by the generous use of contrasting white paper. This book is noteworthy for its page layout, for example, the parallel placement of the figures on facing pages (the two little girls drawn for "Little Polly Flinders" and "Curley Locks" both have their backs to the reader). In another place, Wildsmith arranges three blocks of space on each of two facing pages to create a formal balance, as shown below.

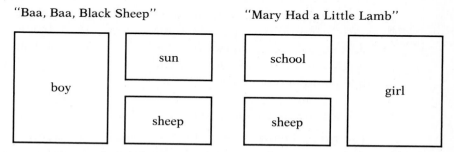

"Baa, Baa, Black Sheep"    "Mary Had a Little Lamb"

Another old counting rhyme children have enjoyed for years is John Langstaff's *Over in the Meadow,* described more fully on page 281.

---

[3]According to William S. Baring-Gould and Ceil Baring-Gould in *The Annotated Mother Goose* (New York: Bramhall House, 1962), this was a clapping game played by children on cold days to keep their hands warm.

### 3. Some rhymes help children learn numbers, letters, and other designations.

An example is a description of the months of the year, which is included in *Mother Goose*, illustrated by Tasha Tudor. It begins:

*January brings the snow,*
*Makes our feet and fingers glow.*
*February brings the rain,*
*Thaws the frozen lake again.*

It concludes with:

*Dull November brings the blast,*
*Then the leaves are whirling fast.*
*Chill December brings the sleet,*
*Blazing fire and Christmas treat.*

This collection features almost eighty verses. Soft pastel illustrations alternate with black-and-white pencil sketches.

Children can learn the days of the week from *Solomon Grundy*, in which the title character's life extends just seven days. Full-page, full-color paintings by Susan Ramsay Hoguet illustrate each phrase, for instance, "married on Wednesday." Interspersed with these are an additional double-page spread and a single picture between each of the phrases. These additional pages add extensive details to the bare-bones plot of the verse itself.

### 4. Some rhymes are lullabies, prayers, and songs.

Several examples of this type are found in *Book of Nursery and Mother Goose Rhymes*, by Marguerite de Angeli. She includes rhymes whose first lines are "Hush-a-bye, baby, on the tree top," "Bye, baby bunting," and "Hush, baby, my doll, I pray you don't cry." The book features full-color paintings of round-faced, pleasant children daintily dressed in styles from an undefined historic period.

### 5. Some verses are riddles and tongue twisters.

The riddle below is part of *Chinese Mother Goose Rhymes*, by Robert Wyndham, a collection of rhymes Chinese mothers have taught their children for hundreds of years.

*My boat is turned up at both ends;*
*All storms it meets it weathers.*
*On its body you'll find not a single board,*
*For it's covered all over with feathers.*

*Daily we fill it with rice;*
*It's admired by all whom we meet*
*You will find not a crack in my boat,*
*But you'll find underneath it two feet!*

What is it?[4]

This Caldecott honor book contains humorous, highly patterned pastel illustrations by Ed Young. Two lines of calligraphy in pale blue are arranged down the outside edge of each page. In addition, the pale blue line is used as an encompassing and unifying feature in that the figures are segmented by it, creating an effect similar to cloisonné.

### 6. Some verses are nonsense-humor rhymes.

The following comes from *Mother Goose; or the Old Nursery Rhymes:*

*Here am I, little jumping Joan,[5]*
*When nobody's with me,*
*I'm always alone.*

Kate Greenaway's illustration for this poem shows a demure, bonneted girl, gowned in blue with a sash flowing behind. The picture of Joan jumping between rocks is typical of the portrayals of children throughout the book, comporting themselves with dignity in pastoral settings. The book features forty rhymes, with a picture above and a verse beneath on each page.

A teacher might ask children to compare the illustration of Joan in Greenaway's book with the one by Michael Hague in *Mother Goose.* Despite her more modern appearance, Hague's Joan seems strangely motionless, in contrast with the energy of Greenaway's.

### 7. Some Mother Goose rhymes are ballads commemorating actual occurrences.

An example of this type is the story of "Good King Arthur" in *Ring O' Roses,* illustrated by L. Leslie Brooke. Two full-color and two black-and-white drawings accompany this three-stanza poem about the king, some stolen barley meal, and the queen. The small details in the pictures set the scene realistically in a particular time and place.

---

[4]It is a duck.
[5]In *The Annotated Mother Goose* (New York: Bramhall House, 1962), Baring-Gould says that "jumping Joan" was originally a cant term for a woman of easy virtue.

### 8. Some of the rhymes are political or religious diatribes.

*Hector Protector*, for example, has identifiable historical antecedents. Hector was the Earl of Hertford, sent to invade Scotland by King Henry VIII. All of this is lost in the mists of time; what remains is a simple plot and ear-tickling rhymes. In Maurice Sendak's version, Hector is an obstreperous little boy who is sent by his mother to take a cake box to the queen. On his way, he subdues a lion and a snake. The queen, reading a Mother Goose Book on her throne, is enraged by Hector's intrusion. She sends him home; Hector is put to bed, and his pet crow happily feasts on the forgotten cake. Sendak fleshed out the minimal five-line verse into a full-color, twenty-page retelling. The pictures are crammed with details that enrich the story. As Nodelman (1983) points out, it is precisely the discrepancy between the "vague words" and the pictures, which tell a different and far more specific story, that accounts for the success of this book.

**MOTHER GOOSE VARIATIONS.** Testimony to the popularity of Mother Goose rhymes is the frequency with which contemporary authors create books based on the originals. In *Mother Goose Riddle Rhymes*, illustrator Joseph Low has created a variant for children who understand the rebus principle.[6] The twenty-two rhymes presented in rebus form are accompanied by a glossary of picture/word equivalencies. The book also includes a complete word version of each rhyme. The freshness of the illustrations is striking; more than thirty years after publication, they are still vibrant and full of life.

A similar collection is *The Rebus Treasury*, compiled by Jean Marzollo, which includes a section of rebus rhymes (for instance "Little Boy Blue") and a second one of rebus songs (for example, "Ring Around the Rosy"). Artist Carol Carson derived the stamp art used in this book from nineteenth-century line engravings and more recent line drawings.

In *The Charles Addams Mother Goose*, the original verses are used. The artist's usual macabre humor is softened a bit—but only a little. His humorous illustrations show a small, toothy lizard emerging from the shell of Humpty Dumpty, the farmer's wife wielding an electric knife, the old lady under the hill occupying a fallout shelter, and so on.

In *Ms. Goose*, Tamar Hoffs attempted to change the stereotypical views of girls presented in some of the original poems. For example, the stanzas

---

[6]The rebus principle is a way of recording ideas in which a picture of an object is used in place of a word that is pronounced the same way. For example, a picture of a bee replaces the word "be."

of one original Mother Goose rhyme begin "What are little boys made of?" and "What are little girls made of?" and end by attributing quite different qualities to the sexes. To avoid this sexism, Hoffs used the original beginnings but ended both stanzas identically: in his version, both boys and girls are made of "lots of muscles and red corpuscles." Although technically more accurate, this altered version lacks the sparkle and interesting use of language found in the original.

Another attempt to update Mother Goose concentrates on modernizing the visual images rather than the words. *Mother Goose Comes to Cable Street*, by Rosemary Stones and Andrew Mann, illustrates the verse "Little Tommy Tittlemouse" with a black child fishing from the pier at London's wharf and being threatened away by a contemporary bobby. This book was produced by the Children's Rights Workshop, a group concerned with "reassessing and extending the intellectual . . . choices available to children in a modern society, including their literature." The picture for "There was an old woman, And nothing she had" shows her over a pint of ale in a pub. That for "Girls and boys come out to play" depicts black, Indian, and other minorities at a carnival. "I do not like thee, Doctor Fell" is illustrated with a female physician. The bright, detailed pictures are very broadly executed.

**EVALUATING MOTHER GOOSE BOOKS.** Collections of Mother Goose rhymes are most typically presented in picture-book format, so the criteria given in Chapter 4 are also appropriate for selecting Mother Goose books. There are some additional criteria specifically related to Mother Goose books.

1. What is the balance between familiar and unfamiliar rhymes? The number of Mother Goose rhymes is great, but the number children actually encounter is small. Some of the better-known rhymes are reprinted in every collection; other equally interesting ones languish unnoticed.
2. What is the total number of rhymes included in the collection? Although it is pleasant to have full-page illustrations for each rhyme, this results in fewer rhymes.
3. If there are many illustrations, does the page layout facilitate understanding? Is the illustration right next to the verse it illustrates?
4. Are there reference aids, such as an index or table of contents, so adults or children can easily find rhymes they wish to read or reread?
5. Does the arrangement in some way enhance the rhymes? Are the verses grouped in some way to illustrate similarities or differences in topic, form, or main characters?

**COMPARING VARIATIONS.** Like other traditional literature, Mother Goose rhymes are available in many editions. The artwork in different editions is often worth comparing and contrasting. Teachers can stimulate oral-language development by sharing several illustrations for the same verse and asking children to note similarities and differences in the pictures.

This technique can be used with some verses about London Bridge. Peter Spier chose a very complete text with all the repetitions for his book-length version, *London Bridge is Falling Down!* It opens with two related stanzas not usually included: "See-saw, sacaradown"[7] and "See-saw, Jack in the hedge," which precede the title page. The title page is crammed with architectural and other details, depicting the exact moment at which the medieval bridge falls. The crowds of people watching from other bridges and on boats give an impression of a bustling London. The drawings bristle with detail: wash hangs from the windows, slop pails are emptied into the river, and vendors in rowboats beguile ships' passengers with fresh fruits and vegetables.

Ed Emberley's version of *London Bridge Is Falling Down* is more fanciful than Spier's. Emberley uses pastel colors and a more decorative, circular line. The refrain is reduced to a bare minimum:

> *Build it up with iron bars.*
> *Iron bars will bend and break.*

This contrasts with the extended form in Spier:

> *Build it up with iron and steel,*
> *Iron and steel, iron and steel,*
> *Build it up with iron and steel,*
> *My fair lady.*

Instead of ending the rhyme with the dog running away, as Spier does, Emberley includes four more stanzas, ending with a prisoner carrying his ball and chain to jail. Although Emberley's illustrations are whimsically elaborate, they provide no feeling of the crowded, busy nature of the city as Spier's do.

Variations of "Yankee Doodle" in books of that title by Edward Bangs and Dr. Richard Schackburg are also appropriate for comparison purposes. Versions of *The House That Jack Built* by Antonio Frasconi and by Paul Galdone, as well as the one included in *R. Caldecott's Picture Book (No. 1)*, can also be compared and contrasted.

---

[7]This verse is also included in Phillip Reed's *Mother Goose and Nursery Rhymes* (New York: Atheneum, 1963). This Caldecott honor book includes simple wood engravings in a variety of arrangements around the verses.

Although Mother Goose rhymes are most often used with young children, Poe (1981) describes using these verses as the core of an elective children's literature course she teaches in high school. She finds the verses help students understand poetic devices such as rhyme, rhythm, assonance, and alliteration. In addition, the students respond favorably to the orderly word patterns and sound repetitions.

## POEMS SET TO MUSIC

A pleasant way to introduce conventionally rhymed poetry is through the use of folk songs. Most of these have been set to music that can be easily played on a piano or guitar.

John Langstaff illustrated many well-made books. *Over in the Meadow* is a popular staple in kindergarten classrooms. This set of verses about mother and baby animals is handsomely bedecked with realistic lithographs of the animals in their natural habitats. Mother froggie, spider, robin, and bee give instructions to their young for appropriate activities. Langstaff's illustrations for this song can be compared with those by Ezra Jack Keats, which are rendered in both paint and cut-paper. Keats's pictures bleed to the edge of the pages, and the print is superimposed on them. Another version of this song by Olive A. Wadsworth features pleasantly large, soft-edged illustrations by Mary Maki Rae that fill the pages to the edges with swirling designs.

Another folk song illustrated by John Langstaff is one that was written down more than four hundred years ago in Scotland. It also features animals, but this time the main character is a debonair frog who takes his demure bride on a honeymoon to France. *Frog Went A-Courtin'* was told and sung, rather than read, before it was brought to the United States. Therefore, it is particularly appropriate to help children learn to sing this, using the simple music Langstaff provides. Chris Conover uses different music in her edition, featuring considerably brighter and more fanciful full- and double-page pictures. Mary O'Hara presents another variant in *Traditional Irish Folk Songs* (Everest Records, #FS 344), which ends: "The big duck came and 'gobobbled' him up."

Other titles by Langstaff in folk song format include *Oh, A-Hunting We Will Go*, featuring animal characters, and *The Swapping Boy*, with a human main character. Rhodes (1981) recommends the former title because its rhyme and rhythm make it a highly predictable and thus effective resource for reading and writing instruction.

Christine Price tells of Tom Pearse's efforts to regain his grey mare in poetry set to music in *Widdecombe Fair*. Soft grey-green woodcuts accom-

*The device of the crooked road, appearing to narrow as it goes deeper into the picture, creates a sense of deep space.* Illustration by Beth and Joe Krush reproduced from *The Swapping Boy* by John Langstaff, copyright © 1960 by John Langstaff and Beth and Joe Krush, by permission of Harcourt Brace Jovanovich.

pany this English song. Tom's seven companions try to help but to no avail, so on stormy nights along the lee, people still search for a gashly white horse, as the refrain continues, "All along down along out along lee." Another version is *On to Widdecombe Fair*, by Patricia Lee Gauch. Plainly bordered, full-color pictures by Trina Schart Hyman are set above the text on pages that alternate with pages containing black-and-white drawings above and below centered text. There is an abundance of historic detail, but viewers are not overwhelmed by elaboration for its own sake. The music is provided at the end for eight verses.

Many old folk songs feature heroines with unusual abilities. "Sweet Betsy," a ballad written in the 1850s, tells of the strength one heroine needed to get her family to the west coast from Missouri. On the long, exhausting trip, Betsy wards off marauding Indians, hunger, and disillusionment until finally she and her husband accidentally discover gold. The illustrations in *Sweet Betsy from Pike*, by Roz Abisch and Boche Kaplan, are done in felt on burlap with other materials used as decoration.

Other heroines in folk songs include the "young thing [who] cannot leave her mother" in *Billy Boy*, by Richard Chase, and Lou in *Skip to My Lou*, by Robert Quackenbush. The main character in *Go Tell Aunt Rhody*, by Aliki, is an older female. Bright-colored endpapers in a patchwork-type design introduce this song, which came to the United States after beginning as part of an opera in France. Words are arranged below full-color pictures on facing pages. At the end, resourceful Aunt Rhody retrieves the dead goose and takes it home, where she plucks it and uses the feathers to make a quilt.

The two-volume *Songs of Innocence* includes poetry about both animals and people. Ellen Raskin composed music for and illustrated William Blake's poems. The first volume has only the poems and Raskin's simplified, decorative woodcuts in steel blue, dull gold, green, and burnt orange. The second volume, whose illustrations complement but do not duplicate those in the first, adds piano music with guitar chords to the poems. Children will enjoy learning some of the songs. They might profit from comparing the companion pictures for the same poem.

*In the Trail of the Wind*, a collection of Indian poems, includes primarily songs but also other forms such as prayers and incantations. This poetry is quite unlike the cheerful, rhyming folk songs described above. These verses originated in oral sharing among people who came to North America about 12,000 B.C. John Bierhorst presents them in literal translations with some words rearranged and a few added or subtracted to make the meaning comprehensible. The result is simple, expressive, nonrhyming poetry.

> *From the place of the south*
> *They come,*
> *The birds.*
> *Hear the sound of their passing screams.*
> > (*Chippewa*)
>
> *In time of rain I come:*
> *I can sing among the flowers:*
> *I utter my song: my heart is glad.*
> > (*Aztec*)

Locating further poems set to music can be facilitated by consulting the book by Peterson and Fenton (1979), a subject, title, and first-line index to 298 books of children's songs.

## POETRY IN PICTURE BOOKS

Many poems for intermediate-grade children are available in books by themselves. *The Warmint,* by Walter de la Mare, captures the delight and frustration of knowing a spirited child. With a conventional rhyme scheme and a strong rhythm, the poem relates the misadventures of the otherwise unnamed "little thing" whose pranks annoy and aggravate adults. Evaline Ness's black-line drawings, printed on blue with some added grey, evoke the poem's Victorian era.

Two criteria are important for evaluating picture books whose text is poetry.

1. Are both the art and the poetry good? Does the artwork function as effective art? Is the poetry strong enough to stand on its own? Would it be interesting poetry without the pictures?
2. Does the art match the poetry in level of sophistication? Although each may be good in itself, the words and pictures may not fit together well. Complex, richly imaginative pictures with many details to be studied are not appropriate with simple poems, for example.

*The Charge of the Light Brigade* has as its text the poem by Tennyson with a very traditional rhyme scheme, yet the book is illustrated with quite imaginative contemporary paintings by Alice and Martin Provensen. Notably unrealistic pictures accompany a markedly realistic poem. The contrast is uncomfortable, and it raises a question about the book's potential audience. The poem itself seems appropriate for at least fifth- or sixth-grade readers/listeners, but the format (full-color pictures on every page) suggests a much younger audience.

An even more perplexing problem is presented when either the art or the poetry is inferior. Illustrated poetry books must combine good poetry and fine art. *Tonight at Nine,* by Janosch, is an example that has good art but poor poetry. Paintings boldly done in opaque tempera have a certain slapdash charm. The pleasant array of colors is simple and appealing. The poetry, however, is mundane at best, and not worth sharing with children. The rhyme scheme in one four-line stanza about a rooster crowing to announce an animal concert is *might/tonight* and *nine/fine,* and the rhythm of the lines is predictable and almost sing-song.

## NARRATIVE POETRY

Narrative poetry tells a coherent, sequential story in rhyme. Because it is based on sophisticated rhythm patterns and requires that the rhymes make sense, it is highly complex poetry to write. As such, it is probably not appropriate for children to attempt writing it themselves unless they have had extensive experience writing other poetry. Nevertheless, students should hear narrative poetry so they become aware of it as one of the various forms available to poets.[8]

All sorts of topics can be treated in narrative verse. *In the Middle of the Night*, by Aileen Fisher, is a charming story about a small girl who wants only one thing for her birthday: to be able to stay out at night and see all the things there are to see. Finally, her family consents; she and her father take a night walk together. The many small creatures fascinate them both, though she doesn't realize how pleased her father is until the very end of their walk. Pleasant casein paintings by Adrienne Adams accompany the verses.

*The Winter Bear*, by Ruth Craft, is a realistic account of three children who set out to explore the countryside in a rural area and rescue a knitted bear and bring it home. The stone fence, the style of the houses, and the openness of the landscape make the setting appear British. The rhyme scheme is conventional, and its familiarity is comforting. Erik Blegvad did artwork suited to the verses: uncomplicated illustrations with no self-conscious stylistic intrusions. The same kind of pleasantly understated style serves equally well in two collections of nursery rhymes chosen by Lenore Blegvad: *This Little Pig-A-Wig* and *The Parrot in the Garret*.

Not all stories told in poetry are realistic. The narrative poem in *The Woman Who Lived in Holland*, by Mildred Howells, is based on an unrealistic but humorous premise. An old lady is so scrupulously clean that she polishes the faces off the children and her doorstep into the ground. When last seen, she is sailing into the evening sky to polish the stars. The black, gray, and white illustrations have an unusual emptiness. Despite some architectural details—steeply pitched roofs, a stone wall, and a windmill—there is no real sense of being anywhere in particular.

Equally improbable happenings occur in *Always Room for One More*,

---

[8]For example, see *In Granny's Garden*, by Sarah Harrison and Mike Wilks (New York: Holt, Rinehart and Winston, 1980), in which the narrator reminisces about his childhood wanderings through the garden, "jungly wild." Pages of text with minimal black-and-white decorations are interspersed with wordless double-page spreads in full color. The calm, even detached, illustrations contrast effectively with the text action.

Sorche Nic Leodhas's story of Lachie MacLachlan, his wife, and their ten bairns. They live comfortably in their wee house in the heather until Lachie's openhearted hospitality results in too many guests. The teacher should practice alone before reading this rhymed story out loud to children because of the number of unfamiliar words and the pronounced rhythm.

Two versions of Eugene Field's poem "Wynken, Blynken and Nod" demonstrate that the same unrealistic narrative can be illustrated both fancifully and realistically. *Wynken, Blynken and Nod* with pictures by two-time Caldecott-Medal winner Barbara Cooney, features white chalk on very dark blue/black paper, creating pleasantly nubby drawings that emphasize the fantasy in the words. In contrast, in another version, artist Susan Jeffers shows her three children (and an orange cat) in a more specific context than does Cooney. The details, the environment, and the characterizations all make this a much more realistic rendition of the poem than Cooney's cool, more distant interpretation.

Narrative poetry can be used to motivate experiences in plot completion. What children write need not be in rhyme. One teacher used Arnold Lobel's *The Man Who Took the Indoors Out*. She read the poem to the place where eccentric Bellwood is trying to solve the problem of his runaway furniture, which escaped when he invited it out to take the air. Two second-grade children wrote the following solutions:

A few weeks later Bellwood Bouse went for a swim. Then he saw his things. He was not mad at them. He was double mad at them! Then the piano played a tune on itself that calmed Bellwood down. They all went home and they lived happily ever after.

*Adam*

One fine day Bellwood Bouse was sitting in his white wicker rocker. He heard a knock at the door. So he opened it, and in walked his pictures. They said, "Sorry, but we need our fun, too." A few days later his chair, sofa and bed came in, and they said, "Sorry, but we need our fun, too." Then the next day all his dishes came back and they said the same thing. Bellwood Bouse was so happy he could cry!

*Lynn*

In addition to such narrative poems as those discussed above, there are some that appeal to middle-school students. For example, Lewis Carroll's imaginative language in "Jabberwocky" is available in book form illustrated with Jane Breskin Zalben's watercolors. The language, including many words that Carroll simply made up, requires listeners sophisticated enough to not be confused by it. In Zalben's pictures, background details are minimal and are grouped to leave extensive white space that contrasts

**An eerie, full-color painting is full of details that both support the strangeness of the words and break through and surround the narrow white frame.** Illustration by Gillian McClure from *Tog the Ribber or Granny's Tale* by Paul Coltman. Copyright © 1985 by Gillian McClure. Reprinted by permission of Farrar, Straus & Giroux, Inc.

effectively with the details. The poem is set in the prose context from which it is taken and is followed by a section entitled "Annotations by Humpty Dumpty," in which Humpty Dumpty explains what Carroll's words mean.

Another longer narrative poem for intermediate-grade readers/listeners is Paul Coltman's *Tog the Ribber or Granny's Tale*. Like Carroll's poem, Coltman's has nonce (or made-up) words. The unfamiliar vocabulary tickles the ear: "glazering glom," "sibble on my lones," and "hobbled clitter clotter after." What makes the eerie tale come to vivid life are the full-color, full-page paintings by Gillian McClure. In addition to the full-page pictures facing the text, the text pages are also decorated. This book provides an invigorating experience for teachers and students—it can be listened to and looked at again and again.

## LIMERICKS

Because of their appealing nonsense, limericks delight children of all ages. However, the form itself is highly controlled, which means that writing limericks is appropriate only for upper-grade students. Teachers lay the groundwork for later writing experiences when they begin reading limericks to primary-grade youngsters. *The Golden Book of Fun and Nonsense*, by Louis Untermeyer, includes many limericks to delight young listeners:

> *There was an Old Man of Peru,*
> *Who watched his wife making a stew;*
> *But once by mistake,*
> *In a stove she did bake*
> *That unfortunate man of Peru.*

Edward Lear is most often associated with this form; many of his best are included in *Limericks by Lear*. These are accompanied by Lois Ehlert's semiabstract drawings in flat, bright colors. The illustrations incorporate ink-stamped designs and much dry-brush work. Some of Lear's limericks, as well as funny poetry by Lewis Carroll, Mother Goose rhymes, and an English version of the German poem "Struwwelpeter" ("Shock-Headed or Slovenly Peter") are found in *A Book of Nonsense*, by Ernest Rhys.

Some limericks depend on word play only older children, who understand homonyms, can respond to, for example:

> *There was a young girl, a sweet lamb,*
> *Who smiled as she entered a tram.*
> *After she had embarked*
> *The conductor remarked,*
> *"Your fare!" and she said, "Yes, I am."*

**A whimsical watercolor in pastel shades is sharpened with pen line and set formally on the page within ruled borders.** Illustration from *The Book of Pigericks* by Arnold Lobel. Copyright © 1983 by Arnold Lobel. Reprinted by permission of Harper & Row, Publishers, Inc.

This is one of many selections in *Merriment! A Treasury for Young Readers*, by Sean Manley and Gogo Lewis, which features both prose and poetry that appeal to older readers. The poems, riddles, and quotes are small gems. The prose, by such writers as James Thurber and O. Henry among others, requires a longer attention span than do the poems.

Several limericks in *They've Discovered a Head in the Box for the Bread* appeal deliciously to children's sense of the macabre. Fernando Krahn's black line drawings accompany this varied collection by John E. Brewton and Lorraine A. Blackburn.

The popular artist/illustrator Arnold Lobel turned his hand to this tightly constrained poetic form, and the result was a thoroughly delightful collection, *The Book of Pigericks*. This volume features a single limerick on each page, with one to three pictures above it, all formally set off with ruled lines and corner decorations. One porcine inhabitant, the "fast pig from East Flushing," is followed on the next page by the "slow pig from Decatur"; the "young pig from Schenectady" is followed by the "old pig from South Goshen." Lobel's pictures and words demonstrate that a firmly defined poetic form does not have to inhibit a truly creative person.

## FREE VERSE

Free verse is not readily accepted by children because it is characterized by a lack of rhyme and a subtle and less predictable rhythm. A major reason for reading such verse to students is that it contradicts the inaccurate stereotype of poetry as always containing strong, easily identifiable rhyme and rhythm.

*Black Is Brown Is Tan*, a book-length poem about family life written in free verse, is suitable for primary-grade children. Poet Arnold Adoff provides a gentle, lyric description of life in his household. The lines of poetry are of varying lengths but the internal rhythm will draw children along. Adoff's *i am the running girl* is a free verse tribute to running. The female main character narrates the preparation, the actual race, and the resulting exhilaration. Careful preparation is necessary if the teacher is to read this work effectively to children; Adoff's word placement often makes more than one interpretation possible. Olexer (1985) comments on this characteristic, but notes that "the kinetic meter and powerful statement will reward those who persevere." In her book, Olexer annotates more than three hundred poetry books, summarizing why each is unique, listing other books by the same poet, and including a brief excerpt.

Teachers whose children enjoy free verse can read to them Adoff's *make a circle keep us in*. This simple circle story recounts events from the time daddy wakes the child in the morning until daddy is holding the child as "the thunder grumbles" after a night storm. One of the most appealing illustrations in the book is the one in which artist Ronald Himler presents the visual metamorphosis from "a great big singing bear i know from yesterday" to the daddy hugging his child. Teachers might also read children parts of *OUTside INside Poems*, by Adoff, for the contrasts shown. For example, outside are shoes, inside are socks and toes. Child listeners should also be encouraged to notice the nesting: inside a house is a room, inside the room is a bed, inside the bed is the narrator. Black-and-white illustrations by John Steptoe accompany the poetry. More recently, black-and-white illustrations by Steve Kuzma accompany Adoff's poetry in *Sports Pages*, about many different sports.

*The Trees Stand Shining* will both introduce free verse to children and expand their appreciation of another culture. This book of native American poetry features one to four poems arranged on each page opposite a full-page, full-color illustration. Hettie Jones selected short poems that briefly describe a moment, an encounter with an animal or person, or a reaction to nature. These poems were gathered from tribes that lived as far east as the Chippewa and as far west as the Zuni. The impressionistic transparent and opaque watercolors are by Robert Andrew Parker, who uses a thin black pen line to give definition to the shapes.

Many times the line between prose and poetry is tenuous. The language may be as evocative as poetry is, but contains few conventional poetic devices. In *Between Cattails*, Terry Tempest Williams presents effectively spare language that is poetic:

> *The marsh*
> *is a watery world*
> *where living things*
> *mingle and mix—*
>
> *where frogs leap*
> *and snakes slither,*
>
> *where pikes spawn*
> *and bitterns yawn,*
>
> *where egrets wait,*
> *and racoons wash,*
>
> *where toads croak*
> *and marsh wrens sing.*

The stylishly minimal drawings by Peter Parnall prove once again that he understands the effectiveness of white space better than most other children's book illustrators working today.


## CONCRETE POETRY

In concrete poetry, the way words and phrases are arranged on the paper is an important elaboration of the meaning; the words look like the idea expressed. This form is not new; Lewis Carroll and others used it (see Carroll's mouse tail/tale in *The Annotated Alice*, edited by Martin Gardner). A helpful book for introducing concrete poetry is *Concrete Is Not Always Hard*, by A. Barbara Pilon. If teachers wish to work extensively with poetic ideas given physical, visual form, *Words and Calligraphy for Children* (Cataldo, 1969) is an exceptionally fine resource. The book is now out of print, but is well worth searching out in library collections. Also, *Seeing Things*, a book of poems written and designed by Robert Froman, is again available. A teacher might share some of these poems with intermediate-grade children and then encourage them to write their own.

# *SHARING POETRY WITH CHILDREN*

As children grow, they too often develop an indifferent or less enthusiastic response to poetry. Intermediate-grade teachers report difficulty in finding poems children will like. Examining why children develop negative attitudes toward poetry can help teachers at all grade levels plan experiences that will engender a lasting appreciation of this literary form.

## CHILDREN'S MISCONCEPTIONS ABOUT POETRY

Children are generally exposed to poetry throughout elementary school. They frequently and inadvertently develop three misconceptions as a result of this exposure.

### 1. *Children believe all poetry must rhyme.*

This is undoubtedly the most universal misconception children have about poetry. Ask any group of randomly selected students to define poetry, and rhyme will figure in most of their definitions. Since so many fine collections of rhymed poetry are available, it is easy to see why this misconception arises. Poems like those in *Circus*, by Jack Prelutsky, provide memorable images and a strong example of the value of rhyme:

> *Tall clowns and short clowns and skinny and fat,*
> *a flat-footed clown with a jumping-jack hat . . .*
> *How quickly a clown can coax smiles out of frowns!*
> *Make way for the merriment . . . bring on the clowns!*

Prelutsky continues his exploration of this type of rhyme in *Ride a Purple Pelican* with full-color illustrations by Garth Williams. Most of the poetry in *Out in the Dark and Daylight*, by Aileen Fisher, is rhymed. The book includes 140 new poems by this winner of the 1978 National Council of Teachers of English Award for Poetry for Children. Another collection containing many fine rhymed poems is *Poem Stew*, by William Cole.

Despite the bounty of fine rhymed verse, teachers should share some unrhymed poetry with children at all grade levels, even though such poetry, often characterized by irregular rhythms, is more difficult for teachers to read and children to enjoy.

---
#### In the Fog
---

*Stand still.*
*The fog wraps you up*
*and no one can find you.*

**The accentuated contrast between light and dark is possible because of the technique used—wood engraving. The sharp edges and clearly defined lines are also characteristic of this medium.** Illustration by Fritz Eichenberg from *Rainbows Are Made* by Carl Sandburg. Copyright © 1982, reprinted by permission of Harcourt Brace Jovanovich.

*Walk.*
*The Fog opens up*
*to let you through*
*and closes behind you.*

This poem, from a collection entitled *I Feel the Same Way*, by Lilian Moore, could be used as a contrast to Carl Sandburg's better-known "Fog." "Fog" is one of more than sixty of Sandburg's poems presented in an elegantly designed format illustrated with wood engravings by Fritz Eichenberg, in *Rainbows Are Made*. Anthologist Lee Bennett Hopkins grouped the poems in six sections, each introduced by a quote from Sandburg and prefaced by full-page, strongly textured engravings. The heavy cream stock contrasts pleasantly with the blackness of the ink.

Some collections include both rhymed and unrhymed poetry. A particularly wide-ranging collection for mature listeners/readers is *Some Haystacks Don't Even Have Any Needle*, by Stephen Dunning et al. For example, John Updike's "The Mosquito" begins "On the fine wire of her whine she walked" and is an intensely descriptive rhymed poem. After the narrator has slapped the mosquito, ". . . as side by side we, murderer and murdered, sleep." On the facing page, an unrhymed poem, "The Orb Weaver" by Robert Francis, is accompanied by a full-color reproduction of Odilon Redon's painting *The Spider*.

## 2. Children think all poetry must be pretty.

For many children, this misconception limits their interest. Too often students think of poems as being only concerned with delicate images of beautiful, fragile things. There are many lovely visual images in the following poem from *Peacock Pie*, by Walter de la Mare, but it will probably not appeal to most children:

---
Silver
---

*Slowly, silently, now the moon*
*Walks the night in her silver shoon;*
*This way, and that, she peers, and sees*
*Silver fruit upon silver trees;*
*One by one the casements catch*
*Her beams beneath the silvery thatch . . .*

Although this poem may appeal to adults, teachers must make sure that a group is ready for its evanescent imagery, unfamiliar vocabulary, and personification before attempting to use it with children.

The teacher has an obligation to choose poetry that deals honestly with a wide variety of topics, some of which may not seem at first consideration to be suitable for children. For example, junior high students should hear "Richard Corey" from *Poets' Tales*, by William Cole. The poem is effective because of the shock in the last line, which destroys dramatically the image created until then. You might use the Simon and Garfunkle recording of the poem on *Sounds of Silence* (Columbia Records, CS 9269).

Sometimes it is not only the topic but the treatment that is shocking:

---
Relative Sadness
---

*Einstein's eyes*
*were filled with tears*

*when he heard about Hiroshima.*
*Mr. Tamiki*
*had no eyes left*
*to show his grief.*

This poem, by Colin Rowbotham, is one of many fine poems selected by Griselda Greaves for inclusion in *The Burning Thorn.*

### 3. Children have the impression that nothing much happens in poetry.

Many modern poetry collections have fortunately minimized or eliminated the lyric but static images that once predominated in such books. However, children today are still too often exposed only to descriptive poetry, in which little conflict and resolution occur. An example of a descriptive poem is "Cirrus," by Mary O'Neill, from her book *Winds.* Despite the accompanying watercolor paintings, this particular poem is probably of limited appeal to children. It describes silky, detached cirrus clouds, made of ice crystals that swerve with a feathery plume. The poem is an effective word picture, but nothing much happens. Similarly, few eight-year-olds will have much interest in a field of dandelions where "lightly pass the feet of spring," an image from "Casual Gold" in *The Year Around,* by Alice Hazeltine and Elva Smith.

A corollary of the second and third misconceptions is the idea, unfortunately too pervasive among intermediate-grade boys, that poetry is essentially for girls. Teachers who present a sequence of poems about "pretty" topics, described in detail, run the risk of losing the interest of both boys and girls. Children need to be exposed to the work of such poets as David McCord,[9] James Reeves,[10] and Harry Behn[11], who present fresh alternatives to much poetry now in anthologies.

## CHANGING POETRY'S IMAGE

What can teachers and librarians do to change children's misconceptions about poetry? Teachers and librarians must examine the kinds of poems

---

[9]In *Every Time I Climb a Tree* (Boston: Little, Brown, 1971), David McCord's vigorous and direct poetry gives unique views of commonplace things and events. The book is boldly illustrated by Marc Simont. A more recent presentation of McCord's poetry is in *All Small* (Little, Brown, 1986), with illustrations by Madelaine Gill Linden.

[10]"Mick," about James Reeves's mongrel dog, is one of many poems included in *Round About Eight,* edited by Geoffrey Palmer and Noel Lloyd (London: Frederick Warne, 1972).

[11]Harry Behn's poems are newly available in *Crickets and Bullfrogs and Whispers of Thunder,* selected by Lee Bennett Hopkins (San Diego: Harcourt Brace Jovanovich, 1984). Fifty poems, along with Behn's original drawings printed in a pleasant blue, are arranged in three sections.

they share with children and the nature of the poetry-sharing experience. A teacher or librarian should ask the following questions when choosing poetry to read to students:

### 1. Is the poem something I can read effectively?

Even if a poem is topical or written by a famous poet, a teacher must make sure he or she likes it. A reader must enjoy a poem to read it well.

### 2. Is the poem different in form or content from other things I've read recently?

All teachers have preferences, even if unexamined. Teachers need to look analytically at what they choose to make sure a wide variety of ideas and styles are presented.

### 3. Will the poem appeal to both boys and girls?

All children are interested in verses that present a clear and unusual view, poems in which something active happens, or poems with humor. Nonsense poems are particularly popular with both girls and boys, who respond to incongruous situations or comparisons, meaningless but amusing words, and exaggerated descriptions of improbable people.[12] In *Beastly Boys and Ghastly Girls*, William Cole capitalized on these characteristics in collecting poems describing two universal qualities of children: being naughty and being disobedient. "Jemima" is an expanded version of Long-fellow's poem about the naughty girl with the curl in the middle of her forehead. "Sarah Cynthia Sylvia Stout," by Shel Silverstein, is about a girl who learns the consequence of disobedience when she refuses to take the garbage out. Role reversal—the child punishing the adult—is a universal fantasy described in Elizabeth Godley's "Extremely Naughty Children." Humorous pen drawings by Tomi Ungerer add to the delights of this collection.

Improbable happenings occur in *Alligator Pie*, by Dennis Lee:

> *I went to play in the park.*
> *I didn't get home until dark.*
> *But when I got back I had ants in my pants*
> *And my father was feeding the shark.*

---

[12]"Nonsense! Nonsense!" is one of the sections in *The Random House Book of Poetry for Children* (New York: Random House, 1983). In fact, funny poems are included in most of the other sections of this compendium selected by Jack Prelutsky and illustrated with Arnold Lobel's usual humorous characters.

*The sly grin, half-closed eyes, and cocked eyebrow are marks of a caricaturist of great talent.* Edited by William Cole. Illustration by Tomi Ungerer. Reprinted by permission of Philomel Books from *Beastly Boys and Ghastly Girls*, copyright © 1964 by William Cole.

Lee includes similar delightful nonsense in *Garbage Delight. I Made a Mistake*, by Miriam Nerlove, is another appealing book of nonsense rhyme. The heroine is constantly doing the wrong thing: "I went to the well to make a wish, I made a mistake . . . and kissed a fish."

### 4. *Have I included poetry by child poets?*

There are increasing numbers of anthologies of student poetry, including verse by children from other countries and minority groups.[13] An example is the poetry composed by Arab and Jewish children and collected by Jacob Zim in *My Shalom My Peace*. The poems are all written on one topic, but this apparently put no limits on the writers' imaginations. Brilliant, boldly executed paintings and drawings illustrate the verses. One by a thirteen-year-old, entitled "The Paint Box," discusses its colors: "Each color glowing with delight." The child poet goes on to describe imaginatively how she would use both colors she had ("pink for dreams and rest") and colors she didn't have ("white for the face of the dead").

---

[13]See Richard Lewis's *Miracles* (New York: Simon and Schuster, 1966) and *The Wind and the Rain* (New York: Simon and Schuster, 1968), which are collections of poems from children of many lands, enhanced by their sensitively designed formats.

Many poems in *I Heard a Scream in the Street,* selected by Nancy Larrick, were written by black children. The book includes selections from thousands of students in grades 4 through 12, who are "deeply concerned with the urban world that engulfs them, a world where streets are littered, neighbors are starving, and violence is normal." Black-and-white photographs illustrate poems about the aspects of everyday life for these children. These aspects can be unfortunate or lyric; for example, one child wrote about staggering junkies and the scent of whiskey and in the same poem wrote that "the street is at a starlight star bright stand still." Two other collections edited by Larrick are *Somebody Turned on a Tap in These Kids* and *Green Is Like a Meadow of Grass.*

## INCIDENTAL AND ORGANIZED EXPERIENCES

When an excited class of first-graders tumbles into the room after recess, led by a child with a caterpillar cupped in her hand, it is time to read "The Caterpillar," by Christina Rossetti. The poem appears in *Magic Lights and Streets of Shining Jet,* edited by Dennis Saunders.

> *Brown and furry*
> *Caterpillar in a hurry,*
> *Take your walk*
> *To the shady leaf, or stalk,*
>     *Or what not,*
> *Which may be the chosen spot.*
>     *No toad spy you,*
> *Hovering bird of prey pass by you;*
> *Spin and die,*
> *To live again as butterfly.*

Another poem appropriate for the same moment is the following from David McCord's *Far and Few:*

> *The little caterpillar creeps*
> *Awhile before in silk it sleeps.*
> *It sleeps awhile before it flies,*
> *And flies awhile before it dies,*
> *And that's the end of three good tries.*

At such times, the immediacy of the experience challenges the teacher's ability to choose memorable words to relate to a memorable event. Such linking builds an interest in poetry and an awareness that poets catch ephemeral experiences in words to be savored again and again. The teacher must be able to quickly and unobtrusively find the poem and share it with children. For this reason, many teachers constantly add to a poetry file, attaching poems to recipe cards for permanence and filing them according to topic. Some teachers like to use margin tabs in anthologies they own, making it possible to turn quickly to appropriate poems.

The teacher or librarian should also plan a poetry curriculum, an organized sequence of poems to share regularly. Reading a poem a day will expose children to more than a hundred poems during a year. Some will make lasting impressions; others will be forgotten before the day is over. In such an extensive selection, each child is sure to find something with deep individual meaning.

Another approach to structuring a poetry curriculum is to feature a "poet of the month." One kindergarten teacher plans her curriculum to acquaint children with the work of a few writers, using many poems by a single author each month. For example, the teacher features David McCord one month, talking briefly with the children about his life and work as an introduction. A bulletin board displays his picture.[14] This teacher shares many poems by various poets with the students during the following month, but concentrates on McCord. Part of the classroom sharing includes eliciting the children's reactions to what they like about a poem. The books the teacher reads from are left out for children to look at in their leisure time. Most boys and girls of kindergarten age cannot read the books themselves, but they seem to enjoy looking at the illustrations that remind them of poems they have heard. As the month goes on, the teacher rereads some of the poems children especially enjoyed, at their request.

It is important for children to understand that a poem is an individual reaction to something. Although some topics have inspired many poets, each poet's response is unique. To instill this idea, the teacher can read several poems about the same subject by different poets. Cats have evoked a variety of poetical responses. Eleanor Farjeon's poem juxtaposes sounds:

Cat!

*Scat!*
*After her, after her,*
*Sleeky flatterer,*
*Spitfire chatterer,*
*Scatter her, scatter her,*
*Off her mat!*
*Wuff!*
*Wuff!*
*Treat her rough!*

[14]Upon written request, trade book publishers will often supply photos of and bibliographic information about their children's poets and authors. Address information is given in *Children's Books in Print.*

This is one of several poems included in the collection *Round About Eight*, by Geoffrey Palmer and Noel Lloyd.

Repetition and rhythm are apparent in T. S. Eliot's "The Song of the Jellicles," from *Old Possum's Book of Practical Cats*:

> *Jellicle Cats come out to-night,*
> *Jellicle Cats come one come all:*
> *The Jellicle Moon is shining bright—*
> *Jellicles come to the Jellicle Ball.*

This is one of a wide variety of poems included in *Listen, Children, Listen*, edited by Myra Cohn Livingston, herself a respected American poet. The other thirteen poems in Eliot's *Old Possum's Book of Practical Cats* will also interest children. Several of these poems by Eliot are now available on the soundtrack recording of the musical *Cats* (Geffen Records, #2GHS2031).

A teacher can use other cat poems for comparison and contrast, including "Catalogue," by Rosalie Moore; "Poem," by William Carlos Williams; "On a Night of Snow," by Elizabeth Coatsworth; and "For a Dead Kitten," by Sara Hay. These poems are all included in *Reflections on a Gift of Watermelon Pickle*, edited by Steve Dunning, Edward Lueders, and Hugh Smith. Another useful resource is Richard Shaw's *The Cat Book*. In addition to Farjeon's poem, this volume includes Moore's "Catalogue" and twenty other selections, both poems and very short folk tales. "Cat's Menu," by Winifred Crawford, and "Puss Leaves Home," by Gwendolyn Griswold, both comment humorously on cats' finicky eating habits. Seventeen artists with widely differing styles illustrated the volume. *I Am the Cat*, by Lee Bennett Hopkins, has twenty-four poems, including some mentioned above, accompanied by realistic black-ink line drawings by Linda Rochester Richards.

## READING POETRY EFFECTIVELY

For a teacher to read effectively requires practice. Because it is condensed, verse is more difficult to read than prose is. Nuances of meaning are often expressed more subtly in verse. Minor changes in *paralanguage*, that is, in pitch, stress, and juncture can subtly signal meaning.

Teachers who want to read poetry effectively should practice different ways of interpreting a poem. After choosing a poem, a teacher should practice it several times, varying pitch (the pattern of high and low sounds), stress (the pattern of emphasis), and juncture (the pattern of pauses and complete stops). One of the most common mistakes made when reading poetry aloud is stopping at the ends of lines rather than at the ends of thought units. For example, in *Suppose You Met a Witch?*, by Ian Serraillier,

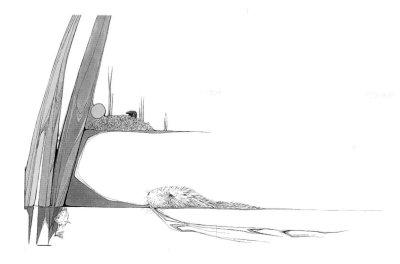

**PLATE I.** *In this illustration from her third Caldecott winner, Marcia Brown achieved interesting effects by layering lighter transparent colors over darker ones. Brown combined the techniques of woodcut and cut paper in these collages, resulting in typically angular outlines.* Illustration from *Shadow,* by Marcia Brown. Copyright © 1982 Marcia Brown. Reprinted with the permission of Charles Scribner's Sons.

**PLATE J.** *This watercolor illustration is bled to the edges of the page and features ink line that gives definition to the forms.* Illustration from *Grandpa* by John Burningham. Copyright © 1984. Reproduced by permission of Jonathan Cape Limited.

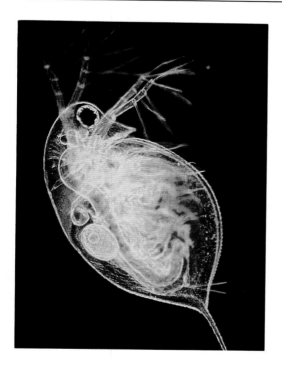

**PLATE K.** *This full-color photograph is of a daphnid, a common freshwater flea about the size of a pinhead. This and other photos in the same book (some color, some black and white) show aspects of the world often overlooked because they cannot easily be seen with the unaided eye.* Illustration by John C. Walsh from *Hidden Worlds* by Seymour Simon. Copyright © 1983. Published by William Morrow and Co., Inc.

"**M**andrill, your face

is sad and long,

How shall I cheer you?

Sing a song?"

PLATE L. *Joseph Low used a varying line width and a color wash—the basic visual elements of line and color—to create an imaginative effect.* Illustration by Joseph Low from *Adam's Book of Odd Creatures.* Copyright © 1962 Joseph Low. Reprinted with the permission of Atheneum Publishers.

PLATE M. *Maurice Sendak expanded a four-line poem into a series of creative images, of which this is one.* Illustration from *Hector Protector* by Maurice Sendak. Copyright © 1965 by Maurice Sendak. Reprinted by permission of Harper & Row, Publishers, Inc.

***The strong pattern of concentric circles and the elaborate feather design reinforce the feeling of fantasy.*** Illustration by Ed Emberley from *Suppose You Met a Witch?* by Ian Serraillier. Copyright © 1973. Reprinted by permission of Little, Brown and Company.

the poetry is irregular both in rhythm and rhyme. The teacher should read this book aloud because it is beyond the difficulty level of many students.

> *"Hi!"*
> *Ho!"*
> *shrieked she,*
> *and "Tickle-me-thistle!" and "Prickle-de-dee!"*
> *And battered she was as she trotted and tripped,*
> *and her clothes were torn and tattered and ripped*
> *till at last,*
> *all mingled and mangled,*
> *her right leg entangled,*
> *her left leg right-angled,*
> *firm as a prisoner pinned to the mast,*
> *she*
> *stuck*
> *fast.*

Just as complex as the poetry are the illustrations. Ed Emberley's designs, heavily accented in black, are full of curves and swirls. It is not only the black that establishes the rhythm of the illustrations; apparently plain areas contain paler pastel images that are likewise twisted and coiled.

Poetry written in dialect is especially likely to require practice. For example, effective reading of *The Gobble-Uns'll Git You Ef You Don't Watch Out!*, by James Whitcomb Riley, depends on ease in reading the dialect.

Having chosen a piece, a teacher might find it useful to record the poem on a tape or cassette to see how it sounds. A few analytic sessions with a tape recorder can improve a teacher's poetry-reading skills immensely.

The most effective way to introduce poetry is to read it aloud to children. Even those students with well-developed reading skills will respond more positively if they first encounter poetry as a flow of sound extending through time, rather than as a line of words across the space of a page. There are instructional purposes that are well served when children see how a poem looks on paper, but such experiences should follow hearing the poem as sound.

## INSTILLING POSITIVE CONCEPTIONS ABOUT POETRY

An appreciation of poetry develops slowly; results of planning, selection, and sharing are sometimes not readily apparent. Yet a diversified experience and a thoughtful approach to verse are both important in fostering children's appreciation of poetry. Long-range goals of a poetry program might include replacing the misconceptions mentioned earlier with some positive conceptions of poetry.

**POETRY AS AN EXPRESSION OF HOW WE FEEL.**  Children need to understand that poetry expresses deeply felt emotions concisely and that they can express their own feelings in poetic form (Lopate, 1975). Mary O'Neill's poem about the word *forget* in her book *Words Words Words* is a compelling journey toward the memorable last line:

Forget

*Forget is a hider*
*In a long black cape,*
*A thing that has happened*
*And wants to escape. . .*
*Then what you forgot*
*Jumps up to say:*
*"You saw me, or felt me.*
*Or heard me one day.*
*Nothing that happens*
*Goes truly away. . . ."*

Poets have cast innumerable shades of feeling into poetry. Some of these feelings children have had; others they may not yet have experienced.

Contact with poetry helps boys and girls reflect on their own feelings and share vicariously what others have felt.[15]

Sometimes feelings expressed in poetry are negative, and that is acceptable. "I'm stupid" in *City Green*, by Eleanor Schick, captures effectively the sense of worthlessness all children have experienced at one time or another because they couldn't do something others could. Some poets contrast good and bad experiences. For example, the author of "Just Remember" tells children that yells are loud but float away, but hugs are solid as the arms that hold you in the quiet time. Black-line illustrations by Ronald Himmler accompany this and other poems in *make a circle keep us in*, by Arnold Adoff.

**POETRY AS A UNIQUE VIEW OF SOMETHING ORDINARY.** It is true that writers sometimes deal with extraordinary events. But a distinguishing quality of poetry is that it can make us see something commonplace in a new way. This might be an experience, an object, or a feeling. Because of this fresh insight, we perceive our world in new and more sensitive ways. According to literary critic Alfred Kazin (1984), it is the poet's ability to look at life in an "indescribably distinctive way" that accounts for this new vision. Kazin is talking about the adult poet Emily Dickinson, but the comments are appropriate nonetheless. He concludes: "That gift of individual vision is something no one has ever been able to explain away."

An example of this unique view is found in Aileen Fisher's poem "Growing," from her *In One Door and Out the Other*. Three four-line stanzas detail a young child's perplexity about what is happening to him. The child narrator asks his mother what makes him grow; he asks his father what has made him stop growing; in the end, he still doesn't have an answer. The book features small black-ink drawings by Lillian Hoban of round-faced children who are appealing without being self-consciously cute.

Elizabeth Coatsworth also shows commonplace things from an uncommon point of view in *The Sparrow Bush*. She talks of a "flowering of cows" in May, of houseplants like "prisoners staring through bars," and a "tiptoe fox" searching for ducks.

In a poem from *Sam's Place*, Lilian Moore concentrates on rural images, sharing her sense of the drama to be found in quiet places.

---

[15]To emphasize the idea that poetry expresses feelings, Gloria T. Blatt and Jean Cunningham encourage children to respond to a poem through movement ("Movement: A Creative Approach to Poetry," in *Elementary School Journal*, May 1975, 490–500). Many helpful ideas about starting a poetry/movement program are included.

### September

*Something is bleeding*
*into the*
*pond,*
*the stains are freshly*
*red.*

*Look—*
*beyond*
*and overhead.*
*The maple*
*is crimson spattered.*
*Summer is fatally*
*wounded.*
*Soon, soon*
*dead.*

What lifts this poetry above its commonplace topic is the poet's ability to use words imaginatively, to create phrases that are unusual, and to take a viewpoint that is unexpected. When asked what she sees as characteristic of her work, Moore replied: "I try to tell the truth. It is the truth of accurate observations, without sentimentality" (Glazer, 1985). The truthfulness is always, however, enriched by her unusual view. At another point in Glazer's interview with Moore, the poet says: "Poems should be like fireworks, packed carefully and artfully, ready to explode with unpredictable effects." There could be no better distillation of her poetry than that.

Not all poets are successful in giving a unique view of the ordinary. In writing about familiar things—often in an attempt to communicate with the youngest listeners—some poets make the mistake of being condescending. "Good Morning" by Muriel Sipe, found in *Sung Under the Silver Umbrella*, collected by the Literature Committee of the Association for Childhood Education, says nothing original and uses pedestrian rhyme and predictable rhythm:

*One day I saw a downy duck,*
*with feathers on his back;*
*I said, "Good morning, downy duck,"*
*And he said, "Quack, quack, quack."*

Even the very youngest listeners deserve better poetry than this.

Elizabeth Coatsworth's "The Mouse," included in the same collection, is unusual and memorable because of its form. Stanzas vary in length and number of lines and contain a combination of both rhymed and unrhymed lines, making this a poem that young children will want to hear again:

*I heard a mouse*
*Bitterly complaining*
*In a crack of moonlight*
*Aslant on the floor—*

*"Little I ask*
*And that little is not granted.*
*There are few crumbs*
*In this world any more.*

*"The bread-box is tin*
*And I cannot get in.*

*"The jam's in a jar*
*My teeth cannot mar.*

*"The cheese sits by itself*
*On the pantry shelf—*

*"All night I run*
*Searching and seeking,*
*All night I run*
*About on the floor,*

*"Moonlight is there*
*And a bare place for dancing,*
*But no little feast*
*Is spread any more."*

Coatsworth's poem illustrates that it isn't the topic but rather the treatment that is critical. Writing about mice—a topic used extensively in both prose and poetry for children—Coatsworth was able to produce a unique poem.

Another example of a unique treatment comes from Ted Hughes's book *Season Songs*. The image of a black-and-white calf might seem trite and commonplace, yet in his poem "A March Calf," Hughes creates a memorable image:

*Right from the start he is dressed in his best—his*
*blacks and his whites.*
*Little Fauntleroy—quiffed and glossy.*
*A Sunday suit, a wedding natty get-up.*
*Standing in dunged straw . . .*

The unusual poems are accompanied by watercolors by Leonard Baskin.

**POETRY AS A VARIETY OF FORMS.**  Verse encompasses a vast array of forms and styles, of models and meters. It is crucial that children understand that the forms of poetry are limitless. Too often students leave elementary school thinking that end rhymes and an insistent rhythmic "thump" are inevitable in poetry. Broadening children's exposure to include a multiplicity of forms helps them understand that they needn't communicate their ideas in conventional *abab* form, in which the first and third, as well as the second and fourth lines rhyme.

## POETRY AND CULTURAL DIVERSITY

As teachers read widely to acquaint themselves with poetry suitable for children, they should seek out poetry by members of minority groups (Larrick, 1969). By sharing expressions of cultural diversity, teachers can enhance children's understanding of poetry's varied nature.

For example, many collections by black poets are available. In *Spin a Soft Black Song*, by Nikki Giovanni, poems of varying lengths and forms are set in black and brown type and the illustrations are done in the same colors by Charles Bible. These poems are highly personal evocations of family life, depicting with sympathy a variety of people. *My Daddy Is a Cool Dude*, by Karama Fufuka, also speaks of familial joys. There is tenderness in "Daddy," admiration in "Basketball Star," and affection in 'Lil' Bro'." But these poems also present the realities of life for poor black children growing up in the city. Jerry Lee's big brother "O-Deed," and the "Park People" are homeless. Pencil illustrations by Mahiri Fufuka enhance this book.

*Listen Children. An Anthology of Black Literature*, edited by Dorothy S. Strickland, comprises a variety of poetry styles in works by such poets as Gwendolyn Brooks, Eloise Greenfield, Don Less, and Lucille Clifton. These poems are interspersed with longer prose selections by famous black writers.

It is also valuable for children to be exposed to the poetry of more remote cultural groups. *I Breathe a New Song* offers insights into the Inuit culture (the Eskimos of northern Alaska, Canada, and Greenland). Ninety poems from nine Inuit groups show the same freshness and simplicity as the title poem. A detailed introduction explains the importance of poetry to the Inuit and the traditional forms they use.

Poems of ancient Mexico, presented in both English and Spanish by Toni de Gerez, are available in *My Song Is a Piece of Jade*. Most of the poems face full-page illustrations. The artist, William Stark, a resident of Mexico, did oversized, pleasantly splashy watercolors defined with intermittent line of varying width. These unrhymed poems are full of memorable images, for example, "The turtledove has bells of gold in his throat."

## FEMALE ROLE MODELS IN POETRY

New female images are being stressed in some anthologies of poetry about girls. The fact that not all girls are sweet, docile creatures is voiced in a collection titled *Amelia Mixed the Mustard*. In subtly humorous woodcuts, Evaline Ness illustrates these poems about characters who live vigorously, enjoying life to its fullest. A. E. Housman's title poem is traditional in its rhyme scheme but not in Amelia's desire to experiment on her mother. "Isabel," in which the title character encounters a bear, has been widely included in anthologies; nowhere is the confrontation as effectively depicted as in Ness's nose-to-nose version. The title character of "Jumping Joan" uses her big feet to propel herself energetically through the events of this Mother Goose rhyme (see page 277). In all, this anthology presents an interesting collection of females.

Some of the poems included in *Girls Can Too!*, by Lee Bennett Hopkins, are really neuter, except for their illustrations. For example, "Samuel," by Bobbi Katz, is about a child's friendship with a salamander that "died very quietly during spelling" and could be about a girl or a boy. A few others, like "Naughty Donna" and "Tricia's Fish," both by Hopkins, describe little girls who do things most girls didn't do in the past.

To introduce nonsexist roles, a teacher might read the title poem from *The New Kid on the Block*, by Jack Prelutsky, a delightful upsetting of expectation. It begins "... that kid is tough," relates all the bad things the kid does, and concludes with "that new kid's really bad, I don't care for her at all." "Be Glad Your Nose Is on Your Face" (instead of between your toes) is typical of Prelutsky's usual, absurdist ideas. James Stevenson's black-and-white cartoons are pleasantly disheveled, which nicely complements the poetry.

## CHORAL SPEAKING

A teacher can encourage children's appreciation of poetry by asking them to repeat it aloud. The teacher first writes the lines on the chalkboard or perhaps on a transparency for an overhead projector; then both teacher and children read the lines aloud. This activity, saying together a piece of verse (or, less frequently, prose), is called *choral speaking*, or sometimes *choral reading*. This ancient language art, the subject of renewed interest (Schiller, 1973), has deep roots extending back to choral renditions in Greek drama. Its antecedents are the parts for the chorus in dramas presented at Dionysian festivals hundreds of years before the birth of Christ.

Doing choral speaking with children is of value in several ways. Choral reading has personal value: students learn to appreciate literature by participating, instead of listening passively to the teacher read. Choral speaking has social values: students learn to work together to achieve a result. Children contribute their ideas and cooperate with one another as they select interpretations and discard others. Especially today, when there is a pervasive emphasis on individualization in elementary schools, children need to learn cooperation. Choral speaking also has psychological value: the experience of participating as a group member is important to boys and girls. Choral speaking provides a group experience without the self-consciousness of a formal presentation.

**ELEMENTS OF CHORAL SPEAKING.**   Voices can be used to produce a wide range of effects to enhance an oral interpretation. At first, and especially with primary-grade children, the teacher will make decisions about how students should speak the poem to make it interesting. Later, and especially with intermediate-grade groups, the teacher can seek suggestions from the students. The class can experiment with the following elements:

*Tempo.* Should a line be said fast or slowly? Do some lines need to begin fast and then slow down, or begin slowly and increase in speed (Moore, 1968)?

*Rhythm.* Given the tempo selected for any line or stanza, how should the heavily stressed words fall to establish a predictable "beat" or movement? Rhythm (or meter) is important, but it must not be emphasized for its own sake. One author comments that rhythm is "sometimes worshipped as a fetish, forcing the poem to jerk along a bumpy road and lose the load of beauty with which the author invested it" (Provenmire, 1974).

*Stress.* Which words in a line or which lines should be said louder?

*Juncture.* Where should the voices stop to mark the ends of thoughts? Is each stop a full one or only a momentary pause within a thought? (Juncture does not necessarily occur at the end of a printed line.)

**ARRANGEMENT.**   Before beginning the choral experience, the teacher should decide who is to say what. She or he should study the poem to determine the best assignment for each verse. There are several possible alternatives.

*Unison.* Speaking in unison is difficult to do effectively, although it seems deceptively simple. It is almost impossible to avoid the singsong monotony that usually results when many inexperienced speakers read together.

*Antiphonal.* In an antiphonal arrangement, different small groups are responsible for different parts of the poem, for example, alternate lines or stanzas. A teacher can begin by dividing students into two groups; children will quickly become able to work in even more groups. Two groups can easily alternate lines in "Snail," by Maxine Kumin.[16]

*Cumulative.* In a cumulative arrangement, more voices are added as the poem gathers momentum. "Trains," by James Tippett, lends itself to a cumulative arrangement. As more voices join in, the effect is created of the train coming closer.

*Single Voices.* An arrangement using single voices works best when children have gained enough confidence to speak a line alone. A good poem for single voices is "Mice," by Rose Fyleman. All the children can say the first and last two lines together. The teacher can assign the remaining twelve lines to eight individual speakers (the last three will each say two lines).

A collection of poems for junior high students that is specifically designed to be read by single voices is *I Am Phoenix,* by Paul Fleischman. The two columns of print on each page are for two readers, who at times read the same words together, at times read different words at the same time, and at times read in sequence. The poems are about birds that are mythical (phoenix), extinct (passenger pigeon), and commonplace (owl).

A fourth-grade class recently evolved the following method of dividing Rose Fyleman's poem "The Goblin," included in *Poetry for Holidays,* by Nancy Larrick.

### The Goblin

| Group 1: | *A goblin lives in our house,* |
|---|---|
| Groups 1 and 2: | *in our house,* |
| Groups 1, 2, and 3: | *in our house.* |

---

[16]The poems in the rest of this section, unless otherwise indicated, are from "Time for Poetry," in *The Arbuthnot Anthology of Children's Literature,* edited by Zena Sutherland (New York: Lothrop, Lee and Shepard, 1976, pp. 4–145). (There is a 1984 edition of this text, but it does not include these poems.) To locate a particular poem elsewhere, consult *Index to Poetry for Children and Young People* by John E. Brewton et al. (New York: H. W. Wilson, 1942; supplements in 1957, 1965, 1972, 1978, 1983). Also see *Subject Index to Poetry for Children and Young People, 1957–1975* by Dorothy B. Frizzell Smith and Eva L. Andrews. (Chicago: American Library Association, 1977; updated by Violet Sell in 1982).

| | |
|---|---|
| **All children:** | *A goblin lives in our house all the year around.* |
| **Bob:** | *He bumps* |
| **Jane:** | *And he jumps* |
| **Mary:** | *And he thumps* |
| **Ted:** | *And he stumps.* |
| **Tim:** | *He knocks* |
| **Allen:** | *And he rocks* |
| **Liz:** | *And he rattles at the locks.* |
| **Group 1:** | *A goblin lives in our house,* |
| **Groups 1 and 2:** | *in our house,* |
| **Groups 1, 2, and 3:** | *in our house.* |
| **All children:** | *A goblin lives in our house all the year around.* |

**SCORING THE POEM.** A composer decides which instrument will play a specific part in a musical score and how the part will be played. The teacher decides—at least at the beginning—which voices will say which lines and how the lines will be said. Older or more experienced children can have a hand in these decisions.

Once teacher and children have agreed on the scoring, they may find it helpful to go through the poem and mark it, so they will remember how they want to read it. A group of fifth-graders also enjoyed "The Goblin." The teacher helped them mark it so they could remember how they wanted to say it. They worked out the following rudimentary marking system:

a slight pause /

a complete stop //

a continuation of the voice (so the thought is continued to the next line) ⌣

a heavy stress on the word ∧

a lighter stress on the word ∨

Then they used it to mark the poem as follows:

*A gŏblin lives in oŭr house,/ in oŭr house,/ in oŭr house,/*
*A gŏblin lives in oŭr house all the year arŏund.//*
*He bumps⌣*
*And he jumps⌣*
*And he thumps⌣*
*And he stumps.//*
*He knocks⌣*
*And he rocks⌣*

*And he ràttles at the lòcks.//*
*A gòblin lives in oŭr house,/ in oŭr house,/ in oŭr house,/*
*A gòblin lives in oŭr house all the year aroŭnd.//*

Other poems about goblins (as well as ghosts, witches, monsters, and trolls), suitable for choral speaking, are included in *In the Witch's Kitchen*, compiled by John E. Brewton, Lorraine A. Blackburn, and George M. Blackburn.

After children have had some experience with choral speaking, they may enjoy trying Arnold Adoff's *MA nDA LA*. A semiabstract "resonant soundings" poem, this deserves to be brought to aural/oral life. There are no recognizable words, but the syllables ("MA" is mother; "DA" is father; "LA" is singing, etc.) can be parceled out to groups or individuals. The spaces between the syllables—indicated by their relative placement on the printed page—should be indicated by pauses of varying lengths when the poem is said. The intense watercolors by Emily McCully make ample and effective use of black silhouettes for the characters.

**CREATING VERBAL OBBLIGATO.** The musical term *obbligato* means a persistent background motif. Usually it refers to a repeated theme played by an instrument against the major melody in a piece of music. In choral speaking, an obbligato is created when some students repeat, at patterned intervals, words or sounds appropriate to heighten the mood of the poem or evoke the image more clearly.

Many poems lend themselves to the creation of verbal obbligato. For example, for James Tippett's "Trains," some children may repeat the words "clickety-clack" in a rhythm they have created as the rest of the children say the poem. The teacher may have a group of children with high-pitched voices repeat the words in one rhythm while a group with lower-pitched voices says the same words at a different rhythm. This provides a background for the group saying the poem.

## EXPERIENCES IN WRITING POETRY

After experiences in listening to and saying poetry, children can write their own poems. Students should have opportunities to write structured, unrhymed poetry such as haiku and cinquain because these forms provide an organizational structure within which they can work. Students need some structure, and these forms are easy to learn if not applied too rigorously. Valuable suggestions for how to work with children in composing these forms of poetry are included in books by Applegate (1965), Arnstein (1962), and Walter (1962).

In the beginning, children do better working with unrhymed forms in which thoughts do not need to be fit to specific sounds. Experts on poetry writing concur that rhyme should be minimized when children are asked to compose poems. Mearns (1958) said:

> Rhyme is a marvelous but unnecessary ornament; a great thing, no mistake, when done by expert artists, but a weak thing and an obstruction of the spirit oftentimes in the hands of any but a technician.

More recently, an American authority on children's poetry writing, Nancy Larrick, stated in the introduction to *Green Is Like a Meadow of Grass:*

> At no time did we suggest the use of rhyme. In fact, we discouraged attempts at rhyming lines because at this stage rhyme seems to force a child into goose-step thinking.

The results of overemphasizing rhyme are sadly and typically evident in a poem written by Mark, a second-grade child:

> *The sun is bright*
> *just like a light.*
> *It is so bright,*
> *If we look at it,*
> *it hurts our sight*
> *like a bite*
> *in a metal kite!*

This poem is clearly not a "thing of astounding beauty," as Myra Cohn Livingston (1973) maintains rhymed poetry can be at its best. Rather, the use of rhyme here resulted in a poem that is forgettable and dishonest, for the ideas probably do not really reflect Mark's thinking.

As an alternative to rhymed verse, either of the following syllabic, structured forms, haiku or cinquain, can be used by teachers to motivate writing.

**HAIKU.** Haiku is a seventeen-syllable, three-line Japanese form of poetry. The first line usually has five syllables; the second, seven; and the third, five. Haiku is frequently characterized by a nature theme and often contains seasonal references. Many books are available to introduce the form to children.[17] The collage illustrations for Richard Lewis's *In a Spring Garden* were done by Ezra Jack Keats and are boldly simple, elegant accompaniments to the haiku. For intermediate-grade children, the books by Harold Henderson, including *An Introduction to Haiku,* are useful.

When introducing haiku to children, it is important to point out the

---

[17]In addition, *Haiku Posters* (#AQ 71514) are available from the Perfection Form Company (Logan, Iowa 51546). Each 17-by-22-inch poster features a poem, explains a figure of speech, and includes an example of oriental calligraphy.

required number of syllables and lines. However, it is equally important to remember that this poetry was originally written in Japanese, *not* English. Because of this, children should be encouraged to notice that in translations the number of syllables is sometimes more or less than seventeen. When writing their own haiku, children must be allowed freedom in meeting the syllable count. Although seventeen is the desired number, children must be told that that is a flexible requirement. Perhaps saying exactly what they want to say in a poem will require more or less syllables. For example, fifth-grade children composed the following haiku:

*A fire fly, a speck*
*of light in a deep black sky.*
*Why tote a lantern?*
                              John

*Broad unbending oak*
*roadway to the nervous*
*scampering squirrel.*
                              Cheryl

Some authorities may think that the above poems are not really haiku. One reason is that each of the above lines is not "as complete a unit of thought as possible within the unity of the whole poem" (Harr, 1974). Nonetheless, the experience of expressing their ideas in nonrhyming poems is a valuable one for children. It shows them that poetry is language, compressed and distilled, communicating ideas in a personal way.

CINQUAIN. Cinquain is another relatively simple yet structured form that can be part of a poetry-writing curriculum. One of the few books of this form for children is *City Talk*, by Lee Bennett Hopkins. This collection of forty-two poems written by urban children is illustrated with striking black-and-white-photographs by Roy Arenella. Teachers can also use poems by Adelaide Crapsey, the American inventor of the cinquain form; teaching suggestions are given by Hopkins (1966, 1967).

Like Haiku, cinquain is a syllabic verse form. The pattern in cinquain involves increasing the number of syllables in each line until the last line, which returns to two syllables:

_____ two syllables

_____ four syllables

_____ six syllables

_____ eight syllables

_____ two syllables

An example is the following:

First Sign

*I see . . .*
*the pale snowdrop,*
*bravely seeking the sun.*
*Be gone, winter winds: stay away—*
*It's spring.*

One teacher of fourth- and sixth-grade children alters the form somewhat. Dearmin (1965) recommends the following pattern:

First line—one word, giving the title.

Second line—two words, describing the title.

Third line—three words, expressing an action.

Fourth line—four words, expressing a feeling.

Fifth line—another word for the title.

**POETRY AS A SOURCE OF IDEAS.** Kenneth Koch, a poet and playwright, developed another approach to poetic composition. His procedures focus on the content rather than on the form of the poems.

The process begins with group composition—different children contribute lines. In writing group poems, the teacher encourages children to use repetition. Koch believes that repetition is more natural to children's speech than rhyme, which he believes is inhibiting. Working in New York City with disadvantaged children, Koch found they could effectively write comparison poems, among others. The students, who had marked reading and writing problems, wrote insightful comparisons, such as these:

*A person's whisper is like a soft pillow.*

*Bad weather is gloomy like our school paint.*

Koch (1970) expressed his point of view that most poetry written especially for the young was

> . . . too often condescending and cute and almost always lacked that clear note of contemporaneity and relevance, both in subject and in tone, which makes the work of a writer's contemporaries so inspiring for him.

Koch presented adult poetry to children as a source of poetry ideas, "suggestions I would give to the children for writing poems of their own in some way like the poems they were studying" (1973). The children are not asked to engage in pointless imitation but rather to find and recreate in themselves the main feelings of the adult poems. The advantages of this approach to poetic compositions are (1) the poems are easy to write, (2) the rules are gamelike, and (3) children can enjoy the experience without the anxiety of competition.

A teacher of fifth-graders recently used Koch's approach with her class. She read "This Is Just to Say," by William Carlos Williams to her class.[18] The poem's real-life situation, in which the narrator apologizes for something he or she has done but is really glad to have done it, is immediately appealing to children. After hearing and discussing the poem, students wrote their own poetry, for example:

*This is just to say*
*I have hit*
*my dog*
*when she*
*was bad*
*and that*
*you would*
*probably do*
*it anyways.*
*Forgive me, Mom,*
*but it felt good.*
             *John*

After reading Carl Sandburg's "Arithmetic" to the group, the teacher asked them to use it as a poetry idea. The following poem was among those that resulted:

### Reading

*Reading is words flying by your eyes.*
*Reading is having a good imagination.*
*Reading is once you're done, you have to start all over again.*
*Reading is books, books, books, and making reports on them.*
*Reading is figuring things out, sounding out new words once, remembering all*
    *the rules.*
*Reading is listening to the teachers say, "Take out your workbook and do ten*
    *pages."*
*Reading is having some fun by exploring into new worlds every time you read a*
    *book.*
*Reading is basically all right.*
                        *Lynn*

---

[18]Unless otherwise noted, poems in this section can be found in *Reflections on a Gift of Watermelon Pickle . . .* , edited by Stephen Dunning, Edward Lueders, and Hugh Smith (Glenview, Ill.: Scott, Foresman, 1969).

Koch's approach is recommended by Sloan (1980), who discusses why writing experiences must be an integral part of the literature program she recommends.

**WRITING LIMERICKS.**  Earlier in this chapter, it was mentioned that limericks, a very highly controlled form of poetry, are difficult for children to write. A curriculum guide published by the Canadian Ministry of Education (1984) tells how to help boys and girls with this form. The guide suggests that students be given this set of descriptions before they try to write their own limericks:

1. One character is usually introduced in the opening line.
2. The second line adds an important detail about the character.
3. The third and fourth lines produce an action or situation in which the character is involved.
4. The fifth line resolves the matter and ends it humorously.
5. The rhyme scheme is *a a b b a.*
6. The first, second, and fifth lines contain no more than nine syllables, and the third and fourth lines have no more than six syllables.

**EVALUATING CHILDREN'S POETRY WRITING.**  Poetry is more difficult to evaluate than prose. Teachers must assess children's understanding of poetry and their ability to write it with a more gentle hand than they would use in assessing prose.

The primary goal of evaluation should be to determine whether children are still responding positively. As teachers read and occasionally discuss poetry with children, they must be constantly alert for signs of boredom or disinterest. In examining the poems children write themselves, the teacher should look consciously for answers to such questions as these:

*1.  Does the topic the child chose to write about seem an authentic choice?*

The goal is to reinforce the idea that the poem must be about a topic of genuine concern to the child.

*2.  Is there a word or phrase the teacher can recommend to the student?*

It is important to look for an unusual word choice or a unique use of a common word.

*3.  Is the topic treated honestly within the context of the situation?*

This is, of course, a subjective judgment.

#### 4. Is there an unusual perception of a commonplace object or event?

Very young children view the world with a freshness that often amazes adults. A teacher's task is to nurture that fresh viewpoint as boys and girls grow older and become more susceptible to peer pressure.

#### 5. Does the poem tell something about how the child feels?

Beyond simply giving information about some object or event, does the poem also include some indication of the child's reaction to the object or event?

#### 6. Is the child becoming aware of the need to edit his or her poetry?

Because of poetry's compact nature, students should come to understand that each word, sentence, and thought must be carefully chosen.[19]

In addition to looking at individual poems, however, teachers should carefully examine children's general responses to writing poetry. In attempting to build a year-long poetry curriculum, a teacher must reflect on two questions:

1. Are children becoming more willing to express themselves in poetic form?
2. Can students express themselves in different kinds of poetry?

Only by continually assessing both the success of the program and the success of individual children can teachers shape and reshape the poetry program to make it more effective.

## EVALUATING BOOKS OF POETRY

The three conceptions about poetry that teachers should try to instill in children (see pages 302–306) can serve as criteria in evaluating individual poetry books. Teachers and librarians can ask themselves such questions as the following:

#### 1. Does this poetry express how the poet feels in a way that will be clear to children? Will this expression of feeling encourage children to express their own feelings?

---

[19]Editing is the process of examining carefully the words chosen, the arrangement of the words (syntax), and the ideas expressed to determine if they can be made more effective. Conversely, editing is *not* cosmetic correction of such elements as spelling and capitalization.

Jean Vallario's illustrations combine fine black ink line and tiny ink dots to create a three-dimensional effect in her realistic pictures of both imaginary and real creatures. By Elinor Parker. Illustration from *Echoes of the Sea* by Elinor Parker. Copyright © 1977 Elinor Parker. Reprinted with the permission of Charles Scribner's Sons.

The poet's feelings are very clearly depicted in *Cold Stars and Fireflies*, by Barbara Juster Esbensen. Many children have experienced making snow angels, depicted so well visually in *The Snowy Day*, by Ezra Jack Keats. Two poems in Esbensen's collection capture this experience in ways that will be vivid for children: "Snow Print One: Mystery" and "Snow Print Two: Hieroglyphics." In the first, the narrator is wondering who made the snow angel with the "big-booted feet." The second makes a link to the patterns left by birds, "printing the new snow with a narrow alphabet."

### 2. Does this poetry present a unique view of something ordinary?

Poetry need not be about exotic things, but it should present an unusual perception about something children know. Not all books of poetry present unhackneyed views. *Poems to Read to the Very Young*, selected by Josette Frank, suffers from cuteness, in both its words and pictures. Such poems as Robert Louis Stevenson's "The Cow" might have been fresh when written but are not today. The illustrations are sweet, not adding to but simply decorating the page. In contrast, in *Rabbits, Rabbits*, Aileen Fisher manages to offer new views on a very overworked subject. Her poem "But Rabbits" makes an interesting point about muteness, for example.

Poets write about things many people would never think of as subjects for poetry. For example, many children have ridden through an automatic car wash. Yet few, if any, will have thought about it in the way Myra Cohn Livingston did in her poem "Car Wash." Included in *A New Treasury of Children's Poetry*, selected by Joanna Cole, this description of the "broad flapping fingers of a mechanical genie" is a unique view of something commonplace. Livingston's poems usually provide such insightful perceptions; her *Worlds I Know and Other Poems* looks freshly at childhood. For example, "Doll" captures the perversity of an older sister in a particularly credible way.

### 3. Does this poetry reinforce the idea that poetry is multiple in topic, in form, or in style? Will the book expand children's understanding of poetic diversity?

For example, children should experience the contagious silliness of John Ciardi's *You Read to Me, I'll Read to You*, and *The Man Who Sang the Sillies*. In contrast, the seriousness in *Echoes of the Sea*, by Elinor Parker, is also effective.

## SUMMARY

As teachers of prereaders read Mother Goose to their students, they are providing an introduction to both the oral tradition and poetry. After using Mother Goose rhymes, teachers can choose from an array of poetic forms, including poems in folk songs or picture books, narrative poetry, limericks, free verse, and concrete poetry.

Despite their early enthusiasm for verse, by the middle grades too many children lose interest in poetry. It is important to instill three conceptions about poetry: (1) poetry expresses personal feelings; (2) poetry gives a unique view of something ordinary; and (3) poetry is multiple.

Teachers base poetry selections on two types of circumstances. They choose poetry appropriate for the moment, to reinforce and extend an incident that occurs in the classroom. And, they choose poetry appropriate for an organized, sequential program of poetry that continues throughout the year. This program can be planned around a poem-a-day format, or it can be planned around individual poets and their works.

Choral speaking is an effective oral technique for interpreting poetry. Experiences in writing haiku, cinquain, or other forms that place minimal emphasis on rhyme can help children build on the teacher's reading of poetry. Koch's "poetry idea" approach to poetic composition focuses on content rather than form. Teachers must ask themselves specific questions about the results of their poetry composition program in order to evaluate its success.

## Suggestions for Further Study

1. It is always enlightening and frequently amusing to read one artist's comments on another's work. Maurice Sendak is at his candid best in "Mother Goose's Garnishings," in *Children and Literature,* edited by Virginia Haviland (Glenview, Ill.: Scott, Foresman, 1973, pp. 185–195). Read the article, then look at some of the books Sendak criticizes. Do you agree or disagree with his comments?

2. Many editions of Mother Goose rhymes are available. Joan Walsh Anglund's *In a Pumpkin Shell* (New York: Harcourt Brace Jovanovich, 1970) is done in her usual quasi-historical, idealized style. Beni Montresor takes a more adventuresome approach in *I Saw a Ship A-Sailing* (New York: Knopf, 1967). *The Random House Book of Mother Goose* (New York: Random House, 1986) features several rhymes and small pictures, by Arnold Lobel, on most pages. A few pages are devoted to one rhyme and an accompanying picture; all pictures are in full color. Look at these three volumes, compare them with some of the ones mentioned in this chapter, and decide which you would choose to share with children. Describe the reasons for your choice.

3. There is much adverse reaction to television violence today. Some collections of Mother Goose rhymes feature violent verses (see page 272). Read what some authors in the field have to say about violence in children's books. Can you defend sharing such verses with children?

4. This chapter advocates teaching children to write haiku. Ann Terry (see "Related Reading for Adults") reports that students she surveyed responded negatively to haiku. Select one of the haiku books available, and share some of the poems with children. What kind of reaction do they have to this form?

5. Explore the role of viewpoint in poetry with

children. After reading several of the cat poems mentioned in this chapter to children, ask them to write a poem in which the point of view is that of a cat, its prey (a mouse), its adversary (a dog), its proud owner, a guest who tolerates but doesn't like cats, a mean child who sees an opportunity for devilry, or a cat-food manufacturer.

6. To emphasize that poets deal with emotional responses, you might read Mary O'Neill's "Forget" (in *Words Words Words*) to children and ask them to make a picture of something they would like to forget. Talking about these things can lead to poem making.

7. This chapter contained no definition of poetry; that task has taken entire books to accomplish. Assuming you have by now evolved your own definition of poetry, read *The Poet's Eye*, by Arthur Alexander (Englewood Cliffs, N.J.: Prentice-Hall, 1967). The author has done an impressive job of describing many facets of poetry in easy-to-read language. With a group of intermediate- or upper-grade children, use this book as an introduction to poetry writing. See if this facilitates their writing.

8. *Where the Sidewalk Ends* (New York: Harper and Row, 1974) and *A Light in the Attic* (New York: Harper and Row, 1981), by poet Shel Silverstein, are immensely popular with young readers. Silverstein deals with topics not often dealt with in poetry for children. Also, through his use of the pronoun *we*, Silverstein suggests the complicity of an adult not afraid to laugh at adult silliness. To find out why children think his poetry seems funny, share these books with students and then discuss their reactions. Then read Myra Cohn Livingston's "The Light in His Attic" (*The New York Times*, March 9, 1986, pp. 36–37). Her reason for thinking that Silverstein is significant is probably entirely different from the reasons children will give. Despite Silverstein's occasionally "metrically mangled lines, use of shoddy form and . . . poor grammar," Livingston believes his new kind of morality is essential for youngsters.

## Related Reading for Adults

Baskin, Barbara, Karen Harris, and Colleen Salley. "Making the Poetry Connection." *The Reading Teacher*, December 1976, pp. 259–265.

The authors believe children should learn that not all questions have a single right answer. They advocate using poetry to help children understand this idea because of its subjective responses, diversity, and wide participatory base. They give reasons for children's dislike of poetry and criteria for selecting poems children will like.

Carlson, Ruth Kearney. *Enrichment Ideas*. Dubuque, Iowa: William C. Brown, 1976.

This volume is a collection of diverse art projects related to Oriental poetry forms. Emphasis is on ideas well within the reach of any classroom teacher. The author is especially well informed on tanka and haiku.

Carter, John Marshall. "Transforming the Self Through Poetry." *The Clearing House*, February 1985, pp. 256–260.

Immersing eighth-grade students in reading and writing poetry is the goal of Carter's six-week poetry unit. Carter shares his own poetry with students as an initial activity to establish credibility, since a teacher's involvement gives value to an activity. Then exercises, conferences, and drama all contribute to students' improved attitude toward poetry. A book of students' poetry—complete with title page and table of contents and including both edited and original versions of students' poems—is the culmination of the unit.

Collom, Jack. *Moving Windows. Evaluating the Poetry Children Write.* New York: Teachers and Writers Collaborative, 1985.

The author, who published eight books of his own poetry, reports on six years of experience leading poetry workshops in New York City schools. Working with kindergarteners through twelfth-graders (though mostly third- through sixth-graders), he helped children explore a variety of forms, including poems modeled on those of William Carlos Williams. Many of the resulting poems are included in their entirety, along with the poet's comments about why they are good. This last idea is similar to the approach of Kenneth Koch. A major problem in Collom's book is the lack of an index: the ideas are scattered throughout various chapters, and it is impossible to find all there is about any single form.

Curtis, David. "With Rhyme and Reason." *Language Arts*, October 1975, pp. 947–949.

The author contends that traditional nursery rhymes should not be eliminated from school curricula after the third grade as they currently are. Older children will be interested in the allegory behind each rhyme. Also, although young children interpret the rhymes literally, older children may gain "whimsical insights into a few interesting historical events."

Hopkins, Lee Bennett. "Report of a Poet-in-Residence." *English Journal*, February 1973, pp. 239–243.

The poet reports on a month spent at a high school in New Jersey, where he tried a variety of ideas to get adolescents to read, write and enjoy poetry. The program began with poetry for children, then proceeded to lyrics of popular songs and poetry written by the students' peers about contemporary problems. A fuller report of Hopkins' work with children at a variety of grade/age levels is included in his *Pass the Poetry, Please!* (New York: Harper and Row, 1987). This revision of an earlier edition of the book makes this valuable resource available again.

Hurst, Carol. "What to Do with a Poem." *Early Years*, February 1980, pp. 28–29ff.

The author gives guidelines for selecting poems, including how to search for subjects interesting to children. Pointers on presenting the poems verbally are also included. Hurst does not feel that children should be required to memorize poems. However, if they keep an anthology of their favorites, which can be illustrated by them, it may lead to natural learning of the poems. The author suggests several other techniques for encouraging students' interest in poetry. The selection of poetry deserves particular care: few people are going to attempt to bring poetry into children's lives.

Kennedy, X. J. "Go and Get Your Candle Lit!" *The Horn Book*, June 1981, pp. 273–279.

Kennedy, criticizing the practice of praising all poetry that children write, says teachers must teach that writing is a skill, both frustrating and difficult. Exposure to quality poetry should precede writing quality poetry. Kennedy is skeptical of Kenneth Koch's practice of introducing difficult adult poetry to elementary school children. The author suggests ways to keep analysis of poetry alive and recommends bringing back rhyme and memorization of poetry. He states that not everyone is a poet, but everyone has the right to enjoy poetry.

Knorr, Mary. "Treasuring Poetry." *Early Years*, March 1980, p. 35ff.

Knorr began a poetry unit by reading *Where the Sidewalk Ends*, by Shel Silverstein. Children became excited about the poems, and she suggested they could stage a poetry recital for parents and friends. Each student chose a poem. Four weeks of memorization, practice of gestures and the use of the microphone, and creation of related artwork led up to the recital. The author reports that she often heard children practicing their poems together on the playground during free time and memorizing their friends' poems.

Livingston, Myra Cohn. "But Is It Poetry?" (two parts). *The Horn Book*, December 1975, 571–580; February 1976, 24–31.

Livingston is highly critical of early adulation of child poets because of the effect such praise may have in diminishing their drive to improve. She criticizes those who accept children's work as finished; to her mind, it is not. She strikes out against the bastardization of haiku and cinquain forms by "well-meaning but stifling teachers" who do not understand how to help children express themselves poetically. Livingston continues this theme in another article, "Beginnings" (*Language Arts*, March 1978, pp. 346–354). She asserts that a teacher can only make children aware of their sensitivities and help them learn the forms, the basic tools of poetry, into which they can put their own voices. Livingston encourages the use of journals, walks and observations, praise for good things and improvement for the bad, and good models.

Lowry, Charlene. "Poetry for Basics." *Educational Leadership*, December 1978, pp. 183–186.

Lowry, an artist-in-residence for a public school system and a published poet, writes of her success with a poetry workshop, in which "barely literate students ... improved dramatically because poetry composition provided them with the motivation to write." Although Lowry does not ignore such mechanics as spelling and punctuation, her first goal is to eliminate fear of writing. Once students have written something, positive reinforcement is essential. The article encourages teachers at any level to teach poetry. Student writing samples included are convincing proof that poetry can teach the basics and does encourage writing.

Lukasevich, Ann. "Making Poetry a Natural Experience for Young Children." *Childhood Education*, September/October 1984, pp. 36–42.

Reading poetry to children preserves their natural love of rhyme, rhythm, and words. Lukasevich suggests, among other techniques, reading Mother Goose, and such poets as A. A. Milne and Robert Louis Stevenson to children. The article, although not presenting novel ideas, serves to remind kindergarten through third-grade teachers of time-tested ones that work; these are put together in a well-thought-out program. The recommended readings for both teachers and children are sufficient to begin a comprehensive study of poetry.

Opie, Iona, and Peter Opie. *The Oxford Nursery Rhyme Book*. Oxford, Eng.: Oxford University Press, 1955.

Eight hundred rhymes and songs, including several variants for some of the verses, are grouped into nine sections. The Opies comment on the importance of illustrations for children, who will frequently ignore a verse without a picture. The art of Thomas Bewick, who brought wood engraving to its zenith in the seventeenth century, is featured; engravings by contemporary artist Joan Hassel are also included.

Terry, Ann. *Children's Poetry Preferences: A National Survey of Children's Poetry Preferences*. Urbana Ill.: National Council of Teachers of English, 1974.

This is the most comprehensive survey of children's poetry preferences available. Despite the abundance of new realistic poetry, teachers have continued to share traditional poems. The author wished to determine whether this was one reason interest in poetry begins to decline in about fifth grade. Students in fourth through sixth grades were asked to listen to poetry on cassette tapes and respond to it. Haiku and free verse were among the least liked. Narrative poems and those with strong rhythm and/or rhyme were favorites. Liking a poem was strongly linked to understanding it.

Western, Richard D. "A Defense of Kenneth Koch." *Language Arts*, October 1977, pp. 763–766.

The author points out weaknesses he sees in Myra Cohn Livingston's criticism of Kenneth Koch's approach to getting children to write poetry. Western identifies the ways Koch avoids making children study about poetic forms by having them actually work with the forms.

## Related Reading for Children

Hopkins, Lee Bennett. *Moments*. San Diego: Harcourt Brace Jovanovich, 1980.

This anthology includes poems about specific days (for example, Shel Silverstein's "Oh Have You Heard," concerning April Fool's Day) as well as individual months ("Stay, June, Stay" by Christina Rossetti) and seasons ("Winter Dark" by Lilian Moore). These poems can be compared with the holiday poems by Myra Cohn Livingston (see below).

Livingston, Myra Cohn. *Celebrations*. New York: Holiday House, 1985.

Taking as her subject holidays, which are often inundated with tired images, Livingston vivifies them with both rhymed and unrhymed poetry. Of particular interest is her use of varying line lengths. Most of the poems are set on double-page spreads and are printed on top of brilliantly colored paintings by Leonard Everett Fisher.

Merriam, Eve. *Blackberry Ink*. New York: Morrow, 1985.

Seasonal poems are among those included in this book, which is augmented with pleasant watercolor illustrations. The rhymed form of "It fell in the city . . ." contrasts with other snow poems. "Five little monsters . . . ," although not specifically about Halloween, would be good to read then; "Crick! Crack!" would brighten a dark autumn day.

O'Neill, Mary. *Hailstones and Halibut Bones*. Garden City, N.Y.: Doubleday, 1961.

A perennial favorite, this collection of poems about colors is useful in motivating children to write their own poems about their favorite colors. The imagery of the poems can interest child readers/listeners: O'Neill not only describes the color but also how it engages her senses of touch, taste, and smell.

Rossetti, Christina. *What Is Pink?* New York: Macmillan, 1971.

Ideal as a companion piece to Mary O'Neill's *Hailstones and Halibut Bones*, this edition, illustrated by Jose Aruego, will charm small children. This book is useful in motivating children to write their own poetry.

## Professional References

Applegate, Mauree. *When the Teacher Says "Write a Poem."* New York: Harper and Row, 1965.

Arnstein, Flora J. *Poetry and the Child*. New York: Dover, 1962.

Cataldo, John. *Words and Calligraphy for Children*. New York: Reinhold, 1969.

Dearmin, Jennie T. "Teaching Your Children to Paint Pictures with Words." *Grade Teacher*, March 1965, 26–27.

Glazer, Joan I. "Profile: Lilian Moore." *Language Arts*, 62 (October 1985), 647–652.

Harr, Lorraine Ellis. "The 'Timbre' of Haiku." *Instructor*, March 1974, 114–115.

Hopkins, Lee Bennett. "For Creative Fun, Let Them Try Cinquain." *Grade Teacher*, December 1966, 83ff.

———. "From Trudeau's Garden." *Elementary English*, October 1967, 613–614.

Kazin, Alfred. "Writing Is an Old-Fashioned Art in a High-Tech Society." *U.S. News and World Report*, July 23, 1984, 79.

Koch, Kenneth. *Rose, Where Did you Get That Red?* New York: Random House, 1973, p. 4.

———. *Wishes, Lies and Dreams*. New York: Vintage, 1970.

Larrick, Nancy. "Life Ain't Been No Crystal Stair." *Library Journal*, February 15, 1969, 843–845.

Livingston, Myra Cohn. *When You Are Alone, It Keeps You Capone*. New York: Atheneum, 1973.

Lopate, Robert. "Getting at the Feelings." *New York Times Magazine*, August 31, 1975, 14–18, 23.

Lynn, Joanne L. "Runes to Ward Off Sorrow: Rhetoric of the English Nursery Rhyme." *Children's Literature in Education*, 10 (Spring 1985), 3–14.

Mearns, Hughes. *Creative Power*. New York: Dover, 1958, p. 77.

Ministry of Education. *Basically Right. English: Intermediate and Senior Divisions*. Toronto: Ministry of Education, 1984, p. 47.

Moore, William. "Choral Speaking." *The English Quarterly*, Summer 1968, 79–82.

Nodelman, Perry. "How Picture Books Work." In *Festschrift: A Ten Year Perspective*. West Lafayette, Ind.: Children's Literature Association, 1983, pp. 20–25.

Olexer, Maryciele E. *Poetry Anthologies for Children and Young People*. Chicago: American Library Association, 1985, p. 150.

Opie, Iona, and Peter Opie. *The Oxford Dictionary of Nursery Rhymes*. Oxford, Eng.: Oxford University Press, 1951, pp. 3–5.

Peterson, Carolyn Sue, and Ann D. Fenton. *Index to Children's Songs*. New York: H. W. Wilson, 1979.

Poe, Elizabeth. "Our Readers Write: What Is Something I've Taught That Was Fun and Worthwhile?" *English Journal*, October 1981, 60.

Provenmire, E. Kingsley. *Choral Speaking and the Verse Choir*. New York: A. S. Barnes, 1974, p. 140.

Rhodes, Lynn K. "I Can Read! Predictable Books as Resources for Reading and Writing Instruction." *The Reading Teacher*, February 1981, 511–518.

Schiller, Charles. "I'm OK, You're OK—Let's Choral Read." *English Journal*, May 1973, 791–794.

Sloan, Glenna Davis. "Developing Literacy Through Literature." *The Reading Teacher*, November 1980, 132–136.

Walter, Nina Willis. *Let Them Write Poetry*. New York: Holt, Rinehart and Winston, 1962.

## Bibliography of Children's Books

Abisch, Roz, and Boche Kaplan. *Sweet Betsy from Pike*. New York: McCall, 1970.

Addams, Charles. *The Charles Addams Mother Goose*. New York: Windmill, 1967.

Adoff, Arnold. *Black Is Brown Is Tan*. New York: Harper and Row, 1973.

———. *i am the running girl*. New York: Harper and Row, 1979.

———. *make a circle keep us in*. New York: Delacorte, 1975.

———. *MA nDA LA*. New York: Harper and Row, 1971.

———. *OUTside INside Poems.* New York: Lothrop, Lee and Shepard, 1981.

———. *Sports Pages.* New York: J. B. Lippincott, 1985.

Alderson, Brian. *Cakes and Custard.* New York: Morrow, 1974.

Aliki. *Go Tell Aunt Rhody.* New York: Macmillan, 1974.

Bangs, Edward. *Yankee Doodle.* New York: Parents Magazine Press, 1976.

Bierhorst, John (compiler). *In the Trail of the Wind.* New York: Farrar, Straus and Giroux, 1971.

Blake, Quentin. *Quentin Blake's Nursery Rhyme Book.* New York: Harper and Row, 1983.

Blegvad, Lenore. *This Little Pig-A-Wig.* New York: Atheneum, 1978.

———. *The Parrot in the Garret.* New York: Atheneum, 1982.

Brewton, John E., and Lorraine A. Blackburn. *They've Discovered a Head in the Box for the Bread.* New York: Harper and Row, 1978.

Brewton, John E., Lorraine A. Blackburn, and George M. Blackburn III. *In the Witch's Kitchen.* New York: Thomas Y. Crowell, 1980.

Briggs, Raymond. *Fee Fi Fo Fum.* New York: Coward, McCann, 1964.

———. *The Mother Goose Treasury.* New York: Coward, McCann, 1966.

———. *The White Land.* New York: Coward, McCann, 1963.

Brooke, L. Leslie. *Ring O' Roses.* London: Frederick Warne, 1977.

Caldecott, Randolph. *R. Caldecott's Picture Book (No. 1).* London: Frederick Warne, n.d.

Chase, Richard. *Billy Boy.* San Carlos, Calif.: Golden Gate Junior Books, 1966.

Ciardi, John. *The Man Who Sang the Sillies.* New York: J. B. Lippincott, 1961.

———. *You Read to Me, I'll Read to You.* New York: J. B. Lippincott, 1962.

Coatsworth, Elizabeth. *The Sparrow Bush.* New York: W. W. Norton, 1966.

Cole, Joanna (selector). *A New Treasury of Children's Poetry.* Garden City, N.Y.: Doubleday, 1984.

Cole, William (ed.). *Beastly Boys and Ghastly Girls.* Cleveland: Collins World, 1964.

Cole, William. *Poem Stew.* New York: Harper and Row, 1981.

———. *Poets' Tales.* Cleveland: World, 1971.

Coltman, Paul. *Tog the Ribber or Granny's Tale.* New York: Farrar, Straus and Giroux, 1985.

Conover, Chris. *Froggie Went A-Courting.* New York: Farrar, Straus and Giroux, 1986.

Cooney, Barbara (ill.). *Wynken, Blynken and Nod.* New York: Hastings House, 1964.

Craft, Ruth, *The Winter Bear.* New York: Atheneum, 1975.

de Angeli, Marguerite. *Book of Nursery and Mother Goose Rhymes.* Garden City, N.Y.: Doubleday, 1955.

de Gerez, Toni. *My Song Is a Piece of Jade.* Boston: Little, Brown, 1984.

de la Mare, Walter. *Nursery Rhymes for Certain Times.* London: Faber and Faber, 1956.

———. *Peacock Pie.* New York: Alfred A. Knopf, 1967.

———. *The Warmint.* New York: Scribner's, 1976.

Dunning, Stephen, Edward Lueders, and Hugh Smith (eds.). *Some Haystacks Don't Even Have Any Needle.* New York: Lothrop, Lee and Shepard, 1969.

Ehlert, Lois (ill.). *Limericks by Lear.* Cleveland: World, 1965.

Eliot, T. S. *Old Possum's Book of Practical Cats.* San Diego: Harcourt Brace Jovanovich, 1967.

Emberley, Ed. *London Bridge Is Falling Down.* Boston: Little, Brown, 1967.

Esbensen, Barbara Juster. *Cold Stars and Fireflies.* New York: Thomas Y. Crowell, 1984.

Fisher, Aileen. *In the Middle of the Night.* New York: Thomas Y. Crowell, 1965.

———. *In One Door and Out the Other.* New York: Thomas Y. Crowell, 1969.

———. *Out in the Dark and Daylight.* New York: Harper and Row, 1980.

———. *Rabbits, Rabbits.* New York: Harper and Row, 1983.

Fleischman, Paul. *I Am Phoenix.* New York: Harper and Row, 1985.

Frank, Josette. *Poems to Read to the Very Young.* New York: Random House, 1982.

Frasconi, Antonio. *The House That Jack Built.* New York: Harcourt, Brace, 1958.

Froman, Robert. *Seeing Things.* New York: Thomas Y. Crowell, 1974.

Fufuka, Karama. *My Daddy Is a Cool Dude.* New York: Dial, 1975.

Galdone, Paul. *The House That Jack Built.* New York: Whittlesey House, 1961.

Gardner, Martin (ed.). *The Annotated Alice.* New York: Bramhall House, 1960.

Gauch, Patricia Lee. *On to Widdecombe Fair.* New York: G. P. Putnam's, 1978.

Giovanni, Nikki. *Spin a Soft Black Song.* New York: Hill and Wang, 1971.

Greaves, Griselda. *The Burning Thorn.* New York: Macmillan, 1971.

Greenaway, Kate (ill.). *Mother Goose; or the Old Nursery Rhymes.* London: Frederick Warne, 1882.

Hague, Michael. *Mother Goose.* New York: Holt, Rinehart and Winston, 1984.

Hazeltine, Alice, and Elva Smith. *The Year Around.* New York: Abingdon, 1956.

Henderson, Harold G. *An Introduction to Haiku.* Garden City, N.Y.: Doubleday, 1958.

Hoffs, Tamar. *Ms. Goose.* Los Angeles: Avondale Press, 1973.

Hoguet, Susan Ramsay. *Solomon Grundy.* New York: E. P. Dutton, 1986.

Hopkins, Lee Bennett (compiler). *City Talk.* New York: Alfred A. Knopf, 1970.

Hopkins, Lee Bennett. *Girls Can Too!* New York: Franklin Watts, 1975.

———. *I Am the Cat.* New York: Harcourt Brace Jovanovich, 1981.

———. *Rainbows Are Made.* San Diego: Harcourt Brace Jovanovich, 1982.

Howells, Mildred. *The Woman Who Lived in Holland.* New York: Farrar, Straus and Giroux, 1973.

Hughes, Ted. *Season Songs.* New York: Viking, 1975.

Janosch. *Tonight at Nine.* New York: Henry Z. Walck, 1967.

Jeffers, Susan (ill.). *Wynken, Blynken, and Nod.* New York: E. P. Dutton, 1982.

Jones, Hettie (selector). *The Trees Stand Shining.* New York: Dial, 1971.

Keats, Ezra Jack. *Over in the Meadow.* New York: Scholastic, 1971.

———. *The Snowy Day.* New York: Viking, 1962.

Langstaff, John. *Frog Went A-Courtin'.* New York: Harcourt, Brace, 1955.

———. *Oh, A-Hunting We Will Go.* New York: Atheneum, 1974.

———. *Over in the Meadow.* New York: Harcourt, Brace, 1957.

———. *The Swapping Boy.* New York: Harcourt, Brace, 1960.

Larrick, Nancy. *Green Is Like a Meadow of Grass.* Champaign, Ill.: Garrard Press, 1968.

———. *I Heard a Scream in the Street.* New York: M. Evans, 1970.

———. *Poetry for Holidays.* New York: Coward, McCann, 1966.

———. *Somebody Turned On a Tap in These Kids.* New York: Delacorte, 1974.

Lee, Dennis. *Alligator Pie.* Toronto: Macmillan of Canada, 1974.

———. *Garbage Delight.* Boston: Houghton Mifflin, 1978.

Lewis, Richard. *I Breathe A New Song.* New York: Simon and Schuster, 1971.

———. *In a Spring Garden.* New York: Dial, 1965.

Literature Committee of the Association for Childhood Education. *Sung Under the Silver Umbrella.* New York: Macmillan, 1956.

Livingston, Myra Cohn. *Listen, Children, Listen.* New York: Harcourt Brace Javanovich, 1972.

———. *Worlds I Know and Other Poems.* New York: Atheneum, 1986.

Lobel, Arnold. *The Book of Pigericks.* New York: Harper and Row, 1983.

———. *The Man Who Took the Indoors Out.* New York: Harper and Row, 1974.

Low, Joseph. *Mother Goose Riddle Rhymes.* New York: Harcourt, Brace, 1953.

Lubin, Leonard B. *This Little Pig*. New York: Lothrop, Lee and Shepard, 1985.

Manley, Sean, and Gogo Lewis. *Merriment! A Treasury for Young Readers*. New York: Funk and Wagnalls, 1965.

Marzollo, Jean. *The Rebus Treasury*. New York: Dial, 1986.

McCord, David. *Far and Few*. Boston: Little, Brown, 1952.

Miller, Mitchell. *One Misty Moisty Morning*. New York: Farrar, Straus and Giroux, 1971.

Moore, Lilian. *I Feel the Same Way*. New York: Atheneum, 1967.

———. *Sam's Place*. New York: Atheneum, 1973.

Nerlove, Miriam. *I Made a Mistake*. New York: Atheneum, 1985.

Ness, Evaline (ill.). *Amelia Mixed the Mustard*. New York: Scribner's, 1975.

Nic Leodhas, Sorche. *Always Room for One More*. New York: Holt, Rinehart and Winston, 1965.

O'Neill, Mary. *Winds*. Garden City, N.Y.: Doubleday, 1970.

———. *Words Words Words*. Garden City, N.Y.: Doubleday, 1966.

Palmer, Geoffrey, and Noel Lloyd. *Round About Eight: Poems for Today*. London: Frederick Warne, 1972.

Parker, Elinor. *Echoes of the Sea*. New York: Scribner's, 1977.

Petersham, Maud, and Miska Petersham. *The Rooster Crows*. New York: Macmillan, 1945.

Pilon, A. Barbara. *Concrete Is Not Always Hard*. Middletown, Conn.: Xerox Educational Publishers, 1972.

Prelutsky, Jack. *Circus*. New York: Macmillan, 1974.

———. *The New Kid on the Block*. New York: Greenwillow, 1984.

———. *Ride a Purple Pelican*. New York: Greenwillow, 1986.

Price, Christine. *Widdecombe Fair*. New York: Frederick Warne, 1965.

Quackenbush, Robert. *Skip to My Lou*. Philadelphia: J. B. Lippincott, 1975.

Raskin, Ellen. *Songs of Innocence* (two vols.). Garden City, N.Y.: Doubleday, 1966.

Rhys, Ernest. *A Book of Nonsense*. London: J. M. Dent, 1974.

Riley, James Whitcomb. *The Gobble-Uns'll Git You Ef You Don't Watch Out!* Philadelphia: J. B. Lippincott, 1975.

Saunders, Dennis (ed.). *Magic Lights and Streets of Shining Jet*. New York: Greenwillow, 1978.

Schackburg, Dr. Richard. *Yankee Doodle*. Englewood Cliffs, N.J.: Prentice-Hall, 1965.

Schick, Eleanor. *City Green*. New York: Macmillan, 1974.

Sendak, Maurice. *Hector Protector, and As I Went Over the Water*. New York: Harper and Row, 1965.

Serraillier, Ian. *Suppose You Met a Witch?* Boston: Little, Brown, 1973.

Shaw, Richard. *The Cat Book*. New York: Frederick Warne, 1973.

Spier, Peter. *And So My Garden Grows*. Garden City, N.Y.: Doubleday, 1969.

———. *London Bridge Is Falling Down!* Garden City, N.Y.: Doubleday, 1967.

Stones, Rosemary, and Andrew Mann. *Mother Goose Comes to Cable Street*. New York: Puffin, 1977.

Strickland, Dorothy S. (ed.). *Listen Children. An Anthology of Black Literature*. New York: Bantam, 1982.

Tennyson, Alfred, Lord. *The Charge of the Light Brigade*. New York: Golden, 1964.

Tucker, Nicholas. *Mother Goose Lost*. New York: Thomas Y. Crowell, 1971.

Tudor, Tasha (ill.). *Mother Goose*. New York: Henry Z. Walck, 1944.

Untermeyer, Louis. *The Golden Book of Fun and Nonsense*. New York: Western, 1970.

———. *Modern American Poetry*. New York: Harcourt, Brace, 1942.

Wadsworth, Olive A. *Over in the Meadow*. New York: Viking, 1985.

Wildsmith, Brian. *Brian Wildsmith's Mother Goose*. New York: Franklin Watts, 1964.

Williams, Terry Tempest. *Between Cattails*. New York: Scribner's, 1985.

Wright, Blanche Fisher (ill.). *The Real Mother Goose*. Chicago: Rand-McNally, 1916, 1944.

Wyndham, Robert. *Chinese Mother Goose Rhymes*. Cleveland: World, 1968.

Zalben, Jane Breskin (ill.). *Jabberwocky*. New York: Frederick Warne, 1977.

Zim, Jacob. *My Shalom My Peace*. Tel Aviv: Sabra Books, 1975.

# 8

# HISTORIC FICTION: TRIPS THROUGH TIME

In this era of supersonic jetliners, it is possible to be half a world away in just a few hours. We can get to remote places with a minimum of inconvenience. That technology can accomplish these wonders is remarkable. That another kind of wizardry can move us not only through space but also through time is equally remarkable. For example, in *Master Cornhill*, Eloise Jarvis McGraw uses the power of words to transport readers across the ocean and back in time three hundred years to the Great Fire in London. In *An Old Tale Carved Out of Stone*, A. Linevski leads readers to Russia and an epoch long past, to participate vicariously in the adventures of Liok.[1] Erik Christian Haugaard takes readers to seventeenth century Denmark in *The Untold Tale*.

Despite the wonder of such journeys, the very word *history* may deter some readers. For students, historic fiction may not be immediately appealing because it is not *now*. Children live in the present and more readily respond to books of contemporary realism. When first introducing historic fiction to students, teachers should try to find books that speak clearly and compellingly of problems that could be current ones but happen to arise in other times.

For writers, this genre is also difficult; it is not easy to write historic fiction convincingly. The author must first do an inordinate amount of hunting and sifting through the innumerable historical facts. After this hunting and sifting, the writer must incorporate the relevant facts, like the pieces of a mosaic, into the background of an interesting story. In the process, the author must keep the overall design in mind and not allow the many details to obscure the main idea or the plot.

## WHAT IS HISTORIC FICTION?

Historic fiction is basically any made-up story set in the past—very distant or more recent. In such fiction, authors attempt to take readers back to look at different times and life-styles. For instance, *The Stronghold*, by Mollie Hunter, is set in the Bronze Age. Hunter effectively makes an enormous leap back to explain the origins of *brochs*, mysterious circular fortresses on the Orkney Islands of Scotland. She invents the absorbing tale of a young genius who creates circular, hollow-walled structures to defend his people against slave-hunting invaders attacking from the sea.

---

[1]This book won the Mildred L. Batchelder Award in 1975. This award is presented annually for an outstanding children's book originally published in a foreign language in a foreign country but subsequently published in the United States.

In addition to books written expressly as historic fiction, this genre includes books that were written originally as contemporary fiction but have since become historic fiction. *Gone Away Lake,* by Elizabeth Enright, tells of two children who meet a charmingly eccentric couple living in the apparently deserted house on a lake shore. Contemporary at the time of its writing, *Gone Away Lake* portrays a life-style that has all but disappeared from the American scene. Adult readers may indeed have experienced such a way of life when they were young, but for the children of today this is history.

Although Sutherland (1986) states that only works originally written as historic fiction should be included in the genre, this chapter includes both types of works described above. Two other forms are also included here, even though some authorities do not consider them to be historic fiction. This chapter discusses historic retellings (accounts of real events recorded afterward by people who lived through them), such as the works of Laura Ingalls Wilder, and fantasies that involve a trip to a historic time, as in *Cat in the Mirror,* by Mary Stolz.

## TIME-SPECIFIC PROBLEMS

Some historic fiction presents a problem or plot conflict peculiar to the time in which the story is set.[2] In *The Witch of Blackbird Pond,* by Elizabeth George Speare, the heroine is considered a witch because, among other things, she can swim! This dilemma is peculiar to the nineteenth century.

Another character facing problems particular to a time and place is William Wythers in *Roanoke,* by Sonia Levitin. Labeled a pauper and threatened with imprisonment in Britain, William escapes as one of a motley group of settlers bound on an overcrowded ship to the New World. William is among the most successful of the group in adjusting to the new environment. He establishes a genuine friendship with an Indian chief, Manteo, who teaches him many skills necessary for survival. The author shows how William's attitudes toward Indians change during the course of the book. On shipboard, several settlers are discussing the possibility of encountering "savages":

> "I mean—can you imagine getting near a savage?"
> I swallowed, hard. "No." He expected more, and I said, "I mean, a savage is—is not like—like other people."

---

[2]Geoffrey Trease believes that all writers of historic fiction approach their task with one of two orientations: they are fascinated with either the differences or the similarities between bygone times and their own. See "The Historical Novelist at Work," in *Writers, Critics and Children: Articles from Children's Literature in Education,* eds. Geoff Fox et al. (New York: Agathon Press, 1976, pp. 39–51).

**Extending this energetic design across a two-page spread allowed the artist to use a wide horizontal space.** Illustration by John Gretzer from *Roanoke* by Sonia Levitin. Copyright © 1973 Sonia Levitin. Reprinted with the permission of Atheneum Publishers.

The following spring, after clinging to life in the hostile surroundings, William enjoys a quiet talk with his Indian friend:

> "I tell you," Manteo began, spreading his hands, and I thought for an instant how "white" that gesture was. And as I listened soberly, I wondered how "native" my passive expression might seem.

## UNIVERSAL PROBLEMS

Another kind of historic fiction deals with universal problems, ones people face in many different times. *Thy Friend, Obadiah*, by Brinton Turkle, is an example. Someone wants to be his friend, but Obadiah does not want to reciprocate—a problem children in all eras have encountered. The setting and the language are both quite effective, but are only incidental to Obadiah's solution.

Another example of this kind of historic fiction is *A Boy of Old Prague*, by Sulamith Ish-Kishor. Many children have had the experience of initially fearing or disliking someone and then getting over it once they know the person better. In this book, Tomas, an intelligent but quite uneducated peasant boy, grows up believing without question in the feudal system into which he was born; he accepts all the stories he hears about Jews living in the ghetto. This unquestioning belief is shaken after he is caught stealing a roasted chicken for his ill, starving mother and is sentenced to act as a servant for a Jew. Old Pesach and his beautiful granddaughter, Rachel, are both kind to Tomas. As he experiences their kindness, his sensitive nature responds warmly to these people, overcoming his earlier prejudice.

Children's interest in the things around them is the universal theme in a book about a boyhood in pre–World War II Japan. Many children have dawdled on the way home from school, studying intently things that attracted their attention. Taro Yashima has produced a first-person account of why it took him so long to walk home. *Plenty to Watch* is illustrated by Mitsu Yashima in soft colors, applied one over another; the shapes in the illustrations are outlined with pen. The pictures show many details of things Taro and his friends saw: a rice-pounding machine, a camphor factory, the sign painter, and the lantern makers.

The universal challenge of conquering unreasonable fears is handled imaginatively in *One Is One*, by Barbara Leonie Picard. Set in medieval England, this story tells of Stephen, a boy who is branded a coward by his many half-brothers and -sisters because of his fear of dogs. In attempting to ward off a persistent puppy, Stephen inadvertently tumbles it over the edge of a cliff. The pup's cries impel Stephen to rescue it, despite his aversion for dogs.

> It would not be true to say that Stephen overcame and lost his fear of dogs in the course of one September afternoon, for it was a long-drawn-out proceeding lasting several months, going from stage to stage and having its setbacks as well as its advances. But the cure which Stephen unknowingly had begun, he was able, with determination, to continue; going from a small beginning to a triumphant conclusion, using the confidence he had gained with his own small pup to serve him, eventually, with all other dogs.

One problem inherent in using historic fiction with children is that teachers may be tempted to apply the values of their own era. Stephen's decision to return to the monastery after he had learned to function so well outside its walls may seem regressive. Our society puts such a premium on being assertive and responding to new challenges that some readers may question

Stephen's apparent submissiveness. When sharing such historic fiction with children, teachers should be familiar with the values of the time, so they can explain behaviors that may be incomprehensible to child readers. Discussion about differing values is necessary to understanding of a time period.

Finding fulfillment in a chosen destiny is another universal theme presented in historic fiction. The details of *The Maud Reed Tale*, by Norah Lofts, place this story convincingly in England during the days of the Canterbury pilgrimages, but Maud's struggle could occur in any era. She wants to be a wool merchant, something those around her cannot understand. Maud resists her widowed mother's plans to send her to Beauclaire castle to learn "womanly graces."

A venerable theme, common in many genres, is that of a hero's quest or journey to find self-acceptance. In *Brothers of the Heart*, Joan W. Blos fleshes out this theme imaginatively. Complexly written, this story switches from third-person narrative to first-person accounts from letters and journal entries. The author acknowledges that all the "historic" material is made up, but despite this fact the tale has the ring of truth. The careful crafting of language is evident:

> These very weeks of Shem's advancement were extremely difficult for the Fiddler and Mrs. Perkins. Loneliness assailed them, and the loss of many hopes brought on a deep and melancholy state that could not be relieved. The Fiddler's health was much improved, but the mill could offer no employment at this time of year.

In *Four Horses for Tishtry*, Chelsea Q. Yarbro deals with the universal theme of the conflict between the talented and the untalented. Tishtry, a fifteen-year-old slave in ancient Greece, turns out to have a surprising gift for stunt horse racing. Because it will benefit her master, she is encouraged to develop it. Within the narrow confines of her slave's life, she searches for kindness from those who are not put off by her talent. She deals regularly with spiteful, envious people, but does encounter compassion in and get help from a slave boy and her tutor. The book ends on a hopeful note: Tishtry has accomplished an intermediate goal (winning the competition) and now her sights are set on competing in Rome. How that will turn out is not made evident, but it is obvious she is an exceptionally capable young woman.

Yarbro explores a similar theme and time period in *Locadio's Apprentice*, the story of Enecus, a fourteen-year-old boy who puts his newly acquired healing skills to work when Vesuvius erupts. The story begins placidly enough, as Enecus and his sister are growing up and beginning to think about what they would like to do. He would like to be a doctor, and a turn of fate makes this unlikely possibility a reality. Enecus finds that—though difficult—the work of doctor's apprentice is rewarding. His skills are put to a crucial test when he and his master seek refuge in a villa along the road on which people are fleeing the volcano's ravages. The author builds up small details to make the story, though dealing with unfamiliar places, objects, and events, totally believable. (The book includes glossaries, but Latin terms and medical terms are not defined in context.)

## FANTASY AS HISTORIC FICTION

Typically, historic fiction is solidly grounded in one period. The author works from the opening sentence to establish and maintain a sense of the chosen time. But another kind of historic fiction is found in books of fantasy in which characters journey, by any of a variety of means, through time from the present to another age.

*The Story of the Amulet*, by Edith Nesbit, is an old time-travel fantasy whose child characters act and talk in ways contemporary children find understandable. First published in 1907, this book is again available in an edition containing two other Nesbit stories: "Five Children and It" and "The Phoenix and the Carpet." The original illustrations by H. R. Millar will be of interest mostly to teachers; because of their small size and lack of color, they will not immediately appeal to children.

A more recent example of time-travel fantasy is *Cat in the Mirror*, by Mary Stolz. Erin, who lives in a New York City apartment, feels shut out by her busy parents and ignored by her classmates. A class film project involves shooting in the Metropolitan Museum, where she impulsively runs down a corridor and crashes into an Egyptian tomb. She awakens to discover herself in ancient Egypt. From this point, the author weaves superb historic fiction. Irun (Erin) inhabits a different world, but her problems bear a striking similarity to those she faced in modern New York. (For comparison purposes, a teacher might use Andre Norton's *Wraiths of Time*, which is discussed in Chapter 11; the main character is "transported" to Egypt in a similar manner.)

Writers who use historic time periods as part of fantasy frequently transport the main character to the historic period and leave him or her there until the story's end. A more difficult task is to move the main character back and forth between two times. In *The Night Rider*, by Tom Ingram, a gold bracelet is used as a linking device.[3] While fishing early one morning, Laura discovers a strange bracelet entangled with her line.

> . . . it was made of three ears of plaited wheat and in their center a face with bulging eyes and high cheekbones and hair swept back from the forehead. The chin was hidden by a curling beard writhing into the wheat. Sightless golden eyes stared into emptiness. The shining gold was like the innocent surface of a lake, smooth reflecting light hiding something mysterious.

The bracelet causes her to shift between the present and an indeterminate, more primitive past. No longer Laura but rather Merta, she meets handsome young Loen at the river's edge. Other encounters in this past time are interspersed with present-day Laura's uneasy, suspicious dealings with her stepfather, her mother, and her brother James.

Another example of this type of writing features a young boy as the main character. In Jay Williams's *The Hawkstone*, Colin Hyatt lives in contemporary times with his family on three hundred acres of land in rural Connecticut. Exploring one day, Colin finds a hawk pendant, which his sketchy knowledge of local history tells him must be from before 1750. What differentiates this story from others is that the pendant does not transport Colin to one historic time as a single character, but rather to several different eras as different people. First he is transported to a previous era as the Indian Quethepah, "He Who Goes Swiftly." When he returns to his own time, Colin is told by the local historian that there really was an Indian named Quethepah. At this point, he realizes the powers of his pendant. His brief visits to other times as different people continue; he is the chief Weaghinacut, whiteface James, and Sarah Linnett, a widow. In each case, the pendant provides the solution for a problem, as it does eventually in Colin's case. Using the stone ornament to find buried gold, Colin is able to solve the financial problems that threatened to cost his family their farm. The ending seems a bit contrived to adult readers, but students will not necessarily respond that way.

Other authors of fantasy as historic fiction use people instead of objects as the impetus that transports the main character. In *Pageants of Despair*, by Dennis Hamley, the main character is Peter, a twelve-year-old who lives in contemporary London and is sent to a country town to stay with an aunt and uncle. On the train, Peter encounters Gilbert, who describes himself as

---

[3]Another book in which the main characters move back and forth between time periods is Edward Eager's *Knight's Castle* (New York: Harcourt, Brace, 1956). The protagonists have several adventures in a medieval castle, to which they travel with the Old One, a lead soldier.

a scribe who writes down the miracle plays enacted by guild members in the town. Gilbert pleads for Peter's help. He fears the actors are confusing the plays with reality; the actor playing Cain may really kill the one playing Abel, and worse may follow. Peter is incredulous at Gilbert's story, but soon awakens to find himself in the town as it was five hundred years ago. The author includes perceptive material that reinforces the idea of the time transition:

> Gilbert's voice had changed as well. It was harsher, deeper, jagged somehow. And though Peter had been aware of a North-Country accent in the train, he was aware now of something much stranger—not now like the speech he was used to from Uncle Tom and Auntie Elsie, but broader, more difficult to understand—almost foreign. Some sounds Peter had great difficulty in understanding at all.

In *The Sword of Culann,* by Betty Levin, a combination of people and objects act to transport imaginative Claudia and her inquisitive younger brother, Evan, to an earlier time. On an island for a camping trip, the children encounter old Mr. Colman. He is a peculiar recluse living with a pet crow that comes only when he swears at it. Mr. Colman can visit the Other Place; first Evan and then Claudia see this place from a promontory through the fog. Eventually, they find themselves in Stone Age Ireland, where they meet the weaver Fedelm, whose mystical weaving predicts the future. The children encounter chaos, as Queen Medb prepares to attack the enemy Ulidians. As the battle intensifies, Claudia and Evan travel back and forth between the two times. This book is probably most appropriate for skilled readers since it is difficult to follow, especially at the beginning. A helpful three-page author's note following the story contains information about the period and how scribes wrote the manuscripts of the time.[4]

Named Children's Book of the Year for 1981 by the Canadian Library Association, *The Root Cellar,* by Janet Lunn, connects our time with the 1860s. Rose is sent to live with her Aunt Nan. She has spent a rather atypical childhood traipsing around the world, staying in hotels with her grandmother, a businesswoman, after her parents' death. She must make the abrupt transformation from the tightly ordered adults-only world of her grandmother to the more than slightly disheveled household of Aunt Nan and her four sons and husband. Even before the family arrives home from their daily activities, Rose has her first encounter with a past time. Initially

---

[4]The other books in the trilogy are *A Griffin's Nest* (New York: Macmillan, 1975) and *The Forespoken* (New York: Macmillan, 1976).

an unwilling visitor to the past, Rose quickly becomes caught up in the tumult of the Civil War.

Another author who writes effective time-travel fantasy is Margaret Anderson, notably in her *In the Keep of Time, In the Circle of Time,* and *The Mists of Time.*

## FICTION FROM THE PAST AS HISTORIC FICTION

Most of what follows is usually described in texts as modern realistic fiction. The books were originally written by their authors to describe current times and events. Yet if historic fiction is defined as books about a time that is past, such stories have become historic fiction.

The pastoral settings in which Elizabeth Enright's happy family groups enjoy their adventures do not exist any more. Memories of similar environments and experiences may linger pleasantly in the minds of some librarians and teachers who read these books to children, but for the child growing up in a metropolis, perhaps living in a single-parent family, this is indeed historic fiction. Even for a child growing up in a rural family, the details of the environment, for example, a coal chute, will mark the work as coming from a different time.

In *Gone Away Lake,* Enright writes effectively about sensory images in the small town where her story takes place. Describing a house, she writes: "The breath of the house came out to them. It smelled old." Cameron (1984) praises Enright's ability to evoke, with her vivid writing, worlds long gone. She characterizes Enright's style as "precise, ironic, and witty." She also notes Enright's ability to capture a "short time of happiness, of security and reason and humor," and to put her stories into words that children still enjoy today. *Gone Away Lake* depicts a very positive interrelation between generations, but its stylistic qualities are also apparent in the sequel *Return to Gone Away.*

Another story typical of Enright's best work is *The Saturdays.* The Melendy children, ranging from thirteen-year-old Mona to six-year-old Oliver, are growing up in a motherless household near New York City. This book was followed by three more about the same family: *The Four-Story Mistake, Then There Were Five,* and *Spiderweb for Two.* The series is remarkable in that even though the housekeeper is an important part of the family, Mr. Melendy does not abdicate responsibility for his children. Any of these books or *Thimble Summer,* the one for which Enright won the Newbery Medal in 1938, still "[make] the connection between their present childhood and their maturity" for child readers, according to Cameron.

A contemporary of Enright, Eleanor Estes, also wrote pleasant family adventures, two of which are set in the small town of Cranbury. In *The Moffats*, the children live in a fatherless household; their mother ekes out a precarious living as a dressmaker. The description of Rufus's first day at school is very funny.[5] This youngest Moffat is pleased about going, but his friend Hughie is not. At recess Hughie runs away, climbing aboard an empty freight car. Rufus has been warned by the superintendent that he must make sure Hughie stays in school, so he follows, and the two share an adventure, as the train takes them to the next town. Estes's writing recreates another age, notably in her description of the school routine:

> At this moment the bell rang for recess. The teacher carefully explained that recess meant they were all to go out and play in the school yard. It did not mean that they should go home. And after a while the bell would ring again. When it did, they were all to come back to Room One. That's what Miss Andrews said.
>
> "Class, stand," she said.
>
> The class stood up. Then they all had to sit down again because they all hadn't stood up together.
>
> "Class, stand," said Miss Andrews again.
>
> This time they all stood up the way she wanted them to. Rufus stood in the aisle by the window. He looked out, for he heard a train. The train whizzed past.
>
> "Class, march," said the teacher.
>
> The class had to go back to its seats and again the teacher said, "Class, march!" This time Rufus marched right past the desks, out the door, down the steps, and into the school yard with his classmates.

Estes's work as a whole, including this book and two sequels, *The Middle Moffat* and *Rufus M*, is lauded by Smith (1985) as reaffirming "the tradition of the American family story in which every child remains an individual and has a life independent of the family, and yet in which the family remains central." Smith sees these episodic stories as precursors of contemporary work by the popular writer Beverly Cleary.

In *A Prairie Boy's Winter*, William Kurelek has written a hauntingly beautiful and true account of farm life in Canada in the hard-pressed 1930s. To children, this era is as remote as a fairy tale; if grandparents read it with children, they will undoubtedly be struck by its realism.

In a similar vein is *Soup*, a piece of Americana in which Robert Newton

---

[5]Children can compare this account of a first day at school with the one in Beverly Cleary's *Ramona the Pest* (New York: Morrow, 1968) or the one in Rebecca Caudill's *Did You Carry the Flag Today, Charley?* (New York: Holt, Rinehart and Winston, 1966).

**William Kurelek's full-page paintings in fairly somber colors—in this case blues and greys—evoke not particular characters but rather a way of life.** From *A Prairie Boy's Winter* by William Kurelek. Copyright © 1973 by William Kurelek. Reprinted by permission of Houghton Mifflin Company.

Peck recounts childhood adventures with his friend, Soup. Peck is candid about the relationship between two growing boys:

> Soup was my best pal. His real and righteous name was Luther Wesley Vinson, but nobody called him Luther. He didn't like it. I called him Luther just once, which prompted Soup to break me of a very bad habit before it really got formed. As soon as the swelling went out of my lip, I called him Soup instead of Thoop.

Rolling down a steep hill in a barrel, ten-cent movies on Saturday afternoons, the first taste of corn silk smoked in an acorn pipe: these are only some of the activities that occupy the two friends. Although the tone of these reminiscences is often humorous, decisions concerning right and wrong come up frequently.

World War II has served as the context for some fiction for young readers. *Snow Treasure,* by Marie McSwigan, is another example of a book that was modern realistic fiction when it was first published (in 1942) but has since become historic fiction. The suspense-filled story is of courageous Norwegian children who smuggle gold past German soldiers by hiding it on sleds.

*The Bomber's Moon*, by Betty Vander Els, is a fictionalized account of the author's real-life experiences as a child during World War II, first in China and then, after a perilous trip, in India. The war seems for the most part quite remote, as perhaps it did to young children not in the immediate area of the fighting. The author's inclusion of specific details makes her writing vivid:

> By the third day most of us had our sea legs and were well enough to start classes. We sat along the edges of the bunks like swallows on a telephone wire. The feet of the kids on the upper bunk barely cleared the heads of those below.

Although the book is useful for the insights it provides into this historic era, the depiction of the school could be more positive. None of the teachers actually seemed to like the children, and one, Miss Elson, is stereotypical.

Not the war itself but rather one of its consequences is described in *Journey to Topaz*, by Yoshiko Uchida. This story is about the internment of Japanese-Americans following Pearl Harbor. Eleven-year-old Yuki finds her life turned upside down, her parents suddenly "enemy aliens," and life in the barren Utah desert, in a camp enclosed in barbed-wire, frightening and dismal. Uchida writes grippingly of the adjustments young Yuki must make. Her fiction is strengthened by being based on details from Uchida's own true-life story.

## EVALUATING HISTORIC FICTION

It is difficult for many teachers and librarians to assess historic fiction since they lack the adequate knowledge of history. For example, in *The Faraway Lurs*, poet Harry Behn created a prose account of the tragic love between Heather, one of the peaceful forest people, and Stone Wolf, the chief of a warrior tribe. To determine whether or not *The Faraway Lurs* is good, a teacher needs to know something about the Stone Age. Fortunately, reviewers of historic fiction can usually give an assessment of the accuracy of the material. Authenticity is another important aspect of historic fiction. Authenticity is measured by the credibility of the setting, the characters, and the action.

## AUTHENTICITY OF THE SETTING

To evaluate the authenticity of the setting in a work of historic fiction, the teacher should judge how skillfully the author transports the reader through time to another era. Is the author able to describe the smell of a kerosene lamp or how horse-drawn carriages on a road make a different sound from that of automobiles clogging the streets of today? Many authors are able to establish evocative historic settings. For example, *The Three Red Herrings*, by Rosemary Weir, is set in London, a formal city in the days when music hall shows, or vaudeville, was first popular, during the middle of the nineteenth century:

> All the way down the length of Sebastopol Avenue the tall red brick houses stood like soldiers on parade, silent, upright, and grim. From each front door six dazzlingly whitened steps led to the pavement. On every house a number was painted on the fanlight, and every door boasted a polished brass door knocker and an important-looking black iron bell-pull.

After their father's death, the three children seek jobs with a troupe of dancers. They go to the house of Mrs. Tully, who runs the troupe. It is considerably less elegant than their former home:

> The parlor was a small, stuffy room made dim by thick, slightly grubby Nottingham lace curtains over the windows and a large collection of plants in pots and hanging baskets, one of which thrust out long tentacles like an octopus of vegetable origin, and the other, which sprouted curious white hairs as if it were an aged little green man. In a bowl among the greenery a solitary goldfish swam mournfully around and around.

A different type of setting is described in *More Adventures of the Great Brain*, by John D. Fitzgerald. What this author does is evoke briefly yet effectively, through his word choices, a place quite unlike towns today. This title is one of a series of seven books about the escapades of a rising entrepreneur. In one book, the Great Brain charges admission to see his family's "water closet." In all the books, he conducts various slightly shady and always hilarious deals, some of which backfire. The year is 1896; the setting is Adenville,

> . . . a typical small Mormon town but quite up to date. There were electric light poles all along Main Street, and we had telephones. There were wooden sidewalks in front of the stores. Straight ahead I could see the railroad tracks that separated the west side of town from the east side. Across the tracks on the east side were two saloons, the Sheepmen's Hotel, a rooming house, and some stores.

This same quality of homespun nostalgia is found in Robert Newton Peck's eight books about his best friend Soup.

The houses and towns described by Weir and Fitzgerald, though different from what we see today, are somewhat familiar objects. But in writing historic fiction, authors frequently need to describe the totally unfamiliar, for example:

> Fires glittered along the shore in the lambent dusk; flames rose blue and green from the salt-soaked wood, and near the funeral ship, a large rock had been moved into place as an altar.
>
> Now the boy stood back and the men moved to lay their shoulder to the hull, easing the ship through the soft white sand and into the shallow water from where she would float away on the outgoing tide. Briefly [the blazing torch] lay burning on the deck, and then seized greedily on the pitch-smeared timber, licking along the decking to catch the gunwales until the narrow boat was lined with fire, burning scarlet from the pitch, and laced with the sharp, clear blue-green flames of salt.
>
> Out on the fire-streaked purple sea the flames took final hold on the drifting ship, a shivering pillar in the quiet dusk, until nothing remained but a vivid skeleton on the darkening water, which moved gently seaward as the funeral feast was eaten on shore.

This description is typical of the fine writing found in *Beorn the Proud*, by Madeleine Polland. Note how the author effectively uses vivid verbs ("seized greedily") and adjectives ("a livid skeleton") to evoke an unusual scene.

*Secret Lives*, by Berthe Amoss, communicates a sense of the social class and religious orientation of middle-class Catholics living in New Orleans in 1937, a setting that is vividly described. Twelve-year-old Addie, orphaned in a storm that swept through Honduras, wants to find out all about her beautiful mother. Holly, the granddaughter of the black cook, is an amateur witch who tries to help Addie unravel the mystery of her mother's past. When the facts are finally revealed, they are not pleasant, but Addie nonetheless accepts them. The story crackles with interesting, amusing details that do not once delay the plot's forward movement.

## AUTHENTICITY OF THE CHARACTERS

In addition to a realistic setting, a writer of effective historic fiction should also be able to establish believable characters, making people from years long gone come to life. Writers of this type of fiction develop characterizations in three ways: they describe physical appearance, language characteristics (as displayed in dialogue), and thoughts and feelings.

*In this drawing of two children sharing a happy, intimate moment, the absence of background directs the reader's focus to their activity.* Illustration from *Little House in the Big Woods* by Laura Ingalls Wilder. Illustrated by Garth Williams. Illustration copyright © 1953 by Garth Williams. Renewed 1981 by Garth Williams. Reprinted by permission of Harper & Row, Publishers, Inc.

An author tells what the characters look like by providing details of physique and feature. Laura Ingalls Wilder, author of what is probably the most popular series of American historic fiction,[6] provides many such physical descriptions. In *Little House in the Big Woods*, the first book in the series, she describes Pa: "His moustaches and his hair and his long brown beard were silky in the lamplight. . . ." Uncle George "had bold, merry blue eyes. He was big and broad and he walked with a swagger." Ma "looked pretty, with her bare arms plump and white, her cheeks so red and her dark hair smooth and shining. . . ." The eleven books, an imaginative reconstruction of Wilder's own childhood, are beloved because of their balanced presentation of vivid adventure and quiet joys. Life was hard, full of dangers like blizzards and hostile Indians. But life also had its homey delights, like Pa playing the fiddle in the firelight after the day's work was done. A cohesive element in all the stories is the family's sense of unity as they overcame their problems. With almost no didacticism, Wilder presents a testament to the strength of the family.

---

[6]Recognizing the strength of Wilder's contribution, the Association of Library Service to Children (a division of the American Library Association), every three years, gives an award in her name to an author or illustrator whose books, published in the United States over a period of years, have made a substantial and lasting contribution to children's literature. Winners have included Clara Judson, Ruth Sawyer, E. B. White, Beverly Cleary, Theodore Geisel (Dr. Seuss), and Maurice Sendak.

Character description also includes details of apparel, and particularly astute writers show how such details affect behavior. Clothes not only make the man or woman but also affect what he or she can do. In *Hail Columbia*, author Patricia Beatty describes the Baines family as they get ready to meet their relative:

> It was raining hard. The Captain had on his long yellow oilskin coat and black sou'wester hat and Mama her brown ulster. Rowena and I were bundled up to the eyes in mackintoshes, slippery black ones, that made us look like wet sea lions, Mama said. I didn't see how Aunt Columbia would ever know who we were.

As the boat comes in, they see her waving:

> A lady was standing at the top of the gangplank. She had on a gray-and-black-checkered traveling costume, no mackintosh at all, and a black hat with white and blue birds sitting on it like they were on a nest. She held an umbrella over herself, a man's big black one. "Is that our aunt?" I asked mama.

It is indeed Aunt Columbia, younger sister of the Captain and a woman who transcends the limitations of confining female clothing just as she ignores conventional ideas about women's roles. Rowena, Louisa, and Mama find life in their small Oregon town is not tranquil after this suffragette comes to live with them. The story describing Columbia's efforts to fight injustices in the town could have happened at almost any time. The details of the environment are particular, but the struggle against inequities is universal.

Details of apparel are also used to characterize suffragettes marching to get the vote in *Whistle Down a Dark Lane*, by Adrienne Jones:

> Though the stirring music of the military bands had faded away down Peachtree Street, the company of women stepped along with great elan. Some wore their hair bobbed in the daring new style, replicas of F. Scott Fitzgerald girls; their skirts showed a bold amount of leg. Others were as sedate as Mother in high-necked lace shirtwaists, with skirts exposing only a modest glimpse of buttoned shoe and ankle.

The youngest and last of the contingent shouts to the main character, Margy, that times are changing and throws her a kiss. Margy and her sister Blainey are growing up in a well-to-do Southern family. Margy becomes aware that changes in the outside world are paralleling even more significant changes taking place in her personal world. The girls' adored and handsome Daddy leaves the family, so the three females must cope alone. In this book and the sequel, *A Matter of Spunk*, author Jones skillfully uses physical descriptions to bring the main and minor characters to life in a variety of settings.

A second way authors establish characters is through the dialogue. The spoken language in historic fiction should evoke with authenticity the time depicted but should not overwhelm child readers. Having to stumble over too many unfamiliar words that are not decipherable by their context will diminish a reader's interest.[7]

Skilled writers create dialect that bespeaks but does not belabor the time period. Examples are found in the work of Lois Lenski, a prolific writer of regional stories based on her travels to the various areas.[8] Her dialect samples represented a significant accomplishment in recording language when they were first published. *Cotton in My Sack* tells of a family of cotton pickers, who toil endlessly in the fields for the pleasure of spending their small wages on weekends. Lenski includes the following dialogue:

"We'll git the money to foot this bill."

"Thinks we're pore, don't she."

". . . 'cause it might could git antses all over it."

In *Phoebe Fairchild*, the characters also speak in dialect:

"Laws, yes; she's laid in a prime lot of chip straws . . . ."

". . . that always gives you a pain in your maw."

"Shame to spile good hen's eggs . . . ."

Similar effective use of dialect to create character is found in *Thee, Hannah,* by Marguerite de Angeli. This is the appealing story of a small girl who despises her plain Quaker garb until she finds it has unexpected advantages during the Civil War. The Quaker dialect is recreated: "Thee knows, dear, thy father wants thee to be happy . . . ."

In some books, the characters' language changes. For example, in *Abraham Lincoln*, author Genevieve Foster shows how the language of the president changed as he grew older. She provides samples of the dialect Lincoln spoke as a child:

"One two three—I drapped one, Pappy."

"Kaint we go now?"

---

[7]See pp. 50–51 in *Talent Is Not Enough* by Molly Hunter (New York: Harper and Row, 1976). Hunter discusses the writing of several different genres, including historic fiction (on pp. 31–56). Joan Stidham Nist wrote an appreciation of this insightful book in "Too Good to Miss" (*English Journal*, 72, January 1983, pp. 69–70).

[8]Lenski's *Strawberry Girl* won the Newbery Medal in 1946 and is available on a cassette from Random House/Miller-Brody Records (#NAR 3020).

"No, Mammy," Abe replied, "jest sayin' the lesson."

This contrasts with the polished, slightly formal language he used toward the end of his life:

"Are you not overcautious when you assume that you cannot do what the enemy is constantly doing?

"If I know my heart . . . my gratitude is free from any taint of personal triumph."

This is adult language, of course, different from the shorter sentences of a child. It is also, however, a very polished style of speech; Lincoln knew that his home dialect was not appropriate in his new world.[9]

Language is used skillfully to evoke characters in *It Had To Be You*, by Elizabeth Byrd. The Great Depression seems to impinge only minimally on the heroine and her friends. Soup kitchens and apple-sellers in the streets are mentioned, but are incidental, minor worries for Kitty, who attends a wealthy and progressive high school. Some commonalities with the present do appear; for example, the girls wait for the boys they like to notice them. The book is unusual in that Kitty doesn't get her boy: he goes off to Annapolis unaware that she wants him to fall in love with her. It also seems unusual to modern readers that teenagers would interact as formally as these young people do. Byrd includes many details that evoke the time period. Interesting to teachers aware of language is an exchange embedded in a description of a day at school from Kitty's point of view. The English teacher is talking with the group about their language use:

". . . you 'bright children' date yourselves a dozen times a day with stale slang. I have heard the 'cat's meow' since 1926—why can't they be put to rest in some alley, along with their pajamas?"

There were snickers, and he frowned. "You girls are the worst offenders. You'd scorn last year's dress, but you're still using 'vampy,' 'the bee's knees,' 'catsy'—one marvels how cats populate slang . . . why is it 'catsy' to use old-fashioned slang?"

"I guess it's just a habit," I said.

"Well . . . get into some new stuff then. . . . Who knows of any?"

Betty spoke up bravely. "I think the 'kitten's cuffs' is new, sir."

He groaned. "This extraordinary obsession with cats. Well, if it's fresh, use it." He went on to talk about the vividness of the American language that came from localities, like "livin' in high cotton" and "eatin' high on the hog." They'd always seem fresh because they were descriptive. Any questions?

---

[9]All the examples of characterization through language given here represent speakers of American English. Particularly skilled use of British English is found in Hester Burton's *The Flood at Reedsmere* (Cleveland: World, 1968).

I said, "Why can't words we use all the time ever get into the dictionary? Like 'snuck.' It's so natural to say that a cat snuck in."

We couldn't help laughing, and he laughed, too. " 'Sneaked' does sound wrong, doesn't it. But use it in your compositions until the dictionary catches up."

In addition to physical descriptions and dialogue, successful authors of historic fiction also provide psychological insights. To respond fully to characters, readers must know their thoughts and feelings. In *Leopard's Prey*, by Leonard Wibberley, the author reveals what Mr. Treegate is like:

> The door was opened and his nephew Manly appeared. Mr. Treegate had mixed feelings about the boy, whose care he had undertaken, together with his brother and sisters, on the death of their father in a smallpox epidemic two years before. At times he felt the boy was a fine young fellow who would make his way readily in the world. At times he felt the boy was flighty and unstable, quick-tempered and headstrong, and must certainly come to ruin.
>
> Peter Treegate had no children of his own, though married twenty-six years. This was one of the conditions of life which he found hard to bear. He had thought of adopting Manly and the other children but had not done so, delaying because of some obscure reason which he could not quite fathom. He told himself that the children were entitled to their father's identity. But the fact was that, although the children were his brother's, he was hurt that he had none of his own, and, in his hurt, kept a little distance between himself and them.

Wibberly wrote a series of books that chronicles the Treegate family's part in American history from just before the Revolutionary War, in *John Treegate's Musket*, through the War of 1812, in *The Last Battle*.

In the best historic fiction, authors are careful to show thoughts and feelings as they would have been in the era depicted, which is often different from the way they are today. Sometimes characters reveal their inner nature through the things they say about themselves—in first-person narration. At the very beginning of *Hakon of Rogen's Saga*, by Eric Christian Haugaard, Hakon himself says:

> A motherless child is both an object of pity and of scorn. He learns early to depend upon himself, for he is hardened by never having experienced the mother's gift to the child, that love which never asks why. Love came to me only as a reward, something which depended upon my own behavior.
>
> I believe that my father never forgave me for causing my mother's death. I hardly ever remember him smiling and I never heard him laugh. His world was one of gloom, of evil forebodings, of disasters lurking behind each day like hungry wolves behind trees. His birth present to me was a feeling of guilt, which covered me as a cloud does the mountaintop.

***This powerful woodcut employs the crude angularity of the medium to evoke the story's tension.***
Illustration by Leo and Diane Dillon from *Hakon of Rogen's Saga* by Erik Christian Haugaard.
Copyright © 1963 by Erik Christian Haugaard. Reprinted by permission of Houghton Mifflin
Company.

Hakon learns that nothing lasts forever: his father's desire for a new bride drastically changes their lives. This Viking tale, reminiscent of ancient sagas, is full of memorable images revealing the philosophy of the culture. In the sequel, *A Slave's Tale*, author Haugaard describes a journey, undertaken in kindness and to fulfill a vow but ending in tragedy. He uncompromisingly depicts both the heights of honorable behavior and the depths of the treachery that humans are capable of.

Another first-person narrator who reveals both her own character and that of those she observes is Louisa in *Prairie Songs*, by Pam Conrad. This book was the winner of the 1986 International Reading Association's Children's Book Award, given for distinguished fiction to the first or second book by an author. Without making value judgments, the story contrasts the rock-solid character of Louisa and her family, especially her mother, with that of the elegant Emmeline Berryman, the doctor's wife. In the end, after the conflict between life on the prairie and those who seek to live there is played out to its tragic conclusion, Louisa concludes that it is her mother who represents the values she admires.

About this narrator, Hickman (1986) comments: "And Louisa is an uncommonly good first-person narrator, compassionate and articulate without seeming overschooled for the time and place." Conrad uses her child narrator to impressive effect when she has her say, at the book's beginning:

> There are two pictures of Emmeline Berryman I have frozen in my memory for all eternity, and this was the first. She was dressed in the most magnificent violet dress I could ever remember seeing, and across her lap lay a sparkling pink parasol flounced with lace and eyelet.

Louisa then goes on to something else, leaving the reader to wonder about the nature of the second picture and providing incidentally, in the word "frozen," a foreshadowing of later events. In fact, not until 144 pages later is the second picture in Louisa's mind revealed, in one of the most graphic scenes in recent children's literature:

> Mrs. Berryman was sitting in the snow, and this is the second picture I will always have of her in my mind—Emmeline was frozen. She had on only a gingham dress, and her shawl was lying around her skirt. I can't remember much else except her hands and face frozen in great horror. Her fingers were extended, stiff icicles of white flesh, and her face, finely coated with white frost, was captured in a ghastly, silent scream that must have locked her face long before the cold did.

In addition to creating believable characters in the ways described above, authors of historic fiction sometimes show readers how people change as a story progresses. Such changes are an important part of the story of the plain, unhappy wife of the Duke of Milan in *The Second Mrs. Giaconda*, by E. L. Konigsburg. Young Beatrice d'Este is a friend of Leonardo da Vinci and of his incorrigible apprentice, Salai. Salai helps Beatrice gain the self-assurance and grace she needs to transcend her physical imperfections and engage her husband's interest. In the process, however, other changes occur.

> After Beatrice returned from Venice, Salai kept track of all her activities. Her collections of glass and silver and musical instruments grew. Her gowns grew fancier. Her confidence grew. Her conversation and her laughter grew louder. Everything grew, and she outgrew her need for Salai.
>
> Salai missed her, missed what they had had between them. It was inevitable that what they had had between them would become stretched thin as each took up a firmer footing in life. Beatrice outgrew her need for Salai before he outgrew his for her; that, too, was bound to happen.

An articulate describer of her own writing processes, Konigsburg (1976) has written humorously of how this book came into being, in the process analyzing da Vinci's character and commenting extensively on his relationship with Salai.

Another character who changes dramatically as a result of the events in a book is Helena in *When Daylight Comes*, by Ellen Howard. This is one of the most gripping pieces of historic fiction published recently and may strike some readers as grisly. Yet Howard's intent is clearly not to sensationalize but rather to contrast the politely civilized world of white plantation owners and the violence that erupts when the smoldering fury of slaves is released. Although most readers are aware of the problems that slavery caused in the United States, few will know of the revolt that occurred in 1733 in the Danish Virgin Islands. Despite the unfamiliarity of the setting, author Howard vividly recreates the elegance of plantation life and the squalor of the revolutionary camps in which the main character discovers what it means to be cold, hungry, exhausted, and helpless. The transition between the two is brought about when Helena's comfortable home is devastated.

> They were in the dining room. . . . the crystal chandelier that was Mama's pride swung on its chain, unlit, above the table until Philip, annoyed by its swinging near his head, reached up and wrenched it from the ceiling and smashed it on the floor. Slave women fell upon the brilliant prisms of shattered glass, gathering them up with delighted cries, unmindful of the cuts the glass made in their hands. Other women were tearing down the velvet draperies at the win-

dows and wrapping the cloth around their bodies, laughing and, Helena saw, some . . . were crying, tears running down their shining cheeks as they stroked the rich, soft cloth.

Helena felt her captor's grasp relax and twisted frantically to escape him. He hit her so hard on the side of the head her ear buzzed, and dazed, she put her hand to it and felt the wetness of her own blood. Her legs gave out beneath her, and the excruciating pain in her head told her she hung by her hair from his hand. . . . He . . . hurled her at the table.

Howard's skill is impressive. Throughout the next few pages, to intensify Helena's denial of what she has witnessed, the author shows her avoidance reaction (italics added): "She pushed out of her mind the vision of *what* lay on top of . . . [the table] . . . the bloody *thing* on the table at home. . . ." Later, Helena sees a group of slaves pouring down a street: "Before Helena let herself realize *what* was impaled upon the pole. . . ." In each of these instances Helena is unable to deal with death, and therefore her reaction is described using inanimate rather than animate words.

One of the most interesting self-revelations comes to Helena midway through the book. The slave women, including Caroline, Helena's personal slave, are camping apart from the men, and Helena is with them.

Why, Helena suddenly wondered, had it never occurred to her before to ask about Caroline's parents? She had assumed they were among the other Sodtmann slaves. Slaves didn't seem to stay together in families. Perhaps, as Mama had said, they didn't care about each other the way white people did. There was so much she didn't know about Caroline, she thought. She had never really talked to her before, except to give her orders, of course. And yet, Caroline was quite pleasant to talk to—actually quite as pleasant as a Danish girl might be.

Later in the book, when Helena has lived with the slave women in their encampment for some time, she reflects on the role language plays in thinking:

Helena's heart pounded with the renewed realization of her changed station. Lodama is not *my* slave, she thought. I am *hers*. And suddenly Helena realized it had been a long time since she had called the queen by her slave name, Judicia, even in her thoughts. It can mean so much, what a person is called, Helena thought. Perhaps that is why we give slaves new names when we buy them. Their African names belonged to them when they were free. When we give them new names, we make them ours. We make them *feel* like slaves. That was what had struck home to Helena when Lodama called her " 'Lena." So long as black people called her "Missy 'Lena," she felt like a mistress. But just plain " 'Lena" made her *feel* like a slave.

At the end, Helena is left with a dilemma, and author Howard wisely avoids the temptation to spell out a solution. The remnants of the slave uprising, including dignified Queen Lodama, are facing the inevitable reassertion of the planters' superior strength. They will go off into the forest, and leave eleven-year-old Helena to return to her family. Physically still a child, she has matured psychologically during her captivity. In the process, she has learned to stand apart and see herself and the slaves in a larger context. She is not the same person the blacks led away from the plantation house. How can she return to her family as a person they will not know?

## AUTHENTICITY OF THE ACTION

For historic fiction to be good, the events that take place should be plausible for the period and the characters in question. We all live within societal constraints, though in our age these may seem to be rapidly disappearing. Even in our permissive era, some actions are possible or impossible, depending on the circumstances. This was true of any historic time, as well. Readers with twentieth-century sensibilities may wish a story had ended differently, but another ending may not have been possible in another era.

Gordon Cooper writes simply and with affection about his heroine in *An Hour in the Morning*. This gentle story of a twelve-year-old country girl in Edwardian England is not full of roaring adventures but is still likely to live in children's imaginations. Cooper details the daily life of Kate, a general maid to a farmer and his daughters, with hypnotic charm. Perceptive readers will also note the social commentary implicit in Kate's calm acquiescence to the rigid boundaries of class. In the sequel, *A Time in a City*, Kate is employed as a kitchen maid during the beginning years of World War I. She works long, strenuous hours; her pleasures are few but keenly anticipated and enjoyed.

In *The Slave Dancer*, Newbery Medal–winner Paula Fox presents a dramatic story about Jessie, thirteen years old and white, who is abducted to a slave ship. His forced task is to provide fife music for "dancing the slaves," a common practice devised to prevent their muscles from atrophying in the packed quarters during the long trip to America. The slaves' degradation and the inhumanity of those in charge of the ship are presented graphically, but without overt comment by Fox. She has been criticized by some reviewers, such as Hoffman (1974), for what they see as the irresponsibility of her hero in not taking action against the injustices he sees, either as a boy or later as a man. But was it possible for Jessie to do anything, given the times and his position in life? Turning him into a crusader against slavery would have made him a more sympathetic character to contemporary readers, but wouldn't it have undermined the historic authenticity of the novel?

In contrast to the two authors just discussed, Joan Aiken, a master of "history re-arranged," gives many facts a cavalier treatment to suit her own purposes. Authenticity isn't her first concern. In her imaginary England, the Tudor-Stuarts are kings; the House of Hanover has never gained the throne. Much of the action involves Hanoverian attempts to overthrow the government by outrageous means, such as a long-distance cannon fired across the Atlantic. Fast-moving plots, full of improbable events and idiosyncratic characters, are trademarks of this author. Her altering of historic details will not bother children, who will be mostly unaware of it. They will simply enjoy following the adventures of Bonnie and Sylvia as they escape their mean governess (in *The Wolves of Willoughby Chase*), of Simon and his balloon riding over the English countryside (in *Black Hearts in Battersea*), or of Dido in Nantucket, where she is treated as a slave by a wicked aunt (in *Nightbirds on Nantucket*). Such books as these are a useful supplement to more conventional historic fiction, in which the author does less conscious fictionalizing. Aiken's work may well interest reluctant readers; after they have had rewarding experiences reading her books they may be lured into reading less easily accessible historic fiction.

## THE IMPORTANCE OF BALANCE

There is a temptation for the writer of historic fiction to cram in many details, to pack a story with descriptions of objects, people, and environments that lend authenticity. This temptation needs to be curbed by an awareness that the plot must move along. The details must be accurate but cannot overwhelm the action.

Good historic fiction maintains this balance of detail and action. For example, after reading *A Traveler in Time*, by Alison Uttley, most readers probably remember the inexorable sweep of the plot toward its inevitable conclusion. Readers may forget the authentic period details that add richness to the work. At one point, the author describes a portrait that a painter has done of Mary, Queen of Scots:

> She had black, drop earrings, and black jet beadwork on her bosom, and a fine ruff edged in point lace. It had a bunch of pearls to fasten it, not ribbons like ordinary folk. There was a gold crucifix hanging by a velvet ribbon from her neck and a cross and beads at her girdle, all painted glittering and real as life. There was a cloak of lawn on her shoulders, not for warmth, just for beauty, all transparent and made very soft and light.

The details about characters and setting add to readers' enjoyment, but when finished, what readers remember is the tragedy of how Anthony Babington's loyalty to haughty Mary led him to the gallows and her to the block.

Another example of a book that achieves a balance between historic detail and story line is *The Boy Who Loved Music*, by David Lasker. History in picture-book format is rare. In this case, Joe Lasker provides pleasant, accurate watercolor paintings to illustrate this book written by his son. The younger Lasker, himself a musician, tells a probably apocryphal tale of the creation of Joseph Haydn's "Farewell" Symphony. The two Laskers make the period live, without overwhelming readers with too many words or too much visual detail. Teachers should probably read this aloud to a class; the audience suggested by the content and the reading-difficulty level is intermediate-grade students, but they are unlikely to choose a picture book for themselves.

## HISTORIC FICTION FOR YOUNG CHILDREN

Creating authentic, engrossing historic fiction for young readers or listeners is difficult. Few children younger than eleven or twelve have developed any accurate sense of finite time relationships. Yesterday seems "a long time ago," whereas in September, Christmas will arrive "real soon." Most young children are convinced their parents grew up in "the olden days," an assessment not often shared by the parents!

The best books of historic fiction for children under eleven deal with quite specific events in a narrow sequence of elapsed time. Brinton Turkle's series of books about Obadiah are particularly fine examples. In *Thy Friend, Obadiah*, events are commonplace: he goes on errands for his mother, the family goes to meeting (church), and he slides on the ice. The time period that elapses is unspecified but could be as brief as a week. The homely details make this a book even the very young can enjoy, despite its historical setting. This book was preceded by *Obadiah the Bold* and followed by *The Adventures of Obadiah* and *Rachel and Obadiah*.

Books of historic fiction that attempt to deal with larger blocks of historic time are often as uninteresting as many conventional history textbooks. Pleasant black line drawings augmented with orange, red, and yellow washes illustrate *Snorri and the Strangers*, by Nathaniel Benchley, but do not compensate for the lack of effective characterization. The story covers an entire winter, and the characters and their plight never really come alive. "That winter was a bad one and the people had a hard time finding things to eat." This pragmatic language does not convey the drama and the hardship that such a situation would in fact entail.

A more effective treatment of a long period of time is found in *Wagon Wheels*, by Barbara Brenner. In four brief chapters (a total of only sixty-four pages), the author presents the account of a black family, separated and then reunited in Solom City, Kansas Territory, in the 1870s. The story, full of action, develops the characters of Ed, a loving widower, and his three boys. It is a survival story, in which the characters are searching for land where they can live freely.

*The Drinking Gourd*, by F. N. Monjo, successfully creates believable characters and condenses historic events that actually stretched out over a number of years into a brief episode. The story is a fictionalized account of the escape of slaves north to freedom on the Underground Railroad, following the "drinking gourd" (the Big Dipper). Tommy Fuller, enduring day-long church services with too little patience, is tempted into mischief and is sent home. Ousted for misbehavior, he discovers his father is engaged in illegal activity, helping slaves to freedom. Tommy's brief encounter with Big Jeff and his family leads to a frightening moment when discovery seems certain. Only Tommy's quick-witted thinking deflects the marshall and his men.

In *The Secret of the Sachem's Tree*, Monjo retells a popular legend but incorporates created characters: young Jonathon Wadsworth and his friends and poor Goody Gifford, half-crazed with sorrow for her husband who was lost in battle. The story poignantly reflects the bigoted attitudes of people living in the American Colonies during the time of King James II: "Says your fine Sir Edmund: 'The mark of an Indian means no more than the scratch of a bear's paw!'" Other equally engrossing embellishments of fact with fiction are Monjo's *King George's Head Was Made of Lead*, a monologue in which a statue of the king complains about the concerted effort colonists have made to disobey him, and *The Vicksburg Veteran*, a long narrative poem telling of the city's capture from the point of view of General Grant's son.

*This Time, Tempe Wick?*, by Patricia Lee Gauch, is another Revolutionary War story, set two hundred years ago in New Jersey. Brave Tempe Wick singlehandedly prevents disillusioned and defeated Pennsylvania soldiers from robbing her. They want her horse but find that taking it from the young girl is not as easy as they expected. Tempe is unusual: she kept growing long after the time most other girls stopped; she can throw her friend David halfway across the kitchen when they wrestle; she can stay at the plow as long as her father can on a spring night. In addition, she is good-humored and inventive in finding a way to save her horse. In these

*Artist Margot Tomes creates the essential characteristics of the fop—bemused smile, delicate hand gesture, and raised eyebrows.* Illustration by Margot Tomes reprinted by permission of Coward, McCann & Geoghegan from *The Secret of the Sachem's Tree* by F. N. Monjo, illustrations copyright © 1972 by Margot Tomes.

and other ways, Tempe is depicted by the author as a girl who did not fit the conventional mold of the time, when females were expected to be docile homebodies who deferred to males. The author is saying that even in those times there were girls who thought and did for themselves.

*Ox-Cart Man*, by Donald Hall, is essentially a visual presentation with accompanying words. Barbara Cooney created masterful pictures for this gentle account of early colonial life in New England. In the process, she won her second Caldecott Medal, and the book was also named a Notable Book by the American Library Association. The story begins with an unnamed farmer packing the products of a year's work into a cart. Readers will be saddened when the ox itself is sold at the market. The text follows the farmer through a year's cycle. By the story's end, readers realize why the ox had to be sold. Cooney uses a technique reminiscent of early American paintings on wood, and in the pictures gives readers a lot of additional detail that doesn't, therefore, have to be given in words. An imaginative book design shows the pictures to best advantage.

A picture-book format is also used for Phyllis Krasilovsky's *The First Tulips in Holland*. With help from S. D. Schindler's pictures, Krasilovsky gives readers an engrossing look at a very different time. This fictionalized account of how tulips—which first appeared some four hundred years ago—were brought to Holland is handsomely showcased in this large book. The illustrator's knowledge of botany, architecture, and costumes (and skill in depicting the same) is demonstrated to maximum effect. As it is in *Ox-Cart Man*, the passage of time is shown in both words and pictures, a more effective technique than using mostly words (as Nathaniel Benchley did in *Snorri and the Strangers*).

## HISTORIC FICTION FOR OLDER CHILDREN

Children in intermediate grades have better-developed cognitive skills and sense of time relationships; therefore, books of historic fiction for them can be more complex. Historic fiction for older children can deal with less familiar events and cover longer periods of elapsed time.

Historic fiction about England is plentiful, and *A Cold Wind Blowing* is among the best.[10] Barbara Willard provides impressively detailed landscapes showing sixteenth-century England as a place of great hardship for people of low station. Royal caprice caused common heads to roll, and the king's decision to break the power of the Roman Catholic church wrought many changes. Despite all of this, the common folk endured and even found time to enjoy themselves. The author describes the chaos and joys of the times via a history of three families. In the process, she gives immediacy to the era.

---

[10]This is the third in a series of five books following the fortunes of the Medley and Mallory families from the time of Richard III to the English Civil War. The others are *The Lark and the Laurel* (New York: Harcourt Brace, 1970), *A Sprig of Broom* (New York: E. P. Dutton, 1972), *The Iron Lily* (New York: E. P. Dutton, 1974), and *Harrow and Harvest* (New York: E. P. Dutton, 1975).

Writers are becoming more conscious of women's roles in history, as is E. L. Konigsburg in *A Proud Taste for Scarlet and Miniver*. This account of Eleanor of Aquitaine's life is cast in an imaginative frame: Eleanor is sitting on a cloud in heaven, waiting for her husband to arrive. With the queen are her mother-in-law, an abbot, and a knight; to while away the time they tell stories of their lives. Eleanor influenced the politics of the time, helped invent rules of courtly love that still govern modern courtesy, and affected the history of England. Konigsburg makes this period, usually remembered as a list of names and dates, come alive, so readers feel the frustrations and sorrows of seven hundred years ago. Her Eleanor is an ambitious, intelligent, and energetic heroine.

The same heroine is presented in a biography by Polly Schoyer Brooks, *Queen Eleanor. Independent Spirit of the Medieval World*. Brooks recreates an amazing set of adventures in a book that focuses on action. Eleanor, indefatigable in performing her duties, brought about amazing cultural changes. The main character and others are developed through description rather than dialogue. There is no sense of Eleanor's personality; the author would have had to have surmised that. This book makes an interesting foil to Konigsburg's: read together, they give an engagingly complete picture of a complex woman.

Writers of historic fiction often take readers to lands farther away than England. *The Bright and Morning Star*, by Rosemary Harris, is the third of a trilogy of books about royalty in ancient Egypt.[11] The book tells of a woman's love for her unlovable son, made recalcitrant by a mysterious illness that left him deaf and mute. With a cat, the mother journeys to a foreign land, after an omen star suggests the journey.

In addition to tales of distant lands, historic fiction for older children also includes stories of life in America. In *George Midgett's War*, Sally Edwards writes about the Revolutionary War era. Instead of focusing on the well-known and influential people often written about, she writes about a small band of fishermen from the Outer Banks of North Carolina. Independent people, fourteen-year-old George and his father see the war as distant and unimportant. Unimportant, that is, until they are drawn into its very center as they navigate treacherous waterways to deliver needed

---

[11]The first volume, *The Moon in the Cloud* (New York: Macmillan, 1970), concerns Reuben's journey to Kemi (Egypt) in search of two lions and two cats for Noah's ark. The second, *The Shadow on the Sun* (New York: Macmillan, 1971), tells of the rescue of Meri-Mehkmet from the evil Prince of Punt. *The Moon in the Cloud* won the Carnegie Medal, given each year to the outstanding children's book written by a British author and published in Britain.

SALLY EDWARDS

# George Midgett's War

GOWING

*This realistic full-color cover painting by Toby Gowing informs readers of the time period and the environment in which the story takes place.* By Sally Edwards. Cover illustration from *George Midgett's War*. Copyright © 1985 by Sally Edwards. Reprinted with the permission of Charles Scribner's Sons.

supplies to Washington's forces at Valley Forge. The story is set within the context of large historic events but explores the more personal but no less important event of a youngster's coming to terms with his father and with himself.

Erskin Midgett . . . stood at the hearth, a tall, big-boned man with blue-green eyes, mostly green, dark red hair, and a red stubble beard. His eyes never twinkled, but there was warmth, even affection, in his calm, very direct gaze. His skin was as tough as whiteleather, the leather used in harnesses for draft animals, and no amount of bear grease, even if he had used it, would smoothe the calluses on his hands. He was thirty-five years old, but he had never looked young, nor would he ever look old. He lived against the wind, and the wind had scarred him ageless. Even in repose his body seemed to strain against an invisible force. He did not stand to his full height. Only when he was angry did the familiar crouch snap tall and intimidating.

Only when they near the end of their perilous journey does Erskin finally see that George has the courage to make difficult decisions under stress. George's determination carries them through to a successful completion. Commending the book to readers, Sebesta (1985) comments: "But here's the point. Their stories are touched with awareness that their lives are part of the pattern of wider events. They know that whatever the pattern is, they're in it. They're a part of courage."

Troubled times are also the background for *Red Pawns*, by Leonard Wibberley. Set on the brink of the War of 1812, this detailed story extends the chronicles of the Treegate family, mentioned earlier. Young Manly Treegate, not at first expecting adventure along the inland Canadian border, finds battle there with Indians, unfortunate pawns in the struggle between white American colonists, the English, and the French. The book conveys the feeling of the era far more effectively than do most textbook accounts.

America as seen through the eyes of Chinese immigrants in the early nineteenth century is the setting of Laurence Yep's *Mountain Light*. Yep explores with insight the cultural contrasts among the clans in China, and between China and America. Nineteen-year-old Squeaky Lau must come to America to work in the California gold fields. He leaves behind the girl with whom he has fallen in love, of whom his clan disapproves. The clan's influence over Squeaky is all-pervasive:

"No clan?" I gasped. "But that's like . . . like trying to stand on thin air." I tried to picture it, but it was too frightening to spend much time on—like picturing myself climbing a ladder of knives.

When Squeaky is in America, Yep illustrates cultural differences by having him react to unfamiliar objects:

In the middle of the cluttered desk was an odd demonic clicking contraption. Its front was occupied by a white circle divided into twelve parts. Two metal rods projected from the center—the short one didn't move at all while I studied it, but the larger one moved a fraction.

More than clocks are unfamiliar to Squeaky as he tries to adapt to living in the new land.

Set later in the nineteenth century, *I Tell a Lie Every So Often*, by Bruce Clements, evokes the pastoral landscapes along the Missouri River. The book features an engagingly wise and innocent narrator. Henry, fourteen, tells an amiable, absentminded lie that takes him and elder brother Clayton on an unnecessary odyssey miles up river by boat, mule, and wagon. The nineteenth-century midwest is brought beautifully to life.

The extended spaciousness of a Montana cattle ranch in 1885 is contrasted with the claustrophobic closeness of a small town in Maine, in *Third Girl from the Left*, by Ann Turner. Young Sarah rebels against what the conventional women who are her neighbors think it means to be a woman. An opportunity to escape comes in the form of a letter printed in a newspaper, in which a rancher seeks a bride. When she arrives in Montana, she finds that her betrothed has not been completely honest with her. In the end, Sarah finds she will need to learn to live with uncertainty. She doesn't really know if her headstrong decision to follow the crew on a spring roundup has inadvertently caused her husband's death. She forces herself to make a difficult decision that has unknown outcomes, and the book ends at a beginning of a new phase for a more mature Sarah.

Times were not easy for Jews living in Russia in 1904, but a pervasive element running throughout *Dvora's Journey*, by Marge Blaine, is the sustaining love Dvora's mother and father have for their children. As the oldest son reaches the age to be conscripted into the czar's army, the entire family's fortunes are changed by their momentous decision to sell most of their goods and emigrate to America. The author is particularly skillful at describing places: the family's home and village, the train cars, unfamiliar and crowded train stations, and the German steamship office.

## USING HISTORIC FICTION TO DEVELOP CHILDREN'S WRITING SKILLS

Children can easily get caught up by a writer's ability to create characters, settings, and plots that are believable, compelling, and memorable. They respond intensely to the events because of the writer's skill. How can teachers help children begin to develop similar writing skills? One of the useful purposes historic fiction serves is as a base for writing children themselves will do.

### POINT OF VIEW

Teachers may start by helping children understand point of view. Much literature is written in the third person: a narrator who is not involved in the action tells what is happening. In first-person accounts, the narrator uses the pronoun "I" in describing the events. Students should be exposed to books that represent both types of narration, so they will begin to see the range of possibilities each provides and the inherent disadvantages of each.

A worthwhile follow-up activity to any story told in the third person is to have children rewrite part or all of the story from one character's point of view. One second-grade teacher used *Martin and Abraham Lincoln*, by Catherine Coblentz, about a poor family struggling to survive after the father is captured during the Civil War. A chance encounter between young Martin and President Lincoln makes the family's life easier. After listening to the story, which is told in the third person, boys and girls rewrote it as if they were one of the characters. Laura wrote:

> I am Amanda. My two sisters are Anna and Maria. My brother is Martin. My brother Martin thinks he is taking my father's place. My father is a prisoner. He didn't do anything wrong. He is a prisoner in the Civil War. We are poor because my father is gone. The things my mother wanted very much was sugar, flour, eggs and butter.
>
> Our friend Snowden is very kind to us. He gives vegetables to us. Snowden's donkey is named Nellie. One day Snowden, Nellie and Martin went to Washington, D.C. to sell vegetables. Snowden left Martin on the steps of the White house. While Martin was sitting on the steps, President Lincoln came out and talked to him about our father.

This is a simple retelling; the child writer recasts the story. Teachers will find that children first beginning such activities concentrate on maintaining the basic plot elements. After students have had several such retelling experiences, they will be able to elaborate on ideas and to explore characters' feelings.

One fourth-grade teacher shared *John Billington*, by Clyde Robert Bulla, which is about a little boy whose family came to America on the Mayflower. Asked to write a first-person version of the story, Lee produced a long adventure:

> My name is John Billington. I'm always getting into trouble. One day I said to my mom, "I'm going to live with the Indians." "You won't like it, John Billington," she said. "I don't care. I'm going to tell Squanto," I said. So I told him. He said I wouldn't like it. He said, "Indians no live the same as white men, food not same, clothes not same, you not like it." But I still ran away.
>
> That day I heard something behind me. I looked but no one was there. Then I heard something again. This time there were two Indians in back of me. They took me on a trail. We got to the water. Now I knew where we were. The Indians pulled a canoe out of the underbrush. We got in the canoe. They were

going the wrong way. I kept on pointing toward Plymouth, but they kept going to Cape Cod. Then I thought to myself, "When the canoe gets to shore, I will jump out before the Indians can get out." Well, it didn't happen like that at all. The Indians got out before I even moved a leg. They took big steps so it was hard to keep up. Just then I saw the Indian village. When everyone saw me they looked at my clothes, my hair, my shoes. Just then I saw a man eating deer meat. Then a person gave me some deer meat. That night I slept in the chief's house.

In the morning my shoes were gone. I looked outside. There was a little Indian boy wearing them. I got into a fight with him, but I got my shoes back. The chief made a sign for me to come to him. He patted a mat beside him. "Thank you," I said, and sat down to put my shoes on.

Stories such as these by children illustrate one of the strengths of first-person narration: it is direct, simple, and fresh. More personal information can be presented in fewer words than if such information had to be described, as is done in third-person narration. The weakness of first-person narration is that nothing can be included unless it would logically have been thought or spoken by the person telling the story.

Other works of historic fiction besides the two suggested here will work as well in motivating boys and girls to try their hand in recasting from third- to first-person narration. This technique is recommended by Dewees (1986), a classroom teacher who presents a variety of ways to get children to read historic fiction and other genres they might not ordinarily choose.

## DESCRIBING A SETTING

Another crucial composition skill is the ability to create setting. Authors of historic fiction must be able to create a specific sense of place. Each environment should be distinct, unlike any other place the reader has experienced.

One third-grade teacher read the description of Eliza's house from the first chapter of *The Red Petticoat*, by Joan Palmer, a story that takes place during the Revolutionary era. Then, the children discussed the images the author used in giving a sense of what Eliza's house was like. They identified ways her home resembled and was different from their own. The boys and girls were asked to study one room in their own homes that evening. The following day, they were given time to write a description of the room. Andy wrote the following:

When I walk through my door I see a neat thing, my new wallpaper. It is covered with curved stripes. The colors are blue, red, green, and white. In my room I have two beds. My two beds both have head boards and they both have

*A scratchy line creates three-dimensional shapes that visually restate the action in the story.*
From *The Red Petticoat* by Joan E. Palmer. Copyright © 1969 by Joan E. Palmer. By permission of Lothrop, Lee & Shepard Books (A Division of William Morrow).

foot boards. The head and foot boards are painted magenta. Next to the beds are two brown shelves with a pot and other neat things. Going a little deeper in my room . . . oops, I bumped my head on the wall. My dad is going to cork up one of my walls, so I can tack on pictures and notes. Going to the far back of the room, I have a window. My mom has ordered me new blinds for my windows.

This is simple observational writing. However, experiences of this nature, in which the teacher uses a piece of literature to sensitize children to some aspect of writing, can make children more skilled readers and listeners as well.

## DEVELOPING A PLOT

Teachers should engender in students some rudimentary ideas about plot development. Interesting characters and evocative settings are of little final effect unless something exciting happens. Children are fond of action, so it is easy to interest them in plot construction.

A simple, effective way to begin developing an understanding of plot in children is to introduce parallel plot construction. After reading a short piece of historic fiction, the teacher leads a discussion to help students recall, on a basic cognitive level, what happened in the book. Plot summarization is a skill children can use in reading programs. After summarizing the action, teachers can encourage children to dictate their own versions of the story, one in which "the plot follows the same path" (Evertts, 1974).

Fourth-grade children listened to Alice Dalgliesh's *The Bears on Hemlock Mountain*, and then analyzed the plot. The main character, sent to fetch something that is needed from some distance, accomplishes the task but on the way home encounters a danger and is saved by an adult. (The action is summarized abstractly to provide a structure around which children can arrange whatever details they want.) The children's stories based on this plot summary included this one by Bob:

> Once upon a time there was a boy named Mark. Now Mark's mother was a poor cook. When she found out that Mark's great great uncle was dead, she invited everyone over for dinner because they were all so sad. Then Mark said, "Remember, you can't cook very well." "Little do you know," Mother began. "Your uncle left me a recipe, and it is in a brick in the chimney of his house. You must go get it."
>
> So the next day, Mark went to his uncle's house. He climbed up on the roof to look at the bricks in the chimney. What did he do, but meet a Dodo Bird? He decided the safest place was in the chimney, so he climbed in and stayed for an hour. His mother got worried, so she went to the uncle's house. When she saw the Dodo Bird, she climbed up on the roof and hit him on the head with a broom and killed him. Then she helped Mark out of the chimney and took him home. When they got home she gave him a bath.
>
> Mark had found the recipe in a brick inside the chimney. His mother got the recipe which was for Dodo Bird Stew. When all the relatives came they wondered how she had become such a good cook.

Experiences in plot completion work well at all grade levels. In the process of writing an ending for a story, a child is challenged to fit details of characterization and setting into a logical sequence of actions. A first-grade teacher shared Brinton Turkle's *Thy Friend, Obadiah*, a convincing portrayal of a curious, independent Quaker child growing up on Nantucket

Island. Obadiah is pestered by a gull that follows him around and by his brothers and sisters, who tease him about his friend. One day the bird mysteriously disappears. The teacher read the story as far as the line: "Every night Obadiah looked out his window, but the sea gull didn't come back." Then she asked the first-grade children to dictate their own endings. Chris dictated the following, which includes a causality statement and a pleasant concluding turn of phrase:

> Obadiah's mother gave him money, and he went to the store and bought some flour. On the way home he slipped and lost his penny. The bird never came back until spring. It was too cold, and the bird went to a warmer place. When the bird came back, Obadiah's heart was full of joy.

Some third-grade children demonstrated how effectively they can create a sense of being somewhere else at another time. The teacher planned a writing assignment based on *Cowslip,* the story of a young black slave destined to be sold with her sisters on the auction block. Set in the South before the Civil War, Betsy Haynes's account of a slave's problems might have seemed remote to the upper-middle-class children who heard it. Therefore, the teacher gave a brief introduction on slavery, describing the issues concisely but avoiding value judgments so the work of fiction could speak for itself. After this minimal introduction, she read the first chapter. When the story opens, Cowslip is about to be sold at the slave market. The town square is crowded, and through carelessness, Cowslip is not shackled with the rest of the slaves. Suddenly she realizes that no chains hold her. What will she do? Mark included a wealth of small details that make his plot completion remarkably realistic.

> She was there alone. It was cool. She stood quietly as a breeze swept across her yellow bandanna. She started to run. Her bandanna fell off and she was unaware of it. Her new master saw her run. He was wearing blue jeans with gray suspenders. Cowslip noticed he was after her. She ran even faster, so fast she made a sharp turn and lost him. He was nowhere to be seen. Cowslip stopped and glanced nervously to see if anyone was behind her. No one was in sight. She was very tired, and very, very hungry.
>
> It was quiet and cool. It was fall. The leaves were red, yellow, orange, green and brown. A chipmunk scampered through the pretty leaves. She was free. She was also very scared. Cowslip heard the clattering of horses' feet. She started to run again. She ran past trees, houses, and animals. She got tired and hid in a tree. The slave hunters rode past her. She was safe again. She noticed her yellow bandanna was gone. She wouldn't find it again. Her best possession was gone.
>
> Cowslip wondered about the children and Mariah. She wondered and wondered. "What should I do?" She repeated that question over and over again.

She told herself she must go on. It started to drizzle as the cool breeze swept on. The moon came out. It was full that night. So was her head! It was full of ideas. "It's a bitter evening," she said to herself. She hid in the trees and soon fell asleep. She was cold as small drops of rain fell down her back. She had a dream. It was about Mariah and the youngsters. She and the youngsters were happy and free.

Lenore's completion of the story incorporates realistic dialogue between Cowslip and a slave boy:

Cowslip decided that she was going to escape! She went quietly out the door, across the street when she suddenly saw Colonel Sprague. She ran behind a rock and waited until Colonel Sprague went away. Now she would have to be very careful and if she saw anyone coming she would hide behind a bush, or a rock, or anything to hide behind. When she finally couldn't walk any longer she sat down on a log nearby. As soon as she had rested her legs she heard someone crying. When she came a little closer, she saw it was a slave boy crying. She walked a little bit closer but the boy didn't notice.

"What's the matter?" she finally managed to ask. "Well, me and my father . . ." "My father and I," Cowslip corrected, but the boy didn't pay any attention to her. "Me and my father ran away and they caught him, and now he's going to be hanged." "Well, why don't you come with me?" Cowslip suggested. "O.K.," said the slave boy with tears trickling down his cheeks. So they walked together.

Once they came to a woods that had nice clean water in the rivers, and big juicy berries that grew on bushes. Once they almost got caught. Cowslip and the slave boy heard some hoofbeats. It was probably a white man! "Quick, let's hide behind a rock or something!" said Cowslip in a panic. "There is no rock or something," said the slave boy. "Run, run as fast as your legs can go!" shouted Cowslip. They ran pretty fast but the white man saw the last of the slave boy's foot turn the corner. "Runaway slave," thought the man. But when Cowslip turned the corner she saw a pile of leaves. "Quick, cover your self with these leaves," said Cowslip. Meanwhile the white man thought to himself, "The slave is probably going to trick me and go the other way, so I'll just wait here and trick the slave." And then when he saw that the slave wasn't coming, he left.

Much historic fiction can be used as a basis for writing assignments. *Blue Stars Watching*, by Patricia Beatty, tells of Will Kinmot, who discovers his father's farm is serving as a way station on the Underground Railroad. A teacher might ask children who have had a number of previous writing experiences to add a character to the story or to create a new obstacle to the escape of the slaves. The teacher can ask: how would a different character or problem affect the outcome of the story?

Brandishing his shield, Sir Gawain drove his spurs into Gringolet's side and the sparks flew from the horse's hooves as they struck the cobblestones of the castle yard.

*The formally placed figures, arrayed in detailed period costumes, are bordered in this full-color painting by a frame with a different, but related, pattern (see the discussion on page 376).* From *Sir Gawain and the Green Knight* by Selina Hastings. Illustration copyright © 1981 by Juan Wijngaard. By permission of Lothrop, Lee & Shepard Books (A Division of William Morrow).

*Constance*, by Patricia Clapp, is the story of an outspoken girl who goes to America with her father on the Mayflower after her mother's death. Written as a first-person narrative, this book can introduce children to the idea of journal writing. After reading it, a teacher might encourage children to keep their own journals. Also Joan Blos, in *A Gathering of Days*, uses the diary format effectively to capture the flavor of long-ago events. This book might be used to motivate child writers to keep their own diaries.

*Ready or Not*, by Norma Johnston, is the refreshing story of a fifteen-year-old girl who fights to live an active life with her brothers.[12] Her rebellion against others' expectations that she be a "lady" is realistically portrayed. A teacher can read this and *The Maud Reed Tale*, by Norah Lofts, and ask children to write a paragraph telling which character they feel is more effectively depicted and why.

## SUMMARY

Authors of historic fiction transport readers not only to other places but to other times. Most historic fiction deals with either time-specific or universal problems, and it helps readers understand these two kinds of problems.

Fantasy that transports the main character to another period in history and fiction originally intended to be contemporary when it was written in the recent historic past can also be considered historic fiction.

Evaluating the authenticity of historic fiction requires examining the author's ability to create believable settings, characters, and action. Good historic fiction balances accurate detail with the forward movement of the plot.

Historic fiction provides a base for developing students' writing. Students can translate a story from third- into first-person narration, use words to describe a setting, and perform parallel plot construction and plot completion exercises.

In telling about interesting characters who live in vividly described environments and do exciting things, authors of historic fiction create works

---

[12]Mildred Lawrence's *Touchmark* (New York: Harcourt Brace Jovanovich, 1975) has a similar theme. Nabby is determined to be a pewterer and willingly becomes Master Butler's indentured servant. After many frustrations, she realizes her ambition and wins her touchmark, the identifying sign of a pewterer.

of intrinsic literary value. But these works can also be given educational value by teachers.

1. They can be used to provide valuable insights into the nature of universal and time-specific problems. Child readers learn that some problems are universal: they are present despite the outward details of the era. A teacher might, for instance, choose a problem like greed; he or she can select several books, from differing time periods, in which a character exemplifies this problem. In groups, children can discuss various manifestations of this problem and how people react differently to it in different times.
2. Reading works of historic fiction with students, focusing on the techniques authors use for evoking a particular time through descriptions of characters, settings and plots, can motivate students to think about how they can write about another time. This sort of conscious examination of an author's writing, to learn something about the writer's craft, can have positive influences on children's own writing.

## An Integrated Unit of Study

Often teachers and librarians are interested in locating several books on the same topic. Reading books that give different accounts of the same event or books about different aspects of a single topic can give children a richer understanding of the event or topic. For example, if a middle-grade teacher is interested in building a unit on the medieval period, she or he may find it helpful to begin with information books, which will provide basic background on the period.

In *Castle, Abbey and Town*, Irma Simonton Black combines information with stories. She uses paintings, tapestries, historic data, and legends to show how noblemen, churchmen, and common people lived in medieval Europe. Black factually describes each group's role in society, its physical surroundings, its everyday life-style. She then creates a readable story about each class of people. Since she writes so well, the reader scarcely recognizes the transition from the factual to historic fiction.

*Knights in Armor*, one of Shirley Glubok's fine art books, can also be used to introduce this period. For this photographic essay emphasizing types of armor, Glubok wrote a straightforward text that describes a knight's training, weapons of the period, and sieges of castles. Gerald Nook is responsible for the book's design, which effectively incorporates pictures, tapestries, suits of armor (on six full pages) and weapons.

Fon W. Boardman's *Castles* provides a word-and-picture history of these most famous of medieval structures. Boardman discusses the historic importance of castles and the weapons and techniques used to storm and defend them. He also gives a thumbnail history of some of the most famous of these structures. The book is illustrated with photographs, as well as black-and-white drawings. The variety in the sizes, shapes, and placements of the illustrations keeps the book from becoming repetitive. Like other information books, this one does not have to be read in its entirety but can be sampled by teacher and/or children.

R. J. Unstead writes mainly historic nonfiction and is a master at presenting children with information they can enjoy. In *Living in a Castle*, there is the usual description of the physical structure, but the author goes even further and discusses such things as the use of sugar, wine, and ale by the residents. Unstead shows the hardships facing serfs and villagers in *Living in a Medieval Village*, and again the coverage is very complete. The last book in this series, *Living in a Medieval City*, describes all classes of city dwellers, from well-to-do bankers to craftsmen to poor serfs, and provides details about their clothing, work, houses, schooling, and amusements.

In *The Black Death*, Daniel Cohen focuses on the darker side of life during the medieval period. Twelve short chapters (from four to ten pages each) provide statistics (90,000 died in Florence), information (plague is a disease of wild rodents), and related background (an early instance of plague was recorded in 705 B.C.). The text is augmented with woodcuts and line drawings from a variety of sources. The medieval period was an era when most children died before reaching the age of six, when human waste was routinely dumped into the rivers that served as sources of drinking water, and when constant warfare resulted in invading armies swarming through countrysides. However, there were actually a few positive outcomes of the extensive plague: relaxation of prohibitions against dissection led to tremendous expansion of anatomical knowledge in the two centuries following the plague.

After providing factual background, the teacher can introduce historic fiction about the medieval period that meets two objectives:

1. the books should help students learn about the structure of feudal society—the terms related to feudal classes and the economic roles, privileges, and physical surroundings of the different classes.
2. the books should help students recognize that the glory of castles and knights came at the expense of the majority of people. The contrasts between the honor of the knights, the piety of the church, the luxury of the castles, and the miserable existence of the serfs can arouse an awareness of the extreme inequity of the feudal system.

There are simple books for younger, or less able, readers. An example of a book that is set in a particular time by pictures, not words, is *The Man Whose Name Was Not Thomas*, by M. Jean Craig. Formally framed pictures (and elaborate borders for text pages) by Diane Stanley show architectural detail, tools, costumes, and furniture, indicating that this book is set in what is to be interpreted—loosely—as the medieval period. The advantage this approach offers is that it requires virtually no previous knowledge of the period; children can simply enjoy the story and the observation exercises it provides. Such a book, although not really historic fiction, can serve the purpose of leading readers to more serious examples of the genre.

Another accessible book shows the rather brief events of the preparation of a feast for a visiting king and his entourage. In *A Medieval Feast*, by Aliki, the author/illustrator has done full- and three-quarter-page full-color pictures, often incorporating captions that provide additional information not directly related to the ongoing text. The pictures are filled with details that further extend children's learning.

Combining both movable and pop-up features, *Looking Into the Middle Ages*, by Huck Scarry, gives a sense of relative scale and a wealth of detail. Unlike pop-up books designed to be viewed only from the front, Scarry's book is deliberately constructed so that it must be viewed from both sides. Many of the intricate details are visible from only one side.

Books for intermediate-grade or junior-high students include *The Sword in the Tree*, by Clyde Robert Bulla. Shan Weldon, age eleven, is forced to flee from his castle home with his mother. His father is missing, presumably dead, and his evil uncle has taken control. Before he leaves, Shan secretly hides his father's jeweled sword in a hollow tree. After living with some kind peasants, Shan goes to Camelot to speak with King Arthur about getting help to reclaim his family's castle. The sword in the tree proves the truth of the boy's story and sets up a happy ending. This short, fast-moving book will appeal to children who might not attempt a more extended work.

*The Door in the Wall,* by Marguerite de Angeli, takes place in fourteenth-century England, and won the Newbery Medal in 1950. As an effective introduction to this book, a teacher might display a child-sized set of crutches and let students try them out. The teacher should help the children realize two things: certain parts of the body become strong while using crutches; and one's hands are not free to do other things. Robin, crippled son of Sir John de Bureford, is to become a page at another noble's castle. However, before he begins the journey, he is struck with a strange malady. Since his father is away fighting the Scots and his mother is in service to the Queen, Robin is taken to a monastery by Brother Luke and taught hand skills, reading and writing, and swimming. Later, he is accepted by Sir Peter, the lord he was meant to serve, despite his limp and crutches. De Angeli's story describes a young boy, surrounded by medieval traditions and expected to become a knight, who has to find an alternative role in life. Robin exemplifies a typical child's struggle to overcome impatience. The pencil illustrations are quite complete and interesting; two or three paintings add color. This book gives an extensive description of settings, characters, and activities in a readable style. After children have listened to or read this book, some might choose to write a response, perhaps in the form of a dialogue between Brother Luke and Robin or a speech in which Sir Peter thanks Robin for a job well done.

Another courageous medieval boy is portrayed in *Adam of the Road,* by Elizabeth Janet Gray. A teacher could introduce this book by showing children a picture of the harps used by medieval minstrels[13] and acquainting them with the importance of these wanderers to medieval people. Adam, a likable eleven-year-old, searches for his dog and then for his father along the king's highway in thirteenth-century England. Adam knows enough of the art of minstrelsy (his father's trade) to make the road his home. The book is filled with medieval lore and songs, and even includes a miracle play.

A young boy's affection for his horse is evident in *Christopher Goes to the Castle,* by Janice Holland. A teacher might introduce this book by show-

---

[13]An example is found in volume 17 of *The New Book of Knowledge* (New York: Grolier, 1974, p. 439). A picture of musicians, including one playing a harp, is in volume 16 of *Compton's Encyclopedia* (New York: F. E. Compton, 1975, p. 556).

ing children a decorative horse bridle (borrowed from a stable-equipment supply house) and some pictures of medieval bridles. Christopher Chantry was sent to train to become a knight, but when he arrived at the castle a bolt of lightening struck the tower as he rode in. This was considered a bad omen, and his horse was not allowed to stay because the head horseman was superstitious. Christopher saves the duke's life in a tournament, and his reward is the return of his horse and a beautiful jeweled bridle. Although the story is slight, the book incorporates accurate information about castle life, the training of knights, and tournaments. After reading the book, children might write a letter that Christopher could have written, mentioning everyday responsibilities he has, special duties he performs before a tournament, and kinds of training he receives.

Children interested in horses, their care, and equipment, might also like to read *Sir Gawain and the Green Knight*, by Selina Hastings. Shown in several realistically detailed paintings by Juan Wijngaard are the *caparisons* (ornamented coverings for horses) common in medieval times. A version of one of the King Arthur tales, this complex story of courage and chivalry describes Sir Gawain's quest for the Green Knight. The illustrations show King Arthur, among others, on horseback, as well as the richly decorated trappings of the royal court (see the illustration on page 370).

Some children might enjoy comparing the factual account of the plague in Daniel Cohen's information book (discussed earlier in this unit) with the fictionalized story of *Three Wanderers from Wapping*, by Norma Farber. This author tells, in a pragmatic tone and with enough detail to be engrossing, how the plague affected ordinary people in suburban London. In the first chapter, we meet John, his brother Tom, and their cousin Richard; the three decide it is time to flee their homes in Wapping. Their travel is filled with perils both before and after they join forces with a larger group of poor people also seeking shelter from the ravages of the Black Death. Each of the five short chapters is preceded by a set of black-and-white pencil drawings in the usual anatomically accurate, realistically detailed style of illustrator Charles Mikolaycak.

Books of fantasy can also be included in a unit on medieval times. One of Lloyd Alexander's best-known works is a five-book chronicle about the imaginary realm of Prydain. Alexander has been interested in the medieval period ever since he read King Arthur stories, legends, and fairy tales as a boy. *The Book of Three* introduces readers to Taran, assistant pig keeper, who struggles to save Prydain and in the process becomes more capable.

*The High King*, the last of the five chronicles, can be read independently of the others. The story recounts how Arawan, Death-Lord, has gained control of Dyrwyn, Gwydion's sword. In the wrong hands, the sword's power is deadly. This book is superb high fantasy set in a historic time.

Writers of fantasy with a historic setting have two tasks: creating a believable historic period and yet following all the constraints that fantasy writing imposes. The resulting books are seldom easy to read. *The High King*, for example, will probably not appeal to all readers because of the complex vocabulary and syntax. Even the characters' names are unusual and difficult to pronounce. It might be wise for a teacher to read the book aloud, thus ensuring that less able readers will be introduced to this fine writing they might be unable to read themselves.

Although there is no need for every student to complete a follow-up activity after reading or listening to a book, at times a teacher, or librarian, may want to suggest an activity for interested children. A teacher can suggest any of several activities for following up a coordinated unit on medieval times. Children might make pictures showing aspects of feudal life: the knights, their tournaments, castles, villages, or serfs' homes or work. Before beginning to draw, students should consider such questions as these:

1. What will the main person look like?
2. How old will he or she be?
3. What will he or she wear?
4. Where will the picture take place?
5. What time of year will it be?

Students might like to create a diorama in two sections. One section could show the life of a lord, the other could illustrate the life of a serf. The background for each section should be appropriate, and the objects or figures should be arranged in front of it. To help children understand the contrasting life-styles of the Middle Ages, the teacher can share with them *Merry Ever After*, by Joe Lasker. The artist uses full-color illustrations to tell parallel stories of two marriages: one between nobles and one between serfs.

A student can make an individual "movie" by drawing pictures in a series on adding-machine tape that can then be pulled through slits past a window cut in a business-sized envelope. Students can work in small groups to construct a simple "box movie" by attaching dowel rods (or pieces of broom handles) at either edge of a suitable cardboard box. A roll of shelf paper can be used for the illustrations.

Children can plan out a narration relating a story orally in their own words. *The Treasure Is the Rose*, by Julia Cunningham, lends itself well to this treatment. It is the short tale of an unprotected noblewoman who uses her wits to thwart robbers who come to her castle.

Boys and girls might construct a wall hanging presenting a scene from a story they have heard and perhaps incorporating the overall ideas of feudalism. Old sheets or large pieces of burlap make good backgrounds. The figures and settings on the hanging can be attached by stitchery or glue, or they can be cut from iron-on materials. Many scenes described in words by Barbara Leonie Picard in *Lost John* can readily be translated into graphic form. Longer than *The Treasure Is the Rose*, Pickard's book tells of a young outlaw in the Forest of Arden. Selecting one or two scenes to illustrate will work out better than trying to do the entire tale.

Students can make life-sized drawings of themselves dressed in medieval clothing. Two students work together, one lying on a large sheet of butcher paper while the other traces the outline. Students can draw or glue on colored paper or cloth to recreate a costume from this period.

Using *Kings Queens Knights and Jesters. Making Medieval Costumes*, by Lynn Edelman Schnurnberger, students can actually construct some costumes. This fine volume introduces students to the complexity and richness of medieval life through brief sections written in simple but not condescending language. It also provides clear, complete instructions for making medieval costumes, everything from crowns to shoes. Measurements are provided, suggestions for materials are given, and numerous black-and-white photographs clarify the text. The author's enthusiasm and honesty prevent this activity from lapsing into self-conscious cuteness, as costuming efforts with children often do. Schnurnberger is well-qualified to write this book: she has been involved for some time in the Cloisters Festival, which each summer draws children to participate in creating costumes, decorating buildings, and mounting a medieval festival.

## Suggestions for Further Study

1. Read the article by Hester Burton listed in "Related Reading for Adults," paying special attention to her reluctance to use actual historic people as characters. Then read some of her books. Compare them with the work of Jean Fritz, who commonly writes fiction about real characters. Whose do you feel is the more effective writing? Why?

2. Read Jane Langton's *The Majesty of Grace* (New York: Harper and Row, 1961), which is about a plain girl's imaginative dreams of glory during the Depression. What references to objects or events are included that might need to be explained to young readers or listeners today? The sequel is *The Boyhood of Grace Jones* (New York: Harper and Row, 1972).

3. This chapter refers to Genevieve Foster's book *Abraham Lincoln*, a fictionalized account of the president's life. Compare this with books of the same title by Clara I. Judson (Chicago: Follett, 1950) and by Anne Colver (Champaign, Ill.: Garrard, 1960). Which one do you feel is most complete and yet most comprehensible to today's readers?

4. *Plenty to Watch*, by Taro and Mitsu Yashima (New York: Viking, 1954), can be the basis for a composition activity. Read it to children, and discuss with them what the boy in the story saw on his way home from school. Ask them to observe carefully on their way home, and then to record their observations the following day. Two other books about observing (and not observing) are Ellen Raskin's *Nothing Ever Happens on My Block* (New York: Atheneum, 1966) and Dr. Seuss's *And to Think That I Saw It on Mulberry Street* (New York: Vanguard, 1937).

5. An author's ability to capture the mood of the time is crucial to historic fiction. *This Time, Tempe Wick?*, by Patricia Gouch, was described in this chapter. *Rebecca's War*, by Ann Finlayson (New York: Frederick Warne, 1972), features a similarly brave young woman, who responds with courage to having British troops billeted in her home. Which book gives you a more concrete feeling of the tenor of the time?

6. Mary Stolz's historic fantasy *Cat in the Mirror* gives one account of life in ancient Egypt. Read either *Tales of a Dead King*, by Walter D. Myers (New York: William Morrow, 1983), or *The Egypt Game*, by Zilpha K. Snyder (New York: Dell, 1986). In what ways do either of these differ in details? Which gives you a more complete idea of the way people lived at that time?

7. To introduce William Kurelek's *A Prairie Boy's Winter*, have children write about what they like to do best in winter. A sense of history can be instilled by having children ask their parents or grandparents how they enjoyed themselves in winters past. Children might also enjoy exchanging letters with children who live in a much colder climate to see how the weather affects what they do.

8. The book by John Rowe Townsend listed in "Related Reading for Adults" includes his recommendation of Joan Aiken's work. Read one of her books, and compare her writing with that of Leon Garfield, whose work is often mentioned favorably as being similar to Aiken's. You might read Garfield's *Footsteps* (New York: Delacorte, 1980), in which a young man journeys to eighteenth-century London, a town teeming with rogues and blackguards, to appease the spirit of his dead father. Both authors concoct free-wheeling fantasies in which historic accuracy is of secondary importance. Even though the events are improbable, the flavor of the period is there in the richly detailed settings and the language that evokes the past without placing a barrier in front of the reader.

9. The chapter recommends *Prairie Songs*, by Pam Conrad, as one of the most impressive pieces of historic writing published recently. To outward appearances, this book might seem completely unrelated to Whitley Strieber's *Wolf of Shadows*, (New York: Alfred A. Knopf, 1985), a compelling account of survival after a nuclear holocaust. But Anita Silvey points out that they are indeed comparable ("The Literature of Survival," *The Horn Book*, May/June 1986, p. 285). Read the two books to see if you can identify the common concerns that Silvey says unite them. A longer article by Richard Western, "The

Children's Survival Story" (*Wisconsin English Journal*, January 1981, pp. 19–22), deals

more completely with some earlier survival books.

## Related Reading for Adults

Aiken Joan. "Interpreting the Past." *Children's Literature in Education*, 16 (Summer 1985), pp. 67–83.

Aiken maintains that those who write historic fiction wish to either interpret the past and make it visible or take refuge away from the present. History lies all around us, though 90 percent of the time we ignore it. Children are hardly aware of the past at all, but many adults yearn for past scenes with intense nostalgia. Perhaps one reason we often long for the past is that the past isn't as appalling as the possible future. Writers of historic fiction have two jobs: to make children (many of whom are reluctant readers) aware of the past and to make them aware of our debt to it.

Bach, Alice. "Cracking Open the Geode: The Fiction of Paula Fox." *The Horn Book*, October 1977, pp. 514–521.

Included in this perceptive analysis of Fox's work is a brief discussion of why *The Slave Dancer* should be considered a classic tragedy. Bach describes Fox's control over her material. She deals succinctly with the criticisms leveled at Fox by the Council on Interracial Books for Children.

Beatty, John, and Patricia Beatty. "Watch Your Language—You're Writing for Young People." *The Horn Book*, February 1965, pp. 34–40.

This article is a humorous description of the authors' trials while writing a first-person historic novel, *Campion Towers* (New York: Macmillan, 1965). The form presents a unique problem: both conversations and narrative have to be in the language of the era (in this case the seventeenth century). The authors checked more than ten thousand words and give examples of some in common use today that were not used in 1651 and others that were used then but have since been "glamorized."

Burton, Hester. "The Writing of Historical Novels." In *Children and Literature: Views and Reviews*. Ed. Virginia Haviland. Glenview, Ill.: Scott, Foresman, 1973, pp. 299–304.

The author describes ways she answers critics who claim the historic novelist must juggle historical facts and that writers should write about what they know. She never uses well-known historic persons as pivots of stories and when she uses them as minor figures, never has them speak words for which there is no documentary evidence.

Collier, Christopher. "Johnny and Sam: Old and New Approaches to the American Revolution." *The Horn Book*, April 1976, pp. 132–138.

According to Collier, he and his brother, James Lincoln, use a "historiographic" approach, which refers to the methodology of historic research and study of varying historic interpretations. The Colliers have described the lives of blacks during the Revolutionary War in three volumes: *Jump Ship to Freedom* (New York: Delacorte, 1981), *War Comes to Willy Freeman* (New York: Delacorte, 1983), and *Who is Carrie?* (New York: Delacorte, 1984). Although these are primarily adventures, not novels of social commentary, they do give an idea of the times and of the perilous condition of those who sought personal freedom when the country was primarily interested in political reform.

Fritz, Jean. "On Writing Historical Fiction." *The Horn Book*, October 1967, pp. 565–570.

The author relates her reasons for writing

historic fiction, including her desire to bridge the gap between past and present, so readers will not forget what has gone by. She relates sources of ideas for her novels and describes her pleasure in writing stories in which the hero or heroine must take a side or make a decision.

Robertson, Gail R. "An Historical Bibliography for Young Children." *The Reading Teacher*, February 1975, pp. 453–459.

A brief introduction includes some pertinent comments about the need for judicious selection of historical materials, since not all are either accurate or effectively done. The annotations for almost seventy books, both fiction and nonfiction, are only two or three sentences in length.

Smith, Jane F. "The Characters in Historical Fiction." *California School Libraries*, Winter 1975, pp. 20–25.

The author gives a definition of the genre and identifies its characteristics, emphasizing that such books seek authenticity of fact and dialogue while imaginatively re-creating the past. She cautions that writers must not overwhelm readers with the results of their research. She says: "The dialogue should be credible in order to create the right atmosphere, but without anachronistic or archaic phrases."

Townsend, John Rowe. *A Sense of Story: Essays on Contemporary Writers for Children*. Philadelphia: J. B. Lippincott, 1971, pp. 17–21.

Writing about Joan Aiken, Townsend calls her "one of the liveliest and most exuberant of today's writers." He comments on her sense of pace and inventive ability, while acknowledging that some readers may be annoyed by her disregard for probability. Townsend believes that one of Aiken's strongest abilities is her use of dialogue to create minor characters. Townsend expands and updates these essays in *A Sounding of Storytellers* (Philadelphia: J. B. Lippincott, 1979).

Trease, Geoffrey. "The Historical Story. Is It Relevant Today?" *The Horn Book*, February 1977, pp. 21–28.

The author says that one reason interest in historic fiction is declining is the lack of professional guidance most children receive in their reading. Teachers do not compensate for the children's instinctive resistance, which is due to reading difficulties and lack of background.

## Professional References

Cameron, Eleanor. "A Second Look: *Gone-Away Lake.*" *The Horn Book*, September/October 1984, 622–626.

Dewees, Geraldine A. "Something New in Reading Every Month." *The Reading Teacher*, 39 (May 1986), 977–978.

Evertts, Eldonna. "Dinosaurs, Witches and Anti-Aircraft: Primary Composition." In *Language and the Language Arts* (ed. by DeStefano and Fox). Boston: Little, Brown, 1974, pp. 387–395.

Hickman, Janet. "Bookwatching: Notes on Children's Books." *Language Arts*, 63 (January 1986), 85–86.

Hoffman, Lyla. "Reviews of *The Slave Dancer.*" *Interracial Books for Children*, 5 (1974), 4–5ff.

Konigsburg, E. L. "Sprezzatura: A Kind of Excellence." *The Horn Book*, June 1976, 253–261.

Sebesta, Sam Leaton. "Critically Speaking." *The Reading Teacher*, 39 (November 1985), 224–229.

Smith, Louisa. "Eleanor Estes' *The Moffats: Through Colored Glass.*" *Touchstones: Reflections on the Best in Children's Literature* (ed. by Nodelman). West Lafayette, Ind.: Children's Literature Association, 1985, 64–70.

Sutherland, Zena. *Children and Books.* Glenview, Ill.: Scott, Foresman, 1986, p. 404.

## Bibliography of Children's Books

Aiken, Joan. *Black Hearts in Battersea.* Garden City, N.Y.: Doubleday, 1964.

———. *The Cuckoo Tree.* Garden City, N.Y.: Doubleday, 1971.

———. *Nightbirds on Nantucket.* Garden City, N.Y.: Doubleday, 1966.

———. *The Stolen Lake.* New York: Delacorte, 1981.

———. *The Wolves of Willoughby Chase.* Garden City, N.Y.: Doubleday, 1963.

Alexander, Lloyd. *The Book of Three.* New York: Holt, Rinehart and Winston, 1964.

———. *The High King.* New York: Holt, Rinehart and Winston, 1968.

Aliki. *A Medieval Feast.* New York: Thomas Y. Crowell, 1983.

Amoss, Berthe. *Secret Lives.* Boston: Little, Brown, 1979.

Anderson, Margaret. *In the Circle of Time.* New York: Alfred A. Knopf, 1979.

———. *In the Keep of Time.* New York: Alfred A. Knopf, 1977.

———. *The Mists of Time.* New York: Alfred A. Knopf, 1984.

Beatty, Patricia. *Blue Stars Watching.* New York: Morrow, 1969.

———. *Hail Columbia.* New York: Morrow, 1970.

Behn, Harry. *The Faraway Lurs.* Cleveland: World, 1963.

Benchley, Nathaniel. *Snorri and the Strangers.* New York: Harper and Row, 1976.

Black, Irma Simonton. *Castle, Abbey and Town: How People Lived in the Middle Ages.* New York: Holiday House, 1963.

Blaine, Marge. *Dvora's Journey.* New York: Holt, Rinehart and Winston, 1979.

Blos, Joan W. *Brothers of the Heart.* New York: Scribner's, 1985.

———. *A Gathering of Days; A New England Girl's Journal. 1830–1832; A Novel.* New York: Scribner's, 1979.

Boardman, Fon W. *Castles.* New York: Henry Z. Walck, 1957.

Brenner, Barbara. *Wagon Wheels.* New York: Harper and Row, 1978.

Brooks, Polly Schoyer. *Queen Eleanor. Independent Spirit of the Medieval World.* New York: J. B. Lippincott, 1983.

Bulla, Clyde Robert. *John Billington.* New York: Thomas Y. Crowell, 1956.

———. *The Sword in the Tree.* New York: Thomas Y. Crowell, 1956.

Byrd, Elizabeth. *It Had To Be You.* New York: Viking, 1982.

Clapp, Patricia. *Constance.* New York: Lothrop, Lee and Shepard, 1968.

Clements, Bruce. *I Tell a Lie Every So Often.* New York: Farrar, Straus and Giroux, 1974.

Coblentz, Catherine. *Martin and Abraham Lincoln.* Chicago: Children's Press, 1947.

Cohen, Daniel. *The Black Death.* New York: Franklin Watts, 1974.

Conrad, Pam. *Prairie Songs.* New York: Harper and Row, 1985.

Cooper, Gordon. *An Hour in the Morning.* New York: E. P. Dutton, 1974.

———. *A Time in a City.* New York: E. P. Dutton, 1975.

Craig, M. Jean. *The Man Whose Name Was Not Thomas.* Garden City, N.Y.: Doubleday, 1981.

Cunningham, Julia. *The Treasure Is the Rose.* New York: Pantheon, 1973.

Dalgliesh, Alice. *The Bears on Hemlock Mountain*. New York: Scribner's, 1952.

de Angeli, Marguerite. *The Door in the Wall*. Garden City, N.Y.: Doubleday, 1949.

———. *Thee, Hannah*. Garden City, N.Y.: Doubleday, 1949.

Edwards, Sally. *George Midgett's War*. New York: Scribner's, 1985.

Enright, Elizabeth. *The Four Story Mistake*. New York: Holt, 1942.

———. *Gone Away Lake*. New York: Harcourt, Brace, 1957.

———. *Return to Gone Away*. New York: Harcourt, Brace, 1961.

———. *The Saturdays*. New York: Rinehart, 1941.

———. *Spiderweb for Two*. New York: Holt, 1951.

———. *Then There Were Five*. New York: Holt, 1944.

———. *Thimble Summer*. New York: Holt, Rinehart and Winston, 1938.

Estes, Eleanor. *The Middle Moffat*. New York: Harcourt, Brace, 1942.

———. *The Moffats*. New York: Harcourt, Brace, 1941.

———. *Rufus M*. New York: Harcourt, Brace, 1943.

Farber, Norma. *Three Wanderers From Wapping*. Reading, Mass.: Addison-Wesley, 1978.

Fitzgerald, John D. *More Adventures of the Great Brain*. New York: Dial, 1969.

Foster, Genevieve. *Abraham Lincoln*. New York: Scribner's, 1950.

Fox, Paula. *The Slave Dancer*. Scarsdale, N.Y.: Bradbury, 1973.

Gauch, Patricia Lee. *This Time, Tempe Wick?* New York: Henry Z. Walck, 1974.

Glubok, Shirley. *Knights in Armor*. New York: Harper and Row, 1969.

Gray, Elizabeth Janet. *Adam of the Road*. New York: Viking, 1944.

Hall, Donald. *Ox-Cart Man*. New York: Viking, 1979.

Hamley, Dennis. *Pageants of Despair*. New York: S. G. Phillips, 1974.

Harris, Rosemary. *The Bright and Morning Star*. New York: Macmillan, 1972.

Hastings, Selina (reteller). *Sir Gawain and the Green Knight*. New York: Lothrop, Lee and Shepard, 1981.

Haugaard, Erik Christian. *Hakon of Rogen's Saga*. Boston: Houghton Mifflin, 1963.

———. *A Slave's Tale*. Boston: Houghton Mifflin, 1965.

———. *The Untold Tale*. Boston: Houghton Mifflin, 1971.

Haynes, Betsy. *Cowslip*. Nashville: Thomas Nelson, 1973.

Holland, Janice. *Christopher Goes to the Castle*. New York: Scribner's, 1957.

Howard, Ellen. *When Daylight Comes*. New York: Atheneum, 1985.

Hunter, Mollie. *The Stronghold*. New York: Harper and Row, 1974.

Ingram, Tom. *The Night Rider*. Scarsdale, N.Y.: Bradbury, 1975.

Ish-Kishor, Sulamith. *A Boy of Old Prague*. New York: Pantheon, 1963.

Johnston, Norma. *Ready or Not*. New York: Funk and Wagnalls, 1965.

Jones, Adrienne. *A Matter of Spunk*. New York: Harper and Row, 1983.

———. *Whistle Down a Dark Lane*. New York: Harper and Row, 1982.

Konigsburg, E. L. *A Proud Taste for Scarlet and Miniver*. New York: Atheneum, 1973.

———. *The Second Mrs. Giaconda*. New York: Atheneum, 1975.

Krasilovsky, Phyllis. *The First Tulips in Holland*. Garden City, N.Y.: Doubleday, 1982.

Kurelek, William. *A Prairie Boy's Winter*. Boston: Houghton Mifflin, 1973.

Lasker, David. *The Boy Who Loved Music*. New York: Viking, 1979.

Lasker, Joe. *Merry Ever After*. New York: Viking, 1976.

Lenski, Lois. *Cotton in My Sack*. Philadelphia: J. B. Lippincott, 1949.

———. *Phoebe Fairchild*. Philadelphia: J. B. Lippincott, 1936.

Levin, Betty. *The Sword of Culann*. New York: Macmillan, 1973.

Levitin, Sonia. *Roanoke*. New York: Atheneum, 1973.

Linevski, A. *An Old Tale Carved Out of Stone*. Trans. M. Polushkin. New York: Crown, 1973.

Lofts, Norah. *The Maude Reed Tale*. Nashville: Thomas Nelson, 1971.

Lunn, Janet. *The Root Cellar*. New York: Scribner's, 1981.

McGraw, Eloise Jarvis. *Master Cornhill*. New York: Atheneum, 1973.

McSwigan, Marie. *Snow Treasure*. New York: E. P. Dutton, 1942.

Monjo, F. N. *The Drinking Gourd*. New York: Harper and Row, 1970.

———. *King George's Head Was Made of Lead*. New York: Coward, McCann and Geoghegan, 1974.

———. *The Secret of the Sachem's Tree*. New York: Coward, McCann and Geoghegan, 1974.

———. *The Vicksburg Veteran*. New York: Simon and Schuster, 1971.

Nesbit, Edith. *The Story of the Amulet*. London: Octopus Books, 1979.

Palmer, Joan. *The Red Petticoat*. New York: Lothrop, Lee and Shepard, 1969.

Peck, Robert Newton. *Soup*. New York: Alfred A. Knopf, 1974.

Picard, Barbara Leonie. *Lost John*. New York: Criterion Books, 1962.

———. *One Is One*. New York: Holt, Rinehart and Winston, 1965.

Polland, Madeleine. *Beorn the Proud*. New York: Holt, Rinehart and Winston, 1961.

Scarry, Huck. *Looking Into the Middle Ages*. New York: Harper and Row, 1984.

Schnurnberger, Lynn Edelman. *Kings Queens Knights and Jesters. Making Medieval Costumes*. New York: Harper and Row, 1978.

Speare, Elizabeth George. *The Witch of Blackbird Pond*. Boston: Houghton Mifflin, 1958.

Stolz, Mary. *Cat in the Mirror*. New York: Harper and Row, 1975.

Turkle, Brinton. *Adventures of Obadiah*. New York: Viking, 1972.

———. *Obadiah the Bold*. New York: Viking, 1965.

———. *Rachel and Obadiah*. New York: Viking, 1978.

———. *Thy Friend, Obadiah*. New York: Viking Press, 1969.

Turner, Ann. *Third Girl From the Left*. New York: Macmillan, 1986.

Uchida, Yoshiko. *Journey to Topaz*. New York: Scribner's, 1971.

Unstead, R. J. *Living in a Castle*. England: A & C Black, 1971.

———. *Living in a Medieval City*. England: A & C Black, 1971.

———. *Living in a Medieval Village*. England: A & C Black, 1971.

Uttley, Alison. *A Traveler in Time*. New York: Viking, 1964.

Vander Els, Betty. *The Bomber's Moon*. New York: Farrar, Straus and Giroux, 1985.

Weir, Rosemary. *The Three Red Herrings*. Nashville: Thomas Nelson, 1972.

Wibberley, Leonard. *John Treegate's Musket*. New York: Farrar, Straus and Giroux, 1959.

———. *The Last Battle*. New York: Farrar, Straus and Giroux, 1976.

———. *Leopard's Prey*. New York: Farrar, Straus and Giroux, 1971.

———. *Red Pawns*. New York: Farrar, Straus and Giroux, 1973.

Wilder, Laura Ingalls. *Little House in the Big Woods*. New York: Harper and Row, 1932.

Willard, Barbara. *A Cold Wind Blowing*. New York: E. P. Dutton, 1973.

Williams, Jay. *The Hawkstone*. New York: Henry Z. Walck, 1971.

Yarbro, Chelsea Q. *Four Horses for Tishtry*. New York: Harper and Row, 1985.

———. *Locadio's Apprentice*. New York: Harper and Row, 1984.

Yashima, Mitsu, and Taro Yashima. *Plenty to Watch*. New York: Viking, 1954.

Yep, Laurence. *Mountain Light*. New York: Harper and Row, 1985.

# BIOGRAPHY:
# BRINGING
# PERSONALITIES
# TO LIFE

Biographies are but the clothes and buttons of the man.

*Mark Twain*

Despite **Mark** Twain's reservations about the worth of biographies, this literary genre offers a diversity of subjects. Children can read about the multitalented Renaissance artist Benvenuto Cellini, who lived over four hundred years ago (*The Autobiography of Benvenuto Cellini*, by Alfred Tamarin); or they can read about people whose lives are today's news on television and in newspapers (for example, *Kareem: Basketball Great*, by Arnold Hano). They can read accounts of the lives of political figures (*Tom Paine, Revolutionary*, by Olivia Coolidge), scientists (*Michael Faraday: Apprentice to Science*, by Sam and Beryl Epstein), artists (*Paintbrush and Peacepipe: The Story of George Catlin*, by Anne Rockwell), or popular folk heros (*The Story of Johnny Appleseed*, by Aliki).

The teacher or librarian must sift through the many books written about people's lives and select the best available. Getting children to read even fine biography is a problem for teachers and librarians, however. For the most part, biography deals with the lives of people in the past, and children have little interest in history. Until they reach the end of the intermediate grades, few children have a stable sense of time. By third grade, some children are beginning to be interested in stepping outside their own time, but the present moment still remains the most important. Even current biographies are not a favorite reading choice of most children. In a recent study, 134 fourth-graders kept logs of their reading choices; these showed that both historic and contemporary biography were chosen significantly less often than were other genres (Anderson, Higgins, and Wurster, 1985).

For authors, this genre can also present problems. Biographers show their artistry in the way they make the person portrayed believable. A flaw in some earlier biographies for children is that they presented models of behavior child readers could emulate, tending to ignore the humanity of the subject. Today's biographies show a better balance between the public personality and the private person. But in order to achieve this balance, authors must decide whether to attempt a complete biography or to focus on one part of a subject's life. That choice is affected by problematic decisions about what is appropriate or inappropriate for children to read.

A complete biography has the advantage of allowing the writer greater space to present a thorough exposition of the subject. The author can record changes in the person and build up a richness of contrast that only becomes apparent over a number of years. However, honesty demands the author at least mention all details of the subject's life; some of these may be difficult to incorporate into reading for children. Partial biographies give authors the advantage of choosing beginning and ending points, so they can attain more specific focus. Authors may also emphasize the part of the subject's life they consider most significant. But events that happen in one part of a life are almost always shaped earlier; a partial biography may create an artificial segmentation.

# A CHANGING STYLE IN BIOGRAPHY

A trend that has become apparent in biography for children is the inclusion of increasing amounts of fictionalized detail or action. One of the proponents of this newer approach was F. N. Monjo, an author who always included in his books a note clarifying which were actual events and which were fictionalized (but logical) ones. As Monjo explained, there are some questions on which history is silent—there is literally no way to know the answers. If there was a detail about which no accurate historic information was available, Monjo believed he was justified in inventing material, providing it fit logically into the constraints of the time. His rationale for including fictionalized elements was that most child readers will not—at least in the beginning—read purely objective nonfiction. If the author's speculation on the characters' thoughts or dialogues produced a biography appealing to a child who might otherwise avoid the genre, Monjo believed invention was justified. Monjo made a convincing argument, but there are some vocal opponents of this approach (Forman, 1972).

An example of a biography of this type, one combining fact and fiction, is Monjo's *Grand Papa and Ellen Aroon, Being an Account of Some of the Happy Times Spent Together by Thomas Jefferson and His Favorite Granddaughter.* More realistic than earlier idealized biographies of Jefferson, this book deals with his owning of slaves, as most people of Jefferson's class did in his era.

# TYPES OF BIOGRAPHY

Biographies for children fall into two general types: those about a single person and those about a small group of related figures.

## SINGLE-FIGURE BIOGRAPHIES

Probably the most familiar and certainly the most numerous type of biography is the one that features a single central subject. These books are most often arranged chronologically, although authors writing about the same subject may choose to begin and end their accounts at different points in the person's life. The advantage of this type of biography is that the author has the freedom to explore chosen aspects of the person's life and character in depth.

An example of a single-figure biography for primary-grade children is *John Muir*, about the Scottish-born naturalist who crossed the Atlantic to a new home in Wisconsin. The author, Glen Dines, uses terms and incidents accessible to younger children to describe Muir's hard work to farm his family's land. (This book is part of the series *See and Read Biography* published by Putnam for beginning readers.) Muir's love of nature and of labor-saving inventions and his thirst for learning are simply described. Many events in his long life have been telescoped into this brief book. Muir's important work as an author and conservationist has been given limited space—because it would not have been as interesting to very young readers as such anecdotes as the one about his finding a little black dog in the Alaskan wilderness.

A more complex biography of Muir for intermediate-grade children is *From the Eagle's Wing*, written by Hildegarde Hoyt Swift and illustrated by Lynd Ward. The author includes all the facts found in Dines's biography for beginning readers but expands on them and describes events in more detail. In some places, the author's omniscience is intrusive, such as when she writes ". . . if he had only known . . . ." Some of the handling of Muir's love life—including the created dialogue—may turn children off. More important than these weaknesses however, is the book's strength: the author's ability to paint in words the natural beauty that enchanted Muir and the restlessness that rose like a sickness in him, forcing him away from all he loved to open spaces, where he found peace.

## COLLECTIVE BIOGRAPHIES

Another type of biography is the collective one, featuring a brief biographical sketch of several different people. The subjects are linked in some way: they may be all scientists or all blacks or all women. This type of biography can sometimes be useful in engaging reluctant readers. The material is brief enough not to intimidate a child who does not read much but wants to know about a particular person. Such a concise introduction may interest the student sufficiently to lead to further reading.

One example of a collective biography is *Growing Up Female in America*, in which author Eve Merriam provides a brief introduction to each of ten women, arranging materials from the letters, diaries, and journals of the subjects themselves.

*The machine is complex, but the artist's skillful rendering clarifies its structure and function.* By Hildegard Hoyt Swift. Illustration by Lynd Ward from *From the Eagle's Wing*. Copyright © 1962 by Hildegard Hoyt Swift. By permission of William Morrow & Company.

*Lift Every Voice* describes the lives of four important black leaders: Booker T. Washington, W. E. B. DuBois, Mary Church Terrell, and James Weldon Johnson. These leaders made lasting contributions to improving race relations in the United States. The authors, Dorothy Sterling and Bernard Quarles, relate each of their subjects' childhoods, accomplishments, struggles against injustice, and, finally, the dates and manners of their deaths. Washington, born a slave, lived to found the Tuskegee Institute. However, although he and his associates were very influential in black culture, they were criticized for telling whites what they wanted to hear. Almost by chance Washington and DuBois, both of whom truly wanted their people's advancement, found themselves as rivals. DuBois's "militancy," which appears mild by today's standards, became even more pronounced when he learned of black soldiers' mistreatment during World War I. One of the first black women in America to hold a bachelor's degree, Terrell was a teacher, suffragette, author, lecturer, and reformer. Johnson also taught, and, in addition, knew much about music and medicine, practiced law, and worked with the National Association for the Advancement of Colored People; but he was best known as an author and poet. All four subjects in *Lift Every Voice* can serve as models for children of all races, influencing them to persevere despite discouragement and to use their talents to surmount obstacles. The biographies are well written, and point out clearly and compassionately the racial inequity that existed and still exists in this country.

*Fifty Voices of the Twentieth Century*, by Emery Kelen, includes short sketches of notable men and women. Among those profiled are Marian Anderson, Carl Jung, Robert Frost, Mao Tse Tung, U Thant, Golda Meir, Herman Hesse, Albert Schweitzer, and Marianne Moore. The book includes only six women but represents a variety of nations and races. The author provides brief information on the birth, accomplishments, and death of each person. The book also includes quotes from the writings and/or speeches of each subject, to illuminate his or her life work, art, or philosophy. The volume includes both a bibliography and an index.

*Famous Mexican-Americans*, by Clarke Newlon, is one of the series *Famous Biographies for Young People* (published by Dodd, Mead), a series of composite biographies numbering over sixty titles. These books include more text than pictures. Newlon deals with such popular heros as football star Jim Plunkett, leading man Ricardo Montalban, and singer Vikki Carr in fifteen short chapters. Children will not know some figures included, such as educator Henry Ramirez, congressman Henry Gonzales, or businessman Hilary Sandoval, but the range of subjects makes the point that Hispanics in the United States have succeeded in a variety of professions.

The adults featured in *Famous Mexican-Americans* are exemplary of success in their chosen professions. In contrast, in *Small Hands, Big Hands*, Sandra Weiner profiles both adults and children—the youngest not yet twelve. All are Chicano migrant workers, whose stories are presented in their own words and augmented with full-page black-and-white photos.

## VARIETY IN SUBJECT

Within the last two decades, authors have made a conscious effort to provide biographies of people who represent groups too frequently ignored in the past.

## BIOGRAPHIES OF WOMEN

As in some other genres, women have in the past been underrepresented in biography. With the rise of the women's movement in the United States, publishers have responded with more and better biographies of women. Those available depict strong women struggling against many kinds of opposition to achieve their goals.

One such woman, the writer George Sand, is described in *A Mind of Her Own*, written by Tamara Hovey. Born in a prison of prejudice during the first half of the eighteenth century, and heavily guarded by tradition, Aurore Dupin was the daughter of a French nobleman and a commoner. Later, using the pseudonym George Sand, she escaped from women's constraints into an outside world of letters few women even dreamed of. Living as she did at a time when few women ventured outside the home without a husband's or father's permission, none could vote or hold property, and only a small minority were involved in professions, George Sand's accomplishments were exceptional. What is especially remarkable about this woman is that she continued to write despite heavy emotional demands and other personal problems. She earned both popularity with the masses and the critical approbation of such respected writers as Victor Hugo, Honore de Balzac, and Gustave Flaubert. The sheer quantity of her writing—generated because of her always precarious financial condition—is matched by its diversity. Because she is neither a popular contemporary figure like Billie Jean King[1] nor a well-known American historic figure like Benjamin Franklin,[2] George Sand's life will probably not attract many young readers. *A Mind of Her Own* is a valuable book that teachers can recommend to a child—boy or girl—interested in writing and the arts. It gives readers a sense of what a determined, talented woman can accomplish despite seemingly insurmountable obstacles.

*Harriet and the Runaway Book*, by Johanna Johnston, also presents the life of a writer who was constrained by society's limitations on women. American writer Harriet Beecher Stowe, growing up in a family of boys, held her own, even though her father manifested attitudes typical of the day: "If only she'd been a boy." Since teaching was one of few avenues open

---

[1] See *Billie Jean King, The Lady of the Court*, by James T. Olsen (Mankato, Minn.: Creative Education, 1974), or *Billie Jean King: Queen of the Courts*, by Carol B. Church (St. Paul, Minn.: Greenhaven Press, 1976). Other female sports figures are featured in Francine Sabin's *Women Who Win* (New York: Random House, 1975), which deals with the need to compete and includes excellent black-and-white action photographs.

[2] See *Benjamin Franklin*, by Thomas Fleming (New York: Four Winds, 1973), or *Benjamin Franklin. Young Printer*, by Augusta Stevenson (New York: Bobbs-Merrill, 1983).

**Artist Ronald Himler contrasts a dark foreground with a rectangle of light at the top of the stairs to emphasize the danger.** Illustration from *Harriet and the Runaway Book* by Johanna Johnston. Illustrated by Ronald Himler. Illustrations copyright © 1977 by Ronald Himler. Reprinted by permission of Harper & Row, Publishers, Inc.

to women, she taught. Her brothers' impassioned exhortations from their pulpits awakened her to the evils of slavery. Daydreaming in church one day, the beginning of a story came to her. Encouraged by her husband, she continued writing, even though it was inconvenient:

> She wrote at the kitchen table
> while dinner was cooking and pies were baking.
> She wrote on the back steps
> while the children were washing up.
> She wrote in the parlor on a rickety table
> while Calvin wrote his lectures at the desk.
> She wrote and wrote,
> for the story had begun to come to her.

A more recent woman writer, Pearl Buck, was immensely popular during her lifetime but is now largely overlooked. Like children's authors Katherine Paterson and Jean Fritz, Buck grew up in China. Her stay there was so extensive that she saw the culture from the inside, not as an outside observer. Buck is one of a select company of women included in *Winners. Women and the Nobel Prize*, by Barbara Shiels. This collective biography focuses on women who have won the prestigious Nobel Prize, for example, for medicine (Rosalyn S. Yalow), for peace (Mother Theresa), or for chemistry (Dorothy C. Hodgkins). In all, eight women—from among the twenty or more women who have won this prize—are included. Convenient features of this book are a general introduction to the eighty-year-old prizes, a "Suggested Reading" list, a bibliography, and an index.

Another biography of a woman writer is *Judy Blume's Story*, by Betsy Lee. Blume's is a life firmly embedded in the context of her times. Briefly—in 110 pages—with many full-page photographs, a rather superficial view of this popular writer's life is presented: "Judy liked having parties at her house" and "Judy fell in love again, but unlike her high school romances, this one lasted." This book can be recommended to Blume enthusiasts who will read anything about their idol. A better biography would put Blume in the more encompassing perspective of writers and writing and extract for readers what the lasting significance of her work is.

The life of a social reformer is presented in *Susan B. Anthony*, by Matthew G. Grant. This title is one of the Creative Education series *Gallery of Great Americans* comprising thirty books about Indians, frontiersmen, explorers, war heros, and women. All of these volumes are primarily pictorial with accompanying words. This one is illustrated with full-color paintings and black-ink and crayon drawings. The simple text deals primarily with Anthony's public life. Another biography that provides additional details about this reformer's life is *Susan B. Anthony*, by Ilene Cooper.

Biographies are written in the third person, but in an effort to have children respond more deeply to Anthony's life, one teacher of fourth-grade students asked them to rewrite her story as if they were the main character. Heidi retold the story in the form of a diary:

### Diary of Susan B. Anthony

December 9, 1822.   Today is my birthday, and I am three years old. The only present I got is this diary from my parents. I have to help mother cook, clean, sew, wash, iron, and care for the garden and the chickens now.

April 28, 1838.   I'm eighteen today, and am now a teacher. It's Friday, and I just got paid. It was only two dollars, and I'm disturbed about that because men get paid more than women. I'm glad I'm a teacher instead of being a servant or working in a factory.

August 19, 1840.   I attended a meeting tonight against slavery. I made a speech and said that I didn't agree with slavery. I plan for another meeting tomorrow.

January 18, 1849.   I have flu and can barely speak. I've had it for a month already. I only had a bowl of soup today.

September 1, 1851.   They're starting a movement of women's rights and I'm glad. I met Elizabeth Stanton and Lucy Stone at the meeting today. They agree with me. I've had poor food and a sleepless night, worrying about our work. I have a bad cold, too.

May 2, 1865.   Slavery is finally done with. I wish they had let women have their rights, too. Now all the men can vote, but women still can't. It seems like women will never have any rights.

October 11, 1872.   I voted today, and was arrested. I was taken to court, and proved to be guilty. I was fined one hundred dollars. I said I wouldn't pay even one cent of the fine. And the truth is I never will.

Helen Keller, a woman of incredible courage, surmounted the handicaps of deafness, muteness, and blindness. Her success is mainly credited to her tremendous intelligence by Norman Richards in his book *Helen Keller*, but he also acknowledges the selfless devotion of her teacher, Anne Sullivan Macy, and the help of her family and friends. That Keller learned to communicate at all is extraordinary, but in fact she eventually wrote books, graduated from Radcliffe *cum laude*, could read several foreign languages, and even learned to make herself understood vocally. For comparison purposes, children can also read the story of Laura Bridgman in *Child of the Silent Night*, by Edith Fisher Hunter. Bridgman lost both her sight and hearing in a bout with scarlet fever, but at the Perkins Institute in Boston she learned to read and communicate with others.

Few women artists have achieved the eminence of Kathe Kollwitz, German expressionist creator of woodcuts and other graphics. *Kathe Kollwitz: Life in Art* is the first children's biography in English of this talented

artist, whose lithographs, drawings, sculptures, and other works are reproduced on almost every page. Authors Mina C. and H. Arthur Klein provide
a description of the artwork under each picture. The art is set within a social
context; the precariousness of Kollwitz's adult life in Hitler's prewar Germany is graphically described.

Contemporary women are also the subjects of biographies for children,
as in *Sally Ride and the New Astronauts,* by Karen O'Connor. One of thirty-
five candidates (six women) selected from among more than eight thousand
people who applied, Ride went on to become the first American woman in
space in 1982. This book details her grade-school determination to become
an astronaut and her training at NASA. The book also includes technical
information about the space program in general. Child readers will be fascinated by the details about daily life in space: how food is injected with
water before heating and how to take a bath in a low-gravity environment
where drops of water float away.

## BIOGRAPHIES OF MINORITY FIGURES

A legitimate criticism of children's biographies until recently has been that
they have seldom presented positive images of minority groups.[3] It has been
difficult to find biographies of figures representing such groups, but fortunately that situation is changing. More and more biographies of blacks,
Chicanos, and members of other minority groups are becoming available.

One such biography is *W. E. B. DuBois: A Biography,* about a powerful
black man who struggled for over ninety years against prejudice. Newbery
Medal–winner Virginia Hamilton describes DuBois's character simply and
with dignity. Born a free man in Massachusetts, he worked as a sociologist,
historian, and political activist; at the end of his life, he was living in Ghana
and writing essays, articles, and speeches to spread his ideas. Author Hamilton edited a representative selection of these writings and added her own
insightful introductions. DuBois was an eloquent writer on many topics,
including war:

> I believe in the Prince of Peace. I believe that War is Murder. I believe that
> armies and navies are at bottom the tinsel and braggadocio of oppression and
> wrong, and I believe that the wicked conquest of weaker and darker nations
> by nations whiter and stronger but foreshadows the death of that strength.

---

[3]The underrepresentation of minorities continues in all children's books (not just biographies).
Though there were about twice as many books containing at least one black character when
Jeanne Chall did her study ("More Black Characters in Children's Books," *Wilson Library
Bulletin,* February 1978, p. 448) as there were in 1965, 86 percent of the books she surveyed
still reflected an all-white world.

Another black man achieved international renown because of his scientific experiments. *A Weed Is a Flower*, by Aliki, presents a simplified retelling of the life of George Washington Carver, who grew from "a sick, weak, little baby" into "one of the great scientists of his country." These lines are from the first and last pages of this book; the language in between is sometimes stilted, describing, without embellishing conversations, the bare bones of Carver's life. The characters remain essentially two-dimensional—a pitfall of writing biography for beginning readers. The artwork, however, is singularly impressive.

Using flat shapes and simplified decorative patterns, the artist shows, in semi-abstract pages, the events of Carver's life. In many cases exaggeration of form depicts the drama of his life more impressively than the words do. The text describing the night raiders who stole Carver and his mother is mundane language at best; the illustrations are arresting.

The life story of singer *Marian Anderson*, a woman of indomitable spirit and fierce pride, is told by Tobi Tobias. The tender description of Anderson's life is enhanced by Symeon Shimin's illustrations. Anderson achieved fame despite poverty and racial prejudice. Her contralto voice with its incredible range moved all kinds and classes of people. She sang all around the world, to princes and paupers and to the wounded in wartime, but never more impressively than when she had to perform in front of the Lincoln Memorial because the Daughters of the American Revolution refused to let a black perform in their concert hall. Like many other singers, Anderson had to become famous in Europe before American audiences would recognize her talent.[4]

Paralleling their general underrepresentation in literature for children, native Americans do not appear often as subjects in biographies. One exception is Jim Thorpe, dubbed "the greatest athlete in the world" (Reising, 1976) at the peak of his career. Reising recommends several biographies of this charismatic athlete, who excelled in both baseball and football.

A fine composite biography, *American Indian Women*, by Marion E. Gridley, features eighteen women with black-and-white photographs of all of them. The book is unusual in including both historic figures, such as Susan LaFlesch, and contemporary ones, such as the dancer Maria Tallchief.

---

[4]Another biography of an American black woman who had an impressive musical career is Jesse Jackson's *Make a Joyful Noise Unto the Lord!* (New York: Thomas Y. Crowell, 1974). This biography of gospel singer Mahalia Jackson appeared shortly after her death. An analysis of this and of two other biographies about singers Billie Holiday and Bessie Smith is found in an article by Richard H. Miller, "Three Musical Lives," *The Lion and the Unicorn*, 4 (Summer 1980), pp. 71–81.

# BIOGRAPHIES OF CREATIVE PEOPLE IN THE ARTS

School art and music programs have, in the last few years, been curtailed as a result of widespread budget cutting. Therefore, classroom teachers and librarians should be aware of biographies about all kinds of creative artists, which can be used to stimulate children's interest in the expressive arts. In those schools that still have art and music teachers, reading such biographies can be coordinated with experiences planned by those teachers.

Although writing about the work of visual artists is not easy, fascination with the creative process of painting has led several biographers to record the lives of such artists. Well-known children's authors Sam and Beryl Epstein describe a life in colonial times in *Mister Peale's Mammoth*. Charles Willson Peale was a renowned portrait painter whose interest in the new science of natural history led him to open a museum and experiment with taxidermy. He also organized America's first scientific expedition, during which he successfully unearthed a complete mammoth skeleton. Drawings by Martin Avillez catch the ebullient mood of the writing and supply additional wit to a lively biography.

Eminence came early in the life of one American painter, described by Beverly Gherman in *Georgia O'Keeffe*. In 1916, women simply did not compete in the all-male world of "real" artists. O'Keeffe—after rejecting the idea of teaching art—was presented to the New York City art establishment by her mentor, later her husband, Alfred Stieglitz, at his gallery. It was unheard of for a woman to achieve such visibility. O'Keeffe's drive to paint resulted in her becoming the single best-known woman artist in America. Before she died in 1986, at the age of ninety-eight, she had carved a unique position for herself in the annals of art history. Her purposefully understated yet exuberant abstract paintings captured the imaginations of Americans more thoroughly than the work of any other woman artist before or since. Her life story is elegantly presented in Gherman's book: the tall rectangular shape is enhanced by a lavish use of white space and generous leading between the lines of type. Unfortunately, all the reproductions are in black and white, and their small size diminishes their impact significantly since O'Keeffe's paintings are generally quite large. The writing style is utilitarian at best; the characters remain two-dimensional. This is, like too many biographies, one to be read because of the compelling dramatic interest of the subject's life, not because the book is interesting in itself.

Although few women artists have achieved O'Keeffe's eminence, there are biographies of other women in the arts who can serve as useful role models for children. Maria Martinez is a minority woman whose folk art is recognized throughout the art world. Mary Carroll Nelson's *Maria Mar-*

*tinez* tells the life story of this artist, who was born around 1885 in a small New Mexican village. The blackware pottery she produced eventually brought fame to her pueblo. After her work was exhibited at the world's fair in San Diego, she received both accolades (a film was made of her life) and financial rewards.

*Dorothea Lange. Life Through the Camera,* by Milton Meltzer, begins by describing this photographer's early life, including daily trips across the Hudson River from her home in Hoboken, New Jersey, to attend (as a non-Jew) a school in a Jewish ghetto near her mother's work. Just before her death, Lange was overseeing the installation of a one-woman show of her life's work at the Museum of Modern Art. As an inexperienced seventeen-year-old, she approached one of the foremost American photographers of the time and convinced him to take her on as an apprentice. Eventually, she won the first Guggenheim Fellowship ever awarded to a woman photographer. Her photo of a migrant worker mother has been reproduced countless times, becoming in the process, as Meltzer says, "a work of art that has had its own life." In the entire body of her work, Lange was able to submerge the rejections of her early life in an impassioned study of other people's humanity, recording the results in photographs that are indeed works of art.

*Grandma Moses. Painter of Rural America,* by Zibby Oneal, describes another woman who achieved acclaim for visual art. Born Anna Mary Robertson, this well-known figure saw her father decorate the living room walls with his paintings, and with his encouragement she painted with grape juice, carpenter's chalk and other improvised materials as a young child. Married life and business enterprises kept the young woman busy for years. After her children had grown up, she was able to return to the visual art she loved. She first did needlework representations of her childhood memories but turned to painting when rheumatism made holding a needle impossible. After her primitive-style paintings gained wide popularity, she went on to star in a documentary film of her life, write an autobiography, and visit with a president in the White House. Until her death at more than one hundred years of age, she maintained a very practical outlook: "I tell folks if they have ten dollars to spend for a picture, they'd be better to put it in chickens. They multiply."

The books on Dorothea Lange and Grandma Moses just mentioned are both from a series of ten published by Viking, *Women of Our Time.* Other titles in the series deal with sports star Martina Navratilova, humanitarian Mother Theresa, and musician Diana Ross.

Many authors have written books about musicians for children; one of the best of these biographies is *Letters to Horseface,* by F. N. Monjo. Mozart, already a musical genius at fourteen, journeyed in 1769 to Italy. Monjo has created a series of letters telling of this trip. The letters show a beguiling mixture of the boy's carefree spirits on a trip with his father and the young composer's smugness as he displays his musical talents to adoring audiences throughout Italy. This American Library Association Notable Book is good reading, even if children are not familiar with Mozart's life and music.

Many biographies of writers have been written for children, for example, *Mark Twain in Love*, by Albert G. Miller. If young readers are not put off by the title, they will probably enjoy reading about this giant of American letters. After beginning with a description of Twain's boyhood, this book continues through the period when he wooed, wed, and made considerable personal changes to retain the woman he loved. The book is marred somewhat by static, two-dimensional characters, with the exception of Twain himself, whose humor is one of the redeeming factors:

> "How's your head today? Does it hurt much?"
> "Only when I think—so I hardly ever notice it."

Children can be encouraged to compare this biography with May McNeer's *America's Mark Twain*, illustrated by her husband, Lynd Ward, which focuses less on Twain's private life.

Female writers have generally been accorded less renown than male writers, but two women who wrote for children have earned the admiration of many.[5] Dorothy Aldis's *Nothing Is Impossible* is the story of the solitary early life of Beatrix Potter, who was constrained in a third-floor room with barred windows in a large house with more servants than family. This life will seem strange but intriguing to active children of today. Potter apparently thrived on this upbringing; in her teenage years, she was grateful to be able to avoid meeting others her own age at parties, which made her physically ill. Aldis describes what Potter's feelings may have been:

> There was her pet hedgehog Tiggy, that she drew in all different positions. The position she liked best was when he rolled himself into a tight spiney ball so that his enemies couldn't touch—let alone eat—him without being hurt themselves. Beatrix wished she could do the same. Not that she wanted to hurt anybody, but she did like being left alone.

---

[5]Some critics do not agree with the general assessment of Beatrix Potter. See "Miss Potter and the Little Rubbish," by Patrick Richardson, in *Suitable for Children? Controversies in Children's Literature*, ed. Nicholas Tucker (Berkeley: University of California Press, 1976, pp. 173–178). Richardson comments that although Potter's books clearly communicate effectively with their audience, there are doubts about their intrinsic value as fine literature. They "fill a tiny niche in the children's bookshelf," but they are in no way the equal of writing by A. A. Milne or Kenneth Grahame.

*Everything in this drawing is even and controlled; the precision of this portrait of Beatrix Potter reflects the calm and regularity of her life and work.* Illustration by Richard Cuffari from *Nothing Is Impossible.* Copyright © 1969 Mary Cornelia Aldis Porter. Reprinted by permission of Atheneum Publishers.

Although Potter had drawn for a long time, it was not until the age of twenty-six that she began to write stories for children. In a letter sent to a former nursemaid's sick child, Potter combined her writing and drawing skills to create *The Tale of Peter Rabbit.* That book and over a dozen others, including *The Tale of Squirrel Nutkin* and *The Tale of Benjamin Bunny*, have since become staples of early childhood. Older children who enjoyed reading Potter's books when they were younger will respond positively to this biography. Segel (1980), however, points out that this biography presents a uniformly positive view of Potter's life that is not substantiated in her own diaries.

Readers in intermediate grades have long enjoyed Laura Ingalls Wilder's work. Her popularity increased markedly during the 1970s as the result of a television series based on her writings. *West From Home*, edited by Roger MacBride, is a collection of letters Wilder wrote to her husband Almanzo, back home in Missouri, when she visited their daughter in San Francisco. Although this book of correspondence was not intended for children, proficient child readers may find it fascinating. The letters provide valuable historic references to life in the young western city and the Panama Pacific International Exposition occurring then. Child readers who are particularly interested in Wilder may also enjoy *Laura Ingalls Wilder* by Gwenda Blair.

The art of film is represented in the biography *Chaplin, The Movies, and Charlie*, by David Jacobs. This book relates chronologically the great comedic mime's rise from a slum childhood to a career peak as a world-acclaimed comic and movie producer. Chaplin was a sensitive artist. As his films became more involved with social commentary, public opinion turned from adulation to suspicion and criticism. Having begun as the silent tramp, Chaplin returned to silence, refusing to dignify his critics' acccusations concerning his politics and personal life. The book reveals Jacobs's careful analysis of Chaplin's complex genius. At one point, the author describes how Chaplin used objects to create humor:

> Throughout his life on film the Tramp carries on a running war with *things*. In Charlie's hands objects seem to have lives and wills of their own, and their aims are always sinister. Wet mops in Charlie's possession feel solemnly obliged to slap him in the face. Ladders are determined to cuff him around the shoulders. Handles of farm or garden implements sincerely believe that Charlie's face is their punching bag. All the world's folding furniture has entered into a solemn agreement never to set up properly for him. Sometimes objects get him so confused that he loses all sense of which are which. He is known, on occasion, to put his cane to bed and tuck it in and go stand himself in the corner; when he gets thirsty he picks up the telephone and pours himself a glass of water.

## BIOGRAPHIES OF HISTORIC FIGURES

Probably the most common subject matter of biographies is the life story of some well-known historic figure. Although widely available, not all of these are necessarily good, according to Higgins (1971).

One author with a long record of success in writing about historical figures is Jean Fritz, who demonstrates that history need not be dull.[6] In

---

[6] This prolific author was named the 1986 winner of the Laura Ingalls Wilder Medal, given every three years by the Association for Library Service for Children (a division of the American Library Association) to an author or illustrator whose books, published in the United States, have made a substantial and lasting contribution to children's literature.

***George Washington is the main figure in the drawing, but his body and arm frame the boy, who is the main character in the book.*** Illustration by Paul Galdone reprinted by permission of Coward, McCann & Geoghegan from *George Washington's Breakfast* by Jean Fritz, illustrations copyright © 1969 by Paul Galdone.

*And Then What Happened, Paul Revere?* she presents, in lively, conversational style, the life of this silversmith and patriot. Small, quixotic details, such as the fact that Revere once made a silver collar for a pet squirrel, make the character come alive. The illustrations by Margot Tomes reflect Fritz's highly personal style, which holds young readers without resorting to fictionalization. Not typical of conventional biography, however, is the device Fritz employs in *George Washington's Breakfast*. She presents a contemporary child tenaciously searching out facts about the first president's food preferences. The boy unearths myriad details about Washington's life in his quest for the answer, and he finally sits down to "three small Indian

Hoecakes and as many dishes of tea." Other books in similar style by Jean Fritz include *Why Don't You Get a Horse, Sam Adams?, Where Was Patrick Henry on the 29th of May?,* and *Can't You Make Them Behave, King George?*

In her biography of Elizabeth I, titled *Queen of England,* author Helene Hanff successfully transports readers three thousand miles across the ocean and four hundred years back in time to an era quite unlike ours. Only ten percent of the people who lived in England then could read and write; her literacy set Elizabeth apart from the commoners almost as much as her high birth did. Despite their affluence, Elizabeth and her father, Henry VIII, dealt with common problems of life then, and Hanff's details give a vital sense of this:

> Henry had three or four palaces in and around London, and half a dozen more in other parts of England. Since there were no bathrooms, and since there were often a hundred men and women living at court at one time, the king and court had to leave one palace and go to another every few months, so that the buildings could be "aired and cleaned."

The author describes the lives of Elizabeth and her family and friends, as well as the affairs of state and the politics of warfare that consumed so much of their attention. The complicated characters and devious interrelationships are clearly explained, and the court intrigues and beheadings are treated pragmatically. Hanff's characters come alive, as is evident in this account of Elizabeth's being courted:

> Elizabeth was having a wonderful time. All the kings and princes had sent her presents—diamond pins and gold dinner plates and heavy ropes of pearls. Elizabeth was like a child about presents. She loved to get them and show them off to everyone.
>
> Each ruler had also sent Elizabeth his picture. She loved to study each face while she was told how rich and handsome and great each ruler was, and what a fine husband he would be. Then she would spread out all the pictures to see which man had the finest eyes or the warmest smile.

In addition to their intrinsic interest as literature, historic biographies can also be used as the base for writing and dramatizing experiences. One teacher read *Sam the Minuteman,* by Nathaniel Benchley, to his first-graders. The story is told in the third person, from the viewpoint of an omniscient narrator. Following the reading, the teacher asked the class to think about how it would feel to be Sam Brown and to retell the story from Sam's viewpoint. A girl and a boy dictated the following accounts:

> I am Sam Brown. My home is in Lexington. I live on a farm. My mother has to do all the work. She makes us all the things we need. Daddy is a Minuteman. One night I was sleeping. I heard my mother crying. I thought she was frightened, so I went downstairs to see.

***Illustrator Arnold Lobel directs attention toward the mother's bandaging hands by arranging the figures in the composition so they form a closed oval.*** Illustration from *Sam the Minuteman* by Nathaniel Benchley. Illustrated by Arnold Lobel. Illustrations copyright © 1969 by Arnold Lobel. Reprinted by permission of Harper & Row, Publishers, Inc.

"Get your gun, Sam." "Why, Dad?" "We have to fight a war." My mother said, "No, Sam." "We need all the men we can get," said my father.

My best friend is named John. He was there with me. Then we heard, Thump! Thump! Thump! The minutemen started toward the road. "I see the soldiers," said one of our men. "So do I," said another. "I sure hope we win." John got hurt in his leg by a soldier. The second time the minutemen got smart. They hid behind rocks and trees. We won anyway, and that started America.

*Fonna*

I am Sam Brown. I live in Lexington, Massachusetts. Our family moved from England. On our farm, my mom has to make everything we need. One time Paul Revere came running through the town on his horse yelling, "The British are coming. The British are armed with big guns loaded with gunpowder."

My dad is a Minuteman. I took my gun and my dad took his gun and we went out to fight the British. I was very, very frightened. There was my friend, John. (At least I knew that someone else was scared besides me.) The Minutemen got right in front of the British. They shot John in the leg. His mother was sad and I was angry. "The next time I'll kill one of the British," I said. The next time we did win.

*Brian*

In addition to such composition activities, dramatizations of incidents from the lives of famous people can be worthwhile classroom experiences. The abundant action in many biographies means they can provide a base from which teachers can select small episodes for classroom drama. Wright and Allen (1976) describe thoroughly how they used Longfellow's poetic account of Paul Revere's ride, comparing and contrasting it with prose versions. The outcome was a series of drama activities based on the literature.

## POLITICAL BIOGRAPHIES

An inherent problem of political biographies is that they must present complex events spanning long periods of time. Such biographies often attempt to describe to children events whose causes are very involved or even incomprehensible.

Complex events that are spread over a long period of time are difficult to summarize vividly and present almost insurmountable problems when the author is writing for young readers. Some events cannot be elaborated because they are not central to the story. A pivotal event, which only paves the way for the story the author intends to tell, must be summarized quickly. In trying to deal with political figures, many authors condense history and thus fail to adequately explain their subject's actions or accomplishments.

Political biographies serve a useful purpose in presenting role models about which children might otherwise remain unaware. Because of this, they should undoubtedly be available. It is unfortunately true, however, that the writing style in many of these works is pedestrian, and the main figures too seldom come to life.

A drawn-out series of complicated events is presented in *Peter the Great*, by Diane Stanley, whose full-color illustrations effectively portray an unfamiliar culture. Crowned czar of an immense, primitive country when he was only ten, Peter took trips to Europe, at times disguised as a common workman, and brought back ideas to modernize his beloved Russia. Stanley gives details that establish the reality of Peter's determination, which made so many reforms possible. However, her language does not really bring the character himself to vivid life. The paintings accompanying the language add many details about the country at the time.

*Juarez*, by Ronald Syme, is a biography for intermediate-grade readers about Benito Juárez,[7] an Indian orphan from Oaxaca recognized as a founder of modern Mexico. This political biography is typical in its condensing of historical events into simple terms. Describing the downfall of the then governor of Mexico, author Syme writes:

> Santa Anna contrived to restore himself in his nation's eyes, but in 1843 his mismanagement made it necessary for him to leave Mexico in a great hurry for temporary sanctuary in Havana.

A complex and dramatic story is hidden behind these few pragmatic, textbook-style words. What really happened was that the vain, ambitious governor led his troops on a futile foray into alien territory and was roundly defeated, narrowly escaping with his life. Skillfully using his charisma, Santa Anna reversed public opinion and was reaccepted into the volatile arena of Mexican provincial politics. Yet all readers get is the bland sentence above.

A condensed, but nonetheless interesting, biography for intermediate-grade readers is *Margaret Thatcher. Britain's "Iron Lady,"* by Doris Faber. As a child, Thatcher excelled both in school and in hobbies. As a teenager, Thatcher not only got admitted to Oxford—unusual for a woman in those

---

[7]This is one of the more than thirty biographies written by Ronald Syme, many of which attempt the worthy goal of introducing young readers to historic figures that might otherwise remain unknown. Included in the series published by William Morrow are *Benedict Arnold, Traitor of the Revolution* (1970); *Toussaint, the Black Liberator* (1971); and *African Traveler, the Story of Mary Kingsley* (1962).

***The meticulous depicting of details of costume and architecture in Diane Stanley's full-page,
full-color painting evokes a long ago time in a place far away.*** Reprinted with the permission of
Macmillan Publishing Company from *Peter the Great* by Diane Stanley. Copyright © 1986 by
Diane Stanley Vennema.

**The casual posture of the male figures in this drawing is in sharp contrast to the formality of the architecture.** From *Juarez* by Ronald Syme. Illustration by Richard Cuffari. Copyright © 1972 by William Morrow and Company, Inc. By permission of the publisher.

days—but received a scholarship. Thatcher later parlayed her political savvy into a position as the first woman ever elected Prime Minister of England and "first woman ever to head the government of a major country in Europe or America." She has a clear sense of her own ability: when asked by a reporter why she thought she won the election, Mrs. Thatcher replied crisply, "Merit."

Golda Meir was embroiled in some of the most turbulent political action of this century. Mollie Keller's *Golda Meir* begins with a description of a frightened child trying to avoid Cossack soldiers bent on destroying Jews in Russia and closes with a description of the astute political guidance and leadership this woman provided as prime minister of the fledgling state of Israel. Readers' respect for Meir is increased by learning that during the last and most demanding years of her life she suffered from cancer. These facts are all important, yet Meir's personality never springs to life in this book as compellingly as it did in her television appearances during her lifetime.

The same two-dimensional personality depiction is apparent in *Adolph Hitler*, by Edward F. Dolan, which tells competently of complex events before and during World War II. A photo section and a very thorough index make this a useful reference work for students researching a report.

Hitler's persecution of the Jews is widely known; less familiar is the story of the Armenian holocaust, recounted in *The Road from Home: The Story of an Armenian Girl*, by David Kherdian. Veron Dumhjian enjoyed a happy and secure early childhood as a member of a prosperous, respected family living in Turkey. Then, in 1915, the Turkish government began persecuting and deporting its Armenian population. Of the whole family, only Veron, an aunt, and a young cousin were left unharmed and together. Those who read Kherdian's tribute to his mother will marvel at the fierce pride of the Armenian people. Kherdian continued this account in *Finding Home* and *Root River Run*.

## BIOGRAPHIES OF CONTEMPORARY FIGURES

The advantage of writing about contemporary figures is that these people are still living and influencing life today. Because of this, children read such biographies more avidly than they do those of remote historical figures. The disadvantage of writing about such people is that authors (and indeed readers) lack the perspective to understand their contributions in the light of history. Someone who seems vitally important today may be virtually unknown twenty-five years from now.

One example is Ralph Nader, portrayed in *Ralph Nader, Voice of the People*, by James T. Olsen. The intended audience is intermediate and upper-grade readers who do not have strong reading skills. In twenty-nine pages, half of which are illustrations, the author presents a great deal of information and a strong feeling for Nader's drive and altruism. This book cannot be considered a definitive biography, but it can serve a useful purpose. Other books in this series, published by Childrens Press, include biographies of Sugar Ray Leonard (by Bert Rosenthal) and Moses Malone (by Hal Lundgren).

*John Denver*, a simple biography of the folk-rock singer, includes descriptions of his early trials and triumphs, told with more than a hint of hero worship by author Linda Jacobs. Henry John Duetschendorf was the child of an Air Force family always on the move. As a boy, he longed for a permanent home, especially one in the country, "close to nature." This childhood longing was the basis for Denver's songs "Rocky Mountain High" and "Leaving on a Jet Plane." The author does a fine job of tracing elements in Denver's boyhood that seemed to have influenced his later career, but readers will not get much sense of the man as a real human with faults and failures.

Another popular singer is the subject of *Michael Jackson, Superstar!*, by Patricia C. McKissack. This book includes a lot of pictures, some only slightly related: of Fred Astaire, whose choreography Jackson studied; of Charlie Chaplin, whom he admires; and of Jane Fonda, a close friend. The book presents Jackson's early musical development in the context of performing family groups such as the Partridge Family and the Osmond Brothers.

Sports figures are often featured in biographies. *Clemente!* is a complex biography by Kal Wagenheim, one that successfully portrays a convincing, three-dimensional human being. The first Latin American to enter baseball's Hall of Fame, Roberto Clemente won the Gold Glove and Most Valuable Player awards and recorded three thousand hits in his career, breaking or tying numerous National League records. Puerto Rican and black, Clemente was subjected to the injustice of being made to wait out seasons in Montreal because the Dodgers wanted to maintain a racial quota. By the book's end, when Clemente is killed on a mercy mission to help earthquake victims in Nicaragua, the reader feels as though a friend has been lost.

*George Brett* is a profile of a current candidate for baseball's Hall of Fame. S. H. Burchard's book includes black-and-white photographs on almost every page and a chart of Brett's batting record for young statistics enthusiasts. Although Brett has stayed with the Kansas City Royals, baseball players frequently change teams. This is one problem with biographies of contemporary sports figures: they are soon out-of-date because they are incomplete. This may bother young fans.

*Larry Bird, Cool Man on the Court* features a top performer in professional basketball. Bird, former College Player of the Year, was also NBA Rookie of the Year in 1979–1980, winning him many loyal young fans who are potential readers. Bert Rosenthal, the author, is basketball editor for the Associated Press and an editor of *Hoop Magazine,* an official publication of the National Basketball Association. In addition, he has written two other books on basketball and is thus well-qualified to write this biography. One of the series by Childrens Press mentioned earlier, this biography has a brief format, laced with lots of full-page black-and-white photos.

Some authors write about female sports stars, as George Sullivan does in *Mary Lou Retton.* In ten brief chapters, Sullivan describes the success of this outstanding female gymnast as she became—at the 1984 Olympic Games in Los Angeles—the first American woman ever to win an individual medal of any kind in Olympic gymnastics competition. Born into a sports-minded family in a medium-sized Ohio town, this determined young woman overcame early perceptions of herself as short and stocky as well as a painful injury only six weeks before the games.

Paula Taylor records the life of a social reformer in her biography *Coretta King.* A native of the south, Coretta Scott King knows injustice firsthand. Many blacks were not even allowed to finish school at the time, yet Coretta Scott not only graduated from college but also won a degree from the New England Conservatory. Instead of pursuing a promising vocal career, she married a young minister—Martin Luther King—and the two returned south to work for the good of their people. Coretta King's courage is emphasized throughout the book. Despite semipoverty, threats against their lives, bombings, and hateful letters, she, her husband, and their children worked for nonviolent integration. Finally, Martin Luther King gave his life for the cause of black freedom. Coretta King faced that tragedy courageously, and her continued courage and the living memory of her husband are both critical to the movement. In just thirty-one pages, author Paula Taylor leaves readers with the knowledge that racial discrimination is not some long-ago problem but one people continue to face.

Another contemporary female's courage is lauded in *Sandra Day O'Connor,* by Carol Greene. This biography of the first woman appointed to the Supreme Court of the United States includes many black-and-white photographs that enhance the straightforward text.

Finally, religious leaders often have considerable influence on current events. *John Paul II. The Pilgrim Pope,* by Robert W. Douglas, is a slim, thirty-two-page book that includes a chronology and a glossary, as well as fourteen full-color, full-page pictures. There is very little text, mostly factual details with minimal interpretation; this makes the book accessible to interested readers who have limited reading skills.

## BIOGRAPHIES WITH ANIMAL NARRATORS

Several biographical books do not fit easily into the categories discussed so far, but are nonetheless important because of their intrinsic appeal to child readers. *Ben and Me,* by Robert Lawson, is an example of a biography with an animal narrator who sees (and tells) his human friend's foibles.

***The diagonally placed motion lines trailing behind the figure emphasize a feeling of pleasant speed.*** From *Ben and Me* by Robert Lawson. Copyright 1939 by Robert Lawson. Copyright © renewed 1966 by John W. Boyd. By permission of Little, Brown and Company.

Amos, the mouse, takes credit for many of Benjamin Franklin's inventions and ideas: the Franklin stove, the printing press, and electrical experiments were all successful after modifications from Amos. Indeed, Franklin's Revolutionary War career and his ambassadorship to France would not have prospered so well had it not been for the not-so-modest mouse's assistance. Franklin is depicted as fumbling and absent-minded, a rather nice switch from the subject-as-hero approach so common in biographies.

*Mr. Revere and I* is a rollicking story, much like Lawson's other volumes, a combination of delightful fiction about an animal and biography about the human subject. The first forty or so pages tell how a horse named Scheherezade, the pride of the Fourteenth Regiment, was metamorphosed into Sherry, the farm horse. Revere's large, loving family, his silversmithing, the famous tea party, and the equally famous ride are all described from the horse's point of view.

Lawson tells the entire plot of *Captain Kidd's Cat* in the book's subtitle:

Being the true and dolorous chronicle of William Kidd, Gentleman and Merchant of New York. Late Captain of the Adventure Galley . . . of the vicissitudes attending his unfortunate cruise in Eastern Waters, of his incarceration in Newgate Prison, and of his unjust trial and execution as narrated by his faithful cat, McDermott, who ought to know.

The tradition begun by Robert Lawson is continued in *The Remarkable Ride of Israel Bissel*, by Alice Schick and Marjorie N. Allen. Molly the Crow is the wise narrator who relates the adventures of a bumbling human. She tells the story of Bissel's historic ride from Watertown, Massachusetts, to Philadelphia, including all the distractions in between. If not for Molly, according to her, the ride would probably never have been completed. Joel Schick provides black-pen illustrations that are full of rather broad humor but do elaborate and extend the minimal text.

# EVALUATING BIOGRAPHY

A teacher or librarian interested in selecting good biography for students should keep several issues in mind.

### 1. Who is the author, and what are this person's qualifications to write biography?

In some cases, a writer's reputation is well established; his or her books can be relied on to be of uniformly high quality. For instance, Clara Ingram Judson and—more recently—Jean Fritz have established reputations as consistently reliable writers of biography. For an author who is less well-known, the dust-jacket may give a description of his or her background. A teacher can also consult the standard reviewing sources to find critics' reactions.

Related to a writer's qualifications is the ethnic group to which he or she belongs. Serious questions have been raised by the Council on Inter-racial Books for Children, as well as other more moderate groups and individuals, about whether any author can write effectively about a member of a different racial group. Many ethnic biographies are being written, but the majority have Caucasian authors. An examination of *Children's Books in Print* gives the following breakdown:

115 biographies about blacks; 40 written by black authors

37 biographies about native Americans; none by native American authors

4 biographies about Puerto Ricans; none by Puerto Rican authors

24 biographies about Jews; the majority by Jewish authors

0 biographies about Asian-Americans.

## 2. What sources did the author consult in researching the subject?

Many biographies now include an end note indicating the sources and scope of the author's research. An example appears in *Journey Toward Freedom*, by Jacqueline Bernard. In an "Author's Note," Bernard tells how she came to be interested in the life of Sojourner Truth, who grew from an uneducated black slave into one of the most impressive black leaders in the country. The acknowledgments section describes briefly the sources the author consulted, and the book contains other bibliographic aids common to adult biographies: a table of contents, an index, and a selected bibliography.

Jean Fritz, for her *Brendan the Navigator*, went to a wide variety of sources, even though she knew all the pieces of this "history mystery" have not been found. In the lives of many historic figures, there are pieces of missing information, and in some cases conflicting details, that make a completely accurate and verifiable account impossible. Fritz nevertheless exercised her usual careful scholarship to research the life of St. Brendan, born almost fifteen hundred years ago and reputed to have discovered America before the Vikings. Her work demonstrates that in the hands of a superb writer distant times, unfamiliar customs, and unknown people can come alive.

Reference aids are important, especially in extended biographies for readers in upper-intermediate or junior-high grades. In *Louis Pasteur*, the author, John Mann, helps readers approach a complex topic. The book includes not only a table of contents and an index, but also a glossary of terms that may be unfamiliar to readers. In addition, a "Synoptic Calendar" helps relate events in Pasteur's life to events in the world at large. A column of dates runs down the center of the page: to the left are listed significant happenings in the scientist's life; to the right are events of worldwide importance.

## 3. What is the author's style like? Does she or he use words with ease and skill?

Bill Libby demonstrates his ability to recreate dramatic moments in a character's life in *Rocky: The Story of a Champion*. Although the author perhaps overemphasizes the appealing aspects of Rocky Marciano, portraying a simple, warmhearted Italian boy who loved his family and hated to hurt anyone, readers can't help liking "The Champ." Libby traces Marciano's life from his childhood in a close-knit loving family, through his disappointment at not making a success in major league baseball and his early career as a fighter, to his death in an automobile crash in the late 1960s. The book's best feature is how the author grippingly recounts electric

*The fish shape and the waves are rendered in light blue with no variation in hue, and the boat and its occupants are drawn in a black ink line that is superimposed over the blue.* Illustration by Enrico Arno reprinted by permission of Coward, McCann & Geoghegan from *Brendan the Navigator* by Jean Fritz, illustrations copyright © 1979 by Enrico Arno.

moments. At one point, the author is describing the minutes after it becomes apparent that Joe Louis will not be able to get up again, that Rocky has defeated the king of boxing:

> And the crowd had begun to roar. The king was dead now, after all, and a new king was being born. The moments of mourning, the seconds of silent respect, had swiftly come to an end, and suddenly everyone was yelling for this new fellow, this new hero they could idolize. They slapped him on the back and reached out to shake his hand as police escorted Marciano through the mob of well-wishers back to his dressing room, along with his trainer and his manager. While the reporters waited impatiently outside, pounding on the door, Marciano sat, sweaty and sore and weary, and wept.

### 4. How successfully has the author used small personal details to breathe life into the official personage?

In *Beauty Millionaire: The Life of Helena Rubinstein,* all the public details are included about this businesswoman's massive fortune and iron-handed management of a far-flung manufacturing empire, as they should be in a comprehensive biography. In addition, however, author Maxene Fabe has woven a wealth of facts about Rubinstein's private life into the retelling, to create a vivid portrait of a complex human being. Generous to a fault in supporting charities, Rubinstein nevertheless always saw herself as the center of the universe, expecting others to share this view. With a flair for the dramatic, she managed events in her life the way a director might stage-manage a play:

> She was now ninety years old. Her own private suite at New York Hospital was kept in constant readiness. Occasionally she staged a little death rehearsal there. She could be very dramatic. One such morning Weill, "the young lawyer," checked in to confer with her because he was flying to Europe that night on an important business trip.
>
> "Come on, Madame," he said. "You can't die now. You know how confused London is right now. I'm sorry, but you'll have to wait until I get back."
>
> He goaded her for several long minutes until her eyes snapped open. You could see her strength returning. The old woman had thought the better of it.
>
> "Nurse! Nurse!" she shouted, flinging aside the oxygen tent. "Get me out of here."

## SHARING BIOGRAPHY WITH CHILDREN

### COMPARISON ACTIVITIES

One instructional use of biographies is to help children see how a historic figure is treated in several different books. Using more than one account of a famous person's life allows teachers and librarians to help children see the diversity in biographical writing. Books that report identical facts yet represent different final products offer children important insights into the writing process.

Some books about Abraham Lincoln can serve as examples to indicate how comparisons can be made. *Abraham Lincoln,* by James Daugherty, is enhanced with two-color lithographs in a style well suited to their subject matter, for example, the craggy frontiersmen shown in several of the illustrations. The author skips over Lincoln's early years, preferring to concentrate on the presidential years. Daugherty's writing style clearly evokes the times.

The d'Aulaires's Caldecott Medal–winner, *Abraham Lincoln*, is illustrated in soft-edged, full-color lithographs in their usual, easily recognized style. The story begins with Lincoln's birth in a Kentucky cabin and ends before Lincoln is assassinated. The language is simple: at times the use of "reckon" to indicate Abe's father's dialect seems flimsy. Some critics have objected to the illustration portraying blacks rejoicing over Lincoln's visit to Richmond, claiming that it is demeaning.

*Meet Mr. Lincoln*, by Richard Hansen and Donald Hyatt, opens in the city of Washington before the inauguration of the newly elected president in November of 1860. A flashback follows almost immediately, giving a sketchy look at Lincoln's early career. The authors then return to 1860 for an in-depth consideration of slavery and Lincoln's opposition to it. The book also includes details of the Civil War. Striking black-and-white photographs engulf the brief text, showing dramatically the epic struggle. The authors close with: "In the house of strangers, at the end of a strange corridor, Abraham Lincoln finds the end of his road."

Perhaps the best-known children's biography of this famous man is *Abraham Lincoln, Friend of the People*, by Clara Ingram Judson. The author begins with four-year-old Abe helping his father with the planting at their farm in Kentucky. A very complete treatment of his life ends with the train journey of Lincoln's coffin to the prairie state. Judson has been careful throughout, as she states in an introductory note, to rely on her meticulous research to help her exclude or correct various myths about Lincoln's life. The book is fully illustrated with small black-ink drawings and full-color photographs of the three-dimensional dioramas of the Chicago Historical Society.

Less serious in tone, but still effective, is . . . *If You Grew Up with Abraham Lincoln*, a chatty book by Ann McGovern. Strictly speaking, this is not biography, but rather an informal answering of questions children might ask about the era. The author phrases the questions simply and provides answers ranging from four to eleven paragraphs in length. Brinton Turkle's pleasantly relaxed black-crayon drawings of appealing young children and humorous adults fill the margins.

May McNeer opens *America's Abraham Lincoln* with seven-year-old Abe going off to school with his sister and closes it with the assassination. Lynd Ward's lithographic illustrations show his characteristically strong style.

Earl S. Miers wrote two useful books about Lincoln, *Abraham Lincoln in Peace and War* begins when Abe's father brings his new wife to care for the children; *That Lincoln Boy* closes with Lincoln's first attempt at being elected to public office, in which he was defeated. Miers provides more extended treatment of events that are briefly described by other writers.

**In this lithograph, the objects cramming the store have as much importance as the main character.** Illustration by Ingri and Edgar Parin d'Aulaire from *Abraham Lincoln*. Copyright © 1939, 1957 by Doubleday & Company, Inc. Reprinted by permission of the publisher.

***Artist Lynd Ward left the background empty to focus the viewer's attention on the figure of Lincoln.*** Illustration by Lynd Ward from *America's Abraham Lincoln* by May McNeer. Copyright © 1957 by May McNeer Ward and Lynd Ward. Reprinted by permission of Houghton Mifflin Company.

Lloyd Ostendorf's *A Picture Story of Abraham Lincoln* includes many small black-and-white photos as well as the author's pen-and-ink drawings. None of the brief, chronological descriptions are longer than a page, so the book will probably appeal to those intermediate-grade children who have limited reading abilities and short attention spans.

A third-grade teacher made all of the above books about Lincoln available to her students. She read the d'Aulaires' book and *Abraham Lincoln*, by Anne Colver, aloud. Children then read parts of the other books and compared the treatments of specific aspects of Lincoln's life. Each child wrote a statement telling what he or she learned that was new and which book was better, for example:

> They both started when he was a baby. It told in both books he lived in Knob Creek. And they told that he was born in 1809. There were many different things about the books. Like the pictures were different. One was very colorful and one was black and white pictures. I think I like the d'Aulaire better because it has colorfuler pictures and the other book had flashbacks and I didn't like that.
>
> *Kirsten*

> Ann Colver's book started when Abe was seven years old. It started with a funny story.

The way he got to be a lawyer is a man sold him a barrel for one-half dollar. Under some shoes in the barrel he found a law book. He studied very hard. He had an examination and he passed.

1. They both have where he almost drowned.
2. d'Aulaire's book has where he starts out to be a baby. Colver's book started out when he was seven.

Both books said he had three sons and two sons died.

I liked d'Aulaire's pictures. It had colored pictures. They told more about his childhood.

I liked both of them. They tell more about him than I knew.

*Brian*

A teacher doing such a comparison activity could also use Russell Freedman's *Lincoln: A Photobiography.* Seven brief chapters present the president's life from birth in rural Kentucky in 1809 to burial in rural Illinois in 1865. The text presents facts gathered through in-depth research at pertinent historical sites interspersed with brief quotes from important figures of the time and from Lincoln himself. Lincoln's words demonstrate how his sense of humor maintained itself despite personal tragedies and political setbacks. For example, when criticized for being "two-faced" during a political debate, he replied: "I leave it to my audience. If I had another face, do you think I'd wear this one?" The smoothly moving text is augmented by more than ninety photographs and prints. There are three appendixes: a list of historic sites, a list of other books about Lincoln, and "A Lincoln Sampler" of quotations concerning both serious and humorous matters.

## WRITING BIOGRAPHY AND AUTOBIOGRAPHY

Children can create biographies after sharing biographies in class has built up their interest. A valuable source of subjects is children's relatives—grandparents or perhaps aunts and uncles. After pointing out to students that biographers often interview their subjects (if still alive), a teacher could encourage those who are interested to gather material for a biography. Asking questions of their grandparents or other relatives helps children understand the nature of past time. Transcribing what they are told provides children with practice in encoding oral language. Finally, with help from a teacher or librarian, boys and girls can edit the material, choosing those parts that are most interesting and arranging and rewording them.

Another activity, appropriate for junior high students, is writing autobiographies. To introduce this idea, a teacher might read one chapter a day of *Staying Power,* by Peter Barton, to the class. Subtitled "Performing Artists

Talk About their Lives," this book comprises informal and brief accounts (from eight to fourteen pages) of their work by artists themselves. Musicians (both classical and popular), dancers (both ballet and modern), and actors (both Shakespearean and street corner) give interesting insights into their occupations, which are integral to their sense of self.

The teacher might instead use *Self-Portrait: Erik Blegvad*, a delightful pastiche by the artist, incorporating snippets of action ranging in time from his own childhood to that of his children. This autobiography is unencumbered by a sustained narrative and includes visuals by Blegvad, his wife, his friend N. M. Bodecker, and five other artists, in both color and black-and-white. Perhaps a little disorganized, this book has the charming freshness of listening to a talented raconteur talk about himself.

Using either of these books as an introduction, the teacher can help children focus on one part of their own lives that was particularly significant to them and describe it in words for someone who did not know them during that time. Presenting the project in this manner is necessary to help children avoid the kind of superficial summarization so common—unfortunately—when children are asked to write on such trite topics as "What I Did During My Summer Vacation."

## SUMMARY

Teachers can use biography for a variety of purposes, such as:

1. developing children's sense of historic time through books that describe people's attitudes, events both public and private, and artifacts of the time such as clothing. Living conditions, including social, economic, and political changes, are brought to life not as facts to be taught but as settings for the character's life story.

2. satisfying children's curiosity about contemporary figures, capitalizing on interest in sports and music figures, for instance. Such biographies can lead readers beyond the superficial, and sometimes repetitious, media accounts to the more thorough descriptions found in books.

3. serving as a base for language activities. Students can talk and write about their reactions to biographies, comparing and contrasting different accounts of the same person's life or perhaps lives of different people living during the same time period. Discussions focussing on similarities between life today and in some other period can lead children to sense the commonality which links us together as human beings, despite differences in surface detail.

In the process of using biographies for these purposes, librarians and teachers acquaint students with powerful role models at a time in their lives when such models are very important.

## An Integrated Unit of Study

Many biographies for children trace the subject's life over a period of time, emphasizing the changes that occur. A significant part of the life of a person who serves as the subject of a biography is the physical, psychological, emotional, or cognitive change he or she undergoes. Interpreting change generally, teachers can present a unit on the kinds of changes authors depict in books, ranging from easy picture books to complex, long fiction for adolescent readers.

Even preschoolers deal with psychological changes. *Little Rabbit's Baby Brother*, by Fran Manushkin (based on characters created by Lucy Bate) shows that anticipating a new family member may be more pleasant than the actuality—depicted in Diane DeGroat's colored-pencil illustrations. Little Rabbit tries to help, but nothing goes right, so she decides to hop right out of the house. Her journey "around the world" ends when the sun sets and it gets cold; mother and father welcome her back with hugs. After they talk about how big sisters can help, and she succeeds at the effort, her attitudes change; in the end, she dreams happily of holding baby brother's hand and hopping with him. For an interesting comparison activity, this book can be used with *Too Big*, by Holly Keller, in which Henry adjusts to the arrival of baby Jake. The type of animal and the setting are different, but the problem of adjusting to a younger sibling is the same.

For older readers, Patricia MacLachlan deals with the significant changes that affect all the characters in *Sarah, Plain and Tall*. Far from the eastern seaside she loves, Sarah finds adjusting to the flat western land difficult, but she knows that accepting a mail-order wife and mother cannot be easy for her intended family. In the end, she decides that what she gains more than compensates for what she gives up. In only fifty-eight pages, Patricia MacLachlan manages to tell an expansive story that will draw children in. This thoughtfully conceived and well-written book received the Scott O'Dell

Award, given by the University of Chicago for exemplary historic fiction. *Sarah, Plain and Tall* reflects MacLachlan's philosophy (Courtney, 1985):

> I think life is a mixture of humor and sadness and poignancy and grief, all these things mixed in together. . . . There's a great deal in this world that is not happy and yet there are moments here or there that I try to illuminate, the kind of thoughtful, pensive moments.

In *Miss Rumphius*, author/illustrator Barbara Cooney follows the life of her main character from the time she was a "little girl named Alice, who lived in a city by the sea" until she has become the little old Lupine Lady, who lives in a house surrounded by rocks with "blue and purple and rose-colored flowers." Miss Rumphius's grandfather had made major changes, coming to a foreign land. Following his instructions, she travels to faraway places, including a real tropical island, and then she comes back to the seaside. To carry out the third task her grandfather set for her (do something to make the world more beautiful), she becomes the female equivalent of Johnny Appleseed, only she plants lupines. In the end, Miss Rumphius is changing the lives of the neighborhood children as her grandfather changed her life. This book won the 1983 American Book Award.

Mature junior-high students can read of the intersection of two conflicting dreams: a boy's desire to attend college and become an architect, and his parents' lifelong desire to leave the city and relocate on a farm. Alden Carter writes, in *Growing Season*, of Pam and Rick, natural children sharing a home with four adopted younger brothers and sisters. Rick's life has been full of change: first adjusting to the coming and going of foster children, then to the adopted siblings, each of whom has problems. Further changes come in Rick's senior year when the farm his father bought turns out to be in poorer repair than was first apparent. Additional changes come, gradually, as he assumes more and more responsibility for his younger siblings, and for farm tasks. These changes are closely linked to growing up, to becoming a man, to accepting responsibilities even though they may not be choices. Junior-high age readers will find this a compelling book.

A collection of short stories, *Early Sorrow*, selected by Charlotte Zolotow, deals with change, resistance to it, and resulting loss. A teacher might read these aloud, one a day, to an academically gifted class or recommend them to an accomplished individual reader. For the most part the stories are by writers not ordinarily thought of as children's authors: E. L. Doctorow, James Purdy, Elizabeth Bowen, and Katherine Mansfield are better known for adult literature. Even the story by Elizabeth Enright, "A Distant Bell," is quite unlike her usual work for young readers. The precocious narrator, trying to hold on to her newly divorced father, purposely does not carry his message to a female friend. The story ends: "I suppose I knew then that by my action I had lost my father just as truly as Mrs. Fenwick had." Enright tells readers that in trying to hold on too hard we may lose what we want to retain. The messages from the other writers included in this collection deal as honestly with resistance to change.

For further discussion about organizing literature study around topics, such as change, see Chapter 14 (pages 668–674).

## Suggestions for Further Study

1. Author Marilyn Jurich (see the article listed in "Related Reading for Adults") claims many subjects are off limits to biographers because their sexual preferences are unorthodox. This may be changing; biographies of Gertrude Stein for children have been published, despite her lifelong involvement in what is widely assumed to have been a lesbian relationship. Read *Gertrude Stein Is Gertrude Stein Is Gertrude Stein: Her Life and Work*, by W. G. Rogers (New York: Thomas Y. Crowell, 1973). Do you find the handling of that relationship acceptable for young readers? Another treatment of this subject is *Gertrude Stein*, by Howard Greenfield (New York: Crown, 1973).

2. Study several biographies about one member of an ethnic minority. Research the authors to determine which—if any—of them belong to that ethnic group. Are there any differences in authenticity that may be related to the authors' backgrounds?

3. Read a biography of a person who is involved in a sport you play or an art you practice. Based on your own knowledge of the activity, do you see any inaccuracies or omissions in the account? Can you get a feeling for whether or not the author actually participated in this type of activity?

4. Dance, an ephemeral artistic activity, was not mentioned in this chapter. Can you locate enough good biographies of dancers to draw up an annotated list of such books? An autobiography by Robert Maiorano is listed in Chapter 12. To prepare children for that, you might introduce them to either *Backstage*, by Maiorano and Rachel Isadora (New York: Greenwillow, 1978), or *A Little Interlude*, by the same authors (New York: Coward, McCann, 1980). You might also want to read and evaluate the authenticity of George Ancona's *Dancing Is* (New York, E. P. Dutton, 1981).

5. Plan a teaching unit based on Eve Merriam's *Growing Up Female in America*. Can you find an individual biography for each of the ten women featured in Merriam's collective biography? Make a list of women in your own

community who might agree to be interviewed by your students concerning their life accomplishments.

6. Use the film *Woodblock Printer* (ACI Productions, New York) to introduce this graphic technique to upper intermediate-grade students. Share *Kathe Kollwitz: Life in Art*, by Mina C. and H. Arthur Klein, with your students. Then plan a related experience with the school art teacher so the class can learn how to make woodcuts.

7. For a suggestion for using F. N. Monjo's *The One Bad Thing About Father* (New York: Harper and Row, 1970), see *E Is for Everybody*, by Nancy Polette (Metuchen, N.J.: Scarecrow, 1982), a book of ideas for involving children with books. The author annotates 126 new picture books published since the first edition of her helpful manual. She includes a teaching suggestion for each. In addition she provides a second section on art and media activities. Try one of her suggestions with children and evaluate its effectiveness.

8. In *Matters of Fact* (New York: Thomas Y. Crowell, 1972), critic Margery Fisher considers the genre of biography, among others. Read her chapter on Abraham Lincoln (pp. 367–406), which contains commentary on several of the biographies discussed in this chapter. Read the books to see whether you think her comments are justified.

## Related Reading for Adults

Carr, Jo. "What Do We Do About Bad Biographies?" In *Beyond Fact: Nonfiction for Children and Young People*. Chicago: American Library Association, 1982, pp. 119–128.

Carr asserts that in the genre of biography readers are confronted with "sentimentality, unwarranted fictionalization, lack of solid documentation, and distortion of history." The remainder of the article provides examples of these problems and suggestions as to how to remedy them. Carr advises that in selecting books, teachers and librarians read reviews skeptically: reviewers are not as critical of biography as they are of other genres in which books are more plentiful.

Coolidge, Olivia. "My Struggle With Facts." *Wilson Library Bulletin*, October 1974, pp. 146–151.

The necessity of recognizing why facts are important is brilliantly illustrated here. Abraham Lincoln's exact birth date may be in itself an unimportant fact, but when it defines what was or was not possible, the fact becomes crucial. Distinguishing between fact and judgment is an omnipresent problem for biographers.

Fisher, Margery. "Life Course or Screaming Force." *Children's Literature in Education*, Autumn 1976, pp. 107–127.

Fisher contends that readers under the age of twelve are not looking for intellectual exploration of personality, but rather want straightforward, brief introductions to important figures, past and present. Narrative is crucial, and the character in a good biography should be extended through descriptions of personal traits. What a person did and when is more important than why.

Fritz, Jean. "George Washington, My Father, and Walt Disney." *The Horn Book*, April 1976, pp. 191–198.

An informal study of high-school students revealed that less than a fifth of them had ever read or cared to read a biography. They were unaware of the insights into the human condition that can be gained by reading biography. Fritz questions the contention that the purpose of biography is to present lives that young people can emulate. She believes this view limits biographers' consideration of controversial subjects, which might provide those valuable insights.

―――. "Make Room for the Eighteenth Century." *The Horn Book*, October 1974, pp. 177–181.

Here this enthusiastic and prolific writer describes the type of work she has become famous for, citing especially the use of small details to bring a person to life, to reveal a larger picture, and to hint at complexities and paradoxes. She describes some of the difficulties entailed in trying to convince children that the subjects of biographies actually lived.

Groff, Patrick. "Biography: The Bad or the Bountiful." *Top of the News*, April 1973, pp. 210–217.

It is widely assumed by adults that biography gives children new models to emulate, but Groff thinks this is a faulty assumption because so few really good biographies are published. Groff contends that child readers form relationships with peers in order to change. It is not until adolescence that children become eager to join adult society by actively assuming adult roles.

Jurich, Marilyn. "What's Left Out of Biography for Children." *Children's Literature*, 1 (1972), pp. 143–151.

This article opens with an assertion that biography is difficult to write because it is supposed to re-create reality and at the same time provide a guide for success. Jurich believes that the antihero is a legitimate subject for a biographer. She admits that the lives of some famous people may be difficult to present for a child audience, but wonders whether exclusion of sensitive material is not a form of suppression.

Lonsdale, Bernard, and Helen Mackintosh. *Children Experience Literature*. New York: Random House, 1973, pp. 409–439.

The authors provide a useful account of the history of biography writing for children, describing the range of books available. Biographies are grouped according to the subjects' occupations, a helpful arrangement for teachers who need to recommend books to a child with a specific interest. A liberal assortment of black-and-white illustrations is included.

Marcus, Leonard S. "Life Drawing: Some Notes on Children's Picture Book Biographies." *The Lion and the Unicorn*, 4 (Summer 1980), pp. 15–31.

Marcus opens by noting that biographies for children often contain only praise for the subject. He continues by analyzing in some depth the work of successful writers in the picture book genre. The analysis of Ingri and Edgar Parin d'Aulaire's work is useful. He comments on their "energy and fullness of vision." In the concluding section, on humorous biography, Marcus points out the influence of Robert Lawson on the more recent work of Jean Fritz.

Monjo, F. N. "Monjo's Manifest Destiny: Authors Can Claim Any Territory in Literature." *School Library Journal*, 21 (May 1974), pp. 30–31.

A response to another critic's commentary on one of his books, Monjo's article widens into a basic statement about not limiting authors to first-hand experience. He talks clearly about why his book, *Indian Summer* (Harper and Row, 1968), is a valid depiction of the time. Monjo comments on that "huge, untidy, writhing panorama that is American history" and speaks strongly against attempts to revise history to present more positive views of minority groups.

Moore, Ann W. "A Question of Accuracy: Errors in Children's Biographies." *School Library Journal*, 31 (February 1985), pp. 34–35.

Of particular interest to upper-elementary teachers involved in instructing children in the use of resource materials, this article examines three different types of errors common in biography. Moore provides examples of errors in dates, names, and numbers; errors caused by oversimplification; and errors from patently false information. Her suggestions of actions both adults and children can take when they find an error are especially valuable. An incidental benefit of analyzing for errors is that it might encourage children to be more careful in checking facts in what they write themselves.

Wilms, Denise M. "An Evaluation of Biography." In *Jump Over the Moon.* Ed. P. Barron. New York: Holt, Rinehart and Winston, 1984, pp. 220–225.

Wilms maintains that it is important to pay more attention to the crafting of biogra-

phies, as many of these books are marginal literature. Critical to a biography's success is the author's own sympathy and enthusiasm for the subject. Biographies too often get bogged down because authors have paid too much attention to vague questions of what is appropriate for children to read. It is important to deepen the genre beyond the two-dimensional platitudes that abounded in early biographies. Compromises like fictionalization and lack of documentation must be dealt with. The teacher must select biographies carefully, for "there aren't many biographies around that successfully combine everything you'd hope [for]."

## Professional References

Anderson, Gary, Diana Higgins, and Stanley R. Wurster. "Differences in the Free-Reading Books Selected by High, Average, and Low Achievers." *The Reading Teacher,* 39 (December 1985), 326–330.

Courtney, Ann. "Profile: Patricia MacLachlan." *Language Arts,* 62 (November 1985), 783–787.

Forman, Jack. "Biography for Children: More Facts, Less Fiction." *Library Journal,* 97 (September 15, 1972), 2968–2969.

Higgins, Judith. "Biographies They Can Read."

*School Library Journal,* 18 (April 1971), 33–34.

Reising, Robert W. "Jim Thorpe: Bicentennial Hero." *Language Arts,* 53 (January 1976), 27–28.

Segel, Elizabeth. "In Biography for Young Readers, Nothing Is Impossible." *The Lion and the Unicorn,* 4 (Summer 1980), 4–14.

Wright, Jone P., and Elizabeth G. Allen. "Sixth-Graders Ride with Paul Revere." *Language Arts,* (January 1976), 46–50.

## Bibliography of Children's Books

Aldis, Dorothy. *Nothing Is Impossible: The Story of Beatrix Potter.* New York: Atheneum, 1971.

Aliki. *The Story of Johnny Appleseed.* Englewood Cliffs, N.J.: Prentice-Hall, 1963.

———. *A Weed Is a Flower: The Life of George Washington Carver.* Englewood Cliffs, N.J.: Prentice-Hall, 1965.

Barton, Peter. *Staying Power.* New York: Dial, 1980.

Benchley, Nathaniel. *Sam the Minuteman.* New York: Harper and Row, 1969.

Bernard, Jacqueline. *Journey Toward Freedom.* New York: Grosset and Dunlap, 1967.

Blair, Gwenda. *Laura Ingalls Wilder.* New York: G. P. Putnam's 1981.

Blegvad, Erik. *Self-Portrait: Eric Blegvad.* Reading, Mass.: Addison-Wesley, 1979.

Burchard, S. H. *George Brett.* New York: Harcourt Brace Jovanovich, 1982.

Carter, Alden. *Growing Season.* New York: Coward, McCann and Geoghegan, 1984.

Colver, Anne. *Abraham Lincoln.* New York: Scholastic, 1962.

Coolidge, Olivia. *Tom Paine, Revolutionary.* New York: Scribner's, 1969.

Cooney, Barbara. *Miss Rumphius.* New York: Viking, 1982.

Cooper, Ilene. *Susan B. Anthony.* New York: Frederick Watts, 1984.

Daugherty, James. *Abraham Lincoln.* New York: Viking, 1943.

d'Aulaire, Ingri, and Edgar Parin d'Aulaire. *Abraham Lincoln.* Garden City, N.Y.: Doubleday, 1939.

Dines, Glen. *John Muir.* New York: G. P. Putnam's, 1974.

Dolan, Jr., Edward F. *Adolf Hitler.* New York: Dodd, Mead, 1981.

Douglas, Robert W. *John Paul II. The Pilgrim Pope.* Chicago: Childrens Press, 1980.

Epstein, Sam, and Beryl Epstein. *Michael Faraday: Apprentice to Science.* Champaign, Ill.: Garrard Press, 1971.

————. *Mister Peale's Mammoth.* New York: Coward, McCann and Geoghegan, 1977.

Fabe, Maxene. *Beauty Millionaire: The Life of Helena Rubinstein.* New York: Thomas Y. Crowell, 1972.

Faber, Doris. *Margaret Thatcher. Britain's "Iron Lady."* New York: Viking/Kestrel, 1985.

Freedman, Russell. *Lincoln: A Photobiography.* New York: Clarion Books, 1987.

Fritz, Jean. *And Then What Happened, Paul Revere?* New York: Coward, McCann and Geoghegan, 1973.

————. *Brendan the Navigator.* New York: Coward, McCann and Geoghegan, 1979.

————. *Can't You Make Them Behave, King George?* New York: Coward, McCann and Geoghegan, 1982.

————. *George Washington's Breakfast.* New York: Coward, McCann and Geoghegan, 1969.

————. *Where Was Patrick Henry on the 29th of May?* New York: Coward, McCann and Geoghegan, 1975.

————. *Why Don't You Get a Horse, Sam Adams?* New York: Coward, McCann and Geoghegan, 1974.

Gherman, Beverly. *Georgia O'Keeffe.* New York: Atheneum, 1986.

Grant, Matthew G. *Susan B. Anthony.* Mankato, Minn.: Creative Education, 1974.

Greene, Carol. *Sandra Day O'Connor.* Chicago: Childrens Press, 1982.

Gridley, Marion E. *American Indian Women.* New York: Hawthorne, 1974.

Hamilton, Virginia. *W. E. B. DuBois: A Biography.* New York: Thomas Y. Crowell, 1972.

Hanff, Helene. *Queen of England.* Garden City, N.Y.: Doubleday, 1969.

Hano, Arnold. *Kareem: Basketball Great.* New York: G. P. Putnam's, 1975.

Hansen, Richard, and Donald Hyatt. *Meet Mr. Lincoln.* New York: Golden, 1960.

Hovey, Tamara. *A Mind of Her Own.* New York: Harper and Row, 1977.

Hunter, Edith Fisher. *Child of the Silent Night.* New York: Dell, 1983.

Jacobs, David. *Chaplin, The Movies, and Charlie.* New York: Harper and Row, 1975.

Jacobs, Linda. *John Denver: A Natural High.* St. Paul, Minn.: EMC Corporation, 1976.

Johnston, Johanna. *Harriet and the Runaway Book.* New York: Harper and Row, 1977.

Judson, Clara Ingram. *Abraham Lincoln, Friend of the People.* Chicago: Wilcox and Follett, 1950.

Kelen, Emery. *Fifty Voices of the Twentieth Century.* New York: Lothrop, Lee and Shepard, 1970.

Keller, Holly. *Too Big.* New York: Greenwillow, 1983.

Keller, Mollie. *Golda Meir.* New York: Franklin Watts, 1983.

Kherdian, David. *Finding Home.* New York: Greenwillow, 1981.

————. *The Road from Home: The Story of an*

*Armenian Girl*. New York: Greenwillow, 1979.

———. *Root River Run*. Minneapolis: Carolrhoda Books, 1984.

Klein, Mina C., and H. Arthur Klein. *Kathe Kollwitz: Life in Art*. New York: Holt, Rinehart and Winston, 1972.

Lawson, Robert. *Ben and Me: A New and Astonishing Life of Benjamin Franklin as Written by His Good Mouse Amos*. Boston: Little, Brown, 1951.

———. *Captain Kidd's Cat . . .* Boston: Little, Brown, 1956.

———. *Mr. Revere and I*. Boston: Little, Brown, 1953.

Lee, Betsy. *Judy Blume's Story*. Minneapolis: Dillon Press, 1981.

Libby, Bill. *Rocky: The Story of a Champion*. New York: Messner, 1971.

Lundgren, Hal. *Moses Malone: Philadelphia's Peerless Center*. Chicago: Childrens Press, 1983.

MacBride, Roger (ed.). *West from Home: Letters of Laura Ingalls Wilder, San Francisco, 1915*. New York: Harper and Row, 1974.

MacLachlan, Patricia. *Sarah, Plain and Tall*. New York: Harper and Row, 1985.

Mann, John. *Louis Pasteur*. New York: Scribner's, 1964.

Manushkin, Fran. *Little Rabbit's Baby Brother*. New York: Crown, 1986.

McGovern, Ann. *. . . If You Grew Up With Abraham Lincoln*. New York: Four Winds, 1966.

McKissack, Patricia C. *Michael Jackson, Superstar!* Chicago: Childrens Press, 1984.

McNeer, May. *America's Abraham Lincoln*. Boston: Houghton Mifflin, 1957.

———. *America's Mark Twain*. Boston: Houghton Mifflin, 1962.

Meltzer, Milton. *Dorothea Lange. Life Through the Camera*. New York: Viking/Kestrel, 1985.

Merriam, Eve. *Growing Up Female in America*. New York: Dell, 1973.

Miers, Earl S. *Abraham Lincoln in Peace and War*. New York: American Heritage, 1964.

———. *That Lincoln Boy*. Cleveland: World, 1968.

Miller, Albert G. *Mark Twain in Love*. New York: Harcourt Brace Jovanovich, 1973.

Monjo, F. N. *Grand Papa and Ellen Aroon, Being an Account of Some of the Happy Times We Spent Together by Thomas Jefferson and His Favorite Granddaughter*. New York: Holt, Rinehart and Winston, 1974.

———. *Letters to Horseface*. New York: Viking, 1975.

Nelson, Mary Carroll. *Maria Martinez*. Minneapolis: Dillon Press, 1972.

Newlon, Clarke. *Famous Mexican-Americans*. New York: Dodd, Mead, 1972.

O'Connor, Karen. *Sally Ride and the New Astronauts*. New York: Franklin Watts, 1983.

Olsen, James T. *Ralph Nader, Voice of the People*. Chicago: Childrens Press, 1974.

Oneal, Zibby. *Grandma Moses. Painter of Rural America*. New York: Viking/Kestrel, 1986.

Ostendorf, Lloyd. *A Picture Story of Abraham Lincoln*. New York: Lothrop, Lee and Shepard, 1962.

Richards, Norman. *Helen Keller*. Chicago: Childrens Press, 1968.

Rockwell, Anne. *Paintbrush and Peacepipe: The Story of George Catlin*. New York: Atheneum, 1971.

Rosenthal, Bert. *Larry Bird, Cool Man on the Court*. Chicago: Childrens Press, 1981.

———. *Sugar Ray Leonard: The Baby-Faced Boxer*. Chicago: Childrens Press, 1982.

Schick, Alice, and Marjorie N. Allen. *The Remarkable Ride of Israel Bissell*. Philadelphia: J. B. Lippincott, 1976.

Shiels, Barbara. *Winners. Women and the Nobel Prize*. Minneapolis: Dillon, 1985.

Stanley, Diane. *Peter the Great*. New York: Four Winds, 1985.

Sterling, Dorothy, and Bernard Quarles. *Lift Every Voice: The Lives of Booker T. Washington, W. E. B. DuBois, Mary Church Terrell, James Weldon Johnson*. Garden City, N.Y.: Doubleday, 1965.

Sullivan, George. *Mary Lou Retton*. New York: Julian Messmer, 1985.

Swift, Hildegarde Hoyt. *From the Eagle's Wing: A Biography of John Muir*. New York: Morrow, 1962.

Syme, Ronald. *Juarez: the Founder of Modern Mexico*. New York: Morrow, 1972.

Tamarin, Alfred. *The Autobiography of Benvenuto Cellini*. New York: Macmillan, 1969.

Taylor, Paula. *Coretta King: A Woman of Peace*. Mankato, Minn.: Creative Education, 1974.

Tobias, Tobi. *Marian Anderson*. New York: Thomas Y. Crowell, 1972.

Wagenheim, Kal. *Clemente!* New York: Praeger, 1973.

Weiner, Sandra. *Small Hands, Big Hands*. New York: Pantheon, 1970.

Zolotow, Charlotte (selector). *Early Sorrow*. New York: Harper and Row, 1986.

# CONTEMPORARY
# FICTION:
# VIEWS OF LIFE

Ox's family is so rich they can afford to charter airplanes.

*Ox*, by John Ney

Charley's family is so poor he has never seen a water faucet.

*Did You Carry the Flag Today, Charley?*, by Rebecca Caudill

Harriet lives in an apartment in New York City, surrounded by millions of people.

*Harriet the Spy*, by Louise Fitzhugh

Jacqueline lives on a game refuge in Kenya, surrounded by a multitude of animals.

*The Bushbabies*, by William Stevenson

Kevin lives with his sister Sandra, his father, his father's wife, his step-brother Harold and his step-sister Jean.

*Good-bye to the Jungle*, by John Rowe Townsend

Slake lives completely alone.

*Slake's Limbo*, by Felice Holman

The above pairs of quotations illustrate the wide range of contrasting life-styles dealt with in contemporary realistic fiction. To understand what this genre encompasses, it is necessary to understand the words *contemporary* and *realistic*.

## WHAT IS CONTEMPORARY REALISTIC FICTION?

What makes fiction contemporary? The term derives from the Latin words *con* ("with") and *tempor* ("the time"). Thus, contemporary fiction deals with stories set in the present time. In an earlier chapter, some books were classified as historic fiction even though they were originally written as contemporary fiction. The decision as to whether a book is still contemporary is a somewhat arbitrary one, and not all readers will be in agreement in all cases.

What makes fiction realistic? Clearly *The Town Cats and Other Tales*, by Lloyd Alexander, is fantasy because cats cannot talk. Is *A Wrinkle in Time*, by Madeline L'Engle, fantasy? The treatment of the story is naturalistic; however, the idea of traveling through time is not yet a reality. Is *Jennifer, Hecate, Macbeth, William McKinley and Me, Elizabeth*, by E. L. Konigsburg, realistic? Several things happen that may seem improbable, but nothing

*Artist Laszlo Kubinyi uses line to create texture and shadows in illustrations as lighthearted as Lloyd Alexander's prose.* From *The Town Cats and Other Tales* by Lloyd Alexander, illustrated by Laszlo Kubinyi. Illustrations copyright © 1977 by Laszlo Kubinyi. Reproduced by permission of the publisher, E. P. Dutton, a division of NAL Penguin Inc.

actually impossible occurs; since the story takes place in present time, the book can be classified as contemporary realistic fiction. It may be interesting to ask children which elements in Konigsburg's story (or some other one) seem real and which do not. Such discussions frequently give teachers insights into children's cognitive processes.

Trying to group books into genres reveals that many do not fit exactly into one. Some authors combine elements of more than one genre in a single book. For example, in *Heartsease*, by Peter Dickinson, the author creates a story that is difficult to classify.[1] Supposedly set in twentieth-century England, the story includes fantasy elements: people turn against machines; witches (those who use machines) are stoned. Margaret and her cousin Jonathan compassionately try to help one of these witches and seem the

---

[1] *Heartsease* is the second book in a trilogy called *The Changes*. The first book is entitled *The Weathermonger* (Boston: Little, Brown, 1969); the third is *The Devil's Children* (Boston: Little, Brown, 1970). These complex books demand a skilled reader.

only sensible people in a world gone mad. Another example of a book difficult to classify is *Secret of the Andes*, by Ann Nolan Clark, which appears to be realistic fiction but also includes elements of legend and fantasy.

It can be said that what is one person's reality is another's fantasy. What seems real to each of us varies, depending on our gender, age, social class, ethnic group, and geographic location, among other factors. In contemporary realistic fiction, readers can find a multiplicity of realities and contrast them with the actualities of their own lives. Good contemporary realistic fiction presents a consistent point of view. The author makes readers enter into a different reality.

An example of this kind of consistency is present in *Harriet the Spy*, by Louise Fitzhugh. Few child readers will be as precocious as Harriet, have a nursemaid, attend a private school, live in an exclusive (and expensive) apartment building, spy on people, secrete themselves in a dumbwaiter to gather information, and record their findings in a diary. Harriet, planning to be a journalist when she grows up, learns a valuable lesson when the other children discover her diary, containing unflatteringly accurate descriptions of them. She finds out that her nursemaid's advice—sometimes lies are inevitable—is useful. Despite her willingness to compromise by printing a retraction in her school newspaper, Harriet remains indomitable to the end. One reason this engaging story of pugnacious Harriet is fine writing is its reality quotient. The author has observed her environment minutely, has reflected thoughtfully on the possible behaviors of her characters, and consequently has presented a very consistent realism.

Fitzhugh effectively develops characters with a comic touch. An example is the scene where a disgruntled Harriet, assigned the role of an onion in the school play, is practicing her part.[2]

> After supper she tried to practice being an onion. She started by falling down several times, making a great bumping noise. The idea was to fall in a rolling way the way an onion would and then roll around in a complete circle several times, then roll slowly to a stop the way an onion would if you put it down on a table. Harriet rolled around and bumped into a chair, knocking it over.
>
> Her mother came to the door. She looked down at Harriet lying there with the chair on top of her. "What are you doing?" she asked mildly. . . .

---

[2]Because there is so much dialogue in *Harriet the Spy*, middle-grade students might like to dramatize a scene or scenes, making a play of their own that is more sensible than the one Harriet endures.

Mr. Welsch came into the room. "What's going on in here? It sounds like someone hitting a punching bag."

"She's being an onion."

They stood watching Harriet fall over and over again.

Mr. Welsch put his pipe in his mouth and crossed his arms. "According to Stanislavsky you have to feel like an onion. Do you feel like an onion?"

"Not in the least," said Harriet. "I never WANTED to be an onion."

"And it's a good thing. How many parts do you think are written for onions these days?" Mr. Welsch laughed. "I don't imagine you did want to be an onion. For that matter, who knows if an onion does, either."

Mrs. Welsch laughed up at him. "You're so smart. Let's see *you* fall like an onion."

"Don't mind if I do," said Mr. Welsch, and putting down his pipe, he fell solidly to the floor.

"Honey! Did you hurt yourself?"

"No," he said quietly. "But it's not as easy as it looks." He lay there breathing. Harriet took another fall just to keep him company.

"Why don't you get up, honey?" Mrs. Welsch stood over him with a worried look on her face.

"I'm trying to feel like an onion. The closest I can get is a scallion."

Harriet tried to feel like an onion. She found herself screwing her eyes up tight, wrapping her arms around her body . . .

"My God, Harriet, are you sick?" Mrs. Welsch rushed over to her.

It is entirely consistent, given the characterization developed by Fitzhugh, for Harriet's mother to exclaim, "My God, Harriet, are you sick?" The expression elicited some objection from critics,[3] but all prior descriptions of Mrs. Welsch make this a very typical remark.

In *The Long Secret*, the sequel to *Harriet the Spy*, Harriet and her friends grow into teenagers. Most of the books discussed in this text are children's books, but in this chapter some books with teenaged protagonists, usually labeled as being for young adult readers, are described. These books are included because they appeal to, and are read by, students younger than the characters. Psychologists such as Marie Wynn (1983) and David Elkind (1981) have commented in recent books that, because of changes in our society, children are being forced to grow up more quickly than in previous

---

[3]See, for example, "Take Cuss Words Out of Kids' Books," by Eva Nelson (*Wilson Library Bulletin*, October 1974, pp. 132–133). Nelson thinks that Fitzhugh's book started a fad for including profanity as a way of developing reality. She criticizes other books in which she believes the profanity is unnecessary.

*This illustration is a dramatic and purposefully minimal statement of Harriet's pugnacious nature.* Illustration from *Harriet the Spy* by Louise Fitzhugh. Copyright © 1964 by Louise Fitzhugh. Reprinted by permission of Harper & Row, Publishers, Inc.

years. Therefore, the positive images presented in recommended young-adult books should be available to younger readers as they begin the process of dealing with their new awareness of the world.

## CREATING REALITY

Since Louise Fitzhugh broke publishing ground with *Harriet the Spy* in 1964, a large group of writers has been busy creating realistic fiction that accurately depicts modern life. One of these writers is Barthe DeClements. Her *6th Grade Can Really Kill You* makes it obvious that DeClements is a careful listener who can capture on paper the language of the real-life models for her characters. In this particular book, Elsie and her friend, returning from their summer vacation, sound convincingly like thousands of other sixth graders because of the mature language they use, casual in structure and incorporating strong terms.

**DIFFERENT KINDS OF REALITY.**   Reality goes far beyond the words authors have their characters use. Descriptions of settings and of characters' actions are also important in setting up a writer's version of reality. For example, in *Sticks and Stones,* by Lynn Hall, there is the following description of a family dinner:

> A couple of loaves of bread were torn open at the kitchen table, along with the usual clutter of open jelly and peanut-butter jars, cereal bowls with the morning's cornflakes pasted to their sides, pop bottles and beer cans with necklaces of flies at their mouths, curled packages of drying bologna and cheese, . . .
>
> Floyd found a knife on the table, swished it savagely through the air to discourage the fly that rode in its butter, and began elbowing his way through the smaller children toward the bread.
>
> He ate four sandwiches, opened a can of baked beans, dumped them into one of the used cereal bowls, and ate them, then opened a beer and buttered several graham crackers. When they were gone, he began to feel a little better. He belched and brought the kids' giggles to shrieks. Long ago Floyd had mastered the art of swallowing air . . . to produce quite a good belch. It was his claim to fame within the family.

Although some readers may find the scene distasteful, it is undeniably lifelike; Floyd's kitchen, as well as his character, is clearly established through the author's descriptive details.

In sharp contrast to the above dinner scene is the following from *Are You in the House Alone?* by Richard Peck:

> Only the mighty Lawvers would give a dinner party for a bunch of high-school juniors. A real dinner party, with damask dinner napkins and finger bowls, with Lawver Mother at one end of the Duncan Phyfe table and Lawver Father at the other end. And two pairs of edgy sixteen-year-olds facing each other in between, across a bowl of stiff chrysanthemums. There were candles in the dining-room chandelier, and a woman in a uniform to do the serving.

Which of the two dinner scenes is more realistic? Neither can be written off as unreal, even though one or both may be very different from the reader's reality. Both scenes are effective because of the authors' skills in establishing characters and settings that are believable.

**REPORTING OR COMMENTING?**   It is important to keep in mind that in realistic fiction, authors should describe society as it is. Effective writers do not preach at readers but rather avoid didacticism in their presentation of characters and situations.

Some adults may shudder at the idea of children's authors writing about premarital sex. However, in writing *Too Bad About the Haines Girl,* author

Zoa Sherburne, like many other writers who tackle this difficult theme, is not advocating but simply describing premarital sex. Not all authors are able to so restrain themselves.[4]

One authority on children's literature comments on the author's responsibility (Huck, 1979):

> But well-written contemporary literature must do more than mirror society, it must make its own comment about it and help the reader view society in a new perspective.

Yet this same authority also points out the problem inherent in this position, which is that

> ... there is a very real danger that the author will attempt to preach or teach. The book written solely to promote an ideological position ... may be overpowered by its theme, didactic in its approach.

In the final analysis, it is the author's ability to create convincing characters, setting, and plot that results in compelling contemporary fiction. Children read because they care about the characters and want to know what happens to them; in the process, they may also gain insights into the nature of the world through a character's eyes. A didactic book, written only to promulgate certain beliefs, is dishonest. When the promulgation of values or beliefs overpower the characters and what they are doing, fiction fails.

This failure to create convincing fiction is particularly apparent in some recent books about handicapped children, which seem to be tracts designed to inculcate readers with "correct" attitudes. For example, *I Have a Sister, My Sister Is Deaf,* by Jeanne Peterson, recounts some days in the lives of two small girls, one of whom is deaf. The children, depicted in soft crayon drawings by Deborah Ray, swing on monkeybars, have a birthday party, and imagine they are stalking deer. Despite these elements of plot and the dialogue that threads through the first-person narrative, this is not convincing fiction. The hearing sister declares, "My sister can play the piano. She likes to feel the deep rumbling chords. But she will never be able to sing. She cannot hear the tune." This is not authentic first-person narration by a primary-school child, but rather an adult writing about deafness in language she thinks is simple enough for her audience of children. It would

---

[4]See Isaac Bashevis Singer's article "I See the Child as a Last Refuge" (*New York Times Book Review,* November 9, 1969, p. 66). He comments on adults' use of literature to teach lessons: sociological, psychological, or humanistic.

have been far better if the author had cast aside attempts to present this information in fictional format and had simply written a nonfiction book. Any piece of literature encourages differing viewpoints, however, and this book is no exception. The book is commended in reviews by Hoffman (1977) and by Lass and Bromfield (1981).

# FUNCTIONS OF CONTEMPORARY FICTION

Contemporary fiction serves several worthwhile purposes for child readers, ranging from entertainment to growth experiences.

## DESCRIBING LIFE TODAY

Many books of contemporary fiction for children simply depict realistically a slice of life, a bit of action that illuminates a character's existence. For example, in *A Wet and Sandy Day*, written by Joanne Ryder for preschoolers, a young girl frolicking alone on the beach comes home dripping wet from rain and waves. There she finds the comforts of mother's presence and hot chocolate, accompanied by the pleasant drumming of rain on the roof. The lovely watercolor illustrations by Donald Carrick make beach and home seem equally enticing. The book presents no particular problem to be solved but is simply an enjoyable description.

In *Sam*, by Ann H. Scott, the main character—a preschool child—tries to interact with his mother, brother, sister, and father, all of whom are too preoccupied with their own concerns. When Sam resorts to tears, a young child's normal response, the family pays attention. A slight story, but one that young listeners and readers will enjoy because of its familiarity.

A slightly exaggerated, but still basically realistic, description of an episode in a child's life is *How to Eat Fried Worms*, by Thomas Rockwell. Billy wagers with Alan that he can eat fifteen worms in fifteen days. Alan and Joe provide the worms, and Tom sees there is fair play all around. Billy settles the bet by eating worms—with catsup and with mustard, fried, boiled, and grilled.

## HELPING CHILDREN TO UNDERSTAND THEMSELVES

One purpose served by some contemporary realistic fiction is to help children learn to cope with their own problems (Huus, 1973; Olsen, 1973). Some books help children to understand themselves, to gain insights into their

*Watercolor is an appropriate medium for capturing a fleeting moment in a child's exploration of her environment.* Illustration from *A Wet and Sandy Day* by Joanne Ryder. Illustrated by Donald Carrick. Illustration © 1977 by Donald Carrick. Reprinted by permission of Harper & Row, Publishers, Inc.

own natures, to realize that in significant ways they are like other youngsters. Most children sooner or later deal with a number of common problems.

**ACCEPTANCE BY PEERS.** Many children worry about being accepted by their peers, and reading or hearing stories about characters who share this concern may help children deal with it better. Allison, in *Will You Be My Friend?*, by Chihiro Iwasaki, is a typical preschool child, wistfully hoping for a playmate. A moving van stops in her street. She wants to be the new boy's friend, but a series of small disasters prevent the friendship from developing. Finally, the boy, overlooking what has happened, takes the initiative to make friends with Allison, and all is well. The slight but pleasant story is accompanied by low-keyed drawings in crayon and watercolor wash. A teacher might recommend this book to a new child in the classroom. Asking the child to dictate his or her reactions to it can emphasize the teacher's concern.

In *The Hundred Dresses*, by Eleanor Estes, Wanda Petronski, a poor Polish girl, attempts to win acceptance by talking about the many clothes she has. Because she wears the same faded dress to school each day, the other girls ostracize her. Wanda and her family move away, and then the other students discover Wanda's dresses: one-hundred fine drawings. Realizing they have been unkind to her, Peggy and Maddie write to Wanda, and she graciously replies in a friendly note. The story may seem rather obvious to adult readers in the lesson it teaches, but many children will respond with compassion to Wanda's need for acceptance.

The unnamed heroine in *The Popular Girls Club*, by Phyllis Krasilovsky, also deals with the problem of fitting in. She was always included in the group's activities until her "friends" start an exclusive club without her. They start to snicker and whisper behind her back, and the worst part is that she doesn't know why. She learns much about friendship when she really gets to know brainy Clara and shy Amy, with whom she discovers genuine closeness and fun.

Barbara Ware Holmes captures effectively the sound of childhood; her characters ring true because of the simple, direct language she uses. In *Charlotte Cheetham: Master of Disaster*, Holmes focuses on the problem caused by lying to gain acceptance. Intermediate-grade readers will symphathize with Charlotte, who lies not out of any compulsion but simply in order to be liked. She gets away with a simple lie to beautiful Mrs. Arnold, the blond librarian, but gets into real trouble when she tells some girls she wants to impress that her mother knows the owner of a sticker factory. Readers will empathize, having most likely found themselves in situations very similar to Charlotte's, though the details may vary.

As children grow older, their concern about peer acceptance extends to include acceptance by the opposite sex. No one knows better how to write about the resulting boy/girl conflicts than Ellen Conford. This author writes young-adult fiction that is eagerly read by middle-school students, many of whom seek out these books about older students because they look forward to their own adolescence. Conford's *If This Is Love, I'll Take Spaghetti* will ring true to young female readers. One of the nine short stories included, "I Hate You, Wallace B. Pokras," is interestingly derivative of Dorothy Parker's short story for adults titled "A Telephone Call." "Loathe at First Sight" is painful and funny: no teenage boy could possibly try as hard to win a girl's attention as Alan does—or could he? These stories do not attempt to give eternal answers to significant problems. They are simply nine miniature gems that are funny because of Conford's acute ear for the unsolvable contradictions of boy/girl relationships in adolescence.

Conford develops the theme of first adolescent love in a more extended fashion in the full-length book *Why Me?* This story concerns G.G.'s efforts to get Hobie to fall in love with her and his efforts to keep her at bay. Conford's wry humor in tangling such webs is always right on target for her intended audience.

**SIBLING RELATIONSHIPS.**    Relationships with siblings are of concern to most children.[5] The popular writer Judy Blume deals with this problem in *The One in the Middle Is the Green Kangaroo.* This is how Blume introduces her main character:

> Freddy Dissel had two problems. One was his older brother Mike. The other was his younger sister Ellen. Freddy thought a lot about being the one in the middle. But there was nothing he could do about it. He felt like the peanut butter part of a sandwich, squeezed between Mike and Ellen.

This excerpt indicates part of the reason for Blume's popularity: her ability to put into simple yet imaginative language the ways children themselves feel. Many middle children have felt exactly like Freddy, but when the author has him liken himself to peanut butter in a sandwich, she crystallizes these vague feelings for her readers, who may not have been able to put them into language. After reading this book to a class, the teacher might ask those students who have no siblings to describe the advantages and disadvantages of being an only child. Those who do have siblings can write about the joys and burdens brothers and sisters bring.

Jalongo and Renck (1985) describe nearly sixty books that portray sibling relationships and identify three common themes of such books. Because these relationships are "so intense they reverberate throughout the lifespan," it is important to make these books available to children so they can "better understand their own responses."

---

[5]In *The Family Story in the 1960s* (Hamden, Conn.: Anchor, 1970), Anne W. Ellis points out that problems that seem insignificant to adults may have disproportionate significance for children.

*Many of Richard Cuffari's illustrations are distinguished by the thin pen line used alone or in crosshatching to give definition to shapes created by washes. The graceful line never calls attention to itself but unobtrusively makes the page interesting.* Illustration by Richard Cuffari from *Joshua, the Czar, and the Chicken Bone Wish* by Barbara Girion. Copyright © 1978 Barbara Girion. Reprinted with the permission of Charles Scribner's Sons.

**SELF-ACCEPTANCE.** As they become aware of their own individual characteristics, all children need to come to terms with both their positive attributes, such as enthusiasm, helpfulness, and imagination, and their negative ones, such as meanness, envy, and quarrelsomeness. Many books for children deal with the theme of measuring up to one's own self-image.

In *Joshua, the Czar, and the Chicken Bone Wish*, by Barbara Girion, Joshua, the fourth-grade narrator, cannot play baseball and is harassed by his older brother, Benjie. Other kids in school make fun of Joshua's inept-itude, but he finds solace in his newfound friendship with Christopher. Joshua saves the day during a class picnic when he prevents things from getting worse after Christopher falls. This is a slight but pleasant account of coming to terms with oneself.

A notable book for junior high–aged readers about proving oneself is *Slake's Limbo*, a dramatic story by Felice Holman. Out of print for some time but now, fortunately, available again, this is about a thirteen-year-old orphan who does not meet people's expectations. His aunt considers him worthless; his peers have long since given up on him because he is useless as a gang member. Usually a loner, the only attention he receives is when spiteful boys tease him for sport. In desperation, Slake flees underground, taking up residence in a hidden recess in the subway. Slake gradually finds his worth, as he learns to handle a job and deals with an illness and a mishap. The book ends on an optimistic note. Clearly one of the more un-usual characters in contemporary children's fiction, Slake is made con-vincing by Holman's skillful writing, which draws readers into the problems of this pathetic loner.[6] Western (1981) perceptively analyzes the reasons *Slake's Limbo* is such a strong book and compares it favorably with a similar book, *The Lottery Rose*, by Irene Hunt.

**OVERCOMING SELFISHNESS.** Learning to overcome selfishness is a common task for children. Eight-year-old Toe (short for Antonia) gets inside reports from her friend Libby about the disadvantages of having a baby in the house. In *Confessions of an Only Child*, by Norma Klein, both girls ponder the problems presented by Baby Matilda. As a consequence, Toe decides she'd rather her mother weren't pregnant. Later, Toe's mother hurries to the hospital, where the baby is born prematurely. Somewhat predictably, the baby dies, and Toe discovers there are some things worse than having a baby. One of these is losing a baby.

The directness of the language is a characteristic that links Klein's book with others in this genre. Toe, after her mother has given birth, remarks,

> I put my hand on her stomach. It was still a little fat, but not like it was before. It was sort of loose and pouchy.

---

[6]Further proof of Holman's impressive writing range is that she is able to create gentle, bucolic fantasy in *Cricket Winter* (New York: Grosset and Dunlap, 1967) and free verse in "Who Am I?" which is included in *To Look at Any Thing*, selected by Lee Bennett Hopkins (New York: Harcourt Brace Jovanovich, 1978).

It is probably accurate to say that neither such a speech nor even the situation in which a child feels her mother's stomach after a birth ever appeared in earlier children's books. The verisimilitude of this brief passage is typical of contemporary realistic fiction.

**COPING WITH FEARS.**   In *Chasing the Goblins Away*, by Tobi Tobias, Jimmy Richard Evan Powell is troubled by the goblins that appear whenever he turns out the light and tries to go to sleep. The first night his father comes and plays rummy with him. The second night his mother comes and holds his hand. The third night his father tells him he will have to fight his own goblins. He does—and ends up in his parents' room with milk and chocolate chip cookies for a celebration! After reading this story, children might enjoy a group discussion in which they can relate their own fears and how they solved them.

More serious fears are those in *The Testing of Charlie Hammelman*, by Jerome Brooks, a convincing account of how a teenage boy overcomes personal weakness. When the one teacher to whom Charlie can talk freely suddenly dies, Charlie's world at first seems shattered. Eventually, however, he comes to a mature understanding that some limitations are self-imposed. The weekend visit to his girlfriend's camp is touching, yet funny. The book gives a believable portrayal of a teenager who doesn't use drugs or liquor but who is trying to deal with significant personal problems.

In *Otherwise Known as Sheila the Great*, by Judy Blume, Sheila tries to deal with her fears by lying and boasting. She is afraid of many things: dogs and water are high on the list. When her parents rent a house in a small town for the summer, Sheila's anxiety mounts. With the house comes a dog. To add to her troubles, Sheila's parents lovingly, but firmly, insist that she learn to swim. Then Sheila meets Mouse, who likes her despite her fears. A practical girl, Mouse has a matter-of-fact attitude that does much to bolster Sheila's confidence.

**RELATIONSHIPS WITH PARENTS.**   Many books depict the problems of children trying to work out their relationships with their parents as they test their own independence. Often authors use first-person narration to illuminate the child's thoughts. In *It's Like This, Cat*, by Emily C. Neville, Dave describes his relationship with his father, with whom he argues incessantly and with his Aunt Kate, whose eccentricities he admires. In this Newbery Medal–winning book, author Neville presents a realistic portrayal of a child growing to independence and beginning to understand his father. The book will appeal to middle school students who are working on similar relationships.

Continuing in the rich tradition of family stories exemplified by the early works of Elizabeth Enright and Eleanor Estes is Phyllis Reynolds Naylor's *How Lazy Can You Get?* This slender volume presents a conventional family unit of mother, father, and three children. But the offbeat humor, as Timothy, Amy, and Douglas confront their sitter, is anything but conventional. Hildegarde Brasscoat, the sitter, has a stern inhibiting manner. The independent and fun-loving children try to cooperate with Miss Brasscoat but fail. The final truce, brought about by the hilarious appearance of Harold, the hermit crab, rising like a specter from a pot of chipped beef, makes a suitably wacky ending.

One of the most hilarious depictions of family life available is that of Helen Cresswell. She has produced a series of books about the Bagthorpes, a clan of rowdy individualists, each of whom marches to the beat of his or her own invisible drummer. Each is oblivious to anyone else's needs and desires, making the stories an antidote to the typically sweet family stories of the past. Beginning with *Ordinary Jack,* Cresswell went on to add *Absolute Zero, Bagthorpes Unlimited, Bagthorpes v. the World, Bagthorpes Abroad,* and *Bagthorpes Haunted.* The consistent high quality of the slapstick situations and Mr. Bagthorpe's constantly sharp wit enliven each successive tale of misadventures. These books are so funny they may make a teacher who is reading one aloud to the class dissolve in laughter!

Books presenting positive parental images are described by Montgomery-Aaron (1986), who groups them into the five categories of need identified by child psychologists, including the need for a sense of belonging, security, unconditional love, comfort, and closeness to parents. The article provides plot summaries of the nearly two dozen books recommended but does not evaluate the literary worth of the works.

## EXPANDING THE RANGE OF LIFE EXPERIENCES

Contemporary realistic fiction helps children develop empathy for characters who have unfamiliar lives and problems. Because of the widening range of acceptable topics, readers meet a variety of characters who must cope with problems the readers themselves may never have to deal with directly.

**DIFFERENT KINDS OF FAMILIES.**   For children who are growing up in a conventional family unit with two parents and perhaps one or more siblings, it is important to read about characters who live in a different kind of family or who have no family.

Several authors provide accounts of children growing up in single-parent families. *There Is a Tide*, by Elspeth Bragdon, takes a serious look at growing up without a mother. Nat Weston is an adolescent who has been expelled from countless camps and schools, most recently from his father's alma mater. The headmaster, an old friend, suggests to Nat's novelist father that he take his son to a cottage on the coast of Maine to get to know him better. Although the relationship between the two does not seem to improve, Nat does make some friends. Then, when he becomes ill following a boating accident, he realizes that his father really does care for him.

David Morgan and his children must learn to cope with a changed life after his wife and their mother is killed in an automobile accident. In Nancy Bond's *A String in the Harp*, the father takes the younger children, Peter and Becky, with him to Wales, where he has accepted a teaching position. Jen stays behind in Massachusetts to finish the school year; when she arrives in Wales, she discovers that her family is not coping with their loss.

> Parents were supposed to *cope*, Jen thought resentfully. They were supposed to be able to handle crises like this one, but David wasn't. She had never before seen her father and her brother so totally opposed, so irreconcilable.
>
> "I came here," said David slowly, "because I couldn't think what else to do. It wouldn't have been any good to stay in Amherst this year. All I could see was your mother. I thought by getting right away to a place that was new to all of us ... we could straighten ourselves out." He spoke softly, almost to himself. "I wanted life to be as different as I could make it. To break off and start again."
>
> "But you *can't* forget Mother!" Jen protested, shocked.
>
> "I didn't say that." David met her eyes gravely. "But we've got to live without her. Memories are important and we've all got them, but they don't help much with the practical side of things. You're old enough to understand that, even if Peter and Becky aren't. Though I'm disappointed at Peter."
>
> "Maybe it's just harder for Peter," suggested Jen tentatively.
>
> "Harder?" David leaned back in his chair. "My God, do you think it's been easy for me? Suddenly I've got the three of you to cope with on my own as well as losing Ann." His eyes rested on Jen's face and he smiled a little. "Not that I'd rather I didn't have you; I'm just not used to being responsible for the whole show."

The story recounts the characters' progress from the numb shock at sudden death through pain, anger, and resentment, until they finally reach acceptance. They fumble in their relationships with each other in a very realistic and human way.

In *The Night Daddy*, by Maria Gripe, a fatherless girl, whose mother works nights, rejects the idea of a sitter but comes to enjoy having an eccentric young writer as her "night daddy." At first, Julia does not like the situation at all because she feels she is well able to care for herself. However, unlike most people, her night daddy talks to her as though she were an equal. Soon they become fast friends, caring for a rare plant, exchanging confidences, and looking for Smuggler, the writer's crow. Julia begins writing a book because no one in her class will believe she has a night daddy. She and the young man write a book of their own, in which alternating chapters of first-person narration show their growth in understanding and communication.

*Come to the Edge* is a typically challenging book by Julia Cunningham. Gravel's father is inept and alcoholic and puts Gravel in a children's home "for a while." At the home, Gravel forms a friendship with Skin. Throughout the dismal days, Skin shows Gravel the small delights of common things in the environment. Gravel responds with elaborate accounts of how good life was when he and his father lived together. Finally, Gravel must face his father's refusal to take him back:

> It must have been the next day when outside the door a certain voice unclamped his arms and raised his head. It was his father. He suddenly ached to be held, to be shut away inside a warmth he could hardly remember. He got to his knees and pressed against the grey door . . .
>
> Gravel rubbed his cheek hard on the grey wood as if he could hollow out a hole to receive his father's answer and let it pour like sweetness into his ear.
>
> The words came out like bullets. "I can't. I can't support him. Have a hard enough time making out for myself. He'd be like a stone around my neck. The reason I left him here in the first place. Fact is—" and then it came "—I don't want him." The rest was obliterated in deafness. Gravel fell away from the door in a kind of faint, though he could still see the single oblong of the window and the dull and sullen sky beyond. Five hours later, the clouds now blackened into night, the terrible emptiness, the descent beyond being lonely, had begun. Its color was grey. Slowly, slowly a terror arose all around him, chilling his skin and jerking at his muscles.

In *Dark Dove*, by A. C. Stewart, Margaret and Roddy McNeil live with their dour father in a gloomy manse in the Highlands. Reverend McNeil is a pathetic figure, eager to observe God's laws but unloved by his parishioners and without Christian love himself. Lonely since his wife's death four years ago, jealous of his children's closeness, which seems to shut him out, he delights in petty cruelties and finally drives Roddy from home. Margaret, in need of money to keep food on the table, takes a job cataloging a neighbor's library. Her father begins to have dreams that come true with terrifying frequency, until, finally, tragedy strikes close to home. The increasing tension and suspense are effectively contrasted with the lovely scenery. This fine book deserves to be better known among young-adult readers.

Ox has both a father and a mother, but he might as well not have either, given their negligible influence on him. Ox seldom sees his parents because they leave him behind when they go globe-trotting. In *Ox Goes North*, by John Ney, the fifteen-year-old is sent to summer camp in Vermont. He has little enthusiasm for the camp's sports activities and even less for New England. When his bunkmate, a nervous orphan named Campbell, is threatened with the loss of his trust fund, Ox launches a wild and wacky plan to rescue his money from the clutches of his avaricious grandparents.

In some books, children do not live with either parent. In *The Pinballs*, by Betsy Byars, three children—Carlie, Harvey, and Thomas J.—find themselves in Mrs. Manson's foster home through no fault or choice of their own. Improbably tough Carlie can't get along with her third and worst stepfather.

> Once he hit her so hard when she wouldn't tell him where she'd been that she had gotten a concussion. Even with a concussion she had struggled up and hit him with a double boiler. "Nobody hits me without getting hit back," she had said before she collapsed.

Harvey has been taken away from his drunken father, who accidentally ran over his son, breaking both his legs. Thomas J. was abandoned on the doorstep of the twin Benson sisters and is put in Mrs. Manson's home when one of the Bensons breaks her aged hip. Carlie's aggressive behavior covers her desire to be friends with the boys and her need for Mr. and Mrs. Manson's acceptance. Carlie and Thomas J. sense that Harvey may die unless he has something to change his despondent mood, and their efforts to smuggle a newly acquired puppy into the hospital are engaging. There is both deliciously sarcastic humor and touching moments in this book. After living with Harvey and Thomas J. for some time, Carlie finally opens up, initiating a discussion with Harvey about the homes from which they have come. Carlie starts talking about her father:

> "He would have to be your *step* father," Harvey corrected.
> "He was a step *down* anyway," Carlie said. "He was a real bum. Before he left he even stole my babysitting money."
> Harvey was silent.
> "Then my third father—*step* father, if you must—he was the first person who ever wanted to do me real harm. I mean, you're always hearing how dangerous the streets are and how you're going to get mugged or hit on the head? Well, in the streets I was perfectly safe. It was when I got home that I got mugged and attacked."
> Harvey said in a quiet voice, "My father ran over my legs. That's how they got broken."

He spoke so quietly Carlie thought she hadn't heard right. "Ran over them?"
"Yes."
"*Ran* over them?"
"Yes. In the car."
Her shoulders sagged. "Oh, wow."
"He said he couldn't help it."
"Which is supposed to make everything all right."
"He said he got mixed up on forward and reverse. He was drinking."
"Oh, wow."
"Yeah."

*The Pinballs* is one of several books recommended by Munson (1986) for their therapeutic effect. She describes the way books can help the healing process as children read about characters who face significant problems and solve them.

*Foster Child*, by Marion D. Bauer, is a powerful novel about a child trapped within a social-services system that protects an abusive foster father. Twelve-year-old Renny tries to be optimistic about her future as she meets the Becks, her new foster family. To her dismay, Pop Beck, a charismatic fundamentalist, attempts to molest her.

**PROBLEMS WITH DRUGS.**　For older children, trying to avoid the perils of drug use as they navigate an uncertain course toward adulthood, it may be helpful to read about characters who have drug problems and are dealing with them.

Characters who must face the problems that drugs cause are effectively developed in *That Was Then, This Is Now*, by S. E. Hinton.[7] Mark and Byron have been like brothers since childhood, but as their involvement with girls, gangs, and drugs increases, their relationship gradually disintegrates. They have a young friend, a dreamer named M & M. Hassled by his father, M & M runs away, and Byron finds him when he has blown his mind on LSD. The description is strikingly graphic:

"Can we see him?"
"Sure."
We followed him up the stairs. He led us to the same room Mark and I had gone to the last time we were there . . . someone [was] huddled in the corner.

---

[7]Books such as *That Was Then, This Is Now* often spark controversy. This book was positively reviewed by Sheldon Root in "Books for Children" (*Elementary English*, April 1968, pp. 526–527). A negative review by a reader was published in "Books for Children" a year later (*Elementary English*, April 1969, p. 529).

To my surprise, Red walked over to the huddle. "Hey, man, there's people here to see you," he said softly.

"Are they spiders?" The person didn't raise his head, but the voice was M & M's.

"No, man." Red laughed gently. "They're squares."

M & M looked up, and I hardly recognized him. His hair was to his shoulders, he was a lot thinner, he was dirty, and the expression on his face was one I had never seen on him before—suspicion.

"Square spiders?" he said, and his face was contorted in fear. "I don't want to see any spiders." . . .

"I went to my stomach," M & M said in a high, unnatural voice. He was talking too fast. "I went down into my stomach and all these spiders came out. I never knew there were spiders in my stomach. I was there ten years, and all that time these spiders kept chewing on me. They were big spiders. . . ."

"He kept trying to jump out the window," Red said. "All day. We took turns holding him down."

What did the guy want, a medal? He had given him the stuff in the first place.

**DIVORCE.**    Even for children who grow up in intact families, reading about characters who must adjust to the trauma of divorce is important. Experiencing these stories develops empathy for friends who are encountering the problems associated with divorce and gives children a sense of their own good fortune in not having to cope with such problems.[8]

For upper-grade students, *It's Not What You Expect* and *Tomboy*, by Norma Klein, deal with divorce and remarriage. Both are characteristic of her works, in which youngsters must often rely on their adaptability to cope with changes in their lives.

Books about divorce are not limited to those intended for upper-grade readers. Just as psychologists have written about the impact of divorce on young children, writers have also created books above divorce for primary-grade readers. *My Dad Lives in a Downtown Hotel*, by Peggy Mann, shows graphically the bleakness of Dad's life after he leaves the family. Mother is painfully resigned, and Joey is confused, fearing that he may have caused the separation. The effective realism of the first half of the book is somewhat marred by the happy ending, when Joey discovers from a classmate that

---

[8]Joanne Bernstein has written about this common problem in *Books to Help Children Cope with Separation and Loss* (New York: R. R. Bowker, 1983). She recommends using books as therapy and discusses theories and research about bibliotherapy. She also includes annotations of 633 books about different kinds of separation; 400 of the annotations are new to this edition of her book.

there are fifty-three kids in his school and on his block living without a father.

**PHYSICAL DIFFERENCES.** Many books depict children with physical disabilities. Nearly fifty books about special children have been annotated in a report by an ACEI-CBC Joint Committee (1981). The task for teachers is to decide which of the available books are also strong literature.

Blindness is described in *Sound of Sunshine, Sound of Rain.* Florence Parry Heide writes sensitively about one day in the life of a young blind child, who also happens to be black. The perceptive descriptions of how the child uses his senses to gather information are convincing. The book ends on a melancholy, but somewhat hopeful, note. Accompanying the text are some extremely impressive graphics.

A primary-grade teacher used *Sound of Sunshine, Sound of Rain* as an introduction to an experience with a blind child. She arranged for the blind child to visit her classroom, where her students had a chance to discuss with their visitor what it is like to be blind. After the visit, her children corresponded with their new acquaintance using cassette-tape recordings. A teacher might instead have children compare this book with the film of the same title (Filmfair Communication, 10900 Ventura Boulevard, Studio City, CA 91604). The film, nominated for an Academy Award, retains the story but not the original art. Collapsing three episodes into one and considerably softening Heide's original ending, the film, although still valuable, tells a significantly different story than the book does.

*David in Silence,* by Veronica Robinson, was an early book about deafness. Michael, thirteen, befriends David, who has moved into a small town in England, one of the prettier villages in one of the ugliest parts of the island. The village people are unused to strangers. The children are predictably uninformed about deafness and muteness, but the adults, including Mrs. Guest, Michael's mother, are little better. Part of the poignancy of deafness is revealed in Michael's comments early in the book:

> "You know the queer thing about him is that he doesn't look deaf."
> "How do you mean he doesn't look deaf? How could he, anyway?"
> "Well," continued Michael, "people who've got something wrong with them

---

*In the illustration on the facing page, the artist has used the compositional device of placing a deer in the foreground and the main characters in the background framed by the tree trunk and the leaves.* Barbara Corcoran, illustration from *A Dance to Still Music.* Copyright © 1974 Barbara Corcoran. Reprinted with the permission of Atheneum Publishers.

usually show it. If a man's leg's broken, it's in a plaster. If he's got a temperature, he looks hot. Anyone call tell a blind man from yards away. But this boy— we've got no way of knowing he hasn't been having us on."

Once Michael is convinced that David is really deaf, the two devise a way of communicating that includes mime, sign language, and written language. Michael's friends resist including David in their activities. This reluctance is heightened when David monopolizes a soccer game. Some weeks later David is finally included in the group when he discovers a flaw in the raft they have built, showing the boys that deafness is not synonymous with stupidity.

In *A Dance to Still Music,* by Barbara Corcoran, Margaret lives alone with her mother in Key West and cherishes memories of happier days when they lived with her grandfather in Maine. He had been "deaf as a haddock," and Margaret herself becomes deaf in her first year in high school, as a result of an ear infection. In a scene in a crowded Cuban market, the author gives an indication of the feelings of humiliation that make Margaret withdraw into a shell of muteness:

> She jumped as someone grabbed her arm. A man with a four-by-four balanced on his shoulder was trying to get past her. She knew from the look of irritation on his face that he had told her to move.

Margaret's mother spends her days working long, hard hours in a restaurant, eking out a precarious existence. Fourteen-year-old Margaret is not in school and spends her days doing nothing, waiting for night and the oblivion of sleep. Her mother's boyfriend proposes, but with the provision that Margaret be sent to a residential home. Fleeing this dreaded alternative, Margaret meets and is accepted by Josie, a leathery-skinned woman living alone in a houseboat at the edge of a swamp. On the night of a severe storm, Margaret starts to talk and talks for hours about her previous life: "like a great load of ice melting inside her" the talk provides the catharsis that makes it possible for Margaret to start anew. In an article pointing out the need to search for books free of stereotypes, Watson (1981) recommends this book, among others, because of the positive image it presents of the aging character Josie.

To give children a sense of what it is like to be deaf, a teacher might obtain some cotton or wax earplugs, which are available in drug stores. The children can wear them for part of a day, trying to carry on the normal school routine, and then write an account of their reactions.

Another book about a physical handicap, *Deenie,* by Judy Blume, deals with the problems of a girl who has scoliosis. One reviewer of children's books commented negatively on the main character (Lukens, 1986):

> While we do feel sorry for Deenie, she is so close to being a stereotyped adolescent—interested only in boys and beauty—that we soon find her uninteresting. One theme of the book, that even girls with back braces can find friends, seems didactic and unconvincing because we have little interest in or understanding of the relatively flat protagonist.

This particular book points out the need for teachers to be aware that children's reactions to a book may be very different from adults' reactions. Children, even those who have had many previous literary experiences, may well react differently than Lukens did. To test Lukens's assertion, one teacher asked some seventh-grade students to read *Deenie* and react to the character. These children attended a school in which almost all teachers read to classes every day; they had free access to the library; and many of them read extensively on their own. They were not uninformed readers. One child responded as follows:

> I really believe Deenie could be a real person, because she faces many of the problems I have had and dealt with them sort of the way I did.
> She was interesting to read about because it brought her scoliosis out in the open, and I found out how a person that's a *little* different must feel.
> At first Deenie didn't know how to act or feel comfortable in the brace, but after she wore it awhile she began to realize, for her, it was just a part of growing up.
> I would love to have a friend like Deenie because she was so outwardly brave and didn't really want pity from anyone. She seemed so real to me I almost felt like I was there with her.
>
> *Gail*

Gail's positive reaction to this character was typical of other students'. It would be unjustified to generalize about student readers' reactions to this book from this small sample, but a teacher might replicate this informal experiment with other young readers to compare reactions.

## EXPLORING SOCIAL AND ECONOMIC DIFFERENCES

Some contemporary realistic fiction helps children transcend the limitations of their own social class, as they come to understand how economic success or lack of it affects behavior. For example, children from comfortable upper-middle-class backgrounds grow as they read stories of children who live in poverty.

In *The Bears' House*, by Marilyn Sachs, Fran Ellen Smith is nearly ten and tries to cope with two problems: she sucks her thumb, and she smells bad. For these traits, she is ridiculed by the children at school. When Fran stays home from school to care for her infant sister, she must also cope with her mother, who is completely unable to deal with her situation. The father has deserted the family, and the five children try to conceal their problems to avoid being separated. Miss Thompson, Fran's kindly teacher, gives her a beautiful handmade dollhouse because Fran is trying to overcome her faults and attend school regularly. The story is open-ended, leaving the reader with the idea that the teacher will try to help, but that there are no pat solutions to Fran's problems.

In *Gertrude's Pocket*, the Tollivers eke out an existence poor in economic resources but rich in family pride. Author Miska Miles writes about some residents of a dying coal town who must learn to get by from day to day. It is a major occasion when Grammaw cuts down an old red dress to fit Gertrude. The first day she wears her new treasure to school, she is tripped by Watson Pike, a bully and a trickster. Grammaw sews a pocket over the rip in the torn dress, and Gertrude is happy again. *Gertrude's Pocket* accurately conveys to child readers from more comfortable backgrounds the reality of a coal-town existence.

In *The Nature of the Beast*, British author Janni Howker writes of some more people living on the economic fringes of life. Her characters are poor in a crushing way characters in books by American writers seldom are. Billy Coward lives with his father and grandfather in a gritty mill town. The other industries have already closed; with the news that Stone Cross Mill is about to close, the poverty so pervasive in the town seeps to the Cowards' doorstep. Howker's use of British dialect also establishes this as a story of people who are different. Billy "nips round" to the "off-license" for two cans of beer for his grandfather. He has "nicked" fish out of a private stream. He is angry at the "sodding" newspapers for interfering. There is much anger in this story: at one point another character says something, and Billy comments, "That got up my nose!" There is "nowt" to be done about the grinding poverty that overwhelms the town. The ending of this story shows Billy's resolute resistance to succumbing to the expected. In the closing episode, Billy overhears the social worker declaring she must remove him from his grandfather's care, so he sets out to the moors above the town, where he intends to elude his potential captors.

Convincing portrayals of children of affluence are somewhat scarce. Problems in the lives of some rich children form the basis for *Father's Arcane*

*Daughter*, by E. L. Konigsburg.[9] The story is narrated by Winston, the sister of Caroline and Heidi. The three children are closely chaperoned and surrounded by servants because Caroline was kidnapped years before. Heidi is crippled by an unspecified disease. She can hear only certain sound frequencies, she walks with difficulty, and she finds it hard to grasp some objects. The book is noteworthy for its compassionate presentation of Heidi, disabled among the trappings of wealth.

> Heidi began to reach for the flowers, her hand open, her arm moving like a broken clutch across the tablecloth. Caroline watched the hand for a minute, and then lifted the flowers herself to Heidi. Heidi held the small vase as if she were going to drink from it, and some of the water spilled.
>
> "Give the flowers back to Caroline, darling," Mother said. "They are very special." Heidi returned the flowers, . . .
>
> "They don't smell," Heidi said.
>
> Mother lifted the dinner bell, rang it, and dinner was served. When the main course arrived, Father carved and Simmons carried Heidi's portion into the kitchen, returning with it cut up on Heidi's special divided platter. Heidi put her elbow on the table and propped her head on her hand and began the left-handed, wooly operation that transported food from her plate to her mouth. She ate everything with a spoon even though a full setting of cutlery was put at her place. I watched her as I had not watched her in a long time. She ate with a weird kind of concentration, not like a puppy—all eagerness and appetite—but like some lower form of life, something cenozoic.

Another child who is wealthy but nonetheless suffers from a serious problem is presented in *The Carnival in My Mind*, by Barbara Wersba. Harvey Beaumont, the fourteen-year-old main character, is so neglected by his rich mother that until kindergarten he thought the butler was his father! Concerned more with her dogs than with Harvey, she doesn't notice when he runs away with a twenty-year-old woman he has met. The two face the vicissitudes of life together until the young woman acknowledges her failure as an actress and returns to her family. Knowing her has given Harvey the

---

[9]As with many children's books, expert opinion varies about the quality of this book. A review as positive as the comments here was written by Anne Tyler ("Books for Those Awkward, In-Between Years," *National Observer*, December 25, 1976, p. 15). In contrast, a sharply critical opinion is expressed by Mera Sapon-Shevin ("Mentally Retarded Characters in Children's Literature," *Children's Literature in Education*, 1982, pp. 19–31), who faults the book for several inaccuracies in her article analyzing more than twenty books depicting mentally retarded characters.

strength to deal with this loss and to cope with life on his own. This is one of the books recommended by Bernstein (1983), who feels it can help children learn to cope with relationships they know must end.

The contrast between rich and poor families, portrayed in three distinct time periods, is part of what makes *I Stay Near You*, by M. E. Kerr, so interesting. Following the poor Cones and the wealthy Storms through generations, beginning in the 1940s and concluding in the 1980s, provides a panoramic view of how money shapes personality. This is the description of where the Cones live:

> It was an awful house, a ramshackle wooden thing with clutter everywhere, the view from every window showing the back of the laundry. The yard out there was filled with piles of old tires, and seats torn out of cars, the leather ripped and the springs popping. There were any number of broken things scattered around in the dirt: chairs with the rungs hanging down, an old rowboat with a cracked seat . . . even an old white toilet bottom, ringed with filthy stains.

In dramatic contrast, the Storms enjoyed

> . . . the house at Cake [which] seemed to go on for miles. . . . through a wall of windows on the first floor, we looked outside at a lawn filled with people and an enormous red-and-white-striped tent.
>
> As we went through the door, there was the sound of an orchestra playing. There was a large oriental carpet laid across the grass, with guests sitting on it, atop silky cushions, and above them real crystal chandeliers hung from the trees.

As she continues interweaving the lives of an engrossing variety of characters, author Kerr holds readers' interest. Although some of them come perilously close to being as unbelievable as television soap-opera denizens, these are interesting characters, and the reader wants to find out what will happen to them.

## EXPLORING GEOGRAPHIC DIFFERENCES

Where people live dramatically affects their lives. Using realistic fiction, teachers can help children think about two environmental influences: geographic location and, within that context, urban versus rural location. Many years ago, Lois Lenski pioneered the writing of regional fiction.[10] Other writers have described various regions, including Appalachia, the Ozarks, and the Louisiana bayous.[11]

*Mrs. Mike*, by Benedict and Nancy Freedman, illustrates the pervasive effects of winter in the lives of many Canadians.[12] Sixteen-year-old Katharine leaves Boston for a visit with her uncle in Alberta. There she quickly becomes enmeshed in life in the north and falls in love with Royal Canadian Mounted Police sergeant Mike Flanagan. After their marriage, she experiences the local winters as a palpable force: lung-freezing cold predominates, with only a brief, insect-ridden summer as respite. Each day Katharine's bond with the north country strengthens, and she grows to respect her new Indian friends. When their village is threatened by an outbreak of diphtheria, her husband isolates Katharine and the children, but to no avail. The children's tragic death drives Katharine to seek solace in Boston. There she comes to understand the full value of her winter-dominated home, her Indian friends, and the deep love she has for her husband.

Realistic works of fiction can help children see differences between city and country environments. For example, a small dirt farm in the Arkansas hills is clearly evoked in *Spud Tackett and the Angel of Doom*, by Robbie Branscum. Most readers will never have been to Arkansas, but can get a vivid picture of what life is like in its rural areas from this book.

In sharp contrast to such a rural portrayal is the picture of the big city in *The Young Unicorns*. The Austin family has moved from a small New England town to New York City.[13] Author Madeline L'Engle evokes the

---

[10]Lois Lenski's many works include *Camp Girl* (Philadelphia: J. B. Lippincott, 1947), *Prairie School* (Philadelphia: J. B. Lippincott, 1951), and *Texas Tomboy* (Philadelphia: J. B. Lippincott, 1950). Even though her books have been criticized for shallow characters and happy endings, they are still useful with children because they give both introductions to geographic areas and interesting examples of language variation.

[11]Miska Miles, in *Hoagie's Rifle Gun* (Boston: Little, Brown, 1970), describes Appalachia; Vera and Bill Cleaver, in *The Whys and Wherefores of Littabelle Lee* (New York: Atheneum, 1973), describe the Ozarks; George Smith, in *Bayou Boy* (Chicago: Follett, 1965), describes the Louisiana swamp country.

[12]This is one of almost twenty books included in a unit titled "Winter Brutality" in *Action and Adventure: A Resource Guide for the Teaching of Canadian Literature*, by The Writers' Development Trust (Toronto: Ministry of Education, 1977). Ten other units feature mainly fiction, but also information books, poetry, and correlated films.

[13]Madeline L'Engle introduced this family in *Meet the Austins* (New York: Vanguard, 1960). *The Moon by Night* (New York: Farrar, Straus and Giroux, 1963) relates their adventure-packed camping trip. *A Ring of Endless Light* (Farrar, Straus and Giroux, 1980) is a more recent title in this series.

variety of city life through descriptions of minor characters such as the following:

> From up the street came the loud voice of a woman singing "The Old Rugged Cross," exhorting the city to reform, hiccuping, almost falling and bursting into a string of oaths. She wore a man's coat and shoes, and her eyes were bloodshot; she staggered as she walked.

## UNDERSTANDING ETHNIC AND RELIGIOUS DIVERGENCE

One of the most useful purposes served by modern realistic fiction is to help children understand different ethnic groups.

**AFRO-AMERICANS.** Today many children's books feature black characters, but such was not the case over forty years ago when Jerrold and Lorraine Beim pioneered with *Two Is a Team*, a book intended for first- and second-graders that portrays a black child positively.[14] In this simple story, two little boys play together, visit each other's homes, disagree and argue, but remain friends. The Beims make no mention of race or color throughout the book. Only the simple, beautiful illustrations by black artist Ernest Chrichlow reveal that one of the boys is black. In *Two Is a Team*, the experiences are universal; many recent books give more specific portrayals of what is unique to the black experience.

Some stories about blacks do not present problem situations; they are simple descriptions of some aspect of black life. *My Street's a Morning Cool Street*, by Ianthe Thomas, is told in the child narrator's typical vernacular. Most of the pages have only three lines, for example:

> Fruit man coming.
> Them flies follow him like a black umbrella.
> They don't hide the sun, though.

The unnamed narrator enjoys the human and animal inhabitants of his neighborhood, depicted in soft blue, green, and yellow wash drawings outlined in ink.

---

[14] A positive comment about *Two Is a Team* is included in an article by Mavis Wormley Davis, "Black Images in Children's Literature: Revised Editions Needed" (*School Library Journal*, January 15, 1972, pp. 37–39). Davis calls for revision of such older works as *Mary Poppins* and *Dr. Doolittle* or elimination of the books from library collections. She approves of the Beims' book and lists others that present a positive black image.

*Artist Emily Arnold McCully employs ink line to create a panoramic view of an urban milieu, in which the young black narrator is only one feature.* Illustration from *My Street's a Morning Cool Street* by Ianthe Thomas. Illustrated by Emily A. McCully. Illustration copyright © 1976 by Emily Arnold McCully. Reprinted by permission of Harper & Row, Publishers, Inc.

The black narrator in *Sink or Swim,* by Betty Miles, is older than the one in Thomas's book and is, in addition, a perceptive observer. B. J. Johnson is leaving his native New York City and his mostly black friends for a vacation in New Hampshire, sponsored by a group that sends inner-city children to the country. The book records his dialect; for example, at one point B. J. comments on another child on the bus:

> Acting like he a big expert about the country. Just because this his second time with the Fresh Air and my first time. He go to some farm last summer and the people there ask him back. They must be crazy.

In addition to the physical and cultural differences in the rural environment, B. J. notices the speech differences of his hosts: "Mrs. Anderson talk funny, like she got a cold." Later, his hostess

> . . . smile and walk to the front to talk to the driver. I don't know how he can

> make out what she say and drive at the same time. I never hear anybody talk like her before.

Later, B. J. notes a similar speech difference in Norm, the father of his host family for the visit.

> He sound funny, the way he talk. They all talk funny here. I can't explain it. Like they holding rocks in their mouths, trying not to drop them when they say something.

Later in the story, B. J. turns to written language, recording his observations from a day on the farm, so that he will have a record of what it is like in New Hampshire when he returns home to New York City. He finally returns, gratefully, to his mother, who has missed him as much as he has missed her. B. J. has changed, however, in a significant way: he has an increased sense of worth from his interactions with his "adopted" farm family, who are very different from him but want him to return next summer.

Pump Jackson is a teenager who, in Nikki Grimes's *Growin'*, discovers that one of the heartaches of growing up is having to leave friends. She is happy in her urban environment because she has a close friend, Cherry. Cherry's constancy makes up in part for Pump's despair over her father's untimely death and her mother's continuing coolness. Pump, whose secret pleasure is writing poetry, narrates the book in straightforward language, as the following excerpt shows:

> "Movin' is dumb," Cherry grumbled. We'd been playing handball in the school yard and it was way past time for us to be going home. She stuffed the ball in her pocket and we started down the block.
> "Damn," Cherry cussed, sucking her teeth. "You shouldn't go nowhere you can't take your friends." There wasn't anything to say, so I just smiled a little and squeezed her hand. We took the slow way home and kicked a rock back and forth between us all the way. We must've worn that rock out.

The first day at the new school confirms Pump's apprehensions:

> I was the first one in school when the bell rang. I went straight to the back of the room and took the seat nearest the window. When everyone was sitting, the teacher took attendance. She read through all the names, one right after another, until she got to mine.
> "Yolanda Jackson," called the teacher.
> "Here," I said, sucking my teeth. Nobody ever called me Yolanda. Not since I was a baby. They used to call me Pumpkin, then they made it Pump. But nobody knew that here.
> The class was noisy. Mrs. Lee, the teacher, tapped her ruler on the desk. Then she did exactly what I hoped she wouldn't.

"Class," she said, "I want you all to say hello to Yolanda. She's new here, and I want you to make friends."

Oh, Lord, I thought, I wanted to scream. I don't care if you make friends or not. You don't like me, I don't like you. I hate everybody. My daddy's dead and you don't understand and I hate everybody. See? I should have screamed. I didn't.

All of the kids turned in their seats to look at me. Half of them rolled their eyes in my direction and turned away, bored. The others stared me up and down till I felt like a speck underneath a microscope. I wished I really was that small just then so I could hide.

While dusting one day, Pump discovers in a book some poems her mother once wrote, representing an aspiration to be a writer, long since discarded. Pump's mother finds her reading them, and finally real communication begins.

We talked about writing a lot. One day she asked me why I started writing. I told her that I couldn't talk to people out loud too good, but I could always say just what I wanted to on paper. The words and feelings never got jumbled up in a poem. It kept me from hurting people too, I said. Most times when I got mad at somebody, I'd write an angry poem instead of yelling at the person who made me mad. Mama said she liked to write poetry 'cause it was one of the most beautiful things in life.

She showed me the poetry she had kept and I read her mine some nights.

Grimes's book is an insightful account of a black experience that will attract younger, as well as teenaged, readers.

Many other authors have written about numerous kinds of black experiences. Broderick (1973) believes that, even though there have been many individually impressive books about blacks, the general picture of blacks in children's books leaves much to be desired. She makes a clear distinction between tolerance, a passive attitude, and acceptance, a more active attitude free of condescension. MacCann and Woodare (1985) comment on this issue and recommend books they find exemplary.

**HISPANICS.** Hispanics constitute the fastest growing, and may soon be the largest, minority group in the United States. Wagoner (1982) surveyed books about the Mexican-American element of this ethnic group, concluding that there are too few available. Furthermore, many of the available books share several negative characteristics. For example, most present Mexican-Americans living in rural poverty, suggesting that a majority of them are migrant workers, despite statistics showing that 80 percent of Mexican-Americans live in cities. Many early books concentrated on colorful customs, dress,

**This close-up view of head and torso only focuses attention on the young protagonist.** Illustration by Ted Lewin from *Chicano Amigo* by Maurine H. Gee. Copyright © 1972 by Maurine H. Gee. By permission of William Morrow & Company.

and language; urban elements are still missing from most of these books. After a general introduction, Wagoner includes a briefly annotated bibliography of more than twenty books she thinks successfully present the variety of Mexican-American experiences in the United States. Fuller annotations are given for several of the most useful books about this group, and they may be helpful for teachers attempting to expand children's consciousness of Hispanics.

Third- and fourth-graders will empathize with the scrappy independence of Kiki (Jose Francisco Moreno), who wants to be a Cub Scout more than anything else. In Maurine Gee's *Chicano Amigo*, he attaches himself to Marc, a gringo; meanwhile Gonny—son of an upwardly mobile Chicano veterinarian—ignores him. In this book, a series of humorous mishaps precede Kiki's acceptance into the scout troop.

A more traditional story, *From Lupita's Hill*, is another one that intermediate-grade children will find interesting. Bettie Forsman wrote this account of a poor Mexican girl who dreams of having a beautiful white dress. She and her friend, as well as a gringa girl, are convincingly developed characters.

*Chicano Girl*, by Hila Colman, contrasts three young women in a story about sixteen-year-old Donna's growing awareness of her own attitudes. She lives with her family in a small white stucco house forty miles from the Arizona border. At home, the family speaks only Spanish, which annoys her; her television-inspired dream is to be assimilated into the American mainstream. Donna's younger sister cannot imagine life anywhere else than in the shadow of the mountains that Donna feels imprison her. When she is allowed to go to Tucson to stay with her father's cousin, Donna meets Ruby. Ruby's resentment of all gringos simmers continuously, fueled by the senseless treatment of her husband. Of the three young female characters in this book, only Donna consciously thinks about her attitudes and changes her life goals as a result of this reflectiveness. Some of the plot seems fairly predictable to adult readers, but that may not bother students.

More convincing conflict affects a youngster who has spent more than a third of his life in jail, in *Viva Chicano*, by Frank Bonham. At seventeen, Keeny Duran has learned to feel pride in *la raza*, the Mexican heritage. In an accident, Keeny's younger brother falls from a window, and Keeny is pursued by the police. Neighbors assume that he has caused the accident, continuing a pattern of prejudice against the young man. Keeny decides to turn himself in to the police, and placement in a foster home gives him a chance to begin a new life without prejudice.

Puerto Ricans are the main characters in *In Nueva York*, by Nicholosa Mohr. A collection of short stories linked by common characters, this book introduces readers to an urban enclave centering around Rudi's diner, which Rudi was able to purchase only after years of scrimping at menial jobs. The author first introduces Old Mary, an empathic figure, soaking up sun while sipping her beer. Youthful beauty fled with Mary's aspirations, both unable to withstand a drunken husband and a lifetime of hard labor. Mary dreams of a comfortable old age and waits for her long-abandoned first son to return. The rest of the stories introduce, among others, Yolanda, busted for drugs and in rehabilitation; Lali, Rudi's wife, who goes to English class to escape the diner for an hour; Johnny and Sebastian, who are lovers and must cope with Johnny's draft notice; and Jenny, an innocent pre-schooler who escapes a child molester and murderer. A feisty orange cat, mangy but enduring, threads its way through the seven stories. In the end, the cat—bloody but unbowed—and the diner—center of a throbbing neighborhood—remain. All else has changed. Mohr's creation mirrors a society remote from many readers' lives, but the characters are drawn skillfully and the conflict is portrayed accurately.

The books described above depict a variety of kinds of Hispanic realities, and each was evaluated positively. A warning note has been sounded, however, in issues of *Interracial Books for Children Bulletin*, which have analyzed literature about Puerto Ricans (volume 4, issue 1/2, 1972) and about Chicanos (volume 5, issue 7/8, 1975). In each case, the conclusion reached was that an overall pattern of cultural misrepresentation exists; most of the books analyzed were not recommended. In contrast, Schon (1986) annotates a list of only ten books about Hispanics, but comments that they are "well written, objective [and] dynamic . . . ."

**ASIAN-AMERICANS.** Oriental people are chronically underrepresented in contemporary children's fiction. Appropriate for primary-grade listeners or readers is *The Feast of Lanterns*, by Allen Say, about two small boys, Bozu and Kozo, who live on a small Japanese island. They live traditional lives, growing toward their destined futures as fishermen. The island is within sight of the mainland, which they see as filled with unfathomable delights. Frustrated because their father and uncle will not take them along to the mainland, they steal the uncle's boat and row away in search of adventure. This journey turns out to be less pleasant than the boys had anticipated. They encounter a troupe of traveling clowns, are bullied by a group of older boys, watch a fire, and are finally rescued by their father and uncle. Particularly effective are the descriptions of the mainland sights and sounds that are new to the boys, such as a train:

> A black, angry iron monster came charging at them like the War God! The one-eyed, steel-toothed raging hulk roared and hissed. Huge flywheels hammered the rails, steel pounding steel, spitting sparks, steam and smoke. The earth shook, trees trembled. . . . Bozu and Kozo huddled together, choking with smoke and terror. Car after car flashed by in one long deafening thunder.
>
> Clack, clack, clack, the rails quivered and blazed in the sun. The train was gone!

A Chinese girl is the main character in *Child of the Owl*, by Laurence Yep, and narrates the story in first person. She is responsible because she must be: her father, Barney, chases an elusive dream of success at the racetrack. The two live a meager existence in a succession of fleabag hotels, until Barney lands in the hospital, and Casey is sent, protesting, to live with her maternal grandmother, Paw-Paw. She resists because she knows nothing of being Chinese, despite her ancestry. If children enjoy this book, a teacher might direct them to Yep's works of historic fiction (*The Serpent Child*) and fantasy (*Dragon Steel*). Dinchak (1982) gives the reasons why she feels Yep's work deserves attention, identifying the strong points in his writing. She comments on, among other things, Yep's use of metaphors, symbolism, and figurative language, especially in his use of comparisons to make the characters seem believable.

**NATIVE AMERICANS.** A fine, realistic portrayal of a Chinook Indian girl, Plum Langor, is found in *The Potlatch Family*, by Evelyn Sibley Lampman. Plum feels keenly the patronizing attitudes of the popular, cliquish white girls with whom she rides the school bus. Only fat, unpopular Mildred makes a conscientious effort to be friends with Plum. At home, Plum copes with her drunken father and her crippled and cynical brother Milo; her brother Simon is away at war. Plum worships Simon and misses his stabilizing effect on the family. Unexpectedly, Simon comes home visibly weakened, discharged because doctors have been unable to cure an unspecified illness. Immediately, the entire family, including members of its extended clan, is caught up in Simon's plan to stage a *potlatch*, a recreation of their ancestors' friendship celebrations. The first potlatch is an unqualified success, bringing an increase in pride and self-confidence to the family members. At the end of the summer, just before the last potlatch of the season, Simon and a cousin drive into Portland, where Simon dies, having lived far longer than the doctors had predicted. The family's shock is intense, but they realize the spirit of the potlatch is larger now than any one of them, and that Simon would have wanted it to continue. The author's ability to depict characters and settings in words is quite convincing. At one point, the narrator, Plum, describes a relative:

> Great-Grandma Lachance was fat, and so short that when she sat on the kitchen chair her moccasins barely touched the floor. They were real Indian moccasins, and I knew she'd made them herself after tanning the skin that Great-Grandpa had brought home. Because of the fat, her face wasn't very wrinkled, but the skin looked old and dry like it had been smoked over a fire. She had little tiny black eyes shining out from the folds of fat, and her hair was gray and braided into skimpy plaits down her back. On, she was a real Indian all right, the kind you read about but never see. I hoped nobody from Cooperville would catch sight of her while she was here.

An analysis of the good and bad in children's books about native Americans is provided by Fisher (1974). A more extended list is that of Stensland (1979), who annotates nearly eight hundred titles. Gilliland (1980) has also provided an annotated list, and additional chapters on the problems of using these books, suggestions for teachers, and listings of the books by tribe, religion, and subject.

**JEWISH AMERICANS.** Jews constitute less than 5 percent of the total population in the United States today, and they could be better represented in literature for children. This and other points are made by Sadker and Sadker (1977) in a chapter on Jewish American life. These authors do not sufficiently develop criteria for judging excellence in contemporary children's literature, but do present material on various themes such as death, ecology, and minority groups.

One account of modern Jewish family life is *Benny*, by Barbara Cohen. Benny is the youngest in his family, and he frequently finds the going tough because his brother is brainy and his sister is dependable. In a family crisis, however, it is Benny who proves his worth, not only to himself but to all concerned.

The warmth of family life and the caring of an entire neighborhood come through in *My Bar Mitzvah*, by Richard Rosenblum. Clearly defined black-ink line drawings by the author illustrate his story, reflecting his own memories, of the most important event in a Jewish boy's life, becoming a "son of the commandment." Although the religious aspects of the ceremony are treated almost incidentally, detail is piled upon detail in the words as well as the pictures. The book will provide useful insights for non-Jewish child readers.

In *About the B'nai Bagels*, by E. L. Konigsburg, Mark's mother becomes the manager of his Little League team to fulfill her responsibility to her B'nai Brith chapter. Mark's big brother, Spencer, is drafted as coach. Though ostensibly about boys playing baseball, the story is really concerned with Jewish loyalty, family life, and trust. The mother enjoys a running conversation with God as she manages the team's fortunes. A pleasantly humorous tone pervades the book.

Author Bess Kaplan provides a similarly humorous story in *The Empty Chair*, dealing with a common problem set in the context of a lower-middle-class shopkeeper's home in Canada. The problem—adjusting to a new stepmother, feared because of her unfamiliarity—isn't specifically Jewish but the many differences between the Jewish and non-Jewish cultures are interestingly presented. The humor when the meddling aunts bring around their "candidates" to be the new mother is appealing; the evocation of an unfamiliar setting and culture is effective.

***An unvaryingly thin black pen line was used to create decorative, two-dimensional drawings.***
Illustration from *My Bar Mitzvah* by Richard Rosenblum. Copyright © 1985 by Richard Rosenblum. By pemission of William Morrow & Company.

In a more serious vein, *Berries Goodman,* by Emily Neville, raises the ugly issue of anti-Semitism. Berries—who is not Jewish—encounters this bigotry in the suburbs. He has lived in New York City and knows many Jews. When his family moves to a suburb, he finds that Jews are discriminated against there. Berries must deal with the fact that adult weaknesses perpetuate the undesirable situation. The book is interesting because of its narrative technique: the first chapter takes place in the present; the remainder of the book is a flashback to earlier times, when Berries became friends with Sidney, who is Jewish.

Anti-Semitism is a problem that is particular to the Jewish culture.

*A specific time and place are evoked through the use of many small details, rendered in flat shades of gray and black and arranged in a strong composition that is divided into rectangles.*
Illustration from *Yossi Asks the Angels for Help* by Miriam Chaikin. Illustrated by Petra Mathers. Illustration copyright © 1985 by Petra Mathers. Reprinted by permission of Harper & Row, Publishers, Inc.

Some books reflect Jewish culture but highlight universal feelings and experiences. For example, in Miriam Chaikin's *Yossi Asks the Angels for Help*, Yossi is despondent because he has lost his Hanukkah gelt (holiday gift money), which he intended to use to buy a present for his little sister. Chaikin has a fine memory for childlike traits, for example, not paying attention in class or impatience over the slowness of adult rituals. The book's happy ending is too simplistic to be really satisfying, but in only fifty-two pages Chaikin provides an introduction to this Jewish holiday, about which many children may know little.

# CHARACTERISTICS OF CONTEMPORARY REALISTIC FICTION

Authors of contemporary realistic fiction handle literary elements in distinctive ways that characterize the genre.

## CHARACTERIZATION

Characterization concerns all authors, but in contemporary fiction for children, characters are often described more forthrightly than they are in other genres. For example, in *A Girl Called Al*, by Constance C. Greene, the main character is easy to picture from this description:

> Al is a little on the fat side, which is why I didn't like her right at first. . . . She walks stiff like a German soldier, and she has pigtails. She is the only girl in the whole entire school, practically, with pigtails. They would make her stand out even if nothing else did. . . . Al's pigtails look like they are starched. She does not smile a lot and she wears glasses. Her teeth are very nice though, and she does not wear braces. . . . Al is a very interesting person.

The last sentence is the most telling: Al is not pretty but is still intriguing to the narrator and therefore to readers. A sequel is *I Know You, Al*, in which Al and her best friend, the narrator, are blundering into adolescence. They talk about whether Al's mother will marry her boyfriend and whether Al should go to her father's wedding. The narrator has great common sense, and her family provides a sense of cheerful family life. The girls' ongoing friendship gives stability to this lighthearted continuation of Al's adventures.

Writing sequels can present considerable problems for an author. By continuing the adventures of a character who has won a following, the author is assured of an audience. However, maintaining the quality and interest level of the first success can be difficult. Greene managed to do this with *I Know You, Al,* and in *Your Old Pal, Al,* she succeeded again. This time fourteen-year-old Al is infatuated with a boy she met at her father's wedding. She's concerned about losing her best friend and, in general, about coping with the ups and downs of life. Greene has a particularly sensitive ear and manages to reproduce the language of the early teen years flawlessly. Part of the book's charm is that the problems are not crises. Some authors choose to deal with highly topical issues of sex and drugs; Greene establishes characters that are believable precisely because they are living through the events of ordinary life. The most recent title in this series is *Just Plain Al.*

Candor also marks a physical description written by Judy Blume, in *Are You There, God? It's Me, Margaret.* Margaret notices the physical qualities of Laura, the biggest girl in the classroom:

> The teacher wasn't in the room when we got there. . . . There was this girl, who I thought was the teacher, but she turned out to be a kid in our class. She was very tall (that's why I thought she was the teacher) with eyes shaped like a cat's. You could see the outline of her bra through her blouse, and you could also tell from the front that it wasn't the smallest size. She sat down alone and didn't talk to anyone.

Physical descriptions are often used by authors of realistic fiction for children to help readers understand people who are different in some way from the average person. The following is from *Me Too,* in which authors Vera and Bill Cleaver describe Janie, a retarded character:

> A figure stood in the door. It had mop-hair, the color of old dust, which set the stage for a young-old face. Its smile was a child's. Its eyes did not belong to childhood nor yet to the state of adults. They belonged to all in that yet unsettled state where Lornie and all like Lornie lived.

Lornie, who is also retarded, has

> . . . eyes the color of nickel and . . . wore [her] chocolate-colored hair pulled back and up with rubber bands wound around the strands so that it appeared something sprouted from the top of [her] head and [she] . . . had big, white teeth and shoulder blades like chicken wings and knobbly knees.

The authors also provide a description of the way Lornie moved:

> Lornie's walk was peculiar. She went in a queer, limp way with her head pulled down to one side, though there was nothing wrong with it, or any part of her physically.

The story is about how Lydia, Lornie's sister, begins the summer with high expectations of teaching Lornie even though others had failed. But by late

August, she has grown discouraged. After deciding that the key to unlocking Lornie's mind is to love her, she realizes that maybe she does not love her sister enough or in the right way. When confronted by a physical danger, she tries to get Lornie to go for help. Though she has consciously accepted that Lornie is different, she still unconsciously expects her to respond normally.

> Nothing in the way she moved showed any alarm. This might be a game with her. Cannot a six-year-old mind in a twelve-year-old body comprehend the differences between a game and what is real?
>
> Taken with a terrible judgment, probably the purest one she would ever have, Lydia thought, "No, fool, she cannot. She is exceptional. Exceptional. She cannot understand. Will never understand the things normal people understand . . . Girl, you have been spoofing yourself."

It is with this compellingly expressed admission that Lydia is able to move to a more mature acceptance of Lornie as she really is.

*Arilla Sun Down*, by Virginia Hamilton, is recommended for gifted children by Polette and Hamlin (1980) in a chapter about helping such children gain deeper understanding of character development. The authors recommend Hamilton's book, though they acknowledge it may be difficult to read at first, as "many of Arilla's thoughts are expressed in half sentences . . . [which] makes one feel as if one is suspended in mid-air." They provide an extended list of questions to use for group discussion to help children understand Hamilton's characterization. Another author, Pat Rigg (1985) recommends Hamilton's book, *Sweet Whispers, Brother Rush* for the particularly strong portrayal it gives of an independent female heroine. However, British critic David Rees (1984) does not mince words in writing that Hamilton too often produces pages of descriptive prose with little dialogue, slow narrative, and predictable characters.

## FIRST-PERSON NARRATION

A striking characteristic of contemporary fiction for children is the prevalence of first-person narration.[15] In contrast, the third-person, omniscient narrator is almost universal in folk literature and very common in historic fiction.

---

[15]First-person narration is one of several characteristics of this genre identified by Al Muller in "New Reading Material: The Junior Novel" (*Journal of Reading*, April 1975, pp. 131–134). The author comments that this genre is essentially one of incident, rather than of characterization, but he points to several trends indicative of change.

First person narrators can present other characters convincingly. The following, from *Danny the Champion of the World*, by Roald Dahl, is Danny's description of his father:

> You might think, if you didn't know him well, that he was a stern and serious man. He wasn't. He was actually a wildly funny person. What made him appear so serious was the fact that he never smiled with his mouth. He did it all with his eyes. He had brilliant blue eyes and when he thought something was funny, his eyes would flash. . . . But the mouth never moved.
>
> I was glad my father was an eye-smiler. It meant he never gave me a fake smile because it's impossible to make your eyes twinkle if you aren't feeling twinkly yourself. A mouth-smile is different. You can fake a mouth-smile any time you want, simply by moving your lips. So watch out, when someone smiles at you with his mouth but his eyes stay the same. It's sure to be a phony.

Motherless Danny and his father have a loving relationship. They turn a simple poaching expedition to nab Mr. Hazell's pheasants into a grandiose scheme to capture the largest number of birds ever bagged.

Another advantage of first-person narrative is that it gives readers immediate and valuable insight into the character who is speaking. In the following from *The Midnight Fox*, by Betsy Byars, fifteen-year-old Tom reminisces about the summer he was nine. Prior to his spending that summer on a farm, his mother extolled the benefits of such an experience.

> My mom . . . went on about the fun I would have in the garden, especially gathering eggs. . . . I could picture that. I would be running to the house with my egg, see, having all this fun, and then there would be a noise like a freight train behind me. A terrible noise growing louder and louder, and I would look around and there would come about 200 chickens running me down. CHA-ROOOM! Me flattened on the ground while the lead hen snatches the egg from my crushed hand and returns in triumph to the coop.

Readers cannot know whether this anecdote is based on Tom's actual nine-year-old apprehension about what might happen or his since embroidered version of that apprehension. Whichever it is, it serves the purpose of characterizing Tom as a person with a good sense of humor.

First-person narration can be very effective in showing how the narrator deals with changes in his or her life. In *I'll Get There. It Better be Worth the Trip*, by John Donovan, thirteen-year-old Davy has been living with his beloved grandmother and is devastated by her death. The only thread of continuity between that happy existence and Davy's new life with his alcoholic mother is his dachshund, Fred. Davy responds to his mother's New York City apartment.

> Mother's house is in the middle of the block. It was built in 1834 and has high ceilings. There is . . . a nutty-looking porch over the kitchen of the people who live under her. . . . We're all shivering with the cold when we come in, and it's the back porch Mother wants to show us first. She calls it her terrace, and I can see right away that she thinks Fred can live out there. I tell her that Fred loves heat, and if she will show me where I'll live, I'm sure Fred can squeeze in there too.

Davy candidly evaluates his room:

> It's all boy, all right. She has had it paneled and has had some skinny drawers built in a skinny double decker bed. She's got a strange collection of stuff on the walls, and she tells me they are from Childcraft. They're great, of course, but they're for kids about five.

Life with his erratic mother comes to an ugly climax; she fears there is something "unnatural" about Davy's relation with his friend Altschuler. Carelessness results in Fred's death, and Davy must deal with his guilt feelings. He thinks perhaps the dog would not have died if he and his friend hadn't been fooling around. As he comes to accept the death of his dog, Davy leaves behind his childhood existence and begins the journey to adulthood.

In *I'll Love You When You're More Like Me,* author M. E. Kerr alternates two first-person narrators. One is Wallace Witherspoon, Jr., the undertaker's frustrated son, caught in a romantic triangle between Lauralei, a Jewish girlfriend who won't marry him because he isn't Jewish, and Sabra, who won't marry him because she is self-centered. Sabra is the other first-person narrator. The worlds of Wallace and Sabra, though remote from most readers' reality, are interesting partly because of Wallace's sense of humor.

> I was lying on the rope carpet with my feet up on an old steamer trunk the Hrens used as a coffee table. I was studying Harriet, trying to see her through the eyes of Lauralei Rabinowitz, who kept returning to my mind like mildew you can't get off a suitcase no matter how often you set it out in the sun and purge yourself of it. Maybe she was more a disease than simple mildew, a disease so far unrecorded in the annals of medical history. Years hence I would be told, "It's Rabinowitzitis, all right, you've been suffering from it since before your marriage. You have all the symptoms."

Another book with two first-person narrators is *Little Little,* by M. E. Kerr. Sidney Cinnamon—age seventeen—narrates the first chapter, which introduces a dwarf whose career began with appearances as "The Roach," a mascot for a high school football team, and escalated from there. The second chapter is narrated by Little Little LaBelle, who has a penchant for honesty (despite her mother's insistence she say "urinate" instead of "pee"). She and her family live comfortably in the Finger Lakes region of New York, and her mother is determined, as an active POD (Parent of a Diminutive), to make sure her daughter does well in life, despite her size. The alternating narrative pattern continues throughout the book. Two more unlikely characters than these are difficult to imagine. Yet with their fey charm, they become people readers care about.

Alice Childress experiments with even more narrators in *A Hero Ain't Nothing But a Sandwich*, about thirteen-year-old Benjie Johnson, who is black and almost hooked on drugs. His story is told by eleven different narrators, each describing inner-city life from his or her own perspective. The book is narrated by Benjie; his stepfather; his best friend, Jimmy; his grandmother; two teachers (one white, one black); his mother; the school principal; Walter, the pusher; a neighbor; and Jimmy-Lee's father, a street-corner "preacher." Toward the end, Benjie feels wanted and loved for the first time in years and appears to want to go straight, but the conclusion is equivocal. Benjie's stepfather waits for him on the street corner near the drug rehabilitation center—but Benjie does not come. This book is interesting linguistically, but readers must have the patience to cope with the dialect, and some may find the profanity offensive, though it does add realism.

Not everyone is enthusiastic about first-person narration as a stylistic device. Egoff's (1980) sarcastic comments about this way of writing make clear that she feels there are significant inherent disadvantages.

## SETTING

Part of any writer's success with realistic fiction is the ability to transport readers to a place, to show the nature of a specific environment. In contrast to folk literature, which is usually set in indeterminate locations, contemporary realistic fiction is set in a wide variety of definite locations.

Ivan Southall is able to successfully transport readers to Australia in *Ash Road*. A description of the weather is so vivid that it seems to give the air its own personality:

> And he was frightened of the sky. It was so threatening, so ugly, so unlike anything he had ever seen. It was a hot brown mantle over the earth with pieces breaking off it, little black pieces of ash: an oppressive mantle that did not

prevent the penetration of the sun's heat but imprisoned it, added to it, and magnified the hostility of the day.

It was an angry day; not just wild or rough, but savage in itself, actively angry against every living thing. It hated plants and trees and birds and animals, and they wilted from its hatred or withered up and died or panted in distress in shady places. Above all, it hated Peter. It seemed to encompass him with a malevolence that would strike him down if he ventured to defy it.

An equally effective description of setting is found in *Hell's Edge*, by John Rowe Townsend. This time the location is a small industrial town in Yorkshire, England.[16] Ril (short for Amaryllis) Terry comes to "Hell's Edge" to live with her father, and at first she is inclined to agree with the derogatory nickname for the town. Her interest in Caradoc Clough, an ancestor who led a rebellion against the local landed gentry, leads her to an appreciation of her Yorkshire heritage. By the story's end, Ril is well content to be who she is, where she is. The author intertwines a mystery into the main plot, but its solution seems to be too dependent on coincidence.

In dramatic contrast to the grime of a factory town is the pristine cleanliness of the house author Julia Cunningham creates in *Dorp Dead*. After the chaotic noise of the orphanage to which the narrator was sent following his grandmother's death, the orderly calm of his new environment appeals immensely:

> . . . the grey house, so perfectly square of shape and so immaculate it looks as if someone scrubs it every day. . . . I inhale a last lungful of the outer world, step inside, and then let out my breath so fast it clouds the air. I am in the middle of a little palace. This is a house like a very detailed drawing that someone has sketched and resketched, placed and replaced for hundreds of evenings until it is, down to the box of matches on the exact center of the mantel, perfect. And there is a feeling in the exactitude of every table, chair, picture, and kitchen canister, that no carelessness or rearrangement will ever be permitted. . . . I find myself not only understanding but approving. This is manufactured peace, but it's peace and I like it.

In most cases, authors of realistic fiction provide multidimensional descriptions of setting, like those above. But authors sometimes concentrate on one sense in order to focus the setting description. In *Behind the Magic Line*, an appealing book for intermediate-grade children, author Betty K.

---

[16]Other works of contemporary realistic fiction set in Great Britain are Walter Maken's *Island of the Great Yellow Ox* (New York: Macmillan, 1966), Alec Lea's *Temba Dawn* (New York: Scribner's, 1975), and Ruth Arthur's *On the Wasteland* (New York: Atheneum, 1975).

Irwin establishes the setting primarily through sound images. The little girl, Dozie, listens to the night.

> She knew it was late at night. She knew that before she opened her eyes. The sounds at night were very different. The streetcars didn't run very often, and there were no voices outside. Right here, in the heart of this great gray city, with the whole dark blowing night outside, it was quiet. If you listened . . . you could hear a far-away rumbling . . . not heard unless you really listened for it, that was the city traffic . . . the continuous beat of a city that never slept. But here in the big square room it was so still that she could hear her brothers and sisters breathing and could tell one from another.

## THEME

Modern realistic fiction such as Cunningham's *Dorp Dead* can help children begin to think about theme as an element of literature. Unlike such forms as fables, in which a moral is given, modern fiction seldom contains a deliberately stated "message." A teacher can help children discover the theme of a work by asking them to think about what the author is really trying to tell the reader. At first, boys and girls often confuse theme and plot.[17] To make the difference clear, the teacher can tell students that plot is *what* happens, whereas theme is *why* it happens. A fifth-grade teacher read *Dorp Dead* to her group and then asked them to summarize the story's theme. The following are some of the responses.

> People should not be satisfied with the way things are, but they should strive for better. Gilly did not enjoy the orphanage, but he enjoyed the privacy at the castle. Initially he enjoyed Kobalt's house, but he learned to hate it.
>
> *Jeff*

> If you convince yourself that you will make it, you will develop the self-confidence that you need. Gilly always said that he was smart and could do just about anything. He convinced himself that he could make it. The hunter tried telling Gilly he should not accept the atmosphere at Kobalt's house, but Gilly didn't realize what the hunter was saying until later.
>
> *Vincent*

---

[17]When asked what a story is about, most six-year-olds simply retell the plot. Children gradually learn to reorganize elements into superordinate categories and finally develop the ability to paraphrase. This sequence is reported by Arthur Applebee in *The Child's Concept of Story* (Chicago: University of Chicago Press, 1978), an incisive study of the processes children use when telling stories and the responses they give to stories.

I think that Julia Cunningham was trying to show what happens when you hold in your emotions. After you hold in your emotions for awhile, they seem to start fading.

*Tom*

Two points should be made about this activity. First, in helping children begin to think about theme, the teacher should encourage youngsters' statements, even though they may not converge on a single theme. With practice, boys and girls will get better at determining what the theme is—a rather abstract concept. Second, many books have more than one theme. It is not important to identify a single theme, only that what the child suggests seems plausible to the teacher.

## TOPIC

Probably the most striking aspect of modern realistic fiction for children is the range of topics it covers. Children can read about premarital sex and abortion in *My Darling, My Hamburger,* by Paul Zindel; about death in *Grover,* by Bill and Vera Cleaver; about suicide in *A Blues I Can Whistle,* by A. E. Johnson; about senility in *Pigman,* by Paul Zindel; about drugs in *Go Ask Alice,* written by an anonymous author; about poverty in *Where the Lilies Bloom,* by Bill and Vera Cleaver; about mental retardation in *Hey, Dummy,* by Kin Platt; about insanity in *Lisa, Bright and Dark,* by John Neufeld; about divorce in *The Trouble with Thirteen,* by Betty Miles; and about homosexuality in *What Happened to Mr. Forster?* by Gary Bargar. There seems to be no limit to what children can read about in books written expressly for them. This fact is distressing to those parents who feel a major part of their role in life is protecting their children from the realities of the world. However, the nature of the world and the nature of children have both changed significantly in recent decades. With increasing influence from television, changing life-styles, and expanding permissiveness, it is more and more difficult to protect children from life's realities. The books mentioned above simply mirror what is actually going on in the world. The authors of contemporary fiction for children are attempting to present accurate portrayals of the changes occuring in our society; they are not necessarily advocating these changes. Many authors feel it is their responsibility to present the world in such a way that children may have a solid foundation for understanding it.

Some teachers may have reservations about books such as those listed above because they believe they are not intended for children, but rather for preadolescent and adolescent readers. But, as was mentioned near the beginning of this chapter, many of these books *do* attract younger readers.

Children are often interested in, and want to read about, students who are older than they are. It is not uncommon for fourth- through sixth-grade students to read books about teenagers, in the same way that it is not uncommon to find four-year-olds playing house, emulating the roles of adults. Such trying on of roles is a natural part of growing up, and students often do that through reading. It may, in fact, be true that this tendency is increasing today in a world where children are more aware of the problems teenagers face than they once were (Elkind, 1981; Wynn, 1983).

**SEXUALITY.** Readers can find many varieties of sexual experience described sympathetically in realistic children's fiction, reflecting psychologists' understanding that children are interested in sex long before they begin to mature physically.

Girls mature earlier than boys, so it is logical that there are a number of books that describe how girls deal with the physical and psychological changes that occur as they approach puberty. In a sequel that is generally not as funny as the first book, author Louise Fitzhugh takes the characters of *Harriet the Spy* into their preteen years. In *The Long Secret*, Harriet's scientifically inclined friend, Janie, explains menstruation to Harriet and another girl very matter-of-factly.

A more humorous book, *Are You There God? It's Me, Margaret*, by Judy Blume,[18] also presents a female main character. With imagination and verve, Margaret copes with problems of everyday life, including physical maturation. In addition to being concerned about menstruation, Margaret is actively seeking a meaningful relationship with God, an unusual theme in children's books today. Neither her father, whose background is Jewish, nor her mother, who is vaguely Christian, helps her in this quest.

Girls are not alone, however, in facing uncertainties in the maturation process. In *Then Again, Maybe I Won't*, by Judy Blume, the author realistically portrays the embarrassment Tony, a thirteen-year-old boy, feels as he beomes aware of his own sexual development. The adjustments to physical development are interwoven with the psychological changes Tony must make to face a new environment with new problems.

*Freddy's Book*, by John Neufeld, is the humorous story of Freddy's perseverance in finding the meaning of "that" word. Freddy and others his age

---

[18]Besides the five books mentioned in this chapter, several other novels dealing with the problems of adolescence have been written by this prolific and talented author. Among them are *Iggie's House* (Scarsdale, N.Y.: Bradbury, 1970), about racial prejudice; *It's Not the End of the World* (Scarsdale, N.Y.: Bradbury, 1972), about separation; and *Tales of a Fourth Grade Nothing* (New York: E. P. Dutton, 1972), about sibling rivalry.

have seen the four-letter word in graffiti on walls, and it has piqued his curiosity. His search for information leads him, without success, to approach his mother, his friend, and his dad. Finally, he gets a compassionate explanation from his teenaged football coach.

Portraying an awareness of or curiosity about sexuality is less difficult than writing about actual sexual experiences. When Zoa Sherburne wrote about premarital sex in *Too Bad About the Haines Girl* in 1967, the sex act that resulted in the pregnancy was not described. The story about Melinda Haines instead emphasizes her concern over how her pregnancy will affect her sympathetically drawn parents, her younger sisters, and her friend Suky. The skillful development of the minor characters helps move this novel beyond simple formula fiction, although some elements—for instance, Melinda's election as Queen of the Valentine Ball—seem stereotypic. Sherburne wisely avoids a simplistic happy ending or a moralistic judgment about what Melinda and Jeff have done. Instead, the book closes with a suggestion of the possible compromises that Melinda and Jeff will find it necessary to make.

The heroine in *Diving for Roses*, by Charlotte Windsor, is light years away from Melinda, even though the publication dates of the two books are only a decade apart. Jean lives in an isolated old house in the country with her mother, Deirdre, an alcoholic. Deirdre, full of resentment about her divorce from Jean's father, is angry and detached. The two women see few people beside their cook and the doctor who attends to Deirdre's frequent imagined illnesses. Jean's first-person musings show sexual curiosity leading to desire when she discovers a stranger in the forest near the house:

> Something is coming.
> The horse snorts and the thrashing stops. Perhaps whatever it is, it has not expected to encounter horses.
> It emerges from the forest and looks startled when it sees the horse. At first it doesn't see me.
> The creature has a flat stomach that needs no support of hands. It is not short and scrabby crabby but is equipped with long brown legs and arms of reasonable length. It does not look frightening but rather slightly humorous because it is wearing high cutoff shorts and the long legs are really very thin and the boots look too large around the skinny calves. The torso is covered by a white shirt, open at the throat and with the sleeves torn off so that only shreds show where they once were. A pulse beats in the brown throat. The chin is held high, like a frightened doe sensing danger. The thin angular face glistens with heat and is partly covered by copper glinting waves of long hair that fall gracefully from the crown of the head. I can see the eyes moving left and right, poor worried doe waiting for the arrow.

> I refrain from gazing at the space between the legs. That's where the secret place is, the identity that creates the difference.
>
> All at once the creature is near, squatting beside me, very close, too close I think, too soon. I can smell something now, my atavistic senses aware of an odor of sweat. The legs are hairy and I can see faint pricklings of hair on chin and cheeks, a dusky blond moss poking through.
>
> Perhaps it's a changling, perhaps it has two sets of sex to use as it sees fit and according to whim. The shirt billows out and I cannot fathom breasts. The throat looks so vulnerable, so tenderly pulsating life. I am overcome with a desire to touch it, to stroke it with my tongue, to implant a deadly kiss.

In writing this passage, Windsor is tacitly acknowledging the female's interest in, and attraction to, the male. Psychologists assert that this interest is natural, but it has been overshadowed in books, where more often the male's interest in the female is depicted. By describing the young man as a physical object, Windsor reverses the usual role of woman (as the described, not the describer) and achieves a more powerful piece of writing as a result.

Writing convincingly about sexual experiences that diverge from the norm, especially when one has not shared those experiences, is a very difficult task. Lynn Hall accomplishes this task in *Sticks and Stones*. She portrays sensitively the problems Tom faces when insidious gossip labels him a homosexual. Newly arrived in a small Iowa town, Tom feels that he is different from most of his junior-year classmates, largely because of his interest in classical music. He doesn't foresee the problems that result when he ignores the friendship of simple, overweight Floyd. One of many children in an impoverished family, Floyd has failed school once and desperately wants Tom's friendship for the status it will bring. His attraction to Tom is probably latent homosexuality, though he is unaware of it. He strikes back savagely when Tom ignores him. The rumor, started so quietly, spreads quickly and isolates Tom. Worse, the innuendos deprive him of the right to compete at the state music competition, largely because of the school principal's weakness. The cause of the unpleasantness is Tom's friendship with Ward, a young man who has returned home after being dishonorably discharged from the army. Only Ward can help Tom, but Tom blindly denies this assistance when he needs it most. Ward's discretion and careful avoidance of any sexual contact in the early stages of their relationship show him to be a maturing male, at ease with the sexual choices he has made. The final scene in the hospital, when Ward takes the chance of being rejected again by coming to Tom's room, is masterfully understated. Hall carefully avoids the temptation to tie up loose ends—the reader does not know what Tom will do. How will Tom deal with returning to school in the fall? Is he gay, or is his feeling only the platonic affection common among males of his age? *Sticks and Stones* is one of several books on the topic of homosexuality recommended by Jenkins and Morris (1983) in an article that covers both fiction and nonfiction.

Skillful writing about homosexuality is also found in *The Man Without a Face*, by Isabelle Holland. The narrator is fourteen-year-old Chuck, growing up in a female-dominated, fatherless home. Chuck lives with his often-divorced mother (whose hobby is marrying), his older, brighter, unlovable sister, Gloria, and his younger sister, Meg. Chuck has a negative attitude toward women, which is evident in his characterization of Meg:

> Meg is OK because she's still short and fat and wears braces and hasn't even started yet to try to manipulate me. She's eleven. But she's a female, so I am keeping an eye on her, because any day now she may launch on some junior version of the "How could you do this to me?" bit.

Because of an equally negative attitude toward studying, Chuck has failed the admission test to the private prep school he was to attend. The school gives Chuck a chance to retake the test, and at this point he meets Justin McLeod. Chuck knows that Justin, a recluse whose face is hideously scarred on one side, has been a teacher. Justin reluctantly responds to Chuck's desperate appeal for tutoring, and they begin a summer of intense work together. Chuck's respect deepens into love for Justin, an adult with whom he can communicate. When the pressures of the summer come to a climax, Chuck turns naturally to Justin, who provides psychological and physical comforting as the two express their love.

*Sticks and Stones* and *The Man Without a Face*, as well as Sandra Scoppettone's *Trying Hard to Hear You* and M. E. Kerr's *I'll Love You When You're More Like Me*, are analyzed by Wolf (1978). She concludes that "although none of . . . [the books analyzed] is outrageously stereotyped," they do suggest that "gay males are all pretty much alike." She sees a lesbian novel, *Ruby*, by Rosa Guy, as similarly stereotypic.

A brilliant piece of writing that avoids stereotyping is *Dance on My Grave*, by Aidan Chambers. The story is presented in small fragments of direct narration, pages from Hal's diary, and his social worker's reports; few of these extend more than two pages. But despite this apparent choppiness, the overall effect is unified, describing a sixteen-year-old's dealing with his homosexuality and adjusting to his friend's death in a motorcycle accident.

Even when Hal thinks about death, his sexuality gets the upper hand:

> What's it like to be a corpse? Who cares? The point being, presumably, that no one inhabits a corpse, the who having departed. . . . A pity really, I thought; I

rather like my body. I'll be sorry when the time comes to leave it. Or will I? By then, probably, it will be wizened, my skin blotched and creased like old bark. My breath will stink like an incinerator, my body like a sewer. My hair will be thin as the fur on a baboon's bum. . . .

Will thoughts still worm in my cadaverous cranium? Will I still juggle with words? Will I remember enough words to juggle with? Will pictures invade my mind with power to give my body some gyp?

Will anybody make passes at me then? Will geriatric men and women give me the eye?

After an escape from a disastrous encounter with a motorcycle gang, Hal and Barry repair to Barry's bathroom to clean up, and the inevitable occurs. Chambers lets the reader know the two have sex, and yet doesn't either avoid it or dwell on it. After the suitably modest description, Hal cheekily confronts the reader directly: "Wish you were here?"

In this book, the author deals with the tragedy of uneven expectations: two boys, drawn to each other physically and emotionally, acknowledge after seven weeks of bliss that their needs are so different they cannot be resolved. When Barry unfeelingly abandons Hal one afternoon for Kari, Hal's jealousy drives the two apart. After Barry's death, it is, oddly enough, Kari who provides the caring to support Hal through the catharsis he needs to move beyond this tragedy into whatever lies ahead. His grief for his lost mate, and for the childhood ideal he will not find, is tempered by his self-acceptance; he can deal with his homosexuality and not let it rule his life.

Chambers has written *Dance on My Grave* with the consummate skill he usually manifests. The book is full of turns of phrase, comparisons, and descriptions to be savored. Some of the numerous Britishisms will remain incomprehensible to most American readers, but they do add to the believability of the writing. An extended analysis of *Dance on My Grave*, considering both its structure and the author's intent, is given by Chambers (1985). He consistently demonstrates that he is one of the most articulate writers about the writing process. His volume presents extended criticism of several of his own books, frequently relating them to each other and to other books.

Sex as an act of aggression is chillingly described by Richard Peck in his book *Are You in the House Alone?* Gail, the narrator, and her boyfriend, assuming they are unnoticed, are having sex regularly throughout the summer. The relationship between Gail's best friend, Alison, and her fiancé, Phil Lawver, son of one of the most influential families in town, is far more chaste. When Gail begins to be harassed by anonymous notes and obscene phone calls, she tries to ignore them, but they persist and even intensify. When the harassment finally culminates in Gail's rape, she is astounded to discover the attacker is Phil. The rape scene is realistic but not at all sensational. The aftermath of psychic horror is more gripping than the scene itself. Largely through her own efforts, Gail gathers strength to return to school; her mother ineffectually protests that she could as well finish out her senior year with an aunt in another town to avoid the "disgrace" of what has happened. When eccentric Sonia is also attacked, Phil's sickness is so apparent that he is institutionalized. In the end, it is Gail's ability to look beyond what has happened that lets her adjust to the trauma. She has grown into a far more mature woman than she was when the story opened. Author Peck (1978) has described his reasons for writing a single-problem didactic novel. An analysis of this book, as well as others that are apt to be censored, is given by MacLeod (1983).

**AGING AND DEATH.**   Only recently has death become an acceptable topic for children's books. When it was published in 1958, *The Dead Bird*, by Margaret Wise Brown, was a noteworthy attempt to introduce this topic into literature for very young children. Today, there are numerous children's books, for all ages, dealing with aging and death.

One of the most positive pictures of aging is *A Likely Place*. Newbery Medal–winner Paula Fox tells the story of Lewis, age ten, who wants to run away. Berated by teachers, parents, and classmates, Lewis is ineptness personified. When his parents go on a trip, his eccentric babysitter lets Lewis go out. While away from home, he meets old Mr. Madruga. Despite the disparity between their ages, the two become fast friends. In solving his new friend's problem, Lewis discovers himself to be more capable than he had thought.

*The Hundred Penny Box*, by Sharon Bell Mathis, is another effective portrayal of a relationship between a young person and an old one. Michael loves his great-great-aunt, Dew. Dewhet Thomas is one hundred years old and has a box with pennies in it that represent the years of her life. Michael is worried because his mother, modern and practical, wants to get rid of the cracked old box, like she has gotton rid of many of Aunt Dew's things. His mother can't understand the way old people cling to the past. The illustrations by Leo and Diane Dillon are soft, blurred pictures in a sepia tint, like old photographs, that complement the story well.

In *Badger on the Barge*, winner of an International Reading Association Children's Book Award, British author Janni Howker effectively depicts relations between young and old in a collection of short stories. Yet these are not at all sentimental depictions of age. Young Helen Fisher is seeking refuge from her father's oppressive grief over her brother's death. She inadvertently finds companionship with Miss Brady, an unusual and prickly old person.

> Helen did not know what to say. Miss Brady baffled her . . . "You must like somebody . . ."
> "I must, must I? Hmmmph!" the old woman snorted.

Other old people in these stories are equally unusual: Old Reicher, assailed as a Nazi by tormenting boys; the egg-man, whom the girls torment; Jakey, who offers friendship to miserable Steven, temporarily exiled with his daft Aunt Lil; and Sally Beck, who asks a surprised Liz what it is like to be young. Each is presented in a story averaging forty pages. Because of their particularity of detail, these stories remain vividly in the memory long after they have been read.

In Jill Paton Walsh's *Gaffer Samson's Luck*, old Mr. Samson is the only person to befriend displaced James, who hates the vast flatness of his new home in the Fens. School is strange, and the two gangs there are both unfriendly toward this newcomer. A gypsy talisman was given years before to a younger Gaffer Samson by an entrancing, dark-haired beauty. Nearing the end of life, Gaffer sets his new young friend the task of retrieving the charm from its hiding place. In the process of accomplishing this, James must confront his nemesis, the bully Terry. Having proved himself, James is able to show compassion toward Terry by passing on Gaffer's charm. Walsh writes skillfully in a format too little used by others—the short novel for middle-grade readers. At 120 pages, *Gaffer Samson's Luck* is not the intimidatingly long book that is much more commonly published for this age group. The author weaves a compelling and gritty story of families with few resources to cushion life's hardships. The characters are described succinctly, and with compassion. Old Gaffer has a voice like a "fen nightingale" (a frog); James is wrapped in the nearness of his parents but knows Gaffer has no one; and Angie is an opportunistic urchin with a penchant for Mars bars.

Aging leads inevitably to death, and since few adults face that sequence with equanimity, it is no wonder children's authors find it difficult to approach the topic with honesty and compassion.[19] Often books about aging

---

[19]The sequence may indeed be inevitable, but one article warns against sharing only books in which old characters die, which may give an unrealistic picture of old age. Carol Seefeldt, Alice Galper, Kathy Serock, and Richard K. Jantz, in "The Coming of Age in Children's Literature" (*Childhood Education*, January 1978, pp. 123–127), assert that children need to experience the diversity of old age. In addition to vicarious experiences with the aged through books, the authors also suggest ways of establishing direct contact between children and the elderly in their community.

**Sharp ink lines and heavy cross-hatching to create dimension readily evoke the story's setting and characters.** Illustration by Brock Cole from *Gaffer Samson's Luck* by Jill Paton Walsh. Copyright © 1984 by Brock Cole. Reprinted by permission of Farrar, Straus & Giroux, Inc.

will recount a grandfather's or grandmother's death or impending death. In *Mama's Ghosts*, by Carol L. Lorenzo, Ellie's adored and dying grandmother helps her become aware that sometimes even if you love someone you have to let go. The writing, appropriate for readers in grades four through six, is personal, touching, and infused with wry humor. The grandmother in *The Mulberry Music*, by Doris Orgel, is very fond of her granddaughter Libby, and the feeling is mutual. Libby's pain when Grandma dies is poignantly portrayed in this novel about a suburban family.

Sam, the teenaged hero in *The Dream Runner*, by Audree Distad, is a runner; the physical challenge of his sport helps him overlook the inadequacies of his situation. Sam's father long ago deserted the family; his mother ekes out a poor living. Shortly after the story opens, Sam's mother receives word that her husband is dead. Out of some sort of loyalty to the past, she travels by bus to the funeral, to finish things off properly. Left alone, Sam feels more keenly than ever his lack of a father.

> He groped for the table, switched on the light and found a sheet of paper and a pencil. Carefully he wrote: Lawrence McKee, father of Sam. Tall and skinny shadow.
>
> Put in the made-up parts, he thought: Pilot, gold miner, cowboy, ocean explorer, traveler. Put in the real, what I know of it: He left us, he went away, he never came back.
>
> Sam stared at the sheet, until his eyes stung with tears. At last he wrote in shaky letters. Why didn't you come back? I could have tagged after you.
>
> He carried it to the stove, struck a match and set fire to the paper. Flame burst along the edge, yellow flaring, curling into ashes. When it hurt his hand, he dropped the paper into the sink and watched until the flame died.

Old Clete, an Indian, fills a gap in Sam's life by becoming his confidante, entertaining him with traditional tribal tales. A genuine affection grows between them as Sam substitutes Clete for his missing father. After Clete's death, Sam goes to the mountains to seek the circle of tepees and the vision cave Clete had described. Sam sprains his ankle, and his attempts to find his way out of the mountains falter as his physical condition deteriorates. It seems possible that he will not make it out of the mountains alive, but a fossil talisman helps him, as does a mysterious young Indian runner.

Writing about the death of a child poses a different problem for an author than does telling about an old person's death. In *A Summer to Die*, by Lois Lowry, young Meg gradually realizes her lovely sister Molly is struggling with a terminal illness. The inevitability of her sister's death is difficult to accept because Meg is conscious she has fought with, and even envied, Molly. Meg's deep friendship with old Will Banks, her partner in photographic endeavors, helps her to understand her own feelings. When she witnesses the birth of a baby, Meg begins to come to terms with her grief for Molly.

The sudden death of a child is described in *A Taste of Blackberries*, by Doris Buchanan Smith, a dramatic, but nonetheless effective work of realistic fiction. The first two chapters are pleasant descriptions of the joys and frustrations of being best friends. Jamie's character is clearly established when the narrator, his friend, describes how they pretend to be circus dogs: "You could get tired and want to do something else but that stupid Jamie would crawl around barking all afternoon." One day, while the narrator and several friends are debugging grape vines, tragedy strikes without

***Thin black line of unvarying thickness is employed to create a number of different patterns; these contrast with the larger plain areas.*** Illustration by Jenni Oliver from *A Summer to Die* by Lois Lowry. Copyright © 1977 by Lois Lowry. Reprinted by permission of Houghton Mifflin Company.

warning. Jamie is stung by a bee and writhes in pain, but the children, including the narrator, ignore him, thinking he is exaggerating as usual. Allergic to bee stings, Jamie dies quickly. At the funeral parlor, and even when they are back home, the narrator doesn't cry. But later that night, when he sees his mother go across to Jamie's house, he experiences the catharsis of tears as he realizes that some questions have no answers. Smith captures the kind of seemingly irrelevant thoughts that crop up in a child's mind at a tragic time. For example, at the graveside service, the narrator thinks:

> There was the hole. Jamie's hole. It was oblong and nice and even around the edges. If Jamie were here he would nudge me and say, "Look at the neat hole!" We had dug foxholes up in the woods but never could get them squared off as he wanted.

This is one of about fifty books recommended by Holdaway (1981) in an article that considers both positive and negative aspects of bibliotherapy, the technique of using readings to turn the attitudes of readers toward healthy directions.

Equally as unexpected as Jamie's is Joss's death in *Beat the Turtle Drum*, by Constance C. Greene. Joss and her sister Kate are good friends. Throughout the spring, Kate watches affectionately as Joss cajoles, saves, and works to make her dream of having a horse for a week come true. Then, while the

**Artist Donna Diamond uses softly modulated shades of gray, black, and white, highlighting the boy's head in light and allowing the tree trunks in the foreground to become simple silhouettes framing him and his father.** Illustration from *Bridge to Terabithia* by Katherine Paterson. Illustrated by Donna Diamond for Thomas Y. Crowell. Copyright © 1977 by Katherine Paterson. Reprinted by permission of Harper & Row, Publishers, Inc.

two sisters sit high in their favorite apple tree, life changes in a moment as Joss falls to her death. The last chapters recount the stages of the family's grief, from tears to silence. The ending is equivocal: Kate has begun to move back to normalcy, but her parents have not.

Katherine Paterson deals with death, among other topics, in *Bridge to Terabithia*, a complex book examining the relationship between two youngsters, Leslie and Jess. Leslie dies in a tragic accident. The author, in her acceptance speech for the Newbery Medal (1978), detailed the events in her own life and that of her son, that led to the writing of this book. Needing to deal with her own mortality, Paterson came to grips with death through writing about a boy's coming to grips with the death of his friend.

Many of the books considered in this chapter are probably better read individually than shared with a group. However, Kimmel and Segel (1983) recommend group sharing of *Bridge to Terabithia*. These authors annotate each book they recommend, including specific suggestions for handling the reading. For example, concerning *Bridge to Terabithia*, they say, "Longer [reading] sessions toward the end of the book may cushion the impact of Leslie's death with Jess's hopes for the future and the continuation of the kingdom of Terabithia." The authors give a suggested age level for each book cited.

In each of the books described so far in this section, the main character deals with the death of a loved one *when* it happens. A compelling story that is a departure from this pattern is *Blackberries in the Dark*, by Mavis Jukes. In this case, young Austin comes to visit his grandma the summer following the death of his grandpa. All around are reminders of how much each of them has lost in Grandpa's death. The book is as strongly written as Jukes's earlier one, *Like Jake and Me*. What Jukes does so competently here is to write very specifically, in a brief number of text pages (twenty-eight), about a particular, small amount of time (one afternoon) and a very large topic (death) without lapsing into generalities. The specificity of detail is engrossing, and yet Jukes links Austin to all children who have lost a loved grandparent. Would that all authors who deal with such significant topics as death could do it with such enviable precision of language!

Views of death vary from culture to culture. *Annie and the Old One*, by Miska Miles, allows children to experience vicariously a Navajo girl's intense affection for her grandmother. The grandmother speaks calmly of her approaching death, which will occur when she finishes the weaving on her loom. In a desperate attempt to forestall the inevitable, Annie sneaks out at night and undoes the day's weaving, until her grandmother discovers this action and helps Annie understand its futility. The understated but elegant language is admirably matched by Peter Parnall's subtle ink-line

*The composition is tightly controlled: the two strong verticals on either side hold the picture together, and the two characters' arms further unify it.* Illustration by Thomas B. Allen from *Blackberries in the Dark* by Mavis Jukes. Copyright © 1985. Reprinted by permission of Alfred A. Knopf, Inc.

illustrations. This is one of 656 books analyzed by Ansello (1978), who examined picture books and easy-reading books to determine the presence of older characters and concluded that this group is significantly underrepresented in such books.

In Gary Paulsen's *Dogsong*, fourteen-year-old Russel resists the death of old, blind Oogruk, who has taught him many skills. Caught between the traditional Eskimo culture and the uneasy adaptation to white culture (represented by his father's acceptance of standard government housing, snowmobiles, and pictures of Jesus), Russel seeks out Oogruk. The old man willingly shares his knowledge, but in the end demands a dear price: Russel must leave him on the ice to freeze to death when Oogruk's time has come. In the subsequent dog run across the country, Russel matures, learning the limits of his and his dogs' endurance. In the end, he is able to use the skills Oogruk taught him to save the girl he finds on the ice. Between the two there is hope for new life, despite the death of her baby, which neither can prevent.

Paulsen's skill lies in his ability to clearly depict an environment most readers will not have experienced firsthand; he evokes the sights and smells and sounds of the desolate country he describes. Through the character old Oogruk, representing Eskimo tradition, Paulsen gives cultural insights incidentally, but compellingly.

> "Dogs are like white people," Oogruk said, looking at the flame. "They do not know how to get a settled mind. They are always turning, looking for a better way to lie down. And if things go wrong they have anger and frustration. They are not like us. It is said that dogs and white people come from the same place." He snorted—a nasal sound, a kind of *chaa* sound through his nose that could have meant anything from scorn to anger to humor. "I do not know how true that is because white people are clearly not dogs. But they have many of the same ways and so one wonders."

Particularly useful suggestions for involving students with this book are given by Lehr (1986). These include dramatization, observation, writing, and related reading activities.

**MENTAL ILLNESS.** In *The Dream Watcher*, author Barbara Wersba describes the problems of a suicidal teenager. Albert Scully, in his first year of high school, considers himself a "nothing" person and contemplates committing suicide. Before he can act on his idea, he meets Mrs. Woodfin, who tells him she gave up her position as a famous actress because she realized that acclaim and fortune do not bring happiness. Albert comes to an acceptance of himself as he pours out his dreams, hopes, and problems to her. But when Mrs. Woodfin dies, Albert learns that in reality she was an alcoholic who could no longer hold a job. At first he is resentful and angry, but he soon realizes how much he loved her and what she gave him—the gift of his own life.

*The Winds of Time*, by Barbara Corcoran, deals with a consequence of mental illness. Thirteen-year-old Gail's father has run away, and her mentally ill mother is committed to an institution; Gail is assigned to live with her Uncle Chad. Gail is mistrustful of all adults; Uncle Chad's horrible temper and devious reasons for wanting to "help" Gail give her good reason.

After an accident, she escapes to the Partridges, who befriend her. Gradually, Gail loses her suspicious nature and learns to trust again. This is one of over three-hundred books portraying the handicapped, published between 1940 and 1975, that are both annotated and evaluated by Baskin and Harris (1977).

Like Barbara Corcoran, Sue Ellen Bridgers explores the effect one person's mental illness has on others in her book *Notes for Another Life*. Wren and Kevin, who live with their grandparents, have lived with the fact of mental illness for years: their father has been in and out of a state hospital since they were youngsters. Wren understands the nature of the choice her mother faced—between a conventional family life and a career—but she doesn't understand *why* her mother chose a career when it affects the entire family. Trying to serve as a healing influence between her mother, her brother Kevin, and their almost always absent father, Wren is faced with her own dilemma. Her music makes its own demands on her, and her first boyfriend, although more insightful than most teenagers, doesn't know how to deal with those demands. Kevin, meeting the challenge of trying to deal more positively with his father, isn't quite sure how he will deal with his own lost love. This book could have been melodramatic as a result of its heavy load of serious topics (in addition to mental illness the book also deals with divorce and attempted suicide); instead the author transcends these to create a compelling study of characters interrelating as they come to terms, in various ways, with their own lives. Readers care about these characters because of Bridgers's skill in using language to create believable people.

## EQUIVOCAL ENDINGS

Characteristic of a lot of realistic fiction for children is the ending. Rather than tying up all the loose ends of plot, providing a solution to the problems, and specifying what happens to each character, many authors choose to conclude a book with questions left unanswered. In *The Arm of the Starfish*, author Madeline L'Engle leaves readers wondering:

Will coy and reckless Kali Cutter and her evil friend Typhon be brought to justice for their part in the death of the young embassy worker, Joshua?

Will Kali recover from the savage, near-fatal shark attack and reconsider her behavior because of Adam's selfless action in bringing her to safety?

A fine example of a book without a pat ending is *M. C. Higgins, the Great*, by Virginia Hamilton, a widely respected and popular children's author. In the story, the mountain has so much life it seems like one of the characters. M. C. rightly fears that strip miners have endangered his home on that mountain by creating the menacing heap of rubble that looms above his house. The other characters affect the story's action: a strange girl, who travels alone in the hills; M. C.'s strong and loving father, who is unable to face the reality of physical danger to their home; and a man with a tape recorder, who will capture the special voice of M. C.'s mother, perhaps making her a star and thus rescuing the family from their predicament. There is no fairy tale ending here. Readers are left with a memorable set of characters, a haunting sense of place, and a strong feeling that the family won't leave their land without a fight. This is a rewarding book for mature readers who do not require constant action and a resolved ending.

*To the Wild Sky*, by Ivan Southall, is a complex book with an equivocal ending and again is most appropriate for mature readers. Six children set off in a private plane for a weekend visit, but the plans are changed drastically when the pilot dies suddenly of a heart attack. One boy figures out how to fly the plane, but an intense dust storm prevents landing until hours later. High winds have carried the plane hundreds of miles beyond its destination, and the children crash-land on an unknown shore. The remainder of the book recounts the children's attempts to survive. At the end, they have been able to make a fire but have no water and virtually no food. There is no sign of other humans, and what happens to the children is not specified. The author presents a profound ambiguity concerning these children, too civilized to cope with a wild environment. Their fate could be to survive or—as one of the girls fears—to die slowly. The author leaves the story to be finished by the reader.

Despite the increasing incidence of equivocal endings in contemporary realistic fiction, Lukens (1986) contends that among examples of enduring children's literature, few have open endings.

## PUBLIC AND PRIVATE GENRES

Contemporary realistic fiction gives rise to fewer activities for teachers to use with groups of children than the other genres discussed so far. Folk literature and historical fiction can be considered *public genres* because it is entirely appropriate to read most, if not all, of such fiction in a group setting and plan ways to involve children in responding. In contrast, much, though not all, of modern realistic fiction can be considered a *private genre* because the specificity of detail and the sometimes controversial nature of the topics make these books more appropriate for individual reading than for group sharing.

Teachers who use books with children and librarians who select books for children must be aware that the sensibilities of parents deserve respect, at least in regard to their own children. The candor of much contemporary fiction may be considered unsuitable by some parents. This means teachers must be knowledgeable about such books. They should select for group sharing only those that are appropriate in that context. Librarians should include controversial books in the collection and must resist the censorship efforts of others in order to preserve the right of children to read what they wish. A librarian would probably not recommend a book about suicide to most children, for example, but she or he must see that such books are available in the library. Although parents' wishes for their own children must be respected, individual preferences cannot be allowed to dictate the reading material available to all children.

## SUMMARY

A major task of teachers and librarians is to see that children have access to reading material that will help them answer questions they have about themselves and the world in general. Libraries must make contemporary fiction available to students, although it is certainly not necessary or possible that schools carry all the books in each of the categories discussed.

Over the last two decades the scope of contemporary fiction has widened to include topics formerly considered inappropriate to children's literature. Children can now get a realistic view of the world around them from books that deal with very familiar subjects such as social acceptance, as well as possibly unfamiliar subjects such as drug abuse. Some works of realistic fiction will help young readers come to terms with feelings and experiences they have already had, whereas other works will allow them to share, vicariously, feelings and experiences they might otherwise never know. In helping young readers use modern fiction to learn about life, teachers and librarians are helping them develop an ability to cope with the diversity of life today.

# Suggestions for Further Study

1. *Harriet the Spy*, commented on favorably in this chapter, received mixed reviews when it was published. *Book Week* (January 16, 1965, p. 18) commented on the book's vigor and originality. *The Horn Book* (February 1965, p. 74) commented that children would not enjoy the book's cynicism. *Library Journal* (November 15, 1964, p. 4638) described Harriet as one of the "meatiest" heroines in children's fiction. Read the reviews, then the book, and decide which review most accurately describes this work.

2. With a Jewish classmate or friend, read either *Berries Goodman* or *About the B'nai Bagels*. Independently of each other, write an analysis of how effectively the book deals with the problem of anti-Semitism. Then compare what you have written. For another view, read "Jewish Identity in Juvenile Fiction," by Eric Kimmel (*The Horn Book*, April 1973, pp. 171–179).

3. Isabelle Holland's *The Man Without a Face* was recommended in this chapter for its sensitive handling of the difficult topic of homosexuality. In *Of Love and Death and Other Journeys* (New York: Lippincott, 1975), Holland writes of Meg Grant's family, who live in Europe until Meg's mother dies. Read this book and think about Holland's ability to create character. In which of the two books are the characters more believable to you? Can you identify reasons for their believability?

4. Eva Nelson, in "Take Cuss Words Out of Kids' Books" (*Wilson Library Bulletin*, October 1974, pp. 132–133), criticizes *Rooftops and Alleys: Adventures with a City Kid*, by Michael Kaufman (New York: Alfred A. Knopf, 1973), and *A Castle of Bone*, by Penelope Farmer (New York: Atheneum, 1972), because of the profanity they contain. Read these books; with another student, role-play a librarian defending them and a parent objecting to them. What arguments can you each develop to convince the other?

5. Read *Dinky Hocker Shoots Smack*, by M. E. Kerr (New York: Harper and Row, 1972), and then share it with a small group of students. Lead a discussion with them centering on three questions: Do they think the portrayal of Dinky's parents as indifferent do-gooders seems convincing? Do they know of parents who are as insensitive as Dinky's were? What are the factors that make parents insensitive to their own children?

6. Read one of the books mentioned as humorous (or some other book of contemporary realistic fiction). Note carefully the sections you think are funny. Then read the book to children. Summarize the similarities and differences between what made you laugh and what makes the children laugh. Then compare your findings with the comments in "Children's Literature: There's Some Sense to Its Humor" (*Childhood Education*, November/December 1985, pp. 109–114), in which author Mary Renck Jalongo summarizes the findings of an extensive array of other researchers, and cites specific children's titles exemplifying the findings.

7. The selection from *Diving for Roses* (pages 481–482), by Charlotte Windsor, is, of necessity, lifted from context. The act of presenting illustrative material this way may distort the nature of a book. Read the whole book, and assess your reaction to it. Apart from Jean's frankness regarding her sexual awareness, do you find her an interesting character? Why or why not? Alternatively, you might read *The Pumpkin Shell* by James Forman (New York: Farrar, Straus and Gi-

roux, 1981) which is also explicit about sex. Do you think students will find the characters interesting? Should they have access to books such as this?

8. For some reason, the name Harriet seems to evoke visions of devilish little girls, involved in endless escapades, for example, the main character in *Harriet the Spy*, described in this chapter. For comparison purposes, see *Harriet and the Haunted School*, by Martin Waddell (Boston: Atlantic Monthly Press, 1984). Beneath this Harriet's cantankerous exterior beats a heart of gold. She wants to help her friend but in the process she lands in the soup (literally). This is improbably overdrawn fiction, yet it works. Read about this Harriet, whose adventures are continued in *Harriet and the Robot* (Boston: Little, Brown, 1987), and see whether you find her more interesting than the other Harriet.

9. This chapter mentioned bibliotherapy, the technique of using books for the express purpose of making children aware of their negative attitudes and subsequently change to more positive ones. The fact sheet "Bibliotherapy" (available from the ERIC Clearinghouse on Reading and Communication Skills, 1111 Kenyon Road, Urbana, Ill. 61801) is a brief but thorough introduction. A longer article that deals with adjustment to death is "Bibliotherapy: Helping Young People Cope with Death," by Mariel Holdaway (*Wisconsin English Journal*, 23, January 1981, pp. 23–30). A problem with the bibliotherapy approach is that advocates sometimes make statements such as this: "Literary quality, *per se*, was not a criterion [in recommending books] because often the most powerful works are not those that are award-winning or renowned" (see Rhea Joyce Rubin's *Bibliotherapy: A Guide to Theory and Practice*, Phoenix, Ariz.: Oryx, 1978, pp. 119–172). Read these sources to see what your response to this technique is.

## Related Reading for Adults

Babbitt, Natalie. "The Great American Novel for Children—And Why Not." *The Horn Book*, April 1972, pp. 176–185.

This versatile writer of poetry (*Dick Foote and the Shark*), mystery stories (*Goody Hall*), and fantasy (*Kneenock Rise*) here analyzes writing for children. Babbitt finds that picture books and teenage novels are full of vigorous activity, but in comparison nothing much is happening in what she calls "children's novels." One possible reason is that authors refuse to accept reality, seeing childhood as the last repository of the American dream.

Barnum, Phyllis W. "Discrimination Against the Aged in Young Children's Literature." *Elementary School Journal*, March 1977, pp. 301–307.

This article reports the results of a content analysis of one hundred books for children, from preschool level through grade three. Barnum concludes that old people appear infrequently, and when they do, they are depicted as more passive, more sickly, and less self-reliant than other adults. Aged women are more drastically underrepresented than aged men and often appear in stereotyped roles.

Fassler, Joan. "Children's Literature and Early Childhood Separation Experiences." *Young Children*, July 1974, pp. 311–323.

Separation of child and parent is a fact of life in America and is likely to increase, given changing family patterns. Fassler is concerned with the effects of four different types of separations and suggests books to help children deal with each type. She lists the books and provides fairly comprehensive summaries of the plots. Her focus is on the use the book will serve, rather than on its literary quality or lack of it.

Greenfield, Eloise. "Something to Shout About." *The Horn Book*, December 1975, pp. 624–626.

Greenfield lists her aims in writing, and, although her books are mainly directed to black children, her goals could apply to any writer writing for children. She is concerned with sustaining children. Despite the limitations of words, "at the right time, in the right circumstances, falling on the right mind, a word may take effect." Other of Greenfield's goals include engendering in children an appreciation of the arts, developing in children a positive self-concept, and presenting to children alternative methods of coping with life.

Konigsburg, Elaine. "The Double Image: Language as the Perimeter of Culture." *Library Journal*, February 15, 1970, pp. 731–734.

In these reflections on the uses of language, Konigsburg concentrates especially on the ways language shows shape and defines limits. She talks about her use of language in *About the B'nai Bagels* to reflect a culture and its shapes. The author also sees language as a tool to poke holes in a culture's perimeter, to let readers enter deeper into its pattern.

MacCann, Donnarae. "Children's Books in a Pluralistic Society." *Wilson Library Bulletin*, October 1976, pp. 154–161.

Racist and sexist books harm children's self-images because children don't have a developed sense of identity. Some books, for instance, *Little Black Sambo*, can be justifiably censored, whereas others cannot. *Sylvester and the Magic Pebble*, for example, should not be censored because children are not the "target."

Madsen, Jane M., and Elaine B. Wickersham. "A Look at Young Children's Realistic Fiction." *The Reading Teacher*, December 1980, pp. 273–279.

Using a sample of seventy-two works of realistic fiction published between 1976 and 1978, Madsen and Wickersham examine traditional/nontraditional roles and stereotyped behavior among other topics. Only a few protagonists, more females than males, exhibited behavior that was not indicative of a sexual stereotype. There were occasions when the illustrations portrayed characters in either traditional or nontraditional roles that the text alone did not indicate. Children were depicted in a variety of social roles; themes were also varied. The most common ethnic group portrayed was Americans of European descent; 10 percent of the books depicted Afro-Americans, but none showed such other groups as Asians and native Americans.

Mertz, Maia Pank, and David A. England. "The Legitimacy of American Adolescent Fiction." *School Library Journal*, October 1983, pp. 119–123.

Mertz and England present ten characteristics of adolescent fiction, giving several examples of specific books illustrating each characteristic. One of the more interesting points they make is that though writers do in fact deal with many formerly taboo topics, they, somewhat paradoxically, advocate a rather conventional morality.

Peck, Richard. "In the Country of Teenage Fiction." *American Libraries*, April 1973, pp. 204–207.

Writing for adolescents is especially challenging because of the pitfalls involved. For instance, no one who has passed through this stage can reenter it with vision unblurred by personal nostalgia. Peck believes, however, that it is necessary to have books written especially for adolescents. In contrast, Babbitt (see above) contends that teenagers do not need a fiction of their own but are able to read adult literature.

Small, Robert C., Jr. "Research and the Young Adult Novel." *Connecticut English Journal*, 15 (Spring 1984), pp. 1–6.

Small asserts that, after many years, the young-adult novel is still looked down on by many teachers, who feel the form is not legitimate. Focusing on the worst examples of the form, some critics denigrate this category, purposely overlooking the many good examples available. Several researchers, including Small himself, have identified characteristics of this literary form; the best young-adult novels make skilled use of these characteristics. Young-adult readers can identify with problems presented in these novels "in a way they could not identify with adult main characters."

Sullivan, Peggy. "Victim of Success? A Closer Look at the Newbery Award." *School Library Journal*, May 1972, pp. 40–42.

Sullivan examines the effect of the Newbery awards on librarians, children, and books. She contends that award status too frequently is the only criterion for book selection and wonders if the book chosen for each year is always the most distinguished one.

Townsend, John Rowe. "Peering into the Fog: The Future of Children's Books." *The Horn Book*, June 1977, pp. 346–355.

Views of the health of children's book publishing conflict and depend largely on whether one is a "book person," a "child person," or a "cause person." Townsend is optimistic about the quality of the output and believes that declining readership is due to factors other than the books themselves.

## Professional References

ACEI–CBC Joint Committee. "Children's Books About Special Children." *Childhood Education*, March/April 1981, 205–208.

Ansello, E. F. "Ageism—The Subtle Stereotype." *Childhood Education*, January 1978, 118–122.

Baskin, Barbara, and Karen H. Harris. *Notes from a Different Drummer. A Guide to Juvenile Fiction Portraying the Handicapped.* New York: R. R. Bowker, 1977, pp. 156–157.

Bernstein, Joanne E. *Books to Help Children Cope with Separation and Loss.* New York: R. R. Bowker, 1983.

Broderick, Dorothy M. *Image of the Black in Children's Fiction.* New York: R. R. Bowker, 1973.

Chambers, Aidan. *Booktalk. Occasional Writing on Literature and Children.* New York: Harper and Row, 1985, pp. 111–115.

Dinchak, Marla. "Recommended: Laurence Yep." *English Journal*, March 1982, 81–82.

Egoff, Sheila. *Only Connect.* Toronto: Oxford University Press, 1980, p. 356.

Elkind, David. *The Hurried Child.* Reading, Mass.: Addison-Wesley, 1981.

Fisher, Laura. "All Chiefs, No Indians: What Children's Books Say About American Indians." *Elementary English*, February 1974, 185–189.

Gilliland, Hap. *Indian Children's Books.* Billings, Mont.: Montana Council for Indian Education, 1980.

Hoffman, Lyla. "Review of *I Have a Sister, My Sister is Deaf.*" *Interracial Books for Children Bulletin*, 8 (1977), 17.

Holdaway, Mariel. "Bibliotherapy: Helping Young People Cope with Death." *Wisconsin English Journal*, 23 (January 1981), 23–30.

Huck, Charlotte. *Children's Literature in the Elementary School*. New York: Holt, Rinehart and Winston, 1979.

Huus, Helen. "Teaching Literature at the Elementary School Level." *The Reading Teacher*, May 1973, 795–801.

Jalongo, Mary Renck, and Melissa Ann Renck. "Sibling Relationships. A Recurrent Developmental and Literary Theme." *Childhood Education*, May/June 1985, 346–351.

Jenkins, C. A., and Julie L. Morris. "Recommended Books on Gay/Lesbian Themes." *Interracial Books for Children Bulletin*, 14, (1983), 16–19.

Kimmel, Mary Margaret, and Elizabeth Segel. *For Reading Out Loud*. New York: Delacorte, 1983, pp. 69–70.

Lass, Bonnie, and Marcia Bromfield. "Books About Children with Special Needs: An Annotated Bibliography." *The Reading Teacher*, February 1981, 530–533.

Lehr, Susan. "Helping Children Respond to *Dogsong:* A Guide." *The Bulletin*, Spring 1986, 16–18.

Lukens, Rebecca. *A Critical Handbook of Children's Literature*. Glenview, Ill.: Scott, Foresman, 1986, p. 122.

MacCann, Donnarae, and Gloria Woodare. *The Black American in Books for Children*, 2nd ed. Metuchen, N.J.: Scarecrow Press, 1985.

MacLeod, Anne Scott. "Censorship and Children's Literature." *Library Quarterly*, 53 (1983), 26–38.

Montgomery-Aaron, Patricia. "Positive Parental Images in Children's Literature." *Childhood Education*, March/April 1986, 287–291.

Munson, Tunie. "Using Books as Healers and Helpers." *Learning*, March 1986, 63–65.

Olsen, Henry D. "Bibliotherapy to Help Children Solve Problems." *Elementary School Journal*, April 1975, 420–429.

Paterson, Katherine. "Newbery Award Acceptance." *The Horn Book*, 54 (August 1978), 361–367.

Peck, Richard. "Rape and the Teenage Victim." *Top of the News*, Winter 1978, 173–177.

Polette, Nancy, and Marjorie Hamlin. *Exploring Books with Gifted Children*. Littleton, Colo.: Libraries Unlimited, 1980, pp. 87–90.

Rees, David. *Painted Desert, Green Shade: Essays on Contemporary Writers of Fiction for Children and Young Adults*. Boston: The Horn Book, 1984.

Rigg, Pat. "Those Spunky Gals: An Annotated Bibliography." *The Reading Teacher*, 39 (November 1985), 154–160.

Sadker, Myra, and David Sadker. *Now Upon a Time*. New York: Harper and Row, 1977.

Schon, Isabel. "Recent Children's Books on Mexico." *The Reading Teacher*, October 1986, 106–107.

Stensland, Anna. *Literature By and About the American Indian*. Urbana, Ill.: National Council of Teachers of English, 1979.

Wagoner, Shirley A. "Mexican-Americans in Children's Literature Since 1970." *The Reading Teacher*, December 1982, 274–279.

Watson, Jerry J. "A Positive Image of the Elderly in Children's Literature." *The Reading Teacher*, 34 (April 1981), 792–798.

Western, Linda E. "New Realism—A Second Look." *Wisconsin English Journal*, 23 (January 1981), 9–12.

Wolf, Virginia. "Same-Sex Relations in the Contemporary Novel for Adolescents." *Wisconsin English Journal*, 20 (January 1978), 27–32.

Wynn, Marie. *Children Without Childhood*. New York: Pantheon, 1983.

# Bibliography of Children's Books

Alexander, Lloyd. *The Town Cats and Other Tales.* New York: E. P. Dutton, 1977.

Anonymous. *Go Ask Alice.* Englewood Cliffs, N.J.: Prentice-Hall, 1971.

Bargar, Gary. *What Happened to Mr. Forster?* New York: Clarion Books, 1981.

Bauer, Marion D. *Foster Child.* New York: Seabury, 1977.

Beim, Lorraine, and Jerrold Beim. *Two Is a Team.* New York: Harcourt, Brace, 1945.

Blume, Judy. *Are You There, God? It's Me, Margaret.* New York: Dell, 1970.

———. *Deenie.* Scarsdale, N.Y.: Bradbury, 1973.

———. *The One in the Middle Is the Green Kangaroo.* New York: Riley and Lee, 1969.

———. *Otherwise Known as Sheila the Great.* New York: E. P. Dutton, 1972.

———. *Then Again, Maybe I Won't.* New York: Bradbury, 1971.

Bond, Nancy. *A String in the Harp.* New York: Atheneum, 1977.

Bonham, Frank. *Viva Chicano.* New York: E. P. Dutton, 1970.

Bragdon, Elspeth. *There Is a Tide.* New York: Viking, 1964.

Branscum, Robbie. *Spud Tackett and the Angel of Doom.* New York: Viking, 1983.

Bridgers, Sue Ellen. *Notes for Another Life.* New York: Alfred A. Knopf, 1981.

Brooks, Jerome. *The Testing of Charlie Hammelman.* New York: E. P. Dutton, 1977.

Brown, Margaret Wise. *The Dead Bird.* New York: Young, Scott, 1958.

Byars, Betsy. *The Midnight Fox.* New York: Viking, 1968.

———. *The Pinballs.* New York: Harper and Row, 1977.

Caudill, Rebecca. *Did You Carry the Flag Today, Charley?* New York: Holt, Rinehart and Winston, 1966.

Chaikin, Miriam. *Yossi Asks the Angels for Help.* New York: Harper and Row, 1985.

Chambers, Aidan. *Dance on My Grave.* New York: Harper and Row, 1982.

Childress, Alice. *A Hero Ain't Nothin' But a Sandwich.* New York: Coward, McCann and Geoghegan, 1973.

Clark, Ann Nolan. *Secret of the Andes.* New York: Viking, 1952.

Cleaver, Vera, and Bill Cleaver. *Me Too.* Philadelphia: J. B. Lippincott, 1973.

———. *Grover.* Philadelphia: J. B. Lippincott, 1970.

———. *Where the Lilies Bloom.* Philadelphia: J. B. Lippincott, 1969.

Cohen, Barbara. *Benny.* New York: Lothrop, Lee and Shepard, 1977.

Colman, Hila. *Chicano Girl.* New York: Morrow, 1973.

Conford, Ellen. *If This Is Love, I'll Take Spaghetti.* New York: Scholastic, 1983.

———. *Why Me?* Boston: Little, Brown, 1985.

Corcoran, Barbara. *A Dance to Still Music.* New York: Atheneum, 1974.

———. *The Winds of Time.* New York: Atheneum, 1974.

Cresswell, Helen. *Absolute Zero.* New York: Macmillan, 1978.

———. *Bagthorpes Abroad.* New York: Macmillan, 1984.

———. *Bagthorpes Haunted.* New York: Macmillan, 1985.

———. *Bagthorpes Unlimited.* New York: Macmillan, 1978.

———. *Bagthorpes v. the World.* New York: Macmillan, 1979.

———. *Ordinary Jack.* New York: Macmillan, 1977.

Cunningham, Julia. *Come to the Edge.* New York: Pantheon, 1977.

———. *Dorp Dead*. New York: Pantheon, 1965.

Dahl, Roald. *Danny the Champion of the World*. New York: Alfred A. Knopf, 1975.

DeClements, Barthe. *6th Grade Can Really Kill You*. New York: Viking/Kestrel, 1985.

Dickinson, Peter. *Heartsease*. Boston: Little, Brown, 1969.

Distad, Audree. *The Dream Runner*. New York: Harper and Row, 1977.

Donovan, John. *I'll Get There. It Better Be Worth the Trip*. New York: Harper and Row, 1969.

Estes, Eleanor. *The Hundred Dresses*. New York: Harcourt, Brace, 1942.

Fitzhugh, Louise. *Harriet the Spy*. New York: Harper and Row, 1964.

———. *The Long Secret*. New York: Harper and Row, 1965.

Forsman, Bettie. *From Lupita's Hill*. New York: Atheneum, 1973.

Fox, Paula. *A Likely Place*. New York: Macmillan, 1967.

Freedman, Benedict, and Nancy Freedman. *Mrs. Mike*. New York: Coward, McCann and Geoghegan, 1968.

Gee, Maurine. *Chicano Amigo*. New York: Morrow, 1972.

Girion, Barbara. *Joshua, the Czar, and the Chicken Bone Wish*. New York: Scribner's, 1978.

Greene, Constance C. *Beat the Turtle Drum*. New York: Viking, 1976.

———. *A Girl Called Al*. New York: Viking, 1969.

———. *I Know You, Al*. New York: Viking, 1975.

———. *Just Plain Al*. New York: Viking/Kestrel, 1986.

———. *Your Old Pal, Al*. New York: Viking, 1979.

Grimes, Nikki. *Growin'*. New York: Dial, 1977.

Gripe, Maria. *The Night Daddy*. New York: Delacorte, 1971.

Guy, Rosa. *Ruby*. New York: Viking, 1976.

Hall, Lynn. *Sticks and Stones*. Chicago: Follett, 1972.

Hamilton, Virginia. *Arilla Sun Down*. New York: Greenwillow, 1976.

———. *M. C. Higgins, the Great*. New York: Macmillan, 1974.

———. *Sweet Whispers, Brother Rush*. New York: Philomel, 1982.

Heide, Florence Parry. *Sound of Sunshine, Sound of Rain*. New York: Parents Magazine Press, 1970.

Hinton, S. E. *That Was Then, This Is Now*. New York: Viking, 1971.

Holland, Isabelle. *The Man Without a Face*. Boston: G. K. Hall, 1972.

Holman, Felice. *Slake's Limbo*. New York: Scribner's, 1974.

Holmes, Barbara Ware. *Charlotte Cheetham: Master of Disaster*. New York: Harper and Row, 1985.

Howker, Janni. *Badger on the Barge*. New York: Julia MacRae, 1984.

———. *The Nature of the Beast*. New York: Greenwillow, 1985.

Hunt, Irene. *The Lottery Rose*. New York: Scribner's, 1976.

Irwin, Betty K. *Behind the Magic Line*. Boston: Little, Brown, 1969.

Iwasaki, Chihiro. *Will You Be My Friend?* New York: McGraw-Hill, 1973.

Johnson, A. E. *A Blues I Can Whistle*. New York: Four Winds, 1969.

Jukes, Mavis. *Blackberries in the Dark*. New York: Alfred A. Knopf, 1985.

Kaplan, Bess. *The Empty Chair*. New York: Harper and Row, 1978.

Kerr, M. E. *I Stay Near You*. New York: Harper and Row, 1985.

———. *I'll Love You When You're More Like Me*. New York: Harper and Row, 1977.

———. *Little Little*. New York: Harper and Row, 1981.

Klein, Norma. *Confessions of an Only Child*. New York: Pantheon, 1974.

———. *It's Not What You Expect.* New York: Pantheon, 1973.

———. *Tomboy.* New York: Four Winds, 1978.

Konigsburg, E. L. *About the B'nai Bagels.* New York: Atheneum, 1973.

———. *Father's Arcane Daughter.* New York: Atheneum, 1976.

———. *Jennifer, Hecate, Macbeth, William McKinley and Me, Elizabeth.* New York: Atheneum, 1967.

Krasilovsky, Phyllis. *The Popular Girls Club.* New York: Simon and Schuster, 1972.

Lampman, Evelyn Sibley. *The Potlatch Family.* New York: Atheneum, 1976.

L'Engle, Madeline. *The Arm of the Starfish.* New York: Farrar, Straus and Giroux, 1965.

———. *A Wrinkle in Time.* New York: Farrar, Straus and Giroux, 1962.

———. *The Young Unicorns.* New York: Farrar, Straus and Giroux, 1968.

Lorenzo, Carol L. *Mama's Ghosts.* New York: Harper and Row, 1974.

Lowry, Lois. *A Summer to Die.* Boston: Houghton Mifflin, 1977.

Mann, Peggy. *My Dad Lives in a Downtown Hotel.* Garden City, N.Y.: Doubleday, 1973.

Mathis, Sharon Bell. *The Hundred Penny Box.* New York: Viking, 1975.

Miles, Betty. *Sink or Swim.* New York: Alfred A. Knopf, 1986.

———. *The Trouble with Thirteen.* New York: Alfred A. Knopf, 1979.

Miles, Miska. *Annie and the Old One.* Boston: Little, Brown, 1971.

———. *Gertrude's Pocket.* Boston: Little, Brown, 1970.

Mohr, Nicholosa. *In Neuva York.* New York: Dial, 1977.

Naylor, Phyllis Reynolds. *How Lazy Can You Get?* New York: Atheneum, 1979.

Neufeld, John. *Freddy's Book.* New York: Random House, 1973.

———. *Lisa, Bright and Dark.* Chatham, N.Y.: S. G. Phillips, 1969.

Neville, Emily C. *Berries Goodman.* New York: Harper and Row, 1965.

———. *It's Like This, Cat.* New York: Harper and Row, 1963.

Ney, John. *Ox.* Boston: Little, Brown, 1970.

———. *Ox Goes North.* New York: Harper and Row, 1974.

Orgel, Doris. *The Mulberry Music.* New York: Harper and Row, 1971.

Paterson, Katherine. *Bridge to Terabithia.* New York: Harper and Row, 1977.

Paulsen, Gary. *Dogsong.* New York: Bradbury, 1985.

Peck, Richard. *Are You in the House Alone?* New York: Viking, 1976.

Peterson, Jeanne. *I Have a Sister, My Sister Is Deaf.* New York: Harper and Row, 1977.

Platt, Kin. *Hey, Dummy.* New York: Dell, 1973.

Robinson, Veronica. *David in Silence.* Philadelphia: J. B. Lippincott, 1966.

Rockwell, Thomas. *How to Eat Fried Worms.* New York: Franklin Watts, 1973.

Rosenblum, Richard. *My Bar Mitzvah.* New York: Morrow, 1985.

Ryder, Joanne. *A Wet and Sandy Day.* New York: Harper and Row, 1977.

Sachs, Marilyn. *The Bears' House.* Garden City, N.Y.: Doubleday, 1971.

Say, Allen. *The Feast of Lanterns.* New York: Harper and Row, 1976.

Scoppettone, Sandra. *Trying Hard to Hear You.* New York: Harper and Row, 1974.

Scott, Ann H. *Sam.* New York: McGraw-Hill, 1967.

Sherburne, Zoa. *Too Bad About the Haines Girl.* New York: Morrow, 1967.

Smith, Doris Buchanan. *A Taste of Blackberries.* New York: Thomas Y. Crowell, 1973.

Southall, Ivan. *Ash Road.* New York: St. Martin's, 1965.

———. *To the Wild Sky.* New York: St. Martin's, 1967.

Stevenson, William. *The Bushbabies.* Boston: Houghton Mifflin, 1965.

Stewart, A. C. *Dark Dove.* New York: S. G. Phillips, 1974.

Thomas, Ianthe. *My Street's a Morning Cool Street.* New York: Harper and Row, 1976.

Tobias, Tobi. *Chasing the Goblins Away.* New York: Frederick Warne, 1977.

Townsend, John Rowe. *Good-bye to the Jungle.* Philadelphia: J. B. Lippincott, 1967.

———. *Hell's Edge.* Baltimore: Penguin, 1968.

Walsh, Jill Paton. *Gaffer Samson's Luck.* New York: Farrar, Straus and Giroux, 1984.

Wersba, Barbara. *The Carnival in My Mind.* New York: Harper and Row, 1982.

———. *The Dream Watcher.* New York: Atheneum, 1968.

Windsor, Charlotte. *Diving for Roses.* New York: Harper and Row, 1976.

Yep, Laurence. *Child of the Owl.* New York: Harper and Row, 1977.

———. *Dragon Steel.* New York: Harper and Row, 1985.

———. *The Serpent Child.* New York: Harper and Row, 1984.

Zindel, Paul. *My Darling, My Hamburger.* New York: Harper and Row, 1969.

———. *Pigman.* New York: Harper and Row, 1968.

# FANTASY: BUT COULD IT REALLY HAPPEN?

Alice was beginning to get very tired of sitting by her sister on the bank and of having nothing to do.

*Alice's Adventures in Wonderland*, by Lewis Carroll

This is the tale of King Fflewddur Fflam and his truthful harp, as the bards tell it in the Land of Prydain.

*The Truthful Harp*, by Lloyd Alexander

She was alive inside but dead outside, her face a black and dun net of wrinkles, tumors, cracks. She was bald and blind. The tremors that crossed Libra's face were mere quiverings of corruption.

*The Wind's Twelve Quarters*, by Ursula LeGuin

Diverse opening lines such as these introduce readers to the world of children's fantasy, which encompasses simple stories about a few talking animals in a realistic setting, as well as extraordinarily complex tales about large numbers of unusual beings in improbable places. Because of the wealth of fantasy that is available, teachers and librarians should be familiar with its different categories. If one kind does not appeal to a child, perhaps another kind will.

## CHARACTERISTICS OF GOOD FANTASY

In writing fantasy, authors must create characters, setting, and action that are so interesting that the reader is willing to suspend disbelief and enter the world being presented.

Lloyd Alexander has been lauded for his ability to create fantasy, for example, his *The Cat Who Wished to Be a Man*. One of Alexander's strengths is creating believable characters. When the story begins, Alexander shows us a wizard who is stirring a kettle of soup: "A high wizard, Stephanus could have commanded the soup to look after itself; but he preferred to do his own cooking." The wizard shares other human characteristics that make him interesting to readers. When perplexed, he tugs at his beard, a common manifestation of annoyance. When Lionel the cat will not abandon his demands to be changed into a human, Stephanus finally consents, muttering, "So be it. Let's get on, then. I've better things to do then change cats into men." Certain words that Stephanus uses are unfamiliar to Lionel. Talking about the people in the neighboring village, Stephanus says,

"They care for nothing, not even each other. Love? They love only gold."
"What's gold?" asked the cat, more curious than ever.
"A yellow substance. Men treasure it."
"It must be delicious," Lionel said. "I wish I could taste some."

Not only is this misunderstanding humorous, it is also very believable, given the fact that Lionel is a cat. After he is transformed into a man, Lionel doesn't realize that he is naked or that clothes are necessary. Even after Stephanus convinces him he must conform to this human foible, Lionel doesn't know how to put the clothes on.

The more fantastic the story, the more necessary it becomes to supply some firm anchor in reality. In *The Swing in the Summerhouse*, author Jane Langton provides a solid grounding in realistic details, such as squabbles between the children and a description of Eddy's room as a haven for a future junk man.[1] In this story, Aunt Lily and her husband, Prince Krishna, have been called to India suddenly, leaving Eddy and Eleanor at home with absent-minded Uncle Freddy. Prince Krishna has magical abilities and has built the children a six-sided summerhouse. One doorway is unfinished; before leaving for India, Krishna secures this door with a "Keep Out" sign. The fantasy grows from this firmly established realism. The children, Uncle Freddy, neighbor Oliver Winslow, Mrs. Dorian, and her daughter Georgie eventually have all gone through the forbidden door.

> Then they came upon something that was altogether unfamiliar. "Look at that," said Eddy. "I told you this wasn't *our* house. What's that statue doing in our backyard?"
>
> There beside the barn loomed a large marble pedestal, and on the pedestal stood a life-size marble statue. It looked to Eleanor like a piece of Greek sculpture in a museum, and she started forward to study it.
>
> "Don't," said Eddy. "Don't go near it. There's something awful about it." His eyesight was keener than Eleanor's, and he could see something that she could not. . . . The statue was not a likeness of Greek youth, dressed in the loose classic draperies of a piece of sculpture in a museum; it was a statue of their old friend Oliver Winslow, wearing a marble shirt with too-short sleeves that showed his knobby wrists and marble pants that rode halfway up his legs. Eleanor put her hand to her mouth to keep from crying out. Oliver Winslow! But what an amazing portrait. . . .
>
> Eleanor didn't want to look at the sculpture anymore. She stamped her feet because they felt as if they were going to sleep. Eleanor's fingers felt full

---

[1] This is the second in a series of adventures about Eleanor and Edward Hall. The first was *The Diamond in the Window* (New York: Harper and Row, 1962); the third was *The Astonishing Stereoscope* (New York: Harper and Row, 1971). Georgie Hall, a minor character in the earlier books, emerges as a person in her own right in *The Fledgling* (New York: Harper and Row, 1980) and *The Fragile Flag* (New York: Harper and Row, 1984).

of pins and needles, and she held them up and looked at them. The tips were whitish, as if they were frostbitten. But it wasn't even cold. Eleanor blew on them and wiggled them and rubbed her hands together.

"I think I must be getting the flu," she said. "My joints are getting so stiff I can hardly move."

Eddy looked at his sister, and dread filled him once more. "Eleanor, what's the matter with your face?"

"My face?"

"It's so pale." It was; it was a dead-white like paper, like snow, like—like marble.

## LOGIC AND CONSISTENCY IN FANTASY

Logic must pervade within any fantasy from beginning to end. In Lloyd Alexander's *The Cat Who Wished to Be a Man,* it is illogical for Lionel to want to be a man, as Stephanus sees it, "Man, indeed! You're not even a full-grown cat. . . . You are not old enough to know how you feel about anything at all." It has been established that Stephanus could easily change an animal into a human, but the nonsense of a young orange-tawny cat wanting to be a man upsets him. A perfectly logical reaction under the circumstances.

As any fantasy develops, the author faces the difficult task of controlling all the small details so the fantasy is consistent. Nothing can seem out of place or contrary to the imaginary order that has been created. If, in the universe the author has imagined, the frogs can speak English, there had better be a good reason why the horses cannot. Or if the goats are wearing trousers, why are the pigs' bottoms exposed to the air? To use a different example, if a wizard has magic powers in one scene, he cannot lose these powers in a following scene without a convincing reason.

For instance, early in Alexander's story, Lionel retains many catlike abilities. He leaps easily over the tollgate bridge and only after much urging from a fellow fugitive will he escape via the river. Alexander reinforces the cat images, despite Lionel's transformation into a man.

Shuddering as much with distaste as with chill, Lionel shook himself from head to foot, then crouched on the pebbles, dabbed away the water from his face, and rubbed at his water-filled ears.

"I've never been so wet in all my life," he moaned. "I've never gone swimming before, either; and I don't mean to do it again."

But as he remains longer and longer with people, these cat abilities begin to fade. Toward the end, the evil Swaggart is pursuing Lionel and Dr. Tudbelly.

> Lionel . . . lost his footing on the cobble and lurched against the side of a building. In horror, he realized he was nearly blind. Darkness had always been as clear as day to him. Now he could make out only vague shapes and looming shadows. His cat's vision was gone.

In *Up from Jericho Tel*, author E. L. Konigsburg creates an absolutely preposterous fantasy that succeeds because of the consistent characterization. Her two main characters, Malcolm and Jeanmarie, are credible because they sound so much like real children, as in this example:

> "I'm very neat," Malcolm said. "It's a talent I have."
> "Being neat is just something that is easier for some people than for others."
> "That's why I would call it a talent," Malcolm said. "Like playing the piano is easier for some people than it is for others, and that's called a talent."
> I told him that I would call it congenital, like a heart murmur or a strawberry birth mark or a clubfoot.

The two children, both unpopular, are drawn together despite their differences. Their relationship is solidified when they tumble through an opening in the earth, pass through two magical boxes, and encounter a dead actress named Tallulah (Bankhead), who sets them on a task. They pass from the real to the fantasy world with ease, at last completing the task, though not in the way either of them envisioned. They have this special ability to move between worlds, but pragmatic Jeanmarie wants to find out what else, if anything, they can do. So she attempts to walk through a closed door; she cannot do it. Konigsburg has established consistent limits to this fantasy.

## LANGUAGE IN FANTASY

The language used has an important effect on the mood of a fantasy. For example, an author might purposely choose an archaic word, describing horses who are "caparisoned" in silver and gold. "Harnessed" would have conveyed a similar thought, but the older word establishes a sense of the past. Richard Adams went so far as to create an entire language for the rabbits in *Watership Down*. Short of this extreme, there are varied uses of language in fantasy.

Some fantasy writers use unfamiliar names that follow common English phonological patterns. Examples are plentiful in Zilpha Keatley Snyder's *Below the Root*. "Kindar" (similar to the English word *kindred*) is the word for the people of Green-sky. "Pense" is similar to the Latin word

***The uplifting of the eyes and the upward thrust of the arms direct attention to the plant.***
Illustration by Alton Raible from *Below the Root* by Zilpha Keatley Snyder. Copyright © 1975 by Zilpha Keatley Snyder. Reprinted with permission of Atheneum Publishers.

*pensare,* which means to weigh carefully or to consider and is the root of the English word *pensive.* "Pensing" in the story means to know via ESP or telepathy. "Orchardgrund" is used as a place name; the suffix "grund" is similar to the English word *ground.* "Pash-shan" is the name given to those who dwell below the root. Leaders of Green-sky have told the people that the Pash-shan are the embodiment of evil, foreign to the peace-loving ways of Green-sky, where words of violence are unknown. The Pash-shan are supposedly subhuman and are believed to rend (with long claws), in a *passion,* any Kindar who is unfortunate enough to fall to the forest floor.

What makes *Up from Jericho Tel* so readable is E. L. Konigsburg's impressive language skills. She uses modern language to make her fantasy believable. This trenchant comment by the female main character, Jean-marie, is typical:

> Our teacher last year had shown us a film strip of microscopic life in a drop of water, and I thought that it should have had an R rating; I found the unseen world violent, full of sex, and with no redeeming social value.

Malcolm also observes his world with childlike frankness, in this case talking about seeing the Rockettes perform at Radio City Music Hall:

> I liked them for the first ten minutes or so. They did everything very precisely. Then I got bored. I thought it was a lot like coloring and staying inside the lines.

Tallulah's comment on hearing Malcolm has gone to see the Rockettes further establishes her believability.

> "Imagine someone paying to see the Rockettes. It is rather like paying to watch someone stir soup."

An admirable use of language is always characteristic of Konigsburg's work, and throughout this book the many enjoyably evocative lines establish a contemporary mood.

## CHARACTERIZATION IN FANTASY

Like other genres, effective fantasy requires strong characterizations. In *The Wizard in the Tree,* Lloyd Alexander creates Mallory, a strong female heroine, and other characters who oppose her. For example, Mrs. Parsel, with whom Mallory lives, has a low opinion of her:

> "It's the fairy tales. . . . They've chewed away at her mind until there's hardly a rind left."

*The artificiality of the woman is effectively expressed in the crook of her fingers, the tilt of her head, and the crossing of her legs.* From *The Wizard in the Tree* by Lloyd Alexander, illustrated by Laszlo Kubinyi. Illustrations copyright © 1975 by Laszlo Kubinyi. Reproduced by permission of the publisher, E. P. Dutton, a division of NAL Penguin Inc.

The Squire is equally disdainful of Mallory's interest in fairy tales.

> "A heavy burden you bear, Mrs. Parsel. But I fear not much can be done. Once these fancies infect the brain, they're not easily cured. I tell you, Mrs. Parsel, I'd rather a dozen cases of small pox than one case of the fairy tales."

In these two selections, the author is demonstrating a characteristic of good writing. He shows what the characters are like through the dialogue, rather than telling what they are like through narrative.

Effective characterizations can be achieved with descriptions of physical features. In *The Foundling and Other Tales of Prydain*, a collection of six short stories by Lloyd Alexander, the characters are drawn from a classic collection of Welsh legends. In the title story, Witch Orddu is described as "a short, plump woman with a round, lumpy face." She and her three sisters look after Dallben. All is peaceful until he must choose one of their gifts to take into the world. The book of knowledge seems a wise choice, but results in a sad transformation in Dallben.

> His fair, bright curls had gone frost-white and fell below his brittle shoulders. His cheeks, once full and flushed with youth, were now hollow and wrinkled, half hidden by a long, gray beard. His brow, smooth yesterday, was scarred and furrowed, his hands gnarled and knotted, his eyes pale as if their color had been wept away.

Another story in this collection relates the consequences of never growing old, in a humorous way. In "The True Enchanter," a very self-assured princess chooses the least prepossessing of her three suitors. "The Rascal Crow" seems reminiscent of some Aesop fables but is more fully developed.

Grossly improbable happenings are acceptable in fantasy if the characters are believable. One way authors make characters seem real is to have them truly care about something outside themselves or about someone else.

In *The Hobbit* by J. R. R. Tolkien, one of the most famous of all quest stories, the characters all care deeply about succeeding in their quest. Although the quest begins with high intentions—to right an ancient wrong by killing Smaug, the dragon who slaughtered many of the dwarfs and stole their treasure—it rapidly becomes motivated by greed on the part of the dwarf Thorin Oakenshield, leader of the band. For Bilbo, the hobbit, the motive is to live up to the expectations of the wizard Gandalf and the thirteen other members of the company. So strong are the characters' motives (altruism, greed, and the desire to save face) that they bravely face up to goblins, trolls, giants, spiders, the gloom of Mirkwood, and the terror of the Lonely Mountain. Michael Hague's rather dark full- and double-page paintings are packed with details that evoke the otherworldly environment of Tolkien's words.[2]

Two other fantasy characters who believe in something far greater than themselves are Rana and Hekura, in *Light in the Mountain*, by Margaret J. Anderson. Rana's crooked back and limbs make her an outcast, but she is

---

[2]*Poems and Songs of Middle Earth* is available from Caedmon Records (either as a disc, #TC1231, or a cassette, #CP1231).

still chosen to be the victim to be sacrificed to Atua Ahi, the God of Fire. Rana will be cast into the volcano. Matakana has a scheme to prevent her sacrifice and advance himself; when he and his followers set out by boat to seek the new land, they take Rana with them. The frail child regains her strength as old Hekura ministers to her. In the process, they both come to a sense of mission: they must lead the band in following Atua Ahi's precepts and free the group from evil Matakana's influence. Readers are drawn to these characters because of their governing belief in something more important than themselves.

Old and young characters are united, despite their differences, in *Glom Gloom*, by Jo Dereske. The author describes old Wicker Bugle, and youngsters Raymond, Bort, and Merrily in ways that make readers care about their efforts to defend their homeland, Waterpushin. Raymond is an often devilish boy and trouble follows him "like the tail of a mousling." He questions what is "for true" of the fragments of early history surrounding the annual Gloom Day celebration, which commemorates the defending of the Gartergates against the invading Weeuns. Old Wicker Bugle is known to be crazy but harmless, a toothless hag dressed in an assortment of tattered clothes. She declares the truth of the history fragments. Determined to find out what really happened, Raymond steals one of the only two maps of Waterpushin and is drawn into a quest to find the physical location of the Gartergates. With him is Bort, "so skinny his clothes hung as unwrinkled as if they were still on a hanger," as well as Merrily Cumbers. The children discover the Gartergates and in the process find out that the old tales are true. To fend off the Weeuns' planned invasion, the children must have old Wicker Bugle's help. She alone can read the secret language of the accounts of the earlier conflict. Finally, the children's efforts foil the invasion plan. The plot is exciting, the conflict eminently believable, and the setting easily visualized in the reader's mind. But it is in the characterizations that author Dereske's talents become fully apparent. She creates people readers want to see succeed, as they work for a cause larger than their own personal concerns.

## SETTING IN FANTASY

Effective fantasy is characterized by compelling descriptions of setting. Sometimes writers create magical places, unlike any the reader has ever visited. In *The Princess and the Goblin*, by George MacDonald, twelve-year-old Curdie, a miner, enters the goblins' lair to spy on them.

> He was at the entrance of a magnificent cavern of an oval shape, once probably a huge natural reservoir of water, now the great palace hall. It rose to a tre-

> mendous height, but the roof was composed of such shining materials, and the multitude of torches carried by the goblins . . . lighted up the place so brilliantly, that Curdie could see to the top quite well. But he had no idea how immense the place was, until his eyes had got accustomed to it. . . . The rough projections on the walls, and the shadows thrown upward from them by the torches, made the sides of the chamber look as if they were crowded with statues . . . reaching in irregular tiers from floor to roof. The walls themselves were . . . of gloriously shining substances, some of them gorgeously colored besides, which contrasted powerfully with the shadows.

This book has recently been reissued, with an afterword giving details of MacDonald's life and the circumstances of the first publication of the book. This new edition includes Jessie Willcox Smith's illustrations, originally done in 1920.

At other times, writers use compelling descriptions to invest commonplace settings with special mystery. *Nothing Said*, by Lucy M. Boston, is the introspective story of Libby, a preteenaged girl visiting in the country. She thinks she sees a nymph among the trees but isn't really sure until the water of the rising river, the Babble, fells a tree. The nymph comforts Libby over the loss of her tree, and Libby brings the nymph into her bedroom. The next morning the nymph is gone. On the surface, nothing much really happens in the story. Its introspective nature derives from the descriptions of the Babble, the river that dominates the story. This is Libby's first meeting with the river:

> Most wonderful of all, and running through the whole of it, filling it with thrilling sound, was the Babble. It was the kind of river that has gravel and pebbles at each side and flows round and over big stones in the center. Over each smooth boulder it made a waterfall, and under each waterfall there was an eddy with bubbles circling round and round. Little rapids escaped from the eddies in any direction they could find, and hurried along to the next hold-up. The whole stream flashed in the sun and chattered like a swarm of children.

Later, the Babble's character changes.

> When Libby woke in the morning these watery noises were still going on, but the river was no longer chattering. It was laying down the law angrily, and nothing was going to stand in its way. Through every window she heard it as she came downstairs.

After laying in provisions in case the flood should cut off the road to the village, Libby and Julia go to inspect the river.

> It could no longer be called the Babble. No boulders showed about its waters, no waterfalls, no wandering swirls, but a great purposeful rush of deep water making for the sea. There was no laughing chatter now, but a shrill hissing of tearing ripples, and at the sides a slapping, sucking and swallowing.

Strong description of setting is also apparent in *The River Witches*, by Ben Shecter. An unusual array of characters, witches and warlocks, inhabits Wiltwick Landing. Shecter evokes the musty, dim recesses of the shop and the pleasantly languid garden behind the shop in images that make these places seem very real. The garden-party lunch that Andrew, unsuspecting son of a farmer, and Auntie Wixard and Miss Celestial Grace, two witches, enjoy is masterfully described.

Another kind of setting, especially common in ghost stories, is a house that seems to have taken on a life of its own. As repositories of history, houses can become forces for good or evil, profoundly affecting those who shelter within their walls. As an example, in Patricia McKillip's *The House on Parchment Street*, ghosts haunt a house located across from a graveyard. Carol Christopher, newly arrived from California for a visit, sees the first ghost before she unpacks her suitcase. Approaching the house for the first time, she sees

> a massive square house [that] sat firm and ancient beyond the wall, stone-grey beneath a beard of ivy. . . . Her head turned slowly toward the closed gate and the grey house hidden behind it.

This is an ancient structure, as her uncle Harold tells her:

> "This used to be a vicarage, a place where the parish priests lived. . . . Parts of it have been rebuilt from time to time, but other parts, like this stone floor and the great broad beam above the fireplace, suggest that the house was not built three hundred years ago, but rather rebuilt from an even older foundation."

The *Green Knowe* series, by Lucy M. Boston, contains a notable example of a house so strongly drawn that it almost becomes another character instead of simply a setting. Six stories explore the house's role as an enduring bastion against the darkness of evil. Beginning with *The Children of Green Knowe*, the series continues with *Treasure of Green Knowe, A Stranger at Green Knowe, The Enemy at Green Knowe*, and *The Stones of Green Knowe*. *The Guardians of the House*, for intermediate-grade children, is a short fantasy set in the future. One description of the remarkable house is found near the beginning of *The Enemy at Green Knowe*:

> To both of them, it was now home and also the most wonderful place on earth. It was like nowhere else, because while most houses are built to shut out everything but the inmates, to close doors and draw curtains equally against the cold winds . . . and the curiosity of neighbors. . . . Green Knowe was full of mysteries. Certainly it was welcoming and comfortable . . . but one had the feeling that behind the exciting colors and shapes of its ancient self, there might be surprises from the unknown universe; that the house was on good terms with that, too, and had no intention of shutting out the ununderstandable.

## ENDINGS IN FANTASY

The equivocal ending is particularly characteristic of long, complex fantasies for older readers. The author sets up a situation for which more than one ending is possible and does not give the reader a definite indication of what will happen. *The Delikon*, by H. M. Hoover, tells of Varina, a 307-year-old teacher who looks like a child of 10. When the starship arrives, Varina knows it is time to leave Earth and return to her own planet and people, a long-lived race of superintelligent beings. But Earth has long been held in thrall by the Delikon and the seeds of rebellion blossom into revolution, trapping Varina and her two young charges, Jason and Alta, between armies. In the end, Varina is the only one of her race left on Earth, but she sees what may be either a meteor or her planet's starship returning for her. The author purposely leaves the ending open.

> . . . she . . . ran down across the lawn and disappeared behind the hedge of the topiary garden.
>> "Are you coming back?"
>
> She heard Jason call, but she could not answer because she did not know.

In Lucy M. Boston's *The Guardians of the House*, Tom Morgan is newly arrived in a busy factory town from a remote farm in Wales, and he hates the newness and the noise. Near the town center is an old house. Tom sees the old woman who lives there leave, and he enters in her absence. (His motivation for doing so and his lack of concern about trespassing are weaknesses in the book; neither is satisfactorily explained.) Once inside, Tom is amazed by the beautiful things surrounding him—the masks on the walls, the statues, the vases—all having faces. The faces mock him, question him, and lead him on adventures both fantastic and terrible. The author provides an appropriately open ending.

> Tom went out and shut the door behind him. As he walked toward the gate he tried to collect his thoughts. Everything in there was beautiful, everything was dangerous, and nothing was what it seemed, or not itself only. Perhaps the silence was the most powerful thing that made everything else happen.
>
> He reached the gate and was gathering up his fishing things on the bank when the gardener came cycling back. All this in only an hour! His schoolmate, too, came by soon after.
>> "Well," he said, "did you get in?"
>> "Yes," said Tom unwillingly.
>> "Did you bring anything out?"
>> "Yes, this." Tom threw his mac into the river.
>> "What did you do that for? It's your mac."
>> "It's no good to me."

519 を含む CHARACTERISTICS OF GOOD FANTASY

"What's the matter? Did they catch you there?"

"Catch me?" Tom's voice was so queer that the boy looked at him curiously. "What, then?"

"It's unbelievable in there, and full of horrid jokes. I guess I shall have to go back there sometime to see if it's really true."

The reader is left with some questions unanswered: What made the magic? Will Tom come back to the house again? Will he fit into town life?

An equivocal ending also concludes *The Devil's Piper*, by Susan Price. Four children meet a luchorpan (an elflike being but not a leprechaun) named Toole O'Dyna, who has just awakened from a two-hundred-year sleep. With his pipe, Toole ensnares the children, who become his "company." The luchorpan shows himself to be evil when he plays his pipe. He causes an entire forest (with wolves) to spring up; he sours milk and sickens cattle; he changes the seasons. Of all the children, it is Mike who has the strongest mind. He is essential to the luchorpan's never totally revealed plan. Toole offers to bring Mike's ancestor Obadiah to life again at the price of Mike's death. Before Obadiah can protest, Mike is gone. In the end, the Old One (keeper of the dead) and his consort, the Lady Dana (weaver of life), help Mike escape. But, like visitors to fairyland in the old British ballads, Mike is never quite the same.

> His parents were more than pleased to see him. After the girls and Chris had come home, but not Mike, they had thought that he was gone forever. His mother became wet-eyed, and his father silent and embarrassed; and they took him visiting around the family as if he were a new baby or husband or wife that had to be shown off. They were even saving the nagging until later.
>
> Normally Mike would have been angry and shamed by all the fuss, preferring a bawling-out any day, but now he didn't care. Half the time he didn't hear them when they spoke to him. He was listening to something else.
>
> He was alone a great deal after he came home. Partly of his own choice, partly because his friends found his silence boring and didn't like being ignored. His mother worried about him for a while; but she had other children to look after and then another baby. "He'll snap out of it," she comfortably told aunties and grannies and neighbors.
>
> She never noticed whether he did or not.

Equivocal endings have three advantages:

1. **They stimulate the imagination.** Because the author has not tightly developed what he or she thinks is the one appropriate conclusion, readers can imagine what may happen to the characters.

2. **They permit diverse opinions.** Teachers can base classroom discussions or writing assignments on equivocal endings, challenging children

to speculate on possible conclusions. In so doing, children develop the ability to judge which endings seem most logical.

3. **They reflect life as it really is.**   In contrast to the artificially resolved endings common on television and in movies, equivocal endings in books help readers sense that in real life events are rarely resolved that happily.

## THE DIFFICULTY OF READING FANTASY

One problem with fantasy is that it requires a great deal of concentration on the part of the reader. The nature of the genre demands that diverse characters and settings be introduced and described. Sometimes the task of keeping all the threads of the story straight is difficult for the reader. For example, in the first eleven pages of *Save Sirrushany!* by Betty Baker, the reader meets five major characters (Agotha, Princess Gwyn, Lady Esther, Prince Jase, and Prince Everitt) and five minor characters (King Gunjar, Count Bosdick, Quinchard, the wolf, and the celbonite snail). To establish the imaginary land that is the setting, Baker introduces readers to seven locations (Dragon's Weep, Mount Sirruch, Sirrushany, Hot Lands, Thackany, Paphippany, and Port Goodsight). The complexity of this work may be a drawback but Baker's writing is heavily infused with redeeming humor. For example, at one point Agotha wonders about the identity of someone she meets:

> "Who are you?" she said.
> The man drew himself up but it didn't make him much taller.
> "I am Quinchard," he said.
> "The sorcerer?"
> "You know another Quinchard?" said the man.
> "No. I was just expecting an older man."
> "Nobody is born a sorcerer. We all have to start someplace."

A companion volume to *Save Sirrushany!* is *Seven Spells to Farewell*, in which the heroine Drucilla, along with Pitt the talking raven and Humphrey the performing pig, sets off in search of sorcery. Instead of finding a way to make her spells come out right, she discovers friendship, adventure, and a true calling.

Despite the humor in Baker's deftly written books, they—like many other books of fantasy—may not appeal to readers who have moderate reading skills unless a teacher or librarian helps. In sharing a book such as *Save Sirrushany!* with children, the librarian might want to read it to them in its entirety, thus making it easier for them to keep up with all the details. Or, the teacher might make a list of characters and their relationships on the chalkboard to help children follow the action. In some complex fantasies, for instance, Margaret J. Anderson's *Light in the Mountain*, the author provides such a list at the beginning of the book.

Another fantasy that makes serious demands on readers' skills is *Snow-Eyes*, by Stephanie A. Smith. A quartet of women, servants of the mystic Lake Mother, have exceptional powers of their own. After wandering the earth preparing themselves, they return to her villa to minister to her and to grant the common people's wishes. Each in turn passes her gifts to a daughter, who takes her mother's place in the succession. Snow-Eyes discovers that in being true to herself, she can receive the gift of insight from Lake Mother. The ending is convoluted and must be even more carefully read than earlier parts of the book. The vocabulary is somewhat difficult (for example, "nacreous black") and requires a mature reader. Smith further compounds the reading challenge by piling up hard words in some longer passages, for example: "A chittering of minute tree-frog voices and the drizzle of an afternoon rain gave the wishing stone room an ambiance of expectancy."

One fantasy book that is accessible to readers only marginally interested in the genre is *The Maze in the Heart of the Castle*, by Dorothy Gilman. It includes far less description than most fantasy and almost none of those quasi-English names often used in other works. Instead, the author concentrates on the action; the story moves from complication to complication. Occasionally the forward movement of the plot seems to keep the author from developing things sufficiently: neither the king's killing nor the movement of the trees to encircle Colin and Serena (protecting them from pursuing robbers) is entirely convincing because the ground has not been adequately laid for either event ahead of time. Such quibbles as these, however, won't occur to child readers, who will be swept along in the action.

A similarly lightweight fantasy is *Bella Arabella*, by Liza Fosburgh. Arabella Fitzgerald, aged ten, lives in Simon Hall:

> With its soaring towers and battlements, its low balconies and deep terraces, and its rambling wings [it] was more like a castle than a mansion or a big house, and anyone who believed in castles and fairy tales loved Simon Hall.

Although cosseted by a solicitous maid, gardener, chauffeur, cook, and nanny, Arabella grows up unaware of her pampered life. Then the latest of her mother's husbands (whose name the staff cannot at one point recall, there having been so many of them) decides that Arabella must be sent away to school. Desperate to avoid this possibility, Arabella is overjoyed to discover that her cat, Miranda, can talk and will help her become a cat. The transformation is gradual; Arabella doesn't really learn to purr properly until she has become a human again. While a cat, she learns that there are worse things than a new stepfather. Among them are a cat's unvarying diet of fish, some threatening gray male cats, and the real poverty experienced by a policeman's children. However, all ends well, inconsequentially but engagingly, in this lighter-than-air soufflé.

## PURPOSES OF FANTASY

As with most literature for children, the primary purposes of fantasy are to provide an aesthetic experience (the pure pleasure of reading about interesting people, places, and happenings) and to provide insights into self or others (from characters similar to or different from the reader). Fantasy serves the third purpose of revealing, through contrast, the nature of the realistic. While fantasy offers temporary refuge from the real world, at the same time it gives insights into real life. For example, George MacDonald's *At the Back of the North Wind* deals with one universal enigma of life: undeserved pain or loss. All adults must cope with this problem; MacDonald's story helps children begin to understand the need to cope with it. Also, through reading *Charlotte's Web*, by E. B. White, a pleasant animal story of barnyard life, children can begin to comprehend the pervasiveness of seemingly undeserved pain and loss.

Fantasy also allows children to pose philosophical questions. For example, at the opening of *Winnie-the-Pooh*, by A. A. Milne, Pooh wonders what it would be like to be someone else. Asking a "what if" question is central to the creation of fantasy. Children naturally ask this sort of question. The naive playfulness that epitomizes children's thinking is also a characteristic of philosophical thought. One reason children should be exposed to fantasy is that it encourages such thinking.

Using books of fantasy with children can help them develop their ability to fantasize in useful ways. Research has revealed a substantial difference between people who have a high predisposition to fantasize and those who have a low one. In one study (Singer, 1976), when high-fantasy children were frustrated, they responded with little overt anger, little excitement, and a minimum of aggression. In contrast, when low-fantasy children were frustrated, they became overtly angry, indulged in compulsive aggressive action, and remained angry for some time. When adults approach an important event, they tend to rehearse in their minds how it will go, they imagine how people will react, and how the environment will respond. In contrast, delinquent adolescents tend to be less skillful fantasizers who act out their thoughts because they cannot fantasize about them.

Some pragmatic adults worry that when children read fantasy they are retreating from reality. In fact, fantasy is not an escape from reality but a search for the real (Richardson, 1976). Healthy children seem able to make the distinction between fantasy and reality, unconsciously identifying fantasy as just that: an imaginary creation of a fanciful world. Like the little child in Hans Christian Andersen's "The Emperor's New Clothes," who looked carefully at the strutting monarch and candidly declared that he was naked, contemporary children can usually tell whether a story is realistic or fanciful.

Well-written fantasy neither denies emotions nor shows them sentimentally. Because of misplaced pride or embarrassment, many adults throttle their emotions. In fantasy, authors often describe characters' feelings in depth, allowing child readers to vicariously experience healthy emotional responses.

The search for identity is a common adolescent quest. Therefore, adolescent readers can develop empathy in identifying with a character who surmounts various tangible obstacles in pursuit of his or her quest, which is a frequently recurring fantasy motif.

# KINDS OF FANTASY

## SIMPLE FANTASY FOR YOUNGER READERS

Much fantasy requires well-developed reading skills; complex plots revolve around unfamiliar characters and places. Fortunately, some writers have written fantasy books appropriate for younger readers. Sharing these with students helps them develop an interest in fantasy that they might not acquire on their own.

A charming fantasy for first- or second-grade children is *The Dollhouse Caper*, by Jean S. O'Connell. The Dollhouse family comes to life only at night, after the human family goes to sleep. This limited freedom does not altogether please Ruth, the daughter.

> "Pooh," Ruth had said, tossing her head . . . "that means we are controlled by the humans completely, and I am going to jump out and roll myself under the radiator and they will never find me."
>
> "We are *not* completely controlled," Mr. Dollhouse said very firmly. . . . "We do exactly as we please all night. Anyway, if you lived under the radiator, you'd get dusty."
>
> "But it's not fair!" Ruth said. "We only come to life in the *night* time."

> "It's fair," Mr. Dollhouse said.... "The humans only come to life in the *day* time."
>
> "Oh," Ruth said. "I never thought of that!" And off she went to play the piano, quite happy.

Kevin, Peter, and Harry, the human children, are growing up fast; in one scene, Peter responds with typical boyish ambivalence to the dollhouse:

> He went toward the dollhouse ... then stooped and plugged in the electric cord.... In the glare of the tiny bulbs, Peter looked carefully at each room. Finally, under a pile of furniture, he found a framed picture about as big as a postage stamp. He looked at it for a long, long, time.... Very gently, Peter hung the picture over the fireplace in the living room.
>
> Then he picked up Mr. Dollhouse and stuffed him, head down, into the toilet, and joined his brother in the kitchen for a snack.

The members of the doll family are ingenious in attempting to warn the humans about robbers they have seen casing the house, but they are unsuccessful. Not until the human family is on their way to a skiing vacation do the three boys put the clues together and figure out that something suspicious is going on at home. O'Connell writes perceptively, creating effective fantasy but keeping a firm anchor in reality. Though the dolls can move and talk, they are firmly grounded in physical reality. A broom made of straws and a swizzle stick is difficult for the dolls to use because of its great height, and two of them must work together to move it. Such clear limitations of being doll-sized are cleverly incorporated by the author.

*Tatsinda*, by Elizabeth Enright, is another pleasant fantasy that is shorter and simpler than many. The Tatrajanni people dwell on a mountaintop in strife-free tranquility. They all have names that begin with the letters *Ta*; the names of all the animals begin with *ti*, including the "large, friendly tiptod, which was prized for its milk, though it looked nothing like a cow; more like a flounder with fur." Tatsinda, who has golden hair and brown eyes, is happy despite being different from the Tatrajanni, all of whom have white hair and icy green-blue eyes. Evil comes to the mist-shrouded mountaintop when the ugliest and most evil of the Gadblangs, Johrgong, invades the kingdom to acquire Greb, a mineral that is plentiful there but not prized by the Tatrajanni. Johrgong's evil strength is overcome only by the magic of Tandanon, the wise woman, and the cleverness of Tatsinda. The story is convincing, the relatively uncomplicated plot moves along swiftly, and the characters are believable. The book also has a quiet humor. Johrgong decides to take Tatsinda with him back to his house as a doll for his niece,

> ... a seven-year-old giantess named Jongborg. Already she was the size of a small house and ugly enough to startle a cow into convulsions, but since among

**The imaginative design on the old woman's cape and her craggy face announce that she is someone it would be intriguing to know.** Illustration by Irene Haas from *Tatsinda* by Elizabeth Enright. Copyright © 1963. Reprinted by permission of Harcourt Brace Jovanovich, Inc.

the Gadblangs ugliness was considered a mark of the highest distinction, let no one feel sorry for her.

In *Dorrie and the Witch Doctor,* by Patricia Coombs, a little witch with a crooked hat and mismatched socks tries her best to be good. Dorrie's mother goes to pick up critical Aunt Agra, arriving for a visit. Despite Dorrie's resolve, things go from bad to worse. Dorrie becomes sick, and her mother calls the witch doctor. A teacher might read this story to this point and then ask students: What do you think will happen when the witch doctor arrives? A first-grader named Sumi dictated the following response to that question:

> The witch doctor will come and see that she is pretending. Aunt Agra is going to be so mad, she's going to fly out of the house.

Edward, a third-grader, dictated this response:

> "Well, what's the case?" said the witch doctor.
> "Dorrie's turning all different colors, and she's sick in bed with the color flu."
> "She has bad manners," said Aunt Agra. "She doesn't know how to make tea right."
> After he examined Dorrie, the witch doctor said, "It's a bad case of coloritis. Stay in bed, and if she's turning green, give her a green sucker, and if she's turning red, give her a red sucker. And give her some water with her sucker."
> Aunt Agra said, "Suckers are too fattening for little girls. And anyway, they'll make you more sick."
> As the doctor packed his bag to leave, he said, "I'll check her next week and give her suckers." He picked up his bag, and as he did it, it meowed. He had picked up the cat instead.
> Aunt Agra said, "No, no. Don't give her suckers. It will make her sick, and she'll turn into a rainbow colored girl."

In *Pezzettino* (Italian for "little piece"), author/illustrator Leo Lionni tells the story of a small orange square searching for his identity. The little piece looks in vain until a wise one sends him on a quest to the Island of Whom, where he gets the answer. A teacher of first-grade students read this book to them and then asked them to retell the story in their own words. This exercise helps boys and girls understand that the same basic story can be encoded in more than one way. The following example is typical in relating the essential story line, even though the dictated language is different from Lionni's written language:

> Once there was this animal and his name was Pezzettino. He thought he was so little that he must be a piece of someone else. So he decided to find out whose piece he was. He went to someone to ask if he was their piece. It was the one who runs. The one who runs said, "How could I run if I had a piece missing?" So then he went to the one who flys. He said, "How could I fly if I had a piece missing?" He went off to the one who swims. He said, "How could I swim if I had a piece missing?" Then he went to the wise one and he said, "How could I be wise if I had a piece missing?" He said, "But go to the Island

of Whom." There weren't any people and no trees. Suddenly Pezzettino tripped and he broke into tiny pieces. Then he said to himself that they were right; everyone is made of tiny pieces. So he picked himself up and he sailed back on his boat and he said, "You were right; everyone's made out of tiny pieces." But they didn't know what he was talking about. They were happy because he was happy.

*Lisa*

*Simon Boom Gives a Wedding*, by Yuri Suhl, is an absurdist fantasy in picture book format. Readers encounter a simpleton who must have the best of everything, even if it turns out to be inappropriate. Simon buys and wears a lamb's-wool hat in the middle of summer because it is the best hat the storekeeper has. His compulsion leads him into greater and greater silliness. The pictures in shades of gold, pink, brown, and mauve are by Margot Zemach, who is skilled at poking gentle, visual fun at her rotund people.

One sixth-grade language arts teacher asked her students to listen to Suhl's story and then write a funny story about a silly person. The following are two of the resulting stories:

Mrs. B. J. Hemingway was one of the richest ladies in town. She was also a penny pincher. Whenever she got something, it had to be the cheapest. For instance, her jeep she bought in the middle of December was $50.00, and her winter coat that she bought in May was $25.00.

"Oh dear. I am so lonely," she thought. "I think I will invite my bridge club over."

So she sat down, wrote out the three invitations, and then mailed them. It was for the day after tomorrow.

The next day she went shopping for her food. She went to a place where they make hors d'oeuvres. She asked what was the cheapest kind.

"Well," said the clerk, "we have some very inexpensive caviar. Would you like that?"

"No, I want the very cheapest," said Mrs. B. J. Hemingway.

"Well," said the clerk once again, "our cheapest is snake eyes rolled in Tabasco sauce."

"Fine," said Mrs. B. J. Hemingway. "I'll take four servings of that . . ."

That night all three ladies called and asked what they would be having tomorrow.

"Snake eyes rolled in Tabasco sauce," Mrs. B. J. Hemingway did reply.

After that, there was a silence and then each would reply, "Uh . . . I am sorry but ah . . . I can't make it. Bye."

After the third, and last lady called, Mrs. B. J. Hemingway said, "Hmmm . . . they all can't come. Do you think it was something I said?!"

*Mary*

There was a boy named "Never Try Again." That was also his motto, "Never Try Again."

The first night he came home from school, he did all his homework carefully.

The next day during school they corrected their homework. He got nothing wrong. But at the last class of the day he corrected a problem and it was wrong. He crunkeled up his paper and said, "I'll never do homework again!"

During classes, he just sat there and if he was called on he just guessed.

When gym started, they went outside to play baseball. He went up to bat but he happened to miss. So he said, "I'll never try sports again."

If he was great at something and then he once did it wrong, he quit.

When he got home from school he just ate and watched TV. Of course he grew obese. When he fell down, the lights shook.

One day in grade 12, he got stabbed with a pencil. All of his "Never Try Again" attitude spilled out of his fat body.

It all turned out well. Now he is thin, a good athlete, and a good learner. Except it made a awful mess on the floor. How would *you* like to clean up someone else's attitude!

*Craig*

## LITERARY FOLK TALES

One kind of fantasy that captures and holds most children's attention is the literary folk tale. These tales follow patterns set by the oral tradition of folk literature but are written by an identifiable author. Because the writers of literary tales are word stylists, such tales are better read verbatim than told.

One writer of such tales was Rudyard Kipling. Having lived for years in India, he was familiar with the ancient *Jatakas*, animal tales told in prose that often end in verse. Kipling, winner of the Nobel Prize for Literature in 1907, wrote a collection of tales called the *Just So Stories* that explain, in mock serious tone, how animals evolved. These stories require an exact reading because the sounds of the language are so richly varied. For example, in "The Elephant's Child," ". . . the Procession had preceded according to precedent." On his journey, the elephant took "a hundred pounds of bananas (the little short red kind), and a hundred pounds of sugar cane (the long purple kind), and seventeen melons (the greeny-crackly kind)." After traveling, the elephant "came to the banks of the great grey-green, greasy Limpopo River, all set about with fever-trees, precisely as Kolokolo Bird had said."

Twelve of these tales by Kipling are available in a handsome oversized volume illustrated by the Swiss artist Etienne Delessert. Each story has at least one full-page picture, representative of Delessert's unique style. For example, the illustration for "The Elephant's Child" is an immense close-up of just the crocodile's head and the tip of the elephant's trunk. The blood from the sharp teeth is disconcertingly real; one huge crocodile tear reflects the elephant's image.

"The Elephant's Child" is also available as a single tale in picture book format with illustrations by Lorinda Bryan Cauley. Black-and-white pictures alternate with four-color ones in highly realistic style. Another edition of this story, with crayon drawings by Tim Raglin, is available in a slipcase that also contains a tape of the text, narrated by Jack Nicholson. Accompanied by plaintive, rhythmic music done on unfamiliar (and unidentified) instruments, this reading moves at a pleasant, leisurely pace.

Less realistic than Cauley's illustrations, but nonetheless interesting, are the pictures by Quentin Blake for *How the Camel Got His Hump*. This book includes the seven-stanza verse conclusion from Kipling's original version; the concluding verse for "The Elephant's Child" is omitted from Cauley's book. Blake's book is from a series of single-story picture books, done by such noted artists as Charles Keeping, William Stobbs, and Michael Foreman.

Hans Christian Andersen is clearly the master of the literary folk tale. One of the most beloved of his tales is *The Fir Tree*.

> And the little Fir Tree, which was now quite well grown, shuddered with fear, for the great stately trees fell to the ground with a crash, and their branches were cut off, so that the trees looked quite naked.

The little tree wonders at the fate of the other trees, and the sparrows bring him information.

> Yonder in the town we looked in at the windows. We know where they go. Oh! They are dressed up in the greatest pomp and splendor that can be imagined. We have looked in at the windows and have perceived that they are planted in the middle of the warm room and adorned with the most beautiful things . . . .

Andersen's vocabulary is distinctive; neither it nor the syntax is simplified for child readers. Nancy Burkert's equally distinctive and complex illustrations are admirably suited to the text. Her realistic pictures include many details and are outlined with a slender black line. Both words and pictures demand attention.

Andersen's *The Steadfast Tin Soldier* is a melancholy story of unrequited love with an unhappy ending, full of intense emotion. It appears that the story may end moderately happily, but the author dashes our hopes as the soldier finally melts in a lump of tin in the stove. Within the format of a generously sized horizontal rectangle, Alain Vaes provides full-page, full-color illustrations, several of which are eerily ominous. The page on which the soldier is threatened by an oversized rat and the one on which a gaping-mouthed fish approaches effectively communicate the soldier's helplessness. Both right-hand illustrations and facing left text pages are ruled with a plain black line, further enhancing the dignified, important format of this edition.

Soft crayon drawings by David Jorgensen accompany an edition of *The Steadfast Tin Soldier* in a slipcase with a tape narrated by British actor Jeremy Irons, whose resonant voice and accent are generally pleasant, though the interpretation of the Jack-in-the-Box becomes somewhat wearing. The music continues throughout the tape but changes in quality, effectively underlying the relaxed tempo of the reading.

Andersen's *The Snow Queen* is a long, seven-part tale of two small children, Kay (a boy) and Gerda (a girl). A sliver of magic mirror pierces Kay's heart, and he follows the Snow Queen on a sled. Gerda has many adventures while searching for Kay. The mirror, she discovers, changes good to evil.

> The most lovely landscapes seen in this mirror looked like boiled spinach, and the nicest people were hideous . . . and had no stomachs; their faces were so twisted that you wouldn't know them, and if they had only one freckle it appeared to spread all over the nose and mouth.

Sometimes the evil in Andersen's characters is very fully developed.

> "She is fat—" said the old robber woman, who had a long stiff beard and eyebrows that hung down over her eyes. "She'll taste as good as a little pet lamb; my, how good she'll taste!" And she drew out her shining knife, which gleamed in a horrible way.

In an episode centering around some pigeons, Gerda again confronts an evil character.[3]

> "They all belong to me," said the little robber girl. She quickly seized one of the nearest, held it by the legs, and shook it so it flapped its wings. "Kiss it!" she cried, and beat it in Gerda's face.

Characters do change in Andersen's stories, however: this reprehensible little creature later repents and loans Gerda a reindeer to carry her on the search for Kay.

---

[3]In addition to these unpleasant descriptions, the story also includes a pragmatic description of the arbitrary killing of a minor character. This killing off of characters is also exemplified in Roald Dahl's *James and the Giant Peach* (New York: Alfred A. Knopf, 1961).

*In this fantasy scene, dark blues and greens are highlighted by the white in the Snow Queen's gown and the snow drifts; the blackness of the demon seems darker because of this contrast.* Reproduced with permission of Macmillan Publishing Company from Hans Christian Andersen, *The Snow Queen,* retold and illustrated by Richard Hess. Copyright © 1985 by Richard Hess.

*The Snow Queen* is available in a translation by Eva LeGallienne, with pastel illustrations by Arieh Zeldich that are interesting because of the curious proportions of the characters. It is also available in an edition translated by Amy Ehrlich, which features finely crosshatched ink drawings by Susan Jeffers. The abundance of detail in these drawings will lure child readers back for another look to see all that is there. Each page is handsomely designed to provide enough white space to act as a foil to the packed drawings. In another edition of *The Snow Queen,* meticulously detailed, full-page illustrations by Richard Hess are eerily surrealistic, especially, for example, the view of the interior of the ice castle. Of historic interest is the edition of this book containing an afterword by Michael Patrick Hearn and featuring pencil drawings by Kate Greenaway. In Hearn's commentary, he explains Greenaway's special interest in the project of illustrating *The Snow Queen.*

Andersen's *The Nightingale* is a softer tale about an emperor who lives in the most beautiful palace in all the world. The Emperor hears about a nightingale with the most beautiful voice in the world. He demands that she sing for him, and when she does, "it was enough to melt your heart." The Emperor and his court are enchanted, but then the plain-looking bird's place in their affections is pre-empted by a mechanical songbird encrusted with gems. The mechanical bird, however, breaks and cannot be repaired. The Emperor becomes deathly ill, and Death sits on his chest, accompanied by all the good and bad deeds he did during his lifetime. The Emperor pleads for music to drown them out, but the mechanical bird cannot respond as there is no one to wind it up. Suddenly a beautiful song comes through the window. The living nightingale—having heard the Emperor was ill— comes to comfort him. Death leaves, and the Emperor thankfully agrees to let the little bird come and go as it wishes, bringing him news of his kingdom.

For an edition of *The Nightingale* translated by Eva LeGallienne, artist Nancy Burkert did eight full-color pictures in her usual finely detailed and restrained style.[4] A panoramic double-page spread showing the emperor's palace opens the book; a close-up view of the mechanical bird comes later. Middle-distance scenes involving courtiers appear at various points in the story. Text pages are embellished with narrow vertical decorations in the margin, printed in an elegant dull gold.

A teacher might compare Burkert's illustrations for *The Nightingale* with those of two other artists. In another edition of this work, pictures by Lisbeth Zwerger are highly detailed, pastel illustrations that bleed off the page, in contrast to the more formal placement of Burkert's illustrations. Beni Montresor also illustrated this tale, in an edition that has a horizontal rectangular shape. The soft pastel drawings accented with line have less apparent opulence than those in other editions. Burns (1986) comments favorably on his "stunning . . . visual interpretation . . . of the darker side of the story," but notes that the text is not as complete as that offered in other editions.

Erik Blegvad's miniature drawings in ink line and full color embellish

---

[4]"The Nightingale" is also available in other media besides books. Information about stories from books that are available in different formats is compiled by Ellin Greene and Madalynne Schoenfeld in *A Multimedia Approach to Children's Literature* (Chicago: American Library Association, 1972). For the most part the entries are factual, telling the user that the material exists and what it contains; unfortunately, they do not tell what the compilers think of the material.

***Illustrator Anne Rockwell used a thin black line to create humorous details superimposed on a watercolor wash. The designs busily decorate every part of the picture.*** Illustration from p. 16 of *The Emperor's New Clothes* by Hans Christian Andersen, retold and illustrated by Anne Rockwell for Thomas Y. Crowell. Copyright © 1982 by Anne Rockwell. Reprinted by permission of Harper & Row, Publishers, Inc.

Andersen's *The Emperor's New Clothes* and, along with black-and-white illustrations, depict the environment in which the well-known fantasy scandal took place. Children will enjoy this charming miniature book, as well as other versions such as those by Anne Rockwell, who shows a portly, pink emperor and mustachioed thieves, and Janet Stevens, who depicts a blowsy, peruked pig replete with purple high-heeled shoes. The edition illustrated by Stevens is both the largest and the most visually overpowering.

Besides being published as individual stories, Andersen's works are collected in *Hans Christian Andersen: The Complete Fairy Tales and Stories*, translated from the original Danish by Erik Christian Haugaard. This book includes 156 tales and faithfully follows the text and sequence of an 1874 edition that Andersen himself edited. This splendid reference work is a rich source of material for reading aloud to students. In addition, an Andersen scholar, R. P. Keigwin, produced *Hans Christian Andersen. Eighty Fairy Tales* in a convenient paperback edition. Keigwin devoted special attention to the difficult task of conveying the "colloquialisms, special Danish idioms, untranslatable puns, and . . . certain Danish adverbs which defy translation" that characterize Andersen's writing.

Howard Pyle also created literary folk tales. In *King Stork*, a drummer coming home from a war befriends an old man at a stream and helps him across the water. The old man, who turns out to be King Stork, gives the drummer a little bone whistle to blow when he needs help. The drummer hears about a princess who has set three tasks for any suitor seeking her hand—several have lost their heads in the attempt. With the stork's help, the drummer is able to avoid her evil and that of the one-eyed witch, her mother. Monochromatic illustrations by Trina Schart Hyman are full of intriguing medieval details; the costumes are particularly authentic looking.

*The Five Chinese Brothers*, by Claire H. Bishop, is a folklike fantasy told in simple language that eliminates all but the essential elements. This old favorite is now in its thirty-sixth printing, attesting to its longstanding popularity with children.[5] One brother can swallow the sea, another has an iron neck, the third has infinitely stretchable legs, the fourth cannot be burned, and the fifth can hold his breath indefinitely. This book, illustrated by Kurt Wiese, can be contrasted with *Six Chinese Brothers*, which has illustrations done as scissor-cuts by Cheng Hou-tien. These black and red, two-dimensional designs are slightly primitive and highly patterned, distinctly different from the pictures by Wiese.

In *The Transfigured Hart*, Jane Yolen tells the story of two unusual candidates for a friendship. Richard is gravely serious and more fond of books than of people; Heather is open, outgoing, and enjoys life. As the story begins, they are rivals instead of friends because each has seen a white hart (or was it a unicorn?) and wants to tame it.

---

[5]Selma Lanes, in "A Case for the Five Chinese Brothers" (*School Library Journal*, October 1977, pp. 90–91), states her belief that this tale is worth sharing with children. Letters of both condemnation and commendation in response to Lanes's article were printed in *School Library Journal* in December 1977 (p. 2), February 1978 (pp. 2–3), and April 1978 (pp. 4ff).

*Sharp-edged designs in solid black and intense vermilion portray characters against a bare white background.* From *Six Chinese Brothers* by Cheng Hou-tien. Copyright © 1979 by Cheng Hou-tien. Reprinted by permission of Henry Holt and Company, Inc.

When the hunting season opens, they must cooperate to save the white hart. One magical evening, they enter the wood, and a unicorn comes to them. Fall becomes summer, but at the sound of a hunting horn, Heather unties the yellow ribbon from around the unicorn's neck, and it escapes. The unicorn is gone and so is the white hart. Were they one and the same? The reader must decide. Donna Diamond's pen-and-ink drawings add to the dreamlike quality of the book.

## STORIES ABOUT ANIMALS WITH SPECIAL ABILITIES

The main character in a fantasy is often an animal with special abilities—usually humanlike traits. In *The Mouse and the Motorcycle*, author Beverly Cleary uses simple language to create Ralph, a hero who has a no-nonsense approach to the world. A young, impetuous mouse, he lives in the second floor of the Mountain View Inn. Keith and his family arrive to spend the weekend and Ralph notices among Keith's possessions a motorcycle, just mouse size. Ralph tries it out, ending up in a wastebasket, and thus his friendship with Keith begins. Adventuresome Ralph is almost devoured by a vacuum cleaner, is trapped in a laundry hamper, and is imprisoned under a waterglass. Thanks to his quick wits and good luck, he escapes each time. When Keith becomes very ill, Ralph braves all dangers to find him an aspirin tablet to ease his fever. In gratitude, Keith gives Ralph the motorcycle to keep. Author Cleary continued the popular adventures of Ralph in *Runaway Ralph* and *Ralph S. Mouse.*

An unusual animal hero is found in E. B. White's *Stuart Little*, a book for intermediate-grade readers:

> When Mrs. Frederick C. Little's second son arrived, everyone noticed that he was not much bigger than a mouse. The truth of the matter was, the baby looked very much like a mouse in every way.

So begins the story of a mouse born to human parents, whose entrance into the world is recorded in such a matter-of-fact way that the idea of humans having a mouse-child does not seem all that strange. Although Mr. and Mrs. Little and brother George dearly love Stuart, his small size does cause some problems. Once he is rolled up in a window shade; once he is shut into a refrigerator and catches bronchitis; another time he is dumped into a garbage scow and narrowly escapes a messy death. Despite many adversities, Stuart survives to set out on an adventure in search of Margalo, his bird friend. Stuart is intrepid: he sails a boat, drives a car, becomes a substitute teacher, and has a brief outing with two-inch-tall Harriet Ames. As the book ends, Stuart is still searching for Margalo.

The best-known animal heroine of a fantasy story is a large gray spider, the main character in *Charlotte's Web*, by E. B. White.[6] Possessed of human qualities, Charlotte presides over a menagerie that profits from her care. Geese, the wise old sheep, even Templeton the rat, are better for having known Charlotte. It is Wilbur the pig, however, who benefits most. Wilbur becomes hysterical when he discovers he is destined for the butcher's block. Charlotte promises to save him, and does so, though in the end she herself must die. This fantasy shows White's ability to make the incredible credible and to maintain the logic in an illogical situation. Charlotte does not weave just any words into her web; she copies words from newspapers. She tells the farmer, Mr. Arable, that Wilbur is "radiant," "terrific," and "humble."

---

[6]The book is rare in its presentation of the good-and-wise-mother archetype, not common in contemporary fantasy for children. In "Fantasy and Self-Discovery" (*The Horn Book*, April 1970, pp. 121–134, Ravenna Helson discusses three types of fantasies and shows how fantasies written by men differ from those written by women.

In Kenneth Grahame's *The Wind in the Willows*, four animal friends share adventures—some homey, some hilarious, some haunting. The friends are Mole, shy and somewhat uncertain; Rat, adventurous and a good friend; Badger, kind under his gruffness; and Mr. Toad, arrogant toward all. Because of Grahame's complex prose, teachers should probably read this book to their classes so marginal readers can also enjoy it. Reading it aloud is very logical, since the print version grew from stories Grahame originally told to his son and later wrote down in letters sent to him (prudently saved by a family servant). The first edition of the book was illustrated by Ernest H. Shepard; this was later followed by a version with pictures by Arthur Rackham. These two editions have, in the intervening time, become the standard against which other illustrators' versions of this classic are measured.

Several of Michael Hague's pictures for *The Wind in the Willows* show an artistic debt to his mentor, an anthropomorphism also common in Rackham's work. The settings are cozy because of the pleasant clutter of the rooms; the animals are more appealing because of the Victorian fussiness of their clothes. Even more appealing, however, is the indefinable vulnerability of the animals in John Burningham's illustrations for another edition. It features fewer full-color pictures, and these are less distinct—and perhaps therefore more evocative—than Hague's pictures because of Burningham's use of crosshatching.

In *The River Bank*, Adrienne Adams illustrates the first chapter of *The Wind in the Willows* in vital pastel watercolors on almost every page. The paintings are detailed, but the details are always subordinated to the total effect.

*Wayfarers All*, illustrated by Beverley Gooding, is the ninth chapter of *The Wind in the Willows*. The watercolor wash and pen line drawings sometimes fill an entire page and at other times merely decorate the margins. In each case, Gooding supplies plenty of details, and children will come back to look again at these pictures. Gooding also illustrated *Mole's Christmas or Home Sweet Home* and *The Open Road*, each of which presents another chapter from Grahame's book in picture book format. These picture book editions will intrigue child listeners, who may find Grahame's extended prose difficult. He uses, for example, 6 sentences and 211 words to describe Mole and Rat looking in a window and seeing a bird on a perch. This is a more leisurely pace than today's children are accustomed to. Teachers might read one of these shorter books to younger children or use them as an introduction to whet the appetite of upper-grade readers.

Although children may simply enjoy *The Wind in the Willows* for its

*Illustrator Beverly Gooding creates a homey feeling by including many small details, painted in watercolor and then further defined with ink line.* Illustration by Beverly Gooding from *Wayfarers All.* Illustrations copyright © 1981 Beverly Gooding. Reprinted with the permission of Charles Scribner's Sons.

fantasy and exciting plot, C. S. Lewis (1963) has commented that, unconsciously, they can assimilate other things from the book:

> Consider Mr. Badger . . . that extraordinary amalgam of high rank, coarse manners, gruffness, shyness and goodness. The child who has once met Mr. Badger has ever afterwards, in its bones, a knowledge of humanity and of English social history which it could not get in any other way.

A large animal that is a main character is Aljan, prince of the unicorns, in *Birth of the Firebringer,* by Meredith Ann Pierce. The author sets the action of her book—the first in a projected trilogy—in the context of four separate cultures. The balance of power has been upset, and the book is about the resolution of this conflict. A common motif is present: a youngster's rebellion against a parent. High-spirited Aljan (or Jan) finds the constraints of his culture irritating. He, his friend Dagg, and their mentor Tek find themselves in various dangers because of Aljan's impetuosity. The book is enriched by the author's ability to describe sights, sounds, and even odors in a way that makes readers believe in the fantastic setting:

> In the middle of the clearing lay a Circle of stones. A grayish powder lay in little heaps within, along with a few leafless twigs, oddly blackened. It was from one of these that the pungent aroma arose. Jan approached the Circle of stones. He stepped inside.

> The dust felt soft beneath his heels, incredibly fine. The branches, puz-zlingly brittle, crunched and compressed under his feet. Dagg set one hoof inside the Ring as Jan bent to sniff the powdery gray stuff, savoring its acrid, aromatic scent.

The unicorns do not know about fire but have just encountered its effects for the first time. Later in the book is another intense olfactory experience:

> He became aware of a faded odor now—it smelled barely, hauntingly sweet. Yet underneath ran a slight stench, like moldering flowers, or damp rotted leaves. The scent itself was not faint, he realized, but subtle. It had taken him a long time to discover it under the keener, more pungent odor of smoke. But it had always been there. And the scent was old, very old, though lingering.

It is through such vivid descriptions that the author develops a convincing sense of place for readers.

## STORIES INVOLVING UNEARTHLY CREATURES

Sometimes writers of fantasy people their works with beings completely unlike anything readers have ever met. In *Sweetwater*, by Laurence Yep, Pa, Ma, Caley, and Tyree are a close-knit human family living in the hostile environment of a cast-off colonial settlement. Dangers from the sea, from other groups of colonists, and, finally, from within their own group result in the community's dissolution. Tyree's interest in music leads him to Ama-deus, who has eight arms with suction-pad ends, but this doesn't prevent him from teaching Tyree to play the flute. Yep describes Amadeus con-vincingly:

> It was an Argan, an old one, sitting there calmly. The bristly fur on his back and arm-legs was a peppery grey, the flesh on his belly was all wrinkled, and he stooped slightly from old age. He looked very much like a four-foot-high Earth spider, though you would never suggest that to an Argan. They hate to be reminded of their resemblance to their Earth cousins the way humans hate to be reminded that they look like apes. . . .
>
> He stepped back in front of me and examined me boldly, even though Argans usually kept their eyelids low because they knew how their eyes bothered humans. Argans have myriads of tiny eyes on their orbs. . . . it takes some getting used to—it's like being watched by a one-person crowd.

Susan and her brother Colin are pursued by a variety of unearthly creatures in *The Weirdstone of Brisingamen*, by Alan Garner. This novel, like Garner's others, gives readers a sense of being in a particular place, because of his ability to create mood and atmosphere through the use of description. Because Susan has the weirdstone bracelet—a tear-shaped piece of crystal

*Artist Julia Noonan gives tangible form to an eight-legged fantasy creature described by author Laurence Yep.* Illustration from *Sweetwater* by Laurence Yep. Illustrated by Julia Noonan. Illustration copyright © 1973 by Julia Noonan. Reprinted by permission of Harper & Row, Publishers, Inc.

on a silver chain—many who wish to possess the powerful stone also wish the children harm. Among those who chase the children through the mines of Alderley Edge are the blind hounds of the Morrigan, one of which is described as follows:

> It was like a bull terrier; except that it stood four feet high at the shoulder, and its ears, unlike the rest of the white body, were covered in coarse red hair. But what set it apart from all the others was the fact that, from pointed ears to curling lip, its head and muzzle were blank. There were no eyes.

## FANTASIES ABOUT PEOPLE WITH SPECIAL ABILITIES

Tales of fantasy often include human characters who possess special abilities—sometimes used for good, other times for evil. Fantasy is peopled with wizards, sorcerers, and magicians.[7] A trilogy by John Bellairs features magical happenings in New Zebedee, Michigan in 1948. In all three books, *The House with a Clock in Its Walls, The Figure in the Shadows,* and *The Letter, the Witch, and the Ring,* the hero is chubby and timid Lewis. His best friend is fearless Rose Rita. Uncle Jonathan Barnavelt is a mediocre wizard, whose next-door neighbor is Mrs. Florence Zimmerman, a witch with a doctorate. Jonathan and Florence banter affectionately, but when the forces of evil threaten, they unite to vanquish them. Neither is all powerful. Jonathan is more a magician than a wizard, and even Mrs. Zimmerman is almost defeated in the third volume. The characters grow and change, and the magic is so matter-of-fact that readers will accept it without question. The platonic relationships between Rose Rita and Lewis and between Jonathan and Mrs. Zimmerman are especially well depicted.

A girl who learns to fly is the main character of *The Summer Birds,* by Penelope Farmer. Charlotte and Emma meet a strange boy—he has no name—who teaches their whole class to fly. They all enjoy moonlight flights together. To become a bird—flying free, with no more work, school, or restraints—seems attractive, but Charlotte must persuade the others it would be wrong for them to go with the boy, even though she aches to accompany him. Finally, the boy admits that "Charlotte is right. . . . I shall not let any of you come. You must not. It would be bad. I should be a thief stealing lives." In the end, however, he does let Maggot, a lonely girl with no family or other ties, accompany him. Other books in which characters fly include Georgess McHargue's *Stoneflight,* Jane Langton's *The Fledgling,* and Beatrice Gormley's *Mail-Order Wings.* To child readers who enjoy *The Summer Birds,* a teacher can recommend either *Emma in Winter* or *Charlotte Sometimes,* by the same author. These novels are introspective, more concerned with ideas and characters than with plot. Their appeal is to thoughtful readers who enjoy books that proceed in a leisurely fashion.

---

[7]In *The Impossible People* (New York: Holt, Rinehart and Winston, 1972), Georgess McHargue distinguishes among these three types of magic makers. She traces the origin of each term and describes the differences in the abilities of them. Equally fascinating is her description of witches, including a tracing of witchcraft to early sources.

The Ol-zhaan, spiritually gifted leaders of the community of Green-sky, possess supernatural mental abilities. In three books, *Below the Root, And All Between,* and *Until the Celebration,* author Zilpha Keatley Snyder tells the story of Raamo D'Ok, who at thirteen has been chosen to become a member of the Ol-zhaan. The people of Green-sky have been victims of a great conspiracy. The small, secret group that leads the Ol-zhaan have knowledge of a captive race of Kindar, held prisoner below the roots of Wissenvine, which supports the community of Green-sky. The spirit force is waning, and things are not good in Green-sky. Raamo, two of his friends, and his sister take the first tentative steps to reunite the Kindar and the Erdlings into one people. This reuniting, which causes tragedy—including Raamo's death in the third volume—is eventually accomplished, and the people's spiritual gifts once again flourish.

Unlike Snyder's completely unfamiliar environment, Louise Lawrence presents a familiar, realistic environment as the context of her story of a person with unusual abilities. At first, all seems conventional in *Star Lord.* Enid has fled from an unhappy marriage with her two children, Gwyneth and Rhys, to her father's remote Welsh country home at the foot of the Mawrrhyn, a mountain so intimidating it seems like another character. But one day reality turns upside down in an instant. There is an intense crash:

> . . . the feeling of impact came rolling down the valley and spread over her in a great boom of sound that the sky spread. . . . Gwyneth felt it in the ground; the shock waves fled up through her shoes and into her.

Rhys, his mother and sister hurry to the point of impact, where "some kind of machine" has crashed.

> It had been blasted, a whole area of the mountain, like a great black scar on the flank of the Mawrrhyn. Rhys stood at the edge of it. Grass and heather still smoked. Heat devils danced at the center of the fire that had burned and died into bare earth. His boots disturbed puffs of hot ash. He couldn't walk into that black center of heat. Nothing could. There was nothing alive in the pit of the crater. Clouds drifted over it like a shroud. The falling dampness touched and turned to steam. There was a sadness in Rhys. He had never seen such total devastation.

Despite their belief that nothing could have survived a crash of such magnitude, the family discovers that a person named Erlich has. Rhys carries him, bleeding and near death, into grandfather's small house. The security of the house inevitably gives way to mysterious dangers. Rhys leads Erlich from the threat presented by the government forces to the safety available in the mountain itself. The government forces intensify their search for the survivor, so they can suppress the potential danger in the population's finding out that an alien from space has landed. Erlich's special abilities are completely believable. Only occasionally does the author's talent falter: the idea of the opening through the mountain isn't completely convincing, for example. Nonetheless, what happens in the mountain and afterwards is an engrossing story for mature readers.

## STORIES INVOLVING TOYS AND DOLLS

Another device used by fantasy writers is the doll or toy that can talk, move, or perform other unrealistic activities. One such toy is the main character in *The Velveteen Rabbit*, by Margery Williams. The other toys in the nursery look down on the poor rabbit. He is only made of velveteen, after all, and filled with sawdust, which is "out-of-date and should never be mentioned in modern circles." His only friend is the Skin Horse who tells him about being real. The rabbit is real to the little boy who loves him, and in the end he becomes a real rabbit by magic. This story, like most fantasy, can be interpreted on several levels. For the youngest children who hear it, it is the tale of a boy's love for a favorite toy—a feeling all children know. The story poses a deeper question for older readers. The two friends, the rabbit and the horse, discuss this question:

> "What is REAL?" asked the Rabbit one day, when they were lying side by side near the nursery fender. . . . "Does it mean having things that buzz inside you and a stick-out handle?"
>
> "Real isn't how you are made," said the Skin Horse. "It's a thing that happens to you. When a child loves you for a long, long time, not just to play with, but REALLY loves you, then you become Real."
>
> "Does it hurt?" asked the Rabbit.
>
> "Sometimes," said the Skin Horse, for he was always truthful. "When you are Real you don't mind being hurt."
>
> "Does it happen all at once, like being wound up," he asked, "or bit by bit?"
>
> "It doesn't happen all at once," said the Skin Horse. "You become. It takes a long time. That's why it doesn't often happen to people who break easily, or have sharp edges, or who have to be carefully kept."

Both Allen Atkinson and Michael Hague have taken a somewhat sentimental yet realistic approach to illustrating this story. Atkinson opted for more but smaller illustrations, so some full color appears on every page. Hague provided fewer pictures on full- and double-page spreads.

*Miss Hickory*, by Carolyn Sherwin Bailey, is about a plucky doll who perseveres, despite the eventual loss of her nut head. This is an episodic story of the title character's survival through the winter in the forest. Inadvertently left behind when the little girl who cares for her leaves to spend the winter in the city, Miss Hickory must learn to fend for herself. The fifteen loosely linked chapters include charming descriptions of such forest dwellers as a doe, woodchuck, and frog. But the main character is the most fully developed, a three-dimensional person. Miss Hickory is concerned about her appearance:

> She sat down on her toadstool, spreading her skirts neatly to cover her ankles.

She is a creature of habit:

> And Miss Hickory, remembering former springs, decided to clean her house next week.

She is stubborn:

> "I won't move!" she repeated as she stepped across the threshold. . . . Crow, she knew, was right. Her head was undoubtedly hard.

Sometimes she is fearful:

> "Pleasant dreams indeed!" Miss Hickory put on her hat and pulled it down tightly. She had not slept a wink. And ever since that night she had worn her hat to bed.

She is sensorily aware:

> Miss Hickory's nose was as keen as a fox's. The smell of pine trees never failed to go to her head.

A doll is also the focus of action in *Twin Spell*, by Janet Lunn. Twins Jane and Elizabeth Hubbard are both attracted to, and repelled by, an old doll in a dusty antique shop. After buying the doll, they become obsessed with trying to discover its history. Tension mounts, and the twins, formerly inseparable, grow apart. They must unite, however, to defeat a malevolent spirit from the past that is trying to separate them forever. Is the doll an innocent, inanimate object or an evil influence? Was the doll the focus of the evil, or was an ancestor's ghost, guilty of causing a family tragedy, trying to reenact that tragedy? There are many questions still unanswered at the end of the story as Elizabeth and Jane grow closer together.

In another story focusing on a doll with special abilities, *The Oracle Doll*, by Catherine Dexter, all seems uneventful, even boring, to ten-year-old, solitary Rose. As summer approaches, she doesn't mind having no other playmates except her younger sister Lucy (who doesn't count). Then it becomes apparent that the ostensibly common doll that is Lucy's birthday present can say things most talking dolls can't. The discovery of the doll's ability occurs gradually, overcoming the reader's disbelief that the doll's body is the current habitation of the ancient Greek oracle of Delphi. The two sisters are bound together by their discovery and must take action against some other children who kidnap the doll. An odd old man proves to be their ally, and, in the end, Rose gives up the oracle with full knowledge that this difficult decision is the right one.

A doll as the personification of evil is the subject of "Mandy Kiss Mommy," by Lance Salway, one of eight short stories included in Aidan Chambers's book *Shades of Dark*. These are sinister tales indeed, suitable for middle- and upper-grade readers who enjoy sophisticated tales of the supernatural.

Far happier are the well-known stories involving Christopher Robin and his toys that come to life, created by A. A. Milne more than sixty years ago. *Winnie-the-Pooh* has captivated generations of young readers and approached cult status in popularity.[8] The stuffed bear, Winnie-the-Pooh, known as Pooh, has a special brand of humor: mispronunciations, misspellings, and other kinds of confusions with words. Does the book laugh indulgently at the foibles of small children (thus appealing to adults), or does it capture the essence of childhood (thus appealing to children themselves)? Lurie (1976) asserts positively that the book has "universal appeal to any child who finds himself at a social disadvantage in the adult world."

In "Pooh Builds a House," from *The House at Pooh Corner*, Pooh goes to see Piglet, but Piglet is not home. Pooh goes back to his own house and finds Piglet waiting for him.

> "Hallo, Piglet," he said. "I thought you were out."
> "No," said Piglet, "it's you who were out, Pooh."
> "So it was," said Pooh. "I knew one of us was."

Pooh and Piglet decide to build a home for Eeyore and they take wood from where it is lying in a pile. Eeyore complains to Christopher Robin that his house is missing; Pooh and Piglet have taken the pile of wood that was Eeyore's house to build Eeyore a house.

---

[8]How this endearing and enduring childhood favorite is also a reflection of the political and social situation of the time in which it was written is explained by Ruth B. Moynihan, in "Ideologies in Children's Literature" (*Children's Literature: The Great Excluded*, 2, 1973, pp. 166–172).

## STORIES IN WHICH MAGICAL OBJECTS PLAY A MAJOR ROLE

A recurring motif in works of fantasy for children is the magical object or the conventional object with an unusual quality. In a picture book for primary-grade readers, *The Man Who Took the Indoors Out*, Arnold Lobel creates a fanciful tale about Bellwood Bouse, who thoughtfully takes his furniture outside so it can enjoy the pleasant weather. The furniture, unfortunately, has a mind of its own, so Bellwood is soon frantically pursuing his runaway belongings. It was explained in Chapter 7 (page 286) how a teacher might read the story to this point and then ask the children to write an ending. Such plot-completion activities exercise children's imaginations.

Several magical objects affect the outcomes in *The Buried Moon and Other Stories,* by Molly Bang. In "William and Jack . . . ," Jack bests an old man, who gives him a cloak of invisibility and shoes of swiftness. He uses these items while pursuing his future bride, a princess trapped in the body of a milk-white deer. By cutting off the deer's head and flinging it down a well, he releases the princess from her captivity. In "The Mad Priest," the shortest and, in some ways, the least comprehensible story in the collection, the priest owns an umbrella that breaks into pieces that become falcons. The handle turns into a serpent that can devour a person whole. The last tale, "The Buried Moon," personifies the moon as a beautiful woman in black hood and cloak, with shining golden hair. Entrapped by evil creatures who come out when she doesn't shine, she is seemingly powerless to regain her original form.

Whereas some magical objects help, others hinder. In *Save Sirrushany!* by Betty Baker, an enchanted thread of light prevents Prince Everitt and the other boys from entering the Spell Tower.

> Prince Everitt organized a combined assault. The prince waved his sword and yelled, "Charge!"
>
> The boys bounced back as if they'd hit a wall instead of an open doorway. The prince fell heavily. He sat up shaking his head and made aching noises.
>
> "This is all your fault," he told her. "The Spell Tower was never locked before."
>
> Agotha went to look at the Spell Tower door. A thread crossed it at waist height, a thread of light that glowed green and thrummed gently. Agotha pressed a hand against it, then leaned on it with all her weight. It held. She slid her foot forward. With a faint ping, the thread divided, a second one pressing against her ankle. She tried putting hands and head through the doorway. Each time the thread split faster than thought. She soon had the doorway laced with green, glowing threads. When she stepped back, all strands pinged into one, waist high.

In *Quag Keep*, by Andre Norton, miniature dice set with gems move the characters to their next encounter. Milo Jagon is a swordsman with six motley companions: Naile Fangtooth, the were-boar; Ingrge, the elf; Yevele, the battle-maid; Deav Dyne, the cleric; Wymarc, the bard; and Gulth, the lizardman. They are summoned under a wizard's spell to seek out and destroy a nameless evil, in a different time. Each of the band has memories of another life in another place; each, too, has a special, if almost unrecognized, power that he or she can call upon when facing danger. The story is fast-paced but episodic; characters encounter one danger per chapter. Because there are so many characters, readers are unlikely to develop feelings for any one. The group works as an effective unit, and they decide to remain together at the conclusion of their quest. As in Norton's *Wraiths of Time*, the heros and heroine do not return to their own time. The ending is equivocal: as the story ends, Milo is rolling the dice to determine their next adventure. This book can be compared with Diana Wynne Jones's *Homeward Bounders*, in which the travelers don't know why they are going where they go.

## TRIPS THROUGH TIME AND SPACE

Many authors of fantasy experiment with time travel. (Chapter 8, in discussing historic fiction, describes several books in which the main character travels between two different eras.)

Simple time-travel fantasy may be clothed in a dream framework. In picture book format, the nameless heroine of *African Dream*, by Eloise Greenfield, narrates her trip to long-ago Africa. She slips in and out of the present, shopping in a marketplace for pearls and perfume and reading old books, and being welcomed home by her long-ago granddaddy. The hazy, soft-edged drawings in many subtle shades of black and white by Carole Byard complement the fantasy nature of the story.

In *Hangin' Out with Cici*, by Francine Pascal, a bump on the head sends the main character into another time. Thirteen-year-old Victoria, attending a private school she hates in New York City, is always in trouble. After her suspension from the school, she has a severe disagreement with her mother but is finally given permission to go by train to Philadelphia to attend a cousin's party. On the return trip, the train swerves around a corner too fast, and Victoria hits her head. When she awakens, she gradually realizes she is in another time:

> Now all I have to do is get my head together and examine this whole thing calmly and rationally. Later I can get hysterical. Right now I've got to be objective. . . .

**This soft, atmospheric chalk drawing illustrates a dream fantasy.** Illustration from *African Dream* by Eloise Greenfield. Illustration by Carole Byard, for John Day. Illustration copyright © 1977 by Carole Byard. Reprinted by permission of Harper & Row, Publishers, Inc.

Okay, so just say this is the forties. I must be out of my head, whacko. How can I be in the forties, and if I am, what am I doing here and how am I ever going to get home and back to my family in the seventies?

I think some horrendously screwy thing has happened to me and I got zapped back in time. I know this sounds really far out, but just suppose somehow I fell into a time fault. You know, like those faults they have in the earth in California. Well, maybe there's something like that in time and somehow I got sucked into one and zoomed back thirty years.

Within this fantasy device of a time warp, the writing remains resolutely realistic, all of the small details fit together and help to make the 1940s seem like the present. After getting off the train in Grand Central Station in a dazed state, Victoria meets Cici, and they strike up a friendship. Cici takes Victoria home with her because no one answers the phone at Victoria's house. When Cici introduces Victoria to her mother, it begins to dawn on Victoria that Cici, with whom she felt such instant rapport, may be someone she knows.

Then she [Cici's mother] turns to Cici and says, "I know Felicia is delighted to have you stay with us in the meantime."

Felicia! Not Cici. Felicia! I let the thought in now because there's no way to fight it. I turn and stare at Cici.

"Victoria? Is something wrong?" One of their voices comes through to me and I think I shake my head.

Felicia! Cici! My own mother! Holy cow, am I dumb. It had to be. Fantastic! I told you she looked familiar. I mean, she didn't really, but there were things about her that reminded me of someone. Not so much the features, but more like the expressions, the way she talked—I don't know what, something . . .

Victoria returns to her own time one night when she is running downstairs in the dark.

Ohhh, my toe goes over nothing, no floor, hurtling me forward. I grab out for the railing, for anything, but there's nothing but flat wall. My hands slide, my body falls forward and down, and I'm going through the air, . . . and then crashing boom against a solid wall with my forehead. Lightening strikes and painful colors push me farther and farther down until I'm spinning, pulling . . . then suddenly falling free and easy . . . something white . . . is getting bigger and bigger as I get closer. It's round and spreading and it's bright and glaring and yellow and I'm heading right for it . . .

The experience changes Victoria dramatically. Although her relationship with her mother may not always be smooth, there is marked improvement in it. Also, in the sections of the book set in the present time, Victoria's mother is fond of her brother; as adults, they relate very well to each other. In the fantasy section, when the mother is the thirteen-year-old Cici, she and her brother antagonize each other in a realistic way very much like the way Victoria and her younger sister Nina antagonize each other.

In *Tuck Everlasting*, by Natalie Babbitt, the Tuck family travels westward toward the frontier and comes to a forest that seems to go on forever. Angus Tuck, his wife Mae, and their two sons, Miles and Jesse, drink from a spring and think nothing of it until Jesse falls out of a tree onto his head and remains unhurt. Pa Tuck gets snakebite, Jesse eats poison toadstools, and Miles cuts himself, but none of them are harmed. After ten years, then twenty, the Tuck family has to face the fact that none of them is growing any older; they will not die. At this point, Winnie Foster enters the story, running away from home. She meets the Tucks, falls in love with Jesse, and has to choose mortality or immortality and a life with Jesse. Pa Tuck helps her consider the alternatives:

But dying's part of the wheel, right there next to being born. You can't pick out the pieces you like and leave the rest. Being part of the whole thing, that's the blessing. But it's passing us by, us Tucks. Living's heavy work, but off to one side, the way *we* are, it's useless, too. You can't have living without dying. So you can't call it living, what we got. We just *are*, we just *be*, like rocks beside the road.

Tuck's voice was rough now, and Winnie, amazed, sat rigid. "I want to grow again," he said fiercely, "and change. And if that means I got to move on at the end of it, then I want that, too. Listen, Winnie, it's something you don't find out how you feel until afterwards."

She makes her decision. At the end, Tuck looks down at the grave of "Winifred Foster Jackson; Dear Wife; Dear Mother; 1870–1948."

... he straightened his jacket again and drew up his hand in a brief salute. "Good girl," he said aloud. And then he turned and left the cemetery, walking quickly.

In a work for junior-high-age readers, *The Wind's Twelve Quarters*, Ursula K. LeGuin created several tales that treat time differently.[9] The seventeen short stories in this collection represent LeGuin's first ten years as a published writer. In "Semley's Necklace," Semley goes on a journey that proves not to be, as she was led to believe, of one night's duration. Her grief at returning to her own time to discover her husband dead and her daughter grown overwhelms her. Different times coexist in "April in Paris." The unhappy Jehan, caught in his time, is able to draw people to him from the present (Barry), the far distant past (Bota), and the future (Kislik). Because they—like him—are unhappy, his otherwise ineffective spell draws them through time. He helps them all achieve the happiness that previously eluded them.

In *Tom's Midnight Garden*, by Philippa Pearce, Tom is unhappy staying with his boring aunt and uncle—until the old grandfather clock strikes thirteen. Tom opens the door at the end of the hall and finds himself in a garden. He meets Hatty, who is lonely like himself. Tom doesn't realize it at first, but he has gone back to the world of seventy-five years ago. He believes Hatty is a ghost, but when he meets the real Hatty, now an old woman, he realizes she is still young in her dreams, and that he has been sharing them. The episodic quality of the chapters adds to the dreamlike atmosphere.

Authors of fantasy sometimes move their characters through space, as in *The Wonderful Wizard of Oz*, by L. Frank Baum. A tornado transports Dorothy, miraculously unharmed, from her aunt and uncle's farm in Kansas to the magical kingdom of Oz. Dorothy wants to return home, despite the

---

[9]LeGuin is one of many fantasy writers included in a bibliography of periodical works by and about authors. Ruth Nadelman Lynn, in *Fantasy for Children* (New York: Bowker, 1983), annotates, in a single sentence or two, over two thousand fantasy titles. For students interested in learning more about authors, the list of critical articles is a useful research tool.

*A scratchy black ink line is laid on heavily in places to create darker areas. This illustration shows what the words in the story tell but doesn't give much additional information.* Illustration from *Tom's Midnight Garden* by Philippa Pearce. Copyright © 1958 by Susan Eiszig. Reprinted by permission of Oxford University Press.

beauty of Oz. The Witch of the North advises her to seek assistance from the Wizard, who lives in the Emerald City. Dorothy and Toto, her dog, follow the Yellow Brick Road and on the way make three friends, who also have favors to ask of the wizard. Young readers believe this fantasy because of the exciting action. Less apparent, but a significant part of the book's vitality, is the universal theme of self-discovery. The Scarecrow, the Tin Woodsman, and the Cowardly Lion feel incomplete; each seeks what he believes will make him whole. The reader soon realizes, however, that each already possesses what he seeks. The Scarecrow has always been intelligent; the Tin Woodsman, kind; and the Cowardly Lion, brave. The wizard merely gives them visible signs of what each already has.

The illustrations for the original edition of this book, by W. W. Denslow, are unique.[10] A particularly American fantasy, this first of fourteen Oz books

[10]Michael P. Hearn's *The Annotated Wizard of Oz* (New York: Clarkson N. Potter, 1973) is an ambitious effort, lavishly augmented by all of W. W. Denslow's original illustrations reproduced in their original colors. A vast amount of factual material about Baum is given.

**John Tenniel's illustrations are traditionally associated with the classic story of Alice.** From Lewis Carroll, *Alice's Adventures in Wonderland,* illustrated by Sir John Tenniel. Copyright © 1960. Reproduced with permission of Macmillan Publishing Company.

was published in 1900; all are still in print. But is this popular book an American classic or far less than that? Opinions vary dramatically. Dempsey (1957) declares it the "first enduring and truly indigenous American fairy tale." In contrast, Sutherland (1986) reports that other critics think that "the style is flat and dull, and that the inventiveness of the first book was followed by mediocrity and repetition."

## CHANGES IN SIZE

The ability to change in size has intrigued many fantasy writers. In *Alice's Adventures in Wonderland,* by Lewis Carroll, Alice's adventures are possible only because she is able, by using a potion, to enter through the small door. The book appeals to readers on many different levels: sixth-graders follow the plot; adult readers see the commentary Carroll was making on society. According to Jorgens (1972), the work is "at once simple and complex, predictable and unpredictable, humorous and satirical, melodramatic and tragic."[11] As with some other fantasies, however, there is difference of opinion on the actual popularity of the story among young readers (MacCann, 1965; Gardner, 1965).

---

[11] Jorgens also comments that Carroll combined the problems children face in growing up with problems of adult life and composed a work of absurdist traits that ranks with the works of major experimental writers of the twentieth century.

**Illustrator Justin Todd's full-color illustrations have a lot of finely-drawn details and patterns repeated with variation; note how the repetitious wave patterns reflect the encircling curve of the gryphon's wing.** Illustration by Justin Todd from *Alice's Adventures in Wonderland* by Lewis Carroll. Published by Victor Gollancz Ltd., 1984. Copyright © 1984. Reprinted by permission of Victor Gollancz Ltd.

The story begins prosaically enough. Alice is tired of sitting on the river bank. Drowsy in the hot sun, she is considering whether or not a daisy chain is worth the effort when a white rabbit with pink eyes suddenly runs past her. When the rabbit takes a watch out of his waistcoat pocket and looks at it before hurrying on, Alice gets to her feet and follows him. The progression into fantasy from the realistic English countryside is as gentle as falling asleep. After seeing and wanting to enter a beautiful garden, Alice discovers a bottle labeled, "Drink Me." Looking carefully to determine that it is not also marked "Poison," she follows the instructions.

> Alice ventured to taste it, and finding it very nice (it had, in fact, a sort of mixed flavour of cherry-tart, custard, pine-apple, roast turkey, toffy, and hot buttered toast), she very soon finished it off.
> "What a curious feeling!" said Alice, "I must be shutting up like a telescope."
> And so it was indeed: she was now only ten inches high, and her face brightened up at the thought that she was now the right size for going through the little door into that lovely garden. First, however, she waited for a few minutes to see if she was going to shrink any further: she felt a little nervous about this; "for it might end, you know," said Alice to herself, "in my going out altogther, like a candle. I wonder what I should be like then?"

This book, like many other children's classics, is available in several editions. *The Annotated Alice*, edited by Martin Gardner, provides the original text in columns of rather large type down the middle of the pages, with extensive marginal notes in smaller sized type providing information about the work. Though the text remains for the most part the same in the editions for children, the illustrations are quite varied. For instance, in Michael Hague's illustration of Alice falling through the rabbit hole, unattached objects float through an undefined space. More careful study shows that even the chair is actually attached to the wall, though why isn't clear. Alice falls gracefully, with little apparent alarm; her skirt doesn't even float up, but remains demurely at her knees. The oval shelving in Justin Todd's illustration, shaped at regular intervals and loaded with books, clocks, an aquarium, and a ship in bottle, contrasts with the more swirling layers of Alice's skirt and petticoat. Despite the motion implied in her dress, this Alice is even more calm than Hague's. Even when this Alice runs, as she does carrying the pig baby, there is no sense of hurry in her movement. In S. Michelle Wiggins's version, Alice, with arms and legs akimbo, falls past an amazing array of this and that. Books stand beside busts, a clock, framed pictures, a teapot and other desiderata of a compulsive hoarder. It is difficult to decide where to look in this crowded picture. Heins (1984) raises the question of whether there is any need for so many versions of the same book and calls Wiggins's version "ornate, crowded, self-indulgent."

In *Among the Dolls*, by William Sleator, Vicky lives unhappily in a strife-filled home. She wants a new bicycle for her birthday and is disappointed when instead she receives

> . . . a musty antique dollhouse with old-fashioned, faded furniture and dolls. . . . It was nearly as tall as she was, and its dark gray Mansard roof and shadowy little rooms cast an aura of gloom over her bright bedroom. All at once she realized that she would have to be alone with it at night. It was the thought of that thing watching and waiting in the darkness, even more than her disappointment . . . that brought on her tears.

She is placated only when her parents agree to let her add a doll of her own choosing. She selects a plastic baby doll, which she names Danderoo. The fantasy is introduced gradually.

> And it was actually rather amusing to play with the dolls. The mother and the aunt would cook and clean; the father would read and work at his desk; the children played with their toys. . . . It was all very calm and pleasant; until one night at dinner the doll family began to fight.
>
> At first there were nothing but uncomfortable little squabbles. The brother would refuse to eat and the mother would send him to his room. The sister would grab one of his toys and claim it was hers. . . . Gradually, the quarrelsome life in the dollhouse became more dramatic, and day by day more fascinating to Vicky—especially as her own life began to change.

The size transformation takes place very suddenly one morning while Vicky is playing with the dolls. She feels dizzy, closes her eyes, and wakes up inside her dollhouse. The dolls threaten her because they are angry; Vicky treated them indifferently because she assumed dolls could not feel anything. She fears they will do unpleasant things to her. She wants to escape, but the dolls warn her that would be futile.

> "There is a barrier," said the aunt.
>
> "Oh, yes, there is a barrier," the mother agreed, sitting down languidly. "You may try getting through it if you like."
>
> Vicky couldn't resist. She was sure they were right about the barrier, but she could not see it, and the thought of getting away from them was unbearably tempting. Feeling their eyes on her, she stepped toward the edge. But at the threshold it became difficult to move forward, as though some great force were pushing against her. She struggled, using every bit of strength she had, but the force was so strong that, even leaning with all her weight against it, she did not move at all. When she turned back to the room, the pressure was suddenly gone.

With Danderoo's help, Vicky discovers that the key to her transformation is in the dollhouse attic: a miniature dollhouse and dolls that are perfect replicas of her own house and family. She is sure that what she must do to get back to her own house is somehow get into this tiny replica. The aunt tries to stop her, but Vicky sticks her hand into the little bedroom.

> It was like the force she had felt before, but in reverse. She was being pulled into the house, too strongly to resist. The aunt's hand slipped away behind; she felt rushing movement all around her and the odd sensation of shrinking and growing at the same time, of being sucked into a kind of whirlwind. . . . And then she was lying on her own bedroom floor, in the pale dawn light from her own windows.

All ends well, and Vicky gains worthwile insights into her parents' personalities and her own.

The title character in *Colin's Fantastic Video Adventure*, by Kenneth Oppel, eventually changes in size. After befriending the miniscule Drogel and Snogel, tiny humanlike inhabitants of the inside of a video game, young Colin devises a scheme for winning video game contests. On the brink of winning the national championship with the aid of his tiny friends, Colin realizes that they have given him an unfair advantage, and he loses the competition purposely. As the book closes, Colin is following his small comrades into the video screen to new adventures far more exciting than winning contests. The first draft of the story was written when the author was only fourteen, and has been developed into a book sure to attract child readers because of its topic.

## FANTASIES ABOUT OTHER TRANSFORMATIONS

Not a size transformation, but rather a change of identity is featured in *Freaky Friday*, by Mary Rodgers. Annabel, an incorrigible brat, wakes up one morning to find herself inhabiting her mother's body. She discovers that life as an adult is far less free than she had thought. Rodgers's tone is light and her humor deft, and this book is thus a hilarious romp rather than a didactic tract. Rodgers continues exploring the idea of changes of identity in *Summer Switch*. Ape Face Andrews, Annabel's brother, suddenly finds himself on the plane to California in his father's body, on the way to a confrontation with his father's new boss. In the meantime, Mr. Andrews is off to survive a summer session at Camp Soonawissakit. Sometimes the coincidences stretch the credibility: Ape Face (as his own father) discovers that the new boss is his own former teacher. Nonetheless, the second book is, like the first, sprightly, harmless fun.

*Top Secret*, by John Reynolds Gardiner, features off-beat humor that will appeal to boys and girls who feel that adults don't understand them. Allen has a perfect idea for his science project: human photosynthesis, a way to help humans make their own food. The problem is that when he does discover how to make it happen, no one except his grandpop will believe him. The experiment works perfectly for Allen, to the extent that he begins to send out small brown roots from the soles of his feet. What sounds like a wonderful idea, an effective way to end world hunger, turns sour when adults are too shortsighted to change their rigid thinking. Miss Green, the formidable science teacher who at first refuses to consider his idea seriously, eventually tries to help him. As the book concludes, Allen is following her advice, making a record of his experiences, so the future will be able to judge what he did.

## CONFLICTS WITH EVIL POWERS

Frequently writers of fantasy portray a conflict between good and evil. Often the evil is some vague but powerful force, as in *A Wrinkle in Time*, by Madeline L'Engle. This book, which won the Newbery Medal, includes three ladies with supernatural powers: Mrs. Whatsit, Mrs. Who, and Mrs. Which. They are able to help L'Engle's youthful characters defeat the disembodied, pulsating brain named It, the Power of Darkness, and the Black Thing of Hate. (A fuller description of this book is given in Chapter 13.)

One kind of formless, terrifying evil appears in a trilogy: *The Wizard of Earthsea*, *The Tombs of Atuan*, and *The Farthest Shore*, by Ursula LeGuin. The trilogy has been described as "high fantasy . . . the actions depicted in the stories take place in a secondary world of the author's inventing and involve an irreducible element of the 'impossible' or 'unreal'" (Jenkins, 1985). The trilogy follows the adventures of Ged, a young Mage (or wizard), from the time he comes to the Island of Gont as a student, through his life as dragonlord and archmage, to his eventual retirement from the world. In *The Wizard of Earthsea*, a rash young Ged uses the great spell to invoke the shadow of his own death, a shadow that pursues him until at last he meets and defeats it. In *The Tombs of Atuan*, Get meets and helps a maiden priestess, Arha, who has been dedicated to the ancient and nameless powers of the earth. Ged comes as a thief to the tombs in the desert of Atuan, where Arha keeps her lonely vigil. The two young people unite their powers and escape from the dominance of the dark. In *The Farthest Shore*, which won the National Book Award, Ged, now Archmage of Roke, is visited by Arren, Prince of Enlad, who tells him the mages have forgotten their spells. There is no longer true magic in Enlad. Roke is as yet untouched. Young Arren and old Ged meet the weaver of the great spell who tries to control both life and death, drawing to himself all the magic he can to fill his emptiness. During the journey and the struggle, Arren gains confidence and maturity. He finally triumphs over the enervating fear that holds him captive. Ged, on the other hand, like the heros of J. R. R. Tolkien's *Lord of the Rings* trilogy, leaves the world, tired and spent, never again to be seen. But the world is whole again. In each book in this trilogy, the dominant theme varies, according to Jenkins (1985), who asserts that "there is an imbalance . . . in the protagonist that reflects or threatens to contribute to an imbalance in the outer world." The protagonist must take steps to deal with this imbalance.

In writing about her work, particularly the differences between realistic writing and fantasy, LeGuin (1979) discusses why she writes fantasy. She identifies an apparent contradiction: young children need protection and shelter, yet they also need the truth.

> It seems to me that the way you can speak honestly and factually to a child about both good and evil is to talk about himself. . . . That is something he can cope with; indeed his job in growing up is to become himself. . . . He needs to see himself and the shadow he casts. That is something he can face . . . learn to control . . . and to be guided by. . . .

LeGuin contends that the best preparation for reality is fantasy.

Author Susan Cooper adeptly creates formless evil that pervades the environment like a fog.[12] In a series of five books, Cooper tells a continuing story of the never-ending battle between good and evil. The stories can be read separately but have greater impact if read in sequence.[13] In *Over Sea, Under Stone*, Barney, Simon, and Jane Drew, aided by their friend Merry Lyon, search for a grail, linked to King Arthur, that will hold the forces of evil at bay. A continuing thread through the books is that evil forces are always near, just below the surface of everyday activity. In *The Dark is Rising*, Will Stanton, aided by Merry Lyon, seeks six signs to hold the evils, both formless and tangible, in check. Will, the seventh son of a seventh son,

---

[12]Susan Cooper's writing presents a "fine, solid, nasty evil we can get our teeth into, and how welcome that is in these days of moral ambiguity," according to Georgess McHargue in "Leaping into Fantasy" (*American Libraries*, December 1974, pp. 610–611). Herself a writer, McHargue discusses characteristics of effective fantasy, as exemplified in works by Andre Norton, Patricia McKillip, and Cooper, among others.

[13]Cooper's series is available in a filmstrip and cassette format (Random House, #394-77187-7). Judicious editing and a competent cast make this package a useful introduction or supplement to the books. The background effects are well done and not obtrusive. The teacher's guide is useful for helping students with the pronunciation of the unfamiliar Welsh place names.

learns the ways of the old ones. In *Greenwitch*, courageous Susan, as the female protagonist, is alone permitted to see the women of Cornwall as they weave the greenwitch, a fertility symbol. She feels pity for the thing, and her pity helps sway the balance in the contest between the dark and the light. In *The Grey King*, which won the Newbery Medal in 1976, Will goes to the Welsh countryside ostensibly to recover from an illness. Only after arriving does he learn the real reason for his coming: to find the harp that will awaken the sleepers who are to fight the last battle between the dark and the light. Merry Lyon, the strange albino boy, Bram, and a dog with silver eyes help Will in his quest. In *The Silver on the Tree*, the dark is rising, and it takes all the strength of Will, Merriman (his ageless master), Bran of Wales, and the three Drew children to defeat it. In the final battle, when the fate of humanity hangs by a word or a deed, it is the courage of one mortal that makes all the difference.

Cooper describes a variety of confusing and insubstantial evils. For example, in *The Silver on the Tree*,

> . . . the great hall was filled suddenly with a hideous mixture of moaning and mumbling and strident wailing . . . a sound more purely nasty than any he had ever heard . . . then suddenly there was silence. And into the silence a new sound came from somewhere outside, . . . the heartbroken whine of a forsaken dog, calling in panic.
>
> As he looked at the blank stone of the far wall, he saw a door take shape in it. It was not a door like the huge vanished pair by which he had entered, but far smaller; an odd, pinched little door looking totally out of place. But he knew he could open it to help the imploring dog.

Merriman, the first of the Old Ones and Will's teacher and mentor warns him,

> "Wait. If you saw the shape of the poor sad dog, you would be greatly surprised. And it would be the last thing you would ever see."

Then Will hears another voice, which sounds like his mother's.

> "Will? Wiii-iil. . . . Come and help me, Will!" It was unmistakably her voice, but filled with an unfamiliar emotion: there was in it a note of half-controlled panic that horrified him. . . . Will could not bear it. He lurched forward and ran towards the door.

But again Merriman warns him to beware because it is not really his mother. Will ignores him and grabs the door's heavy latch.

> There was a sudden searing pain in his forearm, and he cried out and dropped to the floor, staring at the inside of his wrist where the sign of the quartered circle was burned agonizingly red into his skin . . . in a furious flaring warning against the presence of evil.

He listens to the voice, which

> ... wept, then grew angry, then threatened; then softened again and coaxed and cajoled; then finally ceased, dying away in a sob that tore at him even though his mind and senses told him it was not real.
>
> And the door faded with it, melting like mist, until the grey stone wall was solid and unbroken as before. Outside, the dreadful inhuman chorus of moaning and wailing began again.

This cycle of five volumes is remarkable for its mature and disciplined writing, but, because of its difficulty level, it is not immediately accessible to many children. The characters are fully realized, and Cooper is skilled in using language to create threatening evils. The books are set firmly in life's realities, and this makes them frightening, because they could be true.

The retirement of the heros to a fair land of healing often means the end of an age. Victory against evil has been won, but at a high cost. Like Ged in LeGuin's trilogy, Merry Lyon must leave the world at the end of the great battle between dark and light in *The Silver on the Tree*. The same fate befalls the Sons of Don at the conclusion of Lloyd Alexander's Prydain cycle. It is Taran's decision to stay in the world that finally reveals him to be the High King, foretold in prophecy. At the conclusion of J. R. R. Tolkien's *Lord of the Rings* trilogy, Samwise Gamgee and lighthearted Merry and Pippin remain in The Shire, but Frodo has been too much hurt by his confrontation with the Evil of Modor to live happily in the changing world. In all these stories, the magic powers depart with the heros. The age of magic is over, and the age of humanity has arrived. The passing of an age brings a bittersweetness to the stories, but also a hope that the new age will be able to profit from the mistakes of the old.

In contrast to authors who create purposely vague and formless evils, some authors create very solidly defined evil, such as that found in *The Enemy at Green Knowe*, by Lucy M. Boston. Tolly and his Chinese friend Ping come to visit Tolly's great-grandmother, Mrs. Oldknow. Sympathetically and realistically drawn, the three friends live happily together in the sheltering strength of her ancient stone house. Tolly wonders if there is some magic in the house that has made it last as long as it has. Mrs. Oldknow acknowledges that there may be: "Generally, it was something under the threshold, or on the roof, or perhaps under the hearth—the three most important places." When Tolly asks if she has explored these possibilities, she replies she has not, feeling that the magic—whatever it is—is working well enough. The three soon discover they will need magic to protect them from Dr. Melanie D. Powers, Doctor of Philosophy from Geneva:

> A person who would have passed unnoticed in any crowd anywhere was approaching along the garden path. At first sight the only individual thing about

her was her way of walking. It was neither striding nor tripping nor quietly stepping, but rather as though each foot went separately without a fixed rhythm. Each one seemed to be searching for the right place to come down but, having found it, came down heavily. Children often go along the pavement like that, observing rules to tread only, or never, on cracks between stones. But this was plain gravel. "What is she doing?" asked Tolly. "Is she treading on beetles?"

Dr. Powers is a formidable person. Determined to find books of magic that might have been left behind by the evil Dr. Vogel many years before, Dr. Powers tries to invade Green Knowe. Her threat, "there are more ways of entering a house than through the doors," is soon carried out. Rebuffed, she unleashes various plagues on Mrs. Oldknow and her young companions. Maggots in the rosebuds give way to helpful voracious birds, but these in turn are stalked by vicious cats imported by Dr. Powers.

> She had tied a wash line waist-high between two trees opposite the gate, and on this she was pegging up dead birds by the tail. They hung head down with their wings fallen open . . . the known and loved songbirds, Mrs. Oldknow's darlings, enough already to thin out much of the joy of the garden. Underneath the line a sleek and sinuous cat reached up, boxing the dangling corpses.

At this point, the author asks readers to take a much larger leap away from reality—to believe that Ping is able to summon the ghost of an escaped gorilla. Hanno the gorilla is able to divest Green Knowe of cats, but snakes conjured by the evil Dr. Powers frighten him away. The boys drive the snakes away and later find indications that Dr. Powers is in league with the Devil. Everything comes to a climax during an eclipse of the sun. Before the eclipse,

> the cows on the island moved in long, uneasy question marks, and moved about in a procession to nowhere.

Such pastoral images are superimposed against more fantastic ones for which readers are not adequately prepared.

> What were those *things* working about at the lower edge of the roof just above their heads? It was almost too dark to see, but they looked like fingers, without hand or arm: fingers of some dreadful unknown substance, subphysical or superphysical, projectable gray matter. If hatred could be seen at work, it might look like that.

The destruction of the things is even less convincing.

> Ping and Tolly, awestruck and holding their breaths, saw the powerful white fingers fall one by one onto the balcony, wriggle, snatch, and evaporate into puffs of retreating fog.

Good has triumphed and the evil Dr. Powers is routed. The book has an exciting plot, but if the buildup of evil were a little more gradual it would be more convincing.

Examining a different aspect of Lucy Boston's writing, Anderson (1976) comments on the environments she creates. Speaking of a more recent book in this series, *The Stones of Green Knowe*, Anderson notes "the sweet innocence of Lucy Boston's terrain and the soft rustling of her countryside [that] make these magical books very special ones for children."

## SUMMARY

Fine fantasy makes the unbelievable plausible; it makes readers suspend their disbelief in improbable beings doing unlikely things. Characteristics of effective fantasy include internal consistency, strong characters who care about something or someone outside themselves, and a setting fully described in realistic detail, even if the place is imaginary. Fantasy sharply reveals the nature of reality through contrast with the unreal, and encourages children to make "what if" speculations.

The literary folk tale is simple fantasy patterned after traditional forms but having a single, identifiable author. More complex fantasy often uses such stock devices as animal characters, unearthly creatures, people with special abilities, toys and dolls that come to life, magical objects, trips through time and space, transformations in size or identity, and conflicts with evil powers.

Teachers can encourage students to respond to fantasy in writing by getting them to participate in activities such as story completion, story retelling, and parallel plot construction.

## Suggestions for Further Study

1. Maurice Sendak's *In the Night Kitchen* (New York: Harper and Row, 1970) has been called "a richly detailed, imaginative, witty dream adventure" by Elizabeth Graves, in "Children's Books: A Selected List" (*Commonweal*, 93, November 20, 1970, p. 199). It has also been called "heavy, self-conscious, pointless, and—worst of all—dull" by Sheldon Root, in "Books for Children" (*Elementary English*, 48, February 1971, p. 263).

Read the book, and decide which is the more accurate analysis.

2. In contrast to Eleanor Cameron's (see "Related Reading for Adults") essentially negative comments on Alan Garner's *Elidor* is another writer's positive reaction to it. June S. Terry, in "To Seek and to Find: Quest Literature for Children" (*The School Librarian*, December 1970, pp. 399–404) recommends the book as a way for some children

to escape the limitations of the present. After reading the book, read both articles, and decide which is the more accurate critique.

3. This chapter discussed three authors of literary folk tales. Eleanor Farjeon and Richard Hughes also wrote fantasy for children in this form. Find some stories by these authors and share them with boys and girls to determine how successful they are with today's students.

4. A respected fantasy writer, Ursula K. Le-Guin, writes about adult reactions to the genre in "Why Are Americans Afraid of Dragons?" (*PNLA Quarterly*, February 1974, pp. 14–18). She contends many adults, especially successful men older than thirty, deny fantasy and are afraid of it. Read her article, and then write a position paper responding to her contention.

5. *Among the Dolls*, by William Sleator, features a dollhouse and a child who shrinks to fit into the house. In *Mindy's Mysterious Miniature*, by Jane Louise Curry (New York: Harcourt Brace Jovanovich, 1970), the dollhouse grows. Mindy and a friend enter the life-sized house, and when it shrinks again, they cannot get out. Read both of these books, and decide which is a more effective example of writing about size transformations. A sequel to Curry's book is *The Lost Farm* (New York: Atheneum, 1974).

6. Many fantasy books feature wizards; a few are mentioned in this chapter. Others include *Benjamin the True*, by Claudia Paley (Boston: Little, Brown, 1969), and *Magic in the Mist*, by Margaret M. Kimmel (New York: Atheneum, 1976). In addition, Patricia McKillip has created notable wizards whose evil powers seem to dwarf any magic the forces for goodness can muster. Methran, in *The Forgotten Beasts of Eld* (New York: Atheneum, 1974), plays with human minds, calling souls and enslaving them. In the wizard Ghisteslwchlohm, author McKillip created an evil monster whose treachery and betrayal bring the end of an age, and signal the passing of power from the High One to his heir. This drama unfolds in three volumes: *The Riddle-Master of Hed* (New York: Atheneum, 1976), *Heir of Sea and Fire* (New York: Atheneum, 1977), and *Harpist in the Wind* (New York: Atheneum, 1979). Read several of the books mentioned here to determine which are the more effective depictions of wizards.

7. *Stuart Little* may now seem to be a pleasantly innocuous book. When it was first published, however, it received very negative reviews. See "The Librarian Said It Was Bad for Children" (*The New York Times*, March 6, 1966, Section X, p. 19), in which E. B. White reflects on the reviewers' misgivings. Another account is included in an article by Hopkins (1986). Read what some other textbooks on children's literature have to say about this book to see how critical opinion has changed over the years.

## Related Reading for Adults

Alexander, Lloyd. "Truth About Fantasy." *Top of the News*, 24 (January 1968), pp. 168–174.

Alexander makes an important distinction between fairy tales and fantasy. Fairy tales have existed for generations, and despite much study, their origins are essentially unknown. One recurring theme in fantasy and fairy tales is the dangerous quest in various forms: the journey to a strange land, the descent into an underworld, the storming of an ogre's castle, and the slaying of the dragon. Alexander provides an amusing tally of traditional characters in such tales, devoting special attention to the hero and the servant or close companion.

Babbitt, Natalie. "The Roots of Fantasy." *The Bulletin*, 12 (Spring 1986), pp. 2–4.

Beginning with the common assertion that fantasy is deeply rooted in reality, Babbitt points out that fantasy came first chronologically, with stories to embody it coming later. Fantasy deals with three fundamental human attributes: fear, hope, and the need to be diverted. The author discusses and elaborates each of these in turn. She concludes that fantasies have a way of coming true, even if not in the precise form in which they were first envisioned.

Cameron, Eleanor. *"The Owl Service:* A Study." *Wilson Library Bulletin*, December 1969, pp. 425–433.

A noted critic here compares and contrasts Alan Garner's fourth book with his earlier work and with the writings of William Mayne and Ursula LeGuin. Acknowledging the impressive growth she sees in Garner's work, she also points out the problems in this work: flat characters, monotonous rhythm in dialogue, and a weak ending.

Cameron, Eleanor. *The Green and Burning Tree; on the Writing and Enjoyment of Children's Books*. Boston: Little, Brown, 1969, pp. 71–134.

The chapter titled "The Unforgettable Glimpse" surveys good excerpts from children's fantasy and details the qualities that make fantasy good. "A Realm of One's Own" deals with Cameron's Mr. Bass books. In "The Green and Burning Tree; a Study of Time Fantasy," Cameron speculates about the nature of time. She speaks highly of the famous British fantasy writers beloved by children (Boston, Travers, Nesbit, Lofting, and de la Mare).

Evans, W. D. Emrys. "Illusion, Tale and Epic." *School Librarian*, 21 (March 1973), pp. 5–11.

Using *The Hobbit* as a point of reference,

Evans comments on Tolkien's ability to wield language in order to produce magical separations and syntheses and create a secondary world readers can enter. Evans examines the relation between composed fantasy and folk-memory sources. For another author's very complete analysis of *The Hobbit*, see Jon C. Stott's "A Structuralist Approach to Teaching Novels in the Elementary Grades" (*The Reading Teacher*, November 1982, pp. 136–143). In addition to activities directly related to the book, Stott provides suggestions for an array of experiences leading readers through other books into *The Hobbit*, and suggestions for follow-up experiences with other fantasies.

Holbrook, David. "The Problem of C. S. Lewis." *Children's Literature in Education*, March 1973, pp. 3–25.

C. S. Lewis's work is characterized by a continually aggressive stance: there is often an intense self-righteousness. Holbrook thinks a main message these books convey is that there is no point in being halfhearted about fighting. His psychological analysis of the works emphasizes their deep primitive symbolism, including much sexual imagery.

Hunter, Mollie. "One World." *The Horn Book*, December 1975, pp. 557–563; February 1976, pp. 32–38.

Fantasy expresses two common childhood thrills: the pleasure of scaring oneself and "the feeling that around any corner one might catch a sudden glimpse of something strange and wonderful." Hunter believes that all fantasy is rooted in folklore and examines the use of the supernatural in folklore.

Langton, Jane. "The Weak Place in the Cloth: A Study of Fantasy for Children." *The Horn Book*, October 1973, pp. 433–441; December 1973, pp. 570–578.

All fantasy answers three questions: What if? Then what? So what? Langton identifies eight types of fantasy: (1) the cloth (a screen that separates reality and fantasy) is merely stretched out of shape (all action takes place on the "real-world" side); (2) the cloth is punctured (characters are drawn within the fantasy world by an object); (3) the cloth is invisible and permeable (two worlds exist side by side); (4) only the readers remain on the magic side of the cloth; (5) no real magic exists, just a magical premise; (6) characters go back and forth in time; (7) ghost stories; (8) science fiction.

Lenz, Millicent. "Fantasy and Survival." *Catholic Library World*, September 1976, pp. 56–61.

Analyzing nineteen fantasies, Lenz provides a plot summary and a description of how the idea of survival is treated in each. This is a useful article that must be carefully read because the categorization system is complex.

Lurie, Alison. "Back to Pooh Corner." *Children's Literature: The Great Excluded*, 2 (1973), pp. 11–17.

Opening with a brief summary of A. A. Milne's life, Lurie's article relates Milne's experiences and his relations with family and friends to the safe world he created for Pooh. Extensive parallels are drawn between Milne's childhood and relationships depicted in the book. One reason for Pooh's popularity is that he has the virtues and endearing faults common to all children.

Robbins, Sidney. "A Nip of Otherness, Like Life: the Novels of Lucy Boston." *Children's Literature in Education*, November 1971, pp. 5–16.

The most skillful fantasy writers respect the validity and complexity of children's own inner fantasy world. High standards of reading ability now make it possible for writers to make far more exacting and subtle linguistic demands on readers than were once thought practicable. Robbins analyzes Lucy Boston's books, pointing out their strengths, and identifies the reasons why *A Stranger at Green Knowe* is the book on which her reputation will rest.

Thomas, Jane Resh. "Old Worlds and New: Anti-Feminism in *Watership Down*." *The Horn Book*, August 1974, pp. 405–408.

Fantasy writers have the option of creating the world anew. Thomas criticizes Richard Adams because he remains so deeply rooted in the old world as he fashions his new one. Thomas believes the novel draws on an antifeminist social tradition that, imposed on rabbits, is eerie in its clarity. But despite this fault, Thomas thinks the novel deserves the Carnegie Medal because it is a splendid story, admirable in both its originality and craft.

## Professional References

Anderson, Karen B. "'Tis the Season for Fantasies." *National Observer*, December 25, 1976, p. 14.

Burns, Mary M. "Andersen's *Nightingale*." *The Horn Book*, January/February 1986, 78–79.

Dempsey, David. "The Wizardry of L. Frank Baum." In *Bibliophile in the Nursery*. New York: World, 1957, p. 387.

Gardner, Martin (ed.). *The Annotated Alice*. New York: Bramhall House, 1960.

——— . "A Child's Garden of Bewilderment." *Saturday Review*, July 17, 1965, 18–19.

Heins, Ethel L. "Art and Text—And Context." *The Horn Book*, 60 (April 1984), 158–159.

Hopkins, Lee Bennett. "Profile in Memoriam: E. B. White." *Language Arts*, 63 (September 1986), 491–494.

Jenkins, Sue. "Growing Up in Earthsea." *Children's Literature in Education*, 10 (Spring 1985), 21–31.

Jorgens, Jack. "Alice Our Contemporary." *Children's Literature: The Great Excluded*, 1 (1972), 152–161.

LeGuin, Ursula K. *The Language of the Night.* New York: G. P. Putnam's, 1979, p. 70.

Lewis, C. S. "Three Ways of Writing for Children." *The Horn Book*, October 1963, 459–469.

Lurie, Alison. "Now We are Fifty." *New York Times Book Review*, November 14, 1976, 27.

MacCann, DonnaRae. "Wells of Fancy." *Wilson Library Bulletin*, December 1965, 334–343.

Richardson, Carmen. "The Reality of Fantasy." *Language Arts*, May 1976, 549–551.

Singer, Jerome L. "Fantasy: The Foundation of Serenity." *Psychology Today*, July 1976, 33–37.

Sutherland, Zena, and May Hill Arbuthnot. *Children and Books.* Glenview, Ill: Scott, Foresman, 1986, p. 260.

## *Bibliography of Children's Books*

Adams, Adrienne (ill.). *The River Bank.* New York: Scribner's, 1977.

Adams, Richard. *Watership Down.* New York: Penguin, 1972.

Alexander, Lloyd. *The Cat Who Wished to Be a Man.* New York: E. P. Dutton, 1973.

———. *The Foundling and Other Tales of Prydain.* New York: Holt, Rinehart and Winston, 1973.

———. *The Truthful Harp.* New York: Holt, Rinehart and Winston, 1967.

———. *The Wizard in the Tree.* New York: E. P. Dutton, 1975.

Andersen, Hans Christian. *The Fir Tree.* (Illustrated by Nancy Burkert.) New York: Harper and Row, 1970.

———. *The Steadfast Tin Soldier.* (Illustrated by David Jorgensen.) New York: Alfred A. Knopf, 1986.

———. *The Steadfast Tin Soldier.* (Illustrated by Alain Vaes.) Boston: Little, Brown, 1983.

Anderson, Margaret J. *Light in the Mountain.* New York: Alfred A. Knopf, 1982.

Babbitt, Natalie. *Tuck Everlasting.* New York: Farrar, Straus and Giroux, 1975.

Bailey, Carolyn Sherwin. *Miss Hickory.* New York: Viking, 1962.

Baker, Betty. *Save Sirrushany!* New York: Macmillan, 1978.

———. *Seven Spells to Farewell.* New York: Macmillan, 1982.

Bang, Molly. *The Buried Moon and Other Stories.* New York: Scribner's, 1977.

Baum, L. Frank. *The Wonderful Wizard of Oz.* Chicago: Reilly and Lee, 1956 (1900).

Bellairs, John. *The Figure in the Shadows.* New York: Dial, 1975.

———. *The House with a Clock in Its Walls.* New York: Dial, 1973.

———. *The Letter, the Witch, and the Ring.* New York: Dial, 1976.

Bishop, Claire H. *The Five Chinese Brothers.* New York: Coward, McCann, 1938.

Blake, Quentin (ill.). *How the Camel Got His Hump.* New York: Peter Bedrick, 1985.

Blegvad, Erik (trans.). *The Emperor's New Clothes.* New York: Harcourt Brace, 1959.

Boston, Lucy M. *The Children of Green Knowe.* New York: Harcourt, Brace and World, 1955.

———. *The Enemy at Green Knowe.* New York: Harcourt, Brace and World, 1964.

———. *The Guardians of the House.* New York: Atheneum, 1975.

———. *Nothing Said.* London: Faber and Faber, 1971.

———. *A Stranger at Green Knowe.* New York: Harcourt, Brace and World, 1961.

———. *The Stones of Green Knowe.* New York: Atheneum, 1976.

———. *Treasure of Green Knowe*. New York: Harcourt, Brace and World, 1958.

Carroll, Lewis. *Alice's Adventures in Wonderland*. New York: Macmillan, 1960.

———. *Alice's Adventures in Wonderland*. (Illustrated by Michael Hague.) New York: Holt, Rinehart and Winston, 1985.

———. *Alice's Adventures in Wonderland*. (Illustrated by Justin Todd.) New York: Crown, 1984.

———. *Alice's Adventures in Wonderland*. (Illustrated by S. Michelle Wiggins.) New York: Alfred A. Knopf, 1983.

Cauley, Lorinda Bryan (ill.). *The Elephant's Child*. San Diego: Harcourt Brace Jovanovich, 1983.

Chambers, Aidan (ed.). *Shades of Dark*. New York: Harper and Row, 1985.

Cleary, Beverly. *The Mouse and the Motorcycle*. New York: Morrow, 1965.

———. *Ralph S. Mouse*. New York: Morrow, 1982.

———. *Runaway Ralph*. New York: Morrow, 1970.

Coombs, Patricia. *Dorrie and the Witch Doctor*. New York: Lothrop, Lee and Shepard, 1967.

Cooper, Susan. *The Dark Is Rising*. New York: Atheneum, 1973.

———. *Greenwitch*. New York: Atheneum, 1974.

———. *The Grey King*. New York: Atheneum, 1975.

———. *Over Sea, Under Stone*. New York: Harcourt, Brace and World, 1965

———. *The Silver on the Tree*. New York: Atheneum, 1977.

Dereske, Jo. *Glom Gloom*. New York: Atheneum, 1985.

Dexter, Catherine. *The Oracle Doll*. New York: Four Winds, 1985.

Ehrlich, Amy (trans.). *The Snow Queen*. (Illustrated by Susan Jeffers.) New York: Dial, 1982.

Enright, Elizabeth. *Tatsinda*. New York: Harcourt, Brace and World, 1963.

Farmer, Penelope. *Charlotte Sometimes*. New York: Harcourt, Brace and World, 1969.

———. *Emma in Winter*. New York: Harcourt, Brace and World, 1966.

———. *The Summer Birds*. New York: Harcourt, Brace and World, 1962.

Fosburgh, Liza. *Bella Arabella*. New York: Four Winds, 1985.

Gardiner, John Reynolds. *Top Secret*. Boston: Little, Brown, 1985.

Garner, Alan. *The Weirdstone of Brisingamen: A Tale of Alderley*. New York: Henry Z. Walck, 1969.

Gilman, Dorothy. *The Maze in the Heart of the Castle*. Garden City, N.Y.: Doubleday, 1983.

Gooding, Beverley. *Mole's Christmas or Home Sweet Home*. Englewood Cliffs, N.J.: Prentice-Hall, 1982.

———. *The Open Road*. Englewood Cliffs, N.J.: Prentice-Hall, 1979.

———. *Wayfarers All*. New York: Scribner's, 1981.

Gormley, Beatrice. *Mail-Order Wings*. New York: E. P. Dutton, 1981.

Grahame, Kenneth. *The Wind in the Willows*. New York: Scribner's, 1970.

———. *The Wind in the Willows*. (Illustrated by John Burningham.) New York: Viking, 1983.

———. *The Wind in the Willows*. (Illustrated by Michael Hague.) New York: Holt, Rinehart and Winston, 1980.

Greenfield, Eloise. *African Dream*. New York: John Day, 1977.

Haugaard, Erik Christian (trans.). *Hans Christian Andersen: The Complete Fairy Tales and Stories*. New York: Doubleday, 1974.

Hearn, Michael Patrick (ed.). *The Snow Queen*. New York: Schocken, 1981.

Hess, Richard (ill.). *The Snow Queen*. New York: Macmillan, 1985.

Hoover, H. M. *The Delikon*. New York: Viking, 1977.

Hou-tien, Cheng. *Six Chinese Brothers*. New York: Holt, Rinehart and Winston, 1979.

Jones, Diana Wynne. *Homeward Bounders*. New York: Greenwillow, 1981.

Keigwin, R. P. *Hans Christian Andersen. Eighty Fairy Tales*. New York: Pantheon, 1976.

Kipling, Rudyard. *Just So Stories*. (Illustrated by Etienne Delessert.) Garden City, N.Y.: Doubleday, 1972.

Konigsburg, E. L. *Up from Jericho Tel*. New York: Atheneum, 1986.

L'Engle, Madeline. *A Wrinkle in Time*. New York: Farrar, Straus and Giroux, 1962.

Langton, Jane. *The Fledgling*. New York: Harper and Row, 1980.

———. *The Swing in the Summerhouse*. New York: Harper and Row, 1967.

Lawrence, Louise. *Star Lord*. New York: Harper and Row, 1978.

LeGallienne, Eva (trans.). *The Nightingale*. (Illustrated by Nancy Burkert.) New York: Harper and Row, 1965.

———. (trans.). *The Snow Queen*. (Illustrated by Arieh Zeldich.) New York: Harper and Row, 1985.

LeGuin, Ursula. *The Farthest Shore*. New York: Atheneum, 1972.

———. *The Tombs of Atuan*. New York: Atheneum, 1971.

———. *The Wind's Twelve Quarters*. New York: Harper and Row, 1975.

———. *The Wizard of Earthsea*. New York: Parnassus, 1968.

Lionni, Leo. *Pezzettino*. New York: Pantheon, 1975.

Lobel, Arnold. *The Man Who Took the Indoors Out*. New York: Harper and Row, 1974.

Lunn, Janet. *Twin Spell*. New York: Harper and Row, 1969.

MacDonald, George. *At the Back of the North Wind*. New York: Schocken, 1963.

———. *The Princess and the Goblin*. New York: Morrow, 1986.

McHargue, Georgess. *Stoneflight*. New York: Viking, 1975.

McKillip, Patricia. *The House on Parchment Street*. New York: Atheneum, 1973.

Milne, A. A. *The House at Pooh Corner*. New York: E. P. Dutton, 1961.

———. *Winnie-the-Pooh*. New York: E. P. Dutton, 1926.

Montresor, Beni (ill.). *The Nightingale*. New York: Crown, 1985.

Norton, Andre. *Quag Keep*. New York: Atheneum, 1978.

———. *Wraiths of Time*. New York: Atheneum, 1976.

O'Connell, Jean S. *The Dollhouse Caper*. New York: Thomas Y. Crowell, 1975.

Oppel, Kenneth. *Colin's Fantastic Video Adventure*. New York: E. P. Dutton, 1985.

Pascal, Francine. *Hangin' Out with Cici*. New York: Viking, 1977.

Pearce, Philippa. *Tom's Midnight Garden*. Philadelphia: J. B. Lippincott, 1958.

Pierce, Meredith Ann. *Birth of the Firebringer*. New York: Four Winds, 1985.

Price, Susan. *The Devil's Piper*. New York: Greenwillow, 1976.

Pyle, Howard. *King Stork*. Boston: Little, Brown, 1973.

Raglin, Tim (ill.). *The Elephant's Child*. New York: Alfred A. Knopf, 1986.

Rockwell, Anne (ill.). *The Emperor's New Clothes*. New York: Thomas Y. Crowell, 1982.

Rodgers, Mary. *Freaky Friday*. New York: Harper and Row, 1972.

———. *Summer Switch*. New York: Harper and Row, 1982.

Shecter, Ben. *The River Witches*. New York: Harper and Row, 1979.

Sleator, William. *Among the Dolls*. New York: E. P. Dutton, 1975.

Smith, Stephanie A. *Snow-Eyes*. New York: Argo/Atheneum, 1985.

Snyder, Zilpha Keatley. *And All Between*. New York: Atheneum, 1976.

———. *Below the Root*. New York: Atheneum, 1975.

———. *Until the Celebration*. New York: Atheneum, 1977.

Stevens, Janet (ill.). *The Emperor's New Clothes.* New York: Holiday House, 1985.

Suhl, Yuri. *Simon Boom Gives a Wedding.* New York: Four Winds, 1972.

Tolkien, J. R. R. *The Hobbit.* New York: Ballantine, 1969.

———. *The Hobbit, or There and Back Again.* (Illustrated by Michael Hague.) Boston: Houghton Mifflin, 1984.

White, E. B. *Charlotte's Web.* New York: Harper and Row, 1952.

———. *Stuart Little.* New York: Harper and Row, 1945.

Williams, Margery. *The Velveteen Rabbit.* (Illustrated by Allen Atkinson.) New York: Alfred A. Knopf, 1983.

———. *The Velveteen Rabbit.* (Illustrated by Michael Hague.) New York: Holt, Rinehart and Winston, 1983.

Yep, Laurence. *Sweetwater.* New York: Harper and Row, 1973.

Yolen, Jane. *The Transfigured Hart.* New York: Harper and Row, 1975.

Zwerger, Lisbeth (ill.). *The Nightingale.* Natick, Mass.: Picture Book Studio, 1984.

# 12

## INFORMATION BOOKS: THE DESIRE TO KNOW

NATURAL HISTORY

Children who enjoy reading to find things out often seek books in a genre called nonfiction. Often called information books, some of these works have no story line, and others have only a minimal one, because their major concern is with presenting facts. *Nonfiction* is an unsatisfactory term because it implies the lack of a vital element when, in fact, the best of these books are as engrossing as the best fiction. The term *information books* is not definitive either because children can also glean much information from fiction. Teachers, librarians, and children are therefore left without a term that succinctly describes this large body of diversified literature. The books in this genre are about such ephemeral acts as dance (for example, *Imagine That! It's Modern Dance*, by Stephanie and Daniel Sorine) and such enduring monuments as Egyptian tombs (for example, *Tales Mummies Tell*, by Patricia Lauber). Some are simple enough for the youngest reader (for example, *I Touch*, by Rachel Isadora); others are so complex that only upper-grade readers with the reading skills of adults will be able to understand them (for example, *Handwriting Analysis Self-Taught*, by Joel Engel).

This category of books is the most prevalent kind that children's book publishers produce. One industry survey has shown that about 50 to 60 percent of juvenile books published each year are nonfiction (Duke, 1979). Teachers need to be well acquainted with this kind of book. This knowledge has two aspects: teachers should know the qualities that distinguish really fine information books and should be aware of the range of topics available in such books.

## EVALUATING INFORMATION BOOKS

As in any literary genre, there are both fine and not so fine information books. Information books can be evaluated according to the following criteria: the author's qualifications, the use of language, the accuracy of the material, the illustrations, the organizational and reference aids, and the book's self-sufficiency.

### THE QUALIFICATIONS OF THE AUTHOR

A major concern in evaluating an information book is the author's credentials. What qualifies this person to write a book about this topic? Frequently, dust-jacket material or the book's preface may tell why the author is interested in the topic and the background she or he brings to the writing. Excellent educational or experiential background is not enough, however.

Being knowledgeable about the topic is necessary; being able to communicate effectively with young readers is equally important. Part of evaluating the author's qualifications is judging how well she or he writes *for children.*

## THE USE OF LANGUAGE

Because the primary goal of information books is to convey information, the language used must clarify the topic being presented. Does the author use language to enhance readers' understanding of the subject? Language needs to be especially clear for child readers. Sometimes what seems clear to an adult evaluating the book may actually be confusing to a child.

Particularly clear writing is found in *Spring Comes to the Ocean,* by Jean C. George, a writer distinguished by her ability to describe nature. Here she recounts the distinctive way a hermit crab changes shells:

> First he unhooked the muscle at the spiral end of his old shell. Then he pulled himself out and stood vulnerable, so naked that even a windblown grain of sand could kill him. His exposed belly was so delicate that a nodding grass blade could cut him in half. . . . He slashed his tail through the air and stuck it into a new shell. Backing carefully, he reached his tail down and around until he felt the last coil of the shell. When at last he had a firm hold, he contracted all his muscles and slammed himself deep into the shell.

George does not assume that child readers will know what the word "vulnerable" means—she gives two examples of how vulnerable the crab is. The use of a difficult word is in itself not grounds for criticism. As long as words are explained by the context, an author should not be limited to simplified vocabulary all readers will know. Also, in the last sentence of the excerpt above, a less talented writer might have chosen the word "pushed." By using "slammed," a more powerful word for the same action, George emphasizes the intensity of the motion.

Equally as important as clarity is the imaginativeness of the language. The author of an information book should be able to present facts clearly but also creatively.

The talented writer George Mendoza presents facts in remarkably descriptive language. He begins *The Digger Wasp* by describing the environment:

> The sun is rising, brilliant, as though the plum-red eye of a giant were filling the sky. The sea, cooled by the long night of the summer moon, turns now, creeping back over the low tide rocks, foaming over patches of seaweed scattered like nets along the high white shore. The dunes begin to stir.

*A soft grainy texture recreates the sand on the beach; a firmer line defines the shell and crabs' bodies.* Illustration from *Spring Comes to the Ocean* by Jean Craighead George. Illustrated by John Wilson. Copyright © 1965 by Jean Craighead George. Reprinted by permission of Harper & Row, Publishers, Inc.

Later, Mendoza tells of the wasp's life work, providing food for her yet unhatched offspring:

> Spiraling straight up into the sky, the digger wasp disappears in the direction of a thick weed patch, where she will hunt and kill among the leaves. She hears a fat, green grasshopper singing in the sun. Wheeling in the sky, she dives, thrusting her poisonous stinger into the grasshopper's vulnerable underside. And then she returns, dragging her new victim, quivering, still alive, down the tunnel shaft into the oval chamber. Up and down, up and down, until the oval chamber is filled—five fat, juicy grasshoppers, all numbed, living mounds of flesh for the tiny larva to eat through.

After children have heard how the wasp provides food for her offspring, the teacher might encourage them to talk about how other creatures feed their offspring.[1]

Effective writers are able to use language to convey enthusiasm for a subject. In *Pagoo*, Holling C. Holling describes the first few minutes of a hermit crab's life:

> Little Pagurus—"Pagoo" for short—floated at the surface of the sea. Pagurus (pa-*gu*-rus) would grow into a two-fisted Hermit Crab—if he could make it. Someday he would live near the shore, walking on a sea floor of rock and sand. But before he could walk on the sea's bottom he must drift on its top, as helpless as a tiny fleck of foam. Pagoo's chances of growing up were not very good.
>
> Pagoo was quite small, because he had just been hatched from an egg the size of a pencil dot. You could see part way through him, that is, if you could first find his glassy body to slide under a microscope. His large eyes looked like eyes, but the rest of him was all points and joints and fuzzy places.
>
> Pagoo was lucky to be so small, to have a glass body looking like the water around him, to be almost invisible. In this big ocean, being seen could bring death. Even now, shadows of death swam toward him—gigantic Things almost half an inch long! Behind Pagoo, in front of Pagoo, below, above, on both sides of him the shadowy Things were gliding with mouths wide open. The giant shadows sucked up his shimmering neighbors, somehow passed him by, and little Pagoo was left in the sea with nothing to look at but water.

After hearing this part of *Pagoo*, children might find it interesting to learn about the dangers other young animals encounter. A teacher might arrange for a pet store owner to speak with students about the dangers affecting young pets.

The author's imagination and enthusiasm communicate to the reader a sense of the author as a person. Writing about the communication so essential between writer and reader, one expert has said (Fisher, 1972):

> Color, not lacking in the illustrations of modern topic books, is conspicuously absent from the texts of most of them. To the color of interesting facts we should add the color of unusual presentation of fact.

Meek (1977) comments on criteria for evaluating information books and supplies one of her own. She believes that literary merit is a central issue. A critical factor is how the facts are embedded in language. Her comments on the author's need to be aware of how language is related to the conceptual level of the intended reader are particularly helpful.

---

[1]The suckling of young is depicted in *Monkeys and Apes* (New York: Time-Life Books, 1976, p. 95). Full-color illustrations of the life habits of ten different types of monkeys supplement both factual and fictional material about these animals.

## ACCURACY

Imaginativeness of language must not be pursued at all costs; accuracy is the main criterion in evaluating information books. If the subject area is one with which the teacher or librarian is familiar, he or she can assess a book's accuracy. If the book is on a topic the teacher or librarian is not well informed about, there are two possible avenues for assessing accuracy: another teacher or a subject specialist in the school may be asked to examine the book, or published reviews may be consulted. The following shows how one reviewer assessed the accuracy of a science book (Stubbs, 1976):

> There are some errors, mostly arithmetical, which even a young reader should be able to spot if he has been trained to read critically. On page 71, the figures. . . .
>
> The inconsistency should be obvious to the careful reader. . . .

Despite the best efforts of authors and editors, inaccuracies do find their way into print. Sometimes authors present supposition or theorize in ways that make it seem that the material is supposed to be fact. In doing an information book, an author should clearly label and distinguish between facts and theories. A related problem is that information once considered factual may later turn out to be inaccurate. For example, it has recently been discovered that at least some dinosaurs were warm-blooded, rather than cold-blooded, as had previously been thought. Scientific evidence has been uncovered that suggests some dinosaurs did in fact nurture their young for long periods after birth; this new finding again contradicts information presented as fact in earlier books about dinosaurs. Holmes and Ammon (1985) make this point, as well as other useful ones, in describing ways to help children learn to uncover conflicting statements of fact in the books they read. A final problem is that information is always open to interpretation. This is illustrated interestingly in *A Six Pack and A Fake I.D.*, by Susan and Daniel Cohen. At one place, these authors declare (italics added): "There are many reasons for America's heavy drinking, particularly the drinking of *highly alcoholic* spirits like rum and whiskey." In fact, a can of beer or a glass of wine has the same alcoholic content as a shot of whiskey. That fact is obscured by the above statement.

## THE QUALITY OF THE ILLUSTRATIONS

Drawings, paintings, or photographs used to illustrate information books should be clear without being dull. The illustrations as well as the text must be both accurate and imaginative. The very best of these visuals can stand alone.

David Macaulay's drawings have been widely lauded as models of imaginative clarity. Using only black-ink line, Macaulay often recreates distant places and ancient times, and he does this without confusing readers who are unfamiliar with his topic. A fine example of his work is found in *Pyramid*, which covers the intricate, step-by-step process of constructing these ancient Egyptian monuments.[2] Macaulay's illustrations, printed on very heavy paper, help to clarify the complex building concepts. Definitions follow the more difficult words, for example: "annual inundation . . . was the time between July and November when the river rose and flooded the farmland."

Good illustrations can be in black and white or in color. *Life Story* is one book that is illustrated with full-color paintings. Author/illustrator Virginia Lee Burton provides full-page, opaque watercolor paintings in her usual highly decorative style. The illustrations are framed by curtains, as on a stage, since the book is subtitled "A Play in Five Acts." The history of life on earth from eons ago until today is summarized in six to eight lines of text per page, facing the illustrations. Small sketches of animals in scale with the play's narrators are also presented. The paintings are for the most part darker, and therefore somewhat less immediately appealing, than those this artist did for *The Little House*. *Life Story* is a simplified, but not condescending, treatment of a complex topic that can be difficult for young children to understand. To help students grasp the enormous span of time Burton describes, a teacher might construct a time line using a three-inch strip of tagboard extending around the entire room. Using a convenient unit of measure, the teacher can plot the different ages. This project will help children sense how long life has endured on earth and how relatively short is the period represented by modern life as we know it.

Artist Nonny Hogrogian provides softer, but no less effective, full-color illustrations for *The White Palace*, a book about the life cycle of a Chinook salmon written by Mary O'Neill. Hogrogian's beautifully detailed watercolor paintings are primarily in shades of blue and green. These show Chinook's life from his birth as a one-inch-long translucent sliver to his peaceful death beside Kima, his mate.

Many information books are illustrated with photographs. *The Cloud Book*, by Julian May, includes particularly fine ones that frequently extend across two pages. The black-and-white photographs are integral to the text, enhancing visually the written descriptions of various kinds of cloud for-

---

[2]A social studies unit on Egypt would be enhanced by Macaulay's book and the film *Egypt—Land of Antiquity*, which shows relics and artifacts of the pharohs, hieroglyphs, and temples in the Nile Valley (available from MAR/Chuck Film Industries, Mt. Pleasant, IL 60056).

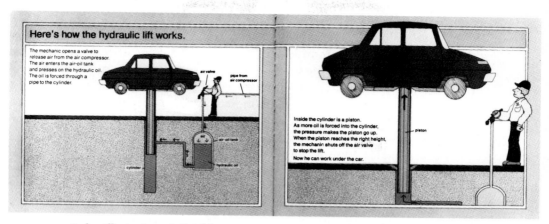

*In her illustrations, Gail Gibbons uses a very straightforward style; line and color do not call attention to themselves but rather serve to convey information.* Illustration from *Fill It Up!* by Gail Gibbons, for Thomas Y. Crowell. Copyright © 1985 by Gail Gibbons. Reprinted by permission of Harper & Row, Publishers, Inc.

---

mations.[3] Placed in a variety of locations on the page, the photos accompany drawings in some cases. The easy-to-read language includes vivid comparisons: "The bird soars only a few hundred feet high. But the clouds, formed of ice crystals, are more than eight miles above the earth."

Some illustrations in information books are in black and white, and others are in color. One reviewer makes the point that there is nothing inherently superior in the use of color. The critical question is whether the illustrations enhance the total effect of the book. Elleman (1981), in discussing *Seeds: Pop, Stick, Glide,* by Patricia Lauber, points out that given the dramatic photographs that effectively highlight shapes, textures, and shading, color would have been irrelevant in this particular book. Teachers and librarians should continually ask an important question as they review books: does this book really need color to make it more effective?

## ORGANIZATIONAL AND REFERENCE AIDS

The organizational and reference aids an author uses can greatly increase an information book's effectiveness. Often an author leads readers through

---

[3]*Clouds* is a black-and-white film showing various types of clouds, low-pressure areas, and the importance of clouds in bringing rain (available from BFA Educational Media, Division of Phoenix Films, 468 Park Avenue, South, New York, NY 10016).

a difficult topic by dividing a book into sections and providing a structural organization that enhances the presentation. The inclusion of such elements as a table of contents, an index, and a list of diagrams also makes it easier to use a book. Students generally use information books quite differently than they do works of fiction. Children usually read a fictional work straight through from beginning to end but often consult a nonfiction book to extract specific information. Therefore, being able to locate or refer back to particular sections is more crucial in an information book.

An especially commendable selection of reference aids is included in *You Can Be a Plumber*, by Arthur Liebers. One of the *Vocations in Trades* series published by Lothrop, Lee and Shepard, this book gives a thorough introduction to the field: what is involved in the work, how to learn the trade, and descriptions of aptitude tests, necessary tools, and apprenticeship training. Special features include the following:

1. detailed contents with main headings and subheads in the body of the texts
2. a list of apprenticeship and training field offices
3. a list of civil-service commission offices
4. a list of state apprenticeship offices
5. a glossary
6. an index
7. plentiful diagrams to illustrate points made in the text

## SELF-SUFFICIENCY

Readers should be able to understand the material being presented in an information book without looking elsewhere for definitions, facts, or concepts. The writer must not have presupposed that readers possess any knowledge about the topic. Information books are not like textbooks, which can sometimes assume that vocabulary and information has been presented earlier. An effective information book is self-contained. Margery Fisher (1972), a British author of children's books, who has written a significant book of criticism of nonfiction, says that

> . . . if a book is the medium of information, it should be as complete as possible within its defined limits. The writer should not rely on any outside agency to make his point clear; it is his duty to use his medium as fully and as expertly as he can.

# SHARING INFORMATION BOOKS

Children generally do not read information books for recreation, nor does a teacher often read an information book to the entire class during the daily literature-sharing period. For some reason, teachers and children seldom think of nonfiction books as literature to be enjoyed for its literary quality, for the aesthetic pleasure it can provide. However, there are ways in which teachers or librarians can promote reading of information books by both individuals and groups.

One function a teacher or librarian can perform is introducing books to a child who has voiced an immediate interest in some object or event. A child's enthusiasm may be short-lived but can be intensified if a teacher or librarian knows a book to suggest. For example, if a student comments on seeing an unusual butterfly on the way to school one morning, the teacher might tell the child about *Butterfly Time,* by Alice E. Goudey. In this book, a two-page introductory author's note provides technical information that helps the reader understand what follows. The text itself is simple, yet graceful—providing information about the forms, habits, and habitats of the butterflies featured. Adrienne Adams provides crayon-and-watercolor drawings. Another book that might be appropriately suggested at such a time is Alice L. Hopf's *Monarch Butterflies.* Black-and-white illustrations by Peter Burchard accompany the text, which tells how to catch, house, raise, and care for a monarch butterfly. Instructions are also given on how to photograph butterflies.

A teacher or librarian can also recommend books to the avid "specialist," the child who wants yet another book in an area of continuing interest. One of the joys of working with children is encountering a child who is intensely interested in some topic, who reads every book she or he can find about the subject. One second-grade boy devoured every book he could find on dinosaurs. He eventually became far more knowledgeable than his teacher about their habits, environments, and struggles to survive. A valuable book to recommend to such a child is *Little Dinosaurs and Early Birds,* by John Kaufmann, part of the *Let's Read and Find Out* series on science published by Thomas Y. Crowell. Drawings in black and white and in three colors help readers visualize how the transformation from dinosaurs to birds might have taken place. Illustrations appear on every page, and the text is set with wide margins. The pronunciation key that follows the introduction of each new term is helpful. As a follow-up to reading about dinosaurs, a child might enjoy making a papier-mâché replica of one. A simple wire armature can support the sculpture, which can be painted authentically and shellacked to ensure permanence.

Knowledge of information books can also be used to broaden the reading habits of a child bogged down in one author or genre. For example, after a fourth-grade girl has read all of Marguerite Henry's fictional horse stories (which are, incidentally, full of valuable information), the teacher or librarian might recommend a nonfiction book on horses to her. Susie Blair's *The Show Ring* follows the life of Easter Pony from spring shearing until her first trip into the ring. Dahlov Ipcar's *Horses of Long Ago* features stylized full-color illustrations and traces horse history back 50 million years. There are almost more black-and-white photos than text in Helen Mather's *Light Horsekeeping,* which regales readers with the delights and trials of owning a horse.

Another function teachers perform is planning group lessons using their knowledge of information books. Much classroom instruction is based on textbook series; many of these are fine and getting better. However, an effective alternative way to extend children's learning is to select related information books that can serve as the foundation for a unit of study. The teacher might read information books or parts of them aloud to the entire class. Such books can also serve as resource material for small-group reports. After introducing the unit, the teacher divides the children into several independent groups; each group chooses the book it will report on. Or, children can expand their competency by reading such books individually and preparing reports to the group.

*The Hidden World: Life Under a Rock,* by Laurence Pringle, would be good material for a small-group report. The vocabulary in this book is simple enough for third-graders to deal with. Pringle's book defines the concept of ecosystem clearly as "a place in nature with all of its living and nonliving parts." The book is divided into two sections: one deals with various creatures and plants that exist on land; the other deals with those in streams, ponds, and lakes. Excellent close-up photographs of such creatures as spiders, sowbugs, and caddis flies provide a visual guide to the "hidden world." Simple pen-and-ink drawings represent other creatures mentioned in the text but not depicted in photographs. A list of further reading is included.

## KINDS OF INFORMATION BOOKS

To make optimal use of information books, teachers and librarians need to be aware of the variety of topics treated by authors of such books. It is possible to find a nonfiction book on almost every topic imaginable. Teachers and librarians must exchange information about which books are needed and which books are available in order to make nonfiction books an integral part of the school curriculum. Lima (1982) makes locating a book on a specific topic easier by providing access to hundreds of books in over two hundred categories. Her reference book includes separate title and illustrator indexes. A larger work, useful in locating books about more elusive topics, is the annual *Subject Guide to Children's Books in Print*, published by R. R. Bowker, which indexes more than 6400 subject categories.

## BOOKS ABOUT THE ARTS

Because of its permanence, the visual art of painting (and to a lesser degree sculpture) has been widely represented in children's books. Extensive annotated bibliographies dealing with the many different kinds of art books are referenced in Chapter 2. Books about color are quite common, for example, *Let's Find Out About Color*, by Ann Campbell. Simple illustrations in intense colors, by Boche Kaplan and Roz Abisch, are on every page. On some pages, the text is printed over the full-page illustration. The book is written for very young children and would be a good introduction to easel painting in kindergarten. The book introduces the concept of mixing colors and the idea that colors can transmit feelings.[4] On a bright red page, the text reads: "Color makes you feel different things. Red makes you feel hot." A vocabulary list at the end of the book augments the content.

Line, another element of art, is introduced in *the lines are coming*, by Hans-Georg Rauch. Done entirely in black and white, this book shows potential artists how to combine lines to create a variety of subjects from different viewpoints and with different perspective.

Art history has received the attention of many writers, and Shirley Glubok is among the best of these (Noyce, 1978). *The Art of the Plains Indians* is illustrated—as are many of Glubok's books—with photographs by her husband, Alfred Tamarin. In this book, the pages are tinted natural shades of buff, gold, tan, and rust except for the parts of the pages where the black-and-white illustrative photographs appear. The author presents artwork found on tepees, buffalo hides, war bonnets, and clothing. Other books by Glubok deal with the art of various native American groups such as the Aztecs, the Incas, and the Northwest, Plains, and woodland tribes. Such books help children begin to differentiate native Americans into distinct

---

[4]The sensory and emotional appeal of color is emphasized in the film *Color*, part of the *Art of Seeing* series (available from Films, Inc., Wilmette, IL 60091).

THE ART OF THE

# PLAINS INDIANS

Shirley Glubok

Pipe bowl, Cheyenne, stone, Denver Art Museum, photograph by Alfred Tamarin

*On this title page illustration, curved lines are used for unity; the circle around the buffalo, the curve of the animal's hump, and the curved lines in the typeface reinforce each other visually.* Reproduced with permission of Macmillan Publishing Company from *The Art of the Plains Indians* by Shirley Glubok, illustrated by Alfred Tamarin. Copyright © 1975 by Shirley Glubok Tamarin.

groups. An intrinsic danger in some social studies programs is that children may end up thinking of "the Indians" as a homogeneous group, despite the physical, linguistic, cultural, political, and religious differences among tribes, which are described by Banks (1984).

Largely anonymous folk artists are the subjects of many of Shirley Glubok's books, but other writers focus on widely known artists. Books about individual artists include the "Artstart" series of paperbound books published by Doubleday. The series includes *Paul Klee, Pablo Picasso,* and *Marc Chagall,* written by Ernest Raboff. These books are distinguished by their large-sized format and the high quality of the reproductions; the fact that a single full-color illustration appears on a page makes these books especially useful for sharing with a whole class at once. Nelly Munthe's *Meet Matisse* is also an impressive book: its large square shape and intensely white coated paper set off the reproductions to their best advantage. Photos of both works on paper and stained glass windows reveal this artist's vivid imagination. In *Pablo Picasso,* Ibi Lepscky focuses on personal details of the artist's life, starting when he was a little boy. The brief text is run below cartoonlike drawings by Paolo Cardoni. Rather than focusing on a single artist, Laurene Krasny Brown and Marc Brown present works by many artists in their book *Visiting the Art Museum*. They unobtrusively use the device of a fictitious family's visit to a museum to tie together the presentation of disparate artworks—ranging from an ancient Egyptian mummy case to works by John Singleton Copley, Auguste Renoir, and Roy Lichtenstein.

Art in the world around us is another subject taken up by many children's book writers. In *New Moon Cove*, Ann Atwood helps readers see the various natural art forms found in and around the sea. Both the color photography and the language are exciting. The author speaks of the "green combers [that] fling off veils of rainbows" and of "a wild fist of water [that] pounds at the rocks." *Inside: Seeing Beneath the Surface*, by Jan Adkins, explores creatively the insides of such unlikely items as an apple pie, a street, and a pencil. Each important object in the detailed drawings is labeled clearly, usually in red. The author emphasizes how the "third eye" works:

> Your third eye can see (or imagine really, though seeing and imagining are very alike) an apple as if it were cut open with all its parts on display.

The book helps readers use their imaginations to see beyond the shell, or outside, of things. The ultimate goal is to be able to view the world from someone else's point of view.

Books about how to complete art projects are often undistinguished; they tend to be craftsy and peculiarly unartistic. A happy exception is *OP-Tricks: Creating Kinetic Art*, by Mickey K. Marks, featuring kinetics by Edith Alberts. Writing for upper-elementary readers, the author gives thorough and understandable instructions. The step-by-step directions show the reader how to create art that tricks the eye and gives the illusion of movement. For teachers seeking a book about a specific craft, Gallivan (1981) indexes over two hundred books according to both the products of the projects and the types of materials used.

Music, unlike the visual arts, is transitory. Once performed it disappears (does not exist except in printed or recorded form) until it is once more reinterpreted. Perhaps because of its ephemeral quality, music is seldom written about by children's authors. Those who do write about it usually write about the instruments that make the music or about the story lines of operas. A third common type of music-related book, the biographies of musicians, was discussed in Chapter 9 (see pages 396, 398, and 410).

*A Rainbow of Sound*, by Herbert Kupferberg, is about the instruments of a symphony orchestra and the music they make. It features photography by Morris Warman, in a pleasing arrangement with lots of open space. Instead of simply describing different instruments, the author shows "how they fit into the beautiful tonal tapestry that constitutes a symphony." A teacher might share this book with children when the school music teacher is doing a unit on instruments or else recommend it to the music teacher for use during music class. If there is no music specialist, the classroom teacher might arrange with the director of a high school orchestra to have some students demonstrate their instruments. Alternatively, a teacher might use the film "Instruments of the Band and Orchestra—the Strings" (available from Coronet Instructional Films, Div. of Random House, 400 Hahn Road, Westminster, MD 21157).

A book incorporating instruments, but really about the people who play them, is *The Philharmonic Gets Dressed.* In this humorous look into the performers' lives, Karla Kuskin describes the homely details about 105 people getting to work as dusk descends on the city one Friday night. There is a great deal of variety in the preparations (some take showers, some take bubble baths), in types of accessories worn (silk socks with clocks, panty-hose), in modes of transportation to work (cabs, subways), and in instruments played (flute, tympany). As she carries this detailing to its conclusion—the musicians working—Kuskin draws readers into a world seldom considered. The delightful, idiosyncratic details of what is involved in this many people coming together to work are shown in simple, cartoonlike illustrations by Marc Simont. This is one of many books recommended by Smardo (1984), who suggests such books can augment the limited music experiences most children now have in school.

A beautiful example of the retelling of an opera is *The Magic Flute,* by poet Stephen Spender, illustrated by Caldecott winner Beni Montresor. The pictures were adapted from Montresor's sets for a production of *The Magic Flute* by the New York City Opera.

Like music, dance disappears once the performance is over, so capturing it in words is difficult. Kellman (1977) annotates a list of books about dance that includes many not discussed here. Authors tend to develop a story line in books about dance in order to interest child readers in this art form. An example is *Opening Night,* by Rachel Isadora, full of house lights, dancers' costume trunks, wardrobe mistresses, stagehands, and other elements integral to young Heather's life. A hybrid between fiction and nonfiction, *Opening Night* emphasizes the pleasures of dance rather than the reality of exhausting physical work.

*A Very Young Dancer,* by Jill Krementz, is told in first-person narration and includes many small realistic details. The narrator, Stephanie, tells readers "I wear size 9" and "I don't eat liver or brussels sprouts"; other minute details accumulate to make this aspiring dancer seem real. Stephanie's life at the School of American Ballet is full of glamorous personalities, the actual stars of George Balanchine's company. The book includes a fair amount of basic information, although there is no glossary. The photographs, which directly reflect the text, are the work of the author, who is primarily known for her fine photography. Krementz used the same format to present the glamour of nine-year-old Tato's life in *A Very Young Circus Flyer*.

In *A Young Person's Guide to Ballet*, by Noel Streatfield, clear black-and-white photographs and line drawings illustrate a series of chapters about ballet, strung together by a fictional account of two children who want to dance. The book provides extended information on the history of ballet, on contemporary ballet dancers, and on the stories told in ballets. The device of the two fictional children could have been better executed; they remain two-dimensional, never really coming to life.

*Dance Me a Story*, by Jane Rosenberg, is a beautifully produced book that will appeal to any child who is interested in ballet. The book has a large trim size and page layouts with impressive amounts of white space. The full-page watercolor paintings tell the stories of twelve classic ballets. The stories are given as they are actually performed in the ballets, not as they are usually told to children. For example, the plot of the ballet "Cinderella" as summarized in this book contains details not usually included in the children's book versions of the story. The book concludes with technical notes by the illustrator and production details of the ballets, which may be of interest even to adults. Recommend this book as individual reading for a child determined to become a dancer.

Currently, there are almost no books about dance designed to appeal to, or even be acceptable to, boys. This undoubtedly reflects the dominant cultural view that dance is less than completely masculine. Rachel Isadora's *Max* does little to dispel this view. A fictionalized account of a boy who wants to both dance and play baseball, this story is unfortunately rather contrived and has a cop-out ending. Max is two-dimensional and never has to deal with the obvious problem: what will his ball-playing buddies think when they discover he is dancing? An energetic dancer such as Edward Villella refutes the notion that dance is not for men; he projects a virile, athletic image. Authors have not yet provided children's books about dance featuring strong, masculine images. One pleasantly positive exception is *Worlds Apart*, by Robert Maiorano, subtitled "The Autobiography of a Dancer from Brooklyn." This book relates the author's experiences, from his early life in a cold-water tenement in the city, to his performance as a soloist during the New York City Ballet's triumphant tour of Europe and Russia. A tough street kid, Maiorano was able, by enduring extensive, physically punishing training, to succeed in the glamorous world of the performing arts.

## BOOKS ABOUT ANIMALS

Books about animals are among the most prevalent of nonfiction works for children, because of children's continuing fascination with animals. Some books about animals are written in simple language that primary-grade students can read to themselves; also available are sophisticated treatments of living creatures written for intermediate-grade boys and girls with well-developed reading skills. The more difficult books can be read aloud by the teacher to a group of young listeners, some of whom might not be able to read them by themselves.

*Dolphin,* by Robert A. Morris, is an interesting book that is part of Harper and Row's series *A Science I Can Read Book,* designed for beginning readers. The language is simple, and there is a lot of repetition in the sentence structure. The short sentences usually contain five to ten words. The pictures by Mamoru Funai are more artistic than many of those found in beginning reading books.

*Wild and Wooly Mammoths,* by Aliki Brandenburg, is one of the *Let's Read and Find Out* series, published by Thomas Y. Crowell. This book presents an interesting account of how the frozen bodies of now-extinct mammoths were discovered in Siberia and studied by scientists. The author describes the life of these animals during the age of dinosaurs, pointing out possible reasons why they became extinct.

Because of primary teachers' common practice of including egg incubation in the science curriculum, *A Chick Hatches,* by Joanna Cole, is a useful book. Cole explains the different parts of an egg and describes the fertilization process. The reader/listener witnesses the chicken's development from conception to hatching. The text is appropriately straightforward and informative. The photographs are integral to the material being presented and are clear and large (usually limited to one per page). Most are in black-and-white, but a few are in color. A pleasant follow-up to Cole's book is the film *Chickens* (available from AIMS Instructional Media Services, 626 Justin Avenue, Glendale, CA 91201), which provides a close-up look at habits and behaviors of these fowls.

*In My Garden,* by Ermanno Cristini and Luigi Puricelli, is unusual in providing information about garden inhabitants in a mostly wordless format. Large, decoratively patterned, yet realistic, pictures bleed to the page edges. On several pages, only part of an animal is shown, which reveals the relative sizes of the creatures quite effectively. The concluding double-page spread contains black-and-white, reduced reproductions of the earlier pages, with the creatures numbered in red and identified by name. A particularly well done introduction to common, garden-variety animals, this book could lead readers to more complex science books.

Intermediate-grade children will enjoy a book written by Carol Carrick, *Sand Tiger Shark*, which tells this shark's story from his birth to his death in a fight with a great white shark. Carrick's storytelling techniques keep the reader interested and in suspense and also provide basic biological information. The artwork, by Donald Carrick, is both beautiful and dramatic; the double-page spreads are done in pastel blues and greens.

*Animals of the Polar Regions*, by Sylvia A. Johnson, is a well-researched information book that opens with a description of the difficult environments in both the North and South polar regions.[5] The book describes the lives and habits of ten animals that live in these areas: emperor penguin, walrus, arctic lemming, musk ox, barren-ground caribou, arctic fox, arctic hare, polar bear, snowy owl, and arctic tern. The text is placed on the left-hand page of each spread, along with a map indicating the region from which the animal comes. The illustrations are on the facing right-hand pages. The book will probably not be read straight through by most children, but it can serve as an excellent research source.

*Animals of the Polar Regions* is from a series of books about the natural sciences published by Lerner Publications. The books illuminate small bits of nature using brilliant full-color photos and lucid text. In contrast to many others, this series seems to be uniformly fine. Another title from it is *Bats*, also by Sylvia A. Johnson. Child readers will be fascinated by the close-up color photos of the ten-day-old horseshoe bat's strong claws and sharp teeth. This picture is an example of how color can enhance a photograph's ability to convey information.

The need for protection is the theme of *How Animals Hide*, by Robert McClung, an exemplary information book published by the National Geographic Society. This book features a simple text printed on glossy, brightly colored paper that complements the accompanying close-up photographs. The author includes a variety of creatures that are able to hide from their

---

[5]A teacher might introduce this book by showing the film *Polar Regions*, which focuses on seals and their constant struggle with enemies. This film is appropriate for intermediate grades (available from CCM Films, 35 MacQuesten Parkway, South, Mt. Vernon, NY 10550).

*John Butler's meticulously executed brush strokes create understated, full-color paintings, with backgrounds that must be studied to notice all the details. The pleasant square illustrations are delicately bordered by thin, unobtrusive lines of two different colors.* From *Panda Climbs* by Derek Hall, illustrations by John Butler. Illustrations copyright © 1984 by John Butler. Reprinted by permission of Walker Books Ltd.

enemies by blending in with their surroundings. One form of protective coloration found on many animals is dealt with in the text as follows, and excellent photos reinforce the information:

> Some creatures have spots that look like eyes but are not eyes at all. The caterpillar and moth may scare their enemies with such eyespots. The bug and the two fishes confuse their enemies with eyespots near their tails.

In *Panda Climbs*, a book by Derek Hall, with illustrations by John Butler, a young panda seeks protection from a leopard. Pages of simple text, telling of a day in the life of this appealing baby animal who is learning about the world, face full-page illustrations. Readers will return again and again to this small book to reexperience a vicarious sense of accomplishment as the panda masters his environment. Similarly modest but enjoyable tales are told in *Tiger Runs* and *Otter Swims*, by the same author and illustrator.

Edward R. Ricciuti explores popular ideas about animals in *Do Toads Give You Warts? Strange Animal Myths Explained*. The book seeks to correct common misconceptions, for example:

Elephants are afraid of mice.

A groundhog tells when spring is coming.[6]

Cobras dance to music.

The author gives biological facts about the animals that explain how these misconceptions might have arisen. At the end of the book, a few pages contain strange-but-true facts about animals, for example: "Some hummingbirds can beat their wings 200 times a second." Children will probably be interested in and remember such facts as these because they are so striking. Equally fascinating little-known-but-true facts are supplied by Jim Aylward in *You're Dumber in the Summer* and *Your Burro Is No Jackass*.

## SCIENCE BOOKS

Most of the many science books for children are about nature, which is an area of study generally emphasized in the elementary school curriculum.[7] Some books help children appreciate the beauty of nature. *We Walk in Sandy Places*, by Byrd Baylor, is a combination of detailed photographs of the desert and elegantly written text. Written from the viewpoint of a repentant intruder, this book tells how to read the tracks left in the sand by insects, birds, and other creatures who live in the desert. Marilyn Schweitzer's photographs capture these imprints, and a few of them tell their own stories. Teachers can use this book to heighten primary-grade students' visual discrimination. It also helps many children understand an environment quite unlike their own. Few boys and girls, except those living in some of the southwestern states, have personally experienced the desert environment. A teacher can help intermediate-grade students share their environment

---

[6]On Groundhog Day, a teacher might have the class compare different treatments of this tradition. Wendy Kesselman's *Time for Jody* (New York: Harper and Row, 1975) is a gentle fantasy of how growing up into responsibility lets Jody help the other animals, who need a groundhog of their own.

[7]Science books are the second most popular type of book among children, according to Sarah B. Granham in "Do Children Read Science Books?" (*Science and Children*, February 1978, p. 29). A year-long survey of books checked out of school libraries by children indicated that fiction was the most popular genre (57 percent), science was second (17 percent), and biography third (7 percent).

with children in another geographic region. Using simple cameras, the class can take snapshots of natural features in their area and write descriptions that elaborate on the pictures. They can then exchange the whole package with students in another part of the country (Jarolimek, 1986).

*Morning Glories*, by Sylvia A. Johnson, is another title in the natural sciences series of Lerner Publications. This book won a New York Academy of Sciences Special Award. The color photos of the outside (stem and leaf structures) and inside (magnified cross section of a seed, showing cotyledon and radicle) of a morning glory are impressive. The book also includes a glossary.

Franklyn Branley has written a distinguished series of scientific books for children, of which *Light and Darkness* is typical. The author explains in concise terms how light helps people see. Several pages are devoted to text and drawings describing how light travels. The three-color and black-and-white drawings by Reynold Ruffins are rather whimsical. Other books by Branley include *Experiments in the Principles of Space Travel*, *Measure with Metric*, and *What the Moon Is Like*. Pleasantly simple, cartoonlike drawings by Holly Keller accompany Branley's *Air Is All Around You*.

A sometimes dangerous element in the physical environment is described in *Fire*, by Gail K. Haines. The cover features wildly dancing fire "creatures" by Jacqueline Chwast. Done in stark black-and-white, but with the fire always a brilliant red, the illustrations reinforce the importance, danger, and mystery of fire. The author lists the uses and characteristics of fire, discusses superstitions about it, and suggests experiments that readers can do with adult supervision. This text is clear, and the vocabulary is simple. Special terms are explained within the context of the sentence or paragraph, for example: "Anything that will burn can be fuel for a fire. These materials are called 'flammable,' which means they can burn."

Science books often include experiments for children to perform. In *Heat and Temperature*, Jeanne Bendick gives instructions for simple experiments that introduce basic concepts about heat and temperature. After each one, she includes short sections titled "What Do You Think?" "Think for Yourself," and "Try This for Yourself." Children can carry out these experiments using easily accessible items. The author has published many books about such diverse topics as the Loch Ness monster, electronics, solids, adaptation, and the environment. She continues her fine work in another book, *Artificial Satellites*.

*Egg-ventures: First Science Experiments*, by Harry Milgrom, contains a variety of simple experiments. The beginning scientist first learns various methods of measuring the egg. Experiments are conducted by rolling, cook-

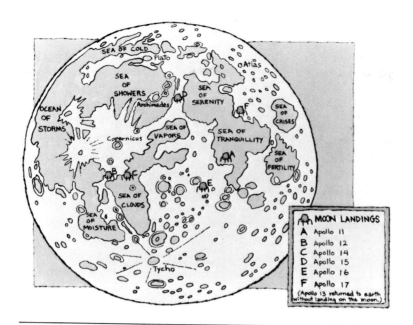

**Color and quality of line are not important elements in a map like this: more critical are readability and accuracy.** Illustration from *What the Moon Is Like* by Franklyn Branley. Illustrated by True Kelley. Copyright © 1986 by True Kelley. Reprinted by permission of Harper & Row, Publishers, Inc.

ing, and beating eggs. On the last page, the author reviews the concepts taught in the experiments. The activities are clearly described and practical; children can perform them with only a minimum of equipment.

It is wise, when using the books discussed above, or similar ones, with children, for the teacher to try the experiments before presenting them to the class in order to anticipate problems that might arise. Although authors of such books are cognizant of the need to eliminate potential dangers from science experiments intended for children, it never hurts to make sure an experiment works safely.

Writing effective science books for children requires a deft touch. As Stubbs (1984) remarks,

> I have a built-in objection to stating scientific information as though it were dogma, but I have to admit that when writing for the young within a limited space, this is a difficult thing to avoid.

The context of this comment is his recommendation of Seymour Simon's *Earth* as a book that skillfully avoids this pitfall. *Jupiter* and *Saturn* continue this series, which has an attractive 10-inch-square format with many full-page, full-color pictures.

## BOOKS ABOUT MATHEMATICS

Many math books currently available for children present complex concepts in comprehensible fashion. One example is *Yes-No; Stop-Go: Some Patterns in Mathematical Logic,* by Judith Gersting and Joseph Kuczkowski. From an imaginary castle surrounded by the friendly Whiffle people and the unfriendly Piffle people, the authors lead readers, via drawbridges over the moat, to an introduction of the "OR pattern" and the "AND pattern" in mathematical logic. After diagramming these ideas, the authors encourage readers to copy and complete the table. Then the authors move on to a modern setting, reexplaining the concept in the context of railroad switching.

Clever drawings in black ink enhanced with pink and brown wash enliven *Solomon Grundy, Born on Oneday,* by Malcolm E. Weiss.[8] Using the old Mother Goose rhyme as the departure point, the author explains the concept of infinite number, contrasting it with the counting system of finite numbers. The book provides simple activities and questions to stimulate the imaginations of primary-grade children.

The concepts of the "mean," "median," and "mode" are explained in an easy-to-understand manner in *Averages,* by Jane J. Srivastava. The examples given and the problems posed are based on situations and experiences familiar to many children. Teachers might use *Averages* to supplement a math program with intermediate-grade students or to introduce primary-grade students to these concepts. The illustrations by Aliki are excellent in their clear, yet imaginative presentation of details.

## BOOKS ABOUT SOCIAL STUDIES

Although some social studies books for children present people stereotypically (for instance, the outdated image of Dutch boys and girls clomping past windmills and tulip fields in wooden shoes), they are fortunately outnumbered by well-written books accurately depicting people today.

A picture book for young readers, *People,* by Peter Spier, deals with an immense topic. Making it accessible is no mean feat, and Spier uses his

---

[8]Another book in this series is David Adler's *3D, 2D, 1D* (New York: Thomas Y. Crowell, 1975), with illustrations by Harvey Weiss. Familiar objects—books, television, and floor tiles—are used to enhance children's understanding through concrete, simple experiments. Fanciful line drawings in black, white, and red, by Wendy Watson, illustrate how to begin the experiments for middle- to upper-primary-grade readers in Clyde Watson's *Binary Numbers* (New York: Thomas Y. Crowell, 1977).

customary watercolor and ink-line drawings effectively to accomplish this task. Some pages detail life's contradictions, for example, wealth and poverty, power and helplessness, the famous and the unknown, wisdom and foolishness. His emphasis is on the ways particularities of a given culture suit that culture.

> All of us want to look our best. Still, what is considered beautiful or handsome in one place is considered ugly, and even ridiculous, elsewhere.

Varieties in skin color and other physical features, where people choose to live, games people play, and how people communicate are all detailed, most often with an array of small drawings that fill the large pages to the margins. The two pages on games, for example, contain twenty-four small drawings covering almost as many different countries. The pages are so filled with information child readers will return to them again and again.

Books that are specifically focused on a certain group of people can enhance middle school students' understanding of many concepts in the field of social studies. One of these concepts is that there are ways all humans are alike and ways they are different. In *An Album of Chinese Americans*, Betty Lee Sung discusses the past history and present customs and problems of this group. The book corrects some prejudices and basic misinformation about Chinese-Americans by presenting a history of anti-Chinese feelings dating back to the nineteenth century. Reference aids include a table of contents, an index, and a section about the author.

Immigration is one topic that is considered in some books, which can be used to augment social studies textbooks. Two long books intended for mature readers provide information about immigrants: *Coming to America*, by Susan Garver and Paula McGuire, and *The Hispanic Americans*, by Milton Meltzer. The book by Garver and McGuire is divided into three sections, describing immigration from Mexico, Cuba, and Puerto Rico. Differences among these groups and their immigration patterns are explored. The text is supported by a section of black-and-white photographs from a variety of sources. Meltzer's book has black-and-white photos interspersed throughout the entire text. The brief accounts of actual Hispanic individuals and families give this book a pleasantly personal feeling; the problems faced by this ethnic group have more impact because the reader sees that they happen to real people.

Migration of people to find work is the subject of *In This Proud Land*, by Bernard Wolf. After a lengthy, though probably necessary, introduction to the plight of Mexican-Americans living in the Rio Grande Valley, the book moves on to consider the life of a particular family in detail. The author describes the annual migration of David Hernandez and his family from their Texas home to find jobs as migrant workers in the sugar-beet fields of Minnesota, where they earn just enough money to survive.

In addition to books about groups of people, books about individuals are enjoyed by children. A book notable for its gritty realism is *Lito the Shoeshine Boy*, a translation of a first-person account of a poor boy's life in a city in Honduras. Author David Mangurian presents the story of Lito, who was abandoned by his family and works ten hours a day shining shoes. Afterward he goes home to the one room he shares with several other children and a woman who allows him to stay there. Lito knows the importance of education, but in order to go to school, he must have an adult register him, and no one will. So he shines shoes and thinks about the future. The narration is dramatic.

> So I walk around, see, with my mouth open catching flies because there's nothing to eat. I feel empty. I get a bad pain in my belly like something hot down there. And when I don't eat, the worms do like this
>
> *brrrrrrrrrrrrrr*
>
> like a motor, asking for food. The worms I have. And when they're full, my guts go
>
> *chee-chee-chee-chee*
>
> in my belly. It's bad.

A striking fact in this book is that Lito's long workday is not considered unusual by others in his community. Laws regulating the age at which children may begin working vary greatly. After reading this book, upper-intermediate-grade students might be interested in getting in touch with local government officials to find out at what age young people are allowed to work and how many hours they may work.

Another way in which some people are different from others is that they must deal with physical or mental handicaps. The books recently produced in large numbers about exceptional children are undoubtedly the work of well-meaning adults. Unfortunately, many feature a paper-thin main character, whose only distinguishing quality seems to be the handicap. These books must be judged on their basic literary qualities, regardless of their utilitarian nature. *Rachel*, by Elizabeth Fanshawe, is not interesting, regardless of one critic's praise (Sapon-Shevin, 1977):

> A colorful picture book for very young children provides glimpses of Rachel's life at home, in school, and on vacation; she has a camera, she belongs to a Brownies troup, and she uses a wheelchair. Rachel has fun and she also has a future; she is a participant in whatever she's involved in rather than an observer.

Western (1978) points out that an author of an information book who chooses to create a fictional character who is a handicapped child must assume the responsibility for making that character live in readers' minds. Western describes the persistence of the didactic tradition, analyzing five books that, she concludes, are neither informative nonfiction nor interesting fiction. Despite the first-person narration common in such books, many remain simple lists of characteristics.

Rather than quasi-fictionalization, Janet Kamien chooses to utilize a pragmatic and direct, but not condescending, approach in *What If You Couldn't . . . ?* She deals with several different types of problems: lack of vision, learning disabilities, physical disabilities, hearing loss, and emotional problems. Highly patterned black-and-white drawings are placed appropriately throughout the text. Complex topics, such as the difference between a conductive and a sensory-neural hearing loss, are explained fully enough so readers can understand them but not in so much detail as to be overwhelming.

Social phenomena of the past are difficult to write about in ways child readers find interesting. In *Medicine Show*, Mary Calhoun writes for upper-grade children with well-developed reading skills and some interest in history. During the era in which these shows were most popular (from 1800 to 1890), there were no pharmaceutical laws. Anyone could mix up anything and declare it to be medicinal. Patent medicines achieved immense popularity; in 1906, eighty million dollars' worth were sold. Such "medicines" were sold via a form of show business in which sellers put on sketchy plays. Between acts, the sellers hawked their wares. The author incorporates extensive accounts from people actually involved in such dealings. She also uses quotes from the advertising of the day:

> . . . if timely taken, it not only cures the griping of the guts and the wind Cholick, but preventeth that woeful Distemper of the Dry Belly Ach [sic].

Calhoun describes the psychology that made people want to buy, to respond to the seller's manipulation:

> In the nineteenth and early twentieth centuries, people were more easily deceived about medicine because they had scanty access to factual medical information. Their schools did not teach details about the human body or how to maintain its health. Nor did magazines and newspapers make a habit of publishing articles on physical health, as they do today. Most people knew little about the internal makeup of their bodies or why their bodies "got out of whack," as they might term disorder. Lacking knowledge, many people feared being cut by the surgeon's knife, and many believed that a person went to a hospital only to die.

One aspect of social history that children often find intriguing is how holidays were celebrated in the past. Children will enjoy *Christmas on the Prairie,* by Joan Anderson, because of the differences from our contemporary celebrations that it describes. Based on a living history museum in Indiana, called Connor Prairie, this book re-creates the particulars of a fictional family—the Curtises—newly arrived in the Midwest from New York State in 1836. Black-and-white photographs by George Ancona illustrate, among other things, a two-foot-high St. Nicholas cookie, Belznickel, the old man who checks to see if children have been good, and the Dutch legend about oranges. The book shows the diversity among people: one family in the town believes Christmas customs to be pagan and adheres only to Biblical injunctions; the young rowdies ride into town, singing and shooting their guns, after "gettin' into the squeezin's." The book makes information about a holiday celebration more vivid than most textbooks can.

*Rosh Hashanah and Yom Kippur,* by Howard Greenfield, is the third in a series of books about Jewish holy days. This book tells, in straightforward language, the meaning of these two religious holidays, neither of which is well-understood, since neither is linked with a historic event or a seasonal celebration. Highly patterned woodcuts frame the text.

The ways adults make a living have been described in many children's books.[9] One such account is *Lumberjack,* by William Kurelek. The story, told in the first person, is based on the author's own experiences in the Canadian woods. He describes twenty-five aspects of life in the lumber camp from "Arrival at Camp" to "The Bunkhouse After Midnight." Beautifully detailed paintings in bold greens, oranges, and blues capture the camp's rugged flavor, the beauty of the woods, and the vigorous life of the lumberjack. However, Kurelek's book is a reminiscence and is not intended to be an up-to-date description of this occupation.

Books that do describe jobs as they are performed today may be compendiums of several different kinds of work or discussions of a single job. *Women in Policing: Fighting Crime Around the World,* by Michael Fooner, describes how women take an active part in police work in such diverse countries as Germany, Israel, Sweden, and Japan. The author writes about the history of job discrimination against women in this line of work. Noting the excellent performance of policewomen, he explodes the myth that

---

[9]See "Occupational Roles in Children's Literature," by Judith S. Hillman, (*Elementary School Journal,* September 1976, pp. 1–4). Hillman examined 120 books from two time periods (1932–1938 and 1965–1971). She found little difference between the two periods in either number of books published or variety of occupations represented.

women cannot competently do the job. He enumerates the duties of police women, including consumer protection (Italy), emergency services during natural disasters (Brazil), and auto traffic control (Israel). To answer the question of inherent danger in the job, the author first points out that violence is the exception, not the rule. In threatening situations, women handle the problem about as well as men; many policewomen are good at discouraging potential violence before it erupts.

Some books focus on a single job that may be a career option of which children are unaware. *Puppeteer,* by Kathryn Lasky, features many black-and-white photos of various sizes by Christopher G. Knight. Child readers follow puppeteer Paul Davis through a year-long process of selecting story material, creating clay-headed puppets, making flats, rehearsing action and dialogue, conferring with the costumer, taking instructions from his director, and, finally, performing for his audience of children.

The idea that people's value systems influence the foods they eat is illustrated in *Corn Is Maize—The Gift of the Indians,* by Aliki.[10] This book describes how Indians discovered and used corn and how it came to be an important food around the world. The text is simple and straightforward. Aliki's pictures clearly show the sequence of planting, growing, and harvesting corn.[11]

People's clothes reflect tradition and the cultural values of the society. A fascinating look at garments as social history is *Figleafing Through History: The Dynamics of Dress,* by Christie Harris and Moira Johnson. The authors spent more than two years researching, writing, and illustrating this comprehensive account of how clothes reflect social conditions. The book opens with a description of the vivid red, yellow, and white painted streaks that primitive hunters in Africa believed enhanced their powers. It closes with a look at the motivation behind unisex fashions. Even though some of the inferences drawn about society (particularly in the section about contemporary life) seem to have the ring of pop sociology, and the "current" fashions are now over fifteen years old, the details about clothing are fascinating. Intermediate-grade students might enjoy visiting a local historic museum where garments are displayed. If such a trip is not possible, sec-

---

[10]This was one of less than a dozen books honored by the New York Academy of Sciences as the best science books published during 1976. Begun in 1971, this awards program encourages the publication of readable, attractive, and informative books on the sciences. The judges are eminent scientists from leading institutions.

[11]See also Arnold Dobrin's *Peter Rabbit's Natural Foods Cookbook* (New York: Frederick Warne, 1970). Grains, fruits, and vegetables are the primary ingredients of the recipes. Illustrations from Beatrix Potter's books brighten the concise, easy-to-follow text.

ondhand shops often sell, at moderate prices, garments dating back to the early decades of this century. Discussing how an older garment differs from what people wear today and what advantages it may have offered to the wearer will help dispel children's common reaction that such clothes are funny. Another approach is to ask children to bring in photographs of their grandparents and to then initiate a discussion about clothing styles.

One important aspect of the social system is economics. Some economic information is interspersed with scientific details in *The Scoop on the Ice Cream* and with manufacturing details in *Sneakers Meet Your Feet*, both by Vicki Cobb. These two books are part of the series *How the World Works*, published by Little, Brown.

## BOOKS DEALING WITH SEX AND PHYSICAL DEVELOPMENT

Psychologists assert that most children are interested in their own physical development, including that of their sex organs, at an early age. Many adults' attitudes toward sex might have been more positive had they received accurate information about sex when they were interested, rather than having had to seek facts from misinformed peers. A variety of books about sex and physical development are available to answer children's questions. Few of these books are appropriate for reading aloud to a class, but teachers should know about them so they can make recommendations to parents.

There are a few bad examples of sex-information books that should be avoided. For instance, *Where Did I Come From?* by Peter Mayle, depicts a sperm as goggle-eyed, wearing top hat and bow tie, sniffing a rose. Children need facts, and the facts should definitely not be obscured by unnecessary silliness. Some comments about Mayle's book and other misleading books about sex are made by Glazer and Williams (1979).

The tone is very different in *Show Me!* by Will McBride, a picture book about sex for children and parents, which some find unacceptable because of its candor.[12] The book features double-page spreads of black-and-white photographs depicting stages of sexual activities progressing from childhood through adulthood. The photography, although pleasantly soft-edged,

---

[12]Many reviewers raised questions about this book. Even before it appeared in bookstores, it was impounded as obscene in Canada; see *School Library Journal*, December 1975, p. 14. It was later judged not obscene in court decisions in Massachusetts, New Hampshire, Oklahoma, and Toronto; see "*Show Me!* Publisher Shows 'em," *American Libraries*, 7 (November 1976), p. 642.

leaves nothing to the imagination. This is clearly not a book for group use, but it may be valuable to parents who are interested in helping children reach an uninhibited understanding of their own sexuality. Explanatory text, by Helga Fleischhauer-Hardt, provides suggestions for parents on how to use the book with children.

More limited in scope is *The New Baby at Your House*, by Joanna Cole, with realistic black-and-white photographs by Hella Hammid. The book begins when the mother is already pregnant, thus avoiding some potentially thorny issues, and concludes when the new baby is brought home. Much of this book deals with physical details (for example, that newborns can't lift up their heads) but some psychological aspects are mentioned (for example, how an older child can feel grown-up when helping to change a diaper).

A franker treatment of conception and birth is found in *A Baby in the Family*, by Althea. Published in Britain, this book uses detailed, but not offensive, drawings to show the parts of the body involved in conception and delivery. The text openly discusses processes American children often remain ignorant of until they learn of them, largely inaccurately, from peers. *A Baby in the Family* is not for group sharing, but it is valuable as a resource for parents concerned about their children's sex education.

*Before You Were Three*, by Robie Harris and Elizabeth Levy, follows the early physical and mental development of a boy and a girl. The book includes text paragraphs that give information about such topics as breastfeeding, colostrum, and antibodies. It traces the development of speech in a way child readers will find both intelligible and interesting.

*Slim Goodbody*, by John Burstein, looks at the structure and functions of the human body, using photographs of the author and light-hearted graphics. Burstein cavorts in flesh-colored leotards imaginatively painted with body parts in the illustrations that accompany the rhymed text. The book includes a large quantity of helpful information packaged in an appealing format.

Sexual abuse of children and their personal safety in an unsafe world have recently become popular subjects in children's books. As is often the case, when an unfilled need is first perceived, books of varying quality have been published to fill the gap. Books on these sensitive topics range from the strident, which could leave children frightened of any and all adults in every situation, to the overly ambiguous, which skirt the topic and do not therefore serve the purpose of educating children about potential dangers. Books written as cautionary guides are seldom great literature, but two books of this type are of acceptable quality and strike a restrained balance in tone. Primary-grade children will be reassured by Sol and Judith Gordon's

*A Better Safe Than Sorry Book,* which confronts the "stranger danger" directly but does not engender paranoia. Intermediate-grade students will benefit from *Feeling Safe, Feeling Strong; How to Avoid Sexual Abuse and What to Do If It Happens to You,* by Susan N. Terkel and Janice Rench. Six chapters present short fictional situations in a nonsensational and matter-of-fact manner and then give clear explanations and facts in a question-and-answer format. This format tends to move the subject from an emotional to an objective plane. In both books, children are reassured: it is the adults who do these things who are the wrongdoers, not the children.

The mind rather than the body is Judith Herbst's subject in *Bio Amazing. A Casebook of Unsolved Human Mysteries.* In ten brief chapters, Herbst writes precisely about such complex topics as communication between twins, stages in sleep, and the mind's role in miracle cures. Other mind-related phenomena discussed include extrasensory perception, hypnosis, the ability to walk on fire, and acupuncture. The book is admirable in being self-contained. All topics are treated dispassionately; the author concedes that in some cases scientific documentation is shaky, but the multitude of examples she uses suggests an inability of science—to date, at least—to explain these mind-body phenomena. Some readers may find the chapter on spontaneous human combustion unsettling; a chapter on near-death experiences deals with a topic of increasing interest. In all, this is a finely crafted example of simple, direct writing about complex topics for upper-grade readers.

## BOOKS DEALING WITH THE CYCLE OF LIFE

*The Golden Circle,* by Hal Borland, is a book that is probably better suited to group sharing than to individual reading because it requires well-developed reading skills. The author provides a two- to three-page description of each month of the year in the wooded hills and cultivated valleys of the rural area in which he lives. He describes effectively the grasses, flowers, vines, and trees, as well as the birds, animals, reptiles, and fish. Exquisite paintings by Anne Ophelia Dowden present close-up views of the wildlife.[13]

---

[13]See "Nature into Art: An Interview with Anne Ophelia Dowden," by Leonard S. Marcus (*The Lion and the Unicorn,* 6, 1982, pp. 28–40). The entire issue is devoted to information books, including an article on criteria for judging science books, an article by a psychotherapist analyzing books on death, and critiques of Bruno Bettelheim's book on reading and Jo Carr's book on nonfiction.

A teacher might read the appropriate description at the beginning of each month and ask children to talk about how the area in which they live differs from the one Borland describes. Each month students could make pictures of how their environment looks. In moderate weather, a teacher might take students on a nature walk to look for plant and mineral materials to bring back to the classroom. These materials could be arranged to create a golden circle for the geographic area in which the children live.

The cyclic nature of animal life is poetically described in *The Mother Owl*. Edith Thacher Hurd, in simple yet graceful language, opens her book with the mother bird sitting on four eggs. Strongly patterned blue, brown, and black woodcuts by Clement Hurd show the turn of the season when the spring-born owlets lose their down and grow to maturity. Summer brings a potentially dangerous encounter with a raccoon. By the time the cold autumn wind blows dry leaves from the trees, the young owls are able to hunt for themselves. The book closes the following spring with mother owl again nesting in the old apple tree. This life-cycle approach can be very effective, but Gagne (1984) points out that fewer recent animal information books incorporate it; more often authors take broader views, considering habits, conservation, and relations with human culture.

A more difficult life cycle to deal with is the human one of birth, growth, and death. Author Eda LeShan, in *Learning to Say Good-by: When a Parent Dies,* addresses children directly—in a warm, personal manner. She talks of the fears, guilts, and confusions that children go through as they worry that they themselves will die. With almost stark honesty, the author shares the depth of sorrow in losing a parent: "The truth is that you will feel a terrible sadness for a long, long time." Recovery, which is slow, comes in stages and is more certain when fortified with love from caring adults. Some children may be too numb to cry, too worried to ask questions; expressing grief seems impossible. The author advises children to keep a record of their parents' activities or of special incidents in their parents' lives to enhance their memory and to pass on later to *their* children. The illustrations and a bibliography of books for children and adults enhance the book's gentle reflectiveness.

A different approach is taken in *The Kids Book About Death and Dying,* by Eric E. Rofes, who produced the book jointly with fourteen of his students, aged eleven to fourteen. The book is thus both a compilation of information about various aspects of death and a record of the unit of study undertaken by Rofes and his class. Students' comments about many related topics make the book seem more personal than does the detached tone in some other books about death. A bibliography is included.

*In a woodcut in strong shades of blue and black, the unyielding wood of the owl's tree home and the owl's features are sharply defined.* From *The Mother Owl* by Edith Thacher Hurd. Illustration copyright © 1974 by Clement Hurd. By permission of Little, Brown and Company.

Students' own words describe their reactions to the loss of a parent in *How It Feels When a Parent Dies*, by Jill Krementz. The book comprises a series of short (four- to fourteen-page) reminiscences by eighteen children who recall losing parents suddenly, through accidents, or foreseeably, after long illnesses. Krementz's photographs are less central to this book than to her other books described earlier in this chapter.

## BOOKS ABOUT CREATED OBJECTS

The fascination with people's creative abilities and the products that result is universal. Many excellent books examine objects men and women have made.

*The Mystery of Masks,* by Christine Price, opens with a description of ancient tribes whose members believed that in putting on a god's mask, the wearer became a god. The mask's power to change the wearer was a belief held by the ancestors of the Pueblo people and by Asian and Siberian prehistoric peoples. Nomadic societies used masks to evoke success in the hunt, cure disease, curse evildoers, and give growing children strength and wisdom. In later agricultural societies, masked gods presided over planting rites, blessed people with children, and danced as ancestors at a person's death. Even though their origins are ancient, masks are still used today. Author/illustrator Price's pencil illustrations in great detail accompany the lucid text showing comparisons and contrasts both within a given geographic area and between widely separated areas. The elephant mask from Nigeria contrasts with one from the neighboring Ivory Coast; the deer mask from Bhutan can be compared with the native American one from Oklahoma. This book supplements older, yet still exemplary, books such as *Masks and Mask Makers,* by Kari Hunt and Bernice Carlson.

Ancient peoples often decorated their dwellings or surroundings. The rock art done by Mongoloid people who moved into and inhabited Texas from 8000 B.C. to 1500 A.D. is described in *The Epic Adventure of Texas,* by Carol Hackney. These hunters lived in caves and "published" stories of their hopes and struggles by enscribing pictographs on the rock walls. The book, covering the history of a diverse state, ends with an account of the space industry in Texas today. Black pencil drawings, with generous crosshatching to create depth, accompany the brief (two- to three-page) descriptions of various topics.

Housing throughout early human history is featured in *The First Civilizations,* by Giovanni Caselli. An encyclopedic work, subtitled "History of Everyday Things," this volume spans eleven cultures from "The Earliest Toolmakers" (4,000,000 years ago) to "The Greeks at Home" (2400 years ago). Most of the cultures are allotted four pages; dealing with tools, transportation, household objects, clothes, and ornaments, as well as housing, in such a brief format is not easy. The many small ink drawings are meticulously detailed and enhanced with—for the most part—monochromatic washes. Interested readers can learn about the bone needles used by "The Ice Age Hunters," the merganser feathers that adorned "The Fisher-Hunters," and the polished obsidian mirrors found at "Catacl Huyuk: the First City." The book's only drawback is one of scale: the Chinese chariot horse is the same size as a bronze knife; a two-pronged hoe is the same size as an Etruscan house. Children will marvel over the multitude of objects but won't get a sense of their relative size. Nonetheless, the book is worthwhile for the insight it offers into a variety of cultures.

The creation of historic structures is admirably described in *Master Builders of the Middle Ages*, by David Jacobs, which might be used to supplement *Cathedral*, by David Macaulay. Unlike Macaulay, who writes about a hypothetical composite structure, Jacobs describes the construction of several actual cathedrals and includes fascinating facts about the power struggle between rulers of the church and secular lords of the time.[14] Many black-and-white and color photographs, reproductions of works of art, and drawings augment the complex but lucid text. Intended for mature readers, this book describes not only the construction of cathedrals, but also the evolution of such related art forms as stained glass, sculpture, and tapestry.

The applied decoration that is a part of many historic buildings is described in *Faces on Places*, by Suzanne Haldane. Subtitled "About Gargoyles and Other Stone Creatures," this book features generously sized photos—both closeups that show details of the creatures and shots that show them in the context of a whole building.

James Cross Giblin deals with one type of modern building in *The Skyscraper Book*. Beginning with the grandfather of all skyscrapers, the Home Insurance Company building in Chicago, designed by William LeBaron Jenny, this book concludes with the controversial postmodernist buildings of such architects as Philip Johnson. As is characteristic of Giblin's nonfiction works in general, the book reflects a careful use of language and an understanding of the potential readers.

*Americans at Home*, by Lee Pennock Huntington, opens with a house built shortly after Spaniards settled St. Augustine, Florida, in 1565 and closes with a solar-heated house built in 1970, with houses from a variety of eras and regions in between. Black-and-white photographs on nearly

---

[14]One of the church rulers described is Abbé Suger, who began the building of St. Denis Cathedral. The story of his determination to create a masterpiece of architecture is also told in Anne Rockwell's *Glass, Stones and Crown* (New York: Atheneum, 1968).

every page range in subject from Thomas Jefferson's Monticello in Virginia to a modern house in California.

Some information books allow students to experience processes that, because of their duration or complexity, children would probably not be able to participate in directly. An example is *Pete's House*, by Harriet Langsam Sobol, which follows the process of home building from blueprint to completed structure. Few children would be able to enjoy as thorough an acquaintance with this process as does Pete. Pete establishes a rapport with the first workers on the scene, bulldozer operators clearing the land. Through the rest of the book, Pete observes and participates in the process until the end, when the kitchen stove is delivered. The photographs are remarkably clear and appear relatively unposed. The book is enhanced by the horizontal rectangular shape and the open page layout. Details such as the difference between mortar and concrete should intrigue mechanically minded readers.

*Building a House*, by Ken Robbins, deals with the same general topic as does *Pete's House* but with less focus on the main characters and more on the processes involved. In a handsome 10-inch-square format with more photographs than text, this book is an elegant production (perhaps to reflect the house itself, which is far more luxurious than most constructed in the United States today). Unfamiliar words are meticulously defined in context, and close-up photographs alternate with more panoramic views to reinforce the word descriptions. In all, this exemplary book effectively depicts a complex process that most children will never witness first-hand in its entirety.

Larger in scope than the building of individual houses is the planning of entire cities, described in *Babylon to Brasilia: The Challenge of City Planning*, by Carl E. Hiller. This volume includes complete reference aids: a table of contents, an introduction, a glossary, sources of illustrations, a bibliography, an appendix, and an index. Black-and-white photographs are abundant; following the introduction is a twelve-page visual answer to the question "What's wrong with our cities?" After the teacher reads this book to intermediate-grade boys and girls, they might make up a list of questions they would like to ask a city planner. The teacher could get in touch with such an official to schedule an interview, and, using a speakerphone, students could ask their questions.[15]

---

[15]Uses of the speakerphone are described by Harlan and Ruth Hansen in "The Speakerphone in the Elementary School" (*Elementary English*, December 1972, pp. 1262–1265). As money for field trips is cut back, teachers may find that the speakerphone is increasingly useful in providing community contacts for students.

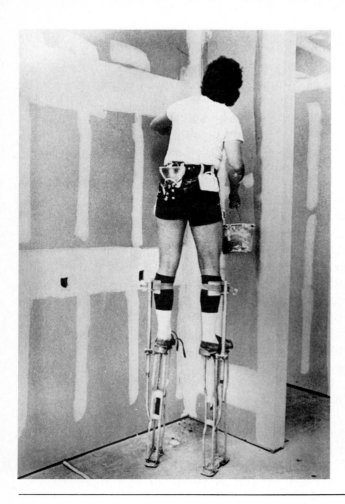

*This is one of the sharply focused black and white photos that show clearly the steps in the process of building a house. Some are grouped in twos or threes; all are placed closely enough to the corresponding text so what they show is apparent.* Reproduced with permission of Four Winds Press, an imprint of Macmillan Publishing Company, from *Building a House* by Ken Robbins. Copyright © 1984 by Ken Robbins.

The opposite of the building procedures described above is the subject of *How to Wreck a Building*, by Elinor Lander Horwitz, a book with large, clear black-and-white photographs. The text concerns the demolition of a seventy-year-old school and is poignant but not sentimental.

Another object that is the result of human ingenuity is the computer. Most of the early books published on this topic were for junior high school students. As more and more schools incorporate computers into the curriculum and more families buy them, books for primary-grade children have also become available. *How to Talk to Your Computer*, by Seymour Simon, is an example. It is part of the *Let's Read and Find Out* series of science books published by Thomas Y. Crowell. The book's brightly colored, cartoon-style drawings are by Barbara and Ed Emberley. The subject is using a language such as BASIC or Logo to make a computer do what is desired.

The popularity of computer books at all reading levels is evident from the three full columns of listings in the most recent *Subject Guide to Children's Book's in Print*. This abundance presents a selection problem. When recommending computer books at any reading level, teachers and librarians need to be aware that all such books very quickly become out-of-date. One way to keep abreast of new books in this subject area is to consult the section titled "Children's Book Review" in *Science Books and Films*, published five times a year by the American Association for the Advancement of Science (1333 H Street, N.W., Washington, D.C., 20005). This column regularly includes reviews of computer books.

The computer is a complex and fascinating tool. Simpler but no less interesting tools are described in *The Toolbox*, by Anne and Harlow Rockwell, who have a long list of books to their credit. Like much of their work, this book is for primary-grade children. To introduce this picture book to her students, one preschool teacher filled a real toolbox, including each of the objects pictured and described by the Rockwells. The teacher's four- and five-year-olds watched in fascination as she demonstrated how to use the tools. With her guidance, the girls and boys were allowed to handle each tool. Later, on a one-to-one basis under the teacher's supervision, students who wanted to were allowed to try using the tools that had attracted their attention.

Fourth- through sixth-grade children will enjoy *Toolchest*, by Jan Adkins, a book that was included in the Children's Book Showcase, a list that used to be compiled annually by the Children's Book Council to acknowledge examples of fine bookmaking. Beginning with a description of the tree itself, the book explains everything readers need to know about how to shape wood: the properties of wood, definitions of "face," "edge," and "end," and the differences in grain. A large section deals with tools. Adkins carefully describes each tool, explains its use, and provides a picture next to the written description.

Tools come in all sizes—from those small enough to hold in the hand to those so large that workers must get into them to use them. The latter class are featured in *Monster Movers*. George Ancona opens his book with a picture of something familiar: a pail of wet sand being moved by children at a beach. He then leads into such unfamiliar things as a walking dragline (with a three-hundred-foot boom), a rotary car dumper (which pours one hundred tons of ore in two minutes), and a rail loader (which fills more than a hundred train cars in three hours). The photographs are very dramatic, but only some of them include people to show the relative size of the objects pictured.

## BOOKS ABOUT LANGUAGE

Language, another human creation, is a rather specialized interest, but a growing number of fine books is motivating children's curiosity about it. For the very youngest readers/listeners are books such as *Our Ollie* and *Just Like Me*, both by Jan Ormerod. Either of these books can be used to introduce the idea of similes to children. The teacher might then encourage them to think of other such language comparisons. In *Our Ollie*, the toddler "sleeps like a cat"; on the left page is Ollie, on the right the cat. In *Just Like Me*, the older sister talks about her younger brother, whose head is "as bald as an egg," and who is "as toothless as a toad."

A book for beginning readers is *Signs*, by Ron and Nancy Goor. Large black-and-white photographs show places where print is an integral part of the environment. A few simple sentences expand the concept, but most of the messages are in the photographs themselves. To follow up, a teacher might take children on a neighborhood walk to find examples of signs.

For older children, *A January Fog Will Freeze a Hog and Other Weather Folklore* is a delightful book of weather ditties. Compiler Hubert David provides a rhyme and a black-and-white illustration on each page. The rhymes are folk sayings having to do with weather, and many of them have a basis in fact. A section in the back of the book gives information about each rhyme: its origins and its reliability as an indicator of weather conditions. The detailed illustrations by John Wallner are eye-catching and humorous.

*Words*, by Jane Sarnoff and Reynold Ruffins, presents etymologies grouped into categories such as "The Family," "Your Right Arm," and "Monsters." Individual entries run about six sentences in length and have been carefully researched. The entries emphasize the unusual or humorous derivations of words in order to capture children's interest.

Word meanings are depicted in full-color, cartoon-style illustrations in *Marms in the Marmalade*, by Diana Morley. Imaginative statements and questions dealing with the perplexities of language provide the format, for example:

> SALTy means having a lot of SALT. So, SKINny means covered with lots of SKIN? I don't think so. Do you?

These and other word paradoxes presented in no particular order will stimulate children's sense of curiosity and humor. Some entries play on a single word, such as "I've seen many ANTs in an ANThill, but in the ANTarctic? I doubt it." Some entries are more complex, embedding several comparisons in one thought: "I've made ROLLerskates ROLL and SNAPdragons SNAP.

### White Elephant

In Siam, white elephants were considered sacred and were not supposed to be put to work. When the king of Siam wanted to ruin someone, he gave that person a gift of a white elephant. The elephant was expensive to feed and care for, but could not be made to work for its keep. Today we use the phrase *white elephant* about a possession that is not worth the expense or the care it needs.

*The blackness of these sharp-edged and two-dimensional illustrations contrasts effectively with the whiteness of the page.* Illustration by Reynold Ruffins from *Words* by Jane Sarnoff. Illustrations copyright © 1981 Reynold Ruffins. Reprinted with the permission of Charles Scribner's Sons.

Do you think I could ask a NAPkin to NAP?" Intermediate-grade youngsters may find it interesting to try to come up with other examples of conflicting meanings for similar words.

One book tells child readers how to disguise what words mean. *The Code and Cipher Book,* by Jane Sarnoff, features humorous three-color drawings by Reynold Ruffins and shows young readers how to both encode and decode messages. It gives clear explanations of twenty-six different ciphers and includes a secret message for children to puzzle out.

*Sending Messages,* by John Warren Stewig, examines twenty-four different kinds of communication, gathered together so that they can be considered in relation to one another. The body language used by dancers, orchestra conductors, mimes, airport ground crews, referees, and television directors is explained. Hand signals used by the deaf and by native Americans are juxtaposed to show how one system is alphabetic and the other is sign. (Alphabetic systems have a different signal for each letter; sign systems convey an entire word with one signal.) The book explains such written, but nonalphabetic, forms of communication as architectural and engineering symbols, music notation, shorthand, hobo signs, and Labanotation (the method of recording dance movements).

*Chinese Writing,* by Diane Wolff, opens with a brief but fairly complex introduction to China. A section on China's two languages is followed by an explication of the written characters. Some of these are simple, one-

RAIN
*(YU)*

雨

The ancient word for rain is a cloud with drops of water falling.

Stroke Order:

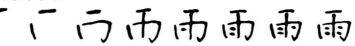

*The calligraphic symbols are shown this way for instructional purposes. Other illustrations in the book are photos of people writing and of tools for writing and samples of different calligraphic styles.* From *Chinese Writing* by Diane Wolff. Copyright © 1975 by Diane Wolff. Reprinted by permission of Henry Holt and Company, Inc.

picture characters, and others are very complex, four-picture characters. A section titled "The Chinese Sentence" closes the first part of the book. The second part of the book is longer and deals with calligraphy, the beautiful handwriting the Chinese consider a great art. Instruction on individual strokes and proper brush use is included, along with a dictionary for practice. The contents are accessible and well laid out on the page. This book is a joy to look at even if one is not—as many children could be—enticed into trying a hand at this ancient art. *Chinese Writing* was an American Library Association Notable Book.

Students old enough to be interested in history may enjoy *Signs, Letters, Words,* by W. John Hackwell, which presents archaeological insights into the development of writing. Beginning with a chapter titled "Before Writing," the author goes on to consider briefly such writing systems as Hittite hieroglyphs, the proto-Canaanite alphabet, and the Etruscan script. Hackwell tells enough about each culture to interest young readers, but not so much that they are overwhelmed with information. Small black-and-white drawings on nearly every page show what the text describes in words.

*Loosely painted areas (as in the water and the sky) and more tightly painted areas (as in the crossing barrier and the sheds) combine in this watercolor illustration, which is bled to the edges of the page. (See the discussion on page 612.)* Illustration from *Ferryboat* by Betsy C. Maestro. Illustrated by Giulio Maestro for Thomas Y. Crowell. Copyright © 1986 by Giulio Maestro. Reprinted by permission of Harper & Row, Publishers, Inc.

## SUMMARY

The diversity of information books is impressive. Covering a vast array of topics at all levels of difficulty and with great imaginativeness in treatment, information books are among the most interesting of children's books. Such books can help students explore the wonders of their world by providing worthwhile vicarious experiences.

Teachers can use information books as related resource materials for units of study or can, indeed, make them the very foundation of a unit of study. For almost any area specified in a curriculum guide, children's interest and knowledge can be extended and expanded by fine information books. Because they are not as constrained by considerations of appropriate language use and of content simplicity and sequence, such books are almost always more interesting than textbooks.

## An Integrated Unit of Study

Building a unit around the topic of ships and boats is an easy task. As an introduction for primary-grade readers, especially for those children living in parts of the country where boats are uncommon, *Boats*, by Anne Rockwell, is particularly effective. The author/illustrator uses very simple descriptive phrases, for example, "Boats float," placed below nearly full-page watercolor illustrations. As is usual in Rockwell's work, the watercolors are mostly flat, outlined with a thin line of unvarying width. The enterprising teacher could easily build on the content of these pictures; neither the kayak shown nor the canals of Venice are identified in the words. There is opportunity here for vocabulary development if a teacher is working with an interested group.

Another picture book appropriate for this unit is *Ferryboat*, by Betsy and Giulio Maestro. Pleasantly casual watercolors are presented on double-page spreads and bled to the edges. (See the illustration on page 611.) The superimposed text describes the daily routine of a ferryboat. Most of the perspectives are head-on, but there is some interesting variation. Focusing on one type of boat and its operation in detail, this book is a pleasant complement to Claudia Lewis's book.

A complete book of poetry, *Up and Down the River*, by Claudia Lewis, features eleven different kinds of boats. Pale blue and orange drawings by Bruce Degen show the "paddle-footed" tug, the Coast Guard cutter "smashing up billows," and the barge that is "a great dark turtle pushing along." Each performs its function, described in Lewis's lyrical nonrhyming poetry.

Four stanzas, with a full-color, double-page spread in watercolor and ink, constitute "I saw a ship a-sailing," from *Over the Moon*. From "comfits in the cabin," to "masts were all of gold," the ship is unusual. It's staffed by mouse sailors, and a duck for a captain. The vocabulary (for example, *packet*) makes this poem more usable with older students than we ordinarily think such rhymes are. The pictures by Charlotte Voake, who illustrates the whole volume, have a pleasantly slap-dash air to them, full of details worth studying.

*Life on a Barge*, an informative book for intermediate-grade students provides a fascinating glimpse into a self-contained world. Author/illustrator Huck Scarry wrote about and pictured his real-life trip through the canals of Holland. The book, in addition to showing present-day life on a barge, also gives a brief historic look at barge life in the seventeenth century. Readers find out about Thalweg markers, ship-to-shore phones, mitersills, and waybills. The barge on which Scarry actually traveled is contrasted with other types of Belgian, French, and early American barges. Some of the pencil drawings are technical and schematic, with careful labeling of components; others are panoramic, without labeling.

*The Amazing Voyage of Jackie Grace*, by Matt Faulkner, is a tale about a young boy and his seagoing companions. The common motif of a child who moves from current reality into fantasy is here impressively developed in full-page, full-color illustrations with containing black-ink line. The pictures are pleasantly exaggerated, yet believable; the use of cross-hatching adds surface enrichment to the underlying watercolors.

*Workboats*, by Jan Adkins, is a fine example of an informative book for older readers. Clear, concise writing is augmented by detailed black-and-white drawings showing such things as a toggle buoy, an oil barge, a C-130 supply plane, and an *Aequipecten irradians* (a bay scallop). The daily activities of fishermen plying the waters off Cape Cod link the different kinds of boats into the narrative.

Even more technical, and thus for a more limited audience, is *The Craft of Sail*, also by Jan Adkins, His handlettered introduction (all the text in the book is in the same lettering) sets the stage for later, detailed explanations of such arcane tasks and terms as heaving to, gybing, halyards, and rigging. The book does not have to be read through consecutively; even those who spot-read will encounter many things well known to sailors but completely unknown to most readers. Adkins's diagrams are admirably clear, and the economy of his line never becomes dull.

Also for intermediate-grade readers, *Tall Ships*, by Kathryn Lasky, provides a lot of information in an attractive, readable format. In five (unnamed) chapters, the author gives readers both historic information on tall ships and details on the recent renewed interest in them. For example, in 1871 alone, more than a thousand tall ships entered the port of Boston. In 1976, most of the ships of this type left in the world came together to participate in a race that ended in a parade up the Hudson River past New York City. The book is enriched with visuals on nearly every page, including contemporary photographs by Lasky's husband, Christopher Knight, historical photos from a variety of sources, and reproductions of paintings.

Such books as those discussed above can give children a good introduction to the world of ships and boats and can show how a variety of authors deal with the same topic in differing ways.

# Suggestions for Further Study

1. A college student once objected strenuously to *The Digger Wasp*, by George Mendoza, contending it was sadistic and therefore not appropriate to read to children. Read the book. Do you agree with the student's contention? Read the book aloud to a group of children. How do they react?

2. In what ways are the illustrations by Virginia Lee Burton in *Life Story* similar to landscape paintings done by Grant Wood late in his career? See *Grant Wood*, by James M. Dennis (New York: Viking, 1975). Compare Burton's artwork with Wood's. Can you list similarities in their uses of color, shape, line, texture, form or space?

3. After children have read or heard *Life Story*, by Virginia Lee Burton, they might enjoy recording their own life stories. Help intermediate-grade students construct individual time lines, on which each student can place events that are personally significant.

4. You might be interested in reading *The Civil Rights of Students*, by David Shimmel and Louis Fischer (New York: Harper and Row, 1975). At what age should such a concept be introduced to children? Or should it be discussed at all? Why or why not? How have ideas about this topic changed since the book was published?

5. *About Dying*, by Sara B. Stein, and *Learning to Say Good-by*, by Eda LeShan, are two books about how to deal with death. Another is *Living with Death*, by Osborn Segerberg, Jr. (New York: E. P. Dutton, 1976). Read these books, and make a list of their literary strong points. Take an informal survey of friends to get the reactions to such books from those who have experienced the death of a loved one.

6. Corn in the life of Indian tribes is the topic of *Corn Is Maize—The Gift of the Indians*, by Aliki. Corn's role in the Spanish culture is described in *Three Stalks of Corn*, by Leo Politi (New York: Scribner's, 1976). Which book gives a more vivid sense of the culture it depicts? What is there about the way each author uses language that enhances the reader's sense of the society?

7. *Show Me*, by Will McBride, was described in this chapter. An important issue related to this book was raised by John Garvey in "Sex, Age, Death, Privacy" (*Commonweal*, June 1976, pp. 376–377). His concern is the erosion of privacy, a gradual disintegration of the belief that some things are too personal for public inspection. He indicts this book for a new level of silliness, "a sappy open-mindedness," that fails to give serious consideration to the possible appropriateness of privacy. Choose a topic you believe is too private to be considered in the public forum of a children's book, and develop an argument supporting your position.

# Related Reading for Adults

Chamberlain, Larry. "Enchantment Isn't Everything: A New Way of Looking at Lands and Peoples." *School Library Journal*, January 1978, pp. 25–26.

Chamberlain rails against series books about foreign countries, saying that too many are stuffed with lists and stilted in tone and encourage child readers to write dull, routine reports. He quotes examples from the type of "dry catalogue" that predominates and argues eloquently for the personalized anecdotes that authors can contribute to make such books more interesting.

Fisher, Margery. *Matters of Fact*. New York: Thomas Y. Crowell, 1972.

This detailed, far-ranging consideration of nonfiction and biography features critical analyses of British and American books. Fisher quotes comparable sections from several works, showing why she feels one is better than the other. Her examples are often set in the context of changes that have occurred in writing for children.

Giller, Pamela R. "Science Books for Young Children." In *Beyond Fact. Nonfiction for Children and Young People.* Ed. Jo Carr. Chicago: American Library Association, 1982, pp. 65–69.

Giller talks about the "recent burgeoning" of science books, which reflects increased respect for the learning capacities of three- to six-year-olds and increased awareness of the need to raise all children's science consciousness. These new books reflect the widening range of children's interests. No longer about just plants and animals, science books now cover very diverse topics. Giller contrasts earlier science books with more recent ones written by the same authors. She also gives specific examples of good and poor writing on the same topic. The article includes criteria for selecting good science books: Giller states that it is important to avoid simplistic language, a condescending tone, and the overuse of questions as an organizing strategy.

Keach, Everett T. "Social Studies Instruction Through Children's Literature." *Elementary School Journal*, November 1974, pp. 98–102.

Modern curricula try to involve pupils in studying how people behave in contemporary cultures. These curricula necessitate the use of a wide variety of media, including trade books. Since no text series can keep abreast of societal changes, it is important to use trade books to supplement the concise presentations in textbooks. The author takes a concept from social studies (such as interdependence) and shows how to build a unit of study based on trade books.

Madden, Peter. "Magazines and Newspapers for Children." *Childhood Education*, April/May 1977, pp. 328–336.

A valuable supplement to information books is the variety of periodicals that provide factual information. The author presents complete bibliographic information, including source and cost, for 125 periodicals. A brief (two- to three-sentence) annotation is given for each. The list includes magazines that are essentially for adults, such as *Dance* and *Ebony*. Updated lists are also available: in "Magazines and Newspapers for Children and Young Adolescents," by Barbara Hatcher (*Childhood Education*, May/June 1983, pp. 367–376), and in "Children's Periodicals Throughout the World," by Nancy Seminoff (*The Reading Teacher*, May 1986, pp. 889–895).

May, Jill P. "The Poetics of Our Natural World." *Juvenile Miscellany*, 16 (Spring 1986), pp. 4–6.

Responding to Meltzer's article (see below), May comments on the prizes that have been awarded since his article was published and concludes: "In fact, prizes have continued to be handed to fiction books rather than to all books." She compares a poem by David McCord with Jean C. George's *All Upon a Stone* (New York: Thomas Y. Crowell, 1971), identifying the similar ways each has of looking at nature. She finds the elements of selection, invention, language, and form are present. What distinguishes George's writing is her ability to draw readers into a compelling drama without resorting to the personification used in too many animal stories. May concludes by using Meltzer's definition of style as "a quality of vision," asserting that George's talent is her ability to create another universe through prose. May continues her examination of this topic in the next issue of *Juvenile Miscellany* (17, Summer 1986, pp. 1–3).

Meltzer, Milton. "Where Do All the Prizes Go? The Case for Nonfiction." *The Horn Book*, February 1976, pp. 17–23.

When this article was written, only five of the fifty-three Newbery Medals had been given to nonfiction, and the ratio was not substantially different from other awards. Textbooks such as those by Isabelle Jan and Sheila Egoff do not even mention nonfiction. Meltzer disagrees with Lillian Smith's contention in *The Unreluctant Years* (New York: Viking, 1953) that the difference between a book of knowledge and a storybook is intent. He feels that, like many others, Smith is guilty of having in mind only the finest writers when discussing fiction and thinking only of run-of-the-mill writers when discussing information books. Meltzer concludes by listing criteria he believes are important in evaluating information books.

Norris, Lynn. "Extending Curiosity: Children's Information Books." *Idaho Librarian*, October 1975, pp. 126–128.

The author comments on the transitory nature of children's interests and the need for books that can extend curiosity beyond the limitations of the original question. Currency of materials and quality of illustrations are two important factors in capturing children's attention. However, there is little research pinpointing the nature of children's reading interests, especially of very young children. Selection of books is complicated because many reviewers do no more than provide plot or content summaries. Norris notes books by Jeanne Bendick, Jean C. George, and Roma Gans as exemplary.

Podendorf, Illa. "Characteristics of Good Science Materials for Young Readers." *Library Trends*, 22 (April 1974), pp. 425–431.

One of twelve articles by different authors in an issue dealing with aspects of writing, editing, and reviewing science books and periodicals, Podendorf's article analyzes what makes an information book effective. The author of many such books for young readers, Podendorf points out that an author must decide if a children's book is the best format for sharing his or her idea.

Spiegel, Dixie Lee. "Using Literature in the Content Areas." *Reading Today*, 3 (June/July 1986), p. 14.

Spiegel suggests using works of literature in science and social studies units. Such books add depth, meaning, and elaboration to concepts usually presented in textbooks, which, for the most part, remain "relatively dry and colorless." She recommends five specific activities, including "What I Learned" cards and ongoing charts made up as children listen to the teacher read. Having children use literature as a model for their own writing is another suggestion.

Sutherland, Zena. "Information Pleases—Sometimes." *Wilson Library Bulletin*, 49 (October 1974), pp. 161–164.

Sutherland takes issue with the point made in Margery Fisher's book *Matters of Fact* that information books must be more than a collection of facts. Sutherland cites the works of Millicent Selsam, each of whose books is a collection of facts in which the whole becomes greater than its parts. She lists criteria for judging excellence. Sutherland deals at length with language use, and she refers to specific authors whose writing style is impressive.

Sutherland, Zena, and May Hill Arbuthnot. *Children and Books*. 7th ed. Glenview, Ill.: Scott, Foresman, 1986, pp. 484–547.

In this most recent edition of a standard reference work first published in 1947, the authors include an unusually complete section on evaluating and selecting information books. They describe the areas in which these books were judged: accuracy, currency, organization/scope, author's responsibility/ competence, format, and style. They also provide a survey of the most significant authors writing information books today, considering twenty-six authors in detail.

## Professional References

Banks, James A. *Teaching Strategies for Ethnic Studies*. Boston: Allyn and Bacon, 1984, p. 145.

Duke, Judith S. *Children's Books and Magazines. A Market Study*. White Plains, N.Y.: Knowledge Industry Publications, 1979, p. 177.

Elleman, Barbara. "From Dream to Reality: Seeing Books from Both Sides." *Booklist*, October 15, 1981, 302–304.

Fisher, Margery. *Matters of Fact*. New York: Thomas Y. Crowell, 1972.

Gagne, Sarah S. "Views on Science Books," *The Horn Book*, June 1984, 368–371.

Gallivan, Marion F. *Fun for Kids*. Metuchen, N.J.: Scarecrow Press, 1981.

Glazer, Joan I., and Gurney Williams III. *Introduction to Children's Literature*. New York: McGraw-Hill, 1979.

Holmes, Betty C., and Richard I. Ammon. "Teaching Content with Trade Books." *Childhood Education*, May/June 1985, 366–370.

Jarolimek, John. *Social Studies in Elementary Education*. New York: Macmillan, 1986, pp. 198–199.

Kellman, Amy. "For Very Young Dancers—A Quickstep Through Recent Books." *School Library Journal*, December 1977, 34–35.

Lima, Carolyn W. *A to Zoo. Subject Access to Children's Picture Books*. New York: R. R. Bowker, 1982.

Meek, Margaret. "What Is a Horse?" *School Librarian*, March 1977, 5–12.

Noyce, Ruth. "Art History for Children: Shirley Glubok." *Language Arts*, May 1978, 626–629.

Sapon-Shevin, Mera. *A Selected List of Recent Children's Books about Exceptional Children*. Madison, Wisc.: Cooperative Children's Book Center, 1977.

Smardo, Frances A. "Using Children's Literature as a Prelude or Finale to Music Experiences with Young Children." *The Reading Teacher*, April 1984, 700–705.

Stubbs, Harry C. "Views on Science Books." *The Horn Book*, April 1976, 181–183; August 1984, 500–502.

Western, Linda. "Books About Handicapped Children." *Wisconsin English Journal*, January 1978, 20–22.

## Bibliography of Children's Books

Adkins, Jan. *The Craft of Sail*. New York: Walker, 1973.

———. *Inside: Seeing Beneath the Surface*. New York: Walker, 1975.

———. *Toolchest*. New York: Walker, 1973.

———. *Workboats*. New York: Scribner's, 1985.

Aliki. *Corn Is Maize—The Gift of the Indians*. New York: Thomas Y. Crowell, 1976.

Althea. *A Baby in the Family*. Cambridge, Eng.: Dinosaur Publications, 1981.

Ancona, George. *Monster Movers*. New York: E. P. Dutton, 1983.

Anderson, Joan. *Christmas on the Prairie*. New York: Clarion, 1985.

Atwood, Ann. *New Moon Cove*. New York: Scribner's, 1969.

Aylward, Jim. *Your Burro Is No Jackass.* New York: Holt, Rinehart and Winston, 1981.

———. *You're Dumber in the Summer.* New York: Holt, Rinehart and Winston, 1980.

Baylor, Byrd. *We Walk in Sandy Places.* New York: Scribner's, 1976.

Bendick, Jeanne. *Artificial Satellites.* New York: Franklin Watts, 1982.

———. *Heat and Temperature.* New York: Franklin Watts, 1974.

Blair, Susie. *The Show Ring.* New York: Ariel, 1960.

Borland, Hal. *The Golden Circle.* New York: Thomas Y. Crowell, 1977.

Brandenberg, Aliki. *Wild and Wooly Mammoths.* New York: Thomas Y. Crowell, 1977.

Branley, Franklyn. *Air Is All Around You.* New York: Thomas Y. Crowell, 1986.

———. *Experiments in the Principles of Space Travel.* New York: Thomas Y. Crowell, 1973.

———. *Light and Darkness.* New York: Thomas Y. Crowell, 1975.

———. *Measure with Metric.* New York: Thomas Y. Crowell, 1975.

———. *What the Moon Is Like.* New York: Thomas Y. Crowell, 1973.

Brown, Laurene Krasny, and Marc Brown. *Visiting the Art Museum.* New York: E. P. Dutton, 1986.

Burstein, John. *Slim Goodbody.* New York: McGraw-Hill, 1977.

Burton, Virginia Lee. *Life Story.* Boston: Houghton Mifflin, 1962.

———. *The Little House.* Boston: Houghton Mifflin, 1942.

Calhoun, Mary. *Medicine Show.* New York: Harper and Row, 1976.

Campbell, Ann. *Let's Find Out About Color.* New York: Franklin Watts, 1975.

Carrick, Carol. *Sand Tiger Shark.* New York: Seabury, 1977.

Caselli, Giovanni. *The First Civilizations.* New York: Peter Bedrick, 1985.

Cobb, Vicki. *The Scoop on the Ice Cream.* Boston: Little, Brown, 1985.

———. *Sneakers Meet Your Feet.* Boston: Little, Brown, 1985.

Cohen, Susan, and Daniel Cohen. *A Six Pack and a Fake I.D.* New York: M. Evans, 1986.

Cole, Joanna. *A Chick Hatches.* New York: Morrow, 1976.

———. *The New Baby at Your House.* New York: Morrow, 1985.

Cristini, Ermanno, and Luigi Puricelli. *In My Garden.* Natick, Mass.: Alphabet Press, 1981.

David, Hubert (compiler). *A January Fog Will Freeze a Hog and Other Weather Folklore.* New York: Crown, 1977.

Engel, Joel. *Handwriting Analysis Self-Taught.* New York: Elsevier/Nelson, 1980.

Fanshawe, Elizabeth. *Rachel.* New York: Bradbury, 1977.

Faulkner, Matt. *The Amazing Voyage of Jackie Grace.* New York: Scholastic, 1987.

Fooner, Michael. *Women in Policing: Fighting Crime Around the World.* New York: Coward, McCann, 1976.

Garver, Susan, and Paula McGuire. *Coming to America.* New York: Delacorte, 1981.

George, Jean C. *Spring Comes to the Ocean.* New York: Thomas Y. Crowell, 1966.

Gersting, Judith, and Joseph Kuczkowski. *Yes-No; Stop-Go: Some Patterns in Mathematical Logic.* New York: Thomas Y. Crowell, 1977.

Giblin, James Cross. *The Skyscraper Book.* New York: Thomas Y. Crowell, 1981.

Glubok, Shirley. *The Art of the Plains Indians.* New York: Macmillan, 1975.

Goor, Ron, and Nancy Goor. *Signs.* New York: Thomas Y. Crowell, 1983.

Gordon, Sol, and Judith Gordon. *A Better Safe Than Sorry Book.* Fayetteville, N.Y.: Ed-U Press, 1984.

Goudey, Alice E. *Butterfly Time.* New York: Scribner's, 1964.

Greenfield, Howard. *Rosh Hashanah and Yom Kippur.* New York: Holt, 1979.

Hackney, Carol. *The Epic Adventure of Texas.* Jefferson, Tex.: Historic Jefferson Foundation, 1985.

Hackwell, W. John. *Signs, Letters, Words*. New York: Scribner's, 1987.

Haines, Gail K. *Fire*. New York: Morrow, 1975.

Haldane, Suzanne. *Faces on Places*. New York: Viking, 1980.

Hall, Derek. *Otter Swims*. San Francisco: Sierra Club, 1984.

——. *Panda Climbs*. San Francisco: Sierra Club, 1984.

——. *Tiger Runs*. San Francisco: Sierra Club, 1984.

Harris, Christie, and Moira Johnson. *Figleafing Through History: The Dynamics of Dress*. New York: Atheneum, 1971.

Harris, Robie, and Elizabeth Levy. *Before You Were Three*. New York: Delacorte, 1977.

Herbst, Judith. *Bio Amazing. A Casebook of Unsolved Human Mysteries*. New York: Atheneum, 1985.

Hiller, Carl E. *Babylon to Brasilia: The Challenge of City Planning*. Boston: Little, Brown, 1972.

Holling, Holling C. *Pagoo*. Boston: Houghton Mifflin, 1957.

Hopf, Alice L. *Monarch Butterflies*. New York: Thomas Y. Crowell, 1986.

Horwitz, Elinor Lander. *How to Wreck a Building*. New York: Pantheon, 1982.

Hunt, Kari, and Bernice Carlson. *Masks and Mask Makers*. New York: Abingdon, 1961.

Huntington, Lee Pennock. *Americans at Home*. New York: Coward, McCann and Geoghegan, 1981.

Hurd, Edith Thacher. *The Mother Owl*. Boston: Little, Brown, 1974.

Ipcar, Dahlov. *Horses of Long Ago*. Garden City, N.Y.: Doubleday, 1965.

Isadora, Rachel. *I Touch*. New York: Greenwillow, 1985.

——. *Max*. New York: Macmillan, 1976.

——. *Opening Night*. New York: Greenwillow, 1984.

Jacobs, David. *Master Builders of the Middle Ages*. New York: Horizon, 1969.

Johnson, Sylvia A. *Animals of the Polar Regions*. Minneapolis: Lerner Publications, 1976.

——. *Bats*. Minneapolis: Lerner Publications, 1985.

——. *Morning Glories*. Minneapolis: Lerner Publications, 1985.

Kamien, Janet. *What If You Couldn't . . . ?* New York: Scribner's, 1979.

Kaufmann, John. *Little Dinosaurs and Early Birds*. New York: Thomas Y. Crowell, 1977.

Krementz, Jill. *How It Feels When a Parent Dies*. New York: Alfred A. Knopf, 1981.

——. *A Very Young Circus Flyer*. New York: Alfred A. Knopf, 1979.

——. *A Very Young Dancer*. New York: Alfred A. Knopf, 1976.

Kupferberg, Herbert. *A Rainbow of Sound*. New York: Scribner's, 1973.

Kurelek, William. *Lumberjack*. Boston: Houghton Mifflin, 1974.

Kuskin, Karla. *The Philharmonic Gets Dressed*. New York: Harper and Row, 1982.

Lasky, Kathryn. *Puppeteer*. New York: Macmillan, 1985.

——. *Tall Ships*. New York: Scribner's, 1978.

Lauber, Patricia. *Seeds: Pop, Stick, Glide*. New York: Crown, 1981.

——. *Tales Mummies Tell*. New York: Thomas Y. Crowell, 1985.

Lepscky, Ibi. *Pablo Picasso*. Woodbury, N.Y.: Barron's, 1984.

LeShan, Eda. *Learning to Say Good-By: When a Parent Dies*. New York: Macmillan, 1976.

Lewis, Claudia. *Up and Down the River*. New York: Harper and Row, 1979.

Liebers, Arthur. *You Can Be A Plumber*. New York: Lothrop, Lee and Shepard, 1974.

Macaulay, David. *Cathedral*. Boston: Houghton Mifflin, 1973.

——. *Pyramid*. Boston: Houghton Mifflin, 1962.

Maestro, Betsy, and Giulio Maestro. *Ferryboat*. New York: Thomas Y. Crowell, 1986.

Maiorano, Robert. *Worlds Apart*. New York: Coward, McCann and Geoghegan, 1980.

Mangurian, David. *Lito the Shoeshine Boy*. New York: Four Winds, 1975.

Marks, Mickey K. *OP-Tricks: Creating Kinetic Art*. Philadelphia: J. B. Lippincott, 1972.

Mather, Helen. *Light Horsekeeping*. New York: E. P. Dutton, 1970.

May, Julian. *The Cloud Book*. Mankato, Minn.: Creative Educational Society, 1972.

Mayle, Peter. *Where Did I Come From?* Secaucus, N.J.: Lyle Stuart, 1973.

McBride, Will. *Show Me!* New York: St. Martin's, 1975.

McClung, Robert. *How Animals Hide*. Washington, D.C.: National Geographic Society, 1973.

Meltzer, Milton. *The Hispanic Americans*. New York: Thomas Y. Crowell, 1982.

Mendoza, George. *The Digger Wasp*. New York: Dial, 1969.

Milgrom, Harry. *Egg-ventures: First Science Experiments*. New York: E. P. Dutton, 1974.

Morley, Diana. *Marms in the Marmalade*. Minneapolis: Carolrhoda Books, 1984.

Morris, Robert A. *Dolphin*. New York: Harper and Row, 1975.

Munthe, Nelly. *Meet Matisse*. Boston: Little, Brown, 1983.

O'Neill, Mary. *The White Palace*. New York: Thomas Y. Crowell, 1966.

Ormerod, Jan. *Just Like Me*. New York: Lothrop, Lee and Shepard, 1986.

———. *Our Ollie*. New York: Lothrop, Lee and Shepard, 1986.

Price, Christine. *The Mystery of Masks*. New York: Scribner's, 1978.

Pringle, Laurence. *The Hidden World: Life Under a Rock*. New York: Macmillan, 1977.

Raboff, Ernest. *Marc Chagall*. Garden City, N.Y.: Doubleday, 1982.

———. *Pablo Picasso*. Garden City, N.Y.: Doubleday, 1982.

———. *Paul Klee*. Garden City, N.Y.: Doubleday, 1982.

Rauch, Hans-Georg. *the lines are coming*. New York: Scribner's, 1978.

Ricciuti, Edward R. *Do Toads Give You Warts? Strange Animal Myths Explained*. New York: Walker, 1975.

Robbins, Ken. *Building a House*. New York: Four Winds, 1984.

Rockwell, Anne. *Boats*. New York: E. P. Dutton, 1982.

Rockwell, Anne, and Harlow Rockwell. *The Toolbox*. New York: Collier, 1971.

Rofes, Eric E. *The Kids Book About Death and Dying*. Boston: Little, Brown, 1985.

Rosenberg, Jane. *Dance Me a Story*. New York: Thames and Hudson, 1985.

Sarnoff, Jane. *The Code and Cipher Book*. New York: Scribner's, 1975.

Sarnoff, Jane, and Reynold Ruffins. *Words*. New York: Scribner's, 1981.

Scarry, Huck. *Life on a Barge*. Englewood Cliffs, N.J.: Prentice-Hall, 1981.

Simon, Seymour. *Earth*. New York: Four Winds, 1984.

———. *How to Talk to Your Computer*. New York: Thomas Y. Crowell, 1985.

———. *Jupiter*. New York: Morrow, 1985.

———. *Saturn*. New York: Morrow, 1985.

Sobol, Harriet Langsam. *Pete's House*. New York: Macmillan, 1978.

Sorine, Stephanie, and Daniel Sorine. *Imagine That! It's Modern Dance*. New York: Alfred A. Knopf, 1981.

Spender, Stephen. *The Magic Flute*. New York: Putnam's, 1966.

Spier, Peter. *People*. Garden City, N.Y.: Doubleday, 1980.

Srivastava, Jane J. *Averages*. New York: Thomas Y. Crowell, 1975.

Stewig, John Warren. *Sending Messages*. Boston: Houghton Mifflin, 1978.

Streatfield, Noel. *A Young Person's Guide to Ballet*. London: Frederick Warne, 1975.

Sung, Betty Lee. *An Album of Chinese Americans*. New York: Franklin Watts, 1977.

Terkel, Susan N., and Janice Rench. *Feeling Safe, Feeling Strong; How to Avoid Sexual Abuse and What to Do If It Happens to You.* Minneapolis: Lerner Publications, 1984.

Voake, Charlotte (ill.). *Over the Moon.* New York: Clarkson N. Potter, 1985.

Weiss, Malcolm E. *Solomon Grundy, Born on Oneday.* New York: Thomas Y. Crowell, 1977.

Wolf, Bernard. *In This Proud Land.* New York: J. B. Lippincott, 1978.

Wolff, Diane. *Chinese Writing.* New York: Holt, Rinehart and Winston, 1975.

# 13

# SPECIAL INTERESTS: CHILDREN'S CHOICES

There are four types of books that appeal especially to those children who will not often read other literature: animal stories, mystery and detective fiction, sports stories, and science fiction. Some books of these types have already been discussed in earlier chapters on specific genres, such as realistic fiction, fantasy, biography, and picture books. But the four categories deserve special attention here because children often read these kinds of books without any encouragement from teachers.

In order to be successful in recommending a book, the teacher or librarian must know what the student already likes to read—or to be aware that she or he doesn't read unless coerced. A nonreader may become interested in one of these special-interest books. A limited reader, who reads only one type of special-interest book, may be encouraged to read more difficult, more rewarding material, if the teacher is aware of this interest.

The first category, animal stories, is universally popular among children, and teachers and librarians should be aware that even the most reluctant reader can usually be enticed by animal characters. The other three categories comprise books often chosen by readers themselves rather than being recommended by adults. These include paperback books children buy in retail outlets and trade among themselves. These types, especially mystery and detective fiction, are often not as well represented as they could be in school library collections.

Schools teach a large percentage of boys and girls the skills necessary to decode print but are not equally successful in making these children readers. Having skills and using them are two different things. Teachers have not paid enough attention to finding out what students are reading on their own before recommending other books to them (Stewig, 1973).

## ANIMAL STORIES

An animal story can usually lure even the most reluctant child reader, no matter what his or her age. A first-grader, unfortunately turned off by the complexities of too much phonics presented too early, may be enticed into reading the amusing adventures of *Harry and Shellburt*, by Dorothy O. Van Woerkom.[1] The clever story is even more delightful if the child is aware of

---

[1] Van Woerkom is one of 239 authors who have contributed brief autobiographical sketches to the *Fifth Book of Junior Authors and Illustrators*, edited by Sally Holmes Holtze (New York: H. W. Wilson, 1983). The section on each author or illustrator concludes with a brief paragraph giving other reference books in which material about the person can be found. In addition, a composite index lists the names of all the people who appear in any of the volumes of this series.

the old tale "The Hare and the Tortoise," on which it is based. An intermediate-grade child, hassled by too many worksheets exacting only convergent answers, may respond to *The Incredible Journey*, by Sheila Burnford. Even if the child does not know every word, the energy in the story will engage his or her attention. A teacher might introduce this book using the excerpt found in *The World Treasury of Children's Literature*, by Clifton Fadiman, which includes a brief introduction to some of the over one hundred authors and poets represented.

One reason for the remarkable appeal of animal stories to children of all reading levels is that there are as many different kinds as there are animals and writers to write about them. Animal stories can be divided roughly into four groups:

1. Stories about animals that behave like humans (for example, *The Story of Babar*, by Jean and Laurent de Brunhoff)
2. Stories about animals that act like animals but are able to think and talk like humans (for example, *Bambi*, by Felix Salten)
3. Stories about animals that behave realistically as animals (for example, *Rascal*, by Sterling North)
4. Stories about imaginary animals (for example, *The Unicorn and the Plow*, by Louise Moeri)

## ANIMAL CHARACTERS THAT SEEM HUMAN

The most common type of animal character in children's books is the animal who behaves like a human. Often such a character personifies a human vice or virtue. Authors seem to find animals particularly adaptable to being used to express ideas about human foibles. In many stories, the animals wear clothes, cook food, sit in chairs, and sleep in beds. They use human language to converse, think human thoughts, and feel human emotions.

George and Martha, two hippopotamuses, both wear clothes in *George and Martha*, by James Marshall.

An elephant chef cooks cream-of-chicken soup in *The Twenty Elephant Restaurant*, by Russell Hoban.

Frances, a badger, resists but finally sleeps in her bed, in *Bedtime for Frances*, by Russell Hoban.

In *The Grouchy Ladybug*, by Eric Carle, the bug, though nameless, clearly personifies this all-too-human trait.

Animals of all sizes act as main characters. *The Biggest House in the*

*World*, by Leo Lionni, is a gentle homily about a tiny snail who imprudently wishes for the biggest of houses. His wise father tells a story within a story—of what happened to an unwise snail who wished for the same thing. In the end, the now wiser little snail appreciates the mobility his small house allows. Unlike other works by this author, this book is not illustrated in collage but in bright, full-color paintings. To children who enjoy this story, a teacher might recommend *Frederick's Fables*, a book in which thirteen of Lionni's stories are collected, with an introduction by the respected child psychologist Bruno Bettelheim. His explication of why rich visual images are critical for children's development is interesting. Unfortunately, some of the best of the illustrations from the original versions of these tales have been omitted. For example, the page in *Swimmy* showing the forest of seaweeds has been left out of this compilation. Nonetheless, this omnibus volume serves a useful purpose in leading children to read more of Lionni's works.

Stories about mice outnumber those about any other animal. In *The Glorious Christmas Soup Party*, by Linda Hale, a mouse family lives behind a bale of hay in the barn. Mrs. Mouse is upset because her children have eaten the bacon pie, and guests are due to arrive momentarily. A unique solution, along the lines of the traditional tale "Stone Soup," is devised. Black-and-white pencil drawings illustrate each page of this small book.

Other books about mice that children have enjoyed include: *Anatole*, by Eve Titus; *Mouse House*, by Rumer Godden; and *Miss Bianca*, by Margery Sharp. Anatole, a most fortunate mouse, holds a respectable position as a cheese taster, is happily married to the lovely Doucette and is the proud papa of six charming children. One day his beloved family disappears. But resourceful Anatole, aided by his friends and lots of catnip, engineers a daring rescue and then all is well again. This is one of several books, both old and new, recommended by Schoenfeld (1985) as particularly effective examples of stories about humanlike animals. In *Mouse House*, little Bonnie is the smallest of the many mice children packed into a flowerpot house in the basement. She is inadvertently responsible for the mouse family's inheriting a beautiful discarded dollhouse from upstairs. In *Miss Bianca*, the dainty title character, accompanied by friends, sets off to rescue little Patience from the clutches of the wicked Diamond Duchess. The scheme's success depends on frightening the duchess's ladies-in-waiting, but they are not human and are therefore immune to fear. The solution is full of high melodrama. Miss Bianca's sentimentality will not appeal to all readers, but the fast action will. Another title in this popular series is *Miss Bianca in the Orient*.

Why are mice so appealing in children's books when they are so much

***Artist Paul Galdone establishes Anatole as a French mouse by dressing him in a beret, smock, and neck scarf.*** Illustration by Paul Galdone from *Anatole* by Eve Titus. Copyright © 1965. Published by McGraw-Hill Book Company.

less appealing in actuality? A noted critic (Blount, 1975) gave the following analysis:[2]

> Mice are small, secret, numerous and usually hidden. They are beautiful and neat and, one must feel, courageous to live with us so closely. . . . perhaps it is easier to imagine them members of their own hidden social systems. . . . Their fur and appearance helps them to win our love . . . ; and they are easy to "dress." Mice have an almost unfair advantage. Under the imagined clothes . . . there is the soft but sexless strokable layer.

Frogs and toads, which have a size and quirkiness that appeal to children, are the main characters in many books. The immensely popular wordless series about a frog, by Mercer Mayer, is a good example (this series was described in Chapter 5). For intermediate-grade readers, *Warton and the Contest*, by Russell E. Erickson, continues the series of six popular books that began with *A Toad for Tuesday*. The language is graceful and more

---

[2]Blount also makes the interesting observation that the best mouse stories are written by women and feature mouse heroines. An exception is Russell Hoban's *The Mouse and His Child* (New York: Harper and Row, 1967).

**The animals and their environment are depicted naturalistically in this ink drawing, although the clothes on the toads reflect the whimsy in the story.** Illustration copyright © 1982 by Lawrence DiFiori from *Warton and the Castaways* by Russell E. Erickson. By permission of Lothrop, Lee & Shepard Books (A Division of William Morrow).

complex than that found in simpler books: "Winds were calm, birds were silent, and most creatures, except those that prowl with stealthy feet and glowing eyes, were asleep." Erickson creates characters who play dominoes, wear woolly bathrobes, and make elderberry jelly. They eat at tables but enjoy humanized versions of toads' real foods: "Just then Morton came to the table. He set out a platter of smoked slug strips, three bowls of mealworm mush, and a tall stack of ryegrass toast." Child readers follow the adventures with excitement, because the toads must deal with natural dangers, such as aggressive crows: "It was noon when he came to a small meadow. After making sure there were no dangerous animals about, he started across." These books by Erickson are particularly appropriate for youngsters who want more text than is found in most picture books but for whom extended novels are not appropriate.

*Lonesome Lester*, by Ida Luttrell, is about a prairie dog who gets himself into predicaments that children will chuckle over. Lester is glad to have company; living in the last house on the last street in the last town on the prairie can be lonely. However, Lester discovers that "greedy, messy, bothersome, rude" ants are not the kind of company he wants. Neither is compulsive Aunt Martha, who is lured from her continual waxing of everything in sight only by the news that a store is having a sale on wax. Neither is the baby rabbit who bawls incessantly until—in an effort to entertain him—Lester nearly incapacitates himself. In the last of four short episodes, Lester settles into the contentment that results from doing familiar tasks at one's own pace, enjoying the comfortable smells, sights, and sounds of home.

Dogs and cats, which are medium-sized animals, have been the subjects of many children's books. A particularly good one is *Benjy's Dog House*, by Margaret Bloy Graham, which tells how Benjy—used to sleeping inside with the family—avoids being banished at night to his doghouse. The story and the pleasant, though undistinguished, cartoonlike drawings will appeal to primary-grade children.

*The Birthday Goat*, by Nancy D. Watson, uses a format very similar to a cartoon strip to recount one day in the life of a family of goats: father, mother, Pam, Bridget, Paulette, and baby Souci. Paulette is celebrating a birthday. When they hear about a kidnapper who is on the loose, her father and mother regret allowing Paulette to celebrate her birthday at the carnival, the very spot where the kidnapper was last seen. The family eludes the kidnapper, baby Souci is lost, the father is instrumental in setting free the kidnapper's victims, and all ends peacefully with a picnic beside a rushing brook. Despite its picture book format, this book is not really appropriate for beginning readers. The pleasant, idiosyncratic watercolor and ink-line drawings demand sustained attention. They are crammed to the edges with so many small details that the book is more appropriate for upper-primary-grade children.

Exceptionally popular with children is Arthur the aardvark in *Arthur's Thanksgiving* and the nine other books in the series. The medium-sized animals who personify humans in this series show that author Marc Brown uses sharp observational skills in detailing how school-aged children relate to one another. Francine, the aggressive female monkey, intimidates Arthur regularly, as does Binky Barnes, the bulldog who is the class bully. In *Arthur's Tooth*, as in most of the other books, the hero somehow muddles through. In *Arthur's April Fool*, he once again eludes Binky. When children make friends with Arthur, they will want to read through the series; to encourage this following, the publisher established an Arthur Fan Club and will send a membership card to any youngster who has read all the Arthur books.

Another medium-sized animal—a pig—is the main character in *Freddy and the Perilous Adventure,* by Walter R. Brooks. There is nothing earthshaking here and no unreasonable demands on the reader's skill—just a gentle, bucolic adventure involving Freddy and his friends from Boomerschmidt's Colossal and Unparalleled Circus. Freddy's stay-at-home friends on the farm include Alice and Emma, the timid (and slightly silly) ducks; Mr. and Mrs. Webb, the spiders; Sanford, the woodpecker; and Zero, the fly. The danger is personified in deceitful Mr. Golcher, owner of the balloon Freddy and his friends inadvertently "steal." Getting it back constitutes the story's main action. The author skillfully incorporates a lot of word play and puns into his writing, for example:

> "Uncle Wesley did not approve of slang," interrupted Alice. "He said it was the empty rattling of a brain too small for its skull."

What makes the book remarkable is how well its story and language have aged: it was first published in 1942. The publisher has also reissued *Freddy Goes Camping, Freddy the Pilot,* and *Freddy the Politician.*

Large animals are encountered less often as main characters, but in *The Great Big Elephant and the Very Small Elphant,* Barbara Seuling provides three short stories about two large beasts who are fast friends. In the first story, the friendship survives the larger elephant's trip, even though his smaller friend worries about him going. In the second story, the smaller friend is in a frenzy about the impending visit of his great aunt, and his large friend solves his problem. In the last episode, the smaller elephant assures the larger that he is a good friend, despite the large elephant's doubts. A teacher might ask a young reader if she or he has ever felt the concerns these friends feel about friendship.

The books discussed so far in this section feature animals that act like humans, but the development of human emotions is minimal in them. In *The Grouchy Ladybug,* Eric Carle's animals express human emotions delightfully. In this clever repeating story, the main character is out to pick a fight, a not uncommon human emotional state. The skillfully planned and executed die-cut pages—elegant and expensive bookmaking—reproduce brightly colored tissue-paper collages. These demonstrate the relative size of the animals encountered, show the time of day by numerals on the clock (also written out in the text), and depict the sun moving along its daytime path.

Reluctant readers who enjoy animal stories can sometimes be encouraged to try related composition activities. In preparation, a teacher might read a story to one or more children, or the children can read it themselves, listen to a recording, or view a filmstrip.

A second-grade teacher had three students who were reluctant readers, so one day she read *Mooch the Messy,* by Marjorie W. Sharmat, to them. Mooch, a rat, lives in (and loves) chaos; the description of his disorganized house brought appreciative chuckles from the children. Mooch "reforms" when his neat father comes for a visit, but what will happen when his father leaves? The teacher read the story to this point and then asked the students what they thought Mooch would do. Two of them created the following endings:

> When he gets back he will mess up his hole again, because he likes messy places. He'll put his shoes on the floor, the sheets in the bathtub, and the books on the chairs, because he likes it that way.
>
> *Ann Marie*

> Mooch will keep his place clean for when his father comes again. He loves his father and misses him so much. If it was messy, his father might not come again. That would make Mooch unhappy.
>
> *Brad*

Another teacher of second-graders read *Owl at Home,* by Arnold Lobel, to two of her children who were reading little themselves. Each morning before the day's activities began, the teacher took the two aside and read them one of the five short tales included in the book. Owl, a comfort-loving homebody, is amiable but not terribly quick-witted. The children smiled knowingly as Owl tried to solve the problem of an unpleasant guest or the mystery of the strange bumps in his bed. On Friday, after reading the last of the five stories, the teacher asked the children to compose another adventure for Owl. These are their responses:

> One day Owl got a letter from Paris. It was an invitation to a wedding from one of his grandsons. So he went upstairs and began to pack his suitcase. Then he went to Paris. When he got there Owl met a girl named Laura. They both of them went sight-seeing and Owl proposed to Laura, and Laura said, "Yes." What joy for Owl! They got married the same time as his grandson. Then both went to Canada for their honeymoon. When they got home they lived happily ever after.
>
> *Christopher*

> Owl went to bed one night and by the window he saw a shadow. He went to turn on the light. It was gone! He wondered. Then he turned off the light. It was there! Again he jumped up and down. The shadow jumped up and down. Owl got so mad. They jumped all night. In the morning Owl found out he was fighting his shadow all night. Then Owl said, "Oh, wasn't that silly of me. I'd better go get some rest."
>
> *Lisa*

*Arthur's Loose Tooth*, by Lillian Hoban, is, like the two preceding books, from Harper and Row's series of *I Can Read Books*. All the books in this series, designed for beginning readers, make use of a limited number of words to provide extra practice as children gain reading fluency. In this seventh book about Arthur, Hoban writes beguilingly about her chimp characters, Arthur and his sister Violet. A loose, but not loose enough, tooth occupies the two, and their baby sister, until the expected ending.

After simple animal stories that flow swiftly, making few demands on reluctant readers, these children may be willing to move on to more complex writing, with the help of a skilled librarian or teacher. William Steig possesses a sophisticated understanding of human foibles and the ability to depict these in animal characters, but his books are not easy to read. His writing is densely textured and contains sophisticated vocabulary. In *Dominic*, the writer capitalizes on children's love of incongruity in presenting a dog hero who has a collection of hats. Dominic wears these

> . . . not for warmth or for shade or to shield him from rain, but for their various effects—rakish, dashing, solemn, or martial.

Dominic also plays the piccolo and sets out to see the world, carrying his belongings in a large bandanna. Funny details are subordinated to the flow of the plot. When Dominic meets the witch-alligator, "it seemed to him that she had many more teeth than were necessary for any ordinary dental purpose." Two pages later, Steig picks up on this idea again. As Dominic leaves, "she smiled, exposing all eighty teeth." Dominic shows he is clever, when he evades the Doomsday Gang who have trapped him; kindhearted, when he frees a yellow-jacket from a spider's web; patient, when he tends Bartholomew Badger (a pig) while Bartholomew is ill; and generous, when he gives away little by little all the inheritance the pig gives him. Readers get a three-dimensional hero, not a flat character invented to move the plot along.

A more serious book by Steig is *Abel's Island*, in which Abel and his ladylove, Amanda, discover that an elegant Edwardian picnic can lead to disaster. Marooned on an island, the little mouse finds his main adversary is the owl.

> It was asleep, but its erect posture, like that of a sentinel of hell, its eyes, which even shut seemed to stare, the tight grasp of its talons on the bough, and the bloody sunset in the sky behind it, filled poor Abel with wintry dread.

This is the kind of sophisticated language that marks Steig's writing. The author alternates this type of involved syntactic arrangement with shorter sentences.

> He hurried home, his heart tripping. What should he do? Could he possibly kill the obnoxious creature while it slept, so it would die as if in a dream? How? With a rock on the end of a rope? With fire? With a burning javelin of wood?

After reading this story, a teacher could ask children to improvise a conversation between Abel and Gower Glackens, a frog who is Abel's only companion for much of his stay on the island.

## ANIMAL CHARACTERS THAT THINK AND TALK

A second general type of animal story is one in which the animals act like animals but are able to think and talk like humans. The prototype of such stories is *Black Beauty*, by Anna Sewell, written in 1877 as a protest against cruelty to horses and still in print. The book seems realistic because the horses lead typically horselike lives. However, critic Rebecca Lukens (1986) thinks that the first-person narration destroys the realism since it is based on a faulty premise—that animals have human feelings.[3] At one point, Black Beauty says:

> Day by day, hole by hole, our bearing reins were shortened, and instead of looking forward with pleasure to having my harness put on . . . I began to dread it.

Having decided to do her duty, despite this harassment, Beauty finds worse things follow: the sharp bit cuts her tongue and jaw, and she froths at the mouth; then she feels "worn and depressed." This story is now available as an oversized volume illustrated with Susan Jeffers's meticulously detailed ink-and-wash drawings. The unusual perspectives in several of these make them more interesting than those with head-on views.

A realistically portrayed small animal, who lives in a real, if somewhat idealized, forest setting, is shown in *Mousekin's Mystery*. This book, by Edna Miller, follows eleven other books about this hero. The simple story revolves around real mushrooms that—when accidentally brushed—transfer their

---

[3]Contrast this critical comment about this book with more favorable ones by Charlotte Huck, Susan Hepler, and Janet Hickman in *Children's Literature in the Elementary School* (New York: Holt, Rinehart and Winston, 1987, pp. 28, 112). Further information about the publishing and distribution of this book is found in Aidan Chambers's "Letter from England: A Hope for Benefit" (*The Horn Book*, June 1977, pp. 356–360).

"living light" to animals temporarily. Mousekin, evicted from his home in a hollow tree when it is struck by lightning, sees a bear, a flying squirrel, a fox, and a raccoon glow. What are these "haunted" creatures, he wonders? The next night the glow helps save him from an owl.

A group of animals that think and talk but in other ways live like animals is described in Robert Lawson's appealing *Rabbit Hill*. These rabbits live in burrows, eat rabbit foods, and instinctively fear humans, but they can talk. Excitement grips them when they discover new folks are coming. Will they be planting folks, or will they be mean folks with guns, traps, dogs, and—worst of all—boys? The book recounts Little Georgie's adventures as he finds out the answer to this all-important question: outrunning dogs, jumping Deadman's Brook (no other rabbit, not even Father, had done that), and when injured, meeting the new folks firsthand. Of all the young rabbits, Georgie is the most beloved. When he is hurt and carried off by the new folks, the hill goes into mourning. The new folks demonstrate their true nature when, on Midsummer's Eve, they set up a statue of Saint Francis surrounded by food. Carved on the stone are the words, "There is enough for all." A more extended analysis of this (and nearly forty other titles) is provided by Brunner (1978), who believes that children's books should promote environmental awareness. He praises author Lawson's ability to "establish a clear insight into the relation between man and nature." Lawson again uses this ability when he extends the adventure begun with *Rabbit Hill* in a sequel, *Tough Winter*.

Rabbits are also featured in stories with an entirely different flavor in *The People Could Fly*, by Virginia Hamilton. In this collection of American black folk tales, readers meet Bruh Rabbit and Doc Rabbit, among other animals, all of whom in most ways retain their animalness but can talk. Some of the tales are in language very close to standard English. Others are in difficult-to-read-aloud Gullah, a combination of American, West Indian, English, and African dialects. These stories should be read to children, so they can hear the flow of language; difficulties with the dialect may prevent unskilled readers from enjoying them on their own.

In *The Tale of Tawny and Dingo*, William H. Armstrong, who also wrote *Sounder*, creates a compelling story about Dingo, the shepherd's dog that is the only one with any compassion for Tawny, the runt of a sheep's litter. Cast aside by his mother, the odd-looking lamb is quickly shunned by the rest of the flock. The friendship between Dingo and Tawny gradually becomes constant companionship. Finally, Tawny saves himself from expected slaughter in an ending that adults may find slightly contrived but that children will cheer. Sensitive sepia illustrations that complement the text are by award-winning artist Charles Mikolaycak.

*Illustrations by Leo and Diane Dillon have sharply defined edges but pleasantly soft interior details. The pictures include an effectively wide range of tone from light to dark and are softer than, yet as heavily patterned as, the Dillons' earlier work.* Illustration by Leo and Diane Dillon from *The People Could Fly: American Black Folktales* by Virginia Hamilton. Copyright © 1985. Reprinted by permission of Alfred A. Knopf, Inc.

*Watership Down,* a more difficult book, will intrigue capable readers. Richard Adams's rabbits are comfortable and secure in their warren, but Fiver feels uneasy. He has a premonition that some undefined doom is approaching. He and his brother, Hazel, try to warn the Chief Rabbit, but they are not heeded. A choice faces them: obedience and death, or rebellion and a chance to live. Resourceful, courageous Hazel makes the difficult decision. He, Fiver, and a band of followers set out to establish a new warren. Only when they have survived the dangerous journey and started building their new colony do they realize that their group includes no does and therefore has no long-term future. The balance of the book is concerned with how they abduct females from an enemy warren, battle General Woundwort, and adroitly overcome the dangers that surround them. Adams's special rabbit vocabulary is intriguing: *fu inle* means "after moonrise"; *ni-Frith* means "noon"; and *Hrair* is any number above four ("a lot," or "a thousand"). The author skillfully maintains the characters' "rabbitness." For example, Hazel, the lead rabbit, does not know what a highway is. Another rabbit does but has no idea what cars are. The author also writes about how the rabbits peer secretly at the humans and talk about the "white sticks" they burn in their mouths (cigarettes). They observe and talk about humans, but their understanding of what they see is limited by their rabbit nature.

## REALISTIC ANIMAL CHARACTERS

In some animal stories for children, the author creates a main character who is consistently and realistically an animal from beginning to end. Everything that happens, every action of the character, is plausible given what is known of animal behavior. These animal characters do not wear clothes or talk; many do not even have names. The author is even careful to avoid attributing human emotions to such an animal character. In the best of such stories, the author succeeds in arousing interest in and developing empathy for the character.

Among the best of this third type of animal story is *The Barn*, by John Schoenherr. The uncannily realistic effect of the illustrations was created using black-ink and dry-brush techniques. The pictures add to the vivid tale of a hunter (a skunk) who becomes the hunted. Double-page spreads effectively portray the skunk's attempt to find shelter in the barn. Schoenherr reproduces the feathers and talons of the owl who hunts the skunk and the fur of the skunk with impressive accuracy.

Similarly convincing is *Wingfin and Topple*, by Evans G. Valens, an account of a winged fish and a herring with long fins. The environment is thoroughly described:

> The sky above was fever-blue, punctured by the white hot circle of the sun. Its arching dome rested like a giant's cup turned upside down upon the great flat saucer of the sea.

Unfortunately, the adventures of the two fish end when the herring becomes trapped in a huge net.

> Topple charged the net. He gnashed his teeth and lashed his tail. He splashed. He smashed. But he couldn't break out of the closing net, or under it, or through it.

In *Nobody's Cat,* Miska Miles uses especially effective language to create a realistic main character and its milieu. This story for intermediate-grade children is about a scruffy alley cat, wise in the ways of his world.

> In the nights, he heard the thud of heavy feet hurrying along the sidewalk, the whine of tires in the street, doors slamming in the alley.

Late one afternoon, the cat hears sounds like "music rocked from a high window." Further on in the book, the alley cat encounters a cat with a saucer of milk. During the resulting fight, "they sprang . . . screaming and biting, thumping and tumbling." The alley cat escapes. "When the alley was quiet, he licked his leg where it was matted with blood." The way the author alternates sound and silence helps establish different parts of the setting and enhances the story's realism.

Cats are also the focus of *The Christmas Day Kitten,* by James Herriot. Though lovingly shown (and, indeed, doted on by their hostess), the cats are realistically depicted. Ruth Brown's watercolor illustrations, sharpened with an unobtrusive ink line, highlight the particularities of gentrified English country life of a few decades ago.

Two other books present animals somewhat differently than do the books described above. The animals are depicted realistically, but their effects on humans are unusual. Cynthia Rylant's *Every Living Thing* is a collection of short stories. In one of these, a turtle helps Leo, a child who was always slow, win a prize and feel better about himself. In another, a parrot helps Harry, who is alienated from his father, understand what he has missed. In yet another, an abandoned cat, whose tail has been amputated, helps Magda discover that true love has nothing to do with money. The twelve minimal stories are short (ranging from three to ten pages) and remarkably understated (no superfluous descriptions here). They still have a dramatic effect far greater than most full-length novels. These strange, unsettling little tales are well worth reading and rereading.

Not an animal story but an exemplary treatment of creatures realistically portrayed is a collection of four small books (less than 4 inches square) slipcased together as *Leonard Baskin's Miniature Natural History.* Baskin uses dark colors and intense contrasts to create dramatic illustrations that are both authentic and imaginative. The books feature wild and domestic animals, insects, birds, and water-dwellers. Each creature is pictured on a single page; on the facing left-hand page, the common name (set in upper case) and the biological name (set in upper and lower case) are elegantly placed between ruled lines in the lower corner. Identical endpapers unify the four books, and the same paper covers the slipcase.

## IMAGINARY ANIMALS

Some children's book authors have written tales about totally imaginary beasts. In *Pea Soup and Sea Serpents,* by William Schroder, Norton and Atherton sally forth in a boat, with ropes and life jackets, to hunt the sea serpent. Thick fog surrounds them, obscuring the monster who rocks the boat, overturns it, and heaves the heros ashore. Schroder also provides pastel illustrations whose mistiness helps establish the setting and whose humor helps carry the dialogue.

In *Dragon Franz,* by Elizabeth Shub, an imaginary beast believes he is a total failure. Unable to produce fire in any form, Franz is discouraged. He visits his godfather, who discovers that Franz has a remarkable attribute that distinguishes him from all other dragons. The full-color, full-page illustrations by Ursula Konopka further develop the book's central idea that every individual is something special.

Imaginary beast stories are not limited to those intended for primary-grade readers. *The Griffin and the Minor Canon,* by Frank Stockton, was first published by Mary Mapes Dodge in *St. Nicholas Magazine.* Stockton, the now largely overlooked author of many elegant literary folk tales, was born in 1834. The story was published in book form in 1963 with art by Maurice Sendak and was reprinted in 1986. Sendak gives some details of Stockton's writing career and describes the process of illustrating this book in its introduction. Sendak's illustrations feature the small, chunky people characteristic of his early work.

The Minor Canon "filled a subordinate position in the old church," where the Griffin's stone image adorned the main door, and "taught a school composed entirely of the bad children in the town with whom nobody else would have anything to do." The Griffin, a changeless, watchful, and soon-to-be-hungry beast, strikes fear into the hearts of all the townsfolk except the sturdy little Canon. The two develop a touching friendship, but the townsfolk, fearing the Griffin's appetite, send the Canon away into the wilderness, in the hope that the affectionate Griffin will follow his friend. The ploy does not work, and in his friend's absence, the Griffin takes on the responsibilities of teaching the school (the children respond amazingly well) and visiting the sick:

> The Griffin now thought that he ought to visit the sick and the poor; and he began to go about the town for this purpose. The effect upon the sick was miraculous. All, except those who were very ill indeed, jumped from their beds when they heard he was coming and declared themselves quite well.

In the end, the modest little Canon receives his reward but only because of the Griffin's selfless sacrifice.

***Pleasant pastel shades of gold and pink watercolor are overlaid with cross-hatched ink lines characteristic of Maurice Sendak's style at that time.*** Illustration from *The Griffin and the Minor Canon* by Frank R. Stockton. Illustration by Maurice Sendak. Copyright © 1963 by Maurice Sendak. Reprinted by permission of Harper & Row, Publishers, Inc.

After sharing *The Griffin and the Minor Canon* with upper-intermediate-grade children, a teacher might ask them to look for examples of stone sculpture on churches or other public buildings in the community.[4] This is one of many books annotated by Baskin and Harris (1980) in their volume about gifted children. Opening chapters on the role of the gifted in society, on identification of the gifted, and intellectual aspects of the reading experience, precede a 175-page chapter that annotates books specifically chosen because they call for "higher stages of cognitive functioning."

## OTHER TYPES OF ANIMAL STORIES

Some animal stories are set in other countries, and such books add variety to children's literary experiences. In *The Cow Who Fell in the Canal*, by Phyllis Krasilovsky, illustrator Peter Spier provides pictures for a humorous animal story set in the countryside and a marketplace in the Netherlands.

Verna Aardema's *Who's in Rabbit's House?* is a brilliantly designed rendition of a humorous Masai folk tale. Rabbit can't get into her house because the Long One, hiding inside, threatens to trample her. After various animals offer unsuccessful solutions to Rabbit's problem, Frog rousts the unknown creature by outwitting him. The bold illustrations by Leo and Diane Dillon present the story in the form of a play performed by actors wearing animal masks. The text skillfully combines repetition of key phrases with authentic African ideophones to produce a rhythmic story for reading aloud or for choral reading. Children will enjoy repeating phrases such as "gdung, gdung, gdung" when the frog laughs and "dilak, dilak, dilak" when the rabbit falls into the water. The book might also be used to inspire a class play to culminate a unit on African culture or African folklore.

Not all animal stories are told in prose. *Bugs: Poems*, by Mary Ann Hoberman, includes statements about a variety of insects—from dragonflys to cockroaches.

> *Spiders seldom see too well*
> *Spiders have no sense of smell.*
> *Spiders spin out silken threads*
> *Spiders don't have separate heads.*

A book of poems for upper-grade readers features creatures of all kinds. *Under the North Star*, by Ted Hughes, contains poems for mature readers

---

[4]*Faces on Places*, by Suzanne Haldane (New York: Viking, 1980), is an elegant book with large black-and-white photographs (many by the author herself) and a clear but brief text describing how gargoyles and other stone creatures carved on buildings came to be. Both historic and modern carvings are shown, and the process is described.

who are attuned to subtle nuances and poetic elements. Some of the creatures are commonplace, for example, the mosquito; others are exotic, for example, the wolverine. All of the poems are accompanied by Leonard Baskin's lushly colored, impressionistic illustrations, whose subtlety requires study.

## MYSTERY AND DETECTIVE FICTION

For adult devotees of mystery and detective novels, vicariously tracking down clues and solving yet another mystery is escape reading at its finest. The satisfying conclusion, when all is neatly wrapped up in a solution, whets the appetite for more reading. So it is for child devotees of juvenile mystery and detective fiction, of which the series of Nancy Drew books are perhaps the best known. Other mystery series are those that feature the Hardy boys, Tom Swift, Cherry Ames, the Bobbsey twins, and the five little Peppers. Such series books have been, and still are, mass produced. Though often published under a single author's name, each series has been, since its inception, written by several different authors. These books unfortunately are typified by quite predictable plots, paper-thin characters, stilted dialogue, and cliché-ridden prose. Nonetheless, they are still immensely popular. Although usually not stocked in libraries, they probably perform a useful purpose, serving as "bait" to reading, stepping stones to better literature.

Mystery stories in series are also available for beginning readers, who may enjoy following a character through several similar adventures. Marjorie W. Sharmat's Nate, featured in *Nate the Great*, for example, attracts readers through his laconic, deadpan delivery. The frantic antics of Elizabeth Levy's Gwen and Jill in the "Something Queer" mysteries, such as *Something Queer at the Library*, prove it is possible to write interesting stories using simple language. Other popular serialized heroines and heros include David Adler's Cam Jansen, in *Cam Jansen and the Mystery of the Television Dog*, for example, and Robert Quackenbush's Piet Potter, in *Piet Potter on the Run*, for example.

Fortunately, there are mystery and detective books that are better written than the popular series titles. Some of those available are at the beginning-to-read level. *Big Max in the Mystery of the Missing Moose*, by Kin Platt, is one example. In sentences of three to eleven words, the author uses simple vocabulary (but rather stilted dialogue) to tell how Big Max, the world's greatest detective, solved a problem for Marvin, who wants to return to Moose Land. Children enjoy the visual image of triangular-shaped Big Max, whose gigantic feet hold him firmly to the ground as he muddles through clues to get to a solution.

An excellent example of a mystery for second- or third-grade readers is *The Case of the Invisible Dog*, by E. W. Hildick. Twelve brief chapters (varying from six to fourteen pages each), tell an engrossing story that sweeps briskly from beginning to end without the distraction of subplots or extensive character development. McGurk and his detective organization, including Wanda, Willie, and narrator Joey, are bemused by, and then determined to solve, the mystery of the dog that is first invisible and then visible. "Brains" Bellingham, the inventor of an invisibility machine, almost uses it to wangle an invitation into McGurk's organization, but the gang discovers his trickery. Then the gang decides to turn the tables on "Brains," in an ending as broadly humorous as the entire story. There is no subtlety here but even indifferent readers will enjoy the abundance of clues and action. There are several other books featuring the same characters; the most recent in the series is *The Case of the Vanishing Ventriloquist*.

*A Summer in the South* is more likely to be appreciated by intermediate-grade readers because the humor is rather subtle. The author, James Marshall, is widely known for his humorous stories about the hippos George and Martha. In this mystery, intrepid Eleanor Owl and her faithful cohort, Mr. Paws, search for the cause of a number of puzzling events that occur at the small seaside hotel where they are vacationing. Other characters in this rollicking mixture of slapstick and parody include fastidious Foster Pig, hypochondriacal Don Coyote, and Mariette Chicken, lately retired from the circus. But who are the mysterious female baboons in the string quartet? Is Maxine the Goose really what she seems to be? And what role can the Cootie family be playing in all this intrigue? Children will follow the unwinding of this tangled skein of characters and events with enthusiasm.

Intermediate-grade readers will also enjoy *The Mona Lisa Mystery*, by Pat Hutchins, a sequel to *The House That Sailed Away*. This time Morgan and his classmates, passports in hand, are off on a trip to Paris. The adventure starts immediately: when the children's bus has just gotten underway, Sacha and Morgan notice that a bearded man, bent over the steering wheel of a black Citröen with a French license plate, is following them. The strange man turns up again in Paris, and thirteen brief chapters later, Jessica is taken hostage by the same man, who is stealing the famous da Vinci painting. All ends well, of course, with the children toasting their success— with bottles of Coca-Cola, nestled in silver ice buckets—as guests at a gala dinner in their honor.

An intriguing book-length mystery story for intermediate-grade or junior high students is *The Famous Stanley Kidnapping Case*, by Zilpha Keatley

Snyder. The Stanley family, who made the author's earlier book, *The Headless Cupid*, a success, here find themselves transported to Italy. Uncle Sid leaves Molly his money, which can only be spent in his native Italy. So the Stanley family **pack up** for a year abroad. Molly and her daughter and Jeff and his four children are comfortably settled in a rambling, slightly decrepit Italian villa, enjoying the lazy late summer, when the mishap occurs. Who are the sinister hooded criminals who kidnap—rather inadvertently—all the Stanley children? The author establishes a remarkable sense of place as she weaves into the story introductory materials about the villa, the Italian countryside, and the array of foreigners who populate the villa. Children who enjoy these characters will be glad to hear that they also appear in *Blair's Nightmare*.

The books discussed so far in this section are mystery stories involving real creatures—animal or human. Also for intermediate-grade readers is a book introducing some supernatural creatures that may interest child readers who are fond of mystery books. *Meet the Vampires*, by Georgess Mc-Hargue, continues the *Eerie Series*. In this volume, she distinguishes between vampires and ghosts, considering both physical and mental qualities. She traces vampires through history and around the world from Greece to Africa. The blood-red cover suitably introduces a book featuring a diversity of art: ancient woodcuts, movie stills, medieval paintings, photographs, and stone busts, as well as eerie drawings by Stephen Gammel.

When a teacher is working with a devoted reader of a series of mystery or detective stories, it may be possible, with careful guidance, to move that child on to more sophisticated writing. Good writing is found in some collections of mysterious short stories. One example is *The Shadow Cage*, by Philippa Pearce, containing ten short tales of the supernatural. Some of the stories have children as main characters (for example, the title story) and some have adults (for example, "The Strange Illness of Mr. Arthur Cook"). There is a beloved grandmother who is behaving peculiarly, a strange ghostly girl who appears when a tree falls on a school, and the ghost of a son lost at war who comes back to help his father one last time. Mysterious attic rooms are closed off to contain unspecified dangers. Sudden death comes to a pair of brothers. In one story, a small boy, hunting for a lost ball, is beckoned into a house by a specter, and as a result a long-estranged daughter returns home.

*Encounters with the Invisible World* consists of ten short stories, drawn from a variety of New England folk tales and embellished and expanded by Marilynne Roach. The language in the stories is as spare as the rocky land in which they originated. They deal with foolish men and clever women who encounter ghosts, witches, and the devil. Sometimes the people win; at other times, the supernatural beings triumph. Jack Fayerweather finds

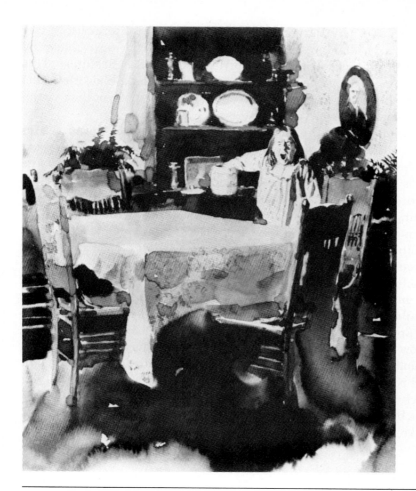

**Impressionistic, loosely rendered ink-wash drawings concentrate not on specificity of form but rather on evocation of feelings.** From *The Shadow Cage and Other Tales of the Supernatural* by Philippa Pearce, for Thomas Y. Crowell. Illustrated by Ted Lewin. Copyright © 1977 by Philippa Pearce. Reprinted by permission of Harper & Row, Publishers, Inc.

that following an angel is hard work. Goody Booker is a genuine witch who still has to spade her own garden. An innocent peddler's ghost finally rests. The stories are distinguished by their exciting turns of plot rather than by their character development.[5]

Fourteen mysterious and diverse stories are collected by Barbara Ireson in *The April Witch and Other Strange Tales*. "Of Polymuf Stock" is a chilling exploration of the ruling and the ruled classes by John Christopher; "The

---

[5]Exciting plot is the feature that wins detective or mystery writing so many devotees, according to Edward Fenton, in "Mystery" (*The Horn Book*, June 1968, pp. 277–280). Fenton believes that the most satisfying mysteries contain an element of the unexpected and avoid pat explanations.

Never-ending Penny," by Bernard Wolf, is an extended literary folk tale about the effects of wishing for something magical. The most charming character is the title character of "The April Witch," by Ray Bradbury. This young girl who can change herself into a tree, a leaf, and a blackbird. One evening when she is out exploring, she enters the body of another young girl and discovers the joy of young love.

*Up the Chimney Down*, by Joan Aiken, is a collection of eleven stories united by the author's use of a wry, unexcited tone to describe the most improbable happenings. The juxtaposition of the commonplace and the exceptional is what makes these stories delectable to mature readers in middle school or junior high. The title story is about a witch and involves child-snatching, as the witch replaces little Clove, the six-month-old baby she lifts from a carriage, with a bunch of celery. Nobody (except Clove's twin sister Cinnamon) notices! In another story, a ballet dancer recovering from a broken leg in her basement apartment has a Nemean lion, which she cannot sell for fear something evil will happen as a consequence. In yet another, an unexceptional mirror makes cantankerous old Cousin Elspeth, who takes cubes of frozen whiskey in her tea, improve remarkably in demeanor and appearance. All of these stories are intended for mature readers, who will know (or choose to look up) such terms as "at quayside," "ramparts of books," and "ye poor ould quadruped." Aiken's imagery will intrigue these skilled readers: a dog "barked himself right off the roof, and fell like a heavy black plum"; another character heaves "a sigh that went all along his bony ribs like a finger along the keys of a piano"; and another has "deep-sunk eyes like holes out of which something nasty might suddenly pop."

## SPORTS STORIES

In sports stories, the plot or action is generally the most important element. Characters usually have one distinguishing trait (for instance, determination or a quick temper) and need no more, since their main purpose is to advance the plot. Because they have such a limited role, these characters are often rather two-dimensional.[6]

Sports stories serve two purposes.

---

[6]Minimal character development is part of the formula in writing sports fiction. The idea of predictable types of story structures, of fiction with certain recurring attributes, is described by Richard D. Western in "Formula Fiction and Literature Study" (*Arizona English Bulletin*, 17, 1975, pp. 97–99). Although he is discussing cowboy stories as formula fiction, the author's assertion that conventions in such literature serve useful purposes for readers seems to apply to sports stories as well.

## 1. *Sports stories present characters with whom readers can identify.*

The people in such books are participating in sports the reader enjoys or would like to take part in. Empathy for the main character or characters, who usually overcome some sort of obstacle in attaining proficiency or success, is very satisfying for child readers.

## 2. *Sports stories provide escape reading.*

Sports stories allow child readers to transcend their own lives and participate vicariously in the achievements of the main characters. These books allow readers to escape into a more satisfying life for a brief interlude.

Some sports stories are written so as to combine high interest and easy reading. *Rod-and-Reel Trouble*, by Bobbi Katz, is part of the *Springboard* series published by Albert Whitman Company. Short sentences, snappy dialogue, and lots of action characterize most sports books, and this book is no exception. Lori has watched the annual fishing contest from afar for years; "boys only" is the rule—until this year. First prize is a spring rod; second prize, a tackle box. Lori and Chris, her friend and fishing partner, enjoy fishing for trout in the creek. One afternoon Chris falls in, hits his head, and loses consciousness. Lori cannot haul him out, but she saves his life by holding his head above water and applying pressure to the wound. They both recover from shock and exposure and enter the contest. Chris wins first prize. Lori wins the second prize but is also rewarded with a rod for saving Chris's life, so all ends happily and tidily. In addition to its fast-moving plot and dialogue, one of the book's assets is that it presents a nonromantic friendship between a boy and a girl.

In *The Meat in the Sandwich*, by Alice Bach, Mike, age ten, has a poor self-image until Kip, a super jock, moves in next door. Mike blooms under Kip's tutelage in hockey but tries to conceal the fact that he spends his spare time doing his share of household chores, the result of his mother's newly raised consciousness. The coach puts them on opposing teams, and their friendship dissolves as they turn rivals. Mike is hurt in a crucial game, but it is his pride that suffers the most significant damage. He resists returning to school and ignores the attempts of his former friend to reestablish contact. When Mike does go back to school, the confrontation between the two former friends is very brief and not—to adult readers—terribly convincing. The hockey details are effectively described, as are the contrasts between Mike's family and Kip's:

> "I've got the picture. Your mom's in the attic [painting] and you're down here doing the wash instead of practicing soccer." I felt ridiculous. I had been wash-

ing dishes, clothes, vacuuming—the whole trip—and Kip was right. I was doing Mom's work.

"Does your dad do laundry too?"

"Sure. He says it only takes a few minutes."

"Woman's work, Mike. Even my mom says so. I help my dad outside. My mom says she wishes she had a daughter to help her instead of a house full of men. She always smiles when she says it, and we know she loves being the only girl surrounded by all of us. Dad calls her the Queen."

"Well, this house is full of queens."

"Then you shouldn't have to do their work." Kip smiled triumphantly. "Boy, they really have you brainwashed. You've gotta remember you're special. Think of it this way. Your sisters are like two slices of bread, but you are a boy—the meat in the sandwich." He slapped me on the back. "Like my dad says, if you don't think you're the best you'll never be the best."

"The meat in the sandwich." I liked the sound of it.

In *Zanbanger*, by R. R. Knudson, Zan narrates the action. She is determined to play basketball with the boys' team, since both the coach and the facilities for the girls' team are inferior. The description of these is devastating:

> We hear Mrs. Butor's voice down the hall but coming nearer. "Gals, you'll simply love your new dressing room. It's divine. Vanity mirrors! Ruffled curtains stitched in our own home ec department. Your lockers alive with glowing color—"
>
> "A wonderful scale to help us keep slim for our menfolks." I heard Mrs. Butor's clunky footsteps at the door. I heard Ooooooo's and Ahhhhhh's from Ruby Jean Twilly, Lurlee Dewey, and Dee-Dee Tupper as they shimmied into Maroon City.

Other humor lightens the intense dose of basketball terms and procedures. Zan's best friend Rinehart is poorly coordinated, has weak vision, and is exceptionally brainy. He works as Zan's coach, supervising her workouts and taking notes on her progress. Upon encountering Mrs. Butor, Rinehart "smiled his brightest smile, the one he usually saved for his pet newt." Zan is temporarily put on the boys' team but denied the right to play. When Rinehart files for an injunction to keep the team from playing without Zan, she is dumped, and the case goes to trial. One chapter is Rinehart's daily log, another is an account of the trial (done in dialogue), and still another is a newspaper article reporting the decision. The boys' coach finally takes the stand and admits that he wants her on the team. With this obstacle removed, Zan works her way up as a sub and then a starter, and the team's original opposition to having to play with a girl begins to diminish. The team battles its way to the finals and, in the last minutes of play, wins by a two-point margin. Clearly, this is the only way the book could end; the author provides a fitting conclusion to a book that is didactic but not oppressively so. This book was preceded by *Zanballer*, in which Zan forms a girls' team, and followed by *Zanboomer*, in which she competes in cross-country running, and *Zan Hagen's Marathon*, in which she trains for an Olympic competition.

The author of *Buddy and the Old Pro*, John R. Tunis, is one of the most respected sports writers for children.[7] Tunis's writing frequently raises fundamental questions about American attitudes toward sports: often characterized by the desire for victory at any cost, the adulation accorded winners, and the ugly atmosphere that can develop when players are encouraged to go to any lengths to win. Tunis emphasizes the finer qualities that sports can encourage: persistence, courage, and a sense of proportion. In this book, the hero is Buddy Reitmayer, captain and shortstop of his elementary-school baseball team, the Benjamin Franklin Tigers. The villain is McBride, Buddy's hero, formerly of the Chicago Cubs and now coaching another team. Buddy is appalled at McBride's behavior. He roars with anger at every adverse decision, encourages his young charges in unsportsmanlike, and even dangerous, practices, and is the antithesis of everything Buddy has learned to value in team sports. The author does not let everything work out all right. Buddy's team loses the big game to the team coached by McBride, a bully and a cheat. Buddy begins to see adults as fallible. Disillusioned, Buddy agrees with his understanding father that sometimes it is better to lose than to win, if winning means hurting others. Tunis's book moralizes, but the author does not make the mistake of portraying characters as all black or all white. Even McBride, unprincipled as he is, gets his share of compassion. Speaking of McBride, Buddy's father says,

> "He's a bully. And everyone in town knows it . . . . Only wait a minute. What made him that way? Remember, he was a poor kid with no home. He had to scrap and fight and scramble the best way he could. No wonder he acts the way he does."

This exciting sports story, with lots of tense action, is also about learning to accept reality and beginning to grow up.

One of the most impressive children's books about sports—a fine piece

---

[7]In "John R. Tunis: A Commitment to Values" (*The Horn Book*, February 1967, pp. 48–54), William Jay Jacobs praises Tunis for "courage, persistence, teamwork, the evaluation of people according to merit instead of race or social class." Tunis's work is distinguished by vivid incidents, realistic characterizations, and an intuitive talent for capturing the fleeting instant or elusive mood.

of writing—is *The Moves Make the Man,* by Bruce Brooks. This book won the Boston Globe–Horn Book Award for excellence in children's literature in 1985. Ostensibly about Jerome Foxworthy's efforts to teach Bix Rivers, the sharpest white athlete Jerome has ever seen, how to play basketball, this story transcends its athletic context. Jerome goes to the biggest white school in Wilmington, North Carolina, to integrate the school, and finds himself inextricably caught up in giving the mysterious Bix hoops lessons. But basketball is only the backdrop. In long sections (for example, the brilliant description Jerome gives of the school communications course) and in small parts of sentences (". . . I was chattering away, a twist above a whisper . . ."), Brooks demonstrates his impressive writing ability. An example is Jerome's commentary on the not yet evident effects of his mother's elevator accident:

> There was only one thing I was worried about, and that was whether she had gotten a little of her smarts knocked out. I did not think so, and I did not draw my worry from anything she showed or did. I drew my worry from knowing how fragile all the ways of being intelligent are. So many things whizzing around in there, ideas and quickness and a smell for the truth, all hooking up the right way to make you do the things you do right. I couldn't help think a crash like Momma's would maybe bust a few quicknesses, cut some of the sense for truth, and you would not be able to notice what was not there any longer. Shifts and misses, you do not see them for themselves probably when they go, like losing a half step in basketball when your ankle is a little stiff. Thought is about something and you pay mind to what it is about, not how quick and right it came.

At other times, the description is less extended, but no less dramatic. After a disastrous trip, Bix and Jerome reach the mental hospital in which Bix's mother is existing.

> The eyes looked out at you and you saw they were deep, but there was nothing behind them, only just an empty room far away waiting to be filled up with whatever fell in front of the gaze.

Child readers may well focus simply on the story's events: the basketball details, the encounter between the railroad men and Jerome over his lantern, the amazingly funny interchange in the home ec room over mock apple pie. These and other details have the ring of truth, even though they concern people, events, and places readers may not be familiar with. But it is in Jerome's private reflections, his thinking things out, that Brooks demonstrates his writing talent so conclusively. This is the kind of work to which teachers should lead students who are interested in sports writing. Additional insight into this author and his work is found in an article he wrote himself (Brooks, 1986).

Probably less familiar than the sports already mentioned here, at least to adults, is BMX (bicycle motocross) racing, described in *Race of the Radical*, by Fanny Howe. It is apparent that the author profited from her son's interest in BMX racing, as the book is a swirl of technical terms. These do not, however, get in the way of the forward movement of the plot. The characters are not especially well-developed, but this lack is hardly noticeable since the action holds the reader's attention. Alex Porter's mother, Marel, is as caught up in BMX racing as her son. She represents a conscious attempt by the author to avoid a stereotyped mother: "She smoked, drank whiskey, ate junk food, and drove a pickup truck around town. She repaired cars for people at home . . . ." Alex's father is equally unexpected—a complete contrast to his wife. The character of Alex, around whom the story revolves, is less distinctive. Some detective work, a scene in a cemetery at night, and a fistfight serve to hold the reader's interest. The language is believable; the author effectively depicts, without much overt talking about it, relations between Alex and his younger brother Robinson. Even readers who have never been to a BMX racetrack can get a clear sense of what such a place is like and what people do there.

Another book about bikes is one of Matt Christopher's well-written sports stories for middle school readers. In *Dirt Bike Racer*, a boy who finds a bike at the bottom of a lake painstakingly restores it to working order. He must take a job in order to earn money to buy the parts he needs. The old man he works for has a nephew who begins to make trouble. As with Christopher's other books, the sports aspect is what attracts readers, but larger themes are also developed.

Stephen Schwandt, in writing *The Last Goodie*, effectively combines sport—in this case, running—with a mystery. A kidnapping tragedy has haunted seventeen-year-old Marty Oliver for twelve years; he only partially deals with his irrationally guilty feeling that he should have done something to prevent his pretty baby-sitter from being abducted. His warm, close relationship with his father and competitive relationship with his friend Ted Harper are effectively portrayed. However, his newly absent mother— off on the middle-class endeavor of "finding herself"—and the extended railing against the incompetence of school administrators and unfair seniority systems are less convincing. Despite this shortcoming, runners will read the book enthusiastically, and even those disinterested in the sport will read to see if the kidnapper will be brought to justice.

*The Sidewalk Racer, and Other Poems of Sports and Motion*, by Lillian Morrison, illustrates effectively that the ability to capture the exhilaration of sports is not limited to writers of prose. In these accomplished poems, which describe how it feels to balance on a surfboard, hurl a spiraling pass, or swerve and dip on a skateboard, Morrison evokes the breathless grace

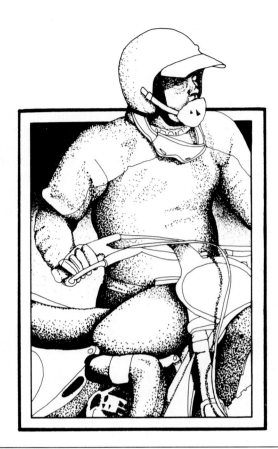

**In this drawing, artist Barry Bomzer makes effective use of dots and large, somewhat abstract shapes that depict both person and machine.** From *Dirt Bike Racer* by Matt Christopher. Copyright © 1979 by Matthew F. Christopher. Illustrations by Barry Bomzer. By permission of Little, Brown and Company.

and joy of movement. Stunning photographs contribute to a distinguished book. This is one of several poetry books recommended by Harms (1982). The poet followed this collection with *The Break Dance Kids*, featuring a similar array of sports, once again augmented with black-and-white photos.

In addition to fiction and poetry, the school library's card catalogue or *Subject Guide to Children's Books in Print* will reveal that many information books about sports are available. These may well appeal to sports-minded children for whom fiction isn't a first choice; such factual books may be an enticement to reading. Three of those available are *Better Roller Skating: The Key to Improved Performance*, by Richard Arnold; *Everybody's a Winner: A Kid's Guide to New Sports and Fitness*, by Tom Schneider; and *Great Beginnings: From Olympics to Superbowl to World Series*, by Stephen C. Turner.

# SCIENCE FICTION

What child could resist the thrill of settling into a spaceship and blasting off toward a distant planet? For many children, particularly those who don't read a lot, science fiction may well be the only kind of book that will be acceptable. In that case, the teacher must be prepared to use this preference as an entrée to more sophisticated literature.

Science fiction and fantasy (a genre described in Chapter 11) are closely related forms of literature, but there are some distinctions that can be made between them. Fantasy can be set in present, past, or future time, whereas science fiction is generally set in the future. In science fiction, what happens is often possible because of mechanical devices or scientific discoveries; in fantasy, what happens is often due to special mental powers of the characters or forces that are not completely understood. Fantasy is often an acquired taste of adept readers who could read any genre; science fiction is often read by students who won't read any other kind of book.

An effective information book for introducing science fiction to primary-grade readers is Franklyn M. Branley's *Is There Life in Outer Space?* Wonderfully whimsical full-color pictures by Don Madden illustrate the kinds of beliefs people used to hold about the inhabitants of other planets. These illustrations are effectively contrasted with black-and-white photographs of real planets and space explorers. Branley concludes by agreeing with those who speculate that somewhere among the billions of stars "there must be plants and animals living on other worlds."

Another book for beginning readers, from Harper and Row's *I Can Read* series, is *The Laziest Robot in Zone One*, by Lillian and Phoebe Hoban. This book features the expected paraphernalia such as robots with control panels and sun shields, as well as some unexpected things, such as a robot dog. Despite the details, the message is familiar: working together can be more productive than going it alone. Although not particularly distinguished in either writing or illustration, this book is one of those that fulfill a very worthwhile purpose for beginning readers, giving them humorous, exciting adventures cast in simple, easy-to-read language.

On a similar reading level is Jane Yolen's *Commander Toad and the Planet of the Grapes* and others in this series, for example, *Commander Toad in Space* and *Commander Toad and the Dis-Asteroid*. In his ship, Star Warts, aided by Lieutenant Lily and Mr. Hop, Commander Toad has a mission to go where no spaceship has gone before.

A robot is a boy's best friend in a series by Marilyn Z. Wilkes. Rodney Pentax and his robot C.L.U.T.Z. meet danger in Wilkes's two books, the first of which was *C.L.U.T.Z.* The second book, *C.L.U.T.Z. and the Fizzion Formula,*

***This line drawing featuring exaggerated facial expressions shows what the author's words tell.***
From *C.L.U.T.Z.* by Marilyn Z. Wilkes, pictures by Larry Ross. Pictures copyright © 1982 by Larry Ross. Reprinted by permission of the publisher, Dial Books for Young Readers.

finds the heros involved in queer goings-on at GalactiCola. Someone is trying to sabotage the plant, steal the Fizzion formula, or even take over the world!

It is possible for even third- and fourth-grade students to read science fiction, although most such books are written for older readers.[8] A fine example for young readers, full of wacky reversals, is *Matthew Looney's Voyage to the Earth*, by Jerome Beatty, Jr. This story opens with the conflict between a small boy (who wants to explore space with his uncle) and his father (who wants his son to work in his factory). Matthew is chosen to be cabin boy on an expedition led by Uncle Lucky. Leaving the moon, they travel to Earth, accompanied by a stowaway, Matthew's pet murtle, Ronald. The official purpose of the trip is to gather geologic samples that will better enable moon officials to determine how to remove this unsightly element in the environment. Uncle Lucky's secret purpose is to test his theory that there may, indeed, be life on Earth. Exploration of the area in which they land appears to be fruitless, but the murtle inadvertently provides evidence that life could exist on Earth by wandering out of the spaceship and breathing the "poisonous" air. Back home, Uncle Lucky is summoned to a hearing held to investigate reports of mishaps during the journey. Matthew bravely answers questions about Ronald's ability to live in oxygen. Since this suggests there may be life on Earth, plans are made for a second voyage, to be taken during school vacation so Matthew can go along.

For intermediate-grade readers, *Miss Pickerell Goes to Mars*, by Ellen MacGregor, features an outspoken heroine who is mildly reminiscent of sharp-tongued Mary Poppins. Miss Pickerell is an engaging blend of determination and homely concern for her simple life. Returning from a pleasant but exhausting visit with her nieces and nephews, she is anticipating a quiet time on her farm when, to her dismay, she discovers a spaceship parked in her pasture. When she attempts to force the captain to move it, she inadvertently becomes a passenger on an interplanetary expedition. She knows nothing about gravity, atmospheric pressure, or, indeed, spaceships.

> Miss Pickerell could see that calibrating an electronic instrument, to make it give the correct reading, must be something like regulating a clock, to make it tell the correct time.

Some explanations by the captain and other crew members tend to be

---

[8]The level of reading difficulty in science fiction is one problem with the genre that is identified by Sonia Brotman in "Out of This World" (*School Library Journal*, December 1976, pp. 30–31). Recent titles are stronger in theme and characterization than earlier ones were, but the books age faster than those in other genres.

preachy, but since most child readers will not know the information, that aspect will probably not bother them. The captain and his crew perceive Miss Pickerell as a nuisance and a danger (her magnetic hammer upsets all the instruments), but later in the trip they find she is useful. Her true bravery and quick resourcefulness become apparent when one of the men, returning to the ship, catches his foot between some rocks. There are seventeen other titles in the Miss Pickerell series; a recent one is *Miss Pickerell and the Blue Whales*.

Another series that is popular with intermediate-grade children is the Danny Dunn books, which combine science, humor, and adventures. *Danny Dunn, Invisible Boy*, by Jay Williams and Raymond Abrashkin, is typical of this series.

Also on an intermediate-grade reading level, *Escape from Splatterbang*, by Nicholas Fisk, is a brief (ninety-four–page) excursion into the world of science fiction gadgetry, entertaining to those who like that sort of thing. Walls that pucker to make door openings, a computer that has a voice with which it can converse, and ecosuits that beep directions to the wearer are examples of the apparatus available to travelers Mykl (thirteen years old), Mags (his mother), and Doggs (his dad).

Also for intermediate-grade readers is *The Trouble on Janus*, by Alfred Slote, the fourth in a series about Jack Jameson and his robot buddy, Danny One. Earlier titles are *My Robot Buddy*, *C.O.L.A.R.*, and *Omega Station*. The books bristle with the paraphernalia of science fiction: the likable robot who thinks and is programmed with a microchip; travel by air cruiser; and communication via laser grams from other planets. Some of the fast-paced action seems contrived, for instance, when the spilling of freckle paint remover results in Jack's pretending to be a robot. Nonetheless, child readers will follow the intrigues with interest. Finding out what happened to the real King Paul and helping the youngster regain his throne from his devious uncle involve Jack in a variety of hairbreadth escapes.

Ellis (1984) comments on the "somewhat sparsely populated territory of science fiction for capable intermediate readers." She recommends the writing of Monica Hughes, whom she describes as Canada's finest author of this genre. Hughes gives the necessary scientific background without getting bogged down in hardware, allowing herself plenty of space to deal with such important themes as the disorientation of the newcomer. Hughes's major work, the *Isis* trilogy, opens with *Keeper of the Isis Light*, set in 2081 and, according to Ellis, showing Hughes's usual delight in invention, "kept firmly in check by a tightly controlled plot."

More readily available than science-fiction books for intermediate readers are science-fiction novels of great complexity for mature readers. These

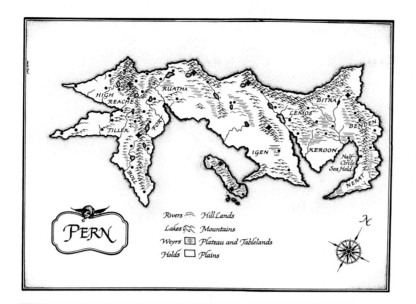

are the works toward which teachers can gradually direct unskilled readers who were originally attracted by the content of the genre. An example is *Beyond the Burning Lands*, by John Christopher, an intense adventure story. Luke, Prince in Waiting, travels from the hushed Seance Hall of the Seers, through the acrid smoke and heat of the wasted burning lands, to the bright garishness of the lands of the Wilsh. The time there seems calm in contrast with the narrow escape from death at the hands of the Sky People and the final treachery of Luke's brother, which is averted only at the last moment. Christopher has proved in this, and in the other books in the trilogy (*The Prince in Waiting* and *The Sword of the Spirit*), that he is able to write intensely convincing science fiction.

Anne McCaffrey wrote three companion volumes, *Dragonsong, Dragonsinger,* and *Dragondrums,* that follow the musically gifted heroine Menolly as she finds fulfillment playing the harp. Youngest daughter of Yanus, Sea Holder, Menolly learned to play from Harper Petiron, to her family's dismay; girls are not allowed to be harpists. She is grudgingly allowed, after Petiron's death, to teach the children their learning songs, but she is forbidden to do any "tuning," songmaking on her own. But before he died, Petiron sent some of Monolly's music to Masterharper Robinton. The new harper comes to Half-Circle Sea Hold with the news that all of Pern is looking for the maker of these songs. Menolly is beaten for her tuning, and she leaves to live on her own. As the first volume concludes, Menolly is discovered to be the sought-after harpist, and she goes with Masterharper Robinton to the harpist's hall as his apprentice. Not only does McCaffrey portray her created world of Pern with stunning clarity, but she also does an impressive character study of a young woman attaining her ambition through perseverance and hard work. This author has also written five adult novels about Pern, to which mature readers might be directed after they have read these three.

A science-fiction fantasy requiring mature reading skills is *A Wrinkle in Time*, by Madeline L'Engle. In it, Meg Murry is wretched: her father has been gone on a "classified" misson for over a year, her mother is lonely and troubled, the kids at school say unkind things about Meg's extraordinary brother Charles Wallace, and Meg herself feels clumsy, unattractive, and stupid. However, matters are somewhat eased for Meg when she meets Calvin O'Keefe and the two become friends. The appearance of Mrs. Who, Mrs. Which, and Mrs. Whatsit catapults Meg, Calvin, and Charles Wallace into fantastic situations. Traveling or "wrinkling" through time lands them on Camazotz, a planet under the domination of a black thing, IT, where the Murry children's father is being held prisoner. Meg had thought, with a younger child's trust, that when they found her father he would make everything right. Having to accept that he is human, and therefore limited, makes her angry and resentful. In the end, Meg must journey alone back to Camazotz and save Charles Wallace.

In a sequel, *A Wind in the Door*, Charles Wallace is very ill: small parts of his cells are dying. Meg and Calvin, accompanied by Mr. Jenkins, the unsympathetic grade-school principal, and Proginoskes, a cherubim, enter one of Charles Wallace's cells and right the wrong there.

In the third volume, *A Swiftly Tilting Planet*, fifteen-year-old Charles Wallace journeys through many layers of time to avert disaster. With the aid of an old rune, given him by Meg's surly mother-in-law, Charles is able to change history by entering into it and averting nuclear war. Hindered by servants of the dark, it sometimes seems as though Charles will fail. Based on the idea that all things are interrelated, L'Engle's story of courage is enthralling but sometimes confusing. So many different things happen, so many difficult concepts unfold, that this book is, even more than the two preceding it, for the special reader who has patience and maturity enough to unravel her plot and philosophy. A belief in morality, right and wrong, is fundamental to L'Engle's writing, but her moralizing is sometimes overwhelming. Her situations are cosmic, but her contrivance is sometimes faulty. Often the ways her characters are tested are trivial and not worthy of their strengths or talents.

Also for mature readers is *The Children of Morrow*, by H. M. Hoover.

Long after the Great Destruction, two isolated outposts exist, each unaware of the other. One is The Base, a militaristic colony ruled by the brutal Major and inhabited by a race of small, sometimes misshapen, people. The other is Morrow, saved during the Great Destruction by an underground system called LIFESPAN. Technocrats and telepaths, the Morrowans are an advanced civilization. Tia and Rabbit, two children of The Base, are—unknown to all—the offspring of the union between a Morrowan and a Base woman. Tia has for years broadcast her dreams. She receives dreams in return that tell her to leave the base with Rabbit and journey to Morrow, but she is uncertain. When Rabbit accidentally kills a soldier who threatens Tia, they have no choice. The journey is long and dangerous, and the children are closely followed. Finally, the children are saved and transported to Morrow. A second volume, *The Treasure of Morrow*, deals with their adjustment to the Morrowans' way of life and their return to The Base as part of an expedition. When they return to Morrow at the end of this book, the children know for sure that they are truly going home.

One of the most talented writers to emerge in this genre, Hoover creates "the sort of stories I write for the simple reason they are the type of stories I liked best when I was a child—that I still like best" (1980). Concluding her comments on writing science fiction, Hoover declares that "good science fiction teaches as well as entertains. It gives you something to think about later." This author certainly does that in her impressive body of writing. Her other works consistently display her talent for science fiction, for example, *The Shepherd Moon*, set in the forty-eighth century and featuring Merry Ambrose, a member of Earth's elite ruling class.

Life after a nuclear holocaust is a frequent theme among science-fiction writers. Like H. M. Hoover, Louise Lawrence has explored this theme in her *Children of the Dust*, a complex, sprawling novel in three parts. There is little character development; as a consequence, readers may feel an appalled compassion but no real empathy for the people in the story. The book's topic suggests an audience of junior-high students, but the characters are so shallowly drawn that it seems unlikely that experienced readers will find them compelling. There are, however, some poignant episodes: the description of the futile attempts by the dog, Buster, to get back inside the house after Veronica has put him outside to fend for himself is heartrending. Her decision is obviously based on a need for rationing of limited nonreplaceable resources, but the scene grabs the reader's attention with its melancholy, nonetheless. The book is unrelentingly depressing, and the author too often slips into telling, rather than showing, as she explores the conflict between those who glorify scientific accomplishments and those who cherish more humane values.

# SUMMARY

In this chapter emphasis has purposely been shifted from what adults think children should read to what students themselves *do* choose to read. Two kinds of reluctant readers concern teachers: those who have not yet mastered the skills of reading, and, as a consequence, aren't able to read; and those who can read well enough but simply choose not to. Despite the contradiction the first kind of problem reader presents, reading programs in this country do teach most children to read. Such programs are, however, far less successful in teaching children to want to read. One reason may be that teachers too often ignore the types of books students want to read, prescribing instead the types of books they think students should read.

Many children are interested in animal stories, mystery or detective fiction, sports stories, or science fiction. Teachers need to make themselves familiar with books of these types so that they can successfully lure readers at all levels into reading more, and better-quality, literature. Teachers often do not recommend mystery or detective stories or sports stories because they assume children will read such books on their own. While true, this assumption disregards the possibilities for teacher guidance: teachers can lead children who read special-interest books to better examples of each type. Science fiction, for example, attracts many reluctant readers who will read little else. Teachers who are aware of the very best of this type of book can lead such readers to discover fine writing in the genre.

## Suggestions for Further Study

1. Critic Margaret Blount (see "Related Reading for Adults") praises Hugh Lofting's *Dr. Doolittle* for containing the best account of the speech of animals that has ever been written. She says his writing is as fine as that of Edward Lear or Lewis Carroll. In contrast, Isabelle Suhl in "The Real Doctor Doolittle" (*Interracial Books for Children*, Spring/Summer 1968, pp. 1, 5–7) blasts Lofting as a racist. Read the book, and then read the critiques by Blount and Suhl. Is there some way to reconcile these two diametrically opposed views? How could you share Lofting's writing with children without promoting racism?

2. Compare Margaret Blount's commentary on Anna Sewell's *Black Beauty* (see "Related Reading for Adults") with the comments in Rebecca Luken's *A Critical Handbook of Children's Literature* (Glenview, Ill.: Scott Foresman, 1986, pp. 84–85, 138–139). Read the book yourself, and see which appraisal you agree with.

3. Matt Christopher has written children's stories about virtually every popular American team sport. This chapter described *The Meat in the Sandwich*, by Alice Bach; Christopher's book on the same topic (hockey) is *Wingman on Ice* (Boston: Little, Brown, 1964). The chapter also described a book on bas-

ketball, R. R. Knudson's *Zanbanger;* Christopher's book about this sport is *Basketball Sparkplug* (Boston: Little, Brown, 1957). Read either of these pairs of books; decide which author's work is more convincing.

4. This chapter mentioned Jean de Brunhoff's *The Story of Babar.* A combination of science fiction with animal main characters is Laurent de Brunhoff's *Babar Visits Another Planet* (New York: Random House, 1973). Critics have much to say about the work of this father and son. In "Jean de Brunhoff's Advice to Youth. The *Babar* Books as Books of Courtesy" (*Children's Literature,* 11, 1983, pp. 76–93), Ann M. Hildebrand compares these books with de Brunhoff's earlier writing that was designed to instill correct behavior. Hildebrand feels the *Babar* books were the first to combine the "systematic content and instructive intent of traditional courtesy books with the narrative and visual organization and delight of modern children's books." A less positive view of de Brunhoff's work is presented by Ariel Dorfman, in *The Empire's Old Clothes: What the Lone Ranger, Babar, and Other Innocent Heroes Do to Our Minds* (New York: Pantheon, 1983). This author asserts that children's books are "a constant secret education" on how not to rebel, inscribing in children's minds the ideological patterns of society. Read these two critiques, and decide which constitutes the more convincing argument about the worth of de Brunhoff's writing.

5. This chapter referred to the writing of John Christopher, which is also described by M. Jean Greenlaw in "Science Fiction: Impossible! Improbable! or Prophetic?" (*Elementary English,* April 1971, pp. 196–202). Read what Greenlaw has to say about Christopher's writing. Then read one of Christopher's books to intermediate- or upper-grade students to get their reactions.

6. Some interesting similarities exist between Andre Norton's *No Night Without Stars* (New York: Atheneum, 1975) and Robert O'Brien's *Z is for Zechariah* (New York: Atheneum, 1975). For instance, in both, the action takes place after a cataclysm has destroyed civilization on the planet. In the first, however, the male and the female are friends; in the second, they are enemies. Read both books. Which more successfully conveys a believable atmosphere of remaining pockets of civilization?

## *Related Reading for Adults*

Barron, Neil. "Launching the SF Collection." *Wilson Library Bulletin,* September 1977, pp. 57–60.

Barron comments that, because many important works of science fiction appear only as mass-market paperbacks, science-fiction books are seldom reviewed in general book-review media. He presents data about how many titles are published each year and a list of publishers most involved in the genre. The main part of this article consists of annotated entries about selection sources.

Blount, Margaret. *Animal Land.* New York: Morrow, 1975.

In this definitive work, Blount presents an exhaustive examination of many kinds of animal stories. A section on animal fables, one on animal fantasy, and one on animal edens make up a thorough summary of how and why authors choose animals as main characters. Blount describes three kinds of writers motivated to use animal characters and analyzes their works.

Dohner, Jan. "Literature of Change: Science Fiction and Women." *Top of the News*, 34 (Spring 1978), pp. 261–265.

A common criticism of science fiction is sexism: few women write science fiction, and few girls read it because most protagonists are male. Writers are remiss in ignoring women's roles in their evolution of, speculation on, and extrapolation to new and different worlds. Dohner includes annotations of works that do include strong portrayals of females. Teachers or librarians interested in this issue might also like to read *Future Females; a Critical Anthology*, by Marlene S. Barr (Bowling Green, Ohio: Popular Press, 1981).

Eaglen, Audrey B. "Alternatives: A Bibliography of Books and Periodicals on Science Fiction and Fantasy." *Top of the News*, Fall 1982, pp. 96–102.

After a brief introduction, Eaglen devotes the remainder of her article to three- or four-sentence annotations on more than three dozen resource books for this genre, as well as briefer annotations on a dozen magazines that publish science fiction and fantasy. This is a useful resource for the teacher or librarian who wants to know where to find more reading material for students who are sci fi or fantasy buffs.

Finch-Reyner, Sheila. "The Unseen Shore: Thoughts on the Popularity of Fantasy." *Journal of Popular Culture*, 18 (Spring 1985), pp. 127–134.

Finch-Reyner asserts that there is a good deal of confusion about the differences between science fiction and fantasy; she reports that there has been a gradual intrusion of fantasy values and methods into science fiction writing. The field has almost as many definitions as it has writers, but generally science fiction is "work that takes as its starting point the presently-known laws of science and extrapolates into the future . . . even though at some time in the future those laws may be called into question or even proved wrong." Both science fiction and fantasy deal with remarkably similar themes, and in fact few works can be neatly classified, for categories are invented, after the fact, by critics, not by writers. Both forms spring from the same roots, use similar techniques, and achieve similar effects. The author considers more generally the functions of myth in our society, and the lack of its representation in school curricula, and comments on the uses of ambiguity in fantasy for mature readers.

Jones, James P. "Negro Stereotypes in Children's Literature: The Case of Nancy Drew." *Journal of Negro Education*, 40 (Spring 1971), pp. 121–125.

Recent editions of the perennially popular Nancy Drew detective stories have been edited to remove the insulting depictions of minorities, including blacks, that appeared in editions published between 1930 and 1941. Jones includes quotes from these racially biased editions, giving special attention to ways black argot was used to reinforce the image that blacks do not talk properly. The problem is that some of the early editions may still be on library shelves.

Mason, Bobbie Ann. *The Girl Sleuth: A Feminist Guide*. Old Westbury, N.Y.: Feminist Press, 1975.

Honey Bunch, the Bobbsey Twins, Nancy Drew, and Trixie Belden are among the series characters examined and found to be blatantly racist and sexist. Many of the more obvious passages are being removed as these books are reissued, yet the entire structure of the stories is suspect.

Moran, Barbara B., and Susan Steinfirst. "Why Johnny (and Jane) Read Whodunits in Series." *School Library Journal*, March 1985, pp. 113–117.

These authors take a much more positive view than Bobbie Ann Mason does (see above) of female heroines in mystery series. In a very complete article, they analyze these series as literature and as sources of psychological benefits to emerging adolescents. The psychologist Erik Erickson says that all adolescents must resolve dilemmas, which results in a corresponding personal recognition of accomplishment. These authors maintain that series books provide models of characters doing that. The authors describe the *Nancy Drew* and the more recent *Doris Fein* series, pointing out similarities and differences. (They do the same for boys' mystery series.) They find these series to be clearly written, highly formulated ". . . fairy tales of the older child." Child readers turn to these series for escape from the trend toward realism so pronounced in today's "problem novel" written by more respected writers. The intellectual challenge of trying to solve the mystery before the protagonist does appeals to many young readers.

Nixon, Joan Lowery. "Clues to the Juvenile Mystery." *The Writer*, 90 (February 1977), pp. 23–26.

Nixon discusses how to write mysteries for eight- to twelve-year-olds. She contends that novels should give readers interesting background information to widen their horizons; well-rounded, three-dimensional, active characters (with a fault or two) are equally important. A little light humor should break the mood occasionally. Child readers delight in finding the obvious clues the main character seems to miss; submysteries are important for maintaining interest.

Oliver, Lin. "The Reading Interests of Children in the Primary Grades." *Elementary School Journal*, May 1977, pp. 402–406.

Little experimental data is available on children's preferences regarding plot, theme, characters, setting, and writing style. Subjects in first and third grades participated in a study that elicited their preference among three kinds of stories. Preference for animal stories decreased substantially from first grade to third grade. Third-graders stated the highest preference for fantasy characters in make-believe settings.

Rayner, Mary. "Some Thoughts on Animals in Children's Books." *Signal*, 29 (May 1979), pp. 81–87.

Opening with a seldom considered contradiction, Rayner reminds readers that we pleasantly anthropomorphize animals, ignoring the reality that, as predators, we also eat some of them. E. B. White's *Charlotte's Web* is unusual because it confronts this contradiction squarely. Authors and illustrators must always decide just how human they will make their animals in order to deal with this problem. Rayner discusses how she dealt with the problem in her *Mr. and Mrs. Pig's Evening Out* (New York: Atheneum, 1976). She contends that children enjoy animal stories because, like themselves, the characters are vulnerable. She further explores this idea in *Garth Pig and the Icecream Lady* (New York: Atheneum, 1977).

Roberts, Thomas J. "Science Fiction and the Adolescent." *Children's Literature: The Great Excluded*, 2 (1973), pp. 87–91.

Roberts describes the intensity with which some children read science fiction, to the virtual exclusion of other types of literature. He lists six different types (pure adventure, horror, sword and sorcery, social satire, scientific speculation, and literary experiment) and gives examples of each. He points out that much of science ficiton is not about science at all; rather it is about the supernatural.

## Professional References

Baskin, Barbara H., and Karen H. Harris. *Books for the Gifted Child*. New York: R. R. Bowker, 1980.

Blount, Margaret. *Animal Land*. New York: Morrow, 1975, p. 152.

Brooks, Bruce. "In Collaboration with My Characters." *The Horn Book,* January/February 1986, 38–40.

Brunner, Mark. "Environmental Literature." *Wisconsin English Journal,* 21 (October 1978), 30–34.

Ellis, Sarah. "News from the North." *The Horn Book,* September/October 1984, 661–664.

Harms, Jeanne McLain. *Comprehension and Literature.* Dubuque, Iowa: Kendall/Hunt, 1982.

Hoover, H. M. "SF—Out of This World." *Language Arts,* 57 (April 1980), 425–428.

Lukens, Rebecca. *A Critical Handbook of Children's Literature.* Glenview, Ill.: Scott, Foresman, 1986.

Schoenfeld, Madalynne. "Mice and Rats." *Day Care and Early Education,* 13 (Fall 1985), 44–45.

Stewig, John Warren. "They Can—But *Do* They? (Read, That Is!)" *Elementary English,* September 1973, 921–925.

## *Bibliography of Children's Books*

Aardema, Verna. *Who's In Rabbit's House?* New York: Dial, 1977.

Adams, Richard. *Watership Down.* New York: Penguin, 1972.

Adler, David. *Cam Jansen and the Mystery of the Television Dog.* New York: Viking, 1981.

Aiken, Joan. *Up the Chimney Down.* New York: Harper and Row, 1984.

Armstrong, William H. *The Tale of Tawny and Dingo.* New York: Harper and Row, 1979.

Arnold, Richard. *Better Roller Skating: The Key to Improved Performance.* New York: Sterling, 1976.

Bach, Alice. *The Meat in the Sandwich.* New York: Harper and Row, 1975.

Baskin, Leonard. *Leonard Baskin's Miniature Natural History.* New York: Pantheon, 1983.

Beatty, Jerome, Jr. *Matthew Looney's Voyage to the Earth.* New York: William R. Scott, 1961.

Branley, Franklyn M. *Is There Life in Outer Space?* New York: Harper and Row, 1984.

Brooks, Bruce. *The Moves Make the Man.* New York: Harper and Row, 1985.

Brooks, Walter R. *Freddy and the Perilous Adventure.* New York: Alfred A. Knopf, 1986.

———. *Freddy Goes Camping.* New York: Alfred A. Knopf, 1986.

———. *Freddy the Pilot.* New York: Alfred A. Knopf, 1986.

———. *Freddy the Politician.* New York: Alfred A. Knopf, 1986.

Brown, Marc. *Arthur's April Fool.* Boston: Little, Brown, 1983.

———. *Arthur's Thanksgiving.* Boston: Little, Brown, 1983.

———. *Arthur's Tooth.* Boston: Little, Brown, 1985.

Burnford, Sheila. *The Incredible Journey.* Boston: Little, Brown, 1961.

Carle, Eric. *The Grouchy Ladybug.* New York: Thomas Y. Crowell, 1978.

Christopher, John. *Beyond the Burning Lands.* New York: Macmillan, 1971.

———. *The Prince in Waiting.* New York: Macmillan, 1970.

———. *The Sword of the Spirit.* New York: Macmillan, 1972.

de Brunhoff, Jean. *The Story of Babar.* New York: Random House, 1933.

Erickson, Russell E. *A Toad for Tuesday.* New York: Lothrop, Lee and Shepard, 1974.

———. *Warton and the Contest.* New York: Lothrop, Lee and Shepard, 1986.

Fadiman, Clifton. *The World Treasury of Children's Literature*. Boston: Little, Brown, 1985.

Fisk, Nicholas. *Escape from Splatterbang*. New York: Macmillan, 1979.

Godden, Rumer. *Mouse House*. New York: Viking, 1957.

Graham, Margaret Bloy. *Benjy's Dog House*. New York: Harper and Row, 1973.

Hale, Linda. *The Glorious Christmas Soup Party*. New York: Viking, 1962.

Hamilton, Virginia. *The People Could Fly*. New York: Alfred A. Knopf, 1985.

Herriot, James. *The Christmas Day Kitten*. New York: St. Martin's, 1986.

Hildick, E. W. *The Case of the Invisible Dog*. New York: Macmillan, 1977.

———. *The Case of the Vanishing Ventriloquist*. New York: Macmillan, 1985.

Hoban, Lillian. *Arthur's Loose Tooth*. New York: Harper and Row, 1985.

Hoban, Lillian, and Phoebe Hoban. *The Laziest Robot in Zone One*. New York: Harper and Row, 1983.

Hoban, Russell. *Bedtime for Frances*. New York: Harper and Row, 1960.

———. *The Twenty Elephant Restaurant*. New York: Atheneum, 1978.

Hoberman, Mary Ann. *Bugs: Poems*. New York: Viking, 1976.

Hoover, H. M. *The Children of Morrow*. New York: Four Winds, 1973.

———. *The Shepherd Moon*. New York: Viking, 1984.

———. *The Treasures of Morrow*. New York: Four Winds, 1976.

Howe, Fanny. *Race of the Radical*. New York: Viking Kestrel, 1985, p. 5.

Hughes, Monica. *Keeper of the Isis Light*. New York: Atheneum, 1981.

Hughes, Ted. *Under the North Star*. New York: Viking, 1981.

Hutchins, Pat. *The House That Sailed Away*. New York: Greenwillow, 1975.

———. *The Mona Lisa Mystery*. New York: Greenwillow, 1981.

Ireson, Barbara (sel.). *The April Witch and Other Strange Tales*. New York: Scribner's, 1978.

Jeffers, Susan (ill.). *Black Beauty*. New York: Random House, 1986.

Katz, Bobbi. *Rod-and-Reel Trouble*. Chicago: A. Whitman, 1974.

Knudson, R. R. *Zanballer*. New York: Delacorte, 1972.

———. *Zanbanger*. New York: Harper and Row, 1977.

———. *Zanboomer*. New York: Harper and Row, 1978.

———. *Zan Hagen's Marathon*. New York: Farrar, Straus and Giroux, 1984.

Krasilovsky, Phyllis. *The Cow Who Fell in the Canal*. Garden City, N.Y.: Doubleday, 1957.

Lawrence, Louise. *Children of the Dust*. New York: Harper and Row, 1985.

Lawson, Robert. *Rabbit Hill*. New York: Viking, 1944.

———. *Tough Winter*. New York: Viking, 1954.

L'Engle, Madeline. *A Swiftly Tilting Planet*. New York: Farrar, Straus and Giroux, 1978.

———. *A Wind in the Door*. New York: Farrar, Straus and Giroux, 1973.

———. *A Wrinkle in Time*. New York: Farrar, Straus and Giroux, 1962.

Levy, Elizabeth. *Something Queer at the Library*. New York: Delacorte, 1977.

Lionni, Leo. *The Biggest House in the World*. New York: Pantheon, 1968.

———. *Frederick's Fables*. New York: Pantheon, 1985.

Lobel, Arnold. *Owl at Home*. New York: Harper and Row, 1975.

Luttrell, Ida. *Lonesome Lester*. New York: Harper and Row, 1984.

MacGregor, Ellen. *Miss Pickerell and the Blue Whales*. New York: McGraw-Hill, 1983.

———. *Miss Pickerell Goes to Mars*. New York: Whittlesey House, 1951.

Marshall, James. *A Summer in the South*. Boston: Houghton Mifflin, 1977.

———. *George and Martha*. Boston: Houghton Mifflin, 1972.

McCaffrey, Anne. *Dragondrums*. New York: Atheneum, 1979.

———. *Dragonsinger*. New York: Atheneum, 1977.

———. *Dragonsong*. New York: Atheneum, 1977.

McHargue, Georgess. *Meet the Vampires*. New York: J. B. Lippincott, 1979.

Miles, Miska. *Nobody's Cat*. Boston: Little, Brown, 1969.

Miller, Edna. *Mousekin's Mystery*. Englewood Cliffs, N.J.: Prentice-Hall, 1983.

Moeri, Louise. *The Unicorn and the Plow*. New York: E. P. Dutton, 1982.

Morrison, Lillian. *The Break Dance Kids*. New York: Lothrop, Lee and Shepard, 1985.

———. *The Sidewalk Racer, and Other Poems of Sports and Motion*. New York: Lothrop, Lee and Shepard, 1977.

North, Sterling. *Rascal*. New York: E. P. Dutton, 1963.

Pearce, Philippa. *The Shadow Cage*. New York: Thomas Y. Crowell, 1977.

Platt, Kin. *Big Max in the Mystery of the Missing Moose*. New York: Harper and Row, 1977.

Quackenbush, Robert. *Piet Potter on the Run*. New York: McGraw-Hill, 1982.

Roach, Marilynne. *Encounters with the Invisible World*. New York: Thomas Y. Crowell, 1977.

Rylant, Cynthia. *Every Living Thing*. New York: Bradbury, 1985.

Salten, Felix. *Bambi*. New York: Grosset and Dunlap, 1929.

Schneider, Tom. *Everybody's a Winner: A Kid's Guide to New Sports and Fitness*. Boston: Little, Brown, 1976.

Schoenherr, John. *The Barn*. Boston: Little, Brown, 1972.

Schroder, William. *Pea Soup and Sea Serpents*. New York: Lothrop, Lee and Shepard, 1977.

Schwandt, Stephen. *The Last Goodie*. New York: Holt, Rinehart and Winston, 1985.

Seuling, Barbara. *The Great Big Elephant and the Very Small Elephant*. New York: Crown, 1977.

Sewell, Anna. *Black Beauty*. Cleveland: World, 1972 (1877).

Sharmat, Marjorie W. *Mooch the Messy*. New York: Harper and Row, 1976.

———. *Nate the Great*. New York: Coward, McCann and Geoghegan, 1977.

Sharp, Margery. *Miss Bianca*. Boston: Little, Brown, 1962.

———. *Miss Bianca in the Orient*. New York: Dell, 1978.

Shub, Elizabeth. *Dragon Franz*. New York: Greenwillow, 1977.

Slote, Alfred. *C.O.L.A.R.* New York: Harper and Row, 1981.

———. *My Robot Buddy*. New York: Harper and Row, 1975.

———. *Omega Station*. New York: Harper and Row, 1983.

———. *The Trouble on Janus*. New York: Lippincott, 1985.

Snyder, Zilpha Keatley. *Blair's Nightmare*. New York: Atheneum, 1984.

———. *The Famous Stanley Kidnapping Case*. New York: Atheneum, 1979.

Steig, William. *Abel's Island*. New York: Farrar, Straus and Giroux, 1976.

———. *Dominic*. New York: Farrar, Straus and Giroux, 1972.

Stockton, Frank. *The Griffin and the Minor Canon*. New York: Holt, Rinehart and Winston, 1986 (1963).

Titus, Eve. *Anatole*. New York: McGraw-Hill, 1965.

Tunis, John R. *Buddy and the Old Pro*. New York: Morrow, 1955.

Turner, Stephen C. *Great Beginnings: From Olympics to Superbowl to World Series*. New York: Julian Messner, 1981.

Valens, Evans G. *Wingfin and Topple*. Cleveland: World, 1962.

Van Woerkom, Dorothy O. *Harry and Shellburt*. New York: Macmillan, 1977.

Watson, Nancy D. *The Birthday Goat*. New York: Thomas Y. Crowell, 1974.

Williams, Jay, and Raymond Abrashkin. *Danny Dunn, Invisible Boy*. New York: McGraw-Hill, 1974.

Wilkes, Marilyn Z. *C.L.U.T.Z.* New York: Dial, 1982.

——. *C.L.U.T.Z. and the Fizzion Formula.* New York: Dial, 1985.

Yolen, Jane. *Commander Toad and the Dis-Asteroid.* New York: Putnam, 1985.

——. *Commander Toad and the Planet of the Grapes.* New York: Coward, McCann and Geoghegan, 1982.

——. *Commander Toad in Space.* New York: Coward, McCann and Geoghegan, 1980.

# 14
## PLANNING  A
## LITERATURE
## PROGRAM

Most of this text is about individual books and their use. Yet separate books, unrelated to one another, do not in themselves have the coherence a planned program does. Beyond the planning each teacher does to bring the right books to the right children at the right time, another kind of planning is necessary: the entire school staff should plan a literature program that will be more than just the sum of its parts.

It is common for curriculum committees to plan sequential and cohesive sets of learning experiences that span the elementary years for such subjects as science, math, or social studies. Groups of teachers within a school system are appointed by a supervisor or director of curriculum. They survey commercial materials, investigate curricula in other school districts, study recommendations in the professional literature, analyze what is currently being done in the school system, and pool their personal ideas about what should be done. Following such research, the committee either recommends adoption of a program and a set of materials, or it writes its own curriculum guide to be implemented. Unfortunately, it is less common for teachers to follow this procedure in setting up a literature curriculum.

When selecting books that will work together to create an effective literature program that stretches from kindergarten through sixth, seventh, or eighth grade, teachers must consider three questions.

### 1. What goals are we trying to achieve?

A statement of the literature program's goals is an important component of the curriculum.[1] Teachers need to think carefully about what they are trying to achieve in sharing books with children in order to formulate precise statements of purpose. Such vague statements as "to help children appreciate good books" are not very helpful. For example, "to share a book of historic fiction so children can discuss ways the life-style depicted is different from their own, thus developing their observation and comparison skills" is a much more useful statement of purpose.

### 2. What will be the program sequence?

On the continuum from kindergarten through the top grade in the school, what will be the order of the literature experiences? Sequential

---

[1] This is one task Kenneth L. Donelson identifies as crucial in "Literature" included in *The Teaching of English, Part I, The Seventy-Sixth Yearbook of the National Society for the Study of Education* (Chicago: University of Chicago Press, 1977). The author surveys changes in literature curricula during the last fifteen years and recommends future directions.

planning is necessary to achieve optimum developmental growth as children move through the grades. The establishment of a program sequence makes it possible for experiences in the later grades to build on what happened in the preceding grades. This kind of cumulative structure is not possible when each teacher follows his or her own plan.

Sequence planning also eliminates overlap, so more than one teacher won't read the same book to the same children. As wonderful as *Charlotte's Web*, by E. B. White, is, it doesn't merit group-sharing time more than once in a literature curriculum, unless teachers coordinate their use to ensure that different activities take place at different developmental levels. With this book, as with other universally known books such as Maurice Sendak's *Where the Wild Things Are*, the possibility exists for overuse.

### 3. What will be the scope of the experiences at any given level?

A literature curriculum—as opposed to random sharing of books—must ensure that children experience diversity. A third-grade teacher may be a fantasy buff, but his or her own personal preferences should not limit children's choices. The teacher needs to share a variety of genres to broaden children's exposure. Planning the scope at each grade level helps teachers provide a balanced program.

## ORGANIZING A LITERATURE PROGRAM

### WHY ADD A LITERATURE PROGRAM?

Some teachers and administrators may wonder why a literature program is necessary, since all schools have a reading program, and most reading programs include at least some literature.

A first answer is that literature selections in basal reading textbooks sometimes bear little resemblance to the original story. For example, *Max*, by Rachel Isadora, deals with a significant dilemma: balancing personal interests against group interests. Max discovers he enjoys ballet and is surprised to find he is quite good at it. What will happen when his ball-playing buddies discover this? Author Isadora draws the conflict convincingly and ends the book without resolving the problem. *Max* thus provides a basis for valuable class discussion of the conflicts between individual and group interests. It is, therefore, a real disappointment to discover that an anthologized version of the story in *Secrets and Surprises*, by Carl B. Smith

*Carefree Max and his leggy sister Lisa are rendered in small black dots, which mass together to create very subtle shades of grey. The irregularly edged drawing is bordered in solid brown.*
Reprinted with permission of Macmillan Publishing Company from *Max* by Rachel Isadora.
Copyright © 1976 by Rachel Isadora.

and Virginia Arnold (New York: Macmillan, 1983) is eviscerated so that no hint of the original conflict remains. Big, bold pictures added by the publishers of this textbook do not compensate for the fact that *Max* has been made into a nonstory. Why would children be interested in reading it in this form, when nothing happens? Neither children nor literature appreciation in general is well served when such "stories" as this are included in basal reading series.

Holbrook (1985) makes the same point in describing a basal adaptation of "The Shoemaker and the Elves" in which the words *shoes, elves,* and *shoemaker* never appear! Removing such words, purportedly because they are too difficult for child readers, removes the vitality of the original story. If children are asked to read such material regularly, it is no wonder that some of them choose not to read at all outside of class.

The second reason a separate, readily identifiable literature strand must be part of language arts programs is that the purpose of a reading program is different from the purpose of a literature program. The purpose of a reading program is to teach children the skills of reading, that is, how to read. The purpose of a literature program is to widen children's exposure to literature and, in the process, to develop their response strategies. Some reading programs claim this second purpose as an objective, but the types of selections included and the treatment given these selections too often show that skill development is paramount. Therefore, it is critical to confront the problem of initiating a separate literature curriculum in elementary schools. How can teachers, with the help of administrative personnel, address this problem?

## PROGRAM DELIVERY

Every day, at every grade level, students should hear a fluent adult reader (the teacher or, perhaps, an aide) present literature by reading it aloud. This assertion—first made in Chapter 1—cannot be overemphasized. With the increased, albeit often misguided, attempts to return to the basics, some teachers may lose sight of how important reading aloud is.

Boothroy and Donham (1981) address this issue, describing a schoolwide oral presentation of literature in a program now several years old. A central theme is chosen for the entire school, to ensure program continuity; individual teachers select books that support this theme and write blurbs describing the books they will read. Each child then selects the story he or she would like to hear and goes to the room of the teacher reading that story. After hearing the story, children engage in response activities with the teacher. The advantages of self-selection are an increased sense of commitment and greater motivation.

Another important part of program delivery is scheduling time for children themselves to read—to read real books, not simply to take part in reading-instruction activities. Under increased pressure to cover more subjects during the school day, some teachers may not feel they have time for individual children to read to themselves. Morrow (1985) comments that many teachers have the attitude that "while promotion of voluntary reading is an important ideal, it is not important enough to detract from emphasis on other subjects." Trying to change this attitude, she conducted field-based research in six elementary classrooms, working with teachers on such subjects as teacher reading and voluntary reading and on the physical setup of the classroom to make such activities easier. Teachers' attitudes toward the value of voluntary reading were much more positive at the end of this research study, undoubtedly because they were involved in the research and could see the benefits for themselves.

## PROGRAM PLANNING BY PUBLISHERS

When a committee meets to plan a curriculum in one of the major subject areas, the task is often a relatively simple one of selecting the best available commercial materials. In such subjects as science, math, and health, many different series are available. Often committees can select from among several excellent programs that represent the most current thinking by experts, ensure continuity with careful sequencing, contain many specific lesson suggestions and supplementary activities, and provide carefully worked-out means of evaluation.

Such is not the case with a literature program, however. A set of commercial materials—a series of sequential books, organized in some thoughtful fashion, marketed by a text-publishing company—is not easy to locate. Many reading or reading-and-language-arts programs recently have incorporated increasingly larger amounts of literature. But, as noted earlier, the major purpose of these series is to teach children skills, not help them to respond more fully to literature.

One series concerned with presenting literature, not with reading instruction, is the *Odyssey* series, by Sam Leaton Sebesta (New York: Harcourt Brace Jovanovich, 1982). Each of the hardbound anthologies contains several selections, followed by questions and suggested activities. In addition, there are content sections about a variety of general topics (for example, "Learn About Pictures in Books," in *Under the Midnight Stars*, pp. 100–103) and about people (for example, "About Eleanor Estes," in *Under the Midnight Stars*, p. 163). What distinguishes the series is the care with which both words and pictures have been chosen.

Included in the volume entitled *Under the Midnight Stars* is the folk tale "Rumplestiltskin," retold by Edith H. Tarcov. Comparing the version in the anthology with the book version from another publisher shows that there have been some word cuts, but these are to shorten the piece, not to make it simpler. Some of the unnecessary repetition in the queen's guessing of names was left out of the anthologized version. None of the cuts eliminates a single interesting vocabulary word, as is sometimes the case in reading-text series. A look at the illustrations for "Rumplestiltskin" is equally reassuring. Eleven (over half) of the pictures from the original book are reproduced at virtually full size in the anthology. In addition, ten of the marginal or text-intervening decorations are also included in their original sizes.

For some selections in the *Odyssey* series, new illustrations have been used. In . . . *and Now Miguel*, a Newbery Medal winner, the original illustrations were by Jean Charlot, in simplified and highly stylized black line. For an excerpt from this book included in *East of the Sun* (pp. 192–205), the publishers of the *Odyssey* series commissioned full-color illustrations from the well-known children's illustrator Don Bolognese. Similarly, *Dragonwings*, by Laurence Yep, published originally without illustrations, appears in *At the Edge of the World* (pp. 234–251), enriched with full-color illustrations by a noted illustrator, Ron Himler.

Only one commercial literature program is discussed here because the only other program available, by Random House, was published too recently for inclusion. Other publishers are currently involved in producing literature programs.

## PROGRAM PLANNING BY TEACHERS

A literature program can be arranged by genres, by literary elements, or by topics, although some authors question this sort of curriculum planning. Purves and Monson (1984) declare:

> Most of the sequences . . . are artificial. Probably the best solution is to arrange the selections in some kind of sequence that uses all of these but none of them in any particular order.

These authors hold that the individual teacher is best qualified to make decisions about which book to read aloud to her or his particular class at a given time. Of course, no matter which approach to curriculum planning is used, children will have opportunities to select books for free-reading purposes.

**ORGANIZING A PROGRAM BY GENRE.** Arranging a literature program by genre ensures that children will have experiences with each genre every year. An advantage of this way of organizing the program is that it helps teachers explore the diversity of each genre. In planning a curriculum this way, teachers need to think about such questions as these: What is an example of a complex picture book that should be shared with sixth-graders? What is an example of a very simple biography that kindergarten children will understand?

The advantages of genre organization are described by Sides (1982), who reports on the implementation of such a program in one public school.

| Sequence of Literature Program | K | 1 | 2 | 3 | 4 | 5 | 6 |
|---|---|---|---|---|---|---|---|
| Picture books | | | | | | | |
| Alphabet books | | | | | | | |
| Historic fiction | | | | | | | |
| Modern realistic fiction | | | | | | | |
| Poetry | | | | | | | |
| Information books | | | | | | | |
| Biography | | | | | | | |
| Folk literature | | | | | | | |
| Fantasy | | | | | | | |

**ORGANIZING A PROGRAM BY LITERARY ELEMENTS.** A literature program can also be arranged by literary elements. Teachers select a story that exemplifies powerful use of each of the following elements: characterization, language use, plot, conflict, setting, point of view, and theme.

| Sequence of Literature Program | K | 1 | 2 | 3 | 4 | 5 | 6 |
|---|---|---|---|---|---|---|---|
| Characterization | | | | | | | |
| Language use | | | | | | | |
| Plot | | | | | | | |
| Conflict type | | | | | | | |
| Setting | | | | | | | |
| Narrator | | | | | | | |
| Theme | | | | | | | |

In addition to identifying the general literary elements, the teacher can identify different types of each element. For example, there are three types of conflict: person versus person, person versus fate, and person versus self. In planning a curriculum organized this way, teachers can select books representing each type of conflict. However, books for mature readers often exemplify all three types of conflict. *Circles in a Forest,* by Dalene Matthee, is a large-scale historic novel, for mature junior-high readers, set in the Knysna forest of South Africa in the nineteenth century, as gold fever is supplanting the greed for wood. Saul Barnard, an introspective woodcutter, is described as being like "a cupboard whose key is lost." Saul fights internal—person versus self—battles in order to come to terms with what is right for him. External—person versus person—conflicts emerge between Saul and MacDonald, a rapacious landowner and entrepreneur whose enterprises go sour, **and** between Saul and others who would rape the forest for their own ends. Finally, a person versus fate conflict emerges as a major theme in the book. The forest exerts a superhuman pull on Saul. Author Matthee skillfully develops these conflicts on an undergirding of historic and geographic details that supports, but does not overwhelm, the compelling story. Such a book could be used to good effect with a group of students who had been exposed to the three separate types of conflict earlier in the elementary school.

In order to demonstrate various points of view, teachers need to show students that a book can be narrated in the third person by an omniscient narrator, in the third person by a narrator with limited knowledge, in the first person, or in the second person. Teachers might share one example of each type of narration each year. Then, in the upper grades, a teacher could use one of the books of contemporary fiction, discussed in Chapter 10 (pages 475–476), that experiment with different narrators. In organizing a curriculum by literary elements, teachers must remember that a wide variety of books from different genres can serve as examples of each element.

**ORGANIZING A PROGRAM BY TOPICS.**   Teachers can also plan curricula around topics, such as horse stories, growing up in other cultures, mysteries, or relations with peers. Such a topical arrangement cuts across all genres.

| *Sequence of Literature Program* | *K* | *1* | *2* | *3* | *4* | *5* | *6* |
|---|---|---|---|---|---|---|---|
| **Friendship** | | | | | | | |
| **Journeys** | | | | | | | |
| **Growing things** | | | | | | | |
| **Interrelationships** | | | | | | | |
| **City and country** | | | | | | | |
| **Seasons** | | | | | | | |
| **Change** | | | | | | | |

## PLANNING A LITERATURE PROGRAM THAT EXPLORES VALUES

One purpose of literature is to help children think about attitudes, beliefs, and values. Teachers in the United States have always taught values. In the early years of American education, it was assumed that the dominant value system was the correct one. From this premise, it followed that one basic purpose of education was to instill the correct set of values. Although other values certainly existed, people accepted the school's role as teacher of the dominant one.

Today, the situation is different. Relatively speaking, more sets of values exist today in our society than ever did before. Although each person may feel his or her own value system is the correct one, there is no general concensus about which values the schools should teach. This situation complicates the school's task, since values expressed consciously or unconsciously by a teacher may conflict with those held by a child's family at home. There is no real escape from the multiplicity of values; children daily see evidence of differing values and are often confused by this. Neither the home nor the school provides much opportunity for children to think consciously about differences in values. If children are given the opportunity to examine values, they can avoid the confusion caused by conflicting values and can better understand and associate with those who hold values different from their own. Teachers can provide experiences that make it possible for children to respond positively to those who value other things. The lack of such experiences may result in students' mistrusting people whose values are unlike theirs. It is thus important to consider how books can help children clarify their values.

Literature can help children reflect on attitudes, beliefs, and values (Harmin, Kirschenbaum, and Simon, 1973). The word *attitude* refers to fairly transient responses. One's attitude about something may vary depending on the given situation. For example, a person's reaction to stealing with respect to a preteen child shoplifting a comic book may be quite different from his or her reaction with respect to a government official embezzling millions of dollars. My attitude may be negative with regard to a particular book of fantasy but more positive with respect to another book in the genre.

On the other hand, beliefs are somewhat more stable and firmly rooted than attitudes. For example, a person who has never lived near or worked with a member of a minority group may believe that all members of that group behave in certain ways. This deep-seated belief may not be challenged if the person never has the opportunity to know a member of that minority group. As another example, I may decide I must read a book about a topic in which I am not paticularly interested because I believe that authors should deal with the total range of life today and that it is my responsibility as the teacher to know about this total range.

Finally, values are the deepest and most meaningful of human feelings. Values are chosen, not imposed. The person holding a particular value is proud of it. Values are manifested in behavior. If a feeling is not supported in action, it is not a value. If one of my values is that children should be able to read about any topic that interests them, then I must speak out in favor of allowing a book to remain in the library collection when a group of parents protests that book, even though I may not personally feel it is great literature.

Children's literature is full of value statements, both tacit and explicit. Authors write about characters' values with respect to individual integrity, family, peers and society, work and leisure, sex, God, religion or sacred ideas, money or possessions, and country.

Children should be encouraged to move through three stages as they think about the values expressed in a piece of literature:

1. *Exploration stage.* Students identify the kinds of values expressed in the particular story. A teacher can help students identify values by asking, "What do you think [character's name] valued in this book?"
2. *Comparison stage.* Children think about and discuss other types of values that might be appropriate in a situation the book describes. In this stage, a teacher might ask, "What is another way someone might respond to this situation?"
3. *Reflection stage.* Students think about and discuss the ways the values in the story are like or unlike the values they hold. The teacher might ask one of these questions: "Do you feel the same way about [this situation] as the character did? Do you feel that what [character's name] did was right?"

Many books can be used by a teacher for exploring with the class the inherent values expressed, and how these compare and contrast with those the students have. This book takes the position that such exploration is an essential part of using literature with children.

**INDIVIDUAL INTEGRITY.** Many books can be used to help children think about their values concerning individual behavior. To reach his consuming goal—to learn how to rope the black horse—the protagonist in *Salt Boy,* by Mary Perrine, must promise not to rope his mother's sheep. Salt Boy does use the rope to rescue the smallest sheep. Seeing his son's brave action, Salt Boy's father realizes he is old enough to learn to lasso the black horse.

Sometimes the author uses animal characters whose actions exemplify values concerning individual behavior. In *Horton Hears a Who!* by Dr. Seuss, the main character is an elephant who values life very highly. He believes that everything, no matter how small or large, has the right to live. When Horton first becomes aware of a small creature living on the speck of dust, he says, "I'll just have to save him. Because after all, a person's a person, no matter how small."

*In much of Leonard Weisgard's work, transparencies add richness—one color shows through another.*
By Alice Dalgliesh. Illustration from *The Courage of Sarah Noble.* Copyright © 1954 Alice Dalgliesh and Leonard Weisgard; copyright renewed © 1984 Margaret B. Franst and Leonard Weisgard. Reprinted with the permission of Charles Scribner's Sons.

Loyalty leading to an act of courage is described in *Seven Magic Orders*, by Shan Mui. This Japanese folk tale tells of people living in the utopian land of Tao Yuen. Chung Shun is a loyal subject of the emperor. He is sent on a quest to vanquish the demon monster and subordinates his own wishes, and his love for his intended bride, to his loyalty. As he learns the meaning of faith, obedience, kindness, and love, Chung Shun triumphs over the monster and regains his beloved.

A complex study of values with respect to individual behavior is found in *The Courage of Sarah Noble*, by Alice Dalgliesh. This is the true story of an eight-year-old girl who accompanied her father to the wilds of Connecticut in 1707. After buying a share of land, John Noble had to travel to New Milford, where he was to build the first house. Because she knew her mother and the sickly baby could not go, Sarah offered to go with her father

**A wide variety of surface patterns decorate this essentially two-dimensional picture, giving a visually complex image.** Reprinted with the permission of Macmillan Publishing Company from *Hitty: Her First Hundred Years* by Rachel Field, illustrated by Dorothy P. Lathrop. Copyright 1929 by Macmillan Publishing Company; copyright renewed 1957.

and cook for him. Except for one other family of settlers, the only people Sarah encountered were Indians, living in bark-covered houses on the hill and along the river. Many times it was necessary for Sarah to call on her faith and courage. Sarah's behavior toward her family and toward the Indians provides opportunities for children to observe how a character manifests what she believes through what she does. Particularly noteworthy is the change that takes place in Sarah's attitudes about the Indians as she gets to know them.

Another book about values and individual behavior is *Hitty: Her First Hundred Years*, by Rachel Field. This appealing story about a doll could be juxtaposed effectively with *Miss Hickory*, by Carolyn Bailey. The teacher could ask the students to think about how the attitudes, beliefs, and values of the two dolls are alike or different.

Carol Ryrie Brink deals with the effects of dishonesty in her book *The Bad Times of Irma Baumlein*. The author's position concerning lying is clearly articulated at the opening of the story:

> Irma Baumlein told a lie. It was the first bad thing that Irma had ever done, and all of the terrible things that she did later grew out of the lie, like poisonous mushrooms out of a rotten log.

Irma told her new friend Judy that she had the biggest doll in the world. After all, Judy claimed she had four brothers, two sisters, a dog, and lots of hamsters and then asked Irma, "What do you have?" What could Irma say? What Irma did have was a father who was too busy helping to manage a department store, a mother who was away at a health spa, an eccentric great-uncle, and a nearly deaf great-aunt. The evil consequences of the lie begin when Irma commits herself to bring "The Biggest Doll in the World" to the school carnival. So she steals a mannequin from her uncle's store, and her bad times really start. Brink does not bludgeon the reader with an explicit moral. Irma's feelings of guilt and discomfort are skillfully depicted, but there is also humor and sly wit.

> She hadn't remembered to bring her usual books home from the library on Friday night, and she now had nothing to read.
> She went downstairs and looked in Uncle Arnold's library. None of the books had pictures and they appeared to be very solid and dull. The first title she noticed was *Crime and Punishment* by an author whose name looked as a sneeze might if you tried to spell it. Irma sighed and went upstairs again.

In Norma Farber's *How Does It Feel to Be Old?*, a book focusing on an older character, the narrator keeps her own counsel, shares her thoughts

**In this line drawing, some parts done in brown (the earlier years) are superimposed on other parts done in black (present time) to suggest the psychological state of the old woman.** From *How Does It Feel to Be Old?* by Norma Farber, illustrated by Trina Schart Hyman. Illustrations copyright © 1979 by Trina Schart Hyman. Reproduced by permission of the publisher, E. P. Dutton, a divison of NAL Penguin Inc.

generously with her granddaughter, and faces the aging process with honesty, seeing both good and bad.

*Old woman, enough!*
*Get up! It's late!*
*I will! But you'll have to wait*
*till I stretch these old, old, old, old knees—*
*I'm getting there, really I am.*
*One foot at a time I'm touching the floor.*
*Soon I'll be standing—*
*but not too fast*
*or I might fall down.*
*I might disgrace*
*this old, old self by landing—*

> *silly old clown—*
> *flat on my face.*
> *I'm up at last!*
> *Like sun! You see?*
> *I'm up! (And only barely recalling*
> *the youngster who long, long ago was me*
> *with never a hint of a fear of falling.)*

Farber wisely avoids describing the inherent integrity of her main character, rather she lets the character demonstrate it. Trina Schart Hyman did without the borders that have become her trademark; May (1986) has commented on these illustrations.

**FAMILY VALUES.**   In *Charlie the Tramp*, by Russell Hoban, Grandfather Beaver repeatedly expresses his attitude toward the "younger generation" of beavers:

> "That is how it is now-a-days," said grandfather. "When I was young, children did not want to be tramps. When I was young . . . children did hard work. Now-a-days all they want to do is little jobs."

And Charlie expresses his beliefs:

> "Tramps don't have to learn how to chop down trees and how to roll logs and how to build dams. . . . Tramps carry sticks with bundles tied to them. They sleep in a field when the weather is nice, and when it rains they sleep in a barn. Tramps just tramp around and have a good time."

Charlie eventually realizes that he shares his parents' values. After living the life of a tramp, he builds a beautiful dam in just the way he'd been taught. He does it simply because he wants to: "Well . . . sometimes I like to tramp around, and sometimes I like to make ponds." In turn, grandfather's attitudes about the younger generation are also modified: "That's how it is now-a-days . . . you never know when a tramp will turn out to be a beaver."

Attitudes concerning the "proper" behavior for a grandmother are explored in *Best Friend*, by Shirley Simon. Jenny wishes her grandmother would be prim, proper, and a good cook and is embarrassed when Grandmother wears blue jeans and sneakers and rides a bike. She is disappointed because her friends Dot and Edythe do not approve of her grandmother; at the time, Jenny needs their friendship. But toward the book's end, Jenny and her friend Ruthie both come to value their own grandmothers.

> "Do you want to trade grandmas?" Ruthie asked, her eyes dancing.
> "No, siree! And neither do you. Maybe it's nice that we have such different

grandmas. We can enjoy them both. You can have fun riding bikes with my Grandma. . . ."

". . . And you can enjoy Grandma Fennerman's cooking and baking."

A conflict in family values is a main theme in *Cinnamon Cane,* by Melinda Pollowitz. Cassie, whose friendship with her grandfather is strong and enduring, is upset when he is forced to move from his beloved farm to a cramped city apartment. The friends she wants so badly are contemptuous of things she and her grandfather enjoy; they make demands on her time, so she has trouble maintaining contact with him. Cassie's affluent mother and father are both too busy with their own affairs to be more than moderately concerned with her problems. Her father feels some guilt about neglecting his own father, but is more than willing to assuage that guilt with material things. As her grandfather's death approaches, Cassie tries to sort out what she feels. In the end, she realizes how important he is to her. She finds that she can share his values and still participate with her peers in their activities.

*Queenie Peavy,* by Robert Burch, is also useful for helping children think about family values. Rebellious Queenie lashes out at those who hurt her. She is a contradiction: a fearsome rock-thrower and tobacco-chewer who plays delightful games and sings and dances with the neighborhood children. She realizes that her father's jail sentence for a post-office robbery is just, but she excuses him on the grounds that he got in with bad company. The father, home on parole, is a shiftless ne'er-do-well, insensitive to his daughter's adoration and her needs. He is put back in jail for breaking his parole. Although the author never moralizes, the difference between Queenie and her mother (who is hard-working and upstanding) on one hand and Queenie's father on the other is very clear.

*Queenie Peavy* might be compared to Katharine Paterson's *The Great Gilly Hopkins.* Lonely and unloved, Gilly prefers dreams to reality and has retreated behind a protective armor of assumed indifference to people and situations. Bruised by life, she lashes out at others before they can hurt her. Living with Maime Trotter helps Gilly realize that even though they are sometimes painful, relationships with others are a necessary and often rewarding part of life. Paterson invests her characters with vigorous individuality; they grow and interact believably. If teachers use questioning strategies to explore the ways Queenie and Gilly respond to problems, students can come to a further understanding of these books.

**SOCIAL VALUES.** Values with respect to peers and society are the focus of many books for children. In *The Two Giants,* by Michael Forman, Boris and

*Artist Jerry Lazare arranges the figures of the people and the dog in a tight oval, an effective compositional device.* Illustration by Jerry Lazare from *Queenie Peavy* by Robert Burch. Copyright © 1966 by The Viking Press, Inc. Reproduced by permission of Viking Penguin Inc.

Sam are steadfast friends who discover what selfishness can do to friendship. A bitter dispute over a seashell turns them into enemies. The disagreement continues for years, until the two have forgotten the reason for the argument. How selfishness can damage a valued friendship is skillfully explored in this humorous tale.

A more serious story for fourth- through sixth-grade children is *A Trainful of Strangers,* by Eleanor Hull. A group of peers with many positive characteristics and healthy attitudes also possess prejudices that prevent them from seeing good traits in one another. The children all live in New York, a city of strangers. Just as city life is compartmentalized, the characters in each chapter inhabit a small compartment of life, separate from the characters in other chapters. The children have a variety of life-styles, living in all types of environments, from the ghetto to suburbia. They meet on a subway train heading downtown. The power fails and, when the train stalls, they talk amongst themselves and discover they are headed for the same destination: a science program at an educational television station. The children realize that, because of the delay, they will miss the program that afternoon but agree to meet to attend it the following week. This sudden change in the course of events allows strangers, who had glanced suspiciously at one another across the aisle, to become friends for a moment, but as the subway starts up again, they return to their silent seats and become strangers again. The narrative deals with the children's thoughts about themselves, their own stations in life, and their perceptions of the other children. By seeing through the eyes of all the children, the reader sees how prejudice blinds each individual to the good in others. The author's style gives a realistic, if somewhat despairing, outlook on human relations, but the story ends hopefully: through small interactions, the children begin to overcome their prejudices and make honest efforts to get to know one another.

Sometimes teachers consider such seemingly complex ideas as overcoming prejudices as being beyond young children's comprehension, but there are books that can help primary-grade boys and girls think about such problems. *The Sneetches and Other Stories*, by Dr. Seuss, deals in the author's usual humorous fashion with the problem of how to relate to people who are externally different. This story is also available in video format as *The Sneetches from Dr. Seuss on the Loose* (from Phoenix/BFA Educational Films and Video, Inc., 468 Park Avenue South, New York, NY 10016).

One writer for middle school children, Nina Bawden (1980), discusses why she believes social values are important for children to consider. Her book, *The Peppermint Pig*, involves some children in a decision as to whether it is right to break into a house (to steal back some money stolen by a confidence trickster). The author makes a convincing argument that social values are vital issues for children to encounter in realistic fiction.

**VALUES CONCERNING WORK AND LEISURE.** Values with respect to work are explored in different ways by many authors.[2] In Leo Lionni's *Frederick*, the mouse is a worker, though what he does is not considered work by the other mice. Later their attitude toward Frederick changes. He brings them warmth and pleasure, and they appreciate his unique contributions. A teacher might ask children questions such as these: "How would you feel, if you were one of the other mice, when you saw the kind of work Frederick was doing? What would you say to Frederick if he were your brother? What

---

[2]An extensive annotated bibliography of books about different kinds of work is included in "Books That Recognize the Joy of Work," by Leland B. Jacobs (*The Instructor*, October 1969, pp. 68–69).

would you tell him to do?" The teacher can ask these questions twice. She or he can read the story to the point when winter has just set in and ask children to respond. Later, after reading the entire book to the class, the teacher can record students' answers to the same questions. A third question can help students move to the reflection stage (in which children think about the ways the values expressed in the story are like or unlike their own): "Does Frederick's work seem like real work to you?" The responses of children who have experienced such a sequential approach to thinking about values should be more thoughtful than the comments made by children in classes where the teacher questions in a less organized way.

*Little Toot*, by Hardie Gramatky, who was at one time the head animator for Disney Studios, is about a tugboat who has no ambition except to relax and enjoy life: "He saw no sense in pulling ships 50 times bigger than himself all the way down to the ocean." This attitude earns him the rancor of the other tugs, who ridicule him as a sissy who knows only how to play. He discovers, when he decides to show them he can work, that they continue to think he is only a nuisance. His opportunity to prove himself comes during a storm, when, because of his small size, he is able to rescue a stranded ocean liner. Little Toot's self-concept has changed by the end of the story: he feels good about himself because he has accomplished something worthwhile. This beloved character also appears in books with different settings: the Mississippi, the Thames, the Grand Canal of Venice, and the Golden Gate. The actor Hans Conreid narrates these stories on a recording (Caedmon Records, #TC1528).

Another book, useful with intermediate-grade children, explores work as a quest. In *Black Pilgrimage*, artist Tom Feelings includes pages from sketchbooks he filled over a period of years as he matured from student to professional illustrator. These illustrations—some full-page, others smaller—accompany a written account of the difficulties in attaining professional competence. Finding that the art school he was attending offered little, Feelings turned to the neighborhood streets, went on assignment in the South, and worked in Ghana. The resulting drawings—in pencil, in ink and wash, and in color—are full of motion, enthusiasm, and, at times, despair. The written account is interesting, but becomes overly preachy at the end. Despite this flaw, the book is a compelling story of a struggle for personal accomplishment in the world of work.

Attitudes toward work and leisure (more specifically, the absence of leisure) are explored in *Friday Night Is Papa Night*, by Ruth Sonnenborn. Everyone works in Pedro's family. Papa is at home only on weekends because during the week he is working two jobs to support his family. He uses what

***Artist Hardie Gramatky uses watercolor in a casual style in this personification of a tugboat; the book is still popular many years after its publication.*** Illustration reprinted by permission of G. P. Putnam's Sons from *Little Toot* by Hardie Gramatky, copyright 1939 by Hardie Gramatky, copyright renewed © 1967 by Hardie Gramatky.

would otherwise be leisure time to make a better life for his family. Each family member has his or her own job to do in joyous preparation for father's homecoming on a particular Friday night. They do the jobs with what may seem, to today's suburban children with few responsibilities, like remarkable compliance.

**VALUES CONCERNING SEX.** Sex is another topic about which people hold various attitudes, beliefs, and values. Many books discussed in Chapter 10 are appropriate as the basis for discussions about sex.

*None of the Above,* by Rosemary Wells, describes the process of molding two families into one, the consequence of which is that some of the people get hurt. When Mr. Hill marries Mrs. Van Dam, Marcia and Sharon Hill move in with John and Christina Van Dam. John is away at college, and Sharon is about to be married. Christina is—or seems—sure of herself. She's extremely intelligent and makes Marcia feel lumpish and stupid. Content with average marks in school, Marcia feels her stepmother is forcing her to compete with Christina; that competition results in an ulcer for Marcia when the two girls enter high school. A part-time job and a new boyfriend bolster Marcia's self-esteem. Raymond's circle of motorcycle-riding friends are "faster" than Marcia is, however, and she feels like a misfit among them. She and Raymond attempt sexual intercourse but are unsuccessful. After months of feeling it is her fault, that she is doing something wrong, Marcia finds out through his own admission that Raymond is impotent. She continues the relationship anyway, and eventually the problem is solved. Because of tensions building at home, Marcia decides to marry Raymond rather than attend the college for which her stepmother has been trying to groom her. The exploration of sexual values is not presented as a moral question: "Should we or shouldn't we?" Rather, it is presented as posing for Marcia one more problem in addition to all the rest. It often seems as if Raymond is using Marcia, especially when he makes her feel the problem in their physical relationship is her fault. Later, she reflects that she is maintaining the relationship to fill her own needs, whereas he is thinking of both of them. Complex relationships—parent/child, sibling/sibling, man/woman—are explored as well as the giving and taking found within them. This book can help readers understand that building relationships is difficult but ultimately rewarding.

**RELIGIOUS VALUES.** Deeply held, but often unexamined, values relate to God, religion, and sacred ideas. This area presents potential problems for teachers because parents and others in the community may not understand the difference between teaching a religion and teaching *about* religions as a sociological phenomena. Certainly it is outside the province of the public schools to advocate a particular religious doctrine. However, it should be one of the concerns of the school to help children examine the religious beliefs expressed by characters in books. Although philosophically this is a defensible position, it is important for teachers to examine the social and religious climate in their own communities before embarking on a classroom discussion of values with respect to God, religion, and sacred ideas.

Many artists have depicted simple Bible stories in picture-book format. Such books can—and should—be used in discussions about illustration techniques and storytelling variations. Whether or not to initiate a discussion of religious values based on them is a decision teachers will have to make individually. *Noah and the Ark and the Animals* is by Bulgarian artist Ivan Gantschev. In this, as in his other distinguished picture books, the illustrator uses watercolor techniques that achieve "remarkable . . . nuances in color variations" (Richard and MacCann, 1985). (See Plate B in the color section.) Teachers might gather several variations on the Noah tale and have children observe similarities and differences in both text and pictures. *Noah and the Rainbow*, by Max Bolliger, contains full-page, full color illustrations, by Helga Aichinger, that do not overwhelm with detail but rather create a mood through their otherworldly symbolism. They make pleasing patterns on the page, although literal-minded children may wonder what is being depicted. *Noah and the Great Flood*, by Warwick Hutton, features full-page and double-page spreads, done in watercolor with pen line, that treat the story seriously and even tragically (one picture shows a drowning man). Very different in mood is Charlotte Pomerantz's *Noah's and Namah's Ark*, in which the author presents the tale in rhymed verse. The realistic, black-and-white, full-page illustrations, by Kelly K. M. Carsen, exhibit accurate historic detail.

Some books explore the religious practices or beliefs of people in other times. In *Christmas on the Mayflower*, by Wilma Pitchford Hays, the Pilgrims have just reached Plymouth Bay and are preparing to build their homes. The story begins the day before Christmas when the Pilgrims are still living aboard the Mayflower. The sailors resent the Pilgrims because of the long delay in getting settled in the new land. The captain acts as mediator between the two groups, and the traditional Christmas message is expressed in the resolving of their differences as they come together on Christmas Eve for a meal and the burning of the Yule log. Children can think about the Pilgrims' religious values and examine how their attitudes toward the Indians reflect their belief that God ordained their superiority. Throughout, the Pilgrims are depicted as very pious; at one point a character remarks, "With God, we shall feel at home anyplace." A teacher could read the story to students and ask them to think about why the Pilgrims were a religious people.

Religious beliefs common to another time period are presented in a biography, *Mozart*, by Reba P. Mirsky. When his son shows outstanding musical talents at age three, Mozart's father says

> "I'm overcome by the great gift and responsibility God has given us. We must do everything possible to fulfill his great talent. I hope we shall be equal to the great task before us."

At another time, a smallpox epidemic is rampant, and the Mozart family has the chance to be inoculated. The father refuses, saying

> "I prefer to leave it all in God's hands. Let Him in His divine mercy dispose as He will of the life of this wonder of nature."

Exactly what time period is being depicted in *The Islanders*, by John Rowe Townsend, isn't clear. A small, closed society living on an isolated island is bound by a strictly prescribed set of teachings (as contained in The Book), an enforcer (the Reader, who, paradoxically, cannot read), and their own enculturated fear of outsiders. Theirs is not like any known religion, but for these believers, adhering to the set of beliefs is crucial. The islanders' tranquil life is first upset by a pair of incomers, found nearly dead with exhaustion from their sea journey. The dilemma of how to deal with them, humanely (as some islanders wish) or according to the teaching in The Book, is not easily resolved. Scarcely has a decision been reached when another boat arrives carrying a whole group of incomers. That problem to be solved is quickly followed by another: deserters from among the islanders' own ranks make the islanders' already precarious existence even more unsure. The revelation that the beliefs they have followed so faithfully are not what is actually written in The Book creates a crisis among the islanders. The book ends equivocally; readers don't know how the islanders will survive, although it is clear they do have the inner tenacity to meet the challenges of their bleak environment and the loss of their faith.

A presentation of religious faith today is central in *The Difference of Ari Stein*, by Charlotte Herman. Ari and his mother and father move to Brooklyn, where Ari makes friends with several boys who are less religious than he is. He wants to be part of their group, but conflicts develop when they demand that he abandon some of his Jewish observances. Temple, the Sabbath, and Hebrew school are important to Ari, who wants to be a cantor. The resolution of the conflict is predictable, but the book is a useful tool for discussing the importance of being true to one's values, whatever they are.

Another treatment of contemporary religious values is *The Long Secret*, the sequel to author Louise Fitzhugh's *Harriet the Spy*. A religious fanatic is leaving anonymous notes throughout the small town where the children are vacationing. Finding out who is responsible occupies the children for most of the summer. At one point, Harriet and her father are talking about religion.

> "Daddy?" Harriet said after a while. "Are you religious?"
>
> "No," said Mr. Welsch. "That is, I do not follow any organized religion. That is not to say I am not a religious man. I don't know how I could look at those stars and not be a religious man. I just mean that I have made up my own set of ethics and don't take them from any organized religion."
>
> "Do you pray?"
>
> "No, I don't."
>
> "I just wondered about very religious people. Do they really mean it?"
>
> "Some of them. Some of them don't. Some of them just say a lot of words and they don't really mean anything. It depends on the person. I do think, though, that we should respect someone's religion whether we share it or not."

Marc Talbert tells an engrossing story of a youngster dealing with serious problems and ultimately finding no solace in the human manifestations of religion in *Dead Birds Singing*. Seventh-grader Matt is trying to come to terms with the sudden deaths in an automobile accident of his mother and sister. The minister who tries to help him is portrayed unsympathetically:

> Matt pictured the minister . . . [whose] name was Untterbach. The preacher had a face that always reminded Matt of a potato. Its shape was irregular and his eyes were uneven. His mouth looked like the gash of a careless paring knife. When Mr. Untterbach talked, his cheeks developed lumps that made him look like he was talking with his mouth full of tough steak. Another thing always struck Matt. The preacher's voice sounded like mashed potatoes felt—thick and mushy.

Later, Matt confronts Mr. Untterbach about the reason for his mother's death, which, understandably, seems senseless to Matt. The minister is inept in helping the boy come to terms with his loss.

> "We were all saddened when we heard of your mother's death," he began. He sounded like his tongue was too big for his mouth. "She was a wonderful, strong woman who overcame so much to bring you and your sister up right."
>
> Matt looked at the preacher. The tangy smell of after-shave mingled with bad coffee breath. "And now, you must be as strong as your mother to overcome this tragedy," he continued.

The minister continues to offer only platitudes, and he doesn't even realize that he isn't getting through to Matt. Finally, the minister retreats into prayer to avoid a more meaningful discussion. In the end, it isn't religion that helps Matt come to terms with his loss. Having trouble sleeping, Matt leaves the house and goes on an extended walk, coming at last to a meadow, where he contemplates his own death:

> This is where I want my ashes scattered, he thought. Here, where my mother and Jeannie and I spent some peaceful afternoons enjoying each other's company.
>
> He looked around at this magical, forgotten field. The light from the moon made everything shimmer, as if the trees and grass were below the surface of a gently rippled pond. For the first time since the accident, Matt thought about swimming and how much he enjoyed racing.

Alone, outside in the dark night, Matt is at last able to say good-bye to his mother and his sister.

Teachers need to be aware that there may be few books that deal with religion, according to Brewbaker (1983). He comments that a 1981 study of American culture revealed that the more than two thousand Americans sampled identified religion as the "element affecting most both their values and actions." A sample of thirty-four recent books for adolescent readers was analyzed to see how much, if any, religious content was present. In summarizing the results, Brewbaker concluded that nearly half of the sample (sixteen books) included "little or no religious content." Titles analyzed ranged from books containing little or no religious content (such as *The Keeping Room*, by Betty Levin), through books including "moderate" religious content (such as *Daughters of Eve*, by Lois Duncan), to books containing a more strongly presented religious dimension (such as *Jacob Have I Loved*, by Katherine Paterson).

Additional comments about such books by Kathleen Baxter (1985) present the point of view of a librarian, who is often asked by parents for books embodying religious values. She contends that, unfortunately, in the area of religion, publishers are not always able to find good-quality manuscripts by talented children's writers. She comments:

> We are in desperate need of quality children's books which deal with religion as a natural part of a child's everyday life—books in which a child prays when faced with problems, books in which faith is viewed as a positive and normal aspect of life.

The extent to which such books should be available in school libraries, or

**The perspective in this illustration emphasizes the length of the walk back to the house.** Illustration by Paul Lantz from *Blue Willow* by Doris Gates, copyright 1940, renewed © 1967 by The Viking Press, Inc. Reproduced by permission of Viking Penguin Inc.

whether they more properly belong in public libraries, is a matter worth discussing.

**MONEY AND MATERIALISM.** Characters' ideas about money or possessions often play a significant part in children's books. "The Contest" is a chapter from the book *Blue Willow,* a Newbery honor book by Doris Gates. It presents episodic accounts of the lives of migrant workers—their families, their problems, and their joys. In this chapter, the Larkin family decides to enter a cotton-picking contest with the help of a neighbor, Mr. Romero. Janey Larkin is best friends with Lupe Romero. The two girls' values with respect to money provide an interesting contrast.

Lupe took a moment to consider the question.

"If I had a thousand dollars, I'd buy an automobile. It would be light yellow with shining wheels. And it would have red leather on the inside and two horns. And I'd drive it anytime I wanted to."

Janey's answer was ready. "I'd have a house built with rooms in it for all of us, not counting the kitchen. And it would be all light inside and clean, and there would be water pipes right inside the house, so you could just turn them off and on whenever you wanted to . . . and we would stay in it always . . ."

Both girls are fantasizing about things they cannot afford because of their poverty, but it is interesting to note the difference in focus: Lupe wants something to bring gratification to herself; Janey wants something to please her whole family.

*The Hundred Dresses,* by Eleanor Estes, shows readers values concerning money. The students in the story discriminate against Wanda because she is so poor. The fact that they value money is expressed when the girls become excited about Cecile's new dress and talk joyously about new dresses they have bought or are planning to buy. This goads Wanda into saying she has one hundred dresses at home hanging in her closet. The statement causes much laughter, as Wanda wears only one dress: "a faded blue dress that didn't hang right." Maddie doesn't agree with these values; she doesn't tease Wanda the way Peggy, the most popular girl in the class, does.

Definite ideas about the value of money are presented in *Where the Lilies Bloom,* by Vera and Bill Cleaver. Roy Luther, an Appalachian tenant farmer, dies, leaving behind four children. His daughter Mary Call promises to maintain and encourage the family as they strive to be independent. Roy, despite a life of poverty, has avoided charity because he believes it

". . . is seldom of real service to those upon whom it is bestowed and those who receive it are always looked upon with suspicion, every need and want scrutinized."

Mary and her family have steadfastly avoided being "happy pappies."

A happy pappy is a poor, no-account mountaineer who sits rocking on the porch of his shotgun shack all day long waiting for the mailman to bring him his charity check. He's so ignorant that's all he knows how to do . . .

As the story unfolds, Mary, armed with her father's basic code of life, must reformulate her own values, compromising and changing some things, cherishing others. The reader will find several incidents throughout the book where Mary leans on her father's teachings. However, she eventually sifts out his traits of stubbornness and uncompromising pride.

A disastrous conflict of values involving two different generations is the focus of *Gentlehands,* by M. E. Kerr. Buddy Boyle, raised in a lower-class police officer's home, is swept off his feet by wealthy Skye Pennington.

**In this unusual character study, the illustrator employs line and dots to convey a sinister feeling.**
Illustration from *Where the Lilies Bloom* by Vera and Bill Cleaver, published by J. B. Lippincott.
Illustrated by Jim Spanfeller. Copyright © 1969 by Vera and William Cleaver. Reprinted by
permission of Harper & Row, Publishers, Inc.

Buddy's long-estranged grandfather represents an attractive kind of life to
Buddy. He can teach Buddy many things that will help Buddy fit into Skye's
life. His mother views the wealthy life-style differently.

> "I was at this dinner party . . . once and I didn't even know what fork to pick
> up," she said, "and I never forgot it. I still wouldn't know. I see what you mean,
> Buddy, don't think I don't see, but those are snob things and your father and
> I aren't raising you to think those things are important."
>
> "You're not raising me to think those things are important because you
> don't know about those things," I said. "You couldn't raise me that way if you
> wanted to, because you don't know."

What Buddy learns from his grandfather is far more significant than which forks to use, how to pour wine, and the plots of operas, however. The old man has ideas about how to live responsibly, how to achieve where others see only obstacles, and how to make decisions that change one's life. When Buddy's world falls apart, he must make a hard choice, and he does so by following his grandfather's advice. In the end, Buddy is reconciled with his family, and the reader wonders if the influence of his grandfather will survive.

**PATRIOTIC VALUES.** Patriotism in a young girl is the subject of *Lotte's Locket*, by Virginia Sorensen. Lotte is the eighth of her name to live in the old Danish farmhouse. She, her mother, and grandmother have lived there alone since the death of Lotte's father in a plane crash during World War II. Well-versed in Danish history, she is fiercely loyal to her country and bitterly resents her mother's marriage to Patrick—who is loud, large, and American. After finishing the school year in Denmark, Lotte will be going to America to join her mother and Patrick. She dreads leaving, especially when she learns that her mother is pregnant. Her mother's courage and her accounts of Pat's kindness help Lotte face the necessity of leaving the country she loves.

## A CAUTION ABOUT EXPLORING VALUES

Teachers who are interested in using books to help students explore values, rather than purely for literary purposes, must be aware of local community mores concerning this matter. The exploration of attitudes, beliefs, and values in the schools is under question. Some parents do indeed want their children to consider their own values and to be exposed to (not inculcated with) other values. But some parents believe that the school intrudes on private concerns when it includes values consciously as part of the curriculum. Often these parents believe that there is a right way and a wrong way to think about most things and that exploring various alternative reactions to events is morally wrong. It is, of course, possible to excuse a particular child from a discussion about values or (in the upper grades) to substitute a less controversial book for the student to read. The problem becomes more troublesome when parents want to restrict the teacher's option to explore attitudes, beliefs, and values with the class, in the process eliminating all children's participation in such experiences.

The root of the problem lies in the confusion between examination and proselytizing. Some parents fear that literature will teach children values that negate home teachings. Even though such fears are based on a misunderstanding of the school's intent, they must nevertheless be dealt with. Before launching a schoolwide program of exploring values through literature, teachers and administrators must clearly define their rationale for such a move. Presentations at parent meetings and letters sent home should help reassure nervous parents that the intent of the program is not to convert students to a single narrow range of values, but rather to inform students of the diverse values found in our society.

A value-based literature program will also help child readers see that authors regularly deal with important issues. Books dealing with values are significant because the characters in them confront real-life questions. Once convinced that reading these books is worth the effort, children will be more likely to read when they are adults.

## EVALUATING BOOKS FOR A LITERATURE CURRICULUM

An advantage offered by schoolwide curriculum planning is that the process allows the staff to draw on a wider base of information in selecting books. If teachers use only their own judgment in deciding to use or exclude a particular book, there is a danger that the decision is based on limited data. When several professionals pool their information, decisions are more likely to have a broader base. Cooperative study and discussion allow individual teachers to move beyond parochial concerns and prevent books from being included or excluded for purely personal reasons.

For instance, suppose one teacher on a literature-selection committee is adamant about excluding any book about a minority group that was not written by an author of that group. There is information to be found and examples to be cited that both support and oppose this stand. Contentions have been made that it is difficult, if not impossible, for any white to write effectively about the black experience. (See Sims, 1982, for this point of view.) This opinion of books about blacks written by whites can be succinctly put: "If you aren't one, you can't write about one," which is patently nonsense. Pushed to its illogical extreme, that statement means writers can write only about what they are. John Rowe Townsend (1983) points out how erroneous that premise is:

> It is not necessary or desirable that writer or critic be restricted to what he knows from direct experiences; otherwise no man could write about women, no middle-aged person could write about old age; no one at all could write about the past. It is the task of the creative imagination to leap across such frontiers.

Townsend does admit that white writers are perhaps more effective when writing stories in which not just blackness but a more universal theme is the issue and the characters' blackness is incidental. *Evan's Corner*, by Elizabeth S. Hill, for example, features a problem that is common to all people; it is not specific to one ethnic group. Hill is not black, but nevertheless writes an effective story about a black child because what she is dealing with is the need for each of us, no matter what age or condition, to have a space of our own.[3]

A book by the respected illustrator Margot Zemach elicited widely varying evaluations because of the issue of racism. Her *Jake and Honeybunch Go to Heaven* was called a "zesty, irreverent look at Heaven and its habitués" (Beavin, 1982). *The New York Times Book Review* commented that "it takes a deft hand to get all this action into the air and keep it going . . . Zemach [is]: strong, nervy, in love with her material . . ." (Kuskin, 1982). Some reviews raised questions: "Is its picture of Depression-era . . . working-class black culture celebratory, or does it perpetuate offensive stereotypes?" (Wilms, 1983). Others were derogatory: "A stiff, flat elaboration on 'black' themes. . . . Unfortunate, because it revives stereotypes without rising above them" (Fretz, 1983). Others were even more derogatory: ". . . the book . . . is offensive and degrading . . . wholly inappropriate for children whether they be black or white" (American Libraries, 1983). A defense by the editor of the book was published to present a countering point of view (Roxburgh, 1983).

James Forman's *Ceremony of Innocence* proves that, with proper research, an author can write about something he did not himself experience. Forman, an American, has effectively written about persecution in Germany during Hitler's reign.

Two questions related to racism, sexism, ageism, or other kinds of perceived discrimination are pertinent to the evaluation of books:

## 1. How does the book relate to its time?

Each book must be reviewed in terms of the era in which it was written or the era it depicts. To evaluate books in terms of the social mores of our own era is unfair. The goal is not to eliminate what appears to be a biased

---

[3]The issue of racism was also raised by some critics concerning *Sounder*, by William H. Armstrong (New York: Harper and Row, 1969). Although this Newbery Medal winner was praised by many, Albert V. Schwartz (1970) said that it does not present "the black perspective" and thus will not be "relevant to black children." Geller (1972) thought it was "aesthetically flawed by its moral limitations."

book from the literature curriculum, but rather to help children explore how the attitudes evinced are different from those prevalent today.

### 2. How does the book relate to the total published output of the author?

In considering any kind of stereotyping, teachers need to examine all the books the author has written. Then they can determine if a specific instance in one book is just that: an isolated example rather than a persisting stereotype, common throughout the author's work.

Teachers need to take a step back from the concerns of the moment. As John Rowe Townsend (1983) says,

> It is a rare individual who can rise above the general insensitiveness of his own day, and none of us can tell what unsuspected sins we may be found guilty of in fifty years time.

*The Sherwood Ring*, by Elizabeth Marie Pope, has been indicted by some as a sexist book. In it, Peggy Grahame comes to live with her irascible Uncle Enos and on the way is given directions by a lovely girl clad in a flowing crimson cape. When she sees the portrait of that same girl hanging in her uncle's home, Peggy knows she has seen her first ghost. One by one, Peggy's ancestors tell her the history of her family and its participation in the American Revolution. Their story of adventure and romance in the eighteenth century somewhat parallels Peggy's own experiences with Pat Thorne in the twentieth century, and the two tales intermingle. The narration moves back and forth between the eighteenth and the twentieth century effortlessly and smoothly. A critic called the book sexist because of "Pat's chauvinistic proposal [and] Peggy's passive acceptance of his description of their future married life" (Klingberg, 1976). Such criticism does not, however, take into account several important factors that mitigate the book's supposed sexism.

1. When the book was written in 1958, less emphasis was placed on the desirability of women having careers. The critic is incensed because Pat speaks of his future career, never mentioning one for Peggy: a situation that is probably quite typical of that era.
2. Peggy has been denied affection by her father and uncle, both cold and selfish men. Pat cares for her, and his proposal, because she cares for him, is psychologically attractive.
3. Peggy's "passivism" must be balanced against the resolution and courage of her ancestor Barbara, who, in the eighteenth century—a time much less sympathetic to women's rights—was able to assert herself in a difficult situation.

*Illustrator Evaline Ness, always masterful in her use of stylized patterns, arranges these figures within a tightly defined shape.* Illustration by Evaline Ness from *The Sherwood Ring* by Elizabeth Marie Pope. Copyright © 1958 by Elizabeth Marie Pope. Reprinted by permission of Houghton Mifflin Company.

4. Elizabeth Pope's work as a whole does not embody the sexist stereotype. *The Perilous Gard*, a Newbery honor book, features a heroine who is remarkable for her courage, handling herself well during many adventures and carrying out the rescue of a male character.

In consideration of the points above, a more balanced view of *The Sherwood*

*Ring* would be that it is not sexist, except in the most extremist view.[4] This whole issue of balance in portraying men and women is a complex one (introduced earlier in Chapter 6). Today, fair presentations of women seem to be on the rise, although unrealistic presentations of men continue to concern experts (Norsworthy, 1973).

## SUMMARY

When focusing on moving beyond recommending individual books to larger program concerns, teachers must formulate techniques for linking or relating books to one another in a unified pattern of experiences. For literature to be appreciated in all its aspects, children must be exposed to books in a program organized at every grade level to span the entire school year. A group of teachers planning a literature curriculum must be concerned about purpose, scope (the range of experiences at any given level), and sequence (the ordering or arrangement of experiences). Four ways in which to organize literature curricula are organization by genres, by literary elements, by topics, or by values. Other organizations are of course possible; some programs might organize according to individual child interests or subject matter correlations. No matter which organization is chosen, the process of organizing is crucial.

Teachers must also develop ways of evaluating the effectiveness of a literature program. Monitoring children's interest in reading and the growing sophistication in their responses to what they have read requires simple, convenient assessment tools. The committee of teachers who decide questions about the nature of the program will also be able to devise ways to assess its effectiveness. A program seldom remains in the curriculum unless it is continually evaluated.

When considering a book for inclusion in the literature program, the committee of teachers should evaluate it in relation to the time in which it was published, the total published output of the author, and other books to be shared in the overall program. Using these criteria, the teachers can make a rational decision about a book's value.

Children also evaluate individual books, using the evaluative criteria given in preceding chapters for individual genres. Part of the purpose of

---

[4]A defense of this book is provided by Ethel L. Heins in "A Second Look; *The Sherwood Ring* " (*The Horn Book*, December 1975, p. 613). Letters about this book appeared in *The Horn Book* in June 1976 (pp. 235, 331) and December 1976 (p. 579).

explaining these criteria to children is to build critical readers who can determine for themselves the value of individual books.

The amount of time teachers or librarians have to share books with children is limited. Even when a fully developed literature program is in place, the number of books a child encounters in the elementary school is a small percentage of those available. Yet the elementary school is where children begin to build lifelong reading habits. By listening to fine literature read aloud, by talking about how books help us understand ourselves and others, and by choosing books to read themselves, children are moving toward adult life as committed readers. To ensure this happens, the two most important decisions the teacher or librarian makes are what books to share and how to share them.

## Suggestions for Further Study

1. One critic labeled *The Sherwood Ring* sexist (see page 698), but editor Ethel Heins says that "the book may not be an undying classic, but it is . . . at the very least an engaging historical romance . . . written with imagination and style" (*The Horn Book*, December 1975, p. 613). Read the book and both critiques, and decide which critique is more accurate.

2. Read Masha Kabakow Rudman's *Children's Literature: An Issues Approach* (New York: Longman, 1984), thinking carefully about your opinion of her suggestions for using literature. Then read "The Ghost of Mrs. Trimmer" by Ethel L. Heins (*The Horn Book*, February 1977, pp. 18–19), which is highly critical of Rudman. Letters of reaction were published in *The Horn Book* in August and October of 1977. Who do you think provides the most accurate analysis of the book?

3. What values should children have about the relation between self, others, and society? In his article "Hidden Within the Pages: A Study of Social Perspective in Young Children's Favorite Books" (*The Reading Teacher*, March 1986, pp. 656–663), Patrick Shannon asserts that teachers need to think about this question, as books contain social values, often covertly rather than overtly expressed. Working with books from the Children's Choices program, Shannon did a content analysis that revealed that "the books showed a clear tendency to espouse the self as the focus for activity, rather than cooperative endeavor or concern for living in harmony with others." Giving several reasons why such self-oriented messages are hidden in books, he concludes this practice may foster individualism to the detriment of society. Read the article, then read several of the books from the list, and formulate your own response.

4. At the conclusion of his article "Reading as Inquiry: An Approach to Literature Learning" (*English Journal*, January 1981, pp. 39–45), Bryant Fillion asks teachers to perform five tasks. He discusses these in the context of high school, though the tasks are appropriate in varying degrees at every grade level. All teachers need to (1) organize units of study around reading and responding activities; (2) encourage students to examine

the role of inquiry in their lives; (3) examine the role of inquiry in reading itself; (4) group selections in a way that stimulates inquiry; and (5) encourage students to generate and to try to answer their own questions. Read this article to get a fuller understanding of the five tasks, then plan a unit based on children's books for a grade level of your choice, including activities that will carry out each task.

5. Interest in the home literary environment has increased recently, and researchers have published extended studies of the literary development of individual young children (see Dorothy White's *Books before Five*, Portsmouth, N.H.: Heinemann, 1984). Researchers have also reported on the value of specific book-presentation techniques used by mothers in broad samples. Writers such as Linda Leonard Lamme and Athol B. Packer ("Bookreading Behaviors of Infants," *The Reading Teacher*, February 1986, pp. 504–509) assert that there is—or can be—a "curriculum in books" before the child encounters formal curricula in school. Visit a nursery school and talk with several of the teachers to find out about the nature and extent of children's familiarity with books before they come to school. If possible, get permission to interview some of the parents to gather more information. How does what you learn relate to what White and Lamme and Packer have written?

## Related Reading for Adults

Berg-Cross, Linda, and Gary Berg-Cross. "Listening to Stories May Change Children's Social Attitudes." *The Reading Teacher*, March 1978, pp. 659–663.

Most of our knowledge about changing young children's attitudes through literature is generalized from findings about older students. These authors used four well-known children's books with 120 children to determine how responses to certain questions differed before and after listening to the books. These four- and six-year-olds changed well over one-half of their answers, indicating a shift in attitudes.

Biskin, Donald S., and Kenneth Hoskisson. "An Experimental Test of the Effects of Structured Discussions of Moral Dilemmas Found in Children's Literature on Moral Reasoning." *Elementary School Journal*, May 1977, pp. 407–416.

This empirical study follows an earlier position paper by the same authors (*Elementary School Journal*, December 1974, pp. 153–157) on how to use literature to affect children's moral development. Fourth- and fifth-grade students read seven stories and participated in structured discussion lessons; their moral maturity scores were determined before and after the lessons (using Kohlberg's procedures). There was a significant difference between mean scores of the control and the experimental groups: discussions of moral dilemmas induced changes in moral judgments.

Bond, Nancy. "Conflict in Children's Fiction." *The Horn Book*, June 1984, pp. 297–306.

Bond identifies three types of conflict: global (external and involving large numbers of people), personal (one person against another), and internal (conflict within a person). (Compare these three types of conflict with the three identified on page 673.) In actuality, most books contain combinations of the three. Bond goes on to contend that conflict is not necessarily bad, even though it is hard for all of us to acknowledge the dark side of ourselves. An author must, with the great specificity characteristic of fine writing, bring her or his book to a conclusion. There are two types of conclusions: resolution and recognition. Some conflicts can be resolved; others are so complex—because of our complexity as humans and the nature of our world—that they cannot be resolved. Having recognized the conflict, characters can begin the complex task of adjusting to it.

Council on Interracial Books for Children. *Human and Anti-Human Values in Children's Books: A Content Rating Instrument for Educators and Concerned Parents.* New York: Council on Interracial Books for Children, 1980.

The council's basic premise is that some books (such as *Bright April*, by Marguerite de Angeli) and characters (such as Hugh Lofting's Dr. Doolittle) set forth an entire ideology. Such books and characters espouse a set of values, and they mold minds. The council questions the source of these values and concludes they are not simply individual but arise from the total society. Children's books generally reflect the needs of those that dominate society. The book includes checklists for evaluating books about Africans, Chinese, Japanese, and native Americans, as well as Filipinos, Puerto Ricans, and women. In addition to this publication, the Council also makes available a small pamphlet entitled "10 Quick Ways to Analyze Children's Books for Racism and Sexism."

Farrell, Edmund J. "Literature in Crisis." *English Journal*, January 1981, pp. 13–18.

Farrell opens this article with an acknowledgment of apparently rosy publishing figures: sales in billions and advances for bestsellers in millions. Despite these figures, a closer look at who reads (percentages of readers compared with total population) and at what is read (the best-seller lists are a revelation) raises questions about the health of literature. Further evidence of Americans' indifference to print culture is found in a poll showing that whereas 96 percent of Americans thought it "very important" that students read well enough to follow an instruction manual, only 33 percent thought it similarly important that students know something of great leaders in art and literature. In addition to noting such popular constraints, Farrell comments on the censorship activities of such people as the Texas Gablers, who censor any school literature that contains a hint of violence or sex despite the fact that preadolescents have ready access to shows on television that are far more violent and salacious.

Goldthwaite, John. "Notes on the Children's Book Trade." *Harper's*, January 1977, pp. 76–86.

Delightfully acerbic, Goldthwaite takes aggressive potshots at many features of children's book publishing, including female editors, the excess of picture books, and the giving of awards. The contentions will arouse the ire of those involved, but they are convincingly stated and deserve careful consideration. Goldthwaite obviously has a wide acquaintance with the books, has spent much time in thoughtful study of them, and writes with the conviction that children deserve only the very best.

Morrow, Lesley Mandel, and Carol Simon Weinstein. "Increasing Children's Use of Literature Through Program and Physical Design Changes." *Elementary School Journal*, 83 (November 1981), pp. 131–137.

Concerned about research findings that young children seldom choose to read literature during free play, Morrow and Weinstein worked in thirteen kindergarten classrooms to change the environments. One group of teachers was involved in program changes (incorporating a wider variety of literature activities into the curriculum), one in physical design changes (setting up library corners), and a third in both types of changes. Researchers noted changes in children's selection of literature activities during free time. All three treatment types significantly increased literature use compared to the preintervention levels; voluntary literature use increased approximately 25 percent in each class. None of the treatments modified sex differences: as early as kindergarten, girls choose reading more often than boys do; at the conclusion of the study, girls still used literature during free play significantly more often than boys. Morrow reported on more work in this area in "Relations Between Literature Programs, Library Designs, and Children's Use of Literature" (*The Journal of Educational Research*, 75, July/August 1982, pp. 339–344) and "Home and School Correlates of Early Interest in Literature" (*The Journal of Educational Research*, March/April 1983, pp. 221–230).

Nelson, Eva. "Why We Hardly Have Any Picture Books in the Children's Department Anymore; A Brief Fantasy." *Top of the News*, November 1972, pp. 54–56.

A humorous picture of the logical consequence of libraries' yielding to any kind of censorship pressure: no books! The cannon in *Drummer Hoff*, the pigs in *Sylvester and the Magic Pebble*, the monsters in *Where the Wild Things Are*, and the large, comfortable mother in *A Snowy Day* are all gone. Only the ABC books remain. No one has objected to a single letter—yet!

Nodelman, Perry. "Thirty Writers Talk About Writing." *Children's Literature*, 12 (1984), pp. 200–205.

In his review of three recent books featuring authors' ruminations about how and why they write, Nodelman concludes that the ability to write for children in no way qualifies the authors to write about that writing. He notes that, at conferences and in print,

writers' comments often take the place of criticism by more objective readers. Nodelman reviews collections of authors' statements compiled by Nancy Chambers, Virginia Haviland, and Betsy Hearne and Marilyn Kaye. He cautions potential users of such volumes to ask what it is the writer is really putting forth: a critique of his or her book, an analysis of the writing process, or gossipy tidbits meant only to entertain fans?

Rudman, Masha Kabakow. *Children's Literature: An Issues Approach*. New York: Longman, 1984.

In the introduction, fantasy author Jane Yolen writes: "Dr. Rudman offers many ways in which an educator can help structure the reading and aid young readers in sorting out conflicting or inconsistent moralities. She does not necessarily throw out a book because its morality is outdated or its characters mouth inhuman statements. Rather she suggests methods of dealing with these problems." Rudman discusses a variety of topics: family (including siblings and divorce), sex, gender roles, heritage (including such ethnic groups as Afro-Americans and Asians), special needs, old age, death, and war.

Singer, Isaac Bashevis. "I See the Child as a Last Refuge." *The New York Times Book Review*, November 9, 1969, pp. 65–66.

This Nobel Prize–winning writer comments that children's literature is gaining in quality and stature while adult literature is going downhill. Writers in the nineteenth and earlier centuries understood the value of a story well told. Twentieth-century adult literature is becoming more and more didactic and utilitarian.

Swinger, Alice K. *Children's Books: A Legacy for the Young*. Bloomington, Ind.: Phi Delta Kappa Educational Foundation, 1981.

In a brief format (forty-five pages), Swinger presents an introduction to the field, designed for a general audience. She includes a section on the value of children's books; a section on genres; a longer, though still brief section on historic trends; and some useful appendixes. This is an ideal pamphlet to give to administrators or share with parents.

Travers, P. L. "On Not Writing for Children." *Children's Literature*, 4 (1975), pp. 15–22.

The respected author of *Mary Poppins* reflects on why she writes and speculates on the motivation of others who write. She concludes that it is probable that few authors consciously write specifically for children. She argues eloquently that labeling books for age levels is ridiculous, for who can judge what child will be moved by what book and at what age? *"Mary Poppins:* Two Points of View" (*Children's Literature*, 10, 1982, pp. 210–217) is an exchange of letters between Travers and Robert B. Moore, director of the Racism Resource Center for the New York City Public Schools. The two debate the issue of whether the book may be damaging to young readers; each makes a convincing argument. This article might be used to stimulate thought and discussion about this question with middle school students.

Wass, Hannelore, and Judith Shaak. "Helping Children Understand Death Through Literature." *Childhood Education*, November/December 1976, pp. 80–85.

Wass and Shaak state a philosophical rationale for a more realistic understanding of death, report research on children's perceptions of death, and consider death education as part of the school curriculum. The article concludes with an annotated list of appropriate books grouped according to age levels.

Williams, Martin. "Some Remarks on Raggedy Ann and Johnny Gruelle." *Children's Literature: The Great Excluded*, 3 (1974), pp. 140–146.

The stories about Raggedy Ann are an interesting example of books that engender a difference in opinion between children's literature experts and children themselves. The books are not deemed critically significant, but they are read voraciously by young readers. Williams identifies reasons for this interest, pointing out the long tradition of stories dealing with the secret lives of dolls. He contends that children like this basic premise and do not mind the repetitiousness of the stories.

## Professional References

*American Libraries.* "Children's Book Fans Smoldering Debate." *American Libraries*, 14 (March 1983), 130–132.

Bawden, Nina. "Emotional Realism in Books for Young People." *The Horn Book*, 56 (February 1980), 17–33.

Baxter, Kathleen. "On Selecting Christian Books." *School Library Journal*, 31 (March 1985), 118–119.

Beavin, Kristi Thomas. Review of *Jake and Honeybunch Go to Heaven. School Library Journal*, 129 (December 1982), 61–62.

Boothroy, Bonnie, and Jean Donham. "Listening to Literature: An All-School Program." *The Reading Teacher*, April 1981, 772–774.

Brewbaker, James M. "Are You There, Margaret? It's Me, God—Religious Contexts in Recent Adolescent Fiction." *English Journal*, September 1983, 82–86.

Fretz, Sada. "Picture Books." *Kirkus Reviews*, 50 (August 15, 1983), 936.

Geller, Evelyn. "Aesthetics, Morality, and the Two Cultures." In *The Black American in Books for Children: Readings in Racism.* Eds. Donnarae MacCann and Gloria Woodard. Metuchen, N.J.: Scarecrow Press, 1972, p. 37.

Harmin, Merrill, Howard Kirschenbaum, and Sidney B. Simon. *Clarifying Values Through Subject Matter.* Minneapolis: Winston Press, 1973.

Holbrook, Hilary Taylor. "The Quality of Textbooks." *The Reading Teacher,* March 1985, 680–683.

Klingberg, Susan. Letter to the Editor. *The Horn Book,* June 1976, 235.

Kuskin, Karla. "The Complete Illustrator." *New York Times Book Review,* 87 (April 25, 1982), 46.

May, Jill P. "Trina S. Hyman." *Children's Literature Association Quarterly,* 11 (Spring 1986), 44.

Morrow, Lesley Mandel. "Field-Based Research on Voluntary Reading." *The Reading Teacher,* December 1985, 331–337.

Norsworthy, James A., Jr. "In Search of An Image: The Adult Male Role in Picture Books." *Catholic Library World,* December 1973, 220–226.

Purves, Alan C., and Dianne L. Monson. *Experiencing Children's Literature.* Glenview, Ill.: Scott, Foresman, 1984, p. 190.

Richard, Olga, and Donnarae MacCann. "Picture Books for Children." *Wilson Library Bulletin,* 59 (March 1985), 482–483.

Roxburgh, Stephen. "On My Mind." *American Libraries,* May 1983, 315.

Schwartz, Albert V. "*Sounder:* A Black or White Tale?" *Interracial Books for Children,* 3 (Autumn 1970), 3.

Sides, Nita K. "Story Time Is Not Enough." *The Reading Teacher,* December 1982, 280–283.

Sims, Rudine. *Shadow and Substance. Afro-American Experiences in Contemporary Children's Fiction.* Urbana, Ill.: National Council of Teachers of English, 1982.

Stavn, Diane G. Review of *Sounder,* by William H. Armstrong. *School Library Journal,* December 1969, 56.

Sutherland, Zena. Review of *Sounder. Bulletin of the Center for Children's Books,* February 1971, 86.

Townsend, John Rowe. *Written for Children.* New York: J. B. Lippincott, 1983, p. 275.

Wilms, Denise M. Review of *Jake and Honeybunch Go to Heaven. Booklist,* 79 (January 1, 1983), 619.

## *Bibliography of Children's Books*

Bailey, Carolyn. *Miss Hickory.* New York: Viking, 1962.

Bolliger, Max. *Noah and the Rainbow.* New York: Thomas Y. Crowell, 1972.

Brink, Carol Ryrie. *The Bad Times of Irma Baumlein.* New York: Macmillan, 1972.

Burch, Robert. *Queenie Peavy.* New York: Viking, 1966.

Cleaver, Vera and Bill Cleaver. *Where the Lilies Bloom.* New York: J. B. Lippincott, 1969.

Dalgliesh, Alice. *The Courage of Sarah Noble.* New York: Scribner's, 1954.

Duncan, Lois. *Daughters of Eve.* Boston: Little, Brown, 1979.

Estes, Eleanor. *The Hundred Dresses.* New York: Harcourt, Brace, 1944.

Farber, Norma. *How Does It Feel to Be Old?* New York: E. P. Dutton, 1979.

Feelings, Tom. *Black Pilgrimage.* New York: Lothrop, Lee and Shepard, 1972.

Field, Rachel. *Hitty: Her First Hundred Years.* New York: Macmillan, 1937.

Fitzhugh, Louise. *The Long Secret.* New York: Harper and Row, 1965.

Forman, James. *Ceremony of Innocence.* New York: Hawthorn, 1970.

Forman, Michael. *The Two Giants.* New York: Pantheon, 1967.

Gantschev, Ivan. *Noah and the Ark and the Animals*. Natick, Mass.: Picture Book Studio, 1984.

Gates, Doris. *Blue Willow*. New York: Viking, 1948.

Gramatky, Hardie. *Little Toot*. New York: G. P. Putnam's, 1939.

Hays, Wilma Pitchford. *Christmas on the Mayflower*. New York: Coward, McCann, 1956.

Herman, Charlotte. *The Difference of Ari Stein*. New York: Harper and Row, 1976.

Hill, Elizabeth S. *Evan's Corner*. New York: Holt, Rinehart and Winston, 1967.

Hoban, Russell. *Charlie the Tramp*. New York: Scholastic, 1966.

Hull, Eleanor. *A Trainful of Strangers*. New York: Atheneum, 1968.

Hutton, Warwick. *Noah and the Great Flood*. New York: Atheneum, 1977.

Isadora, Rachel. *Max*. New York: Macmillan, 1976.

Kerr, M. E. *Gentlehands*. New York: Harper and Row, 1978.

Levin, Betty. *The Keeping Room*. New York: Greenwillow, 1981.

Lionni, Leo. *Frederick*. New York: Pantheon, 1967.

Matthee, Dalene. *Circles in a Forest*. New York: Alfred A. Knopf, 1984.

Mirsky, Reba P. *Mozart*. Chicago: Follett, 1960.

Mui, Shan. *Seven Magic Orders*. New York: Weatherhill, 1972.

Paterson, Katherine. *The Great Gilly Hopkins*. New York: Thomas Y. Crowell, 1978.

——— . *Jacob Have I Loved*. New York: Thomas Y. Crowell, 1980.

Perrine, Mary. *Salt Boy*. Boston: Houghton Mifflin, 1968.

Pollowitz, Melinda. *Cinnamon Cane*. New York: Harper and Row, 1977.

Pomerantz, Charlotte. *Noah's and Namah's Ark*. New York: Holt, Rinehart and Winston, 1981.

Pope, Elizabeth Marie. *The Perilous Gard*. Boston: Houghton Mifflin, 1974.

——— . *The Sherwood Ring*. Boston: Houghton Mifflin, 1958.

Sendak, Maurice. *Where the Wild Things Are*. New York: Harper and Row, 1963.

Seuss, Dr. *Horton Hears a Who!* New York: Random House, 1954.

——— . *The Sneetches and Other Stories*. New York: Random House, 1961.

Simon, Shirley. *Best Friend*. New York: Lothrop, Lee and Shepard, 1964.

Sonnenborn, Ruth. *Friday Night Is Papa Night*. New York: Viking, 1970.

Sorensen, Virginia. *Lotte's Locket*. New York: Harcourt, Brace, 1964.

Talbert, Marc. *Dead Birds Singing*. Boston: Little, Brown, 1985.

Townsend, John Rowe. *The Islanders*. New York: J. B. Lippincott, 1981.

Wells, Rosemary. *None of the Above*. New York: Dial, 1974.

White, E. B. *Charlotte's Web*. New York: Harper and Row, 1975.

Zemach, Margot. *Jake and Honeybunch Go to Heaven*. New York: Farrar, Straus and Giroux, 1982.

# ACKNOWLEDGMENTS

Pages 32 and 301. From *Suppose You Met a Witch?* by Ian Serraillier. Text copyright 1952 by Ian Serraillier. By permission of Little, Brown and Company.

Page 142. Excerpts from *Little Silk*, copyright © 1976 by Jacqueline Ayer. Reprinted by permission of Harcourt Brace Jovanovich, Inc.

Page 144. From *All Us Come Cross the Water* by Lucille Clifton. Reprinted by permission of Henry Holt Inc.

Pages 146–147. Byrd Baylor, excerpted from *The Desert Is Theirs*. Text copyright © 1975 by Byrd Baylor. Reprinted with the permission of Charles Scribner's Sons.

Page 204. Robert Sargent, excerpted from *Everything Is Difficult at First*. Copyright © 1968 by Robert E. Sargent. Reprinted with the permission of Charles Scribner's Sons, a division of Macmillan, Inc.

Page 213. From *Jack and the Beanstalk* by Paul Galdone. Based on *The History of Mother Twaddle and the Marvellous Achievements of Her Son Jack* by B. A. T. published in 1807 by J. Harris, London. Copyright © 1974 by Paul Galdone. Reprinted by permission of Clarion Books/Ticknor & Fields, a Houghton Mifflin Company.

Page 222. "Master Rabbit & the Berries" from *Specimens of Bantu Folk-lore from Northern Rhodesia* by J. Torrends. Reprinted by permission of Routledge & Kegan Paul.

Page 244. "The Cat and Chanticleer" from *Ukrainian Folk Tales* by Marie Halun Bloch. Copyright © 1964 by Marie Halun Bloch. Reprinted by permission of McIntosh and Otis, Inc.

Page 244. "Snowdrop" from *Grimm's Fairy Tales* by Arthur Rackham. Reprinted by permission of William Heinemann Limited.

Page 271. "Baby and I" from *One Misty Moisty Morning: Rhymes from Mother Goose*, illustrated by Mitchell Miller. Copyright © 1971 by Mitchell Miller. Reprinted by permission of Farrar, Straus and Giroux, Inc.

Page 272. From *Cakes and Custard* by Brian Alderson. Reprinted by permission of William Morrow & Company.

Page 273. From *Mother Goose Lost* by Nicholas Tucker. Reprinted by permission of Hamish Hamilton Ltd.

Page 273. From *The Real Mother Goose* by Blanche Fisher Wright. Macmillan Publishing Company.

Page 276. From *Mother Goose* illustrated by Tasha Tudor. Henry Z. Walck, David McKay Co., A Division of Random House, Inc.

Pages 276–277. Rhyme reprinted by permission of Philomel Books from *Chinese Mother Goose Rhymes* selected and edited by Robert Wyndham, copyright © 1968 by Robert Wyndham.

Page 277. From *Mother Goose* by Kate Greenaway. Viking Penguin Inc.

Page 279. "What Are Little Boys Made Of?" from *Ms. Goose* by Tamar Hoffs. Reprinted by permission of Avondale Press.

Page 283. Excerpts from "War Songs" and "Songs of Birds" from *In the Trail of the Wind*, edited by John Bierhorst. Copyright © 1971 by John Bierhorst. Reprinted by permission of Farrar, Straus and Giroux, Inc.

Page 288. "There was an Old Man of Peru" from *The Golden Book of Fun and Nonsense* by Louis Untermeyer. Western Publishing Company.

Page 291. Terry Tempest Williams, excerpted from *Between Cattails*. Text copyright © 1985 Terry Tempest Williams. Reprinted with the permission of Charles Scribner's Sons.

Page 292. *Circus* by Jack Prelutsky. Reprinted with permission of Macmillan Publishing Company from *Circus* by Jack Prelutsky. Copyright © 1974 by Jack Prelutsky.

Pages 292–293. Lilian Moore, "In the Fog" from *I Feel the Same Way*. Copyright © 1967 by Lilian Moore. Reprinted with the permission of Atheneum Publishers.

Page 294. "Silver" from *Peacock Pie* by Walter de la Mare. Reprinted by permission of The Literary Trustees of Walter de la Mare and The Society of Authors as their representatives.

Pages 294–295. "Relative Sadness" by Colin Rowbotham from *The Burning Thorn* by

Griselda Greaves. Reprinted with permission of Macmillan Publishing Company from *The Burning Thorn* by Griselda Greaves. Copyright © 1971 by Griselda Greaves.

Page 296. "On Tuesdays I Polish My Uncle" from *Alligator Pie* © 1974 by Dennis Lee. Reprinted by permission of Macmillan of Canada, A Division of Canada Publishing Corporation.

Page 298. "Cocoon" from *One at a Time* by David McCord. Copyright 1949 by David McCord. First appeared in *The New Yorker*. By permission of Little, Brown and Company.

Page 299. "Cat!" from *Silver Sand and Snow* by Eleanor Farjeon. London: Michael Joseph. Reprinted by permission of David Higham Associates Limited.

Page 300. From *Old Possum's Book of Practical Cats*, copyright 1939 by T. S. Eliot, renewed 1967 by Esme Valerie Eliot. Reprinted by permission of Harcourt Brace Jovanovich and Faber and Faber Ltd.

Page 302. "Forget" by Mary O'Neill from *Words, Words, Words*. Copyright © 1966 by Mary O'Neill. Reprinted by permission of Doubleday & Company.

Page 304. Lilian Moore, "September" from *Sam's Place*. Copyright © 1973 by Lilian Moore. Reprinted with the permission of Atheneum Publishers.

Page 304. "Good morning" from *Sung Under the Silver Umbrella*. Reprinted by permission of The Literature Committee of the Association for Childhood Education and the Association for Childhood Educational International, 11141 Georgia Avenue, Suite 200, Wheaton, MD. Copyright 1935 by the Association.

Page 305. "The Mouse" by Elizabeth Coatsworth. Reprinted by permission of Coward-McCann, Inc. From *Compass Rose* by Elizabeth Coatsworth, copyright 1929 by Coward-McCann Inc., copyright renewed © 1957 by Elizabeth Coatsworth.

Page 305. Excerpt from "A March Calf" from *Season Songs* by Ted Hughes. Copyright © 1968, 1973 by Ted Hughes. Reprinted by permission of Viking Penguin Inc.

Pages 352–353. Ellen Howard, excerpted from *When Daylight Comes*. Copyright © 1985 Ellen G. Howard. Reprinted with the permission of Atheneum Publishers.

Pages 432, 434–435, and 690. From *Harriet the Spy* by Louise Fitzhugh. Copyright © 1964 by Louise Fitzhugh. Reprinted by permission of Harper & Row, Publishers, Inc.

Page 438. From *I Have a Sister, My Sister Is Deaf* by Jeanne Whitehouse Peterson. Text copyright © 1977 by Jeanne Whitehouse Peterson. Reprinted by permission of Harper & Row, Publishers, Inc.

Pages 449–450. From *The Pinballs* by Betsy Byars. Copyright © 1977 by Betsy Byars. Reprinted by permission of Harper & Row, Publishers, Inc.

Page 460. From *My Street's a Morning Cool Street* by Ianthe Thomas. Text copyright © 1976 by Ianthe Thomas. Reprinted by permission of Harper & Row, Publishers, Inc.

Pages 462–463. From *Growin'* by Nikki Grimes. Text copyright © 1977 by Nikki Grimes. Reprinted by permission of the publisher, Dial Books for Young Readers.

Pages 517 and 560–561. From *An Enemy at Green Knowe*, copyright © 1964 by Lucy Maria Boston. Reprinted by permission of Harcourt Brace Jovanovich, Inc. and Faber and Faber Ltd.

Pages 520 and 546. *Save Sirrushany!* by Betty Baker. Reprinted with permission of Macmillan Publishing Company from *Save Sirrushany!* by Betty Baker. Copyright © 1978 by Betty Baker.

Pages 547–549. From *Hangin' Out with Cici* by Francine Pascal. Copyright © 1977 by Francine Pascal. Reprinted by permission of Viking Penguin Inc.

Pages 555–556. From *Among the Dolls* by William Sleator. Text copyright © 1975 by William Sleator. Reprinted by permission of the publisher, E. P. Dutton, a division of NAL Penguin Inc.

Page 639. From *Bugs* by Mary Ann Hoberman. Copyright © 1976 by Mary Ann Hoberman. Reprinted by permission of Viking Penguin Inc.

Pages 680–681. From *How Does It Feel to Be Old?* by Norma Farber. Text copyright © 1979 by Norma Farber. Reprinted by permission of the publisher, E. P. Dutton, a division of NAL Penguin Inc.

# SUBJECT INDEX

# NAME INDEX

# TITLE INDEX